D1108161

# A Heart at
Fire's Center

# A Heart at Fire's Center

*The Life and Music
of Bernard Herrmann*

Steven C. Smith

UNIVERSITY OF CALIFORNIA PRESS
*Berkeley* • *Los Angeles* • *Oxford*

University of California Press
Berkeley and Los Angeles, California

University of California Press, Ltd.
Oxford, England

© 1991 by
The Regents of the University of California


Library of Congress Cataloging-in-Publication Data

Smith, Steven C.
    A heart at fire's center : the life and music of Bernard Herrmann
/ Steven C. Smith.

        p.    cm.
    Includes bibliographical references and index.
    ISBN 0-520-07123-9 (alk. paper)
        1. Herrmann, Bernard, 1911–1975.   2. Composers—United States—
    Biography.   I. Title.
ML410.H562S6   1991
780'.92—dc20
[B]                                                                90–36861
                                                                      CIP
                                                                       MN


Printed in the United States of America

9   8   7   6   5   4   3   2   1

The paper used in this publication meets the minimum requirements of
American National Standard for Information Sciences—Permanence of Paper
for Printed Library Materials, ANSI Z39.48–1984. ♾

Near the snow, near the sun, in the highest fields,
See how these names are feted by the waving grass
And by the streamers of white cloud
And whispers of wind in the listening sky . . .
The names of those who in their lives fought for life,
Who wore at their hearts the fire's centre.

Stephen Spender (from a poem Herrmann<br/>carried in his wallet)

Musically I count myself an individualist. I believe that only music which springs out of genuine personal emotion is alive and important. I hate all cults, fads, and circles. I feel that a composer should be true to his own innate instincts and tastes, and develop these to the best of his ability, no matter what the present vogue may be. . . . I am not interested in music, or any work of art, that fails to stimulate appreciation of life and, more importantly, pride in life.

Bernard Herrmann

# Contents

Acknowledgments      ix

Prelude      1

PART ONE: NEW YORK, 1911–1951

One      7
Two      21
Three      42
Four      59
Five      71
Six      85
Seven      110
Eight      131

PART TWO: HOLLYWOOD, 1951–1971

Nine      163
Ten      191
Eleven      219
Twelve      236
Thirteen      267
Fourteen      292

PART THREE: LONDON, 1971–1975

Fifteen      311
Sixteen      319
Seventeen      336

Postlude      357
Appendix:
  The Music of Bernard Herrmann      365
Notes      377
Selected Bibliography      401
Index      405

*Photographs following page 160*

# Acknowledgments

Without the cooperation of many, the researching of this book would have been impossible. I am most indebted to Norma Shepherd, who, in addition to weeks of her time, gave me total access to Bernard Herrmann's correspondence, library, photographs, and papers. Lucille Fletcher was no less generous in sharing her memories and correspondence, and Lucy Anderson was also extremely helpful.

David Raksin and Norman Corwin were instrumental in giving my research a successful start. My thanks also to the others who shared their recollections with me: John Amis, Lady Evelyn Barbirolli, Victor Bay, Arthur Berger, Elmer Bernstein, Martin Bernstein, Richard Berres, Howard Blake, Ray Bradbury, Elsa Clay, Larry Cohen, Max and Sarah Cohn, the late Aaron Copland, Kathryn Corwin, the late George Coulouris, Don Cristlieb, Tony D'Amato, Oliver Daniel, Ken Darby, James Decker, Georges Delerue, Flora Della Cioppa, Guy Della Cioppa, Margaret Della Cioppa, Meriel Dickinson, Ivan Ditmars, Philip Dunne, the late Len Engel, Mr. and Mrs. Dominic Fera, Raymond Few, Mort Fine, Vivian Fine, Rudolph Firkusny, Sebastian Forbes, Alan Frank, William Froug, Sue Gauthier, Charles Gerhardt, Diane Gleghorn, the late Lud Gluskin, John Goldsmith, the late Benny Goodman, Morton Gould, the late John Green, Bernard Greenhouse, Joan and Henry Greenwood, the late Virginia Gregg, George and Pauline Hamer, W. Clark Harrington, Ray Harryhausen, the late Henry Hathaway, Jack Hayes, the late Irwin Heilner, Dorothy Herrmann, Ruth Herrmann, Paul Hirsch, Buck Houghton, the late John Houseman, Marsha Hunt, Ben Hyams, Ralph Ives, Edward Johnson,

Laurie Johnson, Ben Kanter, Louis and Annette Kaufman, Milton Kestenbaum, Liz Keyes, Dorothy Kirsten, the late Jim Koblenzer, the late Irving Kolodin, the late George Korngold, Diane Lampert, Burt Lancaster, Ernest Lehman, Elliott Lewis, David Licht, Norman Lloyd, Nicholas Meyer, Mitch Miller, Frank Milton, the late Lyn Murray, the late Alan Napier, the late Lionel Newman, Alex North, Christopher Palmer, Abe Polonsky, the late Robert Presnell, André Previn, Martha Ragland, Basil Ramsey, Don Ray, Alastair Reid, Michael Rippon, Peggy Robertson, Alan Robinson, William Robson, Miklós Rózsa, Mr. and Mrs. Sidney Sax, William Schaffer, Charles Schneer, Gerard and Caroline Schurmann, Martin Scorsese, John Scott, the late Jack Sher, Elie Siegmeister, Eleanor Slatkin, Dorothy Spencer, Fred and Shirley Steiner, Fred Stewart, James G. Stewart, the late Paul Stewart, Robert Stone, Suzanne Tarjan, Irbin Theilman, Tony Thomas, Ursula Vaughan Williams, Roger Wagner, John Williams, Richard Wilson, Shimon Wincelberg, Robert Wise, Leslie Zador, and Fred Zinnemann.

Craig Reardon's interviews with Louis Herrmann, John Brahm, Hugo Freidhofer, and others were invaluable. Thanks also to those who provided other important material: Roma Barrin, Rudy Behlmer, the British Film Institute, Wayne Bryan, Sylvia Clay, Roger Dice, Jim Doherty, Kevin Fahey, Dan Haefle, Scott Holton, the Margaret Herrick Academy Library, John Morgan, Pat Hitchcock O'Connell, Howard Prouty, Martin Silver (curator of the Bernard Herrmann collection at the University of California, Santa Barbara), Elwayne Smith, Aubrey Solomon, Adam Stern, and Marc Scott Zicree.

Special thanks to Mike Hamilburg and to Ernest Callenbach, Mark Jacobs, and their fellow editors at the University of California Press for their excellent suggestions, and to Anne Canright for her superb copyediting.

This book is dedicated to my brother and my parents.

# *Prelude*

On Christmas Eve 1906, the unmistakable sounds of music and a cheery human voice crackled through a handful of electric receivers in Brant Rock, Massachusetts. It was the world's first radio broadcast—the most dramatic in a series of breakthroughs in the new century that would shatter all spatial boundaries placed on the arts. At the same time, the phonograph—less than two decades old—was undergoing refinement, and by 1925 its "all-electric" incarnation offered an amazingly wide frequency and clarity of sound.

Artistic sounds that before had reached a few were now available to millions. Not surprisingly, music would benefit most greatly from these inventions: in these early years of the twentieth century, music not only was expanding its tonal language, but through the new media of radio, recordings, and later film and television, it would envelop the world with a diversity of cultural influences.

Not all composers considered these new media artistic; for some, their very accessibility precluded cultural merit. Others saw things differently. No one bridged these new roads more ingeniously than Bernard Herrmann, whose vision of cinema, radio, and television as legitimate artistic tools and whose creative individualism and dramatic insight set him far apart from his contemporaries.

Few American composers followed a more rigid set of personal and creative standards—or lost more friends and work because of them. Explosive, insecure, paranoiac, Herrmann was, as many observed, his own worst enemy. His self-cultivated notoriety is a pity: it obscures a fascinating, often paradoxical array of virtues. No twentieth-century composer championed new and forgotten music so vehemently—and no American composer contributed so much, so brilliantly, to the cinema.

Before Herrmann's first film score, for *Citizen Kane* in 1940, film music in Hollywood was mostly homogenous in style and orchestration. Perhaps Herrmann's greatest achievement in film was his remarkable use of orchestration to reinforce theme and character psychology: each Herrmann instrumentation was uniquely tailored to the subject matter of the film it accompanied. Unlike many of his contemporaries, Herrmann eschewed the use of long melodic ideas in his dramatic scoring,[1] preferring the more succinct short phrase, which he felt could be transformed more effectively throughout a score. Although he did make use of the classic device of the leitmotiv,* this use was often startlingly original: a thematic idea was used not merely for static identification of character, but for psychological enrichment of it. Herrmann's cues also were often shorter, more terse than other composers'; he knew the value of understatement.

Herrmann's use of indigenous American music in film scores was virtually unprecedented in its sophistication. European-trained composers like Dimitri Tiomkin, Cyril Mockridge, and Max Steiner often incorporated traditional American melodies into their scores; but Herrmann, a passionate champion of contemporary American music, was more subtle and experimental in his use of American dance forms and folk themes.

Herrmann remains the most imitated and influential composer in film; yet despite his many innovations in the medium, Herrmann always insisted he was not a "film composer" but a composer who worked in film. The distinction was not a pedantic one: there was no value Herrmann admired more than individualism, in both character and art, and in all aspects of his life—his scoring approach, his passion for the arts, his friendships and his hates—he was an individual.

He was also among the most informed musicians of his generation, a compulsive reader and astute critic of literature, an appreciator of nineteenth-century painting, and a fine, perceptive writer—qualities many had difficulty reconciling with a man of volcanic, often irrational temperament. Close friends saw another, more vulnerable side; observed Ursula Vaughan Williams, wife of composer Ralph Vaughan Williams and Herrmann's friend of twenty years:

Benny was, at first sight, unprepossessing, as if some bad fairy at the christening had given him the wrong face for his character—but once one

---

*A short, recurring musical phrase linked to a specific character or setting.

had seen him talking of paintings, or listening to music or speaking of it, his face became beautiful and noble. He had a sharp eye for character, and could be caustic about anyone whose work he did not respect or whose character or conduct displeased him. In human relationships he tended to take a short cut over susceptibilities and he was frequently impatient; with animals, his own and other people's, his gentleness and patience were endless.[2]

Early in his life Herrmann committed himself to a creed of personal integrity at the price of unpopularity, his philosophy summarized in a favorite Tolstoy quote: "Eagles fly alone and sparrows fly in flocks."[3] Although from childhood until his death he sought out the famous and the obscure to champion and befriend, he often found it impossible to maintain the friendships he began. As great as his generosity was his capacity for self-destruction; the relentless drive that brought him triumphs led to his alienating friends and colleagues. It was a flaw that Herrmann recognized privately but which he felt he could not control. Only death seemed to bring peace.

For despite the many achievements—his film work with Orson Welles, Alfred Hitchcock, and others, his fifteen years as conductor of the CBS Symphony—Herrmann's life was an ongoing battle with demons: lack of recognition as a "serious" composer, his having chosen the high-salary, invisible medium of film to work in; failure to see the performance of the composition he considered his most important; and his inability for twenty-five years to secure a conducting post. There was also a lifelong fascination with—and fear of—death, a subject Herrmann avoided almost pathologically in conversation but studied obsessively in his art.

His life, like his inevitably fragmented film scores, lacked a superficial continuity. Lifelong friendships were few; and professionally, Herrmann was as much a conductor and musicologist as he was a composer. His gift for evoking psychological complexity in music mirrors a personality that was intensely schismatic. Frequently abrasive and slovenly in personal habits, Herrmann idolized the elegance and order of Georgian England. An often dictatorial conductor and perfectionist, he tolerated mediocre playing that pleased him in its overall texture. Despite a vast intellectual sense, he was an instinctual artist who believed that intuition was the heart of creativity. (His intellectual independence also contrasts with Herrmann's childlike reliance on mother figures throughout his life.) And in spite of a sometimes petty suspicion of others' motives, he is recalled by many for acts of touching, often elaborate generosity. In almost every area of Herrmann's life there is a tension of contradiction. (Personal tension,

Herrmann once told a friend, was a necessary element in his creative process; yet he longed to be free of it.)[4]

Binding these many strands was Herrmann's obsessive search for an artistic and personal ideal he could not realize—in friendships, in romance, in his work. Unable to sustain personal happiness, he maintained a faith in the spiritual transcendence of the artist, who could achieve immortality. In the spirit of the Romantic tradition he cherished, he sought an absolute, and was devastated when he found imperfection. Scenarios recur in Herrmann's life like sad leitmotivs: friendships passionately initiated by Herrmann, then ended in anger and suspicion; a zest for work, followed by frustration with his collaborators. His desire to live and create was equaled by a capacity for pain and rejection.

Creatively and personally Herrmann cultivated a vision of life that, like that of the great Romantics in music, art, and poetry, recognized both the beauty and horror in the human condition (elements that often coexist, as in his eerily beautiful "Twilight Zone" music or the sensuous mystery of *Vertigo* and other Hitchcock scores). A passionate, inexhaustible man, Herrmann excelled in capturing the psychological bond between love and anxiety.

His music, almost all of it programmatic, embodied the German Romanticism of Wagner and Mahler as well as the psychological impressionism of the French school (Debussy and Ravel especially)—perceived through the Anglo-American culture Herrmann adored. His music for film, radio, and television not only gave temporal and emotional focus to its subject; it imparted a point of view that was distinctly Herrmann's own.

His idiom was that of a Neo-Romantic schooled in the music of the twentieth century yet most attached to the works that preceded it. A strong element of nostalgia pervades Herrmann's writing, along with a brooding melancholy: the music reflects a divided man who sought more than he could find but reveled in the quest. It is this sensitivity for the separation between possibility and reality—his mastery of "the elemental passions of love, death, pathos and anxiety," as Norman Corwin observed[5]—that gives Herrmann's music its enduring emotional resonance.

Beyond this tension of unrealized fulfillment, a combination of genealogy, artistic ambition, social insecurity, and creative genius helped shape a temperament as critical as it was caring. The result was a man who was constantly seeking, on his own terms, love of the most unconditional kind.

# PART ONE

# New York

## 1911–1951

# ONE

He discovered a great ambition to excel. . . . He was uncommonly inquisitive; and his memory was so tenacious, that he never forgot anything that he either heard or read. . . . In short, he is a memorable instance of what has often been observed, that the boy is the man in miniature.

*Boswell*, Life of Johnson

Bernard Herrmann was a premature baby, born in the seventh month of his mother's pregnancy on June 29, 1911.[1] His early arrival—foreshadowing the tempo of the life to follow—may have resulted in his being born, like many premature infants, without a fully developed nerve-protection system. Or perhaps his sensitized aggression was the legacy of a cultural history marked by persistence. Both of his parents, Abraham and Ida Herrmann, were part of the massive immigration of East European Jews to New York, triggered in the early 1880s by the oppression of their czarist homeland.

In Europe, the Jews were a nation without recognition. Their collectivism threatened by Russia's anti-Semitic Alexander III, the East European Jews began to move westward in search of freedom and a reaffirmation of cultural ties. Their reception in New York was at first one of open hostility, as predictions of "Russian radicalism" and growing crime filled the newspapers and street talk.[2] Gradually more subtle forms of suspicion took hold as an increasing number of skilled workers and intellectuals followed the first wave of settlers. Some, like Abraham Dardick (soon to become Abraham Herrmann), came not from the slums of Russia's Pale of Settlement but from successful professional districts threatened by Russia's political instability.[3] New York promised community, wealth, even intellectualism, values important to the optometrist from Proskourv.

Abraham was one of six Dardick children. Four others—Sonya, Nathan, Lazar, and Hinda—also left for America in the late nineteenth century. Abraham's parents left Russia as well, settling in Palestine at the time of the First World War; they died about fifteen years later.

Abraham Dardick's early years, according to the tales of his children, were the stuff of Melville and Israel Zangwill fiction. After an education in Russia, Dardick left for America around 1880. There he changed his name from Dardick to Herrmann, probably because of the growing success of German Jews in America*—although his son Bernard would have enormous contempt for the "airy" Germans. (This did not prohibit Bernard's admiration, sometimes idolatry, of German composers.)

Abraham sailed to Hawaii to became an assistant overseer of a sugar or pineapple plantation a few years before the overthrow of the Hawaiian monarchy that led to American possession of the islands. After years in Hawaii, Herrmann traveled to Seattle, where he became a whaler aboard the brigantine *Alexander*. During a trip to the Bering Straits the *Alexander* was reportedly shipwrecked, but the crew were saved and made their way to the Ratt Island and Atu.

Herrmann returned to America around 1895, studying optometry through a correspondence course in Chicago. He received his degree in 1896 and moved to Cleveland, opening an optometrist's shop in the Cleveland Arcade. A few years later his wanderlust took him to Watertown, New York, and finally to New York City. There he married another Russian immigrant and fathered two children. The marriage was short-lived, apparently owing to Abraham's temper. The first Mrs. Herrmann returned to Russia with both children. Abraham followed them in an unsuccessful attempt to gain custody of the children.[4] One child died in Russia; the other, Willy, later returned to New York.

By the opening decade of the new century, New York Jews were enjoying their first taste of prosperity. They were becoming bankers and restaurant owners; they inhabited modern downtown apartments, many with that unique symbol of status, the elevator. It was to this upper middle class that Abraham Herrmann belonged, proud of his Russian heritage while cultivating an erudition in Western art, literature, and music. A nonmusician but frequent concertgoer, Herrmann (according to his sons) always purchased two theater seats, even when alone—one for himself, one for his coat and hat.

Abraham Herrmann, with his aristocratic, Edwardian lifestyle, found an opposite in Ida Gorenstein, another Russian immigrant of less well-to-

*Two explanations of Abraham's name change were passed down to the Herrmanns. The first concerned an amatory alliance Abraham sought to escape; the second, a Herrmann family in Pittsburgh with whom Abraham stayed, and which asked Abraham to take their name. Abraham's son Louis believed the first story.

do ancestry. Ironically, the Gorenstein family was from the same Russian city as Abraham, Proskourv;[5] but unlike Abraham, Ida's parents were extremely religious. One of five children, Ida had come to New York with her family at the age of nine, losing most of her native language in the transition. She was uneducated and poor, with only the most basic working skills.

She was also, in 1909, attractive and eligible. Now in her late teens, Ida worked in a New York shop as a gloves salesgirl, supporting her family and introducing her to a leisured, successful class of businessmen. Among the frequent clients was the middle-aged Herrmann, who already had a history of mistresses in the New York area. Soon the gentleman with a diamond stickpin and gold-knobbed walking stick had taken a fancy to the simple young salesgirl, and the first wave of scarves and trinkets was followed by a proposal of marriage to Ida's parents.[6]

His offer was conditional: his fiancée could not be a salesgirl. Since her wages were essential to her family, Abraham agreed to pay her parents to keep her home until he decided it was time for marriage. Ida Herrmann later described herself as "the lady of the district," free from the drudgery of garment labor and protected by a gentleman.[7] Frequently calling for tea and providing tours of the city in his horse and carriage, Abraham insisted on an extended engagement before finally deciding in 1909 it was time—again—to marry. (According to their son Louis, the couple eloped and married in New Jersey.)[8] Ida was nineteen, Abraham in his late forties (even his children never knew his age), as culturally intellectual as Ida was unsophisticated. Recalled a later Herrmann friend, Joan Greenwood:* "Benny always said his mother was a peasant and his father a gentleman."[9]

Ida and Abraham had at least one thing in common: high blood pressure, which their children would inherit. The Herrmann home was rarely calm; Abraham deliberately initiated fights with Ida as an excuse to escape to the Lower East Side and the Café Royal, where Jewish intellectuals could play cards and talk politics.[10] According to Louis, Abraham once brought home a bust of Athena, "goddess of peace," to bring calm to the household.[11] Perhaps it was a joke on Abraham's part. Athena was goddess of war.

The Herrmanns' first home was a spacious brownstone at Second Avenue and 18th Street on New York's East Side, furnished with heavy European furniture and filled with oil paintings, bronze busts, and bookcases. It was a household of clashing extremes; an illiterate mother, insecure about money (despite Abraham's full-time employment), and a well-read

---

*Not the actress.

father who rarely saved his earnings; an Orthodox Jewish mother in perpetual argument with a father who would not tolerate religious discussion.
Outside their community hostility toward Jews remained, in a city whose
police commissioner declared that half its criminals were Jewish.[12]

New York was not the only site of flux. The second decade of the twentieth century was a period of international change, socially, technologi-
cally, and artistically. By 1911 Russia was on the brink of revolution; in
three years the world would be at war. New movements stirred by the industrial revolution swept through business; Einstein and Planck were rewriting classical physics; and in Vienna, Sigmund Freud and Carl Jung offered shocking reappraisals of man's psychological needs and denials.

1911 was also a hallmark year for European concert music. On January
26 the first performance of Strauss's *Der Rosenkavalier* took place in Dres-
den, followed on April 3 by the premiere of Sibelius's Fourth Symphony
in Helsingfors, on May 24 by the first performance of Elgar's Second
Symphony in London, on June 13 by the premiere of Stravinsky's ballet
*Petrouchka* in Paris, and on November 10 by the premiere of Mahler's *Das
Lied von der Erde* in Munich. Music was at a crossroad as Stravinsky,
Schoenberg, Webern, Scriabin, and other modernists challenged the traditionalism of Elgar, Strauss, and Mahler, as well as the more progressive
school of impressionism led by Debussy and Ravel. As Charles Ives, a full-
time insurance salesman and part-time composer, sat in his Connecticut
study writing music not to be heard for decades, the music world mourned
the death of Gustav Mahler at age fifty, his collapse apparently abetted by
New York's artistic politics. It was a fact not lost in later years on 1911's
most distinguished addition to composition, born that June 29 in New
York's Lying In Hospital.

Benny Herrmann—as he was almost immediately known—was the
first of Abraham and Ida's three children. To his mother he was a breathing doll, a plaything to pamper and spoil with attention. His prematurity
was a source of great maternal worry; Ida even wrapped the precious child
in cotton.[13] Pulling and curling his dark hair and rubbing his tiny feet, she
filled the hot afternoon hours with her most precious toy. Another, more
handsome son was born on April 14, 1913—Louis, the practical, athletic
child; and on October 15, 1914, a daughter, Rose, who grew up with a
marked resemblance to Benny. A fourth child died stillborn.[14]

There was no question which of the three children was the favorite. For
the next sixty-four years Ida Herrmann treated her son Bernard with the
constant, excessive nurturing a mother awards a newborn child. Despite

the endless arguments, their relationship was totally supportive. As Freud observed, "A man who has been the indisputable favorite of his mother keeps for life the feeling of a conqueror, that confidence of success that often induces real success."[15] Whether or not Ida was the catalyst, confidence was part of Bernard Herrmann's psychology even before adolescence.

The major trauma of Benny's early years was a battle with St. Vitus's Dance at age five, which he barely survived.[16] This aside, Bernard Herrmann's childhood memories would be a romantic (and no doubt romanticized) collage of carriage rides through New York; of Abraham listening to their extensive gramophone collection as Ida cooked; of young Willy Herrmann appearing at their door and introducing himself as Abraham's son (and receiving a meal from Ida before leaving).[17] Herrmann also remembered literature—especially that evoking the bustling, foggy London of Dickens and Conan Doyle. And he remembered music.

Benny's early passion for the arts was actively encouraged—perhaps initiated—by his extraordinary father, who championed art, literature, and music with a zeal that amazed both friends and family. Recalled Louis Herrmann:

My father was always insistent that we be aware of the adventures that lie before us and that art could fulfill our lives to a larger degree than life itself. We were taken to operas and museums at a very early age—perhaps too early, but who can say? We did not grow up in a permissive attitude. We understood that discipline and obedience were part of the ritual of growing up. We were given the freedom of speaking our minds within the framework of obedience.

My father was basically an agnostic. He gave us no religious training at all. My mother came from a pious but not a particularly learned family. She was very much dismayed by his antagonism to her tradition and her training, but as she had neither the strength nor the ability to cope with my father's dynamism, we grew up basically cultural illiterates as far as religion was concerned. . . . We were not bar mitzvahed, nor did we belong to any organized temple.

My father [so believed] in the necessity to draw from the arts . . . that by the time we were five or six we were already involved in musical activities. Bernard was given the violin, I was given a cello, and my sister, who was probably no more than four, already knew there was a piano in the house. . . . Practice became the rule of the day; an hour or two a day on our instruments was the minimum required. I personally became an avid clock watcher and always heaved a sigh of relief when practice was over. This was not true of Bernard. He took violin lessons to the age of twelve or thirteen, and while he may not have been the world's worst violinist he certainly could have ranked in the lowest strata. He needed a larger field to work with and shifted to the piano. By the time he was about eleven he had already composed an opera, and I was amazed that my brother, only two years older than I, could not only read at such an avid rate but could write music almost as quickly.

Bernard indicated at an early age that he was beyond the capacities of his early teachers. I recall the first teacher we ever had; he charged perhaps fifty cents a lesson, or less. By age ten my brother had already established a very strong recognition in the neighborhood. In those days almost all the barbers were Italians, and while they may have been caricaturized as opera-loving and excitable, they were exceptionally knowledgable; to them, music was another way of life. When my brother entered the barber shop he was hailed as "the young Toscanini." He and the barbers would have animated conversations about Verdi versus Wagner, with the barbers rattling off in a crescendo of voices the operas by Verdi and the Italian school and my brother counterpointing that any one Wagner was worth five "oompa-pahs."

Since we were born at the beginning of the twentieth century, our schoolteachers were all products of the nineteenth century; most were born around 1870, 1880. The result is that we were nineteenth-century people. And if you're a nineteenth-century person, where does your root of art take hold but with nineteenth-century people? This was the root of Bernard's Anglophilia—his love of English poets, English music. We were privileged perhaps in having neither radio nor television; an incentive to read was fulfilling one's imagination. My father bought entire sets of authors; we read Dumas, Zangwill, Tolstoy, de Maupassant, Twain, Balzac, Molière, Ibsen, Dickens. Books were lined from floor to ceiling, and they were read.

In his early grades Bernard was a very good student, because he had a voracious appetite for reading and a remarkable ability to write. His papers were always marked with comments such as "My, what imagination." In my brother's early days at junior high school [the East Side's Public Schools 40 and 50], in the seventh or eighth grade, my father received several communications from the principal, Mr. Franklin, commending my brother and my father on the remarkable ability of Bernard but ruefully indicating that perhaps the mathematics class under Mrs. Lux was not the place to write music. Mrs. Lux was a woman who understood that she had a remarkable student who should be nurtured.[18]

Hampering Benny's school years was his social awkwardness with other children. His scholarly demeanor typed him early as a bespectacled, uncoordinated bookworm. Their taunting abuse left deep scars, shaping Herrmann's artistic empathy with the outcast and strange that would serve him well in later dramatic scores. One group of young toughs particularly enjoyed threatening young Herrmann. Typically, Benny fought back, hiring with his own pocket money an even tougher schoolboy to serve as his protector. One day, when the gang began their usual attack, Benny's bodyguard and his friends seized the tormentors and warned them never to touch Herrmann again. They obeyed.[19]

If Herrmann's memory is to be trusted, some early teachers were almost as brutal. In a 1948 letter to his first wife, Herrmann bitterly recalled an early music lesson, giving a striking glimpse into his perception of his school days:

N.Y. School of Music was the place where when I showed the first songs I ever wrote—they were laughed at and torn up by the bastard that ran the place, Dr. Hearn. There they made fun of my interest in music. And brought in other children—to show me what real talent was. There they showed me what real pupils in harmony did—and there the sour German teacher of the violin hit me with the violin bow—because I would not play the piece of garbage he gave me to learn—it was called "When Knighthood Was in Flower" by Gustave Lange. I ask[ed] to be allowed to play the selections from the "Freuchutz" [Weber's *Der Freischütz*]. How he laughed at me and hit me with his violin bow—but I would not play that lousy piece—and wanted only the Weber piece. He then slapped me hard—and I took my violin and broke [it] square over his head—and ran [out] of the building never to return again. . . .

The songs I showed—and felt so proud of—were settings of Heine—I shall never forget or forgive the laughter and the derision that they were received in. I suppose my hatred of the place—is still there—waiting to be revenged.[20]

Benny's main refuge from harassment was the New York Public Library on 23d Street, a universe of literature that he explored inexhaustibly, complementing the literary scholarship his father expected with an amazing retention of historical detail and quotations. (Even during the summer, when the Herrmanns stayed at a rented bungalow in Rockaway, Long Island, Benny—whose skin and temperament were ill suited to the beach—retreated to the local library. Louis, already a handsome ladies' man, often served as a beach lifeguard.)[21]

Instinctively Herrmann was drawn to authors whose vision was essentially tragic, highly individual, and contemptuous of contemporary mores. For him, "D. H. Lawrence was a man who followed his own personal vision. . . . The last really first-rate writer the world has had. Before him was Hardy, one of the last great titans of English literature. . . . O'Neill was the last distinguished first-class dramatist. . . . You don't have to agree with him, but [his work] was something he felt deeply and wanted to talk about."[22] Herrmann also loved the writings of the iconoclastic artist James McNeill Whistler—especially his collection of essays *The Gentle Art of Making Enemies*.

Benny also studied the moderns. His lifelong fascination with psychology (particularly deviant behavior) took root in Freud. It was Freud who associated anxiety with fear of loss of love, a pivotal theme in Herrmann's best music.[23]

Herrmann's creative disposition was drawn to the brooding poetry of the English Romantics and the socialistic lessons of Dostoyevski, Dickens, and Hardy. One of Herrmann's favorite novels was Hardy's *Jude the Obscure*, a deeply pessimistic study of late-nineteenth-century English society. "I always remember the opening of that book," Herrmann said in 1954, "about little Jude being a young boy: after a rain he goes out onto a road full of puddles, and outside these puddles are worms struggling to get back into the water. Jude hops from rock to rock not to step on them. Hardy says a person of that sensitivity is going to have a very hard and wretched life."[24] That passage, as Herrmann must have realized, was as much a reflection on its admirer as on young Jude. Observed Louis Herrmann, "The poignancy of life was made evident to him very early. He felt the hurts and anguish of life very strongly. You could not value friendships too highly because sometimes they were used for other purposes. As a result he had a tendency to view people slightly from a distance, very cautiously. . . . He was very demanding of other people being able to fill his sense of perfection."[25]

Herrmann also absorbed himself in biographies of artists and composers, learning musical works through the precious 78 rpm recordings Abraham collected and the New York Philharmonic concerts at Carnegie Hall on 57th Street. In 1924, at age thirteen, Benny's literary excavations led him to the *Treatise on Orchestration* by Hector Berlioz, whose work Herrmann knew through the Weingartner recording of the *Symphonie Fantastique*. The *Treatise* became Benny's secret Koran—the book, he later claimed, that convinced him to become a composer.[26] (A CBS press release of the mid-thirties cites a Philharmonic performance of Beethoven's Seventh Symphony as the key factor in Herrmann's career choice. Herrmann's version seems more likely.)[27] Herrmann could not have found a better introduction to the world of orchestration and programmatic music, the areas in which he would excel. Berlioz was, in many ways, his nineteenth-century counterpart—explosive, intuitive, musically and personally adventurous. His work and ideology would be major influences on Herrmann for the rest of his life.

Benny's formal training as a composer reportedly came at the persuasion of a young, nonmusical teacher at P.S. 40, probably the Mrs. Lux recalled by Louis Herrmann. The teacher (whom Herrmann would remember in schoolboy amazement as the first Indian he had ever seen) was so struck by the intensity of Benny's passion for music that she wrote Abraham a letter, urging him to encourage his son's gift. When asked by his father what career he wished to pursue, young Herrmann replied emphatically: "A composer." "You'd better become a good one," Abraham replied.[28]

The next week found Benny, his supportive teacher, and his proud father in a Russian tea room discussing Benny's future. As the teacher stressed the importance of Herrmann's musical education, Father assured her—with a pat on the knee—that he would continue his support of the boy.[29]

While at P.S. 40, both Benny and Louis performed in the school orchestra (as violinist and cellist, respectively) under the leadership of its music teacher, Mrs. Fischer. It was Fischer who invited Benny to give a school lecture on Beethoven—Herrmann's first public speech.[30] Despite the unattractive timbre of his nasal, often high-pitched voice, Herrmann was throughout his life an articulate and compelling speaker. Judging from the pride he took in later speaking engagements in London, New York, and Los Angeles—as well as his frequent monopolization of social occasions—it was an exercise he greatly enjoyed.

In Herrmann's sixteen years the world had changed drastically. Europe had been reorganized, a development that would have great repercussions on the arts, and electronic media had assumed a preeminent place in American society. Radio was about to become a vibrant commercial enterprise. Recording technology was rapidly improving, especially in the record studios of Europe; and motion pictures had been transformed from ten-minute "flickers" to feature-length talking cinema.

In the fall of 1927, Herrmann began his studies at DeWitt Clinton High School, first located at 59th Street and Tenth Avenue on New York's West Side, then after 1928 in the countryside of Mosholu Parkway in the Bronx. DeWitt was in many respects an exceptional high school: it boasted a sixty-piece student orchestra and offered regular productions of operas and plays. (Among Herrmann's DeWitt contemporaries was a young swimming champion, Burton "Burt" Lancaster, whose film directorial debut, *The Kentuckian*, Herrmann would score twenty-five years later.)[31] Again Herrmann found a sympathetic mentor: music department head Harry A. Jennison. To his students, "Pop" Jennison was "a god," Louis recalled: "In the manner of the old schoolteacher we read about now but rarely see, he directed people into paths that served them well for the rest of their lives."[32]

DeWitt's solemn motto—"Men may come and go, but I go on forever"—was especially apt for Benny: his lackadaisical attitude toward school, despite his zest for knowledge, suggested that he might never graduate. Grades in such subjects as history, English, and fine arts—areas in which he would excel throughout his life—were usually C's, occasionally B's. In chemistry, hygiene, drawing, and math, his grades were usually D's. In January 1928, during Herrmann's second year at DeWitt, the principal noted Benny's work as "poor"; by June it had fallen to "unsatisfactory."[33]

Yet Herrmann was not entirely alone. Among the bullies and conformists in his German class Benny found a similarly irreverent youth who shared his passion for music. In 1927 Jerome Moross was fourteen years old, but like Herrmann he had ambitions to be a composer:

I always sat in the back of the class so the teacher wouldn't disturb me while I composed. One day I looked up and saw a boy sitting across the aisle twirling his hair and studying the Mahler Fifth Symphony in a miniature score. He looked at me and said, "D'ya know Mahler?" I said, "Mahler stinks."

He got quite angry, grabbed what I was writing, tossed it back, and said, "Dishwater Tchaikovsky." We started to argue, because I felt he hadn't even looked at it. Suddenly the teacher was calling both of us up and said, "Get out!" She threw us out into the hall. I said to Benny, "There, you got us thrown out of class. We don't even know what the homework is." Benny said, "Forget it. Wanna go to a rehearsal of the Philharmonic?" I asked him how we could. He said, "I know where there's a broken door." I said sure.

From DeWitt we walked the few blocks to Carnegie Hall. We went in the entrance to the studios on the side, climbed up to the dress circle, walked down a hall, and there was the broken door; somehow Benny knew about it. We got on our hands and knees and crawled in. I knew if they saw us they'd throw us out. We peeked over the balustrade, and there was Mengelberg conducting. We watched Mengelberg conduct for the next hour and a half, and Benny and I became friends.[34]

Among the conductors Herrmann and Moross watched from the secret post was the flamboyant Leopold Stokowski, whose conductorship of the Philadelphia Orchestra was Benny's ideal of a musical marriage. There were also Koussevitsky, Furtwängler, and Arturo Toscanini, whose violent rows Herrmann admired more than his music-making—and which he later emulated. On one occasion recalled by Herrmann, the two concert infiltrators were discovered by an angry manager who ordered them to get out. "But I have the score!" Herrmann pleaded. The decision was ultimately the visiting conductor's. Herrmann and Moross were allowed to stay.[35]

The boys also made music on their own. "Benny discovered I was a very good sight reader on the piano, so we began to dig up four-hand music. We played an endless amount of it, and an endless amount of piano/violin music. With Louis on the cello we formed a trio, and even got ourselves a few jobs. That went on for the next few years. Every night we'd take the subway and go to concerts. My life and Benny's were very intimately connected.[36]

Young Herrmann was not just listening to music; he was writing it. From his earliest pencil scribbles, Herrmann's subjects were programmatic and highly theatrical. Among his first pieces was a setting of Paul Verlaine's poem "The Bells," written, Herrmann later claimed, in 1924 (the earliest existing score is dated 1927).[37] It was probably his first musical success, winning a money prize (usually reported as $100)[38] in a De-Witt song competition. (Another Herrmann Opus 1, no. 1 exists—appropriately, a turbulent overture to Shakespeare's *The Tempest* entitled "Tempest and Storm—Furies Shrieking!")[39] Other settings followed, most for piano but some ambitiously orchestral—even the first sketches for an opera, *Herod*. Many pieces were written in the fast bursts of creativity on which Herrmann would pride himself. His later setting of Verlaine's "The Dancing Faun," for example, is dated "April 27 '29, Finished from 9 to 12 A.M."[40]

Coinciding with Herrmann's earliest compositions was the start of his most intense boyhood friendship, with a twelve-year-old would-be writer named Abraham Polonsky. Polonsky—later a successful screenwriter and director—had moved with his family from upstate New York to 11th Street near the Herrmanns. "One afternoon I was skating home from school," Polonsky recalled,

when a young man stopped me on the street. He had been waiting for me, watching for me. He asked, "Did you just move in?" I said yes. He said, "My name is Bernard Herrmann. Your name is Polonsky?" I said yes. "Do you like music?" I said, "Of course I like music." "I love it," he replied. "Let's be friends." No one had ever approached me like that in my life, and no one has since. We were never out of each other's houses after that. This went on until we were about seventeen; he was my closest friend and I was his.

We were both very serious about ourselves. I was going to be a poet or a novelist, or both, and for inspiration we would go up on the roof of my house and recite the poems I had written, and he would make up a tune to go with them—not a pop-type song, but a Brahms-type song. I even wrote music under his influence, although I knew nothing about music. He was so overwhelming—he made music so overwhelming—that he made you want to be a composer.

He also gave me good advice about my writing. Knowing my bent towards abstraction he always said, "You must be concrete! Don't write about ideas, write about things!" I knew literature, but Ben knew literature also; he was the most widely read person I've ever met in my life. The only thing he couldn't read was intellectual stuff; he couldn't stand philosophy, math, physics. But he read biographies, autobiographies, and many a writer I'd never heard of. He was a searcher among books as well as music.

He also taught me composers. I first heard Ives with him. I first heard Berg and *Wozzeck* with him. I went to the Met with him—I don't know how he got the tickets, but he did. We went to concerts of the League of Composers. And Benny knew everybody—famous people, almost-famous people, people who wanted to be famous. He could find his way into the most sacred places; he'd say, "C'mon, we're going to so-and-so's house"— and while we were there we would meet seventeen famous people. But Benny was a musical climber, not a social climber.

Benny's father was not an Edwardian gentleman; that's Benny romanticizing, his admiration and devotion. Abraham was a déclassé Yiddish Russian intellectual. He was certainly educated and had read a lot. Benny and I would make monocles at Abraham's optometry shop, then wear them in class at DeWitt and get thrown out. But we loved working those machines.

As for religion, Benny's father was a semi-demi-socialist who didn't believe in shit about God. Ida Herrmann was a real Jewish mother who loved her children. As far as Benny was concerned God was dog spelled backwards.

By a strange coincidence, when Benny's family moved to 12th and Second Avenue some years later, into a fairly large apartment building with an elevator, my future wife lived in the same building. When I told her Benny was my friend she said, "That's the crazy family. They all play musical instruments they can't play—they do it for the father, I think, and as they're playing their dog barks." Abraham would sit with a glass of port wine eating Roquefort cheese—Benny and I would eat most of it—and he would make the kids play, Benny at the violin, Rose at the piano, and Louis at the cello. Well, Rose couldn't play; Louis had no musical sense whatsoever [here Polonsky must be mistaken; as a result of his playing Louis was awarded a music scholarship at age seventeen]; and I can't tell you how lousy Benny was on the violin. It was all not to be believed.

Benny's first girlfriend was my sister Charlotte. I don't know why that didn't go anywhere—perhaps because he was a composer, or because his peculiarities annoyed her. But the gifts he would spoil on her! Always things he couldn't afford. Benny was a collector from the very beginning, and years later, after his first trip to England, he gave me a Hogarth.

After my name appeared on the blacklist in the late 1940s I didn't see Benny; he had just visited me at my house days before that. About twenty-five years later he told a producer he didn't know me. Obviously something had happened, but the Benny Herrmann I knew as a young man was generous, kind, crazy, warm, friendly, and my best friend for many years.[41]

Benny's first composition teacher was probably Gustav Heine, with whom he began studies around 1927. Heine's musicianship was solid but unadventurous. It was the mysterious, exciting collection of library scores and Philharmonic concerts that introduced Herrmann to two of his greatest influences: Ravel and Debussy, the latter of whom Herrmann once called the greatest twentieth-century composer.

Sharing importance with the impressionists were two composers of disparate cultural backgrounds, one an obscure American, Charles Ives, the other England's most revered composer, Edward Elgar. From adolescence to adulthood many of Herrmann's colleagues were perplexed by his passion for the conservative Elgar and his championing of Elgar works unknown in America. It was acceptable to admire Elgar's *Enigma* Variations or the popular overtures—but the symphonic study *Falstaff*?

Yet for Herrmann, the performance of any Elgar was a spiritual experience, an evocation of the vanished Edwardian culture he adored. "To have lived with and studied Elgar's music has been more than a great musical experience," he wrote in 1957. "It has been an enriching of one's whole life, for it brings in its train not only melodies and harmonies that remain permanently in one's memory, but also a great tranquility and solace, and at the same time the joy and excitement of being on a mountain peak. For Elgar's music is, in the end, an affirmation of the miracle of life and never a negation of it. This accomplishment certainly places him with the very greatest of the masters of music."[42]

At the library Herrmann also found the music of a younger English contemporary, Ralph Vaughan Williams.

As a boy I first heard the "London Symphony"—and at that, only the first two movements—at a concert given by Walter Damrosch. Up to that time I had only been to London through the magic of Dickens' prose and the *Adventures of Sherlock Holmes*. But through the evocative power of this music I was there again. At that time the only full score to be had was in the New York Music Library. I spent days absorbing the contents and reading over and over again the program as delineated by Albert Coates. And all I could do was to wait, with the greatest of impatience and longing, for someone to play the Symphony. This happened about two years later. The second impression, and this time of the full work, only deepened my excitement and fervor for this great poetic work, which not only held me with its individual music-making, but also because of its literary and descriptive powers. I resolved then that whenever I was to have a chance, if I ever did, I would conduct this Symphony.[43]

Another British contemporary had great influence on young Herrmann's development as a musician and iconoclast. The career of Sir Thomas Beecham, England's preeminent conductor, combined iconographic window-breaking and thrilling performances of new music—the former characterized by Beecham's diatribes on "glorified Italian bandmasters" like Toscanini[44] and German "humbugs" like Mengelberg;[45] the latter by premieres of Strauss's *Salome* and the little-heard music of Englishman Frederick Delius (whom Herrmann adored). To biographer Charles Reid, the stately, swaggering Beecham was "Hector Berlioz reincarnated and transplanted."[46] To Herrmann he was an ideological hero.

The first public performance of a Herrmann concert work took place at DeWitt: a concert overture for band (in which Herrmann also reportedly played) based on old school songs. Considering the paucity of his source material, it was not an inspiring endeavor, and after one performance at assembly it was not repeated.[47]

Yet in his studies with Heine, Herrmann had acquired the basics of composition, with which his active imagination was eager to experiment. Genuine inspiration would come not from a high school songbook but from the mavericks Herrmann adored and Heine disparaged—none more than a fiercely obscure American composer whose *114 Songs* Benny discovered one day during his routine exploration of the New York Library.

# TWO

Our day of dependence, our long apprenticeship to the learning of other lands, draws to a close. . . . Events, actions arise, that must be sung, that will sing themselves.

*Emerson*

Charles Ives never could hear properly. One ear, he explained, received sounds one semitone higher than the other.[1] The result of this affliction, real or imagined, were sounds that no other American composer heard quite the same.

Ives was born in Danbury, Connecticut, in 1874, the son of a military band conductor who had served in the Civil War. As with Herrmann, that paternal influence was key to Ives's passion for writing music—music both simple in its reliance on traditional American themes and remarkably complex in its anticipation of twentieth-century dissonance. Childlike and visionary, Ives's music bore the unmistakable stamp of the country he loved.

"The music of Charles Ives is a fundamental expression of America, of the transcendental period—of Emerson, Thoreau and Whittier," Bernard Herrmann wrote in 1932:

It is of New England—the New England of granite puritanism seen through a musical mind unique and extraordinary. His music reveals a brooding introspective and profoundly philosophic temperament, tempered by a keen understanding of men and nature. . . .

In 1890 Ives was writing polytonality, which in 1910 Milhaud introduced in popular garb. In 1902 he was producing polyrhythms, atonality and tone clusters which many years later Stravinsky, Schoenberg and Ornstein received credit for originating. Let it be clearly understood that the above composers were not aware of Ives' work, any more than Ives had been aware of their compositions, 30 years ago. . . .

Ives' music is actually far more logical than Schoenberg or Stravinsky's. His music is not built upon a set of mystical incantations, formulated under gaslight in the suburbs of Vienna, or upon a group of artificial, neo-classic rules.* Ives' modernism is the result of his observation of town and country. "The circus parade comes down Main Street—the old hymn tune that sings to those in the churchyard and haunts the church—with the concert at the Stamford camp meeting and the barn dances on a cold February evening." And the early reproducing of these perceptions brought about a highly complex and dissonant musical style.[2]

It was a style few heard during Ives's lifetime: boyhood shyness and hatred of musical politics kept Ives from championing his works' performance. Ridiculed by music instructors and colleagues, Ives became a successful life insurance salesman, a job that allowed him to compose in total artistic freedom. He died at age seventy-nine in 1954.

Ives's isolationist approach to music resulted in works whose originality and breadth of expression should have placed him at the forefront of American composers. But it was not to be—at least not until composer-pianist Henry Cowell founded the magazine *New Music Quarterly* (in October 1927); until a young conductor from St. Petersburg, Nicholas Slonimsky, began performing Ives's works; and until a curious teenager in the 23rd Street library grew a little older. Recalled Herrmann:

The more I looked at [the *114 Songs*] the more bewildered I became. When I took it to my good teacher Gustav Heine, he just threw it on the floor and said, "This man's a madman—you mustn't even look at it." But I decided there were pieces that I understood. One was a lovely little song called "Serenity"; another was called "Cowboy Rutlage," [published as "Charlie Rutlage,"]. In the back of the book was an essay by Ives in which he said that writing songs was like doing your washing in public—it was all right for your neighbors to see it out on the line. At the end of the essay he gave an address, so I wrote him a note. About a month later, I received a parcel full of big orchestral scores. . . . They were the Third Symphony, the Fourth Symphony, the printing of the Concord Massachusetts Sonata, and various kinds of chamber work.[3]

A long-distance friendship had begun; more letters were followed by more parcels. Jerome Moross was also thrilled by the perplexing, near-illegible scores. As a pianist he tackled the challenging *Concord* Sonata: "At first it was impossible for me to play—but then bit by bit I got to the

---

*Herrmann's early disdain for Stravinsky does not characterize his adult years.

point where I could play some of it. We found other things. . . . I remember that a big thing was to play 'Shall We Gather at the River,' Benny on the violin and I at the piano."[4]

Herrmann's discovery of Ives coincided with important changes in America's social and artistic climate. Music making in America had been dominated by European composers and conductors, whose "old world" roots gave them instant standing. A new wave of immigrants would arrive from Europe in the late 1930s, fleeing Hitler's Germany. But in America of the 1920s there was an unprecedented opportunity for American voices to be heard. By 1928 the "jazz age" had reached its narcissistic peak; within months America would face economic disaster. Already a new spirit of social democracy could be felt, a renewed fascination with the kind of traditionalism Ives's music partly characterized. American composers who had relied on European tradition began to draw from their own country's music and literature. A genuinely American school of music was taking shape.

It was also around 1928 that Herrmann made another important friendship, with a sophisticated composer ten years his senior named Aaron Copland. While Copland's music had little influence on Herrmann's own stylistic development, his role in the young composer's life was significant. Copland's erudition and self-confidence were greatly admired by young Herrmann, who quickly proved his own worth by loaning Copland the 114 Songs.[5] Ives gained another important champion, and within months the Copland-associated Cos Cob Press had published several Ives songs.

New York became a center for musical change and experimentalism; new sounds could be heard not only in the works of Copland (whose bold, jazzy piano concerto had its premiere in January 1927), but also in the music of Virgil Thomson (who collaborated in 1928 with Gertrude Stein on the opera Four Saints in Three Acts), Ernest Bloch, Roy Harris, Walter Piston, and George Gershwin, whose Rhapsody in Blue (1924) and Piano Concerto in F (1925) blended popular and symphonic idioms.

As this new music evolved, Herrmann was eagerly assimilating both past and present. A visitor to classes at New York University and Juilliard, he was now observing such music teachers as Bernard Wagenaar and Rubin Goldmark, whose students at NYU had included Copland, Harris, and Piston. (Gershwin also studied privately with Goldmark.) Soon Herrmann had met them all, including the twenty-nine-year-old Gershwin, then completing An American in Paris. Though he never grasped Gershwin's idiom, Herrmann was fascinated by his work and by Gershwin's sardonic personality. That November, Benny attended the new work's rehearsal and performance under conductor Walter Damrosch.

"Of all the conductors I've know in my life, with the possible exception of Stokowski, Damrosch was the most adventurous conductor that America ever had," Herrmann said in 1971.

If you compare the programs of the New York Symphony at the time the New York Philharmonic was carrying on with Toscanini and Mengelberg, one was an old museum and the New York City Symphony was a vital part of new music. Every other Saturday morning he played two works of young composers so they could have a chance to hear it. He played a work of mine; he didn't play it in public, but he read it through.* Damrosch always said to me, "The world is most likely treating you better than you deserve!" But in spite of the fact, he never allowed his own personal taste to stop young composers from having their say.[6]

While Herrmann was spending afternoons with Gershwin and Damrosch he was failing classes at DeWitt.[7] By the fall of 1929 it was apparent he would not graduate the following January as planned. Fortunately, a school administrator named Abraham Kroll took an interest in the exceptional student's dilemma and encouraged Herrmann not only to focus on school but also to take several previously failed classes again during the same semester.[8]

Although still in high school, Herrmann enrolled in New York University's fine arts school, studying composition with Philip James and conducting with Albert Stoessel. The two classes were equally important to Benny: in addition to his composing aspirations Herrmann was now committed to joining the ranks of Stokowski and Beecham as a world-famous conductor. It was an ambition that would give him more frustration than any other.

Born in 1890 and 1894 respectively, James and Stoessel had both studied and practiced composition before distinguishing themselves as bandmasters in World War I. In 1923 they jointly began NYU's music department, which quickly became one of the world's largest. Herrmann's dislike of formal studies continued at NYU, but Stoessel soon became an admirer of Herrmann's enthusiasm for music—if not of his often graceless conducting. Herrmann, for his part, appreciated Stoessel's support but considered his teacher's conducting "lousy."[9] To most teachers at NYU Herrmann was inexcusably abrasive or, in the words of then-professor Martin Bernstein, "downright crude."[10]

---

*The work was probably either "The Dawn" or "Late Autumn," two moody pieces for full orchestra that already showed Herrmann's affinity for expression through orchestral color. In BH collection, UCSB.

In the "black October" of 1929, Wall Street collapsed and the great American Depression began. Economic catastrophe would actually have a regenerative effect on some aspects of American life, as a sense of national community was reestablished under the new president, Franklin Delano Roosevelt (whom Herrmann considered a brilliant leader).[11] And during the Depression's first years, the Herrmann family's good fortune continued: by manufacturing a highly economical pair of glasses for three dollars, Abraham Herrmann was able not only to maintain but to enhance his business.[12]

More fundamentally, the Depression served as a dividing line between two ages for Bernard Herrmann: the nineteenth-century romanticism that he clung to in literature, painting, and other arts; and the increasingly harsh realities of twentieth-century life, with its economic hardship in America. The Depression reinforced for Herrmann the realization that a career in music would be a battle. His tenacity and confrontational nature were not products of the crash of 1929, but they were almost certainly intensified by it and by the events of the years to follow.

Already by 1930 there existed a schism between the public and private Herrmann which would widen in later years. Both sides were guided by strict principles toward art and an ambition to excel; yet while many people saw only Herrmann's abrasiveness and wild enthusiasm, a more guarded poetic sensitivity was struggling for expression. Herrmann's artistic perspective was crystallizing: melancholy and death-obsessed, it reflected the Romantic literary tradition he loved and the gravity of his own time. A handful of moody entries in Herrmann's private diary reveal his fondness for imagery that was poetic, brooding and musical. Many, in fact, seem written companion pieces to his compositions:

4 P.M. Friday   December 19, 1930

A somber autumnal day. The city is covered with a cloak of weariness and bleakness. The wind brings in its trail the smells of the first winter's snow, the city seems prepared to greet it with a melancholy song of despair and desolation. The mist is of a bluish grey color and hangs above the street with a quiet motion; it fills the dark alleys and is a shroud for the dead trees. In its embrace one smells the odor of decay and futility. Late autumn in its bleakest mood.

Christmas Eve   1 A.M.

A white Christmas day casted [sic] a cloak of ermine over the city, and with it came the extasy [sic] of former days when the stage coaches hurried along the country roads and the snow flakes kissed the passengers a tender Christmas cheer. And the past hours sounded their fanfare of brass which is caught by the wind and echoed and reechoed from the hillside and vale.

At the Tavern sparkling tokay, and sweet meats and a huge turkey.

Afterall this the traditional plum pudding.

Th' memories of a bygone age; how you ring to my soul a symphony of humanity and fellow cheer.

Tonight I was carried back a hundred years. Charlotte [Polonsky] read to me A Christmas Carol, of course it was not possible for her to read it in its entirety; but we reached Marley's ghost. During Charlotte's reading I must confess I sometimes did not listen carefully; but I was carried away to a fog ridden London street and the room of old Scrooge; whos [sic] often looking in the lumber room and under the bed and double bolting the doors prepared to take his evening tea when the ghost appears and with it the bridge players who brought me back to the 20th Century. I shall always remember this evening and shall always be grateful to Charlotte for reading to me on Christmas Eve in a dimly lighted room the Christmas Carol.

For through the intonation of her voice she transported me back into age which will never return save through our imagination and Dickens and of course if one is fortunate to a gentle one to read to you. Truly an evening unique in these years when romance and sentiment seem to be gone.

I only hope that I have not waxed over sentimently tonight.—It has stopped snowing. Good night.

Jan. 5, 1931   2 P.M.

A dismal winter day, rain falls and whispers their song to pavements. It reminds me of the slow movement of Vaughan Williams London Symphony.

During the Christmas holidays I have started my chamber symphony for small orchestra and voice [apparently not completed]. The work shall express the weariness and chagrin of one who life has frustrated. . . .

I long for the spring and for lilacs.

Oh: how dreary the world is in its winters mood and how weary I feel. At this moment I would like to hear the last movement of Mahler's "Lied von der Erde."

From now on I have decided that my compositions will be governed by the following idea. "Art should be an adventure into the unknown" (Secret Glory of Arthur Macken).

I wish that the teacher would stop talking, he is irritating me, he is hardly aware of the fact that in his class some one is listening to the dirge of the winter's rain and not to his verbs and personal pronouns. . . .

I would like at this moment to smell the fresh spring lilacs, to smell their delicate perfume, to let them overpower my senses and release my soul on its extatic [sic] flight toward the stars, where the music of the spheres resound forever and ever. Where one shall embrace his desired one and cleanse his soul, in the early fires of spring, to partake in the sun-lit economics of the body and to live amid the orchids of desire and to kiss the pure white body of his beloved. To kiss her feet, her hips to couch her until you become part of her, part of the purity from which all extasy radiates. Oh lilacs—lilacs of pale blue water—how I desire you.[13]

The Depression notwithstanding, concertgoing, composing, and reading still consumed Herrmann's time: once studied, a score or book was as safe in Herrmann's memory as on the 23rd Street bookshelves. In addition to the Public Library, Herrmann frequented the 58th Street Music Library, a popular research site for composers and musicologists that offered not only a large score collection but also an expanding selection of recordings. Another dweller among the books and manuscripts was Morton Gould, a composer-conductor who, although two years Herrmann's junior, already held a staff position at the Radio City Music Hall. In 1930, after attending a series of Gould's concerts at New York University (where Gould had studied with Vincent Jones), Herrmann introduced himself in typical fashion. Recalled Gould:

I was studying inside the 58th Street Library when Benny appeared from out of nowhere behind a stack of bookshelves. He said, "You're Martin Gould, aren't you? I'm also a composer—I'm Benny Herrmann. I heard your concert—I want to get to know you." I said, "Well, fine." I was a little taken aback. He asked me, "Where do you live?" I said, "Long Island." He said, "I'll come out to see you." I had to rush home to get there before he did!

Benny was very frenetic in those days, full of energy. I vaguely remember him standing on the piano and making a speech about his music and his conducting. He brought a piece of his, "Autumn," which he played for us. He also played the violin—not well, as I recall.

After our meeting, Benny tried to get into Vincent Jones's class at NYU; apparently he walked into the classroom and said, "I know Morton Gould and I want to get into your class." He didn't qualify; they told him he would have to study some more fundamental music forms. But Benny was always boastful. He once said proudly, "My friends tell me I do things that even Toscanini doesn't do!"—to which someone sarcastically replied, "Yeah, I bet!" In those days I don't think he was a very good conductor; subsequently he grew. But Herrmann was very positive about whatever he was doing. He was a strange mix of great talents and short-comings, through which he functioned.

After a short time I had to go out and support my family, and Benny and I lost touch. Many, many years later I saw him in Hollywood, sitting at a café-like setting, and said, "Benny! How are you?" His first words were, "Why do you think . . . " as he immediately picked up whatever musical argument we were having fifteen years before.[14]

Already by 1929, in such early compositions as *Late Autumn, The Forest: A Tone Poem for Large Orchestra,* "Pastoral (Twilight)," and "Requiescat" (after Oscar Wilde),[15] Herrmann was displaying trademarks that would characterize his work: extreme sensitivity to orchestral color (especially the low-register colors of strings and winds); an often static progression of whole- and half-notes to create a brooding, dramatic atmosphere; and a fondness for chromatic patterns, rising and falling without resolution—an unsettling device that Herrmann made his own in virtually every composition. Through orchestral color and a carefully defined harmonic language his music already conveyed individuality, poignance, and psychological resonance.

His style changed little over the years. The early concert works would climax with a handful of large-scale pieces: the cantata *Moby Dick,* his symphony, and the four-act opera *Wuthering Heights.* But most of Herrmann's music would be in smaller forms—radio scores and film and television music. All shared one thing in common: an origin in drama. Herrmann's greatest gift lay in finding dramatic tension in the simplest of devices, the subtle interrelationship of color and rhythm.

His music was also at its best in a supportive yet integral role. While in his teens Herrmann was already fascinated by the idiom of "melo-dram," the integration of music and live drama from ancient Greece that found its modern counterpart in opera, radio, and film—the media to which Herrmann would turn.[16]

In the fall of 1930 Albert Stoessel left NYU to become head of the Juilliard School's new opera and orchestra department and invited Herrmann to continue his studies with him there. A longtime visitor at Juilliard, Herrmann accepted (though he would not graduate from high school until January) and in October began his formal studies there as a fellowship student. Moross joined him the following year: "There was money all over the place there. Since Benny and I were on fellowships, we could have free lunches or free dinners. . . . But we entered after very rigorous examinations; they wanted only talents."[17]

Yet Herrmann's two years at Juilliard were mainly discouraging. Studies with Stoessel and Bernard Wagenaar (his teacher in composition and harmony) were conventional and, to Herrmann's speeding mind, stultifying. ("Bernard had a dim view of teachers," Louis Herrmann recalled. "He felt they were necessary but never creative.")[18] Although his initial grade under Wagenaar was a B, it fell in Herrmann's second year to a D, owing to "too many absences."[19] (Coincidentally, a fellow student in Wagenaar's class was Alex North, later to become one of the few American composers of film music Herrmann openly admired.) Herrmann's interest at Juilliard was gravitating toward its stage and dance departments; he began taking part in ballet and music presentations at the cost of his studies.

At the same time, as the Depression worsened, Abraham Herrmann began to question his son's career choice. Telling him that art, while vital, was rarely lucrative, he persuaded Benny to enroll concurrently at NYU and earn a teaching degree.[20] Out of five classes, Herrmann was soon failing four, including music appreciation. His renewed studies at NYU lasted only the one term.[21]

Despite his lack of money, Benny still dreamed of a successful life as a composer-conductor. He purchased dozens of scores and second hand books. He even frequented a Rolls Royce showroom on the West Side, pretending to be a prospective client (he finally purchased a Bentley-Rolls in 1971).[22]

In January 1931, conductor Nicholas Slonimsky premiered Ives's *Three Places in New England* at the increasingly influential New School for Social Research on West 12th Street. It was the first Ives work Herrmann had heard in concert. Also on the program was another stunning exercise in avant-garde, Edgard Varèse's *Ionization* for large percussion orchestra and ambulance siren. Herrmann later claimed to have performed in the Varèse (a possibility, considering the enormity of the percussion requirements), but his role in the performance is sadly undocumented.[23]

As the Slonimsky concert demonstrated, American composers were finding strength in numbers. The movement's figurehead was the articulate and successful Aaron Copland, who with Henry Cowell had arranged several concerts of contemporary music at the New School. By the summer of 1931 a group of young composers had gathered under Copland's influence, united by a shared passion for modern music and a largely New York Jewish heritage. Modeled after the "French Six" and the "Russian Five" (about whom Herrmann later wrote in a *New Music* article),[24] the

Young Composers Group—as it became officially known in 1932—began meeting at Copland's Manhattan apartment to plan concerts of its members' works and to establish a sense of artistic community at a time when jobs and musical funding were scarce.

The Group was only partly successful. Besides "charter members" Herrmann and Moross, it boasted several other of New York's most promising—and most opinionated—composers: Elie Siegmeister, Henry Brandt, Irwin Heilner, Israel Citkowitz, Lehman Engel, Vivian Fine, and critic Arthur Berger. Agreement among them was rare. Despite Copland's stabilizing presence, Berger recalled, "the sessions became so stormy that even his powers of assuagement were taxed, and on one occasion a card inviting us to a meeting warned us succinctly, 'No polemics.' But when Copland was away, complete disunity was likely to set in among the ranks."[25]

Still, the group was a valuable forum for presentation of its members' music, thanks to Copland's reputation and connections. One visitor to the sessions was Carlos Chávez, whose piano sonatas Copland had performed for the group at an early meeting. After dinner with Chávez at a New York automat, the composers returned to Copland's apartment to perform one original work each for Chávez, who sat through every piece in chilly silence.

The next morning, Heilner eagerly phoned Copland. What, he asked, did Chávez have to say?

"Nothing," Copland replied.

"Nothing all evening?"

Copland thought a moment, then corrected himself. "He said the soup was good."[26]

Elie Siegmeister, who had just returned from studies in Paris with the feisty Nadia Boulanger (who taught Copland, Thomson, and Piston, among others), found Benny Herrmann's contempt for "the old witch" and the entire French school of tutelage uniquely refreshing:

Benny and Jerry represented a brash young American voice to me just back from Paris, and strengthened my interest in exploring our common American roots. Sharply etched in my mind is Benny's "tough guy" talk, his total lack of inhibition in criticizing all and sundry in loud, emphatic yells and yawps—especially the perennial poseurs and phonies endemic to musical groups everywhere.

There were few composers or conductors who escaped Benny's raspy, sardonic, New York–accented abuse. His mocking diatribes against the "Frenchy Frenchy" "tiddlewinks" music confirmed my own feelings and helped me throw off the yoke of preciosity and "uppity" elegance that Boulanger still held over me. Benny helped me get over this illness.

Another debt I owe to Benny and Jerry was their introducing me to the great master, Ives. One night they came over to my house in Brooklyn with a volume of the *114 Songs*. Jerry played quite a few of them, possibly Benny chanted some of the vocal lines (if such vocal paroxysms can be called chanting), and I was immediately hooked—a condition from which I have fortunately never recovered.

There was always lots of talk about Ives, also some about Ruggles, Riegger, Varèse, and other "ultramoderns," as daring composers were called in those days. Strangely enough, it was more Benny's talk than his actual music that had this rough-and-tumble American character; Jerry's was more jazzy and full of a down-to-earth quality. But whenever I got near Benny there were fireworks shooting off.[27]

In the spring of 1932, Herrmann's and Moross's Juilliard studies ended. The circumstances remain unclear. Moross later claimed they were "tossed out" because Stoessel and others disliked their modern compositions;[28] Herrmann cited Juilliard's conservatism as his reason for leaving, adding that he should have left after his first year;[29] while Louis Herrmann said Herrmann had simply completed his fellowship studies there.[30] (The Juilliard record tersely reads; "Dropped May 1932.")

Before leaving, Herrmann co-conducted (with student Charles Lichter) a concert on February 13 with Juilliard's Chamber Symphony Orchestra, which featured the premiere of a perverse little work that Moross proudly titled "Paeans."[31] Herrmann's Juilliard days had also included the performance of Herrmann's miniballet "Congo Rhapsody," about which a Juilliard paper noted: "Using the limited resources of a dance orchestra, Mr. Herrman [*sic*] laid on the colors of the jungle with fine freedom and zest . . . esprit juiced out of it, set flying the body of Blanche Evan who provided the stirring choreography."[32]

1932 was also the year of the Yaddo Festival, a Copland-planned weekend of modern music held in May at the Yaddo resort in Saratoga Springs. Well publicized and respectably attended, the festival became a cause célèbre for musicians outside the group as well, including a young pianist-composer named Oscar Levant.

"At this gathering were two remarkably unpleasant young men, truly possessed of a talent for inimacability—Jerome Moross and Bernard Herrmann," Levant wrote in 1940. "They were present to cast evil spells and mutter curses on everything that was heard at Yaddo, possibly because no works of theirs had been included. They were particularly contemptuous, in a frank and rather charming way, of me; as they interpreted the presence of my sonatina on the program as a cheap Copland trick to leaven the festival with 'Broadway.' " Professional malcontents like Levant, Herrmann, and Moross were destined to become friends, and the result, Levant recalled, was "a little group . . . whose leitmotiv was bad manners."[33]

The Levant-Herrmann friendship also led to one of Herrmann's most important professional relationships. In January, Levant had attended the premiere of *Nightclub: Six Impressions for Three Pianos and Orchestra* by Johnny Green, a twenty-three-year-old Harvard economics graduate turned composer-conductor. Levant and Green found that they shared not only the same publisher (Famous, a New York company managed by Max Dreyfuss) but also an irreverence for the establishment. It was only a matter of time before Herrmann joined this cabal.

"I was at Famous one day in 1932," Green recalled, "when in walked Levant and Herrmann. Oscar had a cigarette hanging out of his mouth, and Benny was wearing a camel's hair coat—which he never took off indoors—and pulling his hair. Oscar asked me to play part of *Nightclub* in one of the publisher's rooms; he thought the four-note timpani ostinato in the fourth movement was terrific. 'Wait till you hear this, Benny,' Oscar said. 'A lot of it I didn't like, but this is *great*.' I played the pattern and the solo piano theme, in octaves à la Prokofiev, and Benny said, 'Nahhh! You shouldn't-a done that! For God's sake.' And he tore it apart. Well, I hated him then—but I loved his honesty, and I loved his perceptiveness."[34]

It was a meeting both would remember.

Another favorite visiting spot for Herrmann and Moross was Dreyfuss's music company Harms, where the young composers met orchestrator-composer Robert Russell Bennett; Vladmir Dukelsky, composer of "April in Paris" and other songs; and others. As Moross observed, "Tin Pan Alley had died and moved to Harms on 45th Street."[35] Although Harms did not publish any of his compositions, Herrmann found some work there as a music editor and arranger for publisher Edwin Kalmus and others. While Herrmann admired some of the musicians at Harms, especially Dukelsky and composer Vincent Youmans, he disdained their "thirdhand" approach to composing, with its reliance on orchestrators and arrangers: "None of them would have been possible without a few talented people who turned it into music."[36]

Herrmann's championing of American music reached its political zenith that July, as Young Composers Moross, Brandt, Fine, and Engel joined him at an artists retreat at Camp Tamiment, Pennsylvania, whose purpose was to attract press attention to the American nationalist cause. Without Copland they were only marginally successful. Herrmann adopted the role of spokesman through both eloquence and decibel level: "The young composer interested in music other than jazz can't get a hearing today," he was quoted as saying (though Herrmann's copy of the article bears the notation "Very inaccurate report of my remarks"). "The reason they haven't a chance is because the conservatories are too conservative and because our great orchestras have European conductors. . . . [They] don't understand American music and, furthermore, they are not interested in it. . . . We are going to stick by the standard set by Charles Ives, Aaron Copland, George Antheil and Henry Cowell."

Inevitably, Ives was the focus of Herrmann's hyperkinetic enthusiasm: "By Golly, Mr. Ives puts cowboy themes and hillbilly songs and camp-meeting hymns into his symphonies. Those are the tunes of our country and we love them. Mr. Ives writes about everything from Nelly, the Poor Working Girl, to the How and Why of Life. One of his sonatas is called 'Concord, Mass.' Now if that isn't American, what is? . . . We know that Mr. Ives belongs among the immortals and some day all the rest of America will know it. America will know it when it can appreciate the meaning of a new American tone, a new dissonance. His music is our music. It is not European."[37]

Despite the disappointment of Juilliard, Herrmann's academic studies were not quite over. In the fall of 1932 he returned a last time to New York University (unofficially) to attend a biweekly lecture course in advanced composition and orchestration. It was the most important of Herrmann's formal studies, largely because of its brilliant, wildly unorthodox instructor.

Percy Grainger was Australia's most innovative advocate of music past and present, from his childhood days as the "flaxen-haired phenomenon" of Melbourne[38] to his years of international fame as folk song collector, composer, and recitalist. At the heart of Grainger's unstable, erratic character was a fixation on truth, a contempt for tradition, and a passion for the outrageous.

Since becoming head of NYU's music department in 1931 Grainger had offered a syllabus of musical eccentricity and frequent brilliance that left many students puzzled and unimpressed. The class of 1932, however, included an important exception. In Grainger, Herrmann saw the qualities he himself was cultivating: individualism and dedication to one's craft and beliefs, however unpopular and unfashionable.

The relationship between the fifty-year-old teacher and the twenty-one-year-old student was one of mutual respect. "Grainger did not place orchestration examples before [his students]," Grainger biographer John Bird wrote; "instead, he allowed them to choose their own pieces and gave them advice where and when needed. Herrmann, for instance, decided to orchestrate MacDowell's 'Celtic' Sonata and felt the need to employ the sonorities of a tenor tuba. The Australian knew little of this unusual piece of plumbing, so, together, they familiarized themselves with the instrument and found suitable moments to include it."[39]

Herrmann and Grainger also discovered a shared love of Whitman and of the music of Delius. One of Herrmann's favorite NYU memories peripherally involved the latter: one morning the gaunt, sprightly Grainger lept onto the lecture stage and announced, "The three greatest composers who ever lived are Bach, Delius and Duke Ellington. Unfortunately Bach is dead, Delius is very ill—but we are happy to have with us today the Duke!" Ellington and his band then mounted the stage and played for the next two hours.[40]

If other Grainger lectures were less dramatic, they were no less influential to Herrmann: ancient monophony, folk music, atonality, polyphony, the indigenous rhythms of Africa, Asia, and the South Seas—each was examined by Grainger with alternating lucidity and jumbled mysticism. When the scholastic year ended in mid-August 1933, Grainger considered his work a failure, as few students had been as responsive as Herrmann;[41] but it cemented a friendship between him and his intense young pupil that affected Herrmann the rest of his life.

Climaxing a turbulent year was Herrmann's professional conducting debut in October. Herrmann's association with dance groups at Juilliard led to his involvement with Charles Weidman and Doris Humphrey, whose ensemble was to appear in the Shuberts' Broadway revue *Americana* that fall. Impressed with Herrmann's work at Juilliard, Weidman asked him to adapt for the program the nineteenth-century music of the Shakers, a religious group that believed in rigid separation of the sexes.[42] Herrmann also wrote original music for the dance number "Amour à la Militaire," performed by Weidman, Cleo Atheneos, José Limon, and Sylvia Manning.

Amid now-forgotten numbers in the revue like "Dividend to You" and "Pooh-Pooh-Pourri" was one song that became a standard: Jay Garney's "Brother, Can You Spare a Dime?" Garney also conducted most of the revue from the Shubert Theater orchestra pit, but he felt uncertain about the more formally academic dance music Herrmann had written. Thus, somewhat by default, Herrmann made his conducting debut, conducting his "Americana" music for the next month and half. (Since the Shuberts had already hired a conductor, Herrmann was contractually listed as a celeste player to receive his conducting fees—$90 a week.)[43] A favorite Herrmann anecdote was that teacher Stoessel, after telling Herrmann he would never be a professional conductor, happened to be in the audience one night and saw his "failed" pupil conducting his own music in the pit.[44]

At about the same time, Herrmann made his last (and perhaps first) appearances as a violinist, performing once or twice as a pit musician at Second Avenue's Yiddish Music Theater.[45] His love for the Jewish theater idiom would reappear thirty-five years later, in his only musical comedy, *The King of Schnorrers*, based on Israel Zangwill's novel, a favorite of the young Herrmann.

By the end of 1932, in the absence of Copland who was traveling through Mexico, Elie Siegmeister and Irwin Heilner were chosen to organize the Young Composers Group's first official concert, "probably because [Irwin and I] could each raise about fifty dollars or so," Siegmeister recalled.[46] They were also the Group's most diplomatic members. As Siegmeister wrote Copland that December:

The best thing about our bunch is nobody likes anybody else's music. Exceptions are me and Irwin—I like *both* his and my stuff and he says he thinks we're both terrible. We've decided the best thing for the success of the concert is to have the group meet as rarely as possible. It always ends up in a fight or in somebody singing songs they heard in a Harlem speakeasy. . . . Two weeks ago the gang got together and Benny showed quite remarkable talents as a "diseuse"—giving Ruth Draper character sketches of the modern composers, from Sibelius through Roger Sessions down to Vivian Fine and Jerome Moross. Then we had a lot of fun going through those songs in the Ives 114 which he marks, "Though there is no danger of it, I hope these songs will not be sung—at least not in public."[47]

Eventually, Siegmeister later noted, "after much debate, scrounging around for performers—all of whom worked gratis—the great night (January 15, 1933) came and we were all introduced to the New York music scene, to the stormy applause of our relations and friends who filled the hall."[48] Their applause was not entirely isolated. The concert was reviewed by most New York arts papers, including Harold Ross's influential *New Yorker*, whose comments on the "Bush League of Composers" were conservatively dour ("There wasn't much played or sung that will resound far beyond 12th Street").[49] Most reviews, however, were marginally encouraging. Typical was the *Musical Leader:* "Eight young composers, banded together for better or worse, gave a first concert on Sunday evening. Much of the music offered . . . shows distinct talent. Time must prove whether their neo-classic tendencies, atonal harmonizations, and definite attempt to eschew any display of personal emotion will form a school, or whether they are merely affectations of an unpleasant phase of life through which we are passing."[50]

Herrmann's string quartet, written during his Juilliard studies but more reflective in its fragmentary lyricism of the impressionist school, received scant mention, two exceptions being the *New York Herald Tribune* ("Mr. Hermann's [sic] quartet dealt atonally and not maladroitly with a sustained, dominating theme and a more energetic subsidiary theme")[51] and the *Musical Courier* ("written in the most approved atonal manner, a little tentative as to form, but with moments of moving sincerity").[52] The more accessible songs of Moross, Fine, and Heilner garnered the bulk of critical praise, adding another divisive element to the struggling group. "After the concert, Irwin and I tried to keep the group together, but it was no go," Siegmeister said. "Everyone went off on his own, the inevitable fights and insults polarized each against the other, and that was it."[53]

During his involvement in the Group, Herrmann had not forgotten his equally cherished goal of becoming a major conductor. His practicing method, according to Heilner, was to stand amid an "orchestra" of empty chairs, each representing a different section, and conduct full scores to the imaginary musicians, carefully cuing each part for what must have seemed the most obedient of ensembles.[54]

The New Chamber Orchestra, while less docile, was almost as inexpensive. An ensemble of thirty unemployed musicians assembled by Herrmann and Harms orchestrator Hans Spialek shortly after the Young Composers concert, the New Chamber Orchestra became Herrmann's first major outlet for the performance of his own music. By May 1933 Herrmann had mounted its premiere concert at the New School for Social Research, with the assistance of Grainger, Vladmir Dukelsky (whose name was soon Americanized by Gershwin into Vernon Duke), Robert Russell Bennett, and Metropolitan Opera tenor George Rasley. The programming, however, showed no hand but Herrmann's, offering several unheard American works (including Herrmann's atypically contrapuntal Prelude to "Anathema," Moross's "Ballet," and the Fugue from the Ives Fourth Symphony), as well as Purcell's obscure Overture to *The Gordian Knot Untied* and excerpts from Elgar's *Falstaff* (Herrmann's first performance of the work, one of his favorites). Uniting these Anglo-American works were their programmatic origins, revealing Herrmann's love of the dramatic.

Scheduled for May 10, 1933, the concert was delayed for one week by the death on May 8 of Abraham Herrmann, who had been bedridden for almost a year after suffering a stroke. In his last moments, Abraham is said to have instructed Louis to "take care of Benny. I fear he will never be able to take care of himself."[55] (For the next forty-two years Louis Herrmann remained staunchly protective and supportive of his brother.)

Abraham's loss was painful and financially calamitous: he had left the family in debt, and Louis—now an optometry student—could not yet take over the family business. Bernard's income was almost nonexistent. Rose was trying to become an artist.

It was Ida who took matters in hand. In addition to taking in an eccentric boarder named Mr. Cohen (who stayed for years in the Herrmann home), Mrs. Herrmann opened an eyeglass concession stand at the department store, Hearn's. Life on 12th Street was never dull: recalled a family friend, Sarah Cohn, "Benny would be banging away at the piano, bathrobe draped around him; Rose was painting; Mr. Cohen was wandering around, trying to get somebody to listen to him; and Ida was screaming from the other room. It was like a scene from 'You Can't Take It With You.' "[56]

The postponed concert was the source of a favorite Herrmann story. According to Benny, one lazy critic panned the concert—even though it had not been held. Rather than exposing and exploiting the gaffe, Herrmann kept silent. From then on, he claimed, he received nothing but praise from the chagrined critic.[57]

In fact, the concert was a success when finally held, and a personal triumph for Herrmann. Although Grainger's fiery reading of his Passacaglia on the folk song "Green Bushes" and Bennett's *Charleston Rhapsody* were the acknowledged highlights, Herrmann's conducting was the most consistently praised element of the evening. "The New Chamber Orchestra conducted by Bernard Herrmann is by far the most competent gathering of its kind that I have encountered upon the present plane of musical enterprise," wrote the *Daily Mirror*. "Mr. Herrmann . . . really thinks it necessary to achieve coherence of tone and discipline in attacks and phrasing. The result is a fine orchestral timbre and unity."[58] The *Herald Tribune* was also impressed: "Mr. Herrmann disclosed a genuine gift for conducting. His technique somewhat recalls Klemperer and his whole approach is that of an earnest, dignified musician."[59]

The *New Yorker* also commended Herrmann as a "maestro of more than conventional talents," but was more skeptical of the music offered: "The program notes illuminated Mr. Heilner as 'the avowed disciple of Charles Ives,' Mr. Herrmann as 'typical of the Schoenberg adherent whose unrestrained romanticism, whose avoidance of the recherché, bring him back to the original source,' and Mr. Moross as having 'taken up the art where Edgar Varèse left off.' These three young men have enough ability not to worry about Ives, Schoenberg or Varese; and their music prompted me to look forward to other concerts, in which we encounter Mr. Heilner as the avowed disciple of Irwin Heilner, Mr. Herrmann as typical of Bernhard [*sic*] Herrmann, and Mr. Moross taking up the art wherever Jerome Moross found it."[60]

Herrmann's foray into Schoenbergian atonality, as characterized by his "Anathema" Prelude, was a brief aberration in his composing. As he soon realized, his most personal idiom, established as early as 1929 in somber, impressionistic works like *Autumn,* owed more to Debussy and the harmonic structure of nineteenth-century Romanticism. In his 1933 book *American Composers on American Music,* Henry Cowell (an early Herrmann supporter) described Herrmann as "an experimenter in the direction of making the orchestra into a more satisfying medium of polyphony, in which he is primarily interested as a composition medium. He attempts varied melodic line and long flowing curves of counterpoint."[61] Soon, however, such elements as polyphony and counterpoint dwindled to minimal importance in Herrmann's writing.

Shortly after the May 17 concert, Herrmann received a short note from 63d Street near Park Avenue. It was a luncheon invitation from Charles Ives.

"If I had met Walt Whitman, I imagine he would have been a lot like Charlie," Herrmann recalled:

When he walked into the room you had a feeling that this was a great man, [even if] you didn't know anything about him. . . . He was a man of tremendous electrical qualities; he had no sense of graciousness or politeness about anything—he said exactly what he thought.

I feel that Ives was a man who never listened to much music in his life. He didn't really care about other people's music; all he cared about was the kind of music that he could make. And the kind of music he was interested in making, at the time he was living, was so completely against all concepts of the performance of music that he found himself driven into a corner by himself. So when he did finally agree that I could visit him, I now understand what a great effort he made towards me.

[Ives] lived in an old Victorian brownstone. I'll never forget the whole feeling of coming in the place, because the whole character of Ives was a very magical one; it was like suddenly meeting Wotan. The nearest thing I've ever seen [to him] was El Greco's self-portrait. He had a very nervous way of speaking, very rapid. He got excited very easily, and he used four-letter words about anything. His home was a very lovely, big house, and should have been a well-furnished one—but it was almost like the cell of a hermit. It had very simple furniture, no ornaments, threadworn carpets, and very few books.

The first thing he said was that I shouldn't waste my time trying to find out about his music, because, he said, "it wouldn't do you any good as a composer if anybody should ever hear you are a friend of mine." Of course, until the very last few years of his life this was true.[62]

It was advice Herrmann steadfastly ignored. Their meetings continued until Ives's death in 1954. Rarely did the two discuss Herrmann's work or even other contemporaries. To Ives, music existed "to enrich people and ennoble them," Herrmann said. "It was a universe, and people became more wonderful because of art. This was the great mission of the artist." The two shared their contempt for the "Toscaninnys" who kept concert halls and listeners' ears as conservative as possible. "He lived across the street from the David Mannes School of Music, and there would be some poor girl practicing in the window. 'Look at that poor thing!' he'd say. 'Look at that fella teaching her ladyfingers—sweet sounds, like all the rest!' "[63]

Two more ambitious concerts were presented by Herrmann that winter. On December 3, 1933, Herrmann conducted the New Chamber Orchestra with Harriet Cohen as guest pianist in Vaughan Williams's *Charterhouse* Suite and Arnold Bax's *Saga Fragment,* as well as Robert Russell Bennett playing the premiere of his Six Variations on a Theme by Jerome Kern. But it was Herrmann's East Coast premiere of Darius Milhaud's *Creation of the World* (written in 1923) that received the most attention. A foreshadowing of the jazz-symphonic idiom of *Rhapsody in Blue*, it painted hedonistically colorful pictures drawn from African legend, provoked and irritated many, and showed Herrmann at his experimental best.

On February 25, 1934, a second concert followed, featuring the Ives Prelude and Fugue from the Fourth Symphony, *Four Episodes* by Ernest Bloch, and the premieres of *Two Irish Fairy Tales* by New York composer Dana Suesse, Roy Harris's *Pastorale*, and Oscar Levant's *Sinfonietta*. The Levant work, its composer recalled, owed its existence entirely to Herrmann's badgering:

Finding that my "Broadway" tendencies did not preclude a sympathetic response to his brashness, Herrmann suggested that I write a piece for the programs. I protested that I had never written anything for orchestra, but he summoned all of his peculiarly inarticulate persuasiveness to convince me that orchestration was a push-over. He gave me daily pep talks, complete with brief biographical sketches of composers who became famous overnight on the strength of one piece. Then he sent me a score, for study purposes, by one Max Trapp (probably because it was the only one he had). [Here Levant was inaccurate: Herrmann had already amassed a large score collection.] On my own, I purchased a small book on clefs. This was my preparation for orchestrating. . . .

Mine was the kind of piece in which nobody knew what was going on—including the composer, the conductor and the critics. Consequently I got pretty good notices. The critics' attitude might in part have been a reaction from the fact that Copland, part of whose First Symphony was included on the program, indignantly denounced the whole project during the intermission. Surrounded by an attentive group of disciples, he tiraded eloquently on the failings of the conductor, the meager talents of the orchestral players and the presumption of both in playing difficult contemporary music. . . . Thus the other composers on the program had the benefit of his protests when the critics came to write their reviews.[64]*

Levant also performed Gershwin's droll "I Got Rhythm" Variations later in 1934, again under Herrmann's direction. (Gershwin had premiered the work that spring.) Gershwin would remain a friend of Herrmann's, respectful of their different musical styles. "George once told me there were two different kinds of music—dry music and wet music," Herrmann said in 1971:

He said, "Herrmann, you like wet music—I like dry music! Look, you even like those 'ius' composers." I said, "What's an 'ius' composer?" He said, "Sibelius, Delius—the 'ius' composers!" I was at the time much taken with the music of Delius and Sibelius, and he wasn't that interested in that kind of music at the time—although, funnily enough, "Summertime" might have been written by Delius; it's full of Delius harmonies. Gershwin as an artist, I would say, was interested in the French school of music—Ravel, Debussy, then [the Russian] Scriabin. He had not much use for Schoenberg and twelve-tone music because he was an instinctive composer.

He lived in the style of a feudal prince. He had cars, chauffeurs, a country home, and an elegant townhouse on 72d Street near Park Avenue.

*Levant later wrote several Hollywood film scores, including delightful, Gershwinesque music for the 1937 comedy *Nothing Sacred*.

[Yet] he was a very modest, simple man. He always regarded himself as a songwriter who was making attempts at vaster forms of music. One day he wanted to see me because he wanted me to hear the song we now know as "Summertime"—only it wasn't called "Summertime" then. He played it for me and said, "It sounds Jewish to me; do you think it sounds Jewish rather that negroid?" I said, "Well, it doesn't make much difference—there's a great deal of similarity." He said, "Well, it sounds to me more like the kind of song a cantor would sing."

He worked very hard on *Porgy and Bess*; he orchestrated the entire [score]. He could have remained a simple songwriter and gotten all the public acclaim and love with his musicals, but he went about the very hard and difficult way to realize the music that was in him. I think *Porgy and Bess* is one of the greatest operas of the twentieth century.[65]

Herrmann had set ambitious goals for his own musical future. His concerts around New York had been personally satisfying and often historically important, but financially unprofitable. Ida's obsessive practicality and the death of his father had taught Herrmann the importance of money—especially in this, the Depression's harshest year. Determined to have both success and artistic satisfaction, Herrmann looked into his and music's future—and decided they were in broadcasting.

# THREE

And as for you, my fine fellow, let me tell you that you make a great mistake in judging from appearances.

*Israel Zangwill*, The King of Schnorrers

By 1933, the young medium of radio, once an experimental novelty, now a sophisticated mass communication form, had become America's great entertainer.[1] Depression-era audiences could no longer afford costly pleasures like the theater or concert hall; but the diversions offered by NBC and its younger rival, CBS, while less sophisticated than film or the theater, were free and accessible. Radio was reshaping attitudes and bridging cultures; and with innovation and professed high ideals came fierce commercial rivalry, particularly between radio's pioneers of the 1930s, David Sarnoff and William S. Paley.

The Columbia Broadcasting System was mostly the product of a mistake in judgment by NBC chief Sarnoff, who in 1926 rejected the idea of a radio production company headed by Arthur Judson, an unsuccessful violinist turned concert promoter. Judson vowed to create a rival network that would eclipse Sarnoff's own. Sarnoff reportedly laughed out loud.[2]

The next summer Judson's United Independent Broadcasters, tenuously supported by the Columbia Phonograph Company, raced to find musical talent to realize its September air debut. Judson, a man of highly conservative taste, asked an obscure New York conductor named Howard Barlow to lead the network's orchestra. On September 18, 1927, the Columbia Phonograph Broadcasting System made its national debut over twenty-two affiliates with a performance of Deems Taylor and Edna St. Vincent's opera *The King's Henchman*, featuring several members of the Metropolitan Opera and the newly formed Columbia house orchestra. West of the Alleghenies, however, listeners heard little but static—an omen of changing ownerships, mounting debts, and disorganization to come.

The chaos ended in 1928, when the Columbia Broadcasting System (deserted by its namesake sponsor) became the property of twenty-seven-year-old William S. Paley, son of a wealthy American cigar manufacturer. Paley moved CBS from New York's Paramount Building to high-rent Madison Avenue, doubled its affiliate numbers, cultivated first-class radio talent, and generally stimulated interest in a costly network enterprise that had excited no one.

For at least its first two decades, profits went hand in hand with admirably diverse broadcasting—comedic, dramatic, and musical programming ranging from Bing Crosby, Jack Benny, and Kate Smith to weekly broadcasts of the New York Philharmonic under Toscanini. Paley's success did not end with the network. In 1930 he formed Columbia Artists, a talent agency headed by Judson (whom Paley quickly removed from network affairs). And in 1938 Columbia Records was launched, soon to be one of the industry's most successful record companies and the developer in 1948 of the 33⅓ rpm LP.

CBS's prosperity was not the work of Paley alone. Paul Kesten, head of promotions, helped create an image of prestige; program director Julius Sebock and his successor, William B. Lewis, hired directors like Irving Reis and William Robson and such writers as Archibald MacLeish and Norman Corwin, all of whom would refine the art of radio drama in the 1930s and 1940s. The erudite Davidson Taylor, supervisor of CBS's growing music department, was instrumental in turning the cramped sound room of the network's Studio One into one of America's most imaginative concert halls.

But it was Paley who hired Johnny Green in the fall of 1933 to arrange and conduct a new CBS series devised by Paley called "Music in the Modern Manner."[3] The program would feature not only "serious" contemporaries like Webern and Schoenberg but also popular composers like Gershwin and Robert Russell Bennett. Accompanying the music would be poetry readings by CBS's top announcer, David Ross, of works ranging from Poe to Edgar Lee Masters. Orchestrations and original music would be written by Green and his arranging partner, Conrad "Connie" Salinger.

By the year's end, Green was also working on *Mr. Whittington*, a musical starring Jack Buchanan that opened in 1934 at London's Hippodrome. Work on both the play and the weekly forty-five-minute broadcasts eventually proved impossible: "One day my secretary Rose Gray and Connie sat me down in my office and said, 'Listen, you're still human. You've got to get an assistant—somebody who's a good musician and can conduct when you're in the booth listening to the sound balance.' Benny Herrmann's name and face flashed into my mind. He had been hanging around the program, coming to rehearsals, and he knew Rose. So I went to Sebock and [division vice-president] Lawrence Lowman and copped a big plea that I needed help, and that I'd found the guy. I think we settled on $85 a week for Benny—I was getting $300—and he came to work for me."[4]

Radio, especially CBS, was the ideal place for Herrmann: an innovative communications medium where a single broadcast could make a career; where Herrmann could conduct, arrange, and program music with little concern for commerciality; and where music and drama were united in concert broadcasts, live plays, and poetry readings. "Within three weeks, Herrmann had the whole building on its ear," Green recalled. "He was remaking the Columbia Broadcasting System, twiddling his hair, criticizing everything, and making himself a total nuisance. Soon I got called up to Lowman's office, and he said, 'Who is this madman you've inflicted on us? Can't you contain him? If he's so valuable to you, keep him in your unit!' Benny was all over the place, and I idolized him."[5]

The early relationship between Green and Herrmann was close outside Madison Avenue as well:

I lived on 86th Street on the East Side, thirty-four blocks from CBS, and my great learning times with Benny were during our walks home. If I opened my mouth it was always to ask, never to tell. He was not only encyclopedic—he out-Groved Grove. I had never heard of Arnold Bax, or Turina; he told me about Ives, Constant Lambert, and shed new light on serialism. I knew a lot about Purcell, but I didn't know the things about him Benny did. He could have *been* one of those early English musicians; he could have been their Boswells, not only biographically but musically.

My first wife, Carol, was very fond of him also. They were as misfit as any two people could be; she stood for a lot of things that were anathema to Benny. She was a very upper class New York Jewish society lady, which he deplored. In fact, German Jewry were anathema to Benny. I came from that same fancy part of New York, and one of the things he loved about me was that I, being one of them, was a renegade.

He deplored the amount of time I gave to arranging other people's music; a fuel line to his ready personal disdain for me was his inability to comprehend how I could have neglected my composing. The thing he hated most was my love of show. I loved telephones and office intercoms where I could flip a switch and talk to the eighteenth floor. "What do you want with all this?" he'd say. "You think people like *me* are peasants. Your friend Mr. Paley, that's who the peasants are. We're the aristocracy."

One of my favorite memories was a lovely dinner at my home on a beautiful autumn day. I had not the pleasure, but the wonder, of being Benny Herrmann's host over his first artichoke. He had never seen one before, didn't know what to do with it, and thought it was crazy. "They should be eaten the way monkeys eat bananas," he said; "ya take the peel and throw it away, and wait till ya get to the—whaddaya call it?" I said, "The heart." So we taught Benny how to eat an artichoke. "This is very good," he said. "But it's too much trouble."[6]

A more significant initiation came several weeks into Herrmann's CBS apprenticeship, in May 1934. One afternoon, Green realized that he had not yet begun his score for the David Ross program—and with his other duties he would not have time to compose one. The poem was Keats's "La Belle Dame Sans Merci," a dramatic poem requiring extensive musical interludes. Green was panic-stricken, until he had an inspiration: "I'll have Herrmann write it; let him earn his keep. That was my attitude, very snotty. To be brief, he wrote it, and it was absolutely brilliant. I never wrote another one. I conducted them, studied them, but I never stuck my neck out again. Connie kept begging to write one, but I said, 'That's between you and Benny. If he wants to write it, no. You and I orchestrate.' Of course, we didn't orchestrate for Herrmann."[7]

A different version of the same event comes from a 1939 article by Lucille Fletcher:

David Ross was reading poetry in a weekly series called the Columbia Variety Hour. Herrmann, then a shy, thin lad of 21 [in fact 23], was working as Johnny Green's assistant. One day in the elevator, Ross saw him with a copy of Emily Dickinson's *Poems* in his pocket.

"Like poetry?" Ross asked. Herrmann nodded his head.

"Why don't you write me a musical background for my poetry reading?" Ross asked him. He never dreamed Herrmann would take him seriously. As far as he knew, the boy was just a jazz conductor. But young Herrmann went home that night, and in two days turned out a symphonic score for Keats' "La Belle Dame Sans Merci." It was then his favorite poem. A week later, he was conducting it on Variety Hour as background to Ross' reading.

It was so successful, so different from any other type of musical background then known, that CBS executives promptly commissioned the youngster to turn out many more.

The melodramas were full of cue music germs—effects like the shrill wind or the scuttering of dead leaves in "La Belle Dame Sans Merci," the moonlight in "Annabel Lee," the mental loneliness of the sightless kings in "The City of Brass."

For example, there were such instructions as these scattered through them: "Harp: Place long strips of paper among strings to soften tone." Or "Piano: Place ruler on 12 notes above high C. Put down damper pedal. Play other notes in score with left hand."[8]

By the summer of 1934 Herrmann was not only scoring "Modern Manner" programs, but he was also writing original music for the "Secone Sketchbook" with Christopher Morley and the Oldsmobile Program with Ruth Etting. He was also the involuntary arranger of Howard Barlow's programs of light music, often seeking the aid of another young CBS employee, Lyn Murray, who specialized in popular music. (Murray, a staunch Herrmann admirer until their rift in 1960, also turned to dramatic scoring at CBS before becoming a successful film and television composer.) As rehearsal conductor of CBS's jazz and "light" orchestras, Herrmann dealt with greats and future greats, in an idiom he never fully mastered. Musicians included Artie Shaw, the Dorsey Brothers, and another distinguished Benny. "Who told you you could play the clarinet?" Herrmann reportedly barked at the visiting musician. "Who told you you could conduct?" replied a young Benny Goodman.[9]

Herrmann's ambitions clearly lay elsewhere. Although he admired the relatively untrained Barlow, the leader of CBS's main orchestra, Herrmann was priming himself as Barlow's successor by focusing attention on his own extensive knowledge of little-known symphonic music. He remained outspoken in his condemnation of most conductors and their conservatism, a stance that only grew more savage in later years. Victor Bay, a fellow CBS conductor, was subject daily to Herrmann's diatribes during their elevator rides to the eighteenth floor: "Benny once turned to me and said, 'You know, I heard a concert of Toscanini's yesterday, and it was very bad.' He paused for a minute. 'And you know, Victor—it wasn't the orchestra's fault!' Everybody looked around and thought, look at Bernard— he talks about *Toscanini!*"[10]

In fact, Herrmann admired Toscanini more than he would admit. Yet the criticism was inevitable, since Toscanini represented the antithesis of the Romantic school of conducting that Stokowski personified and Herrmann emulated. Toscanini's mass popularity underscored another maxim Herrmann spent his life fighting—that successful conductors gave the public what it wanted. Even on radio, in an era before ratings were all-important, concert music had its commercial side. Common at the time were lavish CBS music program auditions (the equivalent of modern television pilots), privately broadcast to the offices of potential sponsors and sometimes costing tens of thousands of dollars. John Green recalled the most memorable—and most unpleasant:

We had an orchestra of sixty players, culled from the forces of the Symphony and the CBS Show Orchestra. The concertmaster was John Corigliano [soon to hold that post for the New York Philharmonic]; Walter Gross was the pianist; it was an unbelievable orchestra. I was on the podium, and Benny was listening for the balance in the control room. He always did this and was great at it, but he never stopped reading the *New York Times* while he was doing it, and it drove me crazy. I don't know if it drove me crazy because I thought it was bad-mannered or because I was envious of the divisibility of his concentrative powers. If you looked in and saw his face, he was devoutly intent on the *Times*, until he'd suddenly push the button and say, "Johnny! The horns are too loud at bar thirty." And he'd be absolutely right.

Well, here we were at the dress rehearsal of the audition, with Paley, Lowman, and all the bigwigs from International Silver. I was getting madder and madder at Benny, who was serving me well. I stopped the orchestra, shushing them, and he didn't even realize it. I leaned down into the talk mike, pushed the button to the booth, and at the top of my voice—I could have deafened him *and* the engineer—I yelled, "Benny Herrmann, for Christ's sake put the GODDAMN NEW YORK TIMES DOWN and stop twiddling your GODDAMN HAIR!"

The minute I had done it—after one look at that face—I was ashamed of myself. He did not walk out of the room, which he had every right to do, but he folded up the paper, took his hand down from his head, folded his hands, and made a monkey out of me. Nobody liked me for it—most of all *I* disliked myself for it—but Herrmann never held that against me.[11]

Despite his duties as arranger, rehearsal conductor, and composer, Herrmann actively continued his concert composing, with increasing skill—and with a ready medium for his music's performance. Two winningly unpretentious works made their radio debuts in 1934–1935: "The Skating Rink" (first broadcast on NBC, curiously, under conductor Erno Rapee) and the *Currier and Ives* Suite, a colorful collage of musical Americana that looked ahead to Herrmann's film scores for *Citizen Kane* and *The Magnificent Ambersons*. A third original work, "Sinfonietta for Strings," was Herrmann's most psychologically provocative to date, with a quietly dissonant Interlude that would resurface twenty-six years later as the "madhouse" theme for his most famous film score, *Psycho*.

Throughout his film career, in fact, Herrmann would reuse themes (or more often thematic fragments) in new works, either weaving them through fresh orchestration into a new entity or retaining them largely intact. The practice was far from unprecedented: Berlioz was particularly fond of reviving early works' themes and movements in later compositions.[12] Yet Herrmann's reputation in later years would suffer from accusations of self-plagiarism, some of it justified: in the mid-1960s, as his life reached a crisis point, Herrmann seemed unable at times to compose new, fresh music.

Yet on the whole, Herrmann's self-borrowings reveal a more complex design. The above-mentioned "madhouse" theme echoes a consistent motif of insanity and horror. Herrmann's music for Cathy and Heathcliff's impossible love in the opera *Wuthering Heights* also defines the spiritual romance between the phantom Captain Gregg and the living Lucy Muir in *The Ghost and Mrs. Muir*. The music of the moors for *Jane Eyre* is recalled in the Brontë-inspired *Wuthering Heights*. Overall, these self-reflexive quotations demonstrate the internal consistency and distinctive personality of Herrmann's work, a sign of artistic maturity rather than fatigue.

Also in 1935 Herrmann realized a key ambition, becoming a staff conductor as well as being named leader of CBS's distinguished "School of the Air" program for the next year. (Also working on the program was a young Edward R. Murrow.) At last Herrmann had his orchestra, and he was committed to exploiting its full value. Within a year he had convinced William Paley to allow him to broadcast much of his favorite musical esoterica on a variety of CBS music programs. When Paley initially balked, Herrmann reportedly said, "You're assuming the public is as ignorant about music as you are."[13] To his credit, Paley accepted the reply, and for the next fifteen years Herrmann had near-unlimited freedom in musical programming at CBS.

Herrmann's unorthodox approach to programming helped define him to some as a troublemaker and non–team player. He had already perfected Whistler's gentle art of making enemies by rejecting convention and often courtesy; yet his iconoclasm was largely supported at CBS. A network press release of February 1938 nicely summarizes Herrmann's philosophies on broadcasting, which would yield greater rewards in the 1940s:

[Herrmann] says he "stands for the very old and the very new." He observes that a tendency to "cling to the romance of the past has placed the greatest emphasis on the nineteenth century and diverted attention from the absolute music of old." He too is a believer in the romantic music of the last century. But this does not prevent him from delving as far as history will take him into other eras, or championing the creativeness that is 1938. "Every period," he states, "has been interested in the music of its own time except the twentieth century. We are interested in twentieth century mechanisms and modes of living but our tastes in music are decidedly nineteenth century. There are as many talented composers today as there ever were. But the modern composer works in a vacuum. He has no contact with his audience because that audience wants the past. Music is the only art whose creations can be repeated over and over again."[14]

Having arrived at CBS, Herrmann was determined to stay there. Even in later years, with his position secure, he could be as unhelpful to prospective CBS conductors as he was magnanimous in championing new composers. Elie Siegmeister, formerly of the Young Composers Group, paid a visit to CBS in the early 1940s looking for a conducting opening but quickly discovered that "Benny obviously didn't appreciate the idea, for when we met in the hall he was most unceremonious and invited me in short to 'get out.' "[15] Yet Herrmann was no doubt instrumental in persuading CBS to hire Jerome Moross in 1935 to write cue music for such programs as "The March of Time."

That same year another young composer-arranger seeking work visited 485 Madison Avenue—David Raksin, who for forty years would battle, befriend, and observe Herrmann as he, too, became a distinguished composer in Hollywood:

When I first entered Johnny Green's office there were two other guys standing with Johnny, neither of whom I had met before. They just stood there like a little cabal, sneering at everything I said to John. At one point John said to me, "I heard you've made a remarkable arrangement of 'I Got Rhythm.' " I said, "Well, I've got it here if you'd like to look at it." I'd made it originally as a jazz band arrangement which counterpointed bits of *An American in Paris* against parts of "I Got Rhythm." Stoki had seen it and was very intrigued. I told Johnny this, which was absolutely true, and these two guys burst into laughter at the idea that I was suggesting Stokowski was going to play it—which never in a million years did I suggest. These two snide individuals were Bernard Herrmann and Jerome Moross.

Later we became friends, but for a while I thought that anybody with that snotty New York quality was not anybody I gave much of a damn about. Before I actually met Benny I used to come from Philadelphia to hear some of the concerts of avant-garde music he gave at Town Hall, and I really didn't understand the connection between that guy and the fellow I met in Johnny's office. Benny was like a child. I used to call him a virtuoso of unspecific anger; he was always furious at everything.

Yet despite his rotten manners, he was, in some ways, a gentleman. Benny modeled himself after Englishmen like Samuel Johnson and others, which led me to call him Sir Shamus Beecham. It's interesting; a lot of the English poets we hear about as having been so beautifully accoutered were guys who physically were something you wouldn't want to have in your living room. Sam Johnson, for instance, had scrofula and was generally a mess. Benny was like that; he was a man who, if he had become an angel, would have soup stains on his vest after the first lunch.[16]

The paradox of Herrmann's intellectual sophistication and frequent social tactlessness struck many of his CBS colleagues as well. Most found the combination an appealing one. "As for books," a CBS press release noted, "there are people who have abandoned the idea of ever finding one Bennie hasn't read. Twirling his hair furiously the while, Bennie can—and does at the slightest provocation—deliver dissertations, complete with quotations, on the works of Trollope, Shaw, Lefanu, the Sitwells, Virginia Woolf, Shakespeare, Dickens, Graham Greene, or almost any other English author you can think of."[17]

One book—or more accurately, its owner—particularly intrigued Herrmann. One day, after restlessly wandering into the office of W. Clark Harrington, head of CBS Music Clearance, Herrmann spotted George Moore's *Memories of My Dead Life* on a desk, borrowed it, and disappeared. He returned the book the following day, but his visits only became more frequent, and it was soon apparent why. Harrington's assistant was Lucille Fletcher, an extremely well read, attractive Vassar graduate and would-be music critic who had recently begun work at CBS as a $15-a-week receptionist.

Herrmann had first met Lucille shortly after his radio composing debut on "Music in the Modern Manner." Two days after the broadcast, which she had attended, Lucille spotted Herrmann at the 14th Street subway station and complimented him on his work. As they were both en route to CBS, Herrmann accompanied her to the building. Although Lucille later forgot most of Herrmann's passionate monologue on their way to 51st Street, she kept a strong impression of the man: "I was so struck by his knowledge and talent and excitement that I really was exhausted. It was like Minerva walking out of Jove's forehead and giving him a terrible headache."[18]

When they parted at CBS, Herrmann forgot to ask her name—then spent the next two weeks searching for her in the giant network. After finding her in Harrington's office, Herrmann barely acknowledged her presence, until one day he saw her crying over the death of her beloved

Boston terrier. Herrmann, a great animal lover, commiserated with her and, that night, walked her to the subway. He also escorted her to her parents' doorstep in Brooklyn—as he would continue to do for the next five years.

Herrmann was shyly old-world in his courtship—as well as extremely patient. Lucille's household, centered on an explosive, intimidating father, extended no invitation to Herrmann. His only meeting with Matthew Fletcher was a disaster. Always critical and suspicious of any young man who came to the house, Fletcher was unimpressed by his political opinions and his piano playing. Lucille's mother found Herrmann's personality abrasive and mystifying. Herrmann was also correct in sensing anti-Semitic prejudice in Lucille's conservative Protestant parents.

But the attraction between Lucille and Herrmann was strong. The two began discussing books, recordings, and story ideas; both relished the macabre and poetic in classic English and American literature. (It was Lucille who convinced Herrmann to open his first bank account. Herrmann soon became very sophisticated in his handling of finances, diagramming his annual earnings with elaborate charts and keeping rigorous track of his ASCAP and BMI residuals.)

Although Lucille was familiar with the traditional symphonic repertoire, Herrmann introduced her to lesser-known American and English composers and obscure music of the eighteenth and nineteenth centuries. "Benny was all the culture I was missing in my CBS job, and all the culture I had not encountered before I met him," Lucille recalled:

It was a return to the very intellectual atmosphere of Vassar College, but in many ways he was far ahead of much that I had learned there. Benny also took it upon himself to encourage my literary career. My first name is Violet, and he liked to say, "I found this violet under a stone."

Benny had a lot of charm for women. Even when he was young, he had other girls who were interested in him, and after he began to rise in the world their numbers increased by leaps and bounds. Very early in our friendship he began pressuring me to marry him, although I had to work to help support my family and he didn't have the money to support me and his mother and sister at the same time. But he never suggested that we live together, or that we go to a hotel together; he was an old-fashioned moralist, conservatively brought up, and so was I.

During our long, devoted, but frustrated relationship, Benny and I loved to go over to Staten Island on the ferry and ride the little train to the remote regions of that island. We would walk through the woods, go along lonely county lanes or to South Beach, which was then wild and deserted. Benny loved its rural atmosphere. We would spend whole days there, eat at a local restaurant, sit on the beach, and walk for miles, always talking incessantly. Benny had very delicate white skin and hated being sunburned, so at the beach he would bundle up in a series of bath towels, wear a big hat, and his socks and shoes!

In the afternoons before I had to go home to Brooklyn he would often take me to the Liberty Music Shop, a very fine record store on, I think, 50th Street across from CBS. They had listening booths then, and he would take a whole armful of records, saying to me, "You really gotta hear this. C'mon." Sometimes we would go spend two hours while he played at least a dozen records! He would usually conduct whatever piece was being played. The first work he ever played for me was Mahler's Second Symphony; he was wild about it. To my shame, even though I was a music minor at Vassar, I had never heard most of the pieces he played me. The second piece Benny played was Delius's *Walk to the Paradise Garden*, and after that I always thought of the walk we took from 51st and Madison over to the subway on 42nd Street and Broadway as our walk to the paradise garden. Poor Liberty Music Shop! But he did buy a lot of their records, and they knew who he was.

I worked in the CBS music library for about a year, and Benny would come down to the library every day to see me. The library was run by a very Germanic, wonderful musicologist, Julius Mattfeld. It wasn't at all like an ordinary music library, but was a huge place humming with activity and all sorts of people. Jazz arrangers, symphony conductors, and bandleaders were going in and out, copyists sat at long tables extracting parts from new scores that had just been composed for the Chesterfield Hour or "Andre Kostelanetz Presents," and in another section stacks and stacks of opera scores, symphonies, and song cycles were kept on file. Over this kingdom Mr. Mattfeld reigned. Benny would come down and head for my desk in the center of the room; Mr. Mattfeld would resent these visits, or else would be entertained by Benny's erudite remarks. Sometimes Benny would start an argument with him about modern music or some leitmotiv of Wagner, and Mattfeld would pick up a window pointer (in those days you opened high windows with a long wooden pointer) and pretend he was Wotan in the scene Benny was describing. Once or twice he invited us to have dinner with him and his wife after office hours.

The subway ride to Brooklyn took an hour every day, and during those rides there was a lifetime of conversation. Benny liked to think of projects for other people, and among other things he suggested that I write a novel about a New England composer who was very gifted but unrecognized in his day. This person's name, we decided, would be Josiah Abbott, and he would live in a small New England village where he was a poor church organist. Under Benny's prodding I started work on the novel, *Idle Thun-*

*der,* and plugged away at it for five or six years, but it never really came off. Actually it was a novel enforced on me by another mind; what the book really came from was Benny's perception of Charles Ives.

Josiah Abbott became a real person to Benny, a man he could identify with deeply. He started to think about what kind of music Josiah Abbott would probably compose. One day, on the BMT subway as we were going past Pacific Street, Benny suggested that Abbott might write a cantata based on Melville's *Moby Dick.* After another station went by he said, "Golly, that's too good an idea to waste on just a novel. I think I'll write that cantata myself." And so he did; he finished it long before I finished *Idle Thunder.*[19]

After two years of CBS staff assignments and several minor compositions, Herrmann was eager to start his first major concert work. Programmatic, literary, and uniquely American, *Moby Dick* was an ideal launching point, but as Herrmann realized, Melville's novel was too vast and complex to adapt without assistance. Herrmann chose as his collaborator Clark Harrington, whose writing and friendship the composer had come to prize:

Benny's usual facial expression was rather forbidding, unsmiling; but in those rare moments when he was content or happy, he managed a faint smile. Somewhere in my diary I wrote a few lines of verse about his habit of twisting a forelock of his hair: "He doth but wind the sprockets of his brain."

He gave me many books which I cherish to this day. [Years after *Moby Dick*] he gave me *The Metamorphosis of Ajax; a New Discourse of a State Subject by Sir John Harrington,* because my namesake Sir John had invented the water closet for Queen Elizabeth. The edition was limited to 450 copies; Benny told me he saw a copy in the private library of a Hollywood producer and sought out another copy. Benny lightly penciled on the flyleaf: "To our own modern Ajax Harrington. Greetings." It shows to what meticulous lengths Benny would go in his research. (Once we were talking on Madison Avenue, and Benny was feeling good about something I had done for him. He put one arm over my shoulders and said, "I like you a lot, Harrington. Too bad you've got the wrong kind of plumbing.")

We often discussed literature during lunches. He asked me if I knew *Moby Dick.* I had read it in 1928 while crossing the Atlantic on a liner. Benny took a gamble and asked me to assist him in keeping track of the passages he would set for the cantata, toward producing a final draft of the libretto. Of course I assented.[20]

Herrmann's research on the Melville novel was thorough to the point of obsession (though by necessity his work on the cantata was subordinate to his nine-month annual duties at CBS). In the summers of 1937 and 1938 he and Lucille drove to Massachusetts with Clark and Amber Harrington, reliving each step of Melville's semiautobiographical journey: a prim white Protestant church in New England, in which Herrmann sat silently and alone in the tall, square-black pews; the Wayside Inn at Sudbury, a century-old hostelry for whalers; and the New Bedford whaling museum, with its massive carcasses and vintage whaling ships.

Herrmann and Harrington would then work on the cantata in New York in the old Juilliard building on 52d Street, now a branch of CBS. Two of the text castings were by Herrmann (the chapel hymn and "Oh jolly is the whale"); the rest were by Harrington: "There were a few instances in the score where Benny had set an accented note or stress to an unaccented syllable of a word (or to an unaccented short word such as *a* or *with*); I tried to have him make adjustments correcting them in the music but was seldom successful."[21] (Herrmann's opera *Wuthering Heights* would suffer from similarly odd accent choices.)

Herrmann's choice of *Moby Dick* for musical setting was astute: Melville's novel is more a metaphysical allegory, rich in brooding and symbolic imagery, than a traditional sea yarn. Mainly static in its drama, it was ideally suited to the cantata form rather than to opera. (Orson Welles took a similar approach years later in his stage version of the play, essentially a dramatic reading.) Reducing the libretto to a concert length was one of Herrmann and Harrington's greatest challenges: "Many characters, such as Queequeg, Stubbs, Flask, Daggoo, many great scenes and wonderful soliloquies had to be omitted," Herrmann wrote in 1940. "However, we feel that the libretto still retains many of the fine highlights of the book, particularly those which depict the strange gloom of the Pequod's last voyage and the violence of Captain Ahab's inner struggle."[22]

Colonialism, religion, and death are scrutinized in the sprawling novel, whose central force is the sea—its deathlike, romantic inescapability. Already one finds the elements that would attract Herrmann again and again: man's pull toward self-destruction, the paradoxical beauty of alien lands (here the remote, empty sea), and above all, an obsessive individualist (here Ahab, to be followed by Charles Foster Kane, Edward Rochester in *Jane Eyre*, Heathcliff in *Wuthering Heights*, Scotty Ferguson in *Vertigo*, and others). In *Moby Dick*, psychological disorder becomes one with the desolate, chaotic ocean, its destructive powers evoked through short, repeated musical devices (but rarely motives) and rich orchestral textures—the aural equivalent of a turbulent Turner watercolor.

Despite its bleak colorations and vocal settings, Herrmann's *Moby Dick* is also persuasive as an inherently dramatic work based on religious subject matter (the novel is at least in part a New England retelling of the Jonah legend). Melville's religious subtext is acknowledged both in the work's declamatory opening for full chorus and orchestra ("And God Created Great Whales") and in the cantata's most moving sequence, the solemn church hymn in which the whalers invoke God as their protector. The song conveys without a trace of irony the faith and pride of Melville's idealistic people.

The heart of the cantata, as of the novel, is psychological. Ahab's character is distilled into two lengthy soliloquies. Like Herrmann's eerie recitative for Ishmael in the cantata's opening, they are unmelodic and freely structured, using impressionistic orchestral commentary to mirror Ahab's alienation and futile quest ("This lovely light, it lights not me. . . . Damned in the midst of paradise"). His obsession finds its antithesis in the high spirits of the *Pequod*'s sailors, who celebrate their whaling adventure in a frenzied jig, a passage based on one of Herrmann's favorite chapters in the novel, "a striking example of Melville's innate musical feeling. A mere glance at the text will show that it is broken up into short ejaculations by various members of the crew, and that these are worked up into a whirling frenzy, the result being a dazzling scherzo in words. With this in mind, I have eliminated the words entirely from this passage—except for a few snatches of a drunken sea chanty—and turned it into a bacchanalian hornpipe."[23]

But the sailors, like Ahab, are doomed. For the climactic sea battle that takes all lives but one Herrmann employs his full ensemble of orchestra and chorus, as the driving bass rhythms of the sea boats crash against the low brass fury of the great whale. Battle cries become a maelstrom of dissonance as the "damned whale" destroys the *Pequod*, an impressionistic timpani roll sending the crew to their deaths (an effect Herrmann scored for radio thunder drum, an instrument never before used in concert music). A sole bass clarinet remains to survey the human wreckage (its three-note device is, again, the *Sinfonietta-Psycho* theme); this too vanishes, leaving only Ishmael's hushed spoken epilogue, "And I only am escaped to tell thee."

Just as Melville dedicated *Moby-Dick* to his mentor, Nathaniel Hawthorne, Herrmann chose as his honoree Charles Ives, "whose music and ideology have always served as an inspiration to me."[24] Ives was touched but remained convinced his reputation would do more harm than good

("When they see my name on it they'll throw bricks at you," he told Herrmann).[25] The dedication remained.

Herrmann began three other concert works between 1936 and 1940; only the nonprogrammatic *Nocturne and Scherzo* (dedicated to Howard Barlow), written in the summer of 1936, was completed. The other, larger-scale pieces (another cantata, based on the story of Johnny Appleseed, and a "fiddle concerto") apparently never satisfied their creator. For Herrmann, the concert idiom was less rewarding, creatively and financially, than the more immediate challenge of dramatic scoring at CBS. Herrmann would spend most of the 1930s writing short, ingenious cues for radio dramas and conducting the network's expanding (and improving) concert orchestra.

Recent additions to the ensemble included the great trumpeter Harry Glans and a young, mischievous oboist named Mitch Miller who, with clarinetist Ben Kanter, delighted in testing Herrmann's short fuse. After one session of playful sabotage Herrmann slammed down his baton, dismissed the orchestra, seized his hair, and shouted, "I knew it! I knew it! There's a strong fascist element in the woodwinds!"[26] Underneath the byplay was genuine admiration between Herrmann and his players, who were regularly astonished by the conductor's vast knowledge.

"Exploring Music," a thirty-minute weekly program of CBS Symphony performances, was among Herrmann's earliest regular offerings of the provocative and obscure. The music of Ives, Delius, and other contemporaries shared airtime with Joachim Raff, Cherubini, and Chabrier, with talented musical amateurs like King Frederick the Great, Samuel Butler, Samuel Pepys, and King Henry IV making appearances as well. Herrmann's faith in the series was justified both by the influx of listeners' letters and by critics' notices. "Herrmann, conducting an essentially thin outfit, manages to get real tonal depth from it, and shows an obvious feeling for the purposes of his composer," wrote *Billboard*. "He handles his light and shade brilliantly—and without any of the resultant sacrifices of content that is so common among most other light and shade boys—notably Toscanini and Stokowski. As a musician he's both brilliant and solid."[27]

"Famous Musical Evenings" blended the historical recreations of CBS's later "You Are There" series with Herrmann's impeccable taste for period music. A typical series entry was "An Evening with the Esterházys," which allowed listeners to "sit in" on an eighteenth-century recital at the home of Haydn's patrons. Another, "An Evening at Versailles," included music by Jean-Jacques Rousseau and Marie Antoinette.

Howard Barlow was also impressed with Herrmann's musicology and compositions, and in October 1936 he broadcast both Herrmann's *Nocturne and Scherzo* (its premiere) and Ives's Fugue and Scherzo from his as-yet unperformed Fourth Symphony. Shortly after the broadcast Herrmann received a letter from the composer's wife, Harmony, in Redding, Connecticut.

Dear Mr. Herrmann:

Mr. Ives wants me to say that he "thanks you from the bottom of his heart for all you have done and that the generosity is all on your side." He says "It doesn't strike me as particularly generous to fill up another man's shelves with [music scores] but to stand up for another man's work, especially when there is a good chance of getting a moving brick for his trouble—now that's not generous but courageous!" . . .

We were very glad that New Music published your String Orchestra Set [in October 1936]. The condition of Mr. Ives' eyes is such that he has not been able to see the music but he hopes it will be played soon.

We suspect to be back in New York next month—and don't feel like letting you come way up here and then strike one of his bad days when he is short of breath and it is difficult for him to talk or have a good visit with you. It would be unsatisfactory to both and it is hard to tell in advance about it. When we get to N.Y. we can telephone you when a good day comes along and I think that will be better. . . .

As you know we have no radio but I went to a friend's and heard the music. I thought it was very fine—to me not too fast—and yours went brilliantly—it was done enthusiastically I thought; Mr. Ives feels Mr. Barlow is to be thanked—we haven't the records yet . . . and as soon as I get some wooden needles will hear them.[28]

Two weeks later Herrmann received another, again in Harmony's handwriting:

Dear Mr. Herrmann:

This morning our aged phonograph was finally persuaded to play the records you so kindly sent last week.

We all enjoyed your music—it is fine, stirring and seemed well played. To me it is natural, strong-moving and spontaneous—inspired by something bigger than nice designs on paper which seems to be the basis of too much music. The scherzo has a real outspoken stride and activity and the Nocturne a dignity and beauty. We hope to hear these someday at a concert as probably all records have some limitations. I don't hear the higher parts well—my ears seem to blur when the upper strings and woodwinds play sustained notes.

The fugue was well played. Please give Mr. Barlow my cordial thanks for playing it.

We send you both thanks and congratulations and look forward to seeing you before many weeks.

Sincerely yours,
Chas E. Ives [Ives's signature][29]

In addition to CBS, the Federal Works programs of the 1930s (a product of Franklin Roosevelt's New Deal) offered listeners the opportunity to hear unusual concert music. In April 1937 Howard Barlow conducted New York's Federal Symphony Orchestra at the Theatre of Music on West 54th Street, in a concert that included the first public performance of Herrmann's *Nocturne and Scherzo*. A perceptive critic of the piece was CBS producer James Fassett, later Herrmann's collaborator on CBS's "Invitation to Music." "The Nocturne is a superior piece of work," he wrote Herrmann. "It creates a distinct mood which . . . I've felt many times before on hearing other compositions, and especially (this may shock you) in Debussy's 'La Mer.' . . . I think its effectiveness lies in its sparse instrumentation . . . economy without thinness. I like the *distant* effects from muted instruments. . . . Best of all, the fact that it is really original music. You can't lay your finger on any single composer, even Debussy."[30]

Herrmann himself later visited the Federal Symphony to conduct Vaughan Williams's *London* Symphony. During its rehearsal Herrmann carefully explained to the players each programmatic episode in the work, recounting at one point its depiction of unemployed workers on the London embankment. Composer Lyn Murray was among those enjoying the irony that "Benny was describing unemployment in great detail to a group of out-of-work musicians."[31]

In three and a half years at CBS, Herrmann had accomplished much. His conducting now was heard by a wide, increasingly receptive audience, and his music received regular performance. But the most famous stage of Herrmann's years at CBS was still to come: his work as a composer with the "Columbia Workshop," Norman Corwin, and Orson Welles, on a path that would carry him to Hollywood.

# FOUR

"Oh, two days! The labour of two days, then, is that for which you ask two hundred guineas?"—Attorney General

"No—I ask it for the knowledge of a lifetime."—Whistler

> James McNeill Whistler,
> The Gentle Art of Making Enemies

In the fall of 1937, Herrmann began work on what was CBS's boldest radio venture to date: the "Columbia Workshop," an experimental vehicle for new, innovative performers. Joining him were directors Irving Reis and William Robson and such writers as Pulitzer Prize–winning poet Archibald MacLeish, Stephen Vincent Benet, William Saroyan, W. H. Auden, Maxwell Anderson, and Lucille Fletcher. (Lucille was now writing publicity for CBS and articles for *Movie Mirror*, the *Detroit Free Press*, and the *New Yorker*.) The series quickly became a symbol of CBS prestige and programming unorthodoxy.

It also secured Herrmann's reputation as radio's fastest and best composer, who, as Lucille wrote, could "wave a fountain pen and turn six notes and two chords into a mountain slide or a fog in no time at all."[1] One "Workshop" script called for the sound of a man turning into a sycamore tree. Sitting at his piano in his sixteenth-floor office, Herrmann decided the experience might be strangely pleasant: "I scored the cue for strings, harp, celeste and flute—all delicate instruments—and composed a theme which was wistful, but not too sad. After all, the man turning into the tree was a postman, and his feet were tired. He was glad to be at peace."[2]

A script by Benet demanded the sound of a Revolutionary army playing "Yankee Doodle" inside a bottle. Herrmann arranged the theme for soft strings, woodwinds, and celeste to create the most delicate of ensembles, then placed the musicians in a separate studio from the actors and had their sounds piped through an electrical filter to complete the effect.

Lucille Fletcher recalled other Herrmann masterstrokes in a 1939 article:

He had to compose a musical representation of [a time clock] when Pare Lorentz presented the industrial drama "Ecce Homo." Lorentz—who was a guest producer—hadn't heard about Herrmann, and at first he planned to use a real sound effect time-clock as background for the show. His friends talked him out of it.

"Get Herrmann to write you a time-clock," they told him. "It'll make the show." It did. Herrmann has never been inside a factory in his life, but he whipped up a cue out of a French horn, a couple of Chinese wood blocks and a piano; and it was better than the real thing. . . .

Herrmann paid little attention to the tradition that if a symphony orchestra was assigned to a program, the full orchestra ought to play all the cues. . . . Once for a script by Irwin Shaw, he scored his cues for a single harmonica player. . . .

Probably the oddest combination he ever wrote music for was an orchestra of saws, hammers and nails. This was used in a script, written by Alfred Kreymbourg, "The House That Jack Didn't Build." It was a play about the Federal Housing Project, and Herrmann conceived the idea of having the rhythm of carpentering substitute for music.

Herrmann and the Sound Effects Department cooperated, too, in a Workshop production of Lord Dunsany's "Gods of the Mountain."

The play was about three Indian beggers who disguise themselves, and pretend to be three stone gods who sit out in the middle of the desert. The populace feeds and worships them, until suddenly the footsteps of the real gods are heard in the distance, striding over the desert toward the town. Herrmann's job was to express these giant stone footsteps in music. . . .

Herrmann and his orchestra—fortified for the occasion with a couple of extra kettledrums and tom-toms—were placed on the twenty-second floor in a studio of their own. Downstairs in another studio, a sound effects man sat, with a huge bag of rocks at his side. But the sound effects man and Herrmann wore earphones which were connected with the main studio where the drama was taking place. At a signal from the producer, Herrmann would bring down his baton, and the orchestra would give out an ominous "rumble" cue. Then, on the off-beat, the sound effects man downstairs would throw his bag of rocks from one end of the studio to the other. Herrmann would pause, and bring his baton down again. Again the rumble would sound, and again the bag of rocks would fly across the studio. On the air, it gave the effect of ponderous feet, moving slowly and terribly across the earth.[3]

Herrmann's and the series' masterpiece was MacLeish's "Fall of the City," the radio drama event of 1937. A verse play inspired by the growth of fascist powers in Europe, it skillfully created rhythm and tension through its interplay of a narrator (twenty-two-year-old Orson Welles), chorus, and sound effects. Director Reis rented the 250-member Seventh Regiment Armory to "portray" the wordless, noisy mob, to which Herrmann added four trumpets, four trombones, and eight drums. The result was brilliantly orchestrated cacophony.

At least one program was devoted entirely to Herrmann's music. "Melodrams," which took its title from the Greek-derived form of combined drama and music, featured four Herrmann poetry settings from his David Ross days (with Ross again narrating): the Chinese poem "The Willow Leaf," in which woodwinds, percussion, harp, and celeste weave a fragile silk frame around a charming five-tone Oriental theme; three poems from A. E. Housman's "A Shropshire Lad," whose folk song opening for horn and orchestra would reappear as the title music of *The Kentuckian* in 1954; the darkly poetic "La Belle Dame Sans Merci," with its plaintive oboe solo depicting Keats's "palely loitering" knight; and "The City of Brass," with its majestic finale that would evolve into Poseidon's theme in Herrmann's *Jason and the Argonauts* film score.

Other adventurous composers contributed to the "Workshop." Marc Blitzstein (whose musical drama *The Cradle Will Rock* was one of 1937's most controversial pieces of theater) wrote an original music play for the series called "I've Got the Tune." Norman Lloyd, a member of Orson Welles's Mercury Theatre, was among the performers: "I had never met Benny before, and I paid very little attention to him until, during the rehearsal, Herrmann slammed the podium with his fist and yelled, 'What is this C doing here?! This should be a C-SHAAP! I'm changing it to a C-SHAAP!' I looked over at Blitzstein, waiting for him to say, 'Listen Benny, stick to your own,' but he went with it. In those days one was always looking for mischief, so after the episode I went up to Benny and kidded him about it, but it fell on deaf ears; he was in no mood for jesting."[4] (Twenty-five years later, as executive producer of Alfred Hitchcock's weekly television series, Lloyd would have many more experiences with Herrmann, who came to enjoy Lloyd's occasional jibes and pranks, countering them with his own acerbic wit.)

Despite the many innovations of Herrmann's "Workshop" music, the composer was careful to maintain its subordination to the scripted performance. "When the audience says 'The orchestra is playing,' the music director has failed of his purpose," Herrmann said in July 1938. "Attention is distracted from the drama, and the whole aim of the cue music is defeated. That is why I rarely use a symphony orchestra for the Workshop, but employ a mixture instead, going easy on the strings. My idea is to disassociate in the minds of the audience from the thought of an orchestral accompaniment, so they can fix all their attention on the drama itself."[5]

By the fall of 1937, Herrmann's three years at CBS had not only allowed him to increase his sizable collection of art, literature, and scores, but they also enabled him to plan his first trip to England—not as a mere tourist, but as a representative American conductor.

Through CBS Herrmann arranged a live conducting performance on the British Broadcasting System, premiering the Prelude and Fugue of Ives's Fourth Symphony. While in England, Herrmann also visited London's major music publishers with a bundle of Ives's most ambitious scores, with Ives's authorization to sell to any interested party. According to Herrmann, every company rejected the offer.[6]

Herrmann also made a brief side-trip to Paris. While attending a concert Herrmann found himself surrounded by Nazis who, he was sure, were contemptuously discussing the Jew in their midst. Herrmann left the auditorium and returned to England the next day.[7]

His time in Britain did yield great pleasures. At last Herrmann could meet many of his musical heroes, including Ralph Vaughan Williams, Arthur Bliss, Constant Lambert, Cecil Gray, Arnold Bax, and the eccentric Lord Berners, an aristocrat composer little known outside England. For Herrmann (probably the only American conductor to have programmed Berners's music), visiting the composer was a memorably odd experience. Berners's large estate was filled with birds dyed in various colors, many sporting tinkling silver bells. The home itself was near freezing, with only a roaring fireplace in the main den to offer a semblance of warmth.[8]

The following year, Herrmann reciprocated the Englishman's hospitality with his own brand of domestic eccentrism. On his first trip to New York, Berners came to the Herrmanns' Second Avenue home for a typical Jewish dinner cooked by Ida. Also present were Louis, Rose, and Abe Polonsky. "Benny wasn't embarrassed by his family at all," Polonsky recalled, "and Berners had a wonderful time. It was like staying in an Arab tent as far as he was concerned."[9]

As CBS work brought weekly challenges, a steady income, and new friendships, Herrmann's network of boyhood friends was disintegrating. After mixed success in concert music and the theater, Jerome Moross left New York for the quick, unsteady work that Hollywood offered. Abe Polonsky soon followed.

"We tried in the worse [*sic*] way to get in touch with Moross but without avail," Polonsky wrote Herrmann in March 1937. "One fine day Syl ran into him in Woolworth and he's been around several times since. He has no contract. He gets assignments from the different studios to write under-music and is getting on pretty well. Most of the time he pals out with Dave Rackson [*sic*]. . . . [Raksin] says you insulted him the last time you met, but . . . quite seriously he said you were probably one of the best young conductors and musicologists of our time. . . . Oscar Levant is the wit in town. In fact all your old acquaintances are out here. All New York is. They sit in Brown Derby every night and insult each other—a corny lot."[10]

Herrmann was about to take his first indirect step toward joining them. It was Davidson Taylor who in 1938 appointed Herrmann composer-conductor of a new CBS drama series "The Mercury Theatre on the Air": "the first time that a complete theatrical producing company has been brought to radio," the network boasted.[11] The Mercury Players had become one of New York's most daring theater companies the previous year with their production of "Julius Caesar," which took place not in the senate houses of Rome but in the meeting rooms of the Nazi Bund. Next came "Voodoo Macbeth," a black actors' rendition of the Scots tragedy reset in the Caribbean.

For their creator, these bizarre, imaginative presentations were but rehearsals for things to come. At twenty-three, Orson Welles was brash, rebellious, brilliant, and maddeningly young for his accomplishments, augmenting his Mercury productions with starring roles on CBS and NBC (most successfully as the deep-voiced, omnipotent "Shadow" who asked each Sunday night, "What evil lurks in the hearts of men?").

In the summer of 1938, Welles, Mercury partner John Houseman, and Davidson Taylor conceived "First Person Singular," a weekly hour-long series of literary adaptations emphasizing Welles's innovative use of the sound medium. Taylor suggested the program's theme, the opening bars of Tchaikovsky's Piano Concerto no. 1 in B-flat Minor—a choice grudgingly accepted by the programming and sales departments, who had hoped for something more "flamboyant" as Welles's theme.[12]

In appointing Herrmann as the Mercury's composer, Taylor was aware of the explosive reaction the two temperamental geniuses might spark. A year earlier Herrmann had scored a Welles-directed production of *Macbeth* for the "Columbia Workshop" that Houseman dubbed "a shambles":

As musical director, [Benny] had composed a score which he had copied
and placed before the orchestra at rehearsal. Orson arrived late, according
to Herrmann, accompanied by an elderly gentlemen in kilts—with a
bagpipe. As soon as the reading began it became evident that the script
was more than twice too long. By the time it had been cut there was no
time for musical rehearsal. When Herrmann protested, Orson yelled, "No
music! No music at all!" standing, as he always did, in the center of the
studio at the main microphone, wearing earphones, which made it impossible for anyone to communicate with him on equal terms. To the bagpiper
he said, "Every time I raise this hand, you come in and play!" To the
trumpets and drums he said, "Every time I lift this hand, you play a fanfare!" And to the infuriated Herrmann, frozen on his podium in front of
his assembled orchestra, he said, "Trust me, Benny! Just trust me!"

"And that's how we went on the air," reported Benny. "Every time
Orson raised either hand, which he did frequently in the role of Macbeth,
trumpets, drums and bagpipes came in fortissimo . . . and so did a whole
lot of sound cues, including wind machines and thunder sheets."[13]*

Things began on a similar footing when Welles and Herrmann reteamed in 1938; but as Houseman observed, "Amid the screaming rows,
snapping of batons, accusations of sabotage and hurling of scripts and
scores into the air and at each other, they came to understand each other
perfectly."[14] Both men deeply respected the other's strong will, noncon-
formity, and old-world romanticism, and in later years Herrmann reflected on his Mercury Theatre days with great affection: "Welles' radio
quality, like Sir Thomas Beecham's in music, was essentially one of spon-
taneity. At the start of every broadcast Orson was an unknown quantity.
As he went along his mood would assert itself and the temperature would
start to increase till the point of incandescence. . . . Even when his shows
weren't good they were better than other people's successes. He inspired
us all—the musicians, the actors, the sound-effects men and the engineers. They'd all tell you they never worked on shows like Welles'.
Horses' hooves are horses' hooves—yet they felt different with Orson—
why? I think it had to do with the element of the unknown, the surprises
and the uncomfortable excitement of improvisation."[15]

The series premiere on July 1—a fast-paced, atmospheric version of
*Dracula*, hastily adapted by Houseman at nearby twenty-four hour Reu-
ben's Cafe[16]—set the standard for most of what followed: a virtuoso

* At least one newspaper critic praised the final effect: "[Herrmann] used trumpet fan-
fares between scenes, each one more hectic, more nervous than the last, to express the growing torture of Macbeth's mind"! (unidentified clipping, probably 1937; from the collection
of Norma Shepherd).

Welles performance (the actor assumed half a dozen roles); a stunning array of sound effects (notably the eerie, distorted reverberation of Dracula's voice); and a sparse, thrilling Herrmann score (the stinging "Dracula" theme for muted brass and graveyard bell, and a crackling variant of the Dies Irae for Jonathan Harker's driverless coachride up the Borgo Pass).

Some of Herrmann's most effective Mercury Theatre music was the briefest. "A Tale of Two Cities," Welles's game attempt to capture Dickens's historical panorama in fifty-five minutes, opens with a droll quote from Berlioz's "March to the Scaffold," a leitmotiv of slaughter heard throughout the broadcast in various guises. For John Buchan's *The Thirty-nine Steps*, Herrmann propels the espionage drama with a charged, minor-key version of "The Bonnie Banks of Scotland," casting an ironic cloud of menace over Buchan's Scottish setting.

One broadcast in late October finally put Welles and his players on the map for millions: the Halloween Eve production of H. G. Wells's *The War of the Worlds*, adapted by writer Howard Koch. By this seventeenth broadcast, Houseman recalled, "a sort of chaotic routine" had been established at Madison Avenue:

Beginning in the early afternoon—when . . . Herrmann arrived with his orchestra of high-grade symphony players—two simultaneous dramas were unfolded each week in the stale, tense air of CBS Studio One: the minor drama of the current show and the major drama of Orson's titanic struggle to get it on. . . . Every Sunday it was touch and go. As the hands of the clock moved relentlessly toward air time the crisis grew more extreme, the peril more desperate. . . . Scheduled for six—but usually nearer seven—there was a dress rehearsal, a thing of wild improvisations and irrevocable catastrophes.

After that, with only a few minutes to go, there was a final frenzy of correction and reparation, of utter confusion and absolute horror, aggravated by the gobbling of sandwiches and the bolting of oversized milkshakes. By now it was less than a minute to air time—

At that instant, quite regularly week after week, with not one second to spare, the buffoonery stopped. Suddenly out of chaos, the show emerged—delicately poised, meticulously executed, precise as clockwork, smooth as satin. And above all, like a rainbow over storm clouds, stood Orson on his podium . . . a giant in action, serene and radiant with the joy of a hard battle bravely fought, a great victory snatched from the jaws of disaster—which, in a sense, it was.[17]

In keeping with the Mercury's last-minute decision making, Koch's *War of the Worlds* script nearly lost its October 30 slot to "an extremely dreary version" of *Lorna Doone* by Houseman;[18] but despite warnings that the Mercury Theatre would be laughed off the air, Welles accepted the challenge of giving the Koch script credibility through faked news bulletins, authentic detail, and eyewitness-style presentation.

While little Herrmann music was involved in the broadcast, the CBS orchestra would play a key role in the show, simulating radio dance bands and concert recitals before and after the fast-paced news interruptions. By this time, New York actor Paul Stewart had joined the series as producer:

We had such a limited budget for the program that we could not get the dance band from CBS, who were suffering our unsponsored show on Sunday night; so we had to use the symphony men, many of whom worked with Toscanini and the New York Philharmonic. To get Benny to conduct the dance songs I had suggested (including "Stardust" and "La Cumparasita") was almost an impossibility. He didn't understand the rhythms at all. I said, "Benny, it's gotta be like *this*" and snapped my fingers—and he got very upset. He handed me the baton and said, "*You* conduct it!"

I got up on the podium. All the musicians understood Benny's personality, so when I gave the downbeat they played it just the way I wanted it. I said, "Now *that's* how to do it!" I handed the baton back to Benny, who was crestfallen.

The moment in the broadcast when Herrmann conducts "Stardust" with the symphony orchestra is one of the most hysterical musical moments in radio.[19]

Hysteria *was* the reaction the broadcast elicited, but Herrmann's conducting was not to blame. At 8:00 P.M. on October 30, Welles not only proved his critics wrong but surpassed even his own expectations, as thousands nationwide fled their homes to escape the Martian invasion of Grover's Mill, New Jersey. Switchboards, highways, bus terminals, and churches filled to capacity as Welles, Herrmann, and company gleefully leveled the East Coast with spaceship death rays.

Perhaps the broadcast's most stunning moment, the death of news reporter "Carl Phillips" in the Martian attack, owed much of its power to Herrmann's musical supervision. Recalled Houseman: "Carl Phillips lay dead, tumbling over the microphone in his fall—one of the first victims of the Martian ray. There followed a moment of absolute silence—an eternity of waiting. Then, without warning, the network's emergency fill-in was heard—somewhere in a quiet studio, a piano, close on mike, playing . . . soft and sweet as honey, for many seconds, while the fate of the universe hung in the balance." After a terse announcement that Trenton had been placed under martial law, "once again, that lone piano was heard—now a symbol of terror, shattering the dead air with its ominous tinkle. As it played on and on, its effect became increasingly sinister—a thin band of suspense stretched almost beyond endurance."[20]

By the time Herrmann was conducting the closing Tchaikovsky theme at 8:58 P.M., panic had broken loose at CBS. Seconds after the sign-off, Studio One was filled with reporters and policemen. (One habitually silent musician noted with pleasure that it was all "quite exciting.")[21] Bustled into a small back office, Welles, Houseman, and Herrmann then "sat incommunicado while network employees were busily collecting, destroying or locking up all scripts and records of the broadcast."[22] Herrmann excitedly called Lucille at home. "He was like a kid, terribly thrilled," she recalled. "He thought Orson was going to be arrested. I think he wanted to be arrested too."[23]

Reporters railed the trio with reports of nationwide fatalities; actually, there were none. In fact, once the anger and embarrassment dissipated, things were better than before for the Mercury Players: their notoriety gained them a sponsor, Campbell Soup. On December 4, the "Mercury Theatre on the Air" became the "Campbell Playhouse" with an adaptation of Daphne DuMaurier's novel *Rebecca* starring Margaret Sullivan. With a rare few weeks' hiatus in the interim, Herrmann had time to write a complete score for the December broadcast: "It was absolutely beautiful," Paul Stewart recalled, "and it was the first time to me that Benny was something more than a guy who could write bridges."[24] It also included themes Herrmann would use as the basis of his 1943 film score for *Jane Eyre*.

One Campbell broadcast became a CBS tradition: Welles's version of *A Christmas Carol*, starring an ideally cast Lionel Barrymore. It gave Herrmann his first of two opportunities to score his favorite Dickens tale. The music is not without charm, especially its music box evocation (for strings and celeste) of a snow-covered Victorian Christmas. Yet its best moments are dark and oppressive: the weird high string harmonics for Marley's ghost (anticipating Herrmann's ingenious sound trickery for 1941's *All That Money Can Buy*), and especially Herrmann's chilling portrait of the Ghost of Christmas Yet to Come, a low pianissimo timpani role and two-note string device as Welles describes "the solemn phantom, shrouded in black, draped and hooded, coming toward him slowly and silently, like a mist upon the ground."

Best of all was Welles's playful coda to the program, in which he as host-director began his weekly sign-off:

WELLES:   And so until next week, from all of us at the Campbell Playhouse,
          I am, obediently yours. . . . [Orchestra begins theme] Oh just a
          minute, Benny—uh, *Benny*. . . . Ladies and gentlemen, it's the
          night before Christmas and all through the Campbell Playhouse
          not a creature is stirring that doesn't join Lionel Barrymore in
          wishing you a merry, merry Christmas. This goes from all of us,
          from myself . . . to Miss Helgren who types the scripts; a merry
          Christmas from Benny Herrmann and his band of merry melodi-
          ans, merry Christmas ["Dracula" theme from Herrmann and or-
          chestra interrupts]—you get the idea. From Max Stair's choristers
          [horses' neighs from singers] and Harry Estman and his crew of
          sound effects [squealing train brakes] thank you, and from Orson
          Welles and his considerable aggregation of dramatic talent . . .

ALL:      Merry Christmas! [Orchestra plays "Hark the Herald Angels
          Sing" to fade]

The year of the Mercury's CBS debut marked the arrival of another exceptional dramatist to the network; but unlike Welles, Massachusetts-
born writer Norman Corwin was the epitome of modesty and grace under
pressure. His eloquent portraits of the American working man, and his
condemnations of fascism, elevated him to the top rank of CBS's writing-
directing staff, and with the 1939 verse drama "They Fly Through the Air
with the Greatest of Ease," a scathing attack on totalitarianism, his national reputation was made.

When the network's best writer and its finest composer began a series
of collaborations that year, the results were happier and smoother than
anyone could have hoped. "I never had any difficulties with Herrmann,"
Corwin said:

He was by all accounts a fractious man, abrasive and testy at times; but
usually he had good grounds. His anger was never petulant—it was always related to his standard of work, his ideals. Herrmann did nothing for
effect; he was almost brutally frank. There was no guise in him, no du-
plicity, no dissembling. In fact, he had contempt for that in others. Benny
was very impatient with hype; he was a sincere, dedicated craftsman, and
his interests lay in great work of all kinds. His reverence for Handel was
particularly conspicuous. While I considered myself fairly well educated
musically, Herrmann helped me appreciate composers whom I had not held
in the highest regard—Chabrier, for one.

There was very little lead time in my CBS productions; I used up all of
it in my first two shows, and therefore my composers, including Herrmann, were under the same constraints that I was. That never seemed to
bother Benny. I would send him pages that involved music, or I would
telephone him and thoroughly explain the premise, the action and devel-

opment I was writing. We were consonant in our approach; he was the perfect collaborator in that sense. Now and then he would make a suggestion that was at variance with my approach, and I would listen to his reasons. He always supported his suggestions very logically. On even rarer occasions, I would make a suggestion that would alter *his* mind, but it was never a question of the use of a veto.

Politically Benny was less involved than I would like to have seen him. While he had great scorn for certain politicians, he never expressed any interest in political action. He was faintly conservative, not in the Bircher sense, but I think he looked upon me as a man who was wasting too much emotion and energy in being liberal. It was the one area in which we did not find common ground. Not that we were ever antagonistic—I don't think we ever found ourselves on opposite sides. It was simply his relative indifference and neutrality that I found not particularly attractive to my mind.

I don't think Herrmann had a high threshhold of patience with humankind, or any optimistic expectations; but neither would I describe him as a pessimist. I may be putting words into his mouth, but I think he felt that so long as there was great art in the world, and artists to express themselves, the world hadn't altogether gone to hell.[25]

A bold, staccato trumpet fanfare opens "Seems Radio Is Here to Stay," a fanciful commemoration of radio's twenty-fifth anniversary and the first of many Corwin-Herrmann collaborations. The playwright's shifting, omnipotent point of view (a Corwin trademark) allowed Herrmann to create an equally broad mosaic of musical styles. Running through each is Corwin's theme of community and shared experience, from the pastoral loveliness of Herrmann's Walt Whitman setting (delicate string tremolos and single woodwinds) to a mystical description of the heavens (a long, vague string line reminiscent of the "Neptune" movement of Holst's *The Planets*). For the program's last soliloquy, a prayer for brotherhood and freedom, Herrmann delivers a patriotic rendition of the Ives favorite "The Red, White, and Blue" ("Oh Columbia the gem of the ocean . . . "), in a clear nod to Herrmann's Danbury mentor.

1939 was a key year for Ives supporters, whose number was steadily growing—owing in no small part to Herrmann's CBS broadcasts. On January 20, pianist John Kirkpatrick gave the first major performance of Ives's *Concord* Sonata at New York's Town Hall, a much-publicized event that led the *New Yorker* to commission an Ives profile from Lucille Fletcher. During their first interview, Lucille recalled,

[Ives] seemed very flushed, very tense and friendly and . . . shaking with excitement. . . . He would get himself terribly worked up to an extent that he would suddenly gasp for breath and then have to lie down. And nobody ever stopped him from carrying on. He seemed to approve having me write the profile, so I set to work to do the research. . . . And that whole year I spent traveling around interviewing people. . . .

I wrote the article and called it "A Connecticut Yankee in Music." The *New Yorker*'s policy was not to submit a profile for anybody to approve, but I submitted mine to Mr. Ives, and it caused a furor—he wanted practically everything taken out. He wanted to put in a great section on an [antiwar] amendment he had, and he wanted most of the piece at the end devoted to his ideas on peace. . . . Well, as time went on, we just couldn't come to any terms at all; the thing was totally emasculated. I decided that he was too old, he was too fine a person, and he was too sick to push it. I couldn't please him, and what I would have left would be nothing. So I said to the *New Yorker*, "I won't submit it—it's not good enough." I withdrew it. It had taken about six months and a lot of legwork, but I told Mr. Ives that he could forget about it. Well, he was very pleased, and he insisted on sending me a hundred dollars.[26]

If Ives was on the brink of recognition, so was his young champion. Months after the Kirkpatrick premiere, the most famous chapter of Bernard Herrmann's career was to begin—in Hollywood.

# FIVE

I believe that the film contains potentialities for the combination of all the arts such as Wagner never dreamed of, and I would therefore urge those distinguished musicians who have entered the world of the cinema to realize their responsibility in helping to take the film out of the realm of hackwork and make it a subject worthy of a real composer.

*Ralph Vaughan Williams*

The fall of 1939 was a season of turning points. On September 1, the "war scare" ended and the war in Europe began, reaffirming Herrmann's anti-German sentiments and his American pride. More indirectly, the war would also hamper Herrmann's opportunities as a concert conductor. A new influx of German émigrés was arriving in New York, and the second era of European dominance in the American arts was about to begin. The war would also inspire much of Herrmann's best radio work—his scores for Corwin's "Untitled" and "On a Note of Triumph," as well as his most affecting concert piece, *For the Fallen.*

It was the season in which, on October 2, Lucille Fletcher became Mrs. Bernard Herrmann, in a small ceremony attended by about forty people, including the Herrmann and Fletcher families. After five years of courtship on and off the New York subway system, Herrmann had given Lucille an ultimatum: marry him or he would leave her life forever. She finally said yes. Lucille's father, long against the marriage, could no longer oppose her: in December 1938 he had suffered a major stroke that left him partially paralyzed and unable to speak. He died in 1948 after ten years as an invalid, during which time Herrmann contributed financially to his support.[1]

The wedding ceremony was performed by Dr. John Paul Jones, a Protestant minister and a friend of Lucille's, and a Brooklyn rabbi. When the newly wed conductor returned to CBS weeks later and gave his first rehearsal downbeat, the CBS Symphony greeted him not with Arnold Bax but with "The Wedding March."[2] An elegant apartment on 57th Street became their home, filled with English furniture, paintings, books, and scores.

It was also the season when Orson Welles asked Herrmann to score his first film—what would become *Citizen Kane*.

It was only a question of time before the twenty-four-year-old Welles tackled film, and before he was given the creative freedom he demanded. The opportunity came from George Schaefer, head of RKO Studios ("Quality Pictures at a Premium Price"), whose history included triumphs (the Astaire-Rogers musicals, *King Kong*) and expensive flops (among them *Bringing Up Baby*, later reappraised as one of Hollywood's best "screwball" comedics). In Welles, Schaefer hoped for both prestige and box office; and to attract the actor-director he delivered the most unconditional contract ever offered to a first-time filmmaker.[3]

From Welles's earliest production meetings at RKO there was no doubt who would score his film. "Orson insisted I go [to Hollywood] despite my protests that I'd never worked on a movie before," Herrmann said in 1975. "He and I have never really had any time for the establishment, and when he did the deal with RKO, they only wanted to pay me a small fee. Orson said 'No—he gets the same as Max Steiner.' RKO, however, protested. 'Who is he? Why should we?' Welles persisted, 'If he's good enough to do my score, he's good enough to get the best price.' (Herrmann received $10,000.) I was very lucky."[4] Still, to many Hollywood executives Herrmann was an unwelcome outsider. "I was told by the heads of many music departments that there was no room for people like me there," he recalled. "They had a tight little corporation going."[5]

If Herrmann was a neophyte to film, it was in practice only. No snob about the cinema, he was familiar not only with American films and film composers but also with their European counterparts—from the well known, like Prokofiev and William Walton, to the obscure, like Alan Rawsthorne (*Uncle Silas*) and Polish composer Karol Rathaus, who scored a 1931 German film version of *The Brothers Karamazov*.* Herrmann once sought out Rathaus at New York's Queens College, where he taught composition. Recalled Herrmann, "The man was one of the absolute geniuses of film music, but for the last 35 years of his life no one ever gave him the opportunity to do any kind of film."[6]

Herrmann knew the obstacles a film composer faced: "I had heard of the many handicaps that exist for a composer in Hollywood. One was the

---

*Ironically, given Herrmann's most famous collaboration in film, one of the first movies that he and Lucille saw together was *The Thirty-nine Steps* directed by Alfred Hitchcock.

great speed with which scores often had to be written—sometimes in as little as two or three weeks. Another was that the composer seldom had time to do his own orchestration. And again—that once the music was written and conducted, the composer had little to say about the sound levels or dynamics of the score in the finished film."[7] But as Herrmann knew, Welles's film would be different—and more than one CBS musician would remember Herrmann's excitement as he announced his leave of absence to go to Hollywood.

Ironically, the project came at a time when Herrmann's career as a concert composer was gaining momentum. In April 1939 Herrmann's *Moby Dick* was selected for performance by the New York Philharmonic. Although its manager, Arthur Judson, had helped begin CBS, it was in spite of Judson that the cantata found a place in the Philharmonic season; the promoter-manager was no admirer of Herrmann's temper, his unorthodox concert programming, or his conducting.[8] It was John Barbirolli, the orchestra's chief conductor since 1936, who championed the work.

If Stokowski represented the thrill of the experimental to Herrmann, Barbirolli was for him the most poetic of conductors.[9] Twelve years Herrmann's senior, Barbirolli shared with him a passion for the English music of Delius, Vaughan Williams, and Elgar (as a young man Barbirolli had played in the cello section in the premiere of Elgar's Cello Concerto, under Elgar's direction). Barbirolli also shared some of Herrmann's excitement for new music and, with the Philharmonic, premiered several American works, usually against much opposition.

"I heard with the most incredulous astonishment that whenever we announce new American works on our programmes, many subscribers asked to have their tickets changed to the next concerts in which these works were not listed," Barbirolli wrote his fiancée, Evelyn Rothwell. "This can only mean one thing: that they are prepared to damn a new work before they hear it."[10] *Moby Dick* was no exception, despite a first-rate performance by the Philharmonic and soloists, including baritone Robert Weede as Ahab. Many critics were put off not only by the work but also by the elaborate, CBS-generated publicity that preceded the April 11 premiere. (Barbirolli's remark that the score was "the most important thing I've seen from any young American composer" probably did not help.)[11] Particularly harsh was *New York Times* critic Olin Downes's assessment of the work: "as pretentious and ineffectually noisy as it is raw, naive and unresourceful in its approach to its tremendous theme."[12] (Downes was one of the most conservative music critics in the 1920s and 1930s, with few good words for any American composers or conductors.)

An exception was the review of Francis D. Perkins in the *New York Herald Tribune*, which astutely perceived Herrmann's strengths: "It reveals a remarkable command of the resources of instrumental color and timbre, an exceptional ability to depict with convincing vividness a wide variety of emotional hues and atmospheres. . . . Mr. Herrmann's power for dramatic suggestion is best revealed in his instruments, although both the singers and the orchestra contributed to the sense of impending tragedy which marked the work as a whole."[13]

Not incidentally, the premiere of *Moby Dick* began one of Herrmann's longest friendships. Recalled Evelyn Barbirolli:

John was always deeply touched that Benny admired him so much and said so to everybody. At a time when John was having a hard time with the New York critics, Benny was always championing him, and John never forgot that; he always felt that Benny's loyalty as a friend and his honesty were completely unpolitical. If Benny felt a thing was right, my god he'd stick to it—and what a lovely quality that is.

Benny never wrapped up anything inside him, and was often to the point of rudeness. He was not an easy guest on social occasions; it was not in him at all to be polite or tactful—which if you loved him was very endearing. Also, Benny would talk enormously of himself and monopolize conversations. If you did love him it was delightful, because his conversation was so fascinating; but John used to say he wished Benny would be a little more careful, because he put people off and prevented them thinking the best of him.

Still, you couldn't alter him—and he was pure gold, really.[14]

After their marriage in October 1939, Herrmann and Lucille left directly for Hollywood on the elegant Twentieth Century. As they boarded the train burdened with luggage, Ida Herrmann made her way to the front of the well-wishers and handed the couple an enormous bowl of strudel. "What'll I do with this?" Herrmann asked. "Eat it!" Ida replied.[15]

As work on *Kane* continued during 1940, the couple made several trips between New York and California, some by plane or train, and one in their 1940 Packard convertible. The most memorable cross-country incident occurred on their drive, when Lucille spotted "an odd-looking man, first on the Brooklyn Bridge and then on the Pulaski Skyway. We never say him again. However, I didn't quite know what to do with the idea until a year later, when . . . I conceived the idea of doing it as a ghost story."[16] The result was "The Hitchhiker," the Campbell Playhouse's best radio play of 1941, which inspired one of Herrmann's most chilling scores. (After the completion of *Kane*, the Campbell Play-

house returned to the air from CBS' Los Angeles affiliate KNX on Sunset
Boulevard.)

On the recommendation of Herrmann's newly acquired agent, the couple rented a furnished Spanish-style home in the Griffith Park area of Los
Angeles. Always a lover of holidays, Herrmann decided to host a Halloween party shortly after moving in. Lucille recalled the result:

Benny found a big tin bucket for bobbing apples and bought packages of
marshmallows to hang on strings from the timbered ceiling of the dining
room. He planned to reproduce the old Halloween custom of peeling an
apple and tossing the peel over your shoulder to see if it would form the
initial of your true love. The refreshments would be hot dogs, potato
salad, cider, and pumpkin pie, but no hard liquor, since neither of us
drank.

We decorated the house with autumn leaves, shocks of corn, pumpkins,
and orange and black streamers. It was perfect, Benny's dream fantasy of a
Halloween party. But the guests, mostly actors from the Mercury Theatre
with their wives and concubines, were used to something livelier in the
way of liquid refreshment, and the party dragged noticeably. Not until my
uncle offered to go down to Los Feliz Boulevard and pick up a case of
"booze" did the party pick up. Soon it became very lively indeed. But
nobody bobbed for apples or ate the marshmallows. They just broke most
of the rented dishes.

Benny was very disappointed.[17]

Orson Welles's film debut was to have been an adaptation of Conrad's
*Heart of Darkness* (one of the Mercury's best radio plays), told in the
first person by using the camera only as the narrator Marlow's point of
view. Welles had begun discussions of the score with Herrmann when the
project was deemed too costly. Welles next considered a light thriller titled
"Smiler with a Knife," which in turn was abandoned for a wholly original
script idea by Welles and Houseman: a multiperspective account of a great
man's life, with industrializing America as its backdrop. Their chief model
was newspaper tycoon William Randolph Hearst; the film was *Citizen
Kane*, the boldest and most innovative American film of its time.[18]

The triumph was, of course, a collaborative one. The screenplay, by
Herman Mankiewicz and Welles, captured not only the feel and sweep of
its time period, but also the personal tragedy of Charles Foster Kane,
whose abuses of power leave him isolated physically and emotionally from
the world he helped to shape. (" 'Kane,' in my opinion, was totally misunderstood," Herrmann said in 1975. "It's not really a picture about
Hearst: it's a picture about wealth and power. It's a composite portrait of

Orson Welles and Harold McCormick, who financed the Chicago Opera Company for a second-rate soprano named Ganna Walska.")[19] Its photographic style was conceived in part by Gregg Toland, a remarkable thirty-six-year-old cameraman. While many of *Kane*'s most stunning techniques (its baroque perspective shots, its deep-focus photography) were not original to this film, no previous work had utilized their dramatic possibilities more brilliantly.

As striking as its visual innovations was *Kane*'s richly layered soundtrack, a result of Welles's radio training. Integral to the film's design, Welles realized, was Herrmann's score—which was why, against all Hollywood precedent, the composer began work on the film from the start of its production. "I was given twelve weeks in which to do my job," Herrmann said. "This not only gave me ample time to think about the film and to work out a general artistic plan of the score, but also enabled me to do my orchestration and conducting. I worked on the film, reel by reel, as it was being shot and cut. In this way, I had a sense of the picture being built, and of my own music being a part of that building."[20] (Herrmann's score was composed in Hollywood and in New York, where Herrmann spent March and April supervising the *Moby Dick* premiere.) Intuitively, Herrmann grasped what *Kane* needed—and what film music in general could achieve. "The real reason for music is that a piece of film, by its nature, lacks a certain ability to convey emotional overtones. Many times in many films, dialogue may not give a clue to the feelings of a character. It's the music or the lighting or camera movement. When a film is well made, the music's function is to fuse a piece of film so that it has an inevitable beginning and end. When you cut a piece of film you can do it perhaps a dozen ways, but once you put music to it, that becomes the absolutely final way. . . . Music essentially provides an unconscious series of anchors for the viewer. It isn't always apparent and you don't have to know, but it serves its function."[21]

By 1940, in the forty-odd years since the Lumière Brothers first matched their flickering images of trains and workhouses with a piano accompaniment, film music had evolved from slipshod blending of popular tunes and sound effects to a highly polished, if often uninspired, medium.[22] Early patchwork scores like Joseph Carl Briel's for D. W. Griffith's *Birth of a Nation* (which cribbed from Liszt, Verdi, Beethoven, Wagner, and Tchaikovsky for this tale of the American South) were joined by original works such as Edmund Meisel's scores for Eisenstein's *Potemkin* (1925) and *October* (1928).

The early 1930s saw the beginning of true innovation in the field: in the Soviet Union, Prokofiev's score for *Lieutenant Kijé* (followed by his collaborations with Eisenstein on *Alexander Nevsky* and *Ivan the Terrible*); in Britain, scores by William Walton (*Escape Me Never*, 1935) and Arthur Bliss (*Things to Come*, 1935); and in America, the earliest masterpieces of Max Steiner (*King Kong*, 1933, *The Informer*, 1934), Alfred Newman (*Street Scene*, 1931), Franz Waxman (*The Bride of Frankenstein*, 1935), and Erich Wolfgang Korngold (*Captain Blood*, 1935).

American-based composers especially set the standard for much of what followed in the next two decades. "Many of these pioneers moved to Hollywood from Europe, and their style was derived from the lush romanticism of the Viennese opera," noted film music historian Mark Evans. For example, Steiner and Korngold "grew up listening to the operas of Wagner, Strauss and Puccini and the symphonies of Mahler. Both were particularly influenced by the harmonic idiom of Richard Strauss. Both preferred large symphony orchestras, with full, lush harmonies, extensive doubling of individual parts and expressive melodic lines."[23]

This style characterized the best and the worst of Hollywood's output in the 1930s, which was often produced assembly line–style by several musicians collaborating on a score. Many of the composers came from Broadway's Tin Pan Alley, their facility for hummable melodies and their accessible styles making them ideal to producers. And while some of the cinema's most memorable scores were written in the late 1930s (e.g., Korngold's *The Adventures of Robin Hood* and Steiner's *Gone with the Wind*), it was an era of virtually homogenous stylistic approach. The year may have been 1940, but in Hollywood recording studios it was usually nineteenth-century Vienna.

With *Citizen Kane*, a musical revolution took place. Undeniably Neo-Romantic in style, Herrmann's score was nonetheless unique in its blend of dramatic scoring and its incorporation of indigenous American music, its innovative orchestration and its pioneering use of bridging musical device. " 'Citizen Kane' was completely different from any other film I ever made," Herrmann recalled. "The score, like the film, works like a jigsaw."[24] Rejecting the then-prevalent Hollywood practice of scoring a film with virtually nonstop music (most typical of Warner Brothers movies of the period), Herrmann instead composed brief aural "bridges" that signaled a quick temporal or scenic transition in the film.

"I used a great deal of what might be termed 'radio scoring,' " Herrmann wrote shortly after *Kane*'s release. "The movies frequently overlook opportunities for musical cues which last only a few seconds—that is, from five to fifteen seconds at the most—the reason being that the eye usually covers the transition. On the other hand, in radio drama, every scene must be bridged by some sort of sound device, so that even five seconds of music becomes a vital instrument in telling the ear that the scene is shifting. I felt that in this film, where the photographic contrasts were often so sharp and sudden, a brief cue—even two or three chords—might heighten the effect immeasurably."[25]

This economy of musical device would be as much a Herrmann trademark in film as it was in radio, as would his use of unique orchestral combinations. "Since the middle of the eighteenth century, the symphony orchestra has always been an agreed body of men performing a repertoire of music," Herrmann said in 1971. "But since a film score is only written for one performance, I could never see the logic in making a rule of the standard symphony orchestra. A film score can be made up of different fantastic groupings of instruments, as I've done throughout my entire career."[26]

For *Kane*'s famous opening sequence—the camera's eerie tour of Xanadu, Kane's imposing estate—Herrmann uses a highly unconventional ensemble to create a "subterranean, strange heaviness of death and futility":[27] twelve flutes, (including four alto and four bass), contrabass clarinets, tubas, trombones, low percussion, and vibraphone. One of the film's longest musical sequences, it gives the two essential pieces of the score's musical puzzle: "I decided that I would use the old musical form of the leitmotiv, in other words a theme that is transferred incessantly. So the very first bars I wrote are a series of few notes that dominate the entire film, no matter what's happening. In my mind it was a sort of variant on the ancient hymn 'Dies Irae,' and seemed to suggest to me what the subject of *Kane* was, which is 'All is vanity.' "[28] Use of leitmotivs in *Kane*, Herrmann felt, was "practically imperative," giving a unity to the film's time-jumping narrative.[29]

The use of a "series of few notes" would be characteristic of Herrmann's essentially nonmelodic style in film. "I think a short phrase has certain advantages," he said in 1975. "The short phrase is easier to follow for audiences, who listen with only half an ear. . . . The reason I don't like this tune business is that a tune has to have eight or sixteen bars, which limits a composer. Once you start, you've got to finish—eight or sixteen bars. Otherwise the audience doesn't know what the hell it's all about."[30]

The second musical clue is heard almost immediately as a visual montage of Xanadu's relics is accompanied by an eerie four-note theme on the vibraphone: Herrmann's motive for Rosebud, Kane's childhood sled and the symbol of his discarded innocence. "Musically, the prelude tells you what the whole film is about," Herrmann noted proudly.[31] "This second theme tells everybody what Rosebud is, even though they soon forget about it. But the music has told them right away."[32]

The funereal tone of Kane's death explodes into the shrill fanfare of "News on the March," Welles's witty parody of the "March of Time" newsreel series and a brilliant expository device to tell the story of Kane's very public private life. None of the music in this sequence was composed by Herrmann; it was culled entirely from RKO's music library and edited by the studio's newsreel department "at Orson's request. He said they had their own crazy way of cutting."[33]

Anthony Collins's stirring "Belgian March" from the film *Nurse Edith Cavell* accompanies the mock newsreel's titles, followed by an excerpt from Alfred Newman's lush *Gunga Din* score as we view Kane's "stately pleasure dome" of Xanadu. Other RKO cues are quoted in the fast-paced montage—Roy Webb's theme from *Reno* for the growing Kane empire, fragments of Webb's ominous *Five Came Back* score to introduce the powerful Thatcher. All are cheerfully obliterated by the rapid sequencing of musical fragment after fragment, reducing the cues to a superficiality that perfectly complements the empty newsreel footage that fails to illuminate its complex subject.

Other non-Herrmann compositions are used in the film for sharp dramatic effect. Charles Barrett and Haven Johnson's "In the Mizz," a bluesy 1933 jazz tune, introduces us to the alcoholic Susan Alexander, and the theme is quietly recalled after her failed suicide attempt. "Oh Mr. Kane," a tune composed by Herman Ruby, serves as Kane's jaunty campaign theme during his failed bid for governor; Herrmann recalls it later in the form of a soft ballad as Kane, alone in the *Inquirer* office, contemplates his political ruin.

*Kane's* supreme musical sequence is Herrmann's grand pastiche of Franco-Oriental opera, *Salammbô*, a work specially written for Susan Alexander's disastrous operatic debut. (The Flaubert novel was also the subject of two genuine operas by Reyer and Mussorgsky, the latter unfinished.) Although Herman Mankiewicz's script cites Massenet's *Thaïs* as the work being performed[34] (*Thaïs* was written for one of William Randolph Hearst's loves, opera singer Sybil Sanderson), the commissioning of an original opera for the film was for neither diplomatic nor budgetary reasons, according to Herrmann:

Our problem was to create something that would give the audience the feeling of the quicksand into which this simple little girl, having a charming but small voice, is suddenly thrown. And we had to do it in cinematic terms, not musical ones. It had to be done quickly. We had to have the sound of an enormous orchestra pounding at her while everyone is fussing over her, and then—"Now get going—go!" they throw her into the quicksand. . . .

How could we achieve this effect musically? If Susan couldn't sing at all, then we know she wouldn't have found herself in this position. But she had something of a little voice. So I wrote this piece in a very high tessitura, so that a girl with a modest little voice would be completely hopeless in it. . . .

We got a very charming singer [Jean Forward] to dub Susan's voice, explaining to her the purpose of the effect. Notice—the reason Susan is struggling so hard is *not* that she cannot sing, but rather that the demands of the part are purposely greater than she can ever meet.[35]

A telegram from Welles to Herrmann in July 1940 supports Herrmann's recollection: "Opera sequence is early in shooting, so must have fully orchestrated recorded track before shooting. Susie sings as curtain goes up in first act, and I believe there is no opera of importance where soprano leads with chin like this. Therefore suggest it be original . . . by you—parody on typical Mary Garden vehicle. . . . Suggest *Salammbo* which gives us phony production scene of Ancient Rome and Carthage, and Susie can dress like Grand Opera neoclassic courtesan. . . . Here is chance for you to do something witty and amusing—and now is the time for you to do it. I love you dearly. Orson."[36]

There remains some confusion as to the authorship of *Salammbô*'s text. Lucille Fletcher recalled preparing it;[37] yet in a 1973 memoir John Houseman (who worked uncredited on the script of *Kane*) claimed he had assembled lines from Racine's "Athalie" and "Phèdre" for the aria. The resulting text, as Houseman acknowledged, was "fairly implausible and unintelligible"[38] but dramatically sound, adding another level of irony to Salammbô/Susan's plight: "Oh cruel one! You have to hear me. . . . It is futile to escape you." The aria itself is among Herrmann's most powerful writing for voice, in both its lyric beauty and its demanding vocal range. Both aspects are heard in the aria's coda, which climaxes in a thrilling high D, hopelessly outside Susan's range. (In 1943, soprano Eileen Farrell did the piece justice on Herrmann's CBS series "Invitation to Music.")

A stunning use of music with visual montage is *Kane*'s celebrated breakfast sequence, which chronicles the collapse of Kane's first marriage through a series of quick time dissolves: "For this montage I used the old classic form of theme and variations. A waltz in the style of Waldteufel [a Welles favorite] is the theme. It is heard during the first scene, then,

as discord crops up, the variations begin. Each scene is a separate variation. Finally the waltz theme is heard bleakly in the high registers of the
violins."[39] Another incisive use of music to integrate images underscores
Kane's early *Inquirer* days. In this "miniature ballet," Herrmann uses period dance forms—gallops, polkas, cancans—to capture the frenetic
rhythms of the young tycoon's adventures.

But it is the two principal motives—the "destiny" and "Rosebud"
themes—that provide the core of Herrmann's musical character study.
They are powerfully united in the film's final sequence, in which Rosebud
is destroyed forever: "The ending of 'Kane' gave me a wonderful opportunity to arrive at a complete musical statement, since the ending contains
no dialogue with the exception perhaps of one or two lines. I wished at the
end of the film to summon forth and draw all the dramatic threads together. . . . I used a full orchestra for the simple reason that, from the
time the music of the final sequence begins to the end of the film, the music has effectively left the film, and become an apotheosis of the entire
work."[40] According to Herrmann, the music was recorded before the
scene was shot "and was used as an enormous playback. . . . [Camera-
man] Gregg Toland followed the music, and we worked together. The music was created first, and camera motion to find the characters followed the
music. But I didn't create it—we all did it together."[41]

By the end of principal shooting, most of Herrmann's score for *Kane*
was completed. As he would throughout his career, Herrmann insisted on
doing his own orchestrating. "Color is very important," he later said.
"This whole rubbish of other people orchestrating your music is so
wrong. . . . I always tell them, 'Listen, boys, I'll give you the first
page of the "Lohengrin" Prelude with all the instruments marked. You
write it out. I bet you won't come within 50% of Wagner.' To orchestrate
is like a thumbprint. I can't understand having someone else do it. It
would be like someone putting color to your paintings."[42]

*Kane's* score was recorded in the fall of 1940. Unlike most studios, RKO
rarely used the "click track" process of score synchronization; but under
the stopwatch supervision of music head Constantin Bakaleinikoff, the result was invariably polished and precise.

Seven years of radio conducting and an innate dramatic sense made
Herrmann a natural for film conducting. Hollywood musicians quickly
learned that orchestral timbre was as important to the conductor as exact
timing. "I never remember him being satisfied with any timpanist's sticks
on the beginning of a date," recalled bassoonist Don Cristlieb, who
worked on virtually all of Herrmann's American films:

Neither was he satisfied with brass mutes, particularly the horns'. He did not like the short, compact, opera-model contrabassoon, preferring it to be extended upwards. He did not want to mix wood and metal flutes and piccolos. While a conductor like Alfred Newman loved high-intensity string playing with a lot of vibrato, Herrmann was just the opposite: he wanted a cool sound with almost no vibrato. He'd abuse the orchestra for half the morning: "Get that hysterical sound outta the strings!"

He also insisted on full-value notes in a score and said triplets should never be hurried, even allowing triplets to extend past the bar. Herrmann never started a date without fussing over these details, and there was always considerable trauma and outright outrage within a new orchestra and its players. But when musicians realized Benny bore no personal grudges and was only interested in performance, things began to improve, and by the end of the day Benny would be enjoying himself and telling jokes.

*Citizen Kane* was a grand experience. The music cutter sitting at the desk monitoring takes would say, "Cues 22 and 23," and Herrmann would answer, "Whaddaya mean? My music has titles! *Use* the titles!" Most of the studios were geared to the breakdown sheet, which they would use to get rid of excess players as they finished their last cue. Obviously, this had been done with these cues, but Herrmann wasn't allowing it.

When it came time for lunch, Benny said, "Let's break, I'm hungry." Bakaleinikoff—Bakki to us—said, "Benny, if you do one more cue we can send some people home." Benny replied, "I'm going to eat. Here's the stick—YOU conduct it if ya want to!"

That delighted the orchestra to no end.[43]

Another professional friendship made on *Kane* began in typically combative fashion, as RKO sound engineer James G. Stewart recalled:

The music for *Citizen Kane* was recorded over a period of time. The picture was not ready for dubbing all at one time, which is normally the case. After one of the early music sessions the music came to the dubbing stage. . . . Without either Welles or Herrmann being present I played the sequence a couple of times with the film. I didn't like the music very much and I think my complaint was mainly about the mechanics of it. It didn't seem to work with the scene. Then Bernard Herrmann came along. I knew nothing about him except that he had come out of the radio field where he'd had considerable success. . . .

I mentioned to him that I didn't think [the cue] was quite right . . . and he simply stormed all over me: I was an idiot, I didn't understand his music, I didn't understand what he was doing with the scene, and so on. . . . He left the stage and returned a little later with Welles.

I had met Welles and talked with him a few times, but I didn't know him at all well. We ran the sequence and Bernard Herrmann made his remark about my incompetence and the fact that I shouldn't even be on the show. Welles's comment was, "Well, I don't like the cue either, so I think we'll have to do something about it!" The music was redone, although I don't recall the cue's subsequent history.

I very much enjoyed my relationship with Herrmann with the exception of that opening incident, and even that passed quickly. But you couldn't be buddies with him. Compliments from Herrmann—and Welles—were very few and far between.* They assumed that your ego was as big as theirs and you know you're good, so why should they go to the trouble to remind you?

One day I was sitting at the sound console with two or three other mixers. The door on that stage was an old one with a heavy latch, like a refrigerator's. All of a sudden there was a big BANG and the door flew open and there was Bernie, enraged. For a minute and a half or two he discussed Orson and Orson's way of dealing with whatever the situation was. Orson had done something to his music, or wanted to do something; it was mostly a personal thing directed at Welles. Finally Bernie stalked out and slammed the door. We just sat there in shock. Then the door opened, and Bernie said, "Understand—I'm talking about Orson the man—not Orson the artist!" SLAM![44]

Another important collaborator was the film's editor, twenty-six-year-old Robert Wise, soon to embark on his own successful career as a director. Wise found Herrmann

bright as hell and irascible as hell—a very rounded person. One time he came into the editing room and started raising heck about something. Finally I just got fed up and told him to go to hell and get out of the room. He said if he didn't get it straight he'd go back to New York, and I said, "Well, the hell with you! Go back to New York. Who needs you?" Half an hour later I went to the commissary to have lunch, and there was Bernie at the table, waving me over, just as friendly as could be.

One thing I was terribly impressed with was his quickness and professionalism, his ability to change things quickly on the set. I suppose this came from his experience in radio. But in those days it was very common for a composer to have a real lock on an edited sequence and say, "That's it, I've got the timing on it." If you fooled around with a scene after Max Steiner, the top man at the time, had scored it, there was hell to pay.

Orson didn't pay much attention to that. Bernie had the timings, and Orson made some changes in a scene. I tried to say this would be very difficult when we got to scoring, but Orson wouldn't hear it. Well, we got to the scoring stage with the new timings, but Benny wasn't upset; he

*Herrmann did acknowledge Stewart in his 1941 *New York Times* article on the score.

said, "Okay, we can cut this bar here, and I'll pull this together . . . ,"
and he very facilely and quickly adjusted his music, with great judgment,
to fit the changes. I had worked with a lot of music directors before, like
Max and Roy Webb, and they wouldn't hear of a change in their music. I
was so impressed with Bernie, that he didn't bat an eyelash.[45]

Welles loved the *Kane* score. Years later he cited Herrmann as one of
his most important collaborators on the film;[46] and not long before his
death in October 1985, Welles told director Henry Jaglom that Herrmann's music was "50 percent responsible" for *Kane*'s artistic success.[47]

After months of editing, threats from the Hearst empire to ban the
film, and a bid from Louis B. Mayer to destroy the film's negative to pac-
ify the tycoon, *Citizen Kane* opened in New York on May 1, 1941, to critical raves. Public response to the film, however, was cool, and Welles was
never again to have the same creative autonomy on a studio film.

"I was fortunate indeed to start my career with a film like *Citizen
Kane*," Herrmann said in 1972. "It's been a downhill run ever since!"[48]
Yet while *Kane* may have been a premature high point for some of its
young participants, for Herrmann—who proved that a gifted outsider
could find recognition in Hollywood—it was just the beginning.

# SIX

I cannot and will not have anything to do with the world of impresarios, directors, businessmen, shopkeepers—all the innumerable varieties of grocer disguised under different names.

*Hector Berlioz*

By the summer of 1941, Herrmann was already scoring his second film.

Since the days of silent film the tale of Faust and his pact with the devil had been a durable theme for Hollywood variations; but none topped *All That Money Can Buy*, Stephen Vincent Benet's sparkling version of the tale, set in nineteenth-century New Hampshire. Filmed at RKO shortly after *Kane*'s completion, the film was another instance of innovative talent working with creative freedom.

Walter Huston gave a wonderful performance as Mr. Scratch, a cunningly folksy Beelzebub, and Edward Arnold was a formidable match as statesman Daniel Webster. German-born director William Dieterle, himself a former actor, was responsible for several of RKO and Warner Brothers' best films, including *The Hunchback of Notre Dame* (1939) and *The Life of Emile Zola* (1937).

But crucial to the film's success was the reuniting of three young collaborators from *Citizen Kane*: editor Robert Wise, sound engineer James G. Stewart, and Bernard Herrmann. Dieterle's choice of Herrmann after his success on *Kane* was not surprising, considering the two films' thematic similarities: both celebrate American independence while recognizing the dangers of unchecked power; both needed a composer sensitive to the musical culture of these period stories. (In 1937 Herrmann had scored the "CBS Workshop" version of "Daniel Webster," though none of his radio music was used in the film.)

Just as Welles had done, Dieterle made Herrmann part of the film during its production. He showed Herrmann each day's rushes and introduced him to actors and technicians. He also trusted Herrmann enough to wait until the first day of recording to hear any of the score.[1] Not surprisingly, Herrmann considered Dieterle a director of rare erudition and musical sophistication. (Stewart, however, regarded Dieterle as an eccentric pedant, whose problems with English and rigorous adherence in later years to horoscope predictions for shooting dates made him a troublesome collaborator.)[2]

One of Herrmann's favorite memories of his association with Dieterle would be recalled over many a dinner and studio luncheon. Evident in it is Herrmann's pride, as well as his love of a sharp-toothed anecdote: "I was at a party at William Dieterle's house which Thomas Mann attended. Also present were a few Hollywood screenwriters—the sort who decided they were the Great American Novelist, but for the moment they were hoping for better things. One of them came up to Thomas Mann and almost bowed as he moaned, 'How can a wonderful writer like you even talk to miserable whores like us?' [Here Herrmann would wring his hands obsequiously, with devastating mimicry.] Mann looked at him for a second and said, 'My dear sir, you are not big enough to make yourself so small.' "[3]

Like *Kane*, Herrmann's second film score is highly American in flavor, empathetic to both nature (here, rustic New Hampshire) and vernacular music. Traditional folk melodies are deftly incorporated into the score: the boisterous "Devil's Dream," which accompanies the film's title and finale; the eloquent "Springfield Mountain" to underscore the farmers' plight;* and, most memorably, a diabolical rendition of "Pop Goes the Weasel" as a fiddle-playing Mr. Scratch turns a barnyard square dance into a devilish free-for-all.

This last sequence was a particular challenge for Herrmann and Stewart, who played a significant role in realizing this remarkable score. Herrmann recalled:

We had to have a fiddle reel nobody else could play. So I had an idea . . . [and] since then it's proven to be very popular: I simply imposed a series of tracks on top of each other. We had a violinist who played "Pop Goes the Weasel"—then he played another version, another one, another one, and another one. Then these were all combined to make one violin, playing the most impossible things that no one violinist could play: harmonic pizzicatos, harmonic pizzicato, and arco simultaneously. . . . As a matter of fact, when I had the final combination, I played it to Heifetz, and we told

---

*Herrmann later claimed to have written Aaron Copland a scathing letter accusing Copland of plagiarism for using "Springfield Mountain" in his 1942 *Lincoln Portrait* (Elmer Bernstein, *Filmmusic Notebook*, no. 2 [1977]: 20).

him we'd engaged a brilliant young Hungarian, and he said, "Quick! Quick! Let me meet him!" When we explained to him what it was, he was so impressed with the technique that he recorded the Bach double violin concerto playing both parts himself. . . .

Of course, people have said to me, you didn't have to do it that way; you could have gotten four violinists. Well, it wouldn't sound like one man playing; it would sound like a quartet of violins. It's only a small point in the film, and yet I feel a composer who doesn't pay as much attention to a small point like that is really being overpaid and ought to be dismissed.

Finding quick solutions that give you the same result is not the same thing. I remember the great care William Dieterle took, and the days that were spent with Walter Huston to synchronize to the track of the violin. . . . William Dieterle never heard of "You've got a schedule."

To create a unique sound to accompany Mr. Scratch's supernatural appearances, "We got out a recording crew and went down to San Fernando [near Los Angeles], and we recorded the [sound of] singing telephone wires—which we used as the background for Mephisto when he first encounters Jabez Stone."[4] The effect was near-subliminal and memorably eerie.

Equally thrilling are the score's purely musical sequences, especially the Ivesian, breakneck scherzo that propels Mr. Scratch on his sleigh ride to Hades (a sequence cut from existing U.S. prints of the film), as well as Herrmann's own favorite scene,[5] the mournful "Miser's Waltz" as Scratch is danced to death by his lovely assistant (Simone Simon). (Other, more nostalgic *valses tristes* appear throughout Herrmann's film and concert music: the wistful "Memory Waltz" from *The Snows of Kilimanjaro*; the love theme from *Obsession*; and the *valse lente* of his string quartet, *Echoes*.) For a chase on horseback, Herrmann complemented Stewart's intricate soundtrack of natural sounds and dialogue with sparse, dramatic kettledrum punctuations.

If *Citizen Kane* marked the arrival of an important composer in Hollywood, *All That Money Can Buy* gave that reputation solid reinforcement. "I feel 'Kane' was the more original of the two, and more completely part of the film," Herrmann later said. "The orchestral combinations in 'Kane' were different for each scene [and] so completely a part of the film [that] it did not make for as effective 'separate hearing' as the 'Money Can Buy' score."[6]

In early 1942 both scores received Oscar nominations, and that February the Academy awarded Hollywood's most coveted honor to the score for *All That Money Can Buy* —the first and last time the notoriously score-deaf Academy would so honor Herrmann. (The film, however, lost money for RKO.)[7] Noted Dorothy Herrmann, the composer's elder daughter, "I remember Charles Ives once said, 'Prizes are for boys, and I'm a grown-up.' I think Daddy had that attitude too. Prizes didn't mean anything to him. If they had, he wouldn't have given me his Academy Award for 'All That Money Can Buy.' He gave it to me when I was a teenager; and in later years, whenever he visited me and saw it, he looked a bit surprised as if he had forgotten he had even won it."[8]

With Herrmann's Hollywood success came a new peak in prestige at CBS and a strengthening of his relationship with the New York Philharmonic. In late 1940, the network and symphony had jointly commissioned a major concert work from the composer for the following season. The result was Herrmann's only symphony, completed on March 29, 1941.

After the innovations of *Kane* and *All That Money Can Buy* and the orchestral originality of *Moby Dick*, Herrmann's Symphony seems in some ways a step back, a retreat to concert Neo-Romanticism. The four-movement work, dedicated to Lucille, would be Herrmann's last piece of nonprogrammatic music: "For the first time I was not confined to the outline of a story. It was not necessary to depict waves, portray the anguish of a lost soul, or look for a love theme. . . . Consequently, working on the Symphony I had a Roman holiday."[9]

Although Herrmann apparently enjoyed the process of its composition ("It's just like writing cues," Herrmann told Lyn Murray),[10] the Symphony illustrates Herrmann's uneasiness working in a rigidly formal structure. It also suffers from the fragmentation that characterizes most of Herrmann's output, a quality ideal for radio and film but not for the concert hall. Yet the Symphony was an impressive achievement for the thirty-year-old Herrmann: a mature, brilliantly orchestrated work whose power increases on subsequent listenings. Its traditional idiom makes it the most accessible of Herrmann's concert works and the most likely candidate for rediscovery (especially in its 1973 revised form).

Like *Moby Dick*, it is almost unremittingly oppressive in tone—"a Sibelian symphony," observed author-composer Christopher Palmer, "all bleak winds and bitter Northern skies with, as Sibelius would have said, nothing of the circus about it."[11] While such stylistic antecedents are evident (the first and third movements, for example, contain a strongly Sibelian "fate" motive for brass and several lyrical string and woodwind passages), Herrmann's personality is equally apparent, especially in the force of the brass writing, the ominous bass rhythms and textures, and the dark brilliance of the second-movement "Hunt Scherzo," which, in Palmer's words, evokes "images of the accursed Huntsman and his pack of wild dogs, the 'wild hunt' of Nordic mythology and a witches' dance on Walpurgis Night all colliding and merging in quasi-surrealistic confusion."[12] Ghostlike string harmonics and pizzicatos are briefly overcome by an eerie graveyard serenity as an oboe beckons from afar (a passage suggested by Milton's "Nymphs and shepherds, dance no more"),[13] but the jocular hunt theme soon returns, bursting with skeletal string tremolos and a demonic fiddle-like violin solo (recalling Mr. Scratch?). The symphony's high point, the scherzo is not coincidentally its most programmatic section.

The work received its premiere on July 27, 1941, not at Carnegie Hall but in CBS's Radio Theatre, under Herrmann's direction. (Its Philharmonic debut took place the following year.) This time CBS mostly avoided the media hype that affected *Moby Dick*; reviews were more consistently favorable. "Mr. Herrmann is a man of ideas and he can keep them going over wide spans in steadily refreshed guise," one critic noted.[14] "Grasp of color is another of his fortes, and his idiom is steeped in rugged modernism under classic control. . . . His known knack for realism in the best style keeps you seeing things."[15]

The Symphony was not the only Herrmann creation to make its debut that afternoon, as another paper noted: "The Bernard Herrmanns celebrated a double-birth yesterday. At 3 P.M., the CBS Symphony Orchestra gave to the listening world Herrmann's new 'Symphony Number One,' a vital, stimulating and original work. Then, just two hours later, Bernard's wife, Lucille Fletcher Herrmann, presented him with a 6 ¾ pound girl, who will be named Dorothy. Both premieres were highly successful."[16]

That Herrmann was attending the musical birth and not that of his first child is significant: work did take precedence in Herrmann's life. His need to be active was compulsive and unending; and while he could enjoy afternoons at the zoo or in Central Park with Lucy and their daughter, Herrmann could not go long without working. His marriage, predictably, would suffer.

Despite his film and concert activities, Herrmann had not abandoned radio scoring. In August and December 1941 he reteamed with Norman Corwin for two outstanding broadcasts.

"Samson," aired on August 10 from New York, was the fourteenth of the "26 by Corwin" series and starred Martin Gabel and Mandy Christians. Although the number of available musicians varied from week to week, "I was able to offer [Herrmann] the resources of a large orchestra," Corwin wrote. "But Herrmann, a rara avis who behaves like a genius and at the same time *is* one, pooh-poohed my idea and scored for four harps, a flute, a mandolin, and a guitar. He was right; and the music was immense. The prelude opened with crashing chords on the harps—a fine patriarchal sound—and under Delilah's 'Lift the curtain' soliloquy was the strange melancholia of a lone mandolin, away off in the Hebrew night. For the last scene Herrmann gave out with a glittering swirl of pagan music, and his seven-piece orchestra sounded like the full Philistine Philharmonic."[17]

Their next broadcast, "We Hold These Truths"—Corwin's salute to the Bill of Rights—was performed under more trying circumstances. With the devastation of Pearl Harbor on December 7 and the American declaration of war, the patriotic broadcast of December 15 acquired a greater resonance. For Corwin the program was a disappointment, owing to mistimings by some of its all-star cast (which included Edward G. Robinson, Lionel Barrymore, Walter Brennan, Walter Huston, James Stewart, and Orson Welles). Yet Herrmann's score "expanded and improved on the basic dramatic ideas," Corwin wrote, adding "color and dimension" to the author's ambitious script.[18] *Variety* also noted Herrmann's "extremely resourceful, imaginative and authoritative [work] . . . a full-scale collaboration in the sense that any would welcome. It was to this production what a good shortstop is to a baseball team."[19]

Another admirer was poet Archibald MacLeish, newly promoted to director of Washington's Office of Facts and Figures. "Your splendid performance and gracious cooperation on the Bill or Rights Program has brought you deserved praise—to which I wish to add my own," he wrote Herrmann on December 29. "Such unselfish team-work as you and others of the radio and motion picture industries have shown is of real aid to your Government and its people in the present war effort. We trust that we may call on you again."[20]

Earlier that year Herrmann and Corwin had joined forces in another sense. During the summer, while Herrmann was scoring *All That Money Can Buy*, Corwin was adapting Lucille Fletcher's story "My Client Curley" into a screenplay for RKO (the film, titled *Once upon a Time*, starred Cary Grant). Since Lucille remained on the East Coast and Corwin was staying in a large Los Angeles apartment owned by RKO's head George Schaefer, Corwin invited Herrmann to share his workplace. "It was a very big apartment," Corwin recalled, "but the walls were very thin, and we were entertained by the sounds of the active connubial life of the people next door. But that was not the chief entertainment—Herrmann was. . . . Living with him was like living with a combination of the *Britannica, Grove's Dictionary,* and the American Society of Anglophiles."[21]

In his first two film assignments, Bernard Herrmann had enjoyed more creative freedom than any other composer in Hollywood. Inevitably, as Herrmann continued to work in the studio system this would change. Yet it was not a major studio but RKO, which had given Orson Welles the movies' freest "train set" one year earlier, that triggered Herrmann's first breach with the Hollywood system.

Despite *Citizen Kane's* tepid box office returns, Welles remained at RKO to make another film. This time, however, he would not have the same "final cut" freedom that made *Kane* such a trying experience for RKO, though he did have the same liberties in casting, shooting, and choice of subject matter—and there is little doubt that only George Schaefer would have approved Welles's decision to film Booth Tarkington's period novel *The Magnificent Ambersons* in war-beleaguered 1941. The choice was a highly personal one for Welles, whose empathy with Tarkington's wistful view of dying American aristocracy came from his own Amberson-like childhood ("Orson was always obsessed with this novel," Herrmann later said).[22] *Ambersons* had been an early Mercury Theatre radio play, and Welles used this program to convince Schaefer of the project's viability. Schaefer reportedly fell asleep during the rebroadcast.[23]

Shooting began on the RKO lot in late 1941. Welles gave the lead role of George Amberson to B-picture star Tim Holt, who turned out a fine performance. Welles also reunited many *Kane* technicians, including Robert Wise and James G. Stewart. Stanley Cortez, a thirty-two-year-old cinematographer, replaced the unavailable Gregg Toland; he later won the Film Critics of America award for his exquisite (but costly) work.[24] As for Herrmann, his knowledge of American literature and his feisty, keen rapport with Welles made him a natural for the project. Again he began work on the film long before post-production, providing important source music and immersing himself in the production's meticulous recreation of turn-of-the-century America.

Welles's screenplay was faithful to most of Tarkington's novel, following the caddish young George Amberson to his inevitable comeuppance with the collapse of his family fortune amid the industrial revolution. Welles did alter the book's finale in letter and in tone, however: in his version, Eugene Morgan (Joseph Cotten), the inventor whose fortunes rise as the Ambersons' fall, pays a last visit to the pathetic Fanny Amberson (Agnes Moorehead, in a performance of chillingly controlled hysteria), now alone in a home for the aged.

Thematically, *The Magnificent Ambersons* completes the quartet of Herrmann's works that, beginning with *Moby Dick*, explore the dark side of American idealism. His *Ambersons* score, however, is closer in spirit to the lovely "Rosebud" theme from *Kane*, recalling a more gentle, traditional era than the present. For this sense of nostalgic romanticism, Herrmann again turned to period sources—most importantly, Waldteufel's "Toujours ou jamais," heard in its original waltz incarnation in the film's opening frames. (This waltz was a favorite of Welles's, whom Herrmann once dubbed "the last of the Victorian gay blades.")[25] The theme is used as much for commentative as for nostalgic purposes: as the lives of the Ambersons disintegrate in the age of the automobile, the nineteenth-century waltz becomes increasingly fragmented and unrecognizable, buried in icy settings for brass and vibraphone.

As in *Kane*, music is used sparingly, often linking visual montages or providing other aural bridges. Two exceptions (at least in the film's original form) were a lovely reverie for solo violin and orchestra that accompanies the first of two porch scenes, in which the Ambersons wistfully acknowledge the passing of their way of life; and the film's haunting ballroom sequence: as Cortez's camera glides across dance floors and up staircases, with Waldteufel's theme accompanying the conversations and flirtations on the soundtrack, an instant of time seems to have been frozen before disappearing forever. For the film's ending, Morgan's visit with Fanny, Herrmann chose a sardonic piece of source music as his final musical comment: "An old gramophone, a wind-up, is playing a record which was very popular in America at that time, 'The Two Black Crows' [a comedic song in dialogue between two Southern men lamenting their imprisonment]. When [Morgan] comes to see Aunt Fanny . . . through the doorway you can hear the inmates listening to this old record. . . . [At the scene's end] he kisses her goodbye, he stands at the doorway on the porch, and he looks all around him. Where before in the film it was all surrounded by beautiful country, we see the city of Chicago being built. And in every direction the Ambersons are being swallowed."[26]

By January 1942 principal shooting was complete, and the painstaking dubbing process began. As Welles prepared for his next RKO project, a semidocumentary to be shot in Brazil, James G. Stewart found his role in postproduction increased considerably. Most challenging was the motorcar sequence, in which George Amberson's carefree sleigh ride is contrasted with Eugene Morgan's troublesome auto. The car sounds, dialogue, and music (including four crisply recorded celestes) took an entire week to finish.[27]

Herrmann's third recording experience with the RKO orchestra was his happiest. Recalled concertmaster Louis Kaufman, "There was one wonderfully nostalgic scene set at dusk, in which the eldest Amberson sat talking about the old times from a rocking chair. Bernard had written a long violin solo—the longest I'd had in any film—and, surprisingly, we did it in one long take.

"The Herrmanns had rented a house not far from where my wife, Annette, and I lived, and after the recording at about 12:30 or 1:00 in the morning there was a knock at our door. It was Bernard; he had been out walking in the neighborhood. 'I want to tell you, Louis, you did a terrific job on that solo,' he said. 'I'm very pleased with the whole score.' We then had a long, rambling talk that lasted until about two in the morning, which ended with his talking, of all things, about the universe and the vast distances of the stars."[28]

The evening began a friendship between Herrmann and the Kaufmans that lasted until the composer's death. "When he was with someone like Norman Corwin or ourselves—someone he knew, who shared his interests and understood him—Benny was absolutely marvelous," Annette Kaufman said. "We used to go to art exhibits and bookstores with him. Benny was a passionate admirer of the Sitwells, and of travel books; he was devoted to everything English—their writing, their furniture, their silver. Benny was also rebellious against things he felt weren't right, and he would express himself very clearly. He offended many people in high circles, for example, with his criticisms of Toscanini. 'He's set music back fifty years!' he'd say. 'Look at his programs—he only plays works by the husbands of the women he slept with in Italy!' "[29]

By early 1942 work on *The Magnificent Ambersons* was finished. The film ran an ominously long 131 minutes, but Welles assured the studio before leaving for Brazil that he would make cuts if necessary. Little was going well for RKO, after a series of box office disappointments (including *Kane*). Then came the first preview of *Ambersons*, in Pomona, California.

The screening was a disaster. There was much derisive laughter; several audience members walked out (though a handful of viewers reportedly cited it as one of the best films they'd ever seen).[30] George Schaefer ordered that the film be recut. Soon Schaefer was replaced by Charles Koerner, former head of RKO's parent theater company. Koerner was appalled at the amount of time and money spent on Welles's first two projects and made it clear that the director's genius temperament had no place in *his* studio. Welles sent his players a telegram telling them not to worry: "We're just passing through a rough Koerner on our way to immortality."[31]

But things only got worse. Wise attempted to take the film to Brazil for Welles to work on, but he and the film were removed from the plane by customs officials. Another preview led to more cutting by RKO, then more, and more. Gone were the gentle porch scenes. Gone was the film's searing conclusion, replaced by a hastily shot saccharine ending that totally subverted Welles's intent.

In all, RKO cut thirty-one minutes of Herrmann's fifty-eight minute score; it then assigned staff composer Roy Webb to score the new finale and other reshot scenes. Though an admirer of Herrmann ("Benny writes the best music in Hollywood, with the fewest notes"),[32] Webb ignored the composer's understated approach and wrote two new sequences of throbbing-violin bathos. On seeing the recut film, Herrmann stormed out of the screening room and demanded that his name be removed from the film.

RKO's initial indecision turned to panic as Herrmann threatened a lawsuit. "Herrmann insists cut [of his credit] be made before trade showing," an East Coast RKO executive cabled the studio that June. "Am convinced in view of man's temperament he will bring injunction proceeding and cause all kind of trouble he can. His theory is that statement is made 'score is by Bernard Herrmann' while it is not entirely so and that this is a deception to the public and injurious to his reputation. Doubt he would ultimately recover on this theory but there is some chance and urge consideration by studio of desirability of making the cut."[33] Herrmann won the battle: no composer received screen credit.

Finally, in August 1942, an eighty-eight minute, marginally coherent version of the film limped to the screen. As RKO's final insult, the movie played as cofeature to a noisy Lupe Valez comedy, *Mexican Spitfire Sees a Ghost*. "It's said that when Orson's final version was first shown, David Selznick wanted RKO to make a copy for the Museum of Modern Art," Herrmann later said. "But [RKO] wouldn't even spend the money to do that."[34] Recalled Martin Scorsese, who worked with Herrmann in 1975: "*The Magnificent Ambersons* was the real heartbreaker. Benny became quite emotional while talking about how the film was ruined. He told me about Welles's ending, all the other details. He just felt it had been destroyed."[35]

Herrmann was eager to put Hollywood behind him, at least temporarily. His film commitments had left little time for other composing or conducting, both of which he was eager to resume. And his estrangement with RKO was decisive, his threats of a legal battle over *Ambersons* having made him new enemies. Welles's relationship with the studio, too, had ended after *Amberson's* financial failure and the termination of *It's All True*, his Brazilian project. It would be years before Welles was to direct another film.

Returning to New York, Herrmann immersed himself in work at CBS, conducting premieres with the network's first-rate orchestra, scoring radio drama (including works for Corwin and the hugely popular "Suspense"), and composing original concert works. Hollywood would have to wait.

1942 was a year of other transitions.

After six seasons of unusual programming but only sporadic public and critical support, John Barbirolli left the New York Philharmonic and returned to his native England, where he became permanent conductor of Manchester's ailing Halle Orchestra the following year. Under his baton it became one of Europe's finest orchestras.

War-theme dramas and escapist variety shows dominated CBS's 1942 programming, replacing the "Columbia Workshop" (revived briefly a decade later) and the now-defunct "Mercury Theatre on the Air." Still, thanks to William Paley's continued support of the unusual and the excellent, CBS remained the most courageous and exciting radio network in America.

"Suspense," the long-running thriller anthology that premiered that summer, may not have been daring, but for sheer goosebump raising it was unmatched. No composer was better suited to its macabre format than Herrmann, whom CBS music head Lud Gluskin commissioned to write the series' theme. Herrmann's shivery signature cue remains one of radio's best remembered, with its eerie harp ostinato, purring flute harmonics, and graveyard bell tolling the arrival of "the Man in Black" and "another tale calculated to bring you to the edge of your chair—to keep you in . . . suspense!" During its early years, Herrmann also composed many original scores for the series, which were characteristically terse but integral to creating tension.

Three months after its June premiere "Suspense" reunited Herrmann and Welles in a four-week-long series of dramas starring, directed, and chosen by Welles. But it was Lucille who gave "Suspense" its most famous half-hour, with her finest radio play: "Sorry, Wrong Number," starring Agnes Moorehead as a bedridden neurotic who overhears a murder plot on the telephone, only to discover too late that she is the victim. The program was performed many times on CBS over the next twenty years, and Fletcher also adapted it into a film that starred Barbara Stanwyck (for which Franz Waxman wrote the score; no music was used on the radio version).

Despite this activity, it was the CBS Symphony that dominated Herrmann's time, in broadcasts that were individual and often outstanding. One program in early August inspired this admiring note from Anthony Collins, a British composer-conductor then working in Hollywood:

My dear Benny:

Your conducting on Sunday was magnificent. You know how I've hated old Schumann. . . . Well, you almost persuaded me otherwise—it was so spirited. You definitely converted me to the "London Symphony." Here again, as you know, I don't like London so I'd made up my mind never to like Uncle Ralph's [Vaughan Williams] portrait of it—but from this distance I've learned to like them both.

Cissie [the Collins family's English companion] was dumbfounded and remained quiet for most of the day. Just before she retired she said—"I think I['ll] buy the records of that symphony Benny conducted."

Bravo Benny—you did and are doing a wonderful job—don't ever think of doing anything in this bloody cul-de-sac but paying it a flying visit.[36]

Herrmann had free rein in programming the Symphony's seasonal broadcasts, offering esoteric programs with little interference. Those who assisted him were invariably subject to rigorous personality tests before gaining his absolute trust, as director Oliver Daniel learned that year:

When I first met Benny, I thought he was so rude and difficult that I dreaded working with him. Davidson Taylor had told me Benny was "a very sweet guy"; I wanted to tell him Herrmann was a bastard. When Benny conducted, he sort of snarled—"NYAHH!"—gesticulating and stopping the men, who were used to him. When we used extra players from the Philharmonic, however, they were not used to this abusiveness and got back at him years later.

The first program I did with Benny featured Eileen Farrell; it included "Amarilli" of Caccini, and the big aria from Korngold's Die tote Stadt. During rehearsal Benny shouted out, "WHO THE HELL MADE THIS PROGRAM?" I was in the control room and pushed the talk-back button and said, "I did." He yelled, "COME OUT HERE!" I thought, I might as well get fired now, I can't stand the man. I pushed down the talk-back again and said, "Listen, shnooks, if you want to talk to me, come in *here*." The entire orchestra burst into a wild guffaw. I saw Benny coming in and thought, Am I going to hit him, or is he going to hit me? He walked in, and to my absolute astonishment he put his arms around me and started to laugh. From then we developed an increasingly warm friendship.

In reference to Benny's conducting, there are men of letter and men of spirit. He was of the spirit. Many people didn't understand him and thought he was just a vulgarian, but he wasn't; he had extreme sensitivity. He was not a time beater à la Toscanini; he saw a grand design, as Stokowski did. He didn't approach conducting using Robert's Rules, but he knew what he was doing, and at his best he was superb. He had what Einstein called the greatest of virtues, curiosity.

Benny could be appalling and explosive and rude to people, but it was only an expression of his intensity. He acted like a Brooklyn street kid, with a toughness that was rather bullish; yet at the same time, in his spirit, he was like an eighteenth-century gentleman from Bath.[37]

That May, Herrmann was awarded a grant of $1,000 by the American Academy of Arts and Letters and the National Institute of Arts and Letters "to further . . . creative work in composition."[38] The Academy's council was a virtual list of Herrmann admirers, among them Stephen Vincent Benet, former teachers Albert Stoessel and Philip James, and colleague Deems Taylor. When asked to select one of his works for performance at the ceremony under the baton of Stoessel, Herrmann chose the first movement of a new vocal work based on the poetry of the Elizabethan Nicholas Breton.

*The Fantasticks,* the five-movement setting of Breton's seasonal cycle of 1626, marked an important turning point in Herrmann's work, away from the American idiomatic settings of *Moby Dick* and *Johnny Appleseed* and toward the English source material (in music and subject) that would typify the next decade of his writing, both in film (*Jane Eyre, Hangover Square, The Ghost and Mrs. Muir*) and in concert work (the opera *Wuthering Heights*). This was less a change in taste than a shift in the composer's own stylistic expression. While the patriotic radio scripts of Corwin would inspire much of Herrmann's best American music, the composer's heart was increasingly drawn to England.

Written for four vocal soloists, chorus, and orchestra, *The Fantasticks* illustrates Herrmann's affinity for English romanticism in its rich orchestral settings and vocal writing. Each of its five movements, charting the transition from bleak January to the warm invitation of May, seems to have been conceived in terms of instrumental color, as Herrmann subordinates vocal parts in favor of shifting orchestral textures.

The first movement, "It is now January," contrasts the brooding recitative of baritone soloist against icy dissonance in strings and muted brass, suggesting in its frozen tones the helplessness of nature and man. "February," for alto and orchestra, is scarcely more animated, although its pool-like vibraphone echoes and a remote oboe solo bring promise of "a better time not far off." At last comes "March," with its vigorous 6/8 rhythms and leaping tenor line; monochromaticism finally gives way to a burst of technicolor, from its prismatic glockenspiel chimes to a coy dialogue between violin and flute, which circle each other like dancing, elusive lovers.

The subdued lyricism of "April," for soprano, solo violin, harp, strings, and woodwinds, shifts the tone to one of bittersweet introspection, a sense that both nature and life are fleeting at best, giving "April" 's final "Farewell" special poignance. Herrmann's last setting, "It is now May," begins in a spirit of gentle celebration, its swaying choral harmonies and string accompaniment evoking a reveler's paradise of sunlit meadows and gardens. But by its middle section an aura of melancholy overcomes the ensemble, darkening the swelling choral passages into muted sighs of reflection. After a traditionally hearty finale, Herrmann, in a revealing touch, adds a brief, wistful coda for orchestra, as if a lone dancer has remained behind to savor the fading pleasures of the day. Unpretentious and heartfelt, The Fantasticks (dedicated to young Dorothy "Taffy" Herrmann) is a gentle valentine to Breton's England of antiquity, revealing, in music critic Royal S. Brown's words, "a moody, sad personality always ready to be led, at least temporarily, into moments of nostalgic warmth."[39]

In November 1942, Herrmann's Symphony was given its concert premiere under Howard Barlow and the New York Philharmonic. Herrmann was especially hoping on this occasion to interest conductors Dmitri Mitropolous and Thomas Beecham in the work, but apparently neither was overwhelmed, though Beecham reportedly did "admire" the piece.[40] Herrmann also sent the symphony score and broadcast recording to Eugene Ormandy, Stokowski's conservative successor with the Philadelphia Symphony Orchestra and a natural subject of Herrmann's disdain and envy. Replied Ormandy:

Dear Mr. Herrmann:

I brought back the score . . . and paged through it on the train yesterday. Being a very frank person I feel that I should give you my honest opinion of the work, and I hope you will understand that I am doing this with sincere admiration for your great talent. . . .

The introductory theme is most powerful and my only regret is that in the last movement you do not build your coda on this theme, which would be a most effective closing. It seems to me that the first movement is a little bit on the longish side, in fact it could stand a considerable cut of perhaps some five or six minutes. . . .

The last two movements could also be cut considerably. The last movement I like least, in fact, in creative power it does not compare to the first. . . . If I may be bold to express my frank opinion, it doesn't seem to get where you would like it to get. If you would consider rewriting part of the last movement and utilizing the opening pages of the first movement in the coda working up a tremendous climax, you might eliminate the last four or six pages, replacing them with the new coda, and I think you would have a very successful work.

My idea is to give this work not only in Philadelphia but in New York as well as on tour . . . and I want to make sure before I accept it that it will be a success. The work as it now stands is, in my opinion, about fifteen minutes too long. In fact, it should not take over thirty minutes. Being an older colleague with long experience, I think I know the public psychology and its reaction, so this is why I am suggesting, in all friendliness, these cuts being fully aware what it means to suggest cuts to a composer. . . .

In view of the fact that my list of novelties for the coming season is almost complete and yours would be the only full symphony I have chosen by an American composer, I would like to make the announcement as soon as I get your decision.[41]

After the Philharmonic performance of September 20 and a dinner meeting with Herrmann in Philadelphia, Ormandy wrote again:

Yesterday I rearranged my schedule in order to hear your symphony. . . . Listening to the work strengthens my first opinion of it . . . that it is a very powerful work worthy of performance by all the great orchestras. My other opinion, however, has been strengthened rather than diminished, and that is the work is entirely too long. . . . I suggest, if you can do so, that you cut the first movement about four minutes, cut three of the third, and about three of the fourth movement, again strongly urging you to utilize the opening horn theme in a brilliant coda, since you are using themes of the first three movements anyhow.

When you were here you told me of some cuts that you could make, but whether they are as long as I suggested to you I don't know. . . . I could possibly perform the symphony on December 26 and 28 in Philadelphia, in Washington on the 29th, and Baltimore on the 30th, also in New York on January 5th. These dates are not final yet but in a few days time I could make them so. Please drop me a note, or still better *send me a wire*, as soon as you receive my letter giving me your decision. . . .

Before closing, may I ask you, in your reply, to give me the name of the Stravinsky work to which you called my attention during dinner, and where I may obtain the score of it.[42]

Herrmann recognized flaws in the symphony but resisted fifteen minutes of cuts. Since neither man would change his mind, the matter went no further, and the Symphony was not heard again until Herrmann's own recording in 1974. It was the first of many times that Herrmann's unwillingness to change his concert music would discourage others from performing it.

The year 1943 saw a continuation of Herrmann's career both as a conductor and programmer for CBS and as a concert composer of increasing stature. It was also a critical year for the war. The political stalemate of the first half of 1943 inspired a new wave of American propaganda, both in Hollywood's patriotic musicals and battle epics, and more subtly, as in the League of Composers commissions for works by American composers based on the theme of war. Herrmann was among those asked to contribute a short work for orchestra, to be performed that fall by the New York Philharmonic. The result, *For the Fallen*, was his most moving and evocative concert work.

Described by Herrmann as a "berceuse for those who lie asleep on the many alien battlefields of this war,"[43] its gentle 6/8 sway echoes Delius's *On Hearing the First Cuckoo in Spring*, while its mood and title recall Debussy's *Berceuse héroïque*, which is subtitled "In Memory of the Fallen." Yet the poignancy of the work is Herrmann's own: the eerie, tenuous beauty of its opening for strings soli; its haunting theme for solo oboe, which hovers above the accompaniment like a phoenix freed briefly from the earth. In its coda, the bleakness of the work is moderated slightly by a delicate woodwind quotation from Handel's "He shall feed his flock" from *Messiah*—a quiet, uncertain benediction.

The work's premiere on December 16 caused a battle in itself when scheduled conductor Barlow took ill and canceled the night before. Ready in the wings were Herrmann and twenty-five-year-old Leonard Bernstein, who weeks earlier had replaced the ailing Bruno Walter in an impromptu debut that included Miklós Rózsa's *Scherzo, Theme, Variations, and Finale*. The concert spoils were split unevenly between the two conductors: Bernstein was given the Beethoven Violin Concerto (with soloist Albert Spalding), Delius's *Paris*, and Brahms's Haydn Variations—and Herrmann was allotted *For the Fallen* and "The Star Spangled Banner."

Naturally Bernstein dominated the reviews of the following morning—one more incident to prey on Herrmann's widening capacity for jealousy and suspicion, an attitude that only deepened when Bernstein later performed Ives to much acclaim.

Another Herrmann concert premiere that season ended in rancor. The *Devil and Daniel Webster* Suite, adapted in 1942 by Herrmann from his film score and dedicated to William Dieterle, was chosen by Eugene Ormandy for the Philadelphia Symphony's 1943 season. Again Ormandy insisted on cuts—here, the "Ballad of Springfield Mountain" movement. Curiously, Herrmann agreed. Yet when Ormandy offered Herrmann the chance to conduct his own work, the composer exploded. "The nerve of him!" Herrmann later said. "I asked Ormandy, 'How about the whole concert?' He said, 'Oh no, it's *my* concert.' How dare he offer me just one piece!"[44]

Herrmann had little reason to be bitter: the suite was extremely well received ("[it] disclosed a composer of keen sensibilities and a gift for expression at once clever and profound," one critic wrote)[45]—and Herrmann's own conducting career was about to enter its most imaginative phase.

Since his first combative weeks at CBS, Herrmann had brought more new and forgotten music to American airwaves than any other individual. "Concert programs on radio should not be run from the box-office standpoint," he told the *Musical Courier.* "The two things have nothing to do with one another. Radio's artistic function, as I see it, is to expose to listeners the literature of music."[46]

"Invitation to Music," which premiered on April 6, 1943, was the artistic highpoint of Herrmann's three-decade career at CBS, a weekly series featuring not only rare concert works but also acclaimed guest conductors and soloists who would perform their own choices from the nonstandard repertoire. Sadly forgotten today, the show and its programming accomplishments can stand against the most adventurous of its concert hall contemporaries. In organizing the series Herrmann was greatly helped by collaborators whose enthusiasm matched his own: producer James Fassett, who planned each program with Herrmann; commentator Ben Hyams; CBS librarian Julius Mattfeld, whose knowledge and wit Herrmann idolized; and the series' director, Oliver Daniel. But Herrmann remained the series' creative guide. "He was the musicologist," Hyams said, "the researcher, the digger."[47]

Another asset to the endeavor was William Paley's management corporation, Columbia Artists, which gave nearly unlimited access to guest conductors and soloists. Equally persuasive was Herrmann's contagious enthusiasm. "Whatever he conducted, whether Delius or Dittersdorf, or a program of Waldteufel waltzes, he did so with a rich sense of discovery and an excitement that infected everyone near," Hyams wrote. "Of music that stirred him he would say, 'It raises a temperature.' "[48]

"Invitation" took on an almost clublike atmosphere. Music notables formed a habit of dropping in. Bartók came one evening when a piece of his was on the program. Some of musicdom's brightest stars were willing, even eager, to participate. . . . Working behind the scenes you could encounter Lotte Lehmann entering the studio like Strauss's Marschallin herself to sing some of the lieder and opera arias she was celebrated for. Wanda Landowska, small and cameolike, came with a companion, equipped with manicure instruments to prepare the baroque hands, and with wraps for Madame's rest period before her performance of a Handel harpsichord concerto.[49]

Other guests included Stravinsky, Villa-Lobos, Darius Milhaud, Paul Hindemith, Erich Korngold, Samuel Barber, and, to Herrmann's special delight, Sir Thomas Beecham. On tour in New York, Beecham conducted a cycle of his beloved Delius and, on another occasion, gave an impassioned performance of excerpts from *Messiah*. During that broadcast, Hyams recalled, "Beecham became so carried away that he 'sang' with the orchestra and the soloists. CBS started getting calls on the switchboard asking if there was a madman in the studio."[50]

Milhaud came from France, at Herrmann's invitation, to conduct his *Creation of the World*, whose East Coast premiere Herrmann had given a decade earlier. Barber gave the radio premiere of his *Capricorn* Concerto. Stravinsky belied his reputation as a fair conductor with intense readings of his *Firebird* Suite and *Apollon Musagete*. (Stravinsky and Herrmann, who first met in New York in 1940, maintained an admiring friendship for over twenty years, once memorably breached when the Russian composer refused to speak to Herrmann for a year. "I [had] conducted a work of his and he was furious with me," Herrmann said. "Stravinsky told me, 'You conducted that section at 88—and it says it's to be at 90!' " It was the kind of behavior Herrmann was fond of emulating.)[51]

Visiting soloists included pianist Claudio Arrau, Rudolf Firkušný, cellist Gregor Piatigorsky, and the fastidious Wanda Landowska, whose eccentricities delighted Herrmann. "I had a most terrible dream last night," she once told him before a performance. "Bach came to me, shook his finger, and said, 'You know, Wanda, I don't like anything you're doing with my music!' "[52]

The series also featured less familiar talents, among them a "plump and cheerful" young soprano from Staten Island named Eileen Farrell.[53] Farrell, who soon became CBS's most celebrated "house soprano," performed Wagner's "Liebestod" under Herrmann's direction, in a rare "Invitation" broadcast of familiar repertoire. On the basis of her performance she was chosen by Leopold Stokowski, a faithful listener to the broadcasts, to record Wagner's Wesendonk Songs.[54]

Another regular soloist was cellist Bernard Greenhouse, who first gained recognition with his mature work on the program. "I was the youngest member of the orchestra, talented but with very little experience," Greenhouse said. "Herrmann encouraged me to play concerti with the orchestra, was most patient when I had difficulty in sight reading, and generally helped to build my confidence. I considered him to be one of the most gifted musicians of my generation."[55]

Among Herrmann's finest broadcasts was that of Gerald Finzi's *Die Natalis*, one of Herrmann's favorite contemporary English works. The performance, which Finzi later received in acetate form, was instrumental not only in getting the work circulated among English broadcasters, but also in initiating a close friendship between Finzi and Herrmann. (Finzi was also a scholarly collector of musical manuscripts, especially of the eighteenth century.) After the broadcast, which featured tenor William Ventura, Finzi wrote Herrmann: "The performance struck me as being *remarkably* good and some of the movements—the Intrada for instance—I have never heard bettered. Everyone present remarked on the care and understanding which had been put into the performance. . . . You and [Mr. Ventura] seem to have got right inside the work."[56]

Another distinguished premiere was the first American performance of the Vaughan Williams Oboe Concerto, played by Mitch Miller under Herrmann's direction. For Ben Hyams it was unforgettable for reasons not entirely aesthetic:

The concerto has a serene pastoral beauty, rolling blithely along like the English countryside. At a particular point there's an orchestral tutti and the oboe rests briefly, a matter of a few bars, a few seconds.

When that time arrived, Mitch instantly snatched off the mouthpiece. He reached for his [whittling] blade and gave the reed a few quick strokes. In another moment he was passing [his cleaning] goosefeather in and out of the tube.

The tutti was rising to its climax. I don't know how many seconds had passed. All I knew was that the oboe was due to come in and Mitch had it in his lap in pieces with a bag of blades and goosefeathers at his feet. I was just about to clamber over three musicians and nudge him when I saw [Herrmann] glance his way.

In an instant he jammed the mouthpiece back on, gave a quick twist and the parts flew back together as in an animated tv cartoon. The conductor's baton jabbed in Mitch's direction and he came in square on the downbeat, sounding a tone of sunlit rapture, and sailed on triumphantly to the close.[57]

Not every performance was as dramatic, but Herrmann's approach to the music helped create a unique excitement. Recalled Annette Kaufman, a frequent visitor to the program: "Bernard had read somewhere that orchestras in Vienna used to stand up during a performance, and he wanted to see what the effect would be. The musicians didn't want to do it, but he pleaded with them: 'Please,' he said, 'Let's just see what it would sound like.' And the effect was amazing. When the violins stood up, they had a completely different quality. Not only acoustically—something entered the spirit. They began to act as free interpreters, and the music had a wonderful quality of vitality."[58]

For four years, "Invitation to Music" offered radio audiences an amazing range of artists and music; but CBS's priorities became less philanthropic. Unsponsored or "sustaining" radio was a costly venture, and when an appeal to colleges for letters of support failed, the series was canceled. It was decades before Herrmann forgave the universities for what he considered their betrayal.[59]

At the time of "Invitation to Music"'s premiere, a more enduring phase of Herrmann's career was beginning in Hollywood. *Jane Eyre*, the film that initiated Herrmann's nineteen-year association with Twentieth Century Fox, owed its inception to producer David O. Selznick, who in March 1941 commissioned John Houseman and an Englishman named Robert Stevenson to adapt the Charlotte Brontë novel for the screen. By April, Houseman recalled, "we finished it and presented it to our leader, only to discover that he had not the slightest intention of producing it. [Selznick vice-president] Danny O'Shea began offering it around . . . at a price so fabulous that it was not until the war boom a year later that he was able to sell it to Darryl Zanuck at 20th Century Fox."[60]

Orson Welles, acting but not directing in Hollywood, was signed to play the mysterious Edward Rochester to Joan Fontaine's Jane; Welles's influence extended to director Stevenson, who used *Citizen Kane*'s deep-focus photographic style, baroque mise-en-scène, and innovative sound techniques to bring Brontë's gothic romanticism to life.

Despite a somewhat superficial script, *Jane Eyre* boasted the high production standards that Zanuck demanded at Fox. A former writer, Zanuck had a gift for hiring first-rate technicians, directors, writers, and actors. It was also Zanuck who appointed Alfred Newman head of Fox's music department in 1940.

"Alfred was the best conductor who ever picked up a stick [in Hollywood]; the sounds he would get from his orchestra were exquisite," David Raksin recalled.[61] "He was a totally remarkable musician with an amazing sense of theater and timing. He was also a taskmaster: he always wanted your best, and no one who ever worked for him for long ever gave him anything else. Al was a self-regenerating man—just when everyone though he had said all he had to say about film music, he would surprise everyone and come up with a great score. He could also be self-deprecating, and he would occasionally refer to himself as a 'hack musician.' It's a strange thing, but if you have any kind of art, there seems to be—in some cases—an inner bargain with yourself not to use it. . . . Newman was a rather reluctant composer."[62]

Yet he was also one of Hollywood's most prolific, acting as musical supervisor, conductor, or original composer on hundreds of Fox releases. Under his direction the Fox orchestra became the finest and best-known Hollywood ensemble (later spawning the famous Hollywood String Quartet), before dissolving in the 1960s as the studio system collapsed. Newman also possessed a sharp instinct for hiring composers who could write excellent scores as well as work with the fast-paced Hollywood system.

In the case of *Jane Eyre*, it was not Newman but the influence of Welles and Selznick that led to Herrmann's being hired. "At luncheon today with Orson, the conversation naturally turned to my deserted child, 'Jane Eyre,' " Selznick wrote Fox vice-president William Goetz in December 1942. "Orson mentioned that he hoped you would have Bernard Herrmann on the score, and by coincidence, he is exactly the man I would have used. . . . I do hope that you will consider this suggestion favorably; and I am sending a copy of this letter to Orson, with the suggestion that he send you a note about Herrmann's work."[63]

Initially, Zanuck had other plans for the score, hoping to entice Igor Stravinsky, then a Los Angeles resident, into making his film scoring debut.[64] But negotiations with Stravinsky collapsed, and Herrmann was offered the film, much to his surprise. In December 1942 Herrmann visited Hollywood alone, where he found "nothing but bad pictures"; regarding *Jane Eyre*, he wrote Lucille (addressed as "Lucy Lockette Gummy Snowdrop Mama"): "There isn't a chance for me to do the score as I am sure that Al Newman will first resign from the studio before he lets me be brought in. . . . Orson says I am to do the picture—but then again he is only hired as an actor. . . . I am sure that they will humor him along and afterward do just as they damn please." (The same letter contains another tantalizing reference: "Saw Hitchcock at the [Brown Derby] and he said he was sorry that I didn't do his picture as he feels it was all his fault as he should have been in closer contact with me from the beginning. Hopes that we do the next one together.")[65]

In fact, Alfred Newman was a great admirer of Herrmann's RKO scores, and, as composer-author Fred Steiner has observed, Newman's support was perhaps the key factor in sustaining Herrmann's career in Hollywood:

Herrmann originally came to Hollywood at the behest of a director, Welles. It's notoriously tough for an outsider to break into the musical colony there, doubly tough for a New Yorker, and triply tough for anybody who's brought in by an outsider. For anyone to make a living there, one had to have certain preconditions: those producers, in this case Welles, then had to have successful careers so that a Bernard Herrmann would continue to work for them. As we know, that didn't happen with Welles.

The only way these composers could do more film scores was in the unlikely event that some other director or producer would hire them because they liked their music. It was unlikely because in those days the studio system was terribly important; musicians or composers were hired mainly by, or certainly with the approval of, the music department. Since Herrmann didn't get any other films at any other studio in the early forties, and since we know that Newman also gave Raksin, Alex North, and Franz Waxman scores to do, I think the evidence is overwhelming that Newman was primarily responsible for Herrmann's career.[66]

Both highly demanding and gifted with a strong sense of the dramatic, Herrmann and Newman were compatible both personally and professionally (if far apart in method). "Newman has never been fully appreciated for his remarkable achievement in film," Herrmann said in 1971, "because he was the first film composer—and in many ways the last—who achieved the highest technical finish and polish of film performance. I think he did a marvellous job on 'The Song of Bernadette' [1943] and 'The Hunchback of Notre Dame' [1939]."[67] At the same time, Newman—a superior conductor—always allowed "Becnie" the rare privilege at Fox of conducting his own scores. If Herrmann's recordings were sometimes imperfect in note readings or screen timings, they were always punctually completed and brilliantly performed by the Fox ensemble. (On the rare occasions when Newman conducted Herrmann's music, Herrmann had only praise: "When old man Newman conducts your music, he brings out things you didn't know were there," he later told composer John Williams.)[68]

Not everyone at Fox was aware of Herrmann's credentials, however. When Herrmann was introduced to *Jane Eyre*'s producer, Kenneth MacGowan, MacGowan made the mistake of asking Herrmann what he had previously done. "Well, I never hearda YOU, either!" Herrmann reportedly snapped before storming out.[69]

*Jane Eyre* is one of Herrmann's most conventional film scores, using a full symphony orchestra and several leitmotivs (Herrmann called the score his first "screen opera");[70] but it was in no way a step down from the quality of his previous film work. *Jane Eyre* returned Herrmann to the world of settings based on English literature, an idiom in which he would write for the next seven years. It is one of Herrmann's longest scores, with almost every scene colored in a dark gothic hue that ideally complements the Brontë text—a mood that is retained, albeit somewhat diluted, in the screenplay. ("On a project like 'Jane Eyre' I didn't need to see the film beforehand," Herrmann said in 1975. "One just remembers the book.")[71]

Three motives dominate the score: the first, a surging theme describing the growing love between Jane and Rochester, is introduced in a propulsive sequence under the opening titles in violins against a driving horn ostinato; it reappears more subtly throughout the film, and resurfaces years later as Cathy's third-act aria "Oh I'm burning" in Herrmann's opera, *Wuthering Heights*. By contrast, Jane's theme—introduced in an oboe solo under Fontaine's opening narration—is one of the most delicate and lovely motives in Herrmann's film work, tinged by its string accompaniment with an aura of darkness, yet essentially warm in its pastoral woodwind color. (Recall that this theme was used in the 1938 radio version of *Rebecca*. The plot and character similarities between *Rebecca* and *Jane Eyre* make Herrmann's reuse entirely understandable, as does the fact that he expected the radio program never to be heard again and the music to be lost.)

Herrmann's Wagnerian approach is most evident in his scoring of Jane and Rochester's first meeting on the moors, which introduces his last important motive, Rochester's theme. Jane walks through the misty countryside, a church bell tolling in the distance; the ringing fades as a defiant, Siegfried-like melody erupts on the soundtrack and Rochester emerges from the fog on horseback. This theme dominates much of what follows in Herrmann's score, a mirror of Welles's engagingly theatrical performance.

Other recurring musical devices appear and blend ingeniously. Herrmann's jaunty gallop for violins, snare drum, and clarinet, which accompanies young Jane's escape from her aunt's home, is later heard against a steely brass "prison" device as Jane awakens in the Lowood Institution for Girls—an eerie polyphonic effect achieved by recording the two cues separately and mixing them into a dreamlike aural wash. A dark variant of the gallop theme underscores a stark, handsome montage of Jane's coach ride to the Thornfield estate; over the fierce bass ostinato Herrmann adds a sinister brass version of Jane's theme as the horses speed across the rugged countryside.

Herrmann uses a similar "building" technique of combined rhythmic and coloristic patterns for his evocation of Rochester's incendiary, mad wife, hidden in Thornfield's towers. As Jane is awakened by a laugh and footsteps, Herrmann introduces a brittle ostinato on piano (an instrument he associates with fire in *Hangover Square* two years later), then adds a tapping snare rhythm (suggesting the stealthy creep of the arsonist); and finally dissonant, screaming violins and horns as Jane finds Rochester's room ablaze.

Herrmann's *Jane Eyre* score was ignored by the Academy of Motion Picture Arts and Sciences the next year, but was praised in a *New York Herald Tribune* article by Paul Bowles: "It contains some of the most carefully wrought effects to be found in recent film scores, and the effects are musical ones of as high a degree of dramatic appositeness as good sound effects. . . . Mr. Herrmann shows a fine understanding of the psychological relationships which exist between drama and music, particularly between mood and orchestral timbre; and this is the determining factor in making the score an outstanding one."[72] (Herrmann was especially fond of Bowles's description of *Jane Eyre*'s "Gothic extravagances and poetic morbidities," a phrase Herrmann later used in his own writing.)[73]

Alfred Newman also was delighted with the score and offered Herrmann another film, which he had turned down: Otto Preminger's *Laura*. Herrmann also declined ("Laura wouldn't listen to Herrmann; she'd listen to Debussy," he told Newman),[74] and the film went to David Raksin, whose theme and score would rank among film music's best. "A couple of times, Benny had the poor grace to remind me that he had passed on *Laura*," Raksin recalled, "and that just tickled me. He'd say, 'Well, if *I'd* done *Laura* . . . ,' and I'd say, 'What? *What* if you'd done *Laura*, Benny?' Herrmann once told me a funny story about Hitchcock. Whenever Hitchcock wanted to needle Benny he'd say, 'Why don't you write me a theme like *Laura?*' And Benny would reply, 'If ya want garbage like that, why don't ya get Raksin?' '[75] On another occasion, however, Herrmann expressed admiration for the score: "Shows you how wrong I could be. Raksin did a brilliant job."[76]

According to a CBS press release of November 1943, Herrmann received another, more unusual offer while in Hollywood: "One producer was planning a sequence for a picture in which Shostakovich would be shown composing his Seventh Symphony and Bennie was picked as a candidate to portray the Soviet composer."[77] Herrmann's alleged response: "I won't be a cut-rate Shostakovich." A better screen role awaited Herrmann in Hitchcock's 1956 film *The Man Who Knew Too Much.*

In fact, Herrmann and Hitchcock met a second time during the composer's 1943 trip to Los Angeles. The circumstance was an extraordinary luncheon at the home of Joseph and Lenore Cotten attended by Herrmann, Lucille, and Taffy, and Hitchcock and his wife, Alma. (A friend of Herrmann's from the Mercury Theatre, Cotten was then starring in Hitchcock's film *Shadow of a Doubt.*) Both conversation and the sumptuous meal, served on the Cottens' terrace overlooking a swimming pool, were overshadowed by a surprise visit from Orson Welles and Rita Hayworth (soon to be Mrs. Welles). Recalled Lucille:

Orson just barged in and said, "Don't let me interrupt your lunch. Rita and I just want to use your pool." They hadn't brought any bathing suits, of course. So Orson just took off his trousers and went swimming in his boxer shorts. Rita vanished upstairs to Joe's bedroom, where she selected two Countess Mara ties, . . . worth about $50 apiece, gorgeous. Rita draped one around her neck and bosoms, tying it in the back, and turned the other tie into a lower bikini part . . . then languidly vanished into the pool.

It was very distracting, I will say, to eat lunch with the others and watch Orson and Rita swim.[78]

By the spring of 1943, Herrmann was eager to leave Hollywood for New York. A new project, inspired in part by *Jane Eyre,* was taking shape in his mind—the most ambitious, and ultimately the most frustrating, of Herrmann's career.

# SEVEN

I accidentally lighted on a MS volume of verse in my sister Emily's
handwriting. . . . To my ear, they had . . . a peculiar music—wild,
melancholy and elevating.

> Charlotte Brontë, "Biographical Notice of Ellis and
> Acton Bell" (introduction to 1850 ed. of Wuthering Heights)

"The only thing I ever did do that was foolhardy was to write an opera,"
Bernard Herrmann said in 1971. "Franz Liszt said that you have to have
the soul of a hero to write an opera and the mentality of a lackey to have
it produced."[1]

In 1943, when his only opera, *Wuthering Heights*, was born, Herrmann thought only of possibilities. During the making of *Jane Eyre* Herrmann had immersed himself in the Brontës' writings, from Emily and
Anne's fantasies of the mythical Gondal to the epic Yorkshire novels like
*Wuthering Heights*; he became obsessed, not only with the works' literary
romanticism and portraits of nineteenth-century rural life, but with the
authors' tragic lives as well. A sense of identification was building, and
soon Herrmann spoke of "Charlotte" and "Emily" as casually and intimately as if they were blood relatives.[2]

Herrmann's first meetings on *Jane Eyre* took place in December 1942.
The next March Herrmann broached the idea of an operatic *Wuthering
Heights* in a letter to the English composer Cecil Gray. Replied Gray:
"*Wuthering Heights* has all the emotional background and atmoshpere
needed in opera, but you might find the construction and writing of the
libretto difficult."[3] By April 1943 Herrmann had begun his first sketches
of the opera. His lively, affectionate *Welles Raises Kane* suite, based on
the two Welles film scores and dedicated to that "last of the Victorian gay
blades," was written "as a relaxation before starting on the serious task
of composing an opera."[4]

Herrmann was brave not only in choosing a novel as intricate as *Wuthering Heights* to adapt, but also in setting it so traditionally. By 1943 Neo-Romanticism had largely given way to the experimentalism of Schoenberg, Stravinsky, and others. Twentieth-century opera (almost an anomaly) was characterized by experimentation: Alban Berg's *Wozzeck*, Stravinsky's 1927 opera-oratorio *Oedipus Rex*, Virgil Thomson's *Four Saints in Three Acts*. Ironically, the new music that Herrmann championed throughout his career would make his own, more conservative idiom seem anachronistic to prospective producers.

Herrmann was not the first to attempt an opera based on *Wuthering Heights*, though he was the first to succeed. Frederick Delius, one of Herrmann's favorite composers, had tried decades earlier and given up. The attraction of the novel to composers is as clear as its problems. In addition to its vivid description of nature, it offers one of literature's most bizarre, fascinating relationships, that of Catherine Earnshaw and the "imp of Satan," Heathcliff, brilliantly incorporated in the text as a natural extension of the moors themselves. The novel's dramatic hazards lie in the characters' complexity and the book's structure: Catherine's death in chapter 16 is followed by eighteen chapters on Heathcliff's plots against his own heirs and those of Catherine, ended only when Heathcliff finds peace himself with Cathy in death. For a composer or dramatist, there is far too much plot.

The adaptation was too great a task for Herrmann alone. For his librettist he chose Lucille, whose knowledge of music and literature was great even before their marriage. Together they agreed that, like the 1939 film of the novel, they would omit the book's second half and end their version with Cathy's death. They also decided that whenever possible, the libretto would quote dialogue from Brontë's text and interpolate descriptions from the novel. Where further material was needed, especially for arias and other soliloquies, Emily's poetry—recently republished, and much of it related in mood to the novel—would be incorporated.

Above all, Herrmann designed the work to be accessible musically, "a straightforward, uncomplicated composition." Avoiding customary operatic recitative, he decided to use "a heightened form of lyrical speech," parlando.[5] Conceived for large symphony orchestra, the score included no chorus, which Herrmann felt was unsuited to the intimate subject matter, but concentrated on eight vocal parts: one soprano (Cathy), two mezzo-sopranos (Isabel Linton and the servant Nelly Dean), one tenor (Edgar Linton), three baritones (Heathcliff, Hindley Earnshaw, and Lockwood), and a bass (the pious servant Joseph). Later the nonsinging child role of Hareton Earnshaw was added, as were carolers for one sequence. All major story elements in the book's first half were included in Fletcher's libretto (a ballroom sequence at Thrushcross Grange was considered but abandoned).[6]

Herrmann's research on the novel was exhaustive (he continued to collect Brontë lore until his death). No English-language opera was more obsessively researched: Victorian esoterica, ranging from the use of the full stop in the English novel to the effect of the corset on Victorian mores, all found their way into Herrmann's library, along with more conventional writings on English literature, art, furniture, painting, and geography. Three years into the writing of the opera Herrmann made his first trip to Brontë country. But it was *Wuthering Heights* itself and the Brontës that gave Herrmann his greatest joy and inspiration. Presenting her husband with a complete set of the authors' works, Lucille wrote, "May the moor winds and heather of these great books blow through his music, and make him the first true singer of the Brontes."[7]

With the opera's form set, Herrmann found composition almost distressingly easy. His experience in setting poetry and prose to music dated to his teens, and his radio and film scores had made dramatic composition second nature. Also, "he was accustomed to working on a deadline," Lucille noted, "and he worked on 'Wuthering Heights' with the same steady concentration he brought to all his music, whether a symphony or a sequence for Twentieth Century Fox."[8] The fact that it took eight years to complete is mainly due to the demands of five film scores, full-time CBS employment, two trips to England, and the emotional upheaval of Herrmann and Lucille's 1948 divorce, all of which occurred during this period.

Predictably, the "oneness of the characters with their environment and also the mood and colors of the day" that attracted Herrmann to the novel inspired his best work in the opera. His evocation of the moors—magnificent, oppressive, and violent—creates a powerful sense of place, enforcing the landscape's role in Cathy's and Heathcliff's lives, even its control of their emotions. "Each act is a landscape tone poem which envelops the performers," Herrmann wrote.[9]

In the richly scored prelude (which like the novel, establishes the story's flashback structure), Herrmann introduces his principal motives with economy and a sense of theater. A thunderous timpani solo opens the work, its pattern echoed by horns and strings fortissimo; in their wake we hear "a short mournful sighing phrase which is associated with the tragedy and the restless spirit of Cathy."[10] Easy to recall, its aura of mystery and sadness comes from Herrmann's shrewd scoring for woodwinds in their lowest register. A four-note bass motive follows, that of Wuthering Heights: again instrumental color adds greatly to the theme's power and sense of menace. This entire opening recurs at the end of the prologue and in the opera's epilogue, a musical full stop to the drama's suspended action.

Herrmann's setting of Emily's poetry, with its musical meter and sharp imagery, is affecting throughout. (Perhaps Fletcher's finest achievement is her seamless combination of these passages with the novel's prose.) Many of the most compact arias come from these interpolations and belie the myth that Herrmann could not write melodies: for example, Edgar's lovely ode to Cathy from "Love's Contentment" ("Now art thou fair my golden June"); Isabel's "Love is like the wild rose briar," a childlike contrast to the lovers' passion; or Cathy's first-act aria "I have been wandering through the woods," a sequence echoing Delius and Warlock without sacrificing Herrmann's own command of orchestration. (Remarkable throughout act one is Herrmann's ability to set Brontë's characters squarely in their own environment, a groundedness illuminated by the stunningly English quality of his scoring; never does the music seem an affectation for atmosphere's sake.)

Fletcher's adaptation of the novel itself put greater demands on Herrmann. Sometimes, as in act one's love duet, the results are wondrous. The duet unites voice and accompaniment in a declamation of Cathy and Heathcliff's affinity with nature, climaxing in an orchestral interlude unmatched in Herrmann's work for its beauty and lyricism: a rapturous, sweeping horn melody over prismatic harp and woodwind arpeggios. Violins embrace the theme, its passion subsiding into a pastoral glow as the couple, "enraptured . . . watch the dying sunset."[11] (This sequence, written in the spring of 1945, appears almost unchanged as the title sequence of Herrmann's 1947 film score for *The Ghost and Mrs. Muir*.)[12]

Throughout *Wuthering Heights*, Herrmann's trademark ostinatos play an important part in creating dramatic tension. The dark valse rhythm of "I have dreamed in my life," as well as its velvet instrumentation for cello, harp, and strings, makes the piece one of Herrmann's most hypnotic and disturbing. And as in many of his radio scores, the steady, persistent beat of a harp, coupled with an agitated pattern for woodwinds, cleverly signals the steady weight of time and Cathy's impatience on act two's "day of fitful changes, of sunlight and clouds, and a gathering thunderstorm."[13]

Herrmann's accompaniment of his singers is usually sensitive and illuminating, from the rushing momentum of the love duet to the Mussorgskian bass churnings of Hindley's drinking ode to Heathcliff's imagined death. Occasionally composer and librettist create powerful sequences based only tangentially on Brontë, as in the act one finale, which ends on a note of superbly quiet menace. As Heathcliff vows to kill Hindley and storms out, a group of carolers arrive outside Wuthering Heights. Against the gentle purity of their song, "It is now Christmastime," with its Christian message of forgiveness, a dissonant bass clarinet whispers portents of death, confirmed by the ominous sustained bass chord that ends the act.

The thrilling inventiveness of such a sequence contrasts with the most tedious of Herrmann's effects, his constant use of parlando—as in act one's meeting of Heathcliff and the elegant Cathy or the subsequent fight with Hindley, where recitative or spoken dialogue would have avoided the awkwardly metered setting Herrmann offers. Here, scrupulous economy of musical device (which makes his best work so compelling) is replaced with melodramatic vocal lines and orchestral excess.

Another problem is the opera's pacing. The prologue succeeds not because it contains the novel's most interesting material but because of the rhythm of its unfolding, from the brooding opening to the magnificent storm music and Heathcliff's plea at its climax ("Oh my heart's darling, hear me this time"). Following acts succeed less consistently, owing to the unevenness of their narrative rhythm.

More controversial are Herrmann and Fletcher's subtle changes in Heathcliff, transformed from "an imp of satan," "a devil," "a cruel man," "a fierce, pitiless, wolfish man," "a lying friend," "a monster," "a madman," "a savage beast," into a misunderstood tragic figure, a characterization suggested in Brontë but explicit in the opera through arias like "I am the only being whose doom no tongue would ask" (itself a lovely piece of melancholia) and "Poor blossoms," neither of which is based on material from the novel. The effect is a softening of Brontë's shocking original, who resists our sympathy and achieves an ambiguity denied his operatic incarnation.

Herrmann's empathy with Brontë's antihero is evident not only in his depiction of Heathcliff, but in the composer's comments of the time. "A devilish part of Heathcliff got to Bernard's inner consciousness," Louis Kaufman recalled. "Benny said that Wagner had such a terrible time writing his operas; Benny was too happy. Life was too easy. He had a marvelous wife, and everything was going fine; but he felt that if he was in such a euphoric state, how could he write a great opera? In a way, he became Heathcliff."[14]

Herrmann's commitment to *Wuthering Heights* cost him far more than his time. Friendships, professional relationships, and his marriage would collapse, along with Herrmann's belief that he would ever see the opera produced. For him, the work was the culmination of his career, the work by which he would be remembered. Posterity has not yet agreed. *Wuthering Heights* was to be a disillusioning reminder that Herrmann's future lay not in concert music or opera, but in the more experimental (and lucrative) media of film and radio.

During this time a change occurred in Herrmann's duties at CBS. His appointment as chief conductor of the CBS Symphony in November 1943, after Howard Barlow's departure to NBC, was a belated recognition of Herrmann's importance in CBS music policies, but it also signaled his diminishing role as a radio composer. It was now easier to turn down programs—like the series about the Royal Air Force, "The Man Behind the Gun," directed by William Robson ("You wanna win the war with music, get Wagner!" Herrmann told the disappointed director).[15] After 1943 new Herrmann scores were reserved mainly for special broadcasts, like the se ries "Columbia Presents Corwin," aired from Hollywood in summer 1944. The programs were among Norman Corwin's best and most diverse, ranging from his synthesis of Sandburg, Wolfe, and Whitman in "An American Trilogy" to the psychological chiller "The Moat Farm Murder," all starring Charles Laughton, whom Herrmann and Corwin greatly admired.

Director and composer worked especially closely that June and July. Recalled Corwin, "We rode together from New York on the Twentieth Century Limited and the Santa Fe Chief as I was writing 'Wolfiana.' We had compartments on the same car, and those pages of script simply made the short transit from my compartment to his. We worked right on the train, so by the time we reached Los Angeles he had the score practically finished. That turned out to be one of the finest scores in the history of the medium."[16]

"The Moat Farm Murder: The True Confession of Herbert Dougal," Corwin's dramatization of a 1903 English court transcript, is Herrmann's most fully realized work for Corwin, and perhaps his best radio score. In this eerie, vivid drama starring Laughton and Elsa Lanchester, Herrmann is at his most nihilistic, weaving a tapestry of evil that anticipates the psychological terror of *Hangover Square* (1945) and *Psycho* (1960). It is also Herrmann's most cinematic score for radio, "morbid as a morgue" (to quote Corwin),[17] its rich instrumental textures—even by Herrmann standards—evoking a precise mental image of madness and death. Much of its effectiveness comes from cold orchestral understatement: rhythmic bass pizzicatos (to reappear in *Psycho* and other Hitchcock scores), dissonant snarls from muted brass, cobweblike piano glissandos, subtle timpani "footsteps," and soft chromatic flute harmonics, as icy as a corpse's fingertips.

Complementing Herrmann's sinister impressionism was Laughton's hypnotic reading of Harry Dougal, the killer of his spinster benefactor. Both music and narration achieve a unique grayness of color that suggests a foggy, indeterminate mind growing cloudier, most memorably during Dougal's account of his victim's death ("My heart almost seemed to stand still as I put my hand inside her dress to see if her heart was beating") paralleled by low falling woodwinds—a device Herrmann later featured in his score for *Torn Curtain* (1966). Also looking ahead to Hitchcock is the hushed processional that accompanies Dougal's disposal of the body, in which high string harmonics and weird timpani effects echo the chill in Dougal's voice ("She was getting cold and stiff, for there was a strong breeze blowing"). Herrmann also uses swirling, high string glissandos (a device that reappears in *Psycho* and 1970's *The Night Digger*) to suggest the damaged workings of Dougal's mind ("I'm sure I aged that night twenty years"). A last foreshadowing of *Psycho* comes at the finale, with the end of Dougal's confession ("I have felt myself standing on the scaffold with a *rope* around my neck"); Herrmann accents this self-pronounced sentence with violent string punctuations, a grim ending for this tragedy without a hero.

"Untitled" is probably the subtlest of Corwin's wartime scripts, a touching character study of a dead G.I., Hank Peters (played by Frederic March), as viewed through the eyes of his friends and enemies, from his fiancée to the German soldier who shot him. Corwin balances each short, often superficial account of the dead man with his own poetic commentary, a requiem for both the fallen soldier and the failed policies that led to World War II.

Herrmann responded strongly to Corwin's eloquent script with a score that was, in the dramatist's words, "austere over most of its pages, but its moments of relief . . . were lyrical and deeply felt. The music managed somehow to superimpose reflections of its own upon what was being said, and did not simply nod and bow before and after every speech."[18] A prime example is the warm violin solo that quietly describes Peters's music teacher, a woman saddened by the young man's death but too removed from him to feel a deeper sorrow. This theme, and the theme for Peters's fiancée, Mary, reappear in expanded form in Herrmann's 1955 score for *The Kentuckian*, just as the program's stirring coda, for brass and orchestra, became the majestic *Jason and the Argonauts* overture in 1962.

In the summer of 1944, Herrmann returned to Twentieth Century Fox for the first time in almost a year, for a film that seemed tailor-made for him. *Hangover Square* was a sequel (in mood and casting) to Fox's 1943 film *The Lodger*, which starred Laird Cregar as Jack the Ripper. The choice of Herrmann (by Alfred Newman) was perfect: like "The Moat Farm Murder," the film allowed Herrmann to create a superb character study of a demented mind. Also, it was a period story, set in the murky, gaslit streets of Victorian London that Herrmann loved; and more than any other film he had worked on, the plot centered on music. Cregar played George Bone, a respected composer writing a piano concerto, who on hearing dissonant sounds becomes a psychotic killer. (Mercifully for the London public, it is years before atonality and Ives.)

*Hangover Square* required a ten-minute concerto for piano and orchestra, to be written before shooting began. Herrmann always enjoyed working on a project from its earliest stage, a privilege few Fox composers shared. His "Concerto Macabre," a diabolical, Lisztian work that compressed the usual three movements into one, was unlike any of the "film concertos" then prevalent in Hollywood, which usually paraphrased existing works in rhapsodic, overscored fashion. Herrmann's concerto uses the romantic idiom as commentary, employing nineteenth-century harmonies to explore the tragic and solitary aspects of Romanticism and to depict the film's doomed Romantic, George Bone. Observed Christopher Palmer, it "not only reflects the distempered state of Bone's mind but is in a sense an apology for it and for his whole life, a logical summation and outcome of all that has preceded."[19]

Just as Bone is unmasked by a contemporary-mannered psychiatrist (George Sanders, typically suave and callous), Herrmann contrasts values in transition by offsetting conventional tonality with shrill dissonant interruptions. The film's murder sequences are accompanied by piercing piccolo screeches until, by the climactic performance of the concerto, the strands of Bone's thoughts and illness meld into a coherent work. But it is too late for Bone, who triumphantly finishes the work as his world crashes down around him—literally—in flames.

Herrmann carefully establishes each thematic strand in his score so that their ultimate presentation makes sense to us, as well as to Bone onscreen. First comes a violent introduction for piano, its leaping, dissonant intervals evoking Bone's dementia; it climaxes with Herrmann's favorite semitone pattern (brutally pronounced by muted horns), a leitmotiv of evil. The concerto's interlude for piano and strings first appears in the film as the melody Bone writes for Netta, the opportunistic dance hall girl (Linda Darnell); wistful and poignant, it mirrors Bone's romanticized vision of Netta and is especially ironic at the finale, since Bone has murdered the girl in a psychotic fit. Culminating each killing is Herrmann's "fire" motive, which becomes the concerto's scherzo. This theme is first heard at the film's opening, as Bone murders a pawnbroker and sets his shop ablaze; it reappears as Bone dumps Netta's body onto a Guy Fawkes bonfire (another morbid, expertly shot sequence), and again as Bone's concert recital becomes his deathtrap. (Another unusual aspect of the "Concerto Macabre" is its coda for unaccompanied piano; by this time the wise musicians onscreen have all fled.)

In director John Brahm's hands, the performance of the concerto in the film was a masterpiece of cutting and photography (as in the vertiginous camera dolly on Bone's hands during the scherzo's glissandos). "The music stimulated me so much," Brahm later said. "For a long time I had been dissatisfied with the photography of music in films. Musicians themselves are uninteresting; it is what they play that should be photographed. I myself could not read a note of music, but when Herrmann came and saw the finished film he could not believe it. I had photographed his music."[20]

As smooth as the final sequence seemed, its shooting was anything but, as British actor Alan Napier (the onscreen conductor) recalled:

George Sanders, who played one of the film's leads, was a curious friend of mine. He had a wonderful sense of humor, but *Hangover Square* was his last picture under contract at Fox, and George hated being under contract to Zanuck. One day he asked me to visit his trailer on the set and said, "Nape, I can't say any of this terrible crap. Write me some decent dialogue." Well, we came to the final scene, filmed at night on the Fox backlot, which was then a vast area. During rehearsal, when it came to his turn to speak, George didn't say a thing. Brahm said, "Come on, George, vat are you vaiting for!" Sanders replied, "I'm not going to speak those silly lines." Brahm said, "Aww, don't be silly. C'mon, George." We then had a dress rehearsal, and George still *wouldn't* say his lines, but no one believed he really meant it.

Finally we got to the take, and the whole bloody backlot of Fox was going up in flames. George came up to me during the scene and just looked at me, poker-faced, not uttering a sound. We tried it again, and exactly the same thing happened. "Now, George!" yelled Brahm, "*Vat* are you doing?!" The shooting was called off for the moment, and Brahm called up the producer, Robert Bassler, who was a little, rather timid man. Bassler finally appeared in a raincoat and went up to George, who was seated in a studio chair. Bassler was yelling at him, calling him a son of a bitch—and George, without moving from his sitting position, hit him in the chin. That ended the shooting that night.

The next day Zanuck, Bassler and Brahm had a meeting and straightened it all out, with George saying slightly different lines. But one must say it takes an extraordinary degree of cool, on an expensive night of an expensive picture, with complete sangfroid, to fuck it all up.[21]

*Hangover Square* was another triumph for Herrmann, whose score was praised in most reviews (if not by the Academy, who again ignored Herrmann). Not long after the film's release Herrmann received an enthusiastic letter from a New York music student praising the concerto. Herrmann responded with a gracious thank-you letter to fifteen-year-old Stephen Sondheim. Recalled Sondheim in 1986, "I can still play the opening eight bars [of the concerto], since they were glimpsed briefly on Laird Cregar's piano during the course of the film, and I dutifully memorized them by sitting through the picture twice."[22] (Herrmann's influence can be heard in Sondheim's musical thriller *Sweeny Todd*, an English melodrama rich in brooding thematic material and dark psychology.)

Despite other film offers from Fox, Herrmann was eager to return to New York and a new series of CBS Symphony broadcasts. That September, two months before scoring *Hangover Square*, Herrmann rejected the most prestigious offer he had received from Hollywood since *Citizen Kane*: Alfred Hitchcock's *Spellbound*, produced by David O. Selznick. A seemingly disinterested Hitchcock left the film's scoring to Selznick, who proposed Herrmann over someone else's suggestion of Leopold Stokowski (conductor of the soundtrack of Disney's *Fantasia*). "I'm not too keen about the Stokowski idea," Selznick wrote production manager Richard Johnston, "because as I understand it, on the last job he did he drove everyone out of their minds as regards time and expense. I still can't see anyone to compare with Herrmann."[23] When Herrmann proved unavailable Selznick hired Miklós Rózsa, whose score won an Oscar in 1945.

Hitchcock's ambivalence regarding the film's music was probably due to his antagonistic relationship with Selznick, who carefully oversaw production of his films. After Rózsa was hired for *Spellbound*, Hitchcock met only briefly with the composer and never came to the scoring stage.[24] A decade later, when acting as his own producer, Hitchcock's attitude toward film music would be very different.

By the spring of 1945, with the collapse of Germany and the defeat of Japan imminent, America was preparing for a new age of prosperity. It was also the end of radio's great era: a new, more literal mass entertainment medium had arrived, and within a few years television had all but destroyed the world of pure sound.

Several fine radio broadcasts would follow, but Norman Corwin's hour-long V-E Day special "On a Note of Triumph," commissioned by CBS and aired on all three networks, was radio's last great masterwork, capturing a half-decade of passion, anger, and patriotism in its prose. Corwin completed the script that January, choosing actor Martin Gabel and Herrmann as his chief collaborators. By the beginning of May Herrmann had completed his score in New York, and he sent copies to Lud Gluskin at Hollywood's KNX in case the program originated there.[25]

It did, on May 8, 1945—the end of the war in Europe. After a quick rehearsal in Los Angeles with the actors, Corwin, and CBS's Hollywood orchestra, under Gluskin's direction, the program was ready to air. Its opening moment—a stirring trumpet-and-percussion fanfare, accelerating into a full-orchestra bonfire—is one of Herrmann's most exultant statements of joy. Against hymnlike string triads, Corwin's script begins:

> So they've given up.
> They're finally done in, and the rat is dead
> in an alley back of the Wilhemstrasse.
> Take a bow, G.I.
> Take a bow, little guy.
> The superman of tomorrow lies at the feet of
> your common men of the afternoon.
> This is it, kid! This is the day!

As Corwin's narrator moves through American kitchens and German prisons, through churches and bomber planes, Herrmann's commentary transforms itself, from a poignant synagogue hymn to a brutal, mechanistic device for brass and percussion that describes the growing prewar Nazi power (in a driving 6/8 rhythm, foreshadowing the *North by Northwest* prelude). The script and score's most affecting moments are at the end, as nervous string tremolos accompany Corwin's cautionary portents like vultures following a trail of blood, and a steadily crescendoing ostinato underscores Corwin's finale:

> Lord God of trajectory and blast . . .
> Sheathe now the swift avenging blade
> with the names of nations writ on it,
> And assist in the preparation of the plowshare. . . .

> Sit at the treaty table and carry the hopes
> of little peoples through expected straits . . .
> And press into the final seal a sign
> that peace will come for longer than
> posterity can see ahead,
> That man unto his fellow man
> Will be a friend . . . forever.

"On a Note of Triumph" was hailed as one of radio's finest hours; the *New York Times* praised Herrmann's score as "a decided and distinguished asset, complementing and strengthening narrative in the best tradition of music written for a play."[26] A second broadcast (in an era before prerecording) was quickly planned. From New York, Herrmann telegraphed Corwin on May 10: "Congratulations on a most magnificent program; am looking forward eagerly to Sunday. May I suggest you carefully discuss all points I spoke to Gluskin about, especially music under final prayer and the conclusion. Feel music under voices just a fraction too low. If it is raised one decibel it will be perfect. . . . Warmest regards, Benny."[27] Four hours later Corwin received another wire· "On hearing record would like to suggest at the very end show conclude with soft pealing of the chimes. Closing credits brought in over it and then orchestra goes into tumultuous finale. If you don't agree, of course forget it. Regards, Bernard Herrmann."[28]

The second broadcast aired three days later (with chimes). A third telegraph followed: "Thought last night's show superior performance to Tuesday's. Heard every word of all. Music balance divine. Deepest admiration for your best to date. Love, Benny."[29]

By 1945, with his radio music for Corwin, Welles, and the Columbia Workshop plus five outstanding film scores, Herrmann had established himself as one of the nation's foremost dramatic composers. Thus, when Erich Leinsdorf, chief conductor of the Cleveland Symphony, targeted film music as "odious . . . absurd and distracting" in the *New York Times*, Herrmann felt compelled to respond. Leinsdorf argued that "those who have stayed in Hollywood have subjected themselves to the demands of standardizations and pattern. . . . Compulsion to write time and again identical scores for identical stories is bound to result in a lifeless pattern which no ambitious and honest musician will be able to stand for any length of time. By and large it is probably unfair to judge an 'industry' on the terms of an 'art.' Art is an individual expression, which is permitted only in cases when a motion picture is produced without the collaboration of dozens of individuals whose only aim is to fabricate another meal along the lines of a proved recipe."[30] Herrmann's response, printed a week later in the *Times*, was a meticulous answer to each of Leinsdorf's generalized points, and remains perhaps the most eloquent defense of the medium's artistic potential:

In last Sunday's *Times*, Erich Leinsdorf indulged in a favorite sport current among many of our interpretive concert musicians—that of belittling film music. As one who is also a conductor of a symphony orchestra, besides being the composer of a considerable amount of film music, I would like to take issue with his criticisms.

In the first place, he seems upset by the fact that music in films must of necessity be incidental. He declares that music in any "subordinate" place is "odious" to a musician. I fail to see what he means by the word "subordinate." If film music is subordinate, so is music in the theatre and the opera house. Music in the films is a vital necessity, a living force. Had Mr. Leinsdorf ever seen a film in the projection room before the music was added, he would understand thoroughly how important the score is.

Music on the screen can seek out and intensify the inner thoughts of the characters. It can invest a scene with terror, grandeur, gaiety, or misery. It can propel narrative swiftly forward, or slow it down. It often lifts mere dialogue into the realm of poetry. Finally, it is the communicating link between the screen and the audience, reaching out and enveloping all into one single experience.

If this role is "subordinate and secondary," then so is the role of opera music, which, no matter how extended, is governed finally by the needs of the drama. So it is with the best film music. It identifies itself with the action, and becomes a living part of the whole. Obviously, few film scores could bear the scrutiny of the concert audience without being radically rewritten. But, similarly, even the Wagnerian excerpts which are performed by our symphony orchestras seem amputated when they are torn from their rightful places on the stage.

Film music is necessarily written to supply a particular moment of drama, and it is memorable only when it remains wedded to the screen. As such, the media has produced masterpieces. Aaron Copland's sardonic commentary on the monotonous supper of the bored married couple in "Of Mice and Men"; the father's hopeless search for work so eloquently expressed by Alfred Newman in "The Song of Bernadette"; the sound of the sinister jungle done almost entirely by percussion instruments by Franz Waxman in "Objective Burma"; Serge Prokofieff's terrifying Battle of the Ice sequence in "Alexander Nevsky"; and the coal delivery scherzo of Anthony Collins in "Forever and a Day"—all classics of their kind.

Mr. Leinsdorf makes a great point, in his article, of criticizing the use of music in scenes of a so-called "realistic" nature. He is annoyed by the presence of an orchestra playing a "nineteenth century romantic piece" during a scene showing a railway terminal, and feels that sound-effects would have sounded much better. He also objects to the use of a musical motif depicting rain in a storm sequence, when the real sound of rain falling could have been used.

Without knowing what scenes in what picture he is discussing, it is a little difficult to answer this point. Certainly the music in the particular scenes he saw might have been ill-chosen. But again perhaps the composer was trying to achieve some purely psychological effect or atmospheric quality which could never have been attained through sound-effects on a dead screen. The examples of film music I have just mentioned above are all cases in point.

Contrary to all rumor, there is no such thing as the "standardization" of motion-picture music. The only "standard" for film music is that it be dramatic. Perhaps this is something Mr. Leinsdorf does not understand when he deplores the fact that many of our modern composers have given up working for the screen. Might it not be, simply, that these composers, though their talents are of sterling quality, lack the dramatic flair?

The whole point I have been trying to make is that screen music is neither industrialized nor insignificant. Indeed the films and radio offer the only real creative and financial opportunities a composer has. He can write a film score for any musical combination and hear it immediately performed. Moreover the film gives him the largest audience in the world—an audience whose interest and appreciation should not be underestimated. A good film score receives thousands of "fan letters" from intelligent music lovers everywhere.[31]*

Film music was not the only topic Herrmann championed in print that summer. In an article for *Modern Music* the four symphonies of Ives received a thoughtful analysis from the composer, who also privately encouraged Ives to find the original lost manuscript of his Second Symphony.[32] Harmony Ives replied:

We have just received the copy of "Modern Music" with your fine article in it. I have just read it to Mr. Ives. He was so deeply moved by it—and I was too—that it is hard to find words to express our feelings.

He says "You instinctively sense the innate something beneath the music, up from which it comes." . . . He sends you his "God bless you" and . . . joins in his father's thanks as do Currier and Ives!—also he says "Your kindly insight into the old hymns and the old lines around them is worthy of Leonard Bacon." He hopes you are having time for your own

*"I read your temperate piece in the Times with great respect," Davidson Taylor wrote his friend. "Who cut out all the vituperation for you? I think you should have blistered the pants off your adversary" (letter to BH, 7–29–45).

composing and we are glad to know that your music is so much performed and hope it is as well played as it deserves to be. . . .

P.S. I wrote Dr. [Walter] Damrosch a few days ago in regard to the Symphony scores and will let you know what I hear from him. It was in 1911 they were sent to him and I fear he has housecleaned them out by now.[33]

Herrmann's characteristic reaction was to find the score himself. Inside Damrosch's brownstone house on 8th Street "was a great, beautiful portrait of Wagner," Herrmann recalled. "It said, 'To my young American friend Walter Damrosch, to whom I entrust my "Parisfal." ' And there was another of Tchaikovsky, and another one of Brahms. There was another of Bruckner, and of Mahler. . . . Damrosch came in and said, 'Ah my boy, how are you? I bet the world is treating you much too good. . . . What can I do for you?' I told him about the symphony. He said, 'The Ives Second Symphony . . . the Ives Second Symphony. . . . Let's look, maybe it's still in the closet.' He went to an enormous closet full of packages, scuttled around, and finally pulled out—still in its wrapping—the Ives Second Symphony. It had been lying for nearly half a century in that closet. He'd never looked at it."[34]

On October 18, 1945, Herrmann and Lucille's second child was born—another daughter, whom they named Wendy. Just as Taffy bore an increasing likeness to her father, the newest family member was clearly in her soft-featured mother's image, with the same quiet temperament. CBS and Hollywood made Herrmann a part-time father at best, but his concern for his children's happiness was genuine; as Taffy later observed, "Daddy's awful about the little things, but he always comes through on the big things."[35] Nevertheless, it was work that consumed Herrmann's time, less of which was spent with Lucille, now a successful writer of radio dramas, journalism, and fiction.

One year after *Hangover Square* Alfred Newman approached Herrmann with another irresistible challenge. *Anna and the King of Siam,* based on Margaret Landon's 1943 biography of the same name, was the (mostly) true story of English governess Anna Leonowens's experiences in the "barbaric" kingdom of Siam, a nation coming to terms with Western cultural influence. Filmed entirely at Fox and starring Irene Dunne opposite Rex Harrison as the Siamese king, the film revealed its Hollywood origins in its juxtaposition of a touching love story with a Westernized version of the Orient.

Newman and Herrmann agreed that the score should act as a geographical tone painting to enhance the story's exoticism. "The music was based on authentic Siamese scales and melodic fragments," Herrmann later wrote. "I tried to get the sound of Oriental music with *our* instruments. The music made no attempt to be a commentary on, or an emotional counterpart of, the drama, but was intended to serve as muscial scenery."[36] If Herrmann's denial of the score's commentative importance is not fully accurate, his claim of stylistic authenticity is. With Louis and Annette Kaufman, Herrmann searched bookshops across Los Angeles for information on Siamese and Balinese music.

That fall the Herrmanns and the Kaufmans exchanged homes for the duration of Herrmann's stay in Hollywood. Shortly before the Kaufmans' departure they held a memorable party, with guests including Harold Clurman, Clifford Odets, and Charles and Oona Chaplin. During a discussion of various composers, Odets casually dismissed the music of César Franck as "the Roxy of serious music." Herrmann flew into a rage; recalled Louis Kaufman: "He demolished Odets, who stayed very quiet after that. Later we played some records of Balinese music we had found with Benny, and Chaplin got up and started to do a marvelous Balinese-style dance, with all the head and wrist motions. It was extraordinary."[37]

Throughout the spring of 1946 Herrmann wrote at the Kaufman home ("The sounds of old Siam echo through the house," Lucille wrote Lyn Murray).[38] The final score was an impressive accomplishment: Herrmann's matching of authentic gamelan recordings by Western instruments was unprecedented in Hollywood.

Rather than writing "pure" Oriental music, Herrmann blends an indigenous musical style—Siamese scales and instrumental timbre—with a more conventional dramatic structure. Herrmann's form remains constant, his idiom refreshingly different. The title music, scored for a large orchestra, is the score's most successful blend of East and West, a Western-structured prelude that sounds like a genuine gamelan piece. In this sequence Herrmann introduces the score's central thematic device, heard throughout the film: a five-tone theme for brass and winds symbolizing the ritualisitic majesty and mystery of Siam.

Later cues—most brief and transitional, some more expansively atmospheric—are characteristic of Herrmann only in the simplicity of their dramatic effectiveness: a charming gamelan-style piece for winds and delicate percussion to accompany the entrance of the king's children; a sensuous woodwind theme for the beautiful Tuptim (Linda Darnell). Gradually Herrmann uses more explicitly Western music as Anna's influence increases. Her first appreciation of the king's kindness is scored with elegant violins soli, a device that expands throughout the score as their relationship grows. The score's emotional development is completed in the king's death scene, with Herrmann's five-tone sources only gently suggested in a restrained setting for alto flute, oboe, English horn, strings, and two harps.

At the recording session Herrmann was intent on "de-Westernizing" the Fox orchestra as much as possible. Richard Berres, a standby cellist (and later head of the music department at Columbia Pictures, where he would work with Herrmann in 1975), recalled a typical incident: "Herrmann wanted a special mute for the tuba—and he had such a remarkable way about him you couldn't be sure the mute actually existed. Benny was twirling his hair and yelling, *"Why* don't I have this mute? I ALWAYS have this mute!" Our short, pudgy stagehand, Mickey, walked up to Herrmann with a wastebasket, and asked, 'Will this do?'—not trying to be funny. That broke up the orchestra that day."[39]

Before returning to New York, Herrmann spoke with columnist Mildred Norton and renewed his defense of his art: "Nobody makes a composer write a poor score. . . . If some film composers aren't writing good music for films, it's because, in nine cases out of ten, they wouldn't be able to write any better music for anything else. There have been plenty of fine film scores written in Hollywood. . . . Take, for instance, the one Aaron Copland did for 'Of Mice and Men.' Or Ernst Toch for 'Peter Ibbetson.' Or Alexandre Tansman for 'Flesh and Fantasy.' These are only a few of the better scores that have been turned out essentially for film use. There are many more."[40]

Years later, as Richard Rodgers and Oscar Hammerstein II began work on their musical based on *Anna, The King and I*, Herrmann reportedly offered Rodgers his research on Siamese music. According to Herrmann, Rodgers declined, saying he was "not interested in Siamese music."[41]* What rare good words Herrmann had had for Rodgers's work were soon replaced with active contempt.

Herrmann's *Anna and the King of Siam* score was nominated for an Oscar in 1947 but lost to Hugo Friedhofer's memorable score for *The Best Years of Our Lives*. Herrmann would not receive another nomination until 1976, when he was nominated twice, posthumously, for *Obsession* and *Taxi Driver*.

Returning to New York in the fall of 1946, Herrmann resumed his CBS Symphony broadcasts in what would be the final year of "Invitation to Music." For the July 4 weekend he scheduled Ives's Third Symphony,

---

*Rodgers elaborates on his lack of interest in idiomatic accuracy in his autobiography, *Musical Stages* (New York: Random House, 1975), p. 273.

"The Camp Meeting," to the composer's delight. Increasingly infirm but encouraged by performances of his works, Ives was having his Second Symphony copied from the retrieved manuscript:

Dear friends . . .

I am sorry to say Mr. Ives isn't atall well lately but he says just as soon as he is able there are four people he wants to see—he says "you know them all, Benny, Lucille, Dorothy and Wendy."

Isn't it joyful that his music is being appreciated so enthusiastically? He says it is to a great extent due to the fine help you have been to it, in playing and in writing in its behalf. Your good article in Modern Music about the Symphonies was a great help. We both appreciate deeply all you both have done.

It interests us that you will broadcast the 3rd Symphony just before the 4th lights up! But we have no radio—Mr. Ives cannot hear over one atall well.

Before Mr. Papano starts copying the 2nd Symphony Mr. Ives hopes to find more of the copy of the old sketch in which there were, as he remembers, a few things mostly in the inner parts which apparently were not put in the score copy. . . . However there is probably no hurry so he says "Just tell Wendy to tell her father not to let this old fellow in Redding's Bass drum keep him awake too long."

We do hope we can see you all before so long again—warmest wishes from us both—

Charles & Harmony Ives[42]

Despite his continued programming of American music, Herrmann's thoughts were increasingly drawn to England and the completion of *Wuthering Heights*. In the fall of 1946, after completing his Symphony duties, Herrmann prepared for his first trip to England in almost a decade. It came at the invitation of John Barbirolli, who realized an earlier promise of inviting Herrmann to conduct the Halle Orchestra. The visit was one of Herrmann's most rewarding, not only because of the superb Halle players, but because of the opportunity it gave him to see the North England countryside he had spent three years imagining. On November 17, after rehearsing a program of Liszt, Schubert, and Copland, Herrmann persuaded the Halle's manager-secretary, Ernest Bean, an Englishman of considerable erudition, to lead him and Lucille on a trek through Brontë country. " 'Persuaded' is perhaps too pallid a word," Bean recalled,

for I remember the day as one of the wettest, mistiest and muggyest days which the Haworth moors can ever have laid on as a backcloth to a Brontë

pilgrimage. In Bernard's mazed eyes, however, the elements were entirely
friendly and propitious. His enthusiasm was wind- and weather-proof,
"the bees humming dreamily among the bloom" as they did to Cathy's
ears.

He had already composed much of the [opera's] music . . . before he
had ever set sight on the scene. . . . His purpose in making the visit was
not, therefore, to "acquire atmosphere" but to assure himself (if such
assurance was needed) that the atmosphere already imagined was true to
the spirit of the author.

As he sang snatches from the opera, the wind playing mocking tricks
with his preposterously unmusical voice, we had our first preview of the
work . . . and against a wild setting that the genius of neither Visconti
nor Zeffirelli could have improved upon.

On the way back from Haworth, notwithstanding that he was due back
in Manchester to conduct a broadcast performance of Liszt's "Faust Symphony," he insisted on making a detour in order that we might visit High
Sunderland Hall—the bizarre ruin of a habitation which first gave birth to
the idea of Wuthering Heights in the mind of Emily Brontë. We
approached the ruin by a muddy cart-track which Bernard no doubt im-
aged to be a carpet of harebells. The rain and mist shrouded the black outline of the derelict building as though the spirit of Hareton Earnshaw still
brooded over the ruin. The Hall was, indeed, in a sorry and shocking state
of disrepair, its windows gone, holes in the roof, blocks of masonary scattered around the carved doorway. But again, Bernard's enthusiasm was
unquenchable.

He tried to persuade me to take away a half-ton carving of a displaced
cherub as a momento of the visit. I settled instead for a negotiable portion
of millstone grit which, for some years afterwards, cast a reproachful eye
at me from my rockery scree until, like High Sunderland itself, it became
submerged in the landscape.[43]

Not far from High Sunderland Herrmann saw three dead trees "standing sentinel at the farmyard gate," Lucille Fletcher remembered. "Benny
said they reminded him of the Brontë sisters, with their 'sad and withered
lives.' "[44]

After three highly successful concerts with the Halle, drawing capacity
audiences and high praise, Herrmann set off on "a brief but intensive"
study of the British musical scene, which he recorded in a *New York Herald Tribune* article that displays his articulateness:

The British musical renaissance, first manifested during the war years, still
flourishes. The public's almost feverish interest in concerts has survived
the blitz, and seems destined to outlast the postwar austerities. Music-

making continues unabated, before vast new audiences who have an insatiable appetite and a wide range of tastes.

In conducting the Halle Orchestra of Manchester, it was my privilege to encounter one aspect of this phenomenon. . . . On a Sunday afternoon in Manchester we played a concert three miles from the center of town, during a bus strike that tied up the entire transportation system. The rain was coming down in torrents, yet an audience of over 5,000 people filled the hall.

This audience is intense, it is fresh. It is a young audience mostly. Steel-workers, cotton-spinners, clerks, shop-keepers and students form its bulk. And what is most exciting, it is open-minded. It wants to hear new, contemporary music, not only of England but of Europe, and it has an enormous curiosity about American music. . . .

The great talent and success of Benjamin Britten is, of course, much discussed in England. Indeed, musical England seems to have fallen into pro and con Britten camps.* However, most British composers seem to feel that though his genius is a little over-publicized at the moment, it is not too bad a thing for English music as a whole. The international entree has been made, and others can follow. . . .

If Benjamin Britten is the present white-haired boy of English music, Vaughan Williams is still its saint. I had a twilight visit with him at his house in Surrey, and found him at 74 intensely interested in contemporary music. He was full of praise for the music of Samuel Barber. He is now completing his sixth symphony. When he told me he was having some difficulty in obtaining music paper, I suggested that I might send him some from America. "That would be fine," he said, "but do not send me too much of it. There must be enough left for the other composers—the young ones. They need it more, and have their work to do." For such fellow feeling, he is much beloved by all British musicians. . . .

In general I would say that the younger generation of English composers falls into two categories. Britten, [William] Walton, [Alan] Rawsthorne and [Constant] Lambert are writing in a more universal modernism. Their music is eclectic, and brilliant, and stands exporting well. [Edmund] Rubbra, [Gerald] Finzi, [Michael] Tippett and [E. J.] Moeran continue the tradition of Vaughan Williams and Elgar. They prefer to find in the English musical past the roots of their texture and their message. English music therefore stands at a most interesting cross-roads. Never before has it had so much variety. Never before has it grown in such an atmosphere so conducive to it. It will be interesting to see what comes of this exciting musi-

---

*Herrmann, an early admirer of *Peter Grimes*, was to tire of Britten's acclaim on both continents. He was also contemptuous of Britten's and Michael Tippett's intellectual (versus emotional) styles, describing them in later years as "airy fairy" composers that "have no guts" (BH to Christopher Palmer; Palmer to SCS, May 1985).

cal environment of the '40s. Will music in England grow more personally English, more insular as time goes on? Or will this new musical virility flower into creations that will have the universality of the greatest English literature?[45]

If Herrmann's implicit hope for a renewed nationalist consciousness in American music went mainly unheeded, his stature as a musicologist and creative programmer did not. Within but a few months Herrmann was honored three times, receiving the George Peabody Citation for bringing to radio "compositions and composers who deserve but might not otherwise have received the hearing"; a $1,000 American Design Award for spreading a wider knowledge and appreciation of the world's music; and, in May 1947, the Henry Hadley Citation from the National Association for American Composers and Conductors for "his unusual programs [at CBS] which adroitly avoid cliché."

But despite the accolades, the thirty-six-year-old Herrmann was becoming emotionally and physically exhausted. The demands of a family, his hypertensive approach to work, his anxiety about *Wuthering Heights*, and a general restlessness were taking a toll few around him realized. However, one triumph—and source of temporary solace—was yet to come that year: a work emotionally linked to his England travels and, for Herrmann, the most fulfilling film score of his career.

# EIGHT

Ghosts and flowers and songs were woven into the texture of those days; music and echoing rooms.

*Constance Sitwell,* Bright Days

Bernard Herrmann considered *The Ghost and Mrs. Muir* his finest film score: poetic, unique, highly personal.[1] It contains the essence of his Romantic ideology—his fascination with death, romantic ecstasy, and the beautiful loneliness of solitude. Superficially it recalls past works—the impressionistic seascapes of Debussy's *La Mer,* Britten's *Peter Grimes;* but beneath an allusive veneer Herrmann paints his most eloquent work, filled with the pain of frustrated desire and the Romantic promise of spiritual transcendence through death.

Such lofty themes seemed unlikely in a film that began typically enough as a Zanuck-commissioned project for an in-house director and writer. Initially John M. Stahl was to direct a Philip Dunne–Fred Kohlmar script based on R. A. Dick's charming novel about the romance between a lovely English widow and the ghost of a sea captain. Zanuck pictured Norma Shearer as Lucy Muir, while screenwriter Dunne imagined Spencer Tracy and Katherine Hepburn in the leads.[2] By the time shooting began in November 1946, Joseph L. Mankiewicz (brother of Herman Mankiewicz, co-author of *Citizen Kane*) was directing, Dunne was the sole screenwriter, Kohlmar was producing, and Gene Tierney and Rex Harrison were the stars.

*The Ghost and Mrs. Muir* became not only the composer's favorite of his films, but also a companion piece to *Wuthering Heights.* Both featured strong-willed, self-reliant heroines with whom Herrmann empathized; both were set in an England of the past, with the turbulence of their natural settings—the sea and the moors—mirrored in their protagonists;

and both offered the promise of spiritual purification after life's disappointments. The two works were wed in Herrmann's mind, his passion for the opera extending to the fantasy film, with the result that several motives and sequences appear in both scores (a fact Herrmann sometimes denied).[3]

Herrmann's music for *Muir* makes extensive (but subtle) use of leitmotivs, more than any other Herrmann score (the composer was said to have half-jokingly called it his "Max Steiner score").[4] Some motives, like the rushing sixteenth notes for woodwinds to evoke the sea's turbulence and beauty, or his eerie three-note device for the haunted Gull Cottage, are oriented more to evoking color than serving as actual themes; but the score also finds Herrmann atypically lyrical, as in his wistful sea shanty for clarinets, echoing Captain Gregg's reflections on his youth, and in the poetic theme for the resilient Lucy Muir (also heard at the climax of the love duet in *Wuthering Heights*). Herrmann's superbly dramatic prelude introduces most of these motives against a montage of the sea sweeping across the English coast, suggesting through image and music one of the film's strongest themes: the inexorability of time and the final release of death. (Mankiewicz and Herrmann reinforce this idea throughout the soundtrack, in the prelude's lovely coda, which ends with the hymnlike tolling of bells, and in the lonely chimes of Lucy's study clock.)

Herrmann's commentary, delicate and unobtrusive, is not limited to scenic transitions; several dialogue scenes are scored as well, lifting Dunne's literate prose into poetry. In one moving scene, dialogue *is* poetry—Keats's "Ode to a Nightingale," which Captain Gregg recites as he and Lucy stand by the study's bay windows, watching the silent flight of gulls above the wave crests outside: "Magic casements, opening on the foam / Of perilous seas in faerylands forlorn." Keats's lyricism is echoed in Lucy's theme, foreshadowing with great delicacy the couple's separation and reunion in death.

Lucy's theme finds its most poignant realization as Lucy and her roguish suitor, Miles Fairley (George Sanders), first kiss—the captain's unseen presence making the moment one of pain as well as fulfillment. "Perhaps he's conceited and erratic, even childish," Lucy says of Fairley in an unscored dialogue scene, "but he's real. . . . I need companionship and all the things a woman needs. I suppose I need love." Gregg agrees; as Miles and Lucy embrace under the stars by the cottage, their themes delicately interacting in a passage for strings soli, the captain watches from a nearby tree, his decision to leave—and his knowledge of Lucy's imminent sadness—heard in Herrmann's passionate climax that adds harps and muted brass and winds to the lovers' themes.

Lucy's destiny is to remain alone. A montage of crashing ocean waves against the Whitecliff coast signals the ebb of time as Lucy's life passes at Gull Cottage, a warm reprise of Lucy's theme recalling the widow's inner strength and solitude. A decade later her daughter, Anna returns; their dreamlike recollections of the captain comprise the film's last main dialogue sequence. Explaining her chosen life of isolation, the aging Lucy tells Anna, "You can be much more alone with other people than you are by yourself—even if it's people you love." An elegiac canon for strings heightens Lucy's sense of remembered loss and looks ahead to her own death (as the same piece does Cathy's in the *Wuthering Heights* fourth-act interlude).

Death finally takes Lucy, as she sits alone in the cottage study that she associates subconsciously with the captain. A glass of milk spills, then falls from her still hand—eerie, hushed string and woodwind colors note the moment of her passing—and Daniel Gregg reappears: "You'll never be tired again. Come Lucia—come, my dear." It is the young, radiant Lucy Muir who takes his arm, passing with him into eternity as her theme becomes a celebratory hymn of triumph, its chiming percussion a happy antithesis of the bells' solemnity in the prelude.

"At Fox, a film could end with an apparition suggesting life after death without appearing to be pietistic," Joseph Mankiewicz's biographer, Bernard F. Dick, noted. "Less talented hands could have transmogrified 'The Ghost and Mrs. Muir' into a supernatural weepie; Mankiewicz, Dunne, and Herrmann made it into a transcendent Love Death. Essentially, Lucy was in love with Death; it was a love that could only be satisfied in myth or in a dreamlike relationship with a visitor from death's kingdom. But mythic roles are difficult to sustain; dreams are evanescent; and art without an artist is impossible. To regain what she had with the captain, she must die."[5]

*The Ghost and Mrs. Muir* was only a marginal success at the box office, but for Herrmann it was a personal triumph second only to his opera. It was also aptly timed: Herrmann had again fallen in love.

It was at his home on Sutton Place in New York that Herrmann first met Lucille's cousin, Kathy Lucille Anderson—better known, ironically, as Lucy Two to Fletcher's Lucy One. A stunning, soft-spoken blonde ten years Lucille's junior, Lucy Anderson had just arrived from Hawaii and a time in the armed services; she knew little about music but she was fascinated with her cousin's husband, who was always at his most charming with an attractive woman.* Anderson's unhappy youth (a lonely childhood, the early death of her much-revered father) struck a responsive chord in Herrmann—and it seems a touch of fate that her first and middle names embraced both *Wuthering Heights* and *The Ghost and Mrs. Muir.* Before long, with the speed and urgency that characterized Herrmann's life, their friendship had become something more intense.

Their meeting came at a particularly precarious time in Herrmann's life. In the last several months, as Herrmann became increasingly restless and engrossed in the opera, his marriage had become strained. Lucille was now successful in her own right (in 1947 she began work on the screenplay of *Sorry, Wrong Number*)—something Herrmann both approved of and resented. A projected "vacation" at the country house of friends Max and Sarah Cohn that summer became, in Lucille's words, "one of the nightmares of my life":

We went with the two children, just when I was approaching my screenplay deadline of September 1. Benny told me time and again, "You don't have to do it for them on time!" But I was sure it had to be in by September 1 or I'd lose the contract and my advance. I had three weeks more work on it, and I was stuck on a really idiotic scene about gangsters that the director, Anatole Litvak, insisted I put into the plot. Every day Benny grew more and more impatient with my constant rewriting. He wanted to tour the countryside, go out to lunch at inns, and enjoy the pleasures of the summer scenery. Instead there were groceries to buy, meals to cook, and our one-year-old baby and our little girl of five to amuse. But Benny still wanted me to sit and talk to him in the evening and give him my full attention. He grew more and more discontent.

Everyone was miserable. I was dead beat and harried, since, according to my contract, I had to finish the script. Benny would go to bed at last after saying bitterly, "I don't know why you don't come to bed. You're killing yourself for that *Litvak!* He's a ghoul, a nothing." Eventually I couldn't lick the gangster scene and it was written by Litvak. I had wasted our entire vacation to no avail and ended up exhausted. I know that those weeks left a very deep scar on our relationship, at a time when I didn't realize how crucial matters stood.[6]

Herrmann was also convinced that his life had settled into an unshakable pattern. He loved his children but tired of the demands they made on

---

*"Women were very attracted to Benny," recalled Alfred Newman's second wife, Martha. "He was interesting, intellectual, and could be mannerly. I first met him with Alfred in 1947, and sensed the electricity of the man right off" (Martha Ragland to SCS, 11–29–85).

his and Lucille's freedom. The temperament that rebelled at boredom or subpar musicianship now rebelled at marriage, and in Lucy Anderson Herrman saw a new beginning.

Another aspect of Herrmann's life was to reach a crossroads that summer. After a decade of hoping, berating, and campaigning (through intermediaries like Davidson Taylor), Herrmann at last received an invitation to guest conduct two New York Philharmonic concerts at New York's Lewissohn Stadium. After seven years as chief conductor of the CBS Symphony, Herrmann had his opportunity to be seen and judged accordingly—and, as the mercurial rise of young Leonard Bernstein had shown, one concert could make a career.

Herrmann's total failure that July was the single most devastating event of his career; for despite selections Herrmann knew and loved (including Vaughan Williams's *London* Symphony, Schubert's *Rosamunde*, and Delius's *Walk to the Paradise Garden*), his appearances were poorly attended and unanimously panned. The critics' viciousness suggests that Herrmann may have been correct in believing he had powerful enemies: "There was, to be sure, no want of external manifestation of his art on display," noted the *Herald Tribune*. "His gestures ran the gamut of every emotion known to the conductor who is also something of an actor; just what kind shall not be specified here. But since many of his cues were inaccurate and his expressive directions inept, the results obtained were seldom musically rewarding."[7] To another critic, Herrmann "jiggled from tip to toe apparently with determined intent. The results, however, did not justify the gymnastics."[8]

The reasons for Herrmann's disappointing performance (conceded by friends as well as critics) were threefold: most critically, the orchestra's personal dislike of Herrmann; his lack of a concise, commanding baton technique (far less detrimental in his work with the CBS musicians, who understood him); and his growing impatience and anger, which all too often masked insecurity—particularly when facing the orchestra unaffectionately known as "Murder Incorporated."

Herrmann's own account placed blame for the concert's failure on his soloist, pianist William Kappell. As Annette Kaufman recalled, "Kappell told Benny, 'It's okay—you know the piece, and I know it.' Benny was very upset by that; he was always ill at ease if he hadn't worked with someone. It wasn't as smooth a performance with Kappell as Benny had wanted, and he was deeply hurt by the bad reviews. Benny was a sort of homemade product, and always lacked a certain polish in his conducting. When he hit it on the head with pieces he liked, he had an insight that

many so-called pros did not have. But generally speaking, he was not of
the same professional stature."[9]

CBS director Oliver Daniel saw the concert's failure as a calculated act
of vindictiveness by the orchestra: "The players resented what they considered Benny's abuse at rehearsals; they themselves were not a gentle
group. During the performance of the concerto, when Benny gave a 2/4
conducting indication instead of a 4/4, the orchestra played the music
twice as fast, creating absolute chaos when the soloist came in; the whole
thing nearly broke down. I consider that literally an act of sabotage by the
orchestra men, because the piece was sufficiently known to all of them."[10]

Herrmann's failure at Lewissohn Stadium and his obsession with
*Wuthering Heights* brought his marital problems to a crux. He began
meeting Lucy Anderson regularly for lunch—something Lucille Fletcher
sensed without needing to be told. One night, as she and her husband sat
reading in their 57th Street apartment, Lucille asked Herrmann about the
meetings. He acknowledged them casually—and was answered by a flying
copy of Edward Arlington Robinson's *Tristan*.[11]

Herrmann could not forget Lucy Anderson. Shortly after she returned
to her home in Minneapolis, he left his family and New York, first on a
cross-country drive to California and back, then to Minneapolis, and finally to Reno.

By late 1947, Herrmann was on the verge of a nervous breakdown.
From his departure for Hollywood to the time of his divorce in the summer of 1948, he wrote his two Lucys long, urgent letters almost daily. His
correspondence with his wife, in particular, provides an extraordinary
glimpse into an agonized personality, split both personally and creatively.
The following excerpts reflect his chief anxieties: his collapsed marriage,
his indecisiveness about his artistic path and talent, and an overpowering
sense of exhaustion, guilt, and frustration.[12]

October 29, 1947

I am . . . doing my best to arrive at some understanding of my feelings
and future. . . . I must try to look at myself honestly . . . as a husband
and as an artist—it may well be that I am a dismal failure at both. But I
wish to face it fairly and not run away from my self. I know that out of
this period of self examination only good can come. . . . Rather face myself as a person of limited talent—and make the most of it. This is not
written in self-pity—but in honesty. . . .

I am most anxious to finish the opera—even if it should only be a 3rd
rate work. Then I should have finished with a part of my musical life that

will then allow me to go forward to a different kind of music. . . . I am comfortable at Tony's [Collins] and achieving a great deal of sleep and rest which I needed so badly. I want you to kiss the girls for me and want you to remember that I am doing all I can to remain your Devoted Benny . . .

Nov. 1947

I now know that I have had many, many false ideas about my self and my work. . . . More and more I feel that perhaps I am not possessed of any real great talent. It is perhaps an echo of a talent—that is why I can conduct and do all kinds of musical activities—they are all echoes—never the real voice. . . . Perhaps I am not in the end a real composer—a real conductor—perhaps just one who will always be on the fringes of the real art. Much of the music that I have written is at best—really unimportant—and my conducting can hardly be considered great. . . . My feelings and yearnings are those of a composer of the 19th century. I am completely out of step with the present. . . . I know that to create really important works one after the other is not given to me.

I am not sad at this realization—I do not deserve any better blessing. I have been much too successfull [sic] at the little things I have done. I have not humbled myself enough before the art—or made enough sacrifices to have had any greater expression granted me. . . . I feel sometimes that perhaps if I left music completely a greater happiness would be allowed me—but then—once one has felt the joy of creating music—could one really ever forsake it. . . . I know that you love me—and that you miss and wish me back—but I wish only to return when I can bring you happiness. . . . I do not believe that anyone can help me—only myself. . . .

By January, 1948, Herrmann was in Minneapolis, staying at the Hotel Nicollet alone, visiting Lucy Anderson and working on the opera. His letters reflect a growing tone of bitterness and a revisionist view of his creative past, prompted by frustration:

January 10, 1948

. . . I at all times tried to make life as comfortable as I could—servants—money—and complete responsibility of my fatherhood. I entered into work that was extremely distasteful to me—movies, commercial radio—to provide some of the things—I never had time for my own reflection and work—only more and more superficial work—and I became more and more exhausted—what I wanted seemed completely unattainable. . . . I always had to go out afterwards alone—everyone else had company— then the prospect of only work—only the piano waiting—only more and more facing of my own lack of achievement—the passing of time—and the hollowness of it all—the onslaught of my enemies. . . .

I am allowing everything to drift. I only wish to finish my opera. . . .

I have just seen a movie called "Sleep My Love" that is lousy—but it uses the 59th Street bridge and Sutton Place as a background—go see it. Please give my poor little girls a million hugs from me and tell them of my love and how I miss them—I miss them so. . . .

January 7, 1948

I have completely recovered my interest in music and am constantly thinking about it. . . . One thing I have made up my mind about—that is that I will never do a movie again. It is completely wasted and expended musical energy that should go into my own work. . . . I now understand that it was the movies that exhausted me and sapped my strength. I sincerely hope that I will never see Hollywood as long as I live. . . .

I spend my time mainly seeking to regain health and peace. . . . This has been a strange Winters Journey for me—but I know that in the end it will bring some sort of contentment and better understanding between us all . . . any hurt that I may cause you—I am deeply sorry for. . . . Do not lose sight of your great talent and genius. . . . Please Please take care of yourself and the little ones. . . .

January 19, 1948

Just a hasty note to tell you that opera is going wonderfully well. . . . The studio at W.C.C.O. [provided by conductor Dmitri Mitropoulos] is a grand place to work. . . . This is the first time in my life that I have enjoyed the advantages of complete concentration on my own music. . . . My head is full of ideas—and my musical invention comes easily. For too long I have led the average life—I must take advantage of this opportunity. . . .

January 25, 1948

I am so sorry that our phone talk had to be of such an angry nature. . . . I have always been frank with you. . . . I now realize that I have been a child about it—a mature man would have continued to be a hypocrite and a liar. . . . For you may as well realize that most men feel that in giving their wife a home—children—security and their part time company—they have done and honestly done their duty. . . . I [have] been the unhappiest of men—since I told you. . . . I can honestly say— that only while working has a peace come over me. The moment I stop— it comes back in a flood, the torment and anguish . . . believe me—I have never betrayed you—. . . .

I now feel that once the opera is done—I shall never write another note again. . . .

You are completely right when you say that I am a neurotic—I cannot be otherwise. You know only a neurotic would have waited and travelled in subways for six years. But I have been an honest neurotic and a loyal one. Some day I shall be psychoanalyzed and I am pretty sure what they will find. That I am pretty much like all other men and that I live all emotions intensely. that I have followed too many paths in my life— whereas one can only follow one. I have no real direction in life and that I am seeking for the intangibles—I look for the poetry and dreams of life— not for the realities. . . .

I know that I am a first rate conductor or at any rate can become one. If my opera is up to my standards well and good—but more than a minor poet in music I can never be. I shall be unable to make a good enough living as a composer to support my family (to have two families is completely out of the picture—for then I shall only have one path open—that of a complete commercial hack). As a conductor I shall become famous in time. . . . But first I shall finish the opera. I must—it is an obbsession [sic] of mine. It will be enough to be remember [sic] by one work—even if only in the history books. . . .

During these coming weeks—try to regain your strength and well being—you now know that I am alone. Let us all try to regain our sanity and health. For without it—all is in darkness and of utmost futility. . . .

March 8, 1948

Wasn't it too bad about Lockridge committing suicide—you know the author of *Raintree County* . . . they say he was just too exhausted by the effort of writing his novel. How well I understand this state of mental being when all purpose of life seems to drop away. I suppose after living for seven years with the creations and characters of his novel, the facing of the reality of the world without them was just too much for him. I know that "Wuthering Heights" has saved me many times and that to finally finish the opera will leave a tremendous void. . . .

March 17, 1948

I feel terribly upset about the world—and I am certain that there will be a war in the next few months with Russia and that all our lives will not be for long. . . . please take care of all the little ones and even be prepared for an (national) emergency. For I believe that Russia will not allow us to arm ourself—but may attack first. I certainly believe that peace is possible—but oh how muddle headed our government is about it. . . . What is it all about anyway . . . what is the use of it all. . . .

[Undated]

I'm sorry our phone call was such a mess . . . don't lose your own self-confidence because of me—after all—I am a neurotic person—restless and unsettled and not really able to adapt to the society of the world. . . . Do not worry about money—if at any time you earn a good deal of money and wish to accept some of this responsibility it is for your own generosity to decide. . . .

I am completely at sea and vainly trying to make a life for myself. I am frank to say that it has been the most agonizing time that I have had in my life. . . . I now fully realize that my devotion and admiration of you—is the same as ever—but that it has been invaded by emotions for some one else. . . .

I wish and desire to be made the center of one's life—I wish to be comforted and babied. I wish to be paid reams of attention. I wish to be regarded as a man first of all. I wish to be loved and cared for. This means more to me than intellectual companionship. I wish to have a sense of my own importance as a being in someone elses eyes. I do not wish to be regarded as an artist . . . or a father—but as a man and being. I hunger for a million small attentions—I do not wish to be apologized for. . . .

It is impossible to get the above—from one as you—because the combination of motherhood—your own creative life—your bondage to your family . . . has always left too little time for you to devote to me. In other words—you quickly became a wife—whereas I wished for a play mate. If the above means that I am a child still—so much the better—all artists are children—that is why they play out the illusions of art. I will never be a mature man—or a well balanced individual. I am willing to assume the responsibilities of life but not to forgo the illusions. . . .

I will not be cheated out of life. . . . I am frank to admit that I never liked your family—and because of the years that they kept us apart. . . . I feel that your efforts at writing and all the time you took from me was not for your own development but because you could earn money to give them. [After nine years as an invalid, full-time nursing care was secured for Lucille's father with the $20,000 she made from the screenplay of *Sorry, Wrong Number.*] She did not come and steal me—I really wish to go. . . .

I am sending Taffy a wonderful book of fairy tales that I read as a boy—"The Wonderful Adventures of Nils." I know that you will enjoy reading it to her. . . . Please keep well. Do not fall into that dark night of the soul from which I am now only beginning to emerge. . . .

After a turbulent month-long visit to New York, during which he battled Lucille Fletcher and his own disapproving family, Herrmann went to Reno in May 1948. There he obtained their "slot machine divorce,"[13] worked part-time as a clerk in a bookstore, and continued work on the opera. He now talked obsessively to anyone—customers, people on the street—about his problems.

May 12, 1948

I am tormented by the great hurt I have given you. . . . I cannot feel that I will be able to bring to Lucille [Anderson] a happy life—I cannot see how one so held by all of the past—by my children—by my life with you—can ever make her happy. . . . What can I bring—only a heavy heart—a deep sense of evading my duties and my fatherhood—my family—and my poor abilities. . . . It is not easy to shut the door on the room—to leave the picture. . . . I am now so alone—I doubt the value of all things I do—not know what to believe in. I do not know if what I follow is a mirage—and I dread the awakening. . . .

I cannot create the past again—or neither can you so—let us remain friends as always. . . . I only wish to help you—I wish you to be a grand fine artist—you must develop and mature—you must have self confidence in yourself. . . .

I have made a friend with a nice chap who runs a bookstore here—we spent yesterday visiting the Ghost Town of Virginia City.

This place once was the biggest city between Salt Lake City and San Francisco. It once had a population of 60,000—to-day about 400. Mark Twain had his first job here—and the silver and gold mines here yielded about $1,000,000,000 in 10 years—then the mines ran dry and all left it. . . . The place is full of decay and death—and the mirage of sudden wealth still hangs over the hills that surround it. How like life it all is— the prospect of happiness—the failure—and the death that follows if it is attained. . . . I went to see the opera house there—now falling into ruins. There once—Patti—Lind—Caruso—Paderewski—played there. There all the great actors of the world played. . . . Now only the wind makes noises through the empty rafters and the vivid red wallpaper sways in the breeze. . . .

May 25, 1948

The hell with Europe and Hollywood and the endless quest for fame— live—for God's sake—live. . . .

I hope to be able to find a new birth and a new full flowering of my talent . . . —but I wish to flower in the tender shade of love—not in the heart of achievement and social world. . . . I feel that I will never again live as formal a life as I have in the past. . . .

May 30, 1948

Such artists as Beethoven—Brahms—Shakespeare—Keats—are full of torment—frustration—and rebellion. Other artists—Bach—Milton—Schu-

mann . . . their art is full of deeper repose and tranquility. But of course
the greatest number of artistic masterpieces have not this repose but are
full of the rebellion of life and destiny. . . . Who is to say which should
be followed. . . . Everyone must do as they can—to live is to suffer. . . .

June 5, 1948

I feel I must do something to preserve my sanity and existence—to
continue to stay on here is impossible—futile—and can only lead on to an
indefinite state of torment and anguish—for nearly one year I have been
in this cell of grief and darkness. I have struggled with all my might and
power to restore myself to you and my little ones—I have battled in
vain—for I cannot surrender this overwhelming love that has flooded
me—I cannot destroy it without destroying both her and myself—and
leaving only a waste land to bring to you. . . .

If life had never sent me this passion I believe I would have remained
content and happy at your side—but since it has been given to me by the
divine power I could not continue to live next to you with a memory and
echo of it in my heart. I would always feel that I was not giving to you
the tributes that you so deserved. . . .

I will always keep in touch with you—I will phone and write you regularly—I believe that in time we can all be friends—that our houses will
be open to each other—that we will view this period of anguish and torment as the birthplace of a new and different life. . . .

June 5, 1948

Be yourself—let some pagan part of you well to the surface—the hell
with this christian piety and purity. Life is only made up of great calls—
calls to participate in the glory of life—not in this small pattern—that you
were brought up in. . . .

To love is to become humble and gentle—the power of love is so overwhelming to stand before—the miracle of witnessing the power of God—it
is great—to stand before—one must kneel before it—with wonderment
and adoration.

Christ was really selfish—for he wished mankind to find in him this
love—and for love to be given to him—but the Jews—were really more
understanding. They said no—in God you will find it—but no one can
see or picture God—therefore in another human being—is God. In your
mate—there is God—in the being to-gether there is God. For God is a
force—a love—not a being on the cross.

God is in every being. . . . we are God—God is love—and love is God.
Christ is human suffering—the torment—the agony—the belief that in
eternity love will be given and received and returned. But Christ is the
symbol of this attempt to find love—and how easily mankind's heart re-

sponses [*sic*] to this suffering and worship it. But not through Christ is love found. . . . He can help one along the bitter paths—but he cannot give you love—for love is within you—that is the God within you. All men are Christ—but the kingdom of heaven is within one—not in the here after. . . . That is why—two sexes were created—not really to continue the race—other ways could have been devised—but because only by two people—becoming one—was fear dispelled—loneliness and questioning destroyed—for love then enveloped and cloaked them—with the grace of God—and his plan complete.

Please forgive this rambling confusing sermon—but I know that you will understand the gist of it. For in the last year—I feel that horizons of life have been spread before me. . . .

June 1948

What is there about you that is so holy so precious—that you must surround it with a high wall. Well I shall not beg—for if I am not worthy of your confidence and love—I shall not plead for it. . . . It is not that I left you because I fell in love—but rather because you did not love me. . . . I was blind all these years. . . .

What am I to do. . . . My children and you pull at my heart. . . . I am truly . . . a drowning man—I began to drown that day—when I first consented to ride you home on the subway—and not enter your house. . . .

You have been unfair and unjust to me—my life has been a mockery— but I shall not think of the past. . . .

You never had to fight for anything in this world. You always got the prizes—the awards—the medals—the head of the class—later on—you were spoiled by me—who did all your fighting—and now you must learn to fight for yourself—for your children—for your work. . . .

You should have let me see your last contract [for a film project with producer Hal Wallis after *Sorry, Wrong Number;* the film was not made]—I would have never allowed you to sign such a contract— especially the clause—that if they did not make the picture—you lost $10,000. Not even a [*sic*] idiot of an agent would let you sign such a clause. . . . Haven't you any sense yourself. . . .

I do not understand you at all—beside all our other problems—your strange attitude whenever I tried to help you in your business deals. . . . If you have chosen to be a writer instead of a housewife—then you must engage in the battle of life—with all the weapons that they use. . . . I hope that in future—you will let me see all of your contracts. . . . But let me warn you—no man can be expected to spend his day—working and fighting through his own business hardships—studying and conducting— and then come home—only to face again the same thing. . . . Is it any wonder—that I fled to the tranquility of Lucille. . . . For in the end you destroyed our marriage—by making me into a lawyer—agent—critic—manager. . . .

I believe that our marriage fell apart because of two full-time careers. Not because we got on each others nerves—but because we drifted apart as human beings. And always I gave in to your desires—the prove [*sic*] of that—is my own neglect of my work. . . . Therefore I say to you—if you are going to be a commercial writer—get your money—and as much as you can. Remember that no one cares really who writes a screen play—than who writes the music. . . . I have working [*sic*] four hours a day in a bookstore here—and let me tell you—people only want to read the utmost trash—the best seller—is it sexy—or if they saw a movie out of it. It is all a big commercial racket—so at least get your money out of them. . . . Call me—when in doubt . . .

Don't be a fool. . . . Live where you are—you will never find another place as cheap and as comfortable or so convenient. . . . Learn to drive a car.

Is it any wonder that you have worn me away—and exhausted me—I must think about a million things in your life—and none of them had to do—with ourselves. You see—it is mostly about yourself. . . .

I am as yet in darkness and alone. . . . .

### June 1948

I sometimes feel—as though I had been living in a carefully tended garden—and that one day—I discovered a secret door in its walls—and then after fighting for months not to open it—I finally did so—and the vista before me was beautiful—but no paths led into it.—that I had to make my own path—but I was afraid—to leave the carefully tended walls of flowers of the garden—but the vistas kept calling—I am still at the gate—and still hesitating to go forth—and still unable to shut the gate upon it. . . .

P.S. Please send me the dress sizes of Taffy and Wendy as I would like very much to send them some Western outfits from here. . . .

### June 8, 1948

20 years of nervous tension and strain leads me to find a simpler life—for if I continue in the past manner—only an early death confronts me. . . . I no longer have the reserve of energy that I once had—I must now conserve it for the music I would like to write. . . .

### June 12, 1948

I would love to be a beachcomber at times—and I also would like to engage in the battle of life—but I insist on languor and idleness as a reward. . . . To appreciate this you would only have to conduct one program to realize the strain and exhaustion—I know that children are very racking at times . . . but then to have you incessantly hammering away with your projects and your high ideals was too much. The sound of the lute and purple waters is as much a part of life as struggle and achievement. . . .

June 14, 1948

I am deeply concerned over your loneliness and understand it completely. . . .

I am glad that slowly my health is improving—mental health—for I was as near to a complete breakdown as one could ever be. It was only an onion skin of thickness that separated me from the chasm. . . . Please do not get too close to the ragged edge. . . .

Remember at all times I will be free to talk to you to help you and advise you. . . . If you wish to destroy me your unhappiness will do it. . . . Give the little ones my love. . . .

By July, the divorce was complete, but Herrmann remained "weary and tired and haunted":

July 1948

The divorce has not separated me from you—or given me the mental freedom to create a new life. You are still my wife . . . until that time the tie is broken I cannot have a new life—let alone marry again. . . . I have no plans—but exist only from day to day. . . .

I have read a book that I have sent to you: *Modern Woman, the Law of Sex*. . . . Certainly, as the book points out, modern woman in search of her own career and ambition at the expense of following her greatest gift, that of being a mother and creating a home and being a sexual mate, has lost her own femininity and happiness. . . .

I wish so tó be loved—to be mothered—to be given a single overwhelming love. . . . But I cannot believe that I shall allow myself to have it . . . all my sense of duty is against it. . . . It is hard to give up a reality for the mirage and unknown future. I do not at all times have this courage.

As one relationship ended painfully, Herrmann attempted to reassure his new love in a series of letters that show him at his most tender. His recovery and new sense of hope may explain the atypical religious references:

My dearest dearest beloved heart: On this twilight of Good Friday— take comfort and hope. Have heart and courage. For before us lies the future—the future of rebirth and new life. Remain at peace with yourself.

Remain tranquil and serene. Remain content. For the Lord is watching
over you—you are very dear and precious to him. You are one of his
most beloved lambs. Believe in Him and his wisdom . . . for a robe of
comfort he has given you my love. My love that now envelops you and
cradles you—and whispers to you—songs of sleep and tenderness. My
love for you is eternall [sic] and all encompassing. I love you for the fragile and beautiful spirit that is your soul. You are an immortal being for a
soul of such beauty as yours—is a part of His being. Remember that. . . .

Behold Beloved—Beloved—it is Easter—it is the day of new life at
rebirth. It is full of the promise of happiness and courage. It is the day
beloved of the Lord. It is the day that he has set aside for his children—
to tell them—that they are immortal and that his great understanding
and love is eternal. It is the day that banishes all shadows and dispells [sic]
all coldness of winter. It is the day that brings all his lambs alone to his
heart. He is now showing his great wonders—his miracle of spring—his
benediction of love—his assurance of life immortal. . . . Therefore my
beloved—to-day he is watching thee and holding you dear and near to
him. He is sending you hope—courage—serenity and love. Therefore let
us both pray now—and thank Him for all the blessings He has showered
upon us. Let us therefore graze like lambs in the spring pastures—knowing that He is guarding the great mountains that surround us. Therefore
let us humbly thank Him for his great gifts that He has bestowed upon
us. Let us sing His songs and be content—and full of the eternal serenity
that He sends for those who love Him. Let us thank him for the great gift
of life—for love—for music—for poetry—for the human heart. Shall
we—beloved—shall we—let us then—now.[14]

Herrmann remained good friends with Lucille Flectcher until his death.
The settlement was amicable, with Herrmann retaining much of his large
collection of art, furniture, and literature. In January 1949, Lucille married writer Douglas Wallop (author of *The Year the Yankees Lost the Pen-
ant*, on which the musical *Damn Yankees* was based). Herrmann often
visited them in Arlington, Virginia, where they lived for thirteen years.
The change was difficult at first for Wendy and especially the older Taffy;
eventually, the girls would visit Herrmann during their summer vacations
from school.

Shortly after her second marriage, Lucille's father died. Herrmann did
not attend the funeral (he avoided funerals throughout his life) but sent
a large wreath of lilies, with a quotation from Matthew Arnold that he
later used as a preface to his opera: "Unquiet souls! In the dark fermen-
tation of earth, In the never idle workshop of nature, In the eternal movement, Ye shall find yourselves again!"[15]

In slow, painful steps, Herrmann was also trying to find himself, discarding one life for another in his search for an ideal companion and inner peace. It would not be for the last time.

During the fall of 1947–1948 Herrmann found himself incapable of work at CBS—or in Hollywood, where he was still listening to offers. The saddest might-have-been was a projected reteaming with Orson Welles, who in October 1947 asked Herrmann to score his exciting, low-budget film of *Macbeth*. (It was the first film since *The Magnificent Ambersons* to remain in Welles's hands long enough for him to choose a composer, unlike *The Stranger* and *The Lady from Shanghai*.)

At first Herrmann was thrilled by the project. "It is a great and wonderful picture," he wrote Lucille Fletcher. "It is by far Orson's best picture (better than Kane) and certainly the finest Shakespeare film ever made. It is set in Scotland in the 2nd Century and looks as if it was painted or rather filmed by Hieronymous Bosch. It is full of a barbaric splendor and decay and all the characters in it are superb. . . . You have no feeling of it being a stage play but only of its horror and doom and the magic of its lines. It is full of darkness and snow and night. I believe that I will be able to do a fine score for it. . . . It know that I will—as I feel that this picture will always be the pinnacle of my movie career."[16]

By November, however, Welles had not finished editing the film and was considering leaving for Europe to start another project. "Unless he stays and works on it himself I am determined not to bother with it," Herrmann wrote Lucille. "I do not care to have another Ambersons pulled on me. . . . I am seeing him this afternoon and we shall have it out. . . . If he goes about his wild orgies of Europe—I prefer to resign."[17]

Welles did not stay. Jacques Ibert scored the film months later in Europe.

Another offer came that fall from the persistent David O. Selznick, who again wanted Herrmann for a Hitchcock film. This time it was *The Paradine Case*, a poorly written courtroom drama that marked the end of Hitchcock and Selznick's combative association. Coincidentally, the film's chief sound and music supervisor was former RKO man James G. Stewart, who doubted that Herrmann and Selznick could ever collaborate:

When Bernie was suggested I said, "Jesus, Mr. Selznick, you don't know what you're going to go through!" "Why do you say that about the man?" Selznick asked. "I'd like to have him see the picture." Well, the picture wasn't finished at that time. I called up Bernie and told him Mr. Selznick wanted him to see some scenes from the film. Bernie didn't want to do it—"Nyah, nyah, nyah . . . I'll look at it when it's finished. I may not even be around then." I said, "C'mon, for God's sake, get me off the hook—he's deviling me to have you do it." Bernie finally said okay.

He came in, and I ran the picture for him; Selznick was not present. All Bernie did during the screening was complain—about the picture, about the way it was shot, about the way it didn't adapt to music. Then he went into the office with Selznick—and he was just charming, absolutely charming. He said he liked the picture—which he didn't—but that he couldn't do it. As Bernie came out of the office I said to him, "You son of a bitch!" He said, "Well, I didn't want to just say I didn't like it." Selznick then came out, all smiles, shook hands with Bernie, and said to me afterwards, "Jimmy, what were you talking about? He's a *charming* man!"[18]

Months later, Selznick asked Herrmann to score his next film, an adaptation of Robert Nathan's romantic fantasy *Portrait of Jennie*. Directed by William Dieterle (*All That Money Can Buy*), the film was largely the vision of Selznick, who heavily rewrote and reshot Dieterle's work. Herrmann turned the film down (telling Lucille he would not accept less than $35,000, nearly three times his usual fee)[19]—but he did contribute an impressionistic love theme for the spirit Jennie, played by Jennifer Jones. (The theme, sung by Jones, is briefly incorporated into the score.) Selznick then hired Dimitri Tiomkin to write a score based on themes of Debussy, whose music "even a Bernie Herrmann could not improve on."[20] A staunch advocate of original music in cinema, Herrmann hated the results.[21]

Contributing, perhaps, to Herrmann's avoidance of Hollywood in 1948–1950 was the advent of McCarthyism and the Communist-hunting sessions of the House Un-American Activities Committee (HUAC). Several of Herrmann's collaborators and friends—including Norman Corwin, Orson Welles, and Abe Polonsky—were branded potential subversives by the self-appointed investigators, and while Herrmann's own politics were moderate, his involvement in WPA activities and vaguely socialist music groups of the early 1930s was a matter of record.

According to blacklisted actress Marsha Hunt, a friend of Herrmann's, "Benny was filled with rage that actors were being denied work. But he was very angry at any of us who protested the [HUAC] hearings. He was asked to lend his name to statements in the press or in ads, and he wouldn't do it."[22] Shortly after Polonsky's name appeared on a list of "Communist sympathizers," Herrmann claimed not to know him.[23]

Over the years, an increasing number of Herrmann's friendships would end with similar abruptness. The reason was usually a sharp defense mechanism: aware that he had made enemies, Herrmann was oversensitive to the threat of betrayal, despite his need for intense friendship. "Beenie was unable to express love to the people he felt very deeply about," recalled Kathryn Corwin (Norman's wife). "I think had he had a sense of his lovely inner quality he would not have been as defensive. He managed to transfer his inability to deal with people to animals: he identified with the independence of cats, their inability to have love thrust at them. When Norman and I visited him, the door would open, and there was Beenie nuzzling a cat—caressing it, kissing it, talking baby talk to it. He usually concealed that sweetness."[24]

Although Herrmann's Hollywood career had reached a hiatus, his interest in the medium was undimmed. Particularly intriguing to him was the commercial release of film soundtracks on (newly invented) long-playing albums—a trend that would have enormous repercussions on Herrmann's career a decade later. In September 1947, it was the topic of a Herrmann article in the *Saturday Review*:

Each month sees the appearance of discs, both from America and abroad, containing background music from a picture. This is not "popular" or "hit" music in any commercial sense. Rather, it is usually turgidly symphonic, often in a modern style, sometimes uncompromisingly dissonant, with nothing to recommend it to the public except its immediate association with a picture. Yet these records prove popular. . . . Listening to them raises several questions in my mind—questions which I am sure the composers must have asked themselves before allowing their efforts to see the light of day.

I say "light of day" in a real sense, for film music, by its very nature, was meant to be heard only in the dark, from the flickering screen. The screen made it, and to the screen it belongs. . . . A montage, a long lyric scene, a span of epic pageantry, a battle—these are things movie composers long for. But even so, they are generally brief and can be interrupted arbitrarily by the cutter. There is not much you can do, musically, with a battle that only lasts a minute on the screen, or a storm that peters out in thirty seconds. But such problems are faced daily by the boys in Hollywood and Shepherd's Bush.

For me, it is a necessity to see a film before judging the quality of a recorded score. Only then can one evaluate the peculiar problems posed, or the subtleties of orchestration and thematic development which the composer has conjured up. Notably such scores as "The Red House" music of Miklós Rózsa . . . and Dimitri Tiomkin's score for "Duel in the Sun." . . . Both were highly effective film scores, wedded to the screen action. Without Tiomkin's music, the fiercely rhythmic Orizaba dance in the Casino scene would have lost half its violence, Pearl Chavez's lonely trek across the desert to her lover would have been without grandeur or

psychological significance. But this same music, which seemed in the theatre to supercharge the screen with its own power, has abstract excitement
only if one can relive the scene, mentally, as it is heard from the record.
The same is true of Rózsa's "Screams in the Night" sequence, as the
frightened boy runs through the twilight woods. This, as I saw it in "The
Red House," seemed a real high point in film music. To hear it alone
without the photography, is to compare the roaring of the ocean with the
rushing noise inside a sea shell. . . .

One of the most satisfying of the year's film music releases is the
handsome album from Walton's "Henry V." . . . It is not a typical film
score in any sense, for music was allotted an important, often paramount
position in this moving, brilliant tapestry of color and sound. But on
records, the music itself shrinks in size, compared to a memory of its brilliance in the theatre. Since the album features the spoken lines of Laurence Olivier, no attempt has been made to doctor the music for the
records. . . . Perhaps we will one day have a reworking of the music by
Walton himself into a suite or perhaps a cantata. The epic nature of the
music, and its great variety—I regret the omission of the lovely music of
Falstaff's death—cry out for a treatment similar in stature to that which
Prokofieff gave to his "Alexander Nevsky" movie music.

Which brings us, perhaps to the proper place for all ambitious film music—the legitimate concert-hall suite. The vogue for the kind of issue discussed herein, with the music in undigested form, gets it out in an accessible form, but hardly in an ideal way. Film composers are busy men, and
scarcely inclined to take time off to assemble their bits and pieces into an
art form. Some of them, too, working as they do constantly with short,
effective episodes have lost the musical stamina to carry through a full-
length piece. But it is only in such a way that a work can be produced
that will stand on its own two feet, without the screen.[25]

Herrmann would follow his own advice twenty years later by arranging
many of his scores into suites for recording.

By the fall of 1948, Herrmann was eager to return to England. Again
the professional means came from John Barbirolli and Ernest Bean, who
wrote Herrmann in October about a return to the Halle Orchestra: "Everyone remembers the pleasure and enjoyment given on your last visit.
If there were any chance of the production of 'Wuthering Heights' with
J. B. conducting the visit would be still more exciting."[26]

The opera was still unfinished, and Herrmann was apparently against
arranging excerpts in an orchestral suite, but the Halle directors did schedule a Herrmann appearance for November 1949. In the meantime, Herrmann returned to the CBS Symphony, where his esoteric broadcasts of

musical Americana, modern European music, and obscure classical works continued to delight discerning listeners in the United States and abroad.

"I wonder if you know how valuable Mr. Bernard Herrmann's 'Treasure Bandstand' is to the Voice of America and to what a large international audience its programs are distributed," wrote Ralph L. F. Combs of the Voice of America to William Paley. "These [broadcasts] have been sent to embassies and consulates throughout the world. They are lent to local radio stations and broadcast as a presentation of the American government. . . . You can appreciate what useful and subtle propaganda this program is, particularly to listeners who tend to think of all Yanks as wholly absorbed in money-making. . . . Mr. Herrmann's programs of American music are widely representative, selected with taste and performed with skill. I marvel at the interest and variety which is consistently maintained. . . . We would be quite lost without the Treasury programs for there is no other source for such excellent brief items of musical Americana."[27]

Inevitably, some Herrmann broadcasts had dissenters. After a performance of a Schoenberg work in June 1949, Herrmann received this badly typed note:

Dear Mr. Herrmann:

To tell you the truth I had a very bad reception with many disturbances; electrical and I think also accoustical. It seems to me that the engineers in the broadcasting station do not like my music and always distort by their mixtures to the sound. Otherwise it is really difficult to understand why the sonority was so poor. Though one must not forget the electrical disturbances.

You will perhaps understand that such an annoyance is really severe and can deprive a composer entirely of the pleasure of hearing his work. But let me thank you for all the good you did to this music. I am sure that you spent much and serious work in rehearsing it and if I may say so, I found especially the second movement very good as regards technique and clarity. The first movement especially was very much distorted in sound so that I had not much pleasure in it.

Now, let me thank you very much for your very kind words and for your great interest in my music and I hope we will meet on these opportunities again.

With cordial greetings I am,

Sincerely yours,
Arnold Schoenberg[28]

After offering Schoenberg a recording of the broadcast, Herrmann received another letter from the composer:

Dear Mr. Herrmann:

> Excuse me answering your kind letter so late. I was a little sick.
>
> I would like to receive the record which you offered to send me. The disturbances, when I heard it over the radio, were very nasty and there came so many ugly noises out of the radio that one could not hear the basses for much of the time. I mean, it was really to the greater part very annoying, especially the second movement. So, if you think your record is better, I would really be grateful if you would send it to me.
>
> Thank you very much.[29]

Herrmann did strive to perform a work as accurately as possible—unlike one of the conductors he most admired, Leopold Stokowski. The paradox becomes less puzzling after one reads a Herrmann essay on Stokowski, which reveals Herrmann's own obsession with orchestral timbre and musical experimentation:

> He is the only great conductor whose ambition was not so much to be a "great interpreter" of music, but rather to create a tonal sound that had never really been achieved before. . . . The orchestra of modern times bears no more resemblance to the orchestra of 1820 than a modern Steinway does to a piano of 1820. So in order to realize a completely vital tone picture, Stokowski swept aside all the traditional aspects of the symphony orchestra and began building anew.
>
> First of all, Stokowski decided to re-seat the players of the orchestra in an unorthodox way. . . . Twenty years ago the first and second violins were divided and placed on either side of the conductor, and so on. Stokowski . . . seated all the strings in a mass on his left and put all the woodwinds on the right so that they projected with greater clarity to the audience, and he placed the brass and percussion at the very back. . . . He did not dissipate his [string] forces with uniform bowing, which divided a phrase of music into short segments, but he introduced free-bowing and as a result achieved a great plastic curve of sound.
>
> Stokowski's search for a flexible sound led him to take a great interest in recordings and that is why his records from the very beginning had a marvellous sonority. I remember when I was a youngster that the old 78 r.p.m. records sounded as wonderful in their way as the hi-fi records of today. . . . All great conductors seem to leave their tonal style on an orchestra—not as markedly as Stokowski does—but it is one of the tragedies that his own particular concept of music has not been emulated. The nearest of all the younger generation of conductors is Karajan. But Karajan

polishes the tone-color very differently—and though much of his conducting has a lovely sheen, that kaleidoscopic effect of color escapes him. . . . Karajan's conducting has a wonderful chromium polish whilst Stokowski's has the iridescence of burnished gold.

One of the great contributions Stokowski has made has been to the music of the twentieth century. . . . When he was a young conductor he made his New York debut conducting Mahler's 8th Symphony—at that time a brand new work. . . . It is very hard to ascertain exactly what Stokowski's own taste is in contemporary music because he is so eclectic and catholic. . . .*

This empathy with the composer is shown in Stokowski's Bach transcriptions. We admit that Bach never heard his Toccata and Fugue in D Minor in the way that Stokowski has realized it, but Bach must have had that kind of sound in his mind. He certainly didn't have the sound of some baroque church organ with a couple of tired little boys trying to pump air in at the back—but rather he must have imagined some great cosmic sound and Stokowski's transcription is a metamorphosis of that sound. Stokowski is not just a conductor or a re-creator; he is a co-creator with the genius to evoke a unique and distinctive orchestral style, and the ability to fully realize the sound in the imagination of the composer.[30]

The year 1949 saw a strengthening of Herrmann's friendship with Stokowski, who listened devotedly to Herrmann's CBS broadcasts and admired the composer's work. "Last Sunday's concert was wonderful in every way," Stokowski wrote Oliver Daniel after a CBS "musical intermission" for a Philharmonic broadcast. "The program was just right for the day and the intermission fitted in perfectly. It was for everyone, and yet it did not sacrifice quality. . . . The conducting of Herrmann was as always a joy to listen to."[31]

In February, Stokowski performed the *Devil and Daniel Webster* suite at three Philharmonic concerts, to Herrmann's and critics' delight. "In power of speech and content Mr. Herrmann's suite from the widely acclaimed film easily dominated the first half of the program," one reviewer wrote. "The racy orchestral writing brought smiles and chuckles from sedate subscribers and several rounds of applause for the bowing composer. . . . Mr. Stokowski seemed to enjoy the Herrmann music as much as last night's crowd."[32]

---

*It was Herrmann who introduced Stokowski to Ives. In 1966, Stokowski gave the world premiere of Ives's Fourth Symphony, portions of which Herrmann had conducted as early as 1933.

Throughout the summer, which Stokowski spent in Greenwich, Connecticut, the two men corresponded often, each offering the other advice and encouragement:[33]

6 June 49
Dear San Bernadino:

We have been away to a friend's farm and just came back here and find the most interesting book on Thibet [sic] you so kindly sent us. The photographs could not be better and what I have read of the text is deeply interesting to me. . . .

I listened with the greatest interest to your concert on the 29th of May and thought the program, including the intermission, was simply perfect. It had unity because the music, Memorial Day, and the intermission all were perfectly appropriate. . . . The two Whitman poems were perfect for that program and I enjoyed so much your music to [Leaves of] GRASS and found your FOR THE FALLEN most original and yet effortless. . . .

It was a delight not to have the symphonic coughing of Carnegie Hall.

Have you any interludes or other symphonic music from Wuthering Heights that I could play?

5 July
Dear San Bernadino:

I was greatly impressed with the beauty of the Prelude to Act 3 of NATOMA that you played. OKLAHOMA is perfect music of its kind. . . . But for me the highest point of the program was Welles Raises Kane. This music is fascinating and interesting every second. It never lets down for a moment. Its musical conception and orchestration are all one. It makes me look forward enormously to your opera because I know it is going to be great.

15 July 49
Dear Bernard:

I think you are right I should make my own ending to the Haydn SPRING OVERTURE. . . .

Whenever you feel ready, and have the time let's discuss what I can conduct from your new opera and perhaps you would play some of it for me.

When you go to England, please give Beecham my greetings. It would be wonderful if you and he and I could work together some day.

Let's meet soon in New York and have a nice time together like last time.

Leopold

Nothing could deter Herrmann from his CBS duties once a concert season had begun—not even his decision, one year after his divorce, to remarry. Witness to the odd, telling occasion of Herrmann's second wedding in August 1949 was CBS director Oliver Daniel:

One afternoon I was sitting in my office, when Benny stormed in and said, "Hey Ollie, whaddaya doin' for lunch?" I said, "I'm sorry, I have plans." "*Cancel* it—ya gotta come with me!" I canceled whatever I had and walked with Benny from CBS to a brownstone house on Lexington Avenue a few blocks away. There was Lucy Anderson, whom I'd met before. Benny said, "C'mon, we're goin' downtown—Lucy, got your flowers?" He put a corsage on her, and we started down to City Hall. Only in the taxi cab did Benny tell me he was getting married.

The wedding was performed in the most antiseptic room you could imagine; it looked like an unused courtroom. The justice of the peace started the ceremony; Benny looked a bit glum, Lucy a bit expectant. The justice said to Benny, "Will you put the ring on her third finger?" Benny put the ring on the middle finger of Lucy's hand. The justice said, "Oh no, her *third* finger." Benny looked up and screeched, "CAN'T YA COUNT? EVERYBODY KNOWS when ya study piano it's one, two, three, four, FIVE! Thumb is number one! If ya want it on her fourth finger say FOURTH FINGER!" It was an incredible harangue.

After the ceremony I suggested we have lunch. It's funny—I recall a photo of Toscanini walking somewhere in Holland, with his wife trailing behind him alone. Well, here was Benny, stalking off alone in the direction of the restaurant; I waited behind and walked arm-in-arm with Lucy. Benny was not insensitive; it was just his way to go ahead and see. We first went to an unpretentious French-Italian restaurant at the base of the Brooklyn Bridge. When we got there Benny said, "Aww, we're not gonna eat here!"—so we took a cab to the Empire State Building and a pleasant restaurant inside.

Afterwards we went back to CBS in a taxi. They let me off, and I thought, The newlyweds are off on their honeymoon. An hour and a half later, Benny was back in my office, discussing new scores and what was going to happen next at CBS! It was the most unromantic occasion you could imagine.[34]

After the CBS concert season ended in late October and his contract as the Symphony's chief conductor was renewed for three more years, Herrmann returned to Manchester and northern Yorkshire for his real honeymoon. Of his Halle performance of Liszt's *Faust* Symphony, the *Manchester Guardian* wrote: "Mr. Herrmann conducted this work (in its original, all-orchestral form) with evident devotion, maintaining a regard for its wealth of fascinating detail without losing sight of the vast span of the whole conception. . . . So finely eloquent a performance of the symphony is indeed exhilarating—indeed, a great—experience."[35]

Again accompanied by Ernest Bean, Herrmann took a second tour of Brontë country. In Halifax, he purchased every available text on the authors and had lunch at Kildwick Hall; he then visited Haworth parish church, the Parsonage Museum, and Ponden Hall (the believed model for Thrushcross Grange). Each site was photographed for the opera's set designs. Throughout his northern travels Herrmann received a hero's welcome, from invitations by the Brontë Society to an official welcome by the mayor and mayoress of Keighley.

"The orchestra are still talking of the great pleasure they had having you with them again and what a stimulating experience it was to play with you so much music that was new to them," Barbirolli wrote his friend weeks later. "I was particularly happy to have the opportunity of hearing you conduct your most sensitive and lovely 'For the Fallen' which moved me very much. We all retain the happiest and most vivid recollections of your company . . . and I hope it will not be too long before we are together again."[36]

1949 had been a year of healing for Herrmann. His conducting ambitions were satisfied through the artistic freedom of CBS and his triumphant Halle performances; the pain of his separation from Lucille and their daughters was replaced by a new, happy marriage; and the following spring Herrmann returned to Hollywood and RKO, for one of his most underrated film projects.

Nicholas Ray, a young director from New York (with the strong drama *They Live by Night* to his credit), was the first to see screen potential in Gerald Butler's novel *Mad with Much Heart,* a psychological thriller RKO considered "unpleasant but powerful. . . . It is likely to emerge as an 'art' production which may receive critical acclaim but no sizeable box-office returns."[37] Their assessment proved half-correct. *On Dangerous Ground,* as the adaptation by Ray and A. I. Bezzerides was retitled, attracted neither popular nor critical acclaim. " 'On Dangerous Ground' was an absolute failure, but I'm still fond of it in some ways," Ray later said.[38] To its producer, John Houseman (now independent after his tenures with the Mercury Theatre and Selznick), the film was "peculiar and strange . . . sort of a mess [but] awfully good."[39]

As in much of Ray's work, the film's conflict was largely psychological, couched in accessible thriller terms. Robert Ryan starred as Jim Wilson, an alienated city cop whose pent-up anger finds release in the beating of suspects. Transferred upstate to investigate a molestation killing, Wilson meets Mary Warden (Ida Lupino), a young blind woman, whose brother Danny, Wilson learns, is the hunted man. Mary's humanity helps Wilson rediscover his own, but he is unable to save her brother: the boy falls to his death after a chase across the mountains. In Mary, however, Wilson has found salvation: his hands, once instruments of pain, are now filled with gentleness as they hold Mary's at the fade out.

*On Dangerous Ground* fell short of realizing its themes of personal redemption and the connection between social alienation and violence; yet its erratic brilliance makes it more compelling than many a conventional "success." The film's first, darkest half is its best, a tour of Boston's alleys as seen through Wilson's anguished eyes. Like Travis Bickle in *Taxi Driver*, a later Herrmann film, Wilson is an urban casualty, filled with longings he cannot articulate.

Director Ray was no stranger to Wilson's problems. According to Houseman, "Nick was a difficult and sometimes disturbing companion. He was inarticulate and garrulous . . . his mind was filled with original ideas which he found it difficult to express in an understandable form. . . . Yet, confronted with a theatrical situation or a problem of dramatic or musical expression he was amazingly quick, lucid and intuitive with a sureness of touch, a sensitivity to human values and an infallible taste I have seldom seen equalled in a director."[40]

Such an artist, and the dark vision he communicated, found an admirer in Herrmann. For the composer, the film's mix of emotional black and whites, of tragedy and optimism, had considerable power. "It's a very good film," he said in 1971. "It's still occasionally shown and I'm always very partial to it."[41] Herrmann strove to give the film an emotional continuity by polarizing its two halves, and he largely succeeded. His score divides good and evil into clearly separate entities—the former represented by a single, expressive instrument (the resonant viola d'amore), the latter by a violent scherzo (the "Death Hunt") that is one of the most exhilarating pieces of film music ever written.

Frequently Herrmann allows images and dialogue to carry themselves. Wilson's mental breakdown in the film's first third is conveyed visually, not musically: Ray's city scenes are strong enough without scoring. After a scherzolike prelude for horns and orchestra (an allusion to the film's climax), Herrmann reserves commentary for Wilson's beating of a suspect, in the film's most violent scene: "Why do you make me do it?" Wilson cries, his fists punching his offscreen victim (at the camera's eye) as Herrmann's metallic brass strike with equal brutality.

A cool pastel of woodwinds signals the beginning of Wilson's journey to the country (and self); yet even this cue brings menace, in a churning triplet device for low strings (which becomes a key motive of danger in Herrmann's *North by Northwest* score nine years later). Soon Wilson's quarry is spotted and the death hunt begins, the unsteadiness of Ray's sometimes handheld visuals mirrored in a spiraling string device that anticipates *Psycho*'s famous rainstorm escape. (Both sequences take their cue from the beating rhythm of car windshield wipers and the emotional frenzy of the drivers—here, Wilson and the dead girl's father, Brent [Ward Bond].)*

What Bezzerides' screenplay lacks in giving Mary's character dimension is compensated for in Lupino's touching performance and Herrmann's compassionate scoring for strings, winds, harp, and viola d'amore to convey Mary's altered perception of the world and her (literally) blind faith. "I felt the instrument had a veiled quality," Herrmann said. "The color of the music was like her character."[42]

There is no score during Wilson's tense confrontation with the killer, Danny, whose repeated threat, "I'll *cut* you," becomes an almost musical, staccato device. For several minutes Wilson and Danny move quietly through the shadows of an empty cabin, their dialogue and Ray's subtle cutting the sole provider of tension—until Brent charges in, rifle in hand, hungry for vengeance. At last, Herrmann's scherzo, heard allusively throughout the score, explodes with terrifying ferocity, its polyphonic rhythms for nine horns propelling the chase to its tragic end. (Years later, Herrmann cited the sequence as his favorite among his work.)[43]

Wilson's reunion with Mary may seem an unconvincing contrivance ("I don't believe in miracles," Ray later said),[44] but musically the resolution is credible and transcendent, pitting Mary's theme for viola d'amore against the brass and basses of Wilson's city music, until the viola theme is embraced by full orchestra—a climax that for Herrmann is inevitable and celebratory.

1951 would be a critical year of births and deaths. On June 30—at 3:45 P.M., according to the score[45]—*Wuthering Heights* was completed after eight years of work. "We shall drink to it to-night, and one day I do so

*From Lyn Murray's 1951 diary: "Benny in the middle of dubbing. . . . Full of anger because in a big chase scene where eight horns are wailing, dogs . . . drown out the horns. He told Constantin Bakaleinikoff that if the dogs covered up the horns he would withdraw the whole score from the picture. A producer said, 'But you've been paid.' Benny said, 'I haven't cashed the checks' " (Murray, *Musician: A Hollywood Journal* [Secaucus, N.J.: Lyle Stuart, 1987], p. 31).

greatly hope to hear it," wrote Evelyn Barbirolli that August. "John looks forward to receiving the score when copies are made, but I think it would be far better if you could deliver it in person!"[46] The orchestral parts having been copied in Hollywood and reduced to a piano score, Herrmann phoned Lyn Murray and invited him to an in-house "performance" of the work. With Murray at the piano and Herrmann approximating the vocal parts in raspy Brooklynese, the two men played the opera from start to finish—then drove to director John Brahm's beachside home for an encore rendition.[47] Noted Murray in his journal: "[Benny] gets into such a lather of recreative excitement, one gets the impression that if one interfered with his trajectory at a time like this he would explode and leave nothing but a smoking crater for miles around."[48]

That same year, the CBS Symphony was disbanded. Television was now the network's main priority and the orchestra was among the first of many casualties in the dying medium of radio. "What fools they will be," John Barbirolli wrote his devastated friend. "What is particularly disturbing is that your splendid influence or rather your unparalleled influence and taste is no longer available to the thousands who badly needed it."[49]

One afternoon at CBS, Herrmann encountered Paley in the men's room and launched a tirade of criticism and frustration with the network leader's decisions. Paley allegedly replied, "The trouble is, Benny, you're wearing the old school tie, and there's no old school anymore."[50]

Herrmann, now forty years old, was no longer conductor-in-chief of a unique symphony orchestra. There would be no more network commissions or broadcast premieres, only a handful of radio scores left to write. The likelihood of guest invitations from East Coast orchestras was slim.

Herrmann's options were narrowing—and pointing west, to Hollywood.

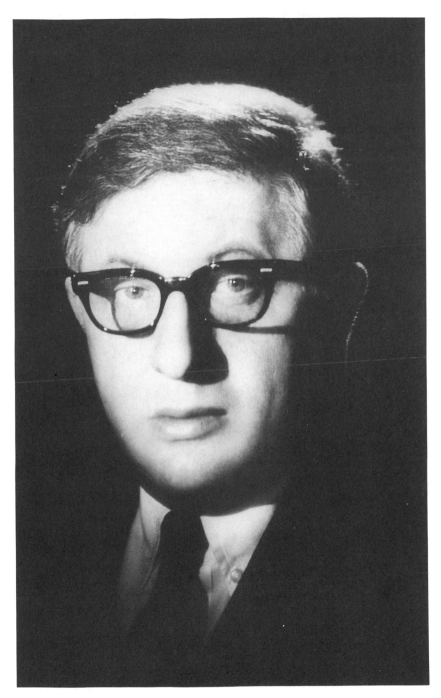
Bernard Herrmann, ca. 1960.

Abraham Herrmann at his office, ca. 1915.

Ida Herrmann with Louis, Rose, and Benny, ca. 1918.

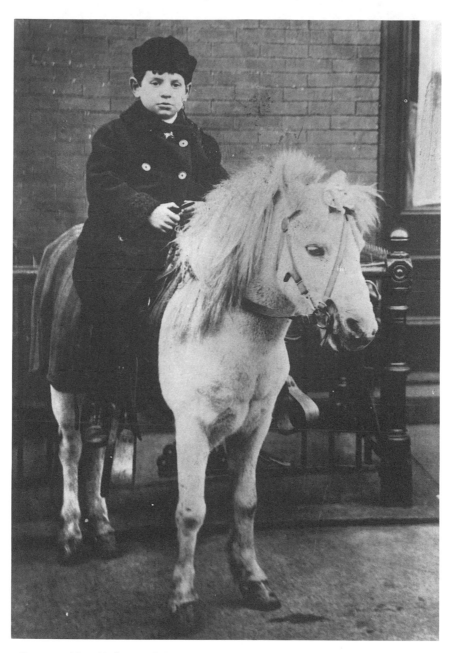

Benny in New York, ca. 1919.

The Young Composers Group and friends (Herrmann in back row), Yaddo, 1932.

Herrmann at CBS, ca. 1937.

With Orson Welles, rehearsing a "Campbell Playhouse" broadcast, 1939.

With John Barbirolli, discussing *Moby Dick*, 1940.

With Orson Welles on the set of *Citizen Kane*, 1940.

Herrmann receiving his Oscar, with Mary Astor, 1942.

"Columbia Presents Corwin," CBS radio, summer 1944: Charles Laughton, unidentified actor, Norman Corwin, and Herrmann.

With Lucille Fletcher, ca. 1945.

At home with Wendy, ca. 1947.

In Yorkshire, at High Sunderland Hall (the inspiration for *Wuthering Heights*) with Lucille, 1946.

At Stonehenge, 1946.

With Wendy, ca. 1951.

At Bluebell Avenue, with Ida, Lucille Anderson, Taffy, and Wendy, ca. 1953.

With Alfred Hitchcock on the set of *The Man Who Knew Too Much*, 1955.

At Bluebell, ca. 1955.

Rehearsing the Glendale Symphony, October 29, 1957. (Courtesy of Don Cristlieb)

After the performance, with Louis Kaufman, left. (Courtesy of Don Cristlieb)

With bassoonist and serpent player Don Cristlieb, recording *Journey to the Center of the Earth* at Fox, 1959. (Courtesy of Don Cristlieb)

With Twi (in a portrait modeled after a photograph of Elgar and his dog), ca. 1960.

With Alfred Hitchcock, ca. 1964.

With Ray Bradbury on the set of *Torn Curtain*, ca. 1965. (Courtesy of Ray Bradbury)

Recording *Wuthering Heights* in London, 1966.

With Norma Shepherd, ca. 1968.

With Twi, ca. 1970.

With Miklós Rózsa (and Charles Gerhardt, upper left) in Kingsway Hall, London, 1974. (Courtesy of Mrs. Sidney Sax)

Recording *Obsession* in London, August 1975; in back, left to right: Paul Hirsch, Brian De Palma, and George Litto. (Courtesy of Paul Hirsch)

# PART TWO

# Hollywood
## 1951–1971

# NINE

He had, from the irritability of his constitution, at all times, an impatience and hurry when he either read or wrote. . . . His most excellent works were struck off at a heat, with rapid exertion.

*Boswell*, Life of Johnson

The decade of 1951–1961 would be Herrmann's most creatively productive and financially successful. Although his days of conducting at CBS were over, compensation lay—temporarily, at least—in a series of distinguished screen offers from some of cinema's best directors, among them Fred Zinnemann and Alfred Hitchcock.

By 1951 Herrmann was committed to leaving New York. A few months after the CBS Symphony disbanded, he and Lucy drove west to start a new life in California. (Throughout the trip Herrmann was seized by violent headaches and often was physically sick, a condition Lucy attributed to the trauma of his severance from CBS.)[1] Instead of settling in high-rent Beverly Hills, Herrmann made his new home in less pretentious North Hollywood, in a modest ranch-style house at 5119 Bluebell Avenue. The decor and furniture were English Georgian; the backyard was ample, containing a small guest house and a large pool and deck area. The area's tranquility and closeness to North Hollywood's parks, with their free-roaming animals, made Bluebell an ideal base for Herrmann for the next twenty years.

Although Herrmann remained susceptible to emotional tantrums, he was extremely proud of Lucy. As with Lucille Fletcher (and third wife Norma Shepherd), all that money could buy was lavished on her. Friends like actress Marsha Hunt "learned to pay attention to what Lucy was wearing; if a comment was not made, Benny couldn't stand it. They made frequent shopping trips to Bullock's in Beverly Hills, where you can drop a fortune on the simplest clothing; and I might not notice Lucy's new clothes because they were so understated. Benny would point out item by item what they had spent the day collecting together. Eventually my eyes were peeled for anything I hadn't seen before, and when I asked, 'Isn't that new?' Benny would just beam with pleasure."[2]

While Herrmann's professional friendships were extensive, his and Lucy's social life was centered on a handful of people. A frequent Bluebell visitor was Lyn Murray, who also had traveled from CBS to a career in Hollywood film scoring. His diary of 1951–1952 includes several amusing notations of life at the Herrmanns':

Lucille, very thin, full of service for Benny. He looks at wrestling on the television, turns off the sound, tunes in KFAC with the good music. I am not interested in wrestling, but he got me to look at one of the matches. KFAC was playing Faust Symphony of Liszt, which Benny conducted right there, calling off all the entrances correctly. . . . [After dinner at Bluebell with director Frank Tashlin,] talking about religion. Two points [Benny] used to attack us, or at least pooh-pooh us, were: what we believe in produces a store of euphoria which won't last. It's all right to have a religion if you are not strong enough to stand the pressures of the world without it.

In a rather hazy way he stated that a musician should have his art for his religion. . . . He includes painters and all creative people as having their art for their god. Frank remarked on the way home that Benny is a quoter. All night it was what Voltaire said, what Anatole France said. Frank said, "It's never what Herrmann said."[3]

One topic Herrmann rarely discussed was politics, except to vilify the liberal activism of friends like Norman Corwin and screenwriter Robert J. Presnell (Marsha Hunt's husband). Recalled Presnell: "Benny would pick up *Saturday Review* and say, 'Awww, it's full of political shit. They don't just do books and music, they take sides! I won't take it anymore!' Magazines I read, like *The Progressive*, really bothered him. To him, politics and the arts were separate. I asked him once what he thought of von Karajan, with his Nazi association. Well, that didn't seem to bother Benny very much, because von Karajan was a great musician. I asked him what he thought about Wagner's authoritarianism. That didn't bother him— only American liberalism. Once, after Benny made many elitist statements and attacked me for being liberal, I said to him, 'You strike me as being like one of those eighteenth-century noblemen'—he brightened at this—'who tosses a bag of gold out the window after his carriage has run over a child.' *That* made him very angry."[4]

Herrmann's first film after his move to California was Fox's *The Day the Earth Stood Still*, a thoughtful, well-produced science fiction film directed by former RKO editor Robert Wise. Their relationship on the new film was unaffected by the outcome of *The Magnificent Ambersons:* Wise greatly admired Herrmann's work and gave him free rein to "do something special."[5]

Herrmann took him at his word. His music was another scoring milestone that anticipated the era of electronic music with its then unheard-of instrumentation for electric violin, electric bass, two high and low electric theremins (a zitherlike instrument used effectively in Rózsa's earlier scores for *The Lost Weekend* and *Spellbound*), four pianos, four harps, and "a very strange section of about 30-odd brass."[6] To this odd ensemble Alfred Newman added one hot water bottle—just "in case."[7]

Herrmann's orchestration puzzled more than one Fox executive, as well as director Wise, who "didn't quite understand what Bernie was talking about. But when we got on the music stage and he started to record the cues, I was thrilled. It was beyond anything I had anticipated."[8] Herrmann realized that the film's drama, in which the peaceful alien Klaatu (Michael Rennie) tries to prevent Earth's self-destruction, worked well with little musical commentary (except for a brief, salutory theme for brass that links Klaatu's philosophy with the best of American thinking— here Lincoln's Gettysburg address). What the film needed was an extraterrestrial strangeness, a sense of the bizarre and unsettling; this Herrmann achieved through his wisely sparse electronic soundtrack. (Fox considered releasing an album of the score before realizing it would barely fill one side.)[9] If the music's impact is lessened today, the reason is not the score itself but the host of inferior imitations its success spawned.

Herrmann's "prelude" illustrates his fresh use of familiar devices in a new context: against a title sequence of star-filled constellations and distant planets, Herrmann blends an ominous rising-and-falling pattern for theremins and tubas with rapid-fire, crystalline harp and piano arpeggios to evoke a sense of alien menace. An eerie harp glissando segues the cue into a brittle dialogue between two pianos soli played octaves apart as radar systems around the world pick up the spaceship's signal.

For the film's title sequence, in which Klaatu stops all electric power worldwide after his efforts to secure peace have failed, Herrmann created a unique electronic montage that surpassed even *All That Money Can Buy* in its overdubbing wizardry. After recording a long cue of brass and vibraphone dissonances, Herrmann augmented the piece with music tracks played backwards (anticipating the studio gimmickry of the Beatles fifteen years later), completing the otherworldly din with the process of oscillator testing, usually used to set studio sound levels. While these techniques were not recognizable to moviegoers, it didn't matter: "What *is* important," said Herrmann, "is what it does for the film."[10]

Herrmann's music did a great deal. *The Day the Earth Stood Still* was one of the most successful science fiction films, artistically and commercially, in its genre. And if Herrmann could complain years later of the "electronic clichés which are so much in vogue" in film music, he could console himself in knowing that he had foreseen the future.[11]

Herrmann's last professional meeting with Wise a year later was typical and amusing. As the director recalled:

While editing my next film, a semidocumentary called *The Captive City*, I ran into Bernie and told him about the movie. He said, "That sounds great. I've talked to a coupla people who've seen it, and they say it's a terrific little film. I'd love to score it." I said, "Come on, Bernie, we can't afford you; we've got a $250,000 budget." He kept going on about it, so I finally made a date—almost reluctantly—for him to see me and the producer. Bernie came and kept making his pitch until he finally said, "Well, how much money do ya *have* in the music budget?" "Bernie," I said, "We have ten thousand dollars." He hit the ceiling. "TEN THOUSAND DOLLARS?! HOW CAN YOU *BELITTLE* THE MUSIC SCORE WITH THAT KINDA THING?!" He frothed at the mouth for ten minutes and stormed out. That was so typical; he was so insulted—not personally, but that that's all we had for the score.[12]

Despite his film commitments, Herrmann was not yet finished with radio, or with creating innovations in the medium. By 1952, many of radio's best directors and writers had moved to CBS's new Television City in Los Angeles, and only a few musicians remained on the radio branch payroll. Still, a few loyalists, like director Elliott Lewis, were convinced there was life left in the old form:

I presented to CBS radio the concept of a show called "Crime Classics," in which the host would narrate true stories of famous crimes. I think we did every one except Cain and Abel—which we wanted to do, but CBS said, "We don't think so." There was nothing in the budget for music; CBS wanted us to use tracked music. I asked, "Could we get three live musicians and a composer-conductor for the same cost of recorded music?" I thought that since this was an anthology show, with a different place and time period each week, the composer could simply change his orchestra. At this point [CBS executive] Guy Della Cioppa said, "Talk to Bernie Herrmann—he'd be perfect."

I told all this to Bernie, who said, "You're crazy!" But he stayed sitting in his chair. I didn't say a word until he finished arguing. Then

I said, "I don't want to argue. I *know* this can be done, and I'd like very much to have you do it." He kept arguing for about half an hour, until after finishing his complaints he said, "Yeah, that's a pretty good idea. Okay!"

Benny would never tell me what his orchestration would be. He would score the whole show, calling me once in a while to ask for a fourth player. If we had the money I said okay. Cast and sound would rehearse for about three hours, then break for lunch for an hour. During lunch, Bernie would come in and rehearse the music, so we didn't know until we came back for dress rehearsal what the orchestra was. This delighted him. He would play all sorts of games and write the most marvelous things.

His scores for old English crimes were usually for woodwinds—oboe, clarinet, English horn. For the death of Jesse James he used four trombones. He asked for a fourth man on the death of Abraham Lincoln but wouldn't tell me what he was doing. When I came into the studio he had four timpanists, with xylophone, tambour, tubular chimes, kettle drums, field drums, snare drums, bass drums; the studio was filled with instruments, and his score was sensational.

He was always very articulate about the sound he wanted from each instrument. Once one of the clarinetists was doubling on bass clarinet. When he played the bass, he rested the instrument on the floor, and Benny went through the ceiling—oh, such a lecture! "Can't ya hear the change in the SOUND?" he yelled. "You're not bringing us the sound of the instrument—you're bringing us the sound of this goddamn STUDIO!"

We mostly used musicians from the L.A. Philharmonic, because Bernie had to have soloists. One week I stayed in the booth during lunch to do some work; Bernie hadn't arrived yet. The stage crew came in and set up four music stands and four chairs. The doors then opened, and in walked four Philharmonic men with trombone cases. They stopped. There were four of them, and there were four chairs. They were wondering, where's the damn orchestra?! You never saw such expressions of consternation.

At first Bernie argued about where to put music in the shows. I'd put music cues in the script and he'd say, "Don't tell ME where to put music!" So I said okay. But once he began to trust me we didn't have any problems. I think Bernie was very suspicious that he'd be working with somebody who didn't know what he was doing, and the result would be less than he wanted. When he found out that you had some idea of what you were doing, that you were working in a professional manner, he relaxed. I was very fond of him, and I think he finally got to be fond of me as well.[13]

During these broadcasts Herrmann made another lasting friendship, with one of the youngest (and last) composers to emerge from CBS radio.

Fred Steiner was also working for Elliott Lewis, on the concurrent program "Cathy and Elliott Lewis on Stage":

By that time, everything was transcribed for broadcast at CBS, but our show was still done live because of various union conditions. Elliott was using the CBS staff orchestra because we didn't have a sponsor, while Herrmann was doing "Crime Classics," which *was* sponsored, and therefore the musicians got paid on a more casual scale. Benny did his show with three players in the studio next to mine, and I had a bigger studio with the staff orchestra of sixteen players. Every once in a while I would drop in to see what Herrmann was doing. I'd always admired his music, but I really didn't know too much about it.

I was absolutely flabbergasted with what he was doing with three players; it was so imaginative and bold. One day while he was working, he took a break and opened the door between our studios. Apparently he listened to our show and liked what he heard. He stormed in in a mock rage and yelled, "What the hell's goin' on in here? Here I am breakin' my ass with three players and you've got the goddamn Philharmonic in here!" From that point, we became rather good friends.

My wife, Shirley, and I started going over to Bluebell and having dinner with Benny and Lucy. Of course, we always dressed up to go over there, because that's the way Benny was. It was always very elegant; Lucy was a fine, gourmet-style cook, and Benny always served nice wine. He drank very little of it himself; he claimed it gave him migraine headaches. Sometimes he'd be short-tempered with Lucy over little things that didn't matter—something was wrong with the meal, or something was misplaced. And each time we could see Lucy getting just a little less patient.

After dinner, Shirley and Lucy would go into the kitchen and start the dishes, and Benny and I would talk. We mostly saw eye to eye on music and literary things. He always made fun of my addiction to Béla Bartók, whom he called Béla Barstow. I think he secretly admired Bartók as a composer, but it was difficult for him to express admiration for anybody except Elgar and Vaughan Williams. He would play transcriptions he'd made with the CBS Symphony which he was very proud of; he played his recording of Elgar's *Falstaff* for me several times. He introduced me to the Elgar symphonies, the Bliss symphonies; he was probably amazed I'd heard of William Boyce or William Lindley. He'd say, "Oh, you know Boyce's symphonies? Look here . . . ," and he'd go into his cupboard and pull out some precious, rare first edition. Every once in a while he'd give me books and music, some of which I found were autographed by their writers.

Benny liked to play piano duets—and if you never played a piano duet with Bernard Herrmann you missed an incredible experience. He loved the

Haydn symphonies, and when he heard that I had them for piano he said, "Pull 'em out, I wanna play 'em." He would insist I play the primo part, the melody, because he said his technique wasn't sufficient. Well, we'd start to play, and no sooner had four bars gone by than Benny would start to conduct; he'd be waving his right hand and playing with his left. Meanwhile, he'd move a little bit to the upper side of the bench, instead of staying down where he belonged. Little by little I was being forced to the edge of the bench with my hands stretched to the *n*th degree trying to get to the keys! And he would start to pound and pound, with no semblance of balance. What with the banging and the singing and the waving and my being forced onto the floor, it was really something to see. But he loved it, and as soon as we got through it—we'd both be wringing wet— he'd say, "Oh, that was great—let's play another one!"[14]

As Shirley Steiner recalled, Herrmann's demanding standards applied to every aspect of their friendship:

I loved Benny very much, but I was terrified of him, as almost all of us were. He was a driver. He wanted perfection—but of course Benny was human, and perfection consisted of what he perceived as perfection. Any trivial mistake, any rationalizations, any dishonesties you had with your-self were blown out of proportion for him; he had no patience for these. I remember commenting once on someone else's success, and I didn't realize that what I was actually doing was complaining. It was really about money; I was enviously saying, "Everybody else gets to do all these won-derful things, and all we do is sit here." Benny turned on me ferociously and said, *"Don't you know* that the only value money has is that it buys time? It's not things; it's not travel; it's *time."* His ferocity shocked me out of my self-pity and gave me something to think about.

Benny could have great polish. He moved in wonderful circles, but he picked and chose when he wanted to display his charm, when it was important to him. You could have Benny as a dinner guest with people whom he wanted to be nice to, and he was as great a gentleman as you could find; but it's incredible how he could put those manners aside when he didn't want to use them. I think he was an opportunist, like all of us.

Benny was frustrated in that he knew, he lived, and he talked the language of abstract composition; there was that kind of emotional involvement in him. While Benny was, at times, able to accept praise and congratulations gracefully, inwardly I felt there was always something else he was striving for. That something else was not necessarily what we saw in his performance but what *he* would consider his performance. Even when he was successful, it wasn't success enough.[15]

The second and last teaming of Herrmann and director Joseph L. Mankiewicz, *Five Fingers*, showed that Hitchcock was not alone in his ability to craft a gripping, sophisticated spy thriller. In fact, the film was a rehearsal of sorts for Herrmann, who would begin his work with Hitchcock two years later.

Like Hitchcock, Mankiewicz was fascinated with the subtle power of long, sustained camera takes and dialogue-free sequences of mounting tension. These techniques, with James Mason's cool performance as "Cicero," the English-bred traitor who steals the Normandy invasion plans in 1944 Turkey, brought a steely impartiality and almost hypnotic intensity to the narrative. Herrmann's score is mainly nonthematic, heightening the largely interior drama with a rich blend of exotic rhythms and orchestral color. His prelude—nervous string and wind tremolos over a vaguely Turkish melodic fragment—is characteristic of this blend of East and West; it sets the stage for the urbane thriller that follows.

Source music not only creates a period ambience; it also serves as an ironic counterpoint to the film's tale of deceit. For Cicero's meeting with the bankrupt Countess Stavinska in a Turkish slum, Herrmann uses several heavily nostalgic recordings, sung by a Piafesque chanteuse—a cynical comment on the loveless business transaction Cicero proposes to the countess. Fragments of one of these themes ("Adieu mon coeur," by Marguerite Monnot, Paul Deuscher, and Henri Content) return as Cicero plans their escape to Rio, and later, bitterly, as he learns of the countess's betrayal. Another subtle use of source music accompanies Cicero's meeting with the Gestapo head von Richter at the countess's château, as two party guests—unaware of a shadowy figure at the window—play "The Erlking," Schubert's song about the lurking specter of death.

Two purely visual suspense sequences showcase Herrmann's skill. As Cicero removes war documents from a study in the British consulate, Herrmann introduces a steady, ticking flute ostinato over hushed, sustained clarinet chords, building tension by the addition of violins to the clocklike rhythm. Dark bass harmonics quietly enter, adding the final color to the sinister cue that reminds us, with subtle intensity, that Cicero's time is short, and diminishing by the second.

For the film's dramatic high point, Cicero's bungling of his last consulate robbery, Mankiewicz and Herrmann demonstrate their awareness of the power of silence. For most of this lengthy sequence (in which Cicero photographs a letter, unaware that a cleaning woman has switched on the safe alarm) Herrmann lets the tense action carry itself, alternating long

stretches of silence with muted strings and tuba harmonies—until the
quiet is shattered by the shrill explosion of the triggered alarm.

Only once does Mankiewicz suggest a touch of humanity in Mason's
character, as Cicero recalls his childhood glimpse of Rio and his ambition
to settle there a wealthy man. Herrmann enhances Mason's monologue
with a wistful, vaguely South American melody on solo clarinet—a theme
that is recalled in the last scene as Cicero fleetingly realizes his dream.
With this brief exception, both Mankiewicz's austere thriller and Herrmann's superb score remain emotionally remote—but always riveting.

Nine of Herrmann's ten film projects to date (*Kane* being the exception)
derived from literary sources, as would his next. Since *A Farewell to Arms*
in 1932, Hollywood had had little success in transferring the writing of
Ernest Hemingway to the screen. His stories were usually trivialized in
the transition, with little of Hemingway's terse, thematically complex
style surviving. *The Snows of Kilimanjaro,* Fox's lavish version of Hemingway's short story starring Gregory Peck as the disillusioned writer
Harry Street, was another ambitious attempt that fell short of total realization; yet as high-gloss adventure and Hollywood-level character study,
it ranks among the best-crafted studio films of the period.

Herrmann's own opinion of Hemingway characterized his ambivalence
about most American writers, as compared to the English. "[Hemingway]
is one of the best examples of an American writer who started out with
much talent, and look at what a complete piece of corn he's been for
twenty-five years," Herrmann was quoted as saying in 1954. "He never
has a pronouncement to make about the world of any interest, he never
has a literary criticism to make, all he's got to do is talk some more about
hunting or getting a new wife, which is his own affair. . . . He's the same
age now or when he wrote *Across the River* as Thomas Hardy when
he wrote *Jude the Obscure.* That shows you the difference between the
two men."[16]

Herrmann enjoyed the change in subject matter that *Kilimanjaro* offered. Unlike the brooding city drama of *On Dangerous Ground* and the
science fiction parable of *The Day the Earth Stood Still,* "the sensitive direction of Henry King gave me many opportunities to create music of a
highly nostalgic nature, inasmuch as the film deals with the tale of a man
who is dying on the African veldt and during the fever of his illness relives
much of his emotional past."[17]

In Hemingway's story, death, not remembrance, fills Harry Street's
ebbing thoughts. It hovers nearby, not merely as the hyena outside
Street's tent, but in the commonplace: "It can be two bicycle policemen

just as easily, or be a bird"[18]—or at the story's end, the illusion of Street's
hunter friend Compton. Not surprisingly, Hemingway's bleakness was
tempered by screenwriter Casey Robinson to allow warmer colors of
Street's life and personality to emerge—most damagingly in Street's climactic rescue from death. But flashes of Hemingway survived, especially
in the film's laconic dialogue and in Herrmann's meticulous, romantic
blend of sentiment with shadowy mortality.

Unlike most of Herrmann's past title sequences (*Five Fingers* excepted),
the film's agitated prelude is unrelated thematically to the rest of the
score; yet, less specifically, "it's related because it presents the turmoil of
the leading character. The idea was that in the film, we had different reso-
lutions of his problems. So you can say that while the prelude presents the
problem, other material has to evoke their solution."[19] That "problem"
reappears in the next cue, a high-register motive for strings, echoing the
circling of vultures over the dying Street, and a plagal, quasi-religious
chord progression, suggesting the mystery of death that looms over the
injured man. At the film's end, this eerie motive returns as Harry's death
vigil begins: its simple repeated pattern, evolving into a creeping ostinato
for low brass and winds as the hyena/reaper nears Harry's tent, conveys
more of Hemingway's mystical subtext than King's direction or Robinson's screenplay.

Like Street's nostalgic reflections, the heart of the score recalls Paris—
the weary accordion solo that transports Harry from his argument with
Helen (Susan Hayward) to the prewar sounds of the Left Bank, or Herrmann's own favorite sequence in the score, the "Memory Waltz," encap-
sulating the beauty of a Paris spring. One of many memorable *valses
tristes* in Herrmann's film work, the "Memory Waltz" proves (with other
Herrmann themes) that, while his melodic facility was limited, Herrmann
could write themes of lyric poignancy and unpretentious charm. (A dis-
senting opinion came from David Raksin: "If Benny ever started a tune,
as in the case of the 'Memory Waltz,' he would obliterate it in no time at
all."[20]

The film was a commercial success despite (or perhaps because of) Hollywood's alterations. (Its fans did not include Hemingway, who retitled it
"The Snows of Zanuck.")[21] *New York Times* critic Bosley Crowther especially praised Leon Shamroy's rich photography (this was Herrmann's
first color film) and Herrmann's "musical score of rich suggestion. . . .
For it is Mr. Herrmann's music, singing sadly and hauntingly, that helps
one sense the pathos of dead romances and a wasted career. A saxophone
and a piano in a Paris studio, an accordion in an old Left Bank bar and an

arrogant guitar in a Spanish café—these are also actors in the film. Perhaps they come closer than any to stating what Hemingway had to say."[22]*

Significantly, the Oscar for best score of 1952 went to neither eligible Herrmann score but to Dimitri Tiomkin's score for the western *High Noon* by Fred Zinnemann. Tiomkin's score was based on his theme "Do Not Foresake Me, Oh My Darlin'," which became one of the year's top-selling records and also won 1952's best song Oscar. The film's score-song interrelationship was not unprecedented, but the scale of its commercial success was. It was a turning point in music for cinema, and one that bode ill for composers like Herrmann who had neither the ability nor the inclination to write hit themes. (Hugo Friedhofer offered an interesting opinion on Herrmann's opposition to songs in scores: "Songwriters were the bane of Benny's existence—but he would *love* to have written a hit song.")[23]

1952 had been a year of stabilization for Herrmann. With more film offers coming his way, Herrmann decided to hire a secretary to assist in correspondence and business matters. Elsa Clay, who became an employee and friend to the Herrmanns for the next twelve years, was the happy choice:

In spite of his reputation for short temper and bellicosity I always found Benny to be appreciative, compassionate, and generous. His vocabulary was extensive and colorful, with many literary allusions; Blake was a favorite. He was always sympathetic to my problems as a single mother and interested in my children's progress, even though he felt the time and attention I devoted to peace and civil rights might have been better spent on something to do with music!
  I believe he felt the same way about Lucy's interest in wanting to prepare herself for a nursing career. I felt that he discouraged any attempt she might make in that direction, wanting her to be at his side at all times. This was pre–women's movement, of course, but I don't believe he undervalued women's abilities or potentialities; rather, [he felt] that to attend to the artist, to stimulate and inspire creativity, should be sufficiently satisfying to any woman.[24]

Although Herrmann's two daughters remained with Lucille Fletcher and her husband, the girls began spending their summers with their father

---

*In fact, the source music Crowther cited came from other hands: the sax and piano theme was Alfred Newman's "Blue Mountain." The saxophonist, incidentally, was jazz great Benny Carter.

and stepmother at Bluebell Avenue. Despite his temper, Herrmann was a sensitive and tolerant parent, and his daughters' visits were a special time for him. Recalled Dorothy Herrmann:

As his daughters, we never thought Daddy did any work, because all of his work was finished by the time we got up in the morning. I don't think he ever slept through the night: he slept about four hours a night and took four or five catnaps a day. And in contrast to other composers, who had to have absolute silence and kept their children locked off in wings of their palatial Hollywood homes, Daddy could work with us around him; the more noise, the more screaming and yelling, the better. Sometimes he worked at the dining room table—he liked to be at the center of things. He was not the kind of person who really enjoyed solitude: if people weren't coming over he would go and visit somebody for the evening.

Wendy and I always watched his score dubbing sessions in Hollywood. Then we'd go to the commissary, which was very exciting in those days because Fox was filming so many different movies. People came in wearing Viking costumes, and there'd be a big star or two, or a friend like Oscar Levant. Daddy had a habit of taking us to the studio, then seeing somebody and wandering off; and there we would be, wandering around by ourselves. He didn't do it maliciously; he just forgot we were there.

When he lived in California, even though on one level he seemed content with his film work, Daddy still had hopes and dreams about conducting. He followed the Los Angeles Philharmonic's politics very closely. Intellectually he lived and breathed the world of classical music. At night he could be writing a score for this picture or that, but friends would come over and they would listen to some symphony recording. He never really fit into the mold of a Hollywood film composer. I think he was caught in the middle between those two worlds.

Daddy was not a morbid person; but behind the outspokenness and outrage he expressed publicly there was a wistfulness that gave him a great hold over people. You always sensed he was very vulnerable. You sensed he felt he had not achieved what he wanted to for himself. There was always more—the Romantic dream. I think one reason for his unhappiness throughout his life was his restlessness. It was part of his nature to never be entirely satisfied.

Daddy hated discussing the subject of death; he had problems talking about it. He avoided funerals. His fear of death was such that he didn't tell you when someone had died. . . . Lucy might encounter someone she hadn't seen for awhile and say, "How's your wife?" and the person would reply, "Didn't Benny tell you? She died months ago"—or sometimes years ago. That put us in a very strange situation; if you cared about the person you felt like crying while the recently bereaved tried to comfort *us*.

As for Daddy's outbursts, I feel that anybody who truly knew him became relatively unaffected by them. They really weren't meant to be taken seriously. Daddy really didn't hold grudges, at least at that time. His explosive fits of anger would subside as quickly as they came, like sudden storms. I didn't know him to brood for long about things. Also, a lot of what he got mad about was valid—things that would irritate most people, except they would politely say nothing or go home and sulk about it. He was just very blunt. It was unlike him to really pick on someone who wasn't able to stand up to him. I think what annoyed him was stupidity.[25]

By the time of *Kilimanjaro's* release, Joseph Mankiewicz had completed a new film, for MGM: *Julius Caesar*, produced by John Houseman. Both Houseman and Mankiewicz were eager for Herrmann to score the film (to be recorded in stereo, cinema's latest attraction); but Metro was loath to hire nonstaff composers. Ironically, the head of MGM's music department was John Green, who had moved from radio to Broadway to Hollywood with increasing success—and mounting contempt from Herrmann. Recalled Green:

I think Benny Herrmann committed suicide. Unwittingly; not with drugs, not with a pistol, but with a four-letter word called hate. I'm convinced that he filled his life with unneeded stress and tension. Having said that, as one of the victims of Benny's hate syndrome, I'll say he was a fair man. . . . One day in 1942 I was having lunch with Benny at Louis and Armand's on 52d Street. Benny said, "Nyaah . . . whaddaya gonna do at MGM? Ya gonna compose?" I said, "It's a kind of omnibus contract. I arrange and orchestrate." He said, "Awww, there ya go again! How is it possible for everybody else to know who you are and YOU don't know?!" He was screaming at me in the restaurant; everybody was looking. Well, it's an awful conceit, but I think Benny was right.

One of Benny's enormous resentments was that, of all the places he felt he had a swath to cut, the Hollywood Bowl was number one. He was never engaged at the Bowl. I was first engaged there in August 1949 and was an instant smash. After two years, my association with Mrs. Norman Chandler was well known. One night my wife, Bonnie, and I arrived at the Bowl in that wonderful twilight period of the evening with our picnic; I wasn't conducting that night. We'd started our "tour" of walking around and visiting our friends when down the aisle came Benny. Bonnie was the first to speak, with her arms outstretched. She said, "Benny! How good to see you." To which his shouted reply—that you could hear to Franklin Avenue—was, "YOU TWO AND MRS. CHANDLER . . . and all your FANCY FRIENDS!" He went on and on; everybody was looking. I couldn't speak, but Bonnie said, "Benny, don't do this. We love you." Tears were coming down her face. But he just brushed by us.

Then came *Julius Caesar*. Dore Schary was head of production then at MGM. I was general music director and executive in charge of music, but I was extremely cooperative with producers. When *Julius Caesar* came along I had a fellow named Miklós Rózsa on my payroll, and he was getting $1,500 a week. I didn't have another picture on the lot that I could hang that kind of a composer's salary on; their salaries have to be proportionate to a picture's total budget. Rózsa had just had his vacation and was available. There was no justification for putting him on leave.

I had a conference with Mankiewicz and Houseman, two men I most respected, and both wanted Benny hands down. When they started to make their pitch I said, "John! How can you sell Benny to me after our CBS background? He's got no bigger admirer in the world than me. Let's see if I can loan Rózsa out."

I cannot tell you the effort I made to loan out Mikki. There was no resistance to him on an aesthetic basis; it's just that nobody needed him at the time. I went so far as to offer Rózsa at what we were paying him, something you just don't do. But I could not make a deal for Rózsa. I called Mankiewicz and Houseman and told them all the things I'd tried. "Please don't tell me Rózsa's not going to do a good score," I said. "Will it be different from what Benny would do? Yes. Will it be less effective? I doubt it. It'll be effective in a Rózsa way. You want a Herrmann way, and Metro can't afford it." They were livid.

Minutes after they left my office, the red line on my intercom was flashing. Dore was saying, "For God's sake, John, what the hell are you doing? Come up here right away." I went, with the film's schedule, the budget, everything, and said, "Dore, put Rózsa on your budget, not mine. Take him off the music department cost sheet, and you've got Herrmann." Schary wouldn't do it.

After the *Julius Caesar* decision I tried to reach Benny, but he avoided me like the plague. Looking back on it now, I was probably solid enough that if I hadn't been so cocky, I could have given them Herrmann and absorbed Rózsa's $25,000 with the enormous budget I had. I think I could have survived that. But I have to confess that I felt I had done a good job.[26]

Although he would tell elaborate tales of Green's alleged betrayal, Herrmann bore no anger toward Rózsa, a more recent acquaintance. Instead, Herrmann not only complimented Rózsa on his *Julius Caesar* score but also recorded selections from it with the National Philharmonic twenty-two years later. "It was terribly touching," Rózsa said. "Benny invited me to his house in London and said, 'I have to play it for you.' He put on the record, played the three pieces—and watched me all the time. When I told him I thought it was great, he was the happiest man on earth."[27]

It was Rózsa who, as a teacher of film music at the University of Southern California (USC), first invited Herrmann to address a college audience. Like his writings, a Herrmann lecture was an opinionated, insightful treat, especially in later years as his popularity reached cult status among young filmmakers. ("At colleges there are thousands of eager youngsters who all love cinema and want to know," Herrmann said in 1975. "But the academics, they have decided that film is an art form beneath them. Of course, young people know differently.")[28]

But as Rózsa discovered in the mid-1950s, Herrmann's instinctive defense shield had to be broken: when arranging a symposium on film scoring at USC, "I rang my friend . . . to invite him; whereupon a species of volcanic eruption took place at the other end of the phone, the gist of which was that the course, the University and everyone connected with them (which presumably included myself) should go to the Devil, and with convenient speed. I knew my Benny and left it at that. Sure enough, in no time at all he called back and, sheepishly and with the greatest show of reluctance, asked for details of what he would be required to do. He came—and absolutely stole the show. He was in top form, and the students adored him. Why then the preliminary tantrum? But that was Benny all over. First the lion had to roar; then he would become as docile as a lamb."[29]

If the doors of MGM were closed to Herrmann—as they would be until Hitchcock interceded in 1959—Twentieth Century Fox was still eager to buy the composer's time. But after three A films in a row, a qualitative change was to occur in Herrmann's Fox career. As the studio decreased its yearly output in favor of fewer but bigger pictures to combat television, first-class pictures grew increasingly scarce.

The first (and best) of Herrmann's B pictures at Fox was *White Witch Doctor*, an absurd, entertaining action movie starring Susan Hayward and Robert Mitchum, directed by Henry Hathaway. The film did offer Herrmann a fresh challenge: its setting, 1907 Africa, required indigenous music unlike any he had previously written. As with *Anna and the King of Siam*, Herrmann immersed himself in regional scales, instrumentation, and rhythms, turned a blind eye to the story's implausibilities, and produced a rousing, dramatic winner.

After a brief onscreen dialogue for talking drums, Herrmann's prelude throws us full force into a fierce jungle dance for large orchestra and a battery of percussion. Much of the score's freshness comes from Herrmann's dazzling use of unusual sounds: the clanging beat of an African break drum, the sensuous vibrations of marimbas, and especially the grotesque moan of the serpent, an obscure baroque reed instrument Herrmann had discovered as a child in Berlioz's orchestration text. Shaped like its namesake, the serpent was described by David Raksin as "sounding like a donkey with emotional problems."[30] To Herrmann, its grossly distorted timbre was the ideal accompaniment for the tarantula that briefly scales Susan Hayward's shoulder.

Nestled among such extrovert sequences is one of Herrmann's loveliest nocturnes, heard as nurse Barton (Hayward) tells adventurer Lonni Douglas (Mitchum) of her past. Like Charles Foster Kane and Lucy Muir, Mrs. Barton mourns a lost love, her husband; Herrmann responds to her mixed emotions of love and regret with great tenderness. (The cue was one of Herrmann's favorites; its delicate woodwind bridge reappears in the love theme from *North by Northwest* six years later.)

Alfred Newman was not alone in his admiration for the score. "I think the musical score on 'White Witch Doctor' is one of the very best we have had on any of our pictures," Darryl Zanuck wrote its producer, Otto Lang. "In every respect this is a wonderful score. It captures realistically the mood and it has great class and distinction."[31]

If the quality of Herrmann's next projects was inferior to that of previous, more selectively chosen ones, the scope of presentation was now greater: all of his subsequent Fox films were made in Cinemascope, whose stereo sound was infinitely better than standard monophonic presentation for showcasing a musical score. A good example was Herrmann's next film, *Beneath the 12-Mile Reef*, a routine sea romance (written, surprisingly, by A. I. Bezzerides, co-author of *On Dangerous Ground*) starring a young Robert Wagner and Terry Moore as the sponge fisherman's Romeo and Juliet. It was one of Fox's dullest releases, except for Leon Shamroy's sumptuous color photography and Herrmann's first stereo score.

The composer's near-obsessive concern for sonic balance at CBS had paid off handsomely in his early film experiences of integrating music and dialogue. Now, with the extended dynamic range of stereo, Herrmann could realize an even more complex, realistic presentation of his craft. (For his stereo scores, Herrmann carefully diagrammed instrument and microphone placement on his manuscript).[32] His inspiration for the new score came not from the script or the film's charmless cast but from its lush photography, especially under water. As in *The Ghost and Mrs. Muir* the sea becomes a poetical force that dominates the relationships of the story's protagonists.

The sea's mysterious beauty had suggested to many composers the liquescent textures of the harp (Debussy's *La Mer*, for example, and many a Hollywood score); but Herrmann outdid his predecessors by using not one or two harps, but nine, each playing a separate part. The result was an orchestral palette of Rimskian vividness, using, as Christopher Palmer observed, "glissandos for the surge of waves, rapid figurations on the low resonant bass notes for the swell and rhythm of the moving water . . . all enhanced by the harp strings' very reverberant properties, which make for a characteristic haze, a film or mist as of water or light."[33]

These properties emerge both as grandly heroic—as in the prelude, each harp glissandoing upward on a separate note, to "sweep us into the main title like a huge tidal wave"—and as mystical and portentous—as in the evocation by harps soli of Gilbert Roland's fatal sponge dive. In *12-Mile Reef*'s climactic exploration of the undersea forest, the harps' pedal-rooted colorations maintain "a shadowy, murmurous continuum against which drums, low winds, electric bass and organ pedals heave and struggle as if to resist the enormous pressure of the water."[34]

The scope of Herrmann's brilliantly orchestrated score was the ideal complement to the film's handsome visuals and soggy story. Again, Zanuck was enthusiastic in his praise: "I thought 'Beneath the 12-Mile Reef' was one of the most original scores I have ever heard. It really gave me a thrill. The manner in which Bernard handled the underwater sequence[s] was simply thrilling. The entire picture has been enormously enhanced by this wonderful score. It gives the picture a bigness it did not originally have—yet the music never interferes but adds to the dramatic values."[35]

Closely observing Herrmann's methods was a new member of the composer's team at Fox, music editor Len Engel, who would work with Herrmann for the next eight years:

From an editor's standpoint, Benny was our idol because of the way he composed. He had a vertical form of four-bar phrases that was so easy to cut. When Fox first got into television there was no definitive contract with the musicians' union about putting music in television shows, so we were able to go into our old films, and I daresay over 90 percent of what we used in those days was written by Benny. Alfred Newman and the others wrote beautiful themes, but they were always interwoven, and you couldn't use long themes in a medium that had to move quickly.

Generally, Benny treated Fox's music editors very well. It's true he
wasn't an accomplished conductor, but he *was* a good conductor in
the sense of hitting cues for a film. One story comes to mind. Alfred
Newman had a very intricate method of showing a film for recording:
we'd give a composer timing sheets, and he would write the music. Then
we'd get a copy of the music back, and only one man was allowed to cue
the film for Alfred. He would go through the complicated mechanical for-
mulations to put this marking system on the film itself.

Benny was the exact opposite; he hardly used any cue marks on a film.
When I first started working with him I found this hard to believe—how
could he catch cues with nothing on the screen? No click tracks, nothing.
On one particular cue, Benny had indicated in his music a line where a
streamer would start on a film, and a line where it would end. The cue
was about two and a half minutes long, and there were to be no marks on
the film in between. The cue had a lot of transitions, a lot of things that
were important to catch. So I called him and said, "Benny, I just wanted
to double-check—do you want any other inner timings besides the first
line and the last line?" He said, "No, that'll be fine."

It was two or three weeks between that phone call and the recording.
Well, right after Benny started conducting at the session, I got a phone
call and walked from the podium to the other side of the Fox stage, which
was quite large. As the playback ended, Benny turned around and looked
for me on the music editor's bench. I wasn't there, so he looked across the
recording stage and saw me on the phone. He pointed at me and in his
loud, screechy voice said, "SEE? *SEE*! I didn't NEED any more lines in
there!" Of course, nobody knew what the hell he was talking about; even
I had forgotten about it. It was amazing that with all that was in his
mind, he remembered our phone call and was so proud that he had caught
everything in the cue.

In those days at Fox each department had its own table at the commissary. It was a very closed group; everyone literally knew everybody
else on the lot. Benny would sit with us, gravy down his tie, and clobber
all his colleagues as well as past composers. The one that knocked me out
was Beethoven; he thought Beethoven's Fifth was the worst thing: "Anybody can do da-da-da-dum! What the hell's so unique about that?" The
music editors always got a kick out of that, so as we were eating, we'd
hum the opening bars of the Fifth; and each time Benny would give us
that look.[36]

Of his next Fox film, *King of the Khyber Rifles*, Herrmann later
quipped, "Everybody's life has some rain in it."[37] Starring Tyrone Power
and the ubiquitous Terry Moore, the film was a dreary action story pitting
British legionnaires against Indian natives circa 1857. The film was report-

edly assigned first to Hugo Friedhofer, who withdrew.[38] Attracted, perhaps, by the *idea* of a British adventure yarn à la Kipling, Herrmann accepted.

Herrmann's instrumentation is again epic, but the fluid, impressionistic textures of *12-Mile Reef* are replaced by the militaristic sheen of brass and timpani (with winds and occasional strings). *Khyber Rifles* opens with a rousing Allegro against a montage of the riding British soldiers: Herrmann's galloping timpani rhythm and crackling brass theme promise excitement and danger (although little will follow). The prelude's tone of dashing heroism returns at the film's finale, with the percussive, polyphonic "Attack on the Mountain Stronghold" and a stirring Herrmann arrangement of the Scottish air "Cock o' the North." In the interim one can enjoy a delicately ethereal *valse lente*, the love theme for Captain King (Power) and his major's daughter (Moore). The theme first appears as source music for an officers' ball honoring Queen Victoria; carefully recorded to seem distant and distilled by the desert air, its major-minor harmonies and velvety string sonorities look ahead to Herrmann's *Obsession* valse twenty-two years later.

What *Khyber Rifles* and *12-Mile Reef* lacked in drama they made up for—at least to Herrmann—in providing the opportunity to write music of widely divergent idioms, in both time period and setting. The apex of this style-over-substance exchange was *The Egyptian*, a lavish adaptation of Mika Waltari's novel set in 1300 B.C. that followed a young physician's path from lust (for the Babylonian Nefer-Nefer) and true love (with a servant girl, Merit) to monotheism. *The Egyptian* was one of Darryl Zanuck's most personal projects; unfortunately, his surprisingly poor decision making caused much of the film's undoing. Zanuck cast his then-inamorata, Bella Darvi, as Nefer-Nefer, causing Marlon Brando, who was then considering the film's lead role, to leave the project. (Edmund Purdom ultimately starred.)[39] Likewise, Michael Curtiz (*Casablanca*, *The Adventures of Robin Hood*) proved a disastrous choice as director. According to co-screenwriter Philip Dunne, Curtiz "was rehearsing the stand-ins instead of the cast, establishing movements which the actors would then have to come in stone cold and duplicate. . . . I was told [by Zanuck] to stay on the set and watch what Mike was doing with the stand-ins, then tip off the actors and rehearse them in the dressing rooms on their moves and lines." Although the film made a profit, in Dunne's memory it "shed no luster on those of us who worked on it."[40]

Two participants felt differently. Alfred Newman was to have scored the 140-minute film alone, but when Fox moved up its release date by nearly three weeks, leaving five weeks for composition, Newman realized the task was impossible. Herrmann learned of the dilemma: "I proposed to Alfred . . . that we collaborate. Fortunately, 'The Egyptian' has three quite distinct stories—the love story of Sinuhe and Merit; the disintegration of Sinuhe through his lust for Nefer-Nefer; and the story of [the pharaoh] Akhnaton's dedication to monotheism. I proposed that I take the Nefer-Nefer portion and that Newman compose for the other two. We sent each other what we wrote so we could smooth out anything that would call attention to our differing styles."[41]

Although Newman receives top billing, more than half of the score was composed by Herrmann. Significantly, Herrmann chose to score the film's darkest sequences and characters: the cruel seductress Nefer-Nefer, the scheming princess Baketamon. Newman scored the more conventional love scenes, as well as the platitudinous religious scenes at the film's end. Nearly all the rest of the score was Herrmann: the prelude and opening scenes, the town music of Thebes, the lion hunt sequence, and the film's finale.[42]

Herrmann and Newman consulted only twice during scoring. The most crucial decision to be made concerned the music's stylistic idiom. "No one knows anything about Egyptian music of that period, so we had to invent it, and I'm proud of the result," Herrmann said in 1971. "I feel that if they did have music, ours would be something like it. I don't feel this intellectually; I feel it emotionally and I feel it so strongly that I believe that in a way it must be so. Alfred felt that way too."[43]

Herrmann and Newman chose to base the score around pentatonic (five-tone) scale patterns, to use a wordless chorus, and, in addition to a symphony orchestra, to employ instruments traditionally associated with ancient Egypt: lute, harp, and exotic percussion. The final score is impressively seamless. Although a discerning ear can recognize trademarks of both composers, their music is truly integrated into a cohesive whole, conveying a sustained musical conception. Indeed, Herrmann and Newman deliberately suppressed their individual styles (more in orchestration than thematic material). The usual exoticism of Herrmann's instrumentation is transferred to the score's harmonies and scale patterns; similarly, Newman downplays his customary lushness of timbre to write love music of moving simplicity and sharply defined color.

Herrmann's *Egyptian* prelude (for full orchestra and mixed chorus) anticipates his 1975 music for *Obsession* in its use of voice and orchestral grandeur to suggest spiritual mystery. It segues into an eerie cue for muffled timpani (beating steadily, inexorably), muted brass (with a sustained, unresolved figure that seems to ask Sinuhe's question "Why?"), and muted strings. The music's static nature suggests both danger and the profound unknown. Later, under the pharaoh's speech against Egypt's impending war with the Hittites, the same music conveys another favorite Herrmann idea: the immutability of life, a sense of waste in the face of mortality.

Herrmann and Newman's handling of scenes involving the two women in Sinuhe's life makes an interesting study in contrasts. Newman's theme for Merit is a plaintive, songlike theme for oboe, winds, and lyric string accompaniment, while Herrmann's music for Nefer-Nefer is more impressionistic, shaded with provocative harmonic colors—a reflection of the unpredictable temptress. Nefer's sedutiveness leads Sinuhe to "The Lotus Pool," a cue of subtle sensuality and grave beauty, its wordless melody sung by soprano Doreen Tryden over lute, harp, and strings.

Zanuck was delighted with both the idea and the result of Herrmann and Newman's collaboration. Herrmann himself considered the experience "a pleasure. . . . I'm very fond of that score."[44] Each composer conducted his own music at the recording session, which was attended by a Decca Records producer who oversaw the score's soundtrack album. Recalled bassoonist Don Cristlieb: "The producer kept patronizing Al, saying, 'I wish you'd done *this* cue.' Al said, without a moment's hesitation, 'Don't sell Bernie short!' "[45] The album was a best-seller, although the score, like all of Herrmann's since *Anna and the King of Siam*, was ignored by the Academy.

Herrmann's next film at Fox was less grand but equally undistinguished. *Garden of Evil* was a leaden rehash of Warner Brothers' *Treasure of the Sierra Madre* seven years earlier, with Gary Cooper, Richard Widmark, and Susan Hayward as explorers in Mexico fighting Apaches and each other. It was another film Herrmann would not have undertaken had the CBS Symphony survived radio's demise; but it was an opportunity to work in a genre new to Herrmann's film career: the western.

Written for large orchestra, the score communicates some feel for the epic voyage that Henry Hathaway's film pretends to be. (As with most Fox releases, the director's role ended in the cutting room; Hathaway and Herrmann never met on the film.)[46] But despite several outstanding cues—a foreboding main theme for brass, pulsating timpani rhythms to suggest the unseen Apaches, and an eerie woodwind chorale on the Dies Irae for an abandoned Mexican church—the film remained tedious and uninvolving. (As Herrmann was fond of telling Zanuck, "I can dress the corpse, but I can't bring it back to life.")[47] Like *12-Mile Reef* and *The Egyptian*, at least, the film was released in stereo.

Herrmann's next film, begun immediately afterward, finally marked the qualitative change the composer deserved. *Prince of Players*, an expensive biography of theater's legendary Booth family, was a labor of love for director Philip Dunne, whose long career as a Fox screenwriter included *How Green Was My Valley*, *Stanley and Livingstone*, and *The Ghost and Mrs. Muir*. On the basis of Herrmann's music for *Muir* Dunne requested him for *Prince of Players*, his directorial debut. The result was another masterful Herrmann score and the start of a twenty-year friendship.

Dunne and Herrmann had met in 1947 during the making of *Mrs. Muir*, but it was not until discussing the new film, about which Herrmann was enthusiastic, that Dunne learned of the composer's passion for theater and English literature. The two men spent a week discussing the score's placement in the film, agreeing (against a suggestion by its star, Richard Burton) that the film's recreations of Edwin Booth's Shakespearean performances would not have music: "Benny and I said, 'Those scenes *are* the musical numbers."[48]

Dunne's own musical sophistication did not always help his relationship with Herrmann. For the film's last scene, in which Booth gazes sadly at the empty theater box reserved in memory of his dead wife, Herrmann gave his expressive main theme to first violinist Louis Kaufman; but Dunne found "the violin theme . . . super sweet. I said to Benny, 'I wonder why you didn't use a solo oboe there—it would have been much more haunting.' Benny replied, 'Well, if ya know so much about it, why didn't YOU write the music?' "[49]

More characteristic of the collaboration is Herrmann's heartfelt score. Although he had rarely set Shakespearean text in the past, his music for the film's dialogue interpolations from the Bard, as well as for its less successful depiction of Booth's life, is confident in idiom and imaginative in its psychological use of orchestral timbre. Herrmann's title overture is unique in his film work, a pageantlike fanfare that announces a propulsive, Rózsaesque march (though its unison string writing is distinctly Herrmann's own). None of this material reappears in the score, but its theatricality sets the tone for what follows.

Herrmann responds strongly to the film's earliest (and best) scenes, which introduce the aging Junius Brutus (Raymond Massey) and the young Edwin, a lonely child whose passions are theater and literature—a character with whom Herrmann could empathize. We see the Booths' dark side, their hereditary madness; again, the sinuous color of low strings becomes a voice of psychological disorder and loss of control. In the film's most intense scene, as Booth Sr. becomes hysterical, Herrmann builds a quiet stepladder of ascending chromatic tones for celli and basses, a question searching for a tonal answer. The scene ends on a note of considerable pathos: trying to soothe his father, young Edwin sings to him, off-key but tenderly; under the boy's voice high strings quietly descend, accentuating the missed pitches in Edwin's song and blending unevenly with the child's voice as the melody ends—a lullaby unnerving in its subtly dissonant lyricism.

Moss Hart's screenplay often enables Herrmann to draw from Shakespearean verse for musical setting; two brief scenes are especially strong. As Edwin listens to his father perform *Lear's* storm scene, Herrmann transports us to the unseen stage with a surging moto perpetuoso device for strings unison, creating a rushing sense of acceleration: the figure is tossed to winds, then back to strings, dark harmonies echoing it violently; we are at the center of Lear's storm. In thirty seconds Herrmann has created a vital sense of the magic in Shakespeare's verse, and a sense of the excitement of theater.

Herrmann's second text setting also has dual meaning. The excerpt is Prospero's act four speech from *The Tempest* ("We are such stuff / As dreams are made on, and our little life / Is rounded with a sleep"), spoken as Junius Brutus bids his acting career farewell. Herrmann's setting for clarinet soli is deeply affecting in its elegiac simplicity, the weary, ethereal contours of descending winds adding a soft countermelody to the verse, echoing Brutus's depression.

In the film's longest set piece, Booth's London debut as Hamlet, Herrmann scores part of Dunne's play-within-a-play: dictating his choice is the appearance of the ghost of Hamlet's father, an entrance most unspectral if not for Herrmann's eerie, sustained whisper of organ and unison strings in their highest register. The cue's importance is as much psychological as atmospheric, with its inference of the madness that plagues the Booths. (In his directing debut, Dunne shows little feel for the story's morbidities, especially in the subplot of Edwin's brother, assassin John Wilkes Booth. Herrmann's music in these scenes is therefore doubly important.)

Hampered by an as yet unknown star and unfamiliar subject matter, *Prince of Players* was a commercial failure, achieving "the dubious distinction of being the first production in Cinemascope to lose money," Dunne recalled.[50] Dunne moved on to another directing project and in

1955 asked Herrmann to score *The View from Pompey's Head*, Dunne's adaptation of Hamilton Basso's novel. Other commitments led Herrmann to decline; but in addition to some perceptive editing criticisms, Herrmann suggested another, less known composer. No one was more surprised than the nominee, a young New York composer named Elmer Bernstein:

I'd had a very strange career in Hollywood by 1955. I'd started off very well in 1950 and then got caught in the political troubles of the time. By 1953–1954 I was fairly graylisted if never totally blacklisted, and I was really down in the mouth about my career. It was in the midst of all this that I got a call from Alfred Newman to score *The View from Pompey's Head*. During the course of our conversation it came out that one of the big factors in his calling me was that I had been recommended by Bernard Herrmann. That absolutely floored me, because I had no idea Herrmann knew anything I'd done; he never really talked about your work unless he didn't like it.

I was so thrilled that I immediately called Herrmann and thanked him—whereupon he blew up at me. In that incredible voice of his he yelled, "Don't bother me—if I didn't think ya had any talent I wouldn't-a recommended you!" and hung up on me. What does one say to that? It was very nice in a reverse sort of way. And it was typical of him. Either he was never secure enough to be really grateful, or it just made him too uncomfortable.

With all that gruffness, I found him very easy to like, and very generous with time. I would go to his home on Bluebell, and he would talk to me about film music and music in general. I found him very generous, provided it was clear that he was the master and you were the student. He was comfortable with that arrangement of characters.

The only real insight I ever had into the way he worked concerned the way he wrote film scores. It seems almost incomprehensible, but he would start with the first piece of music in the film and write a prologue or over-ture—then he'd just write straight through the film, from beginning to end, in ink, on score paper. That tells us about an extraordinary mind. He didn't seem to torture himself a lot creatively; to do the creative process and the orchestration process within the same time that most of the rest of us were writing and using orchestrators shows us he was not slow.

He was also the greatest ostinato writer who ever lived, because he made it work. It wasn't just a question of his being lazy and repeating a figure twenty times; it really works when he does it, because it's the *right* ostinato. It's true that if you don't deal with development you're going to work faster; but I don't think Herrmann made the choices he did because he was incapable of development. His aesthetic told him music was to be integrated into a film, not to be the star.[51]

By 1957, after the commercial success of Bernstein's score for *The Man with the Golden Arm*, Herrmann's support had turned to disdain. The jazz-oriented soundtrack sold very well on record,

and Bernie always felt there was something suspicious about anything that was commercially successful. He was also against jazz in films from the start. At a composers-lyricists dinner two years after the film, I walked in and Herrmann set upon me in public, with a lot of people hanging around, saying, "Oh, here's that great VAMP writer!"—which was funny, coming from the greatest ostinato writer of all time. I was infuriated and wouldn't talk to him for about two years after that; it was totally uncalled for. With the exception of Fred Steiner, I don't think Bernie was talking to any of his Hollywood composing friends by the time he left California in the late sixties. But I don't think he ever went into one of his sallies with the intent of alienating someone.[52]

Although few composers in Hollywood enjoyed his freedom to pick and choose projects, Herrmann was becoming an increasingly bitter man. Neither of his two chief ambitions, seeing his opera produced or getting a major conducting offer, showed promise of being realized. The Chandler family's cultural empire in Los Angeles had little use for Herrmann's temperament, his conducting, or his taste for the esoteric.

As a result, the few hours that Herrmann spent in front of an orchestra outside film studios were in high school auditoriums, with "rehearsal orchestras" of studio musicians playing the classical repertoire for pleasure. For Herrmann, these sessions served as a medium to hear his favorite obscure music as well as an outlet for his seething frustration with musical politics. Often anger overcame professionalism, and the evenings degenerated into savage Herrmann tongue-lashings. One night Lyn Murray joined Herrmann and Lucy for a rehearsal of Tchaikovsky's *Manfred* Symphony. Recalled Murray:

They didn't have the number of musicians needed for the piece; there was an important bass clarinet part in the first movement and only two clarinetists were present. When they stopped for a break, one of the clarinetists said, "Look, I live about ten minutes from here—I'll go home and get my bass clarinet." He left, and when the break was over the orchestra resumed. The musician got back quickly and started setting up his bass.

The second movement opens with two clarinets playing in thirds. While this guy was unpacking his instrument Herrmann started to conduct. He stopped and yelled, "Goddamn it, this is very important! TWO clarinets here! Whaddaya doin' with that goddamn bass clarinet—get the OTHER clarinet!" The musician tried to explain he had just gone home to get his bass for the first movement, but Herrmann just kept tearing his hair out. On the way home I asked him, "Jesus, why did you talk to the guy like that? He was just trying to help." Herrmann said, "Awww, you're gonna be one-a *those*." After I said good night, Lucy said to me, "I hope we haven't lost *another* friend."[53]

Few escaped Herrmann's spontaneous eruptions, which were increasing with time. Even the most devoted, like Norman Corwin, were subject to fierce scrutinies of their loyalty:

Herrmann had in his nature an eyedropper amount of paranoia. He felt he had to be on guard against exploiters and denigrators. He sometimes strained friendships by expectations larger than life size. This sometimes took the form of enlarging on very small, even unintentional offenses. A classic example: we had agreed to have dinner one evening at the Brown Derby. I was always on a very fast, tight schedule. We met promptly, had dinner in good time, and around the second cup of coffee I told him I had to leave for a meeting. Herrmann was silent to that. I left, and didn't hear from him for quite some while. I later learned through a third party that Herrmann had been offended that I had truncated our dinner to go off to something, and that he wasn't speaking to me. Why that should have estranged us, why he could not have said something straight out, I don't know.[54]

The incident, and many like it, stemmed from deep dissatisfactions in Herrmann rather than from superficial grievances. The true initiators were the studio and orchestra heads, whose predecessors, Herrmann felt, had thwarted the careers of such artists as Schubert, Berlioz, and too many others. Occasionally Herrmann's sallies were more amusing than vicious. Recalled David Raksin:

At one point the studios decided composers were getting too much money, so they decided to cut us off at the pockets, and we refused to work for them. Now, Benny *had* been working, and he had been out of work for a grand total of something like three weeks, whereas the rest of us hadn't worked for months. Benny called me one night, really upset about the fact that he wasn't working. I gave him a long spiel from one friend to another, saying, "Benny, they'll come to you." But the conversation went on and on for forty-five minutes—at the end of which there was a silence, and he said, "I'm sorry you're so depressed," and hung up!

Benny could be very loving, but when the chips were down he was like a street fighter and could almost betray you. In the late sixties Herrmann went to a party full of Hollywood people, including producers and directors—the guys who give jobs to composers. When he saw Arthur Knight, who taught cinema at USC where I gave a film music class, Benny walked up to Knight and said in a loud voice, "Is that RAKSIN still teachin' down at USC?" Arthur said yes. Benny said, "Well, what does HE know about film music?" This is my admiring friend who behind my back would say glowing things about me. But he was in a rotten temper that night, and when he was in a rotten temper nothing mattered. The pressure from his discontent was greater than the pressure to be a gentleman.[55]

Herrmann's main solace was work—but as all Hollywood-based composers knew, days or weeks could pass without assignments. To fill the time gaps, Herrmann turned to television, now a fixture in American homes despite its relative crudity. Little original music was written for TV in its early days, but by 1954, when Herrmann composed "A Christmas Carol"—the first of his two "television operas"—producers had begun to perceive the benefit of music specially written for the medium.

It was appropriate that Herrmann, who had scored CBS's radio version of the story, was commissioned to write the music for the network's TV adaptation, which starred a nonsinging Frederic March as Scrooge. Playwright-lyricist Maxwell Anderson's adaptation was superficial and unsatisfying; but if Dickens's 1840s England is diminished in Anderson's book and lyrics, it survives in the rich modal colors of Herrmann's music.

Although billed as an opera, the telecast more closely resembled a musical, with dialogue sequences bridged by songs. Too many of Anderson's lyrics are simple to the point of laziness, as in the repetitious baritone solo "A Very Merry Christmas" or the ponderous "What Shall I Give My Love for Christmas?" But at least two songs stand apart from the mostly forgettable score: "On This Darkest Day of Winter" is a lovely carol sung by chorus and boy soprano accompanied by solo flute, elegantly suggestive of the English folk tunes Herrmann and Dickens drew from. And Tiny Tim's gentle "Dear God of Christmas" is a charming expansion of the "April" movement from *The Fantasticks*, ending with a graceful plagal cadence on Tim's "Bless us every one." Originally written in 4/4, the song was quickly adapted by Herrmann to 3/4 after a suggestion from music supervisor Victor Bay. (On Bay's copy of the score Herrmann wrote, "For Victor, whose superb help and encouragement made the composing of this work a pleasure, and its performance a pleasant and rewarding task. In gratitude, Bernard.")[56]

Herrmann's underscoring is even more evocative. His music for Marley's ghost (Basil Rathbone) is an eerie series of modal progressions (sung by wordless chorus), suggesting a state of timelessness, a glimpse into a frozen, chilling hereafter. And in the rollicking dance music for the festive party at the Fezziwigs, one can hear Herrmann's nostalgic affection for Dickens's England, a time that, with Scrooge, he can perceive only in poignant retrospection.

"A Christmas Carol" was telecast on December 24, 1954, on CBS's "Chrysler Shower of Stars." Conducting the chorus was the distinguished Roger Wagner; among the supporting cast was a little-known mezzo-soprano, Marilyn Horne. (Both were great admirers of Herrmann's talent and knowledge, if not his vocal skill. Recalled Wagner: "Benny was the worst singer in the world.")[57] The program was well received, and aired again the following Christmas.

# TEN

Had Mr. Whistler been the possessor of a more even temper and a
little more common sense, he would have had five or six of his works
on the line in the American department, and nearly twice as many on
exhibition than is actually the case.

*James McNeill Whistler,*
The Gentle Art of Making Enemies

Despite several fine projects, none of Bernard Herrmann's recent film collaborators had matched the genius and imagination of Orson Welles—until November 1954, when Bernard Herrmann's most famous screen association, with Alfred Hitchcock, began. The resulting collaborations—*The
Trouble with Harry, The Man Who Knew Too Much, The Wrong Man,
Vertigo, North by Northwest, Psycho, The Birds,* and *Marnie*—would be
masterpieces of director-composer teamwork, perhaps the greatest such
relationship in film.

For most of their eleven years of collaboration the two men were
friends as well, although with Hitchcock intimacy was possible only on an
artistic level. Yet Herrmann's remark that he and Hitch shared "a great
unanimity of ideas" applied not only to their attitudes toward film but also
to their seemingly disparate personalities.[1]

Born in London's East End in 1899, Hitchcock was the product of a
strict Catholic upbringing, a cultural aberration for a Cockney that, in addition to a lonely childhood, helped shape Hitchcock's adult fears of emotional involvement and death—fears that would inspire his best work.[2]
Herrmann's background was that of another outsider seeking acceptance,
a Russian Jew who, during the Depression, sought recognition at a time
when work was scarce. Both men desired social mobility, Hitchcock aspir-
ing to join the English upper class, Herrmann seeking a place among top-
rank conductors in his own country and abroad.

Professionally there was a similar bond. Both were artists of longevity,
in a medium where sporadic achievement was common. "Many directors

can make one or two good movies, but how many can make 50 great ones like Hitchcock?" Herrmann observed in 1968. "Somerset Maugham once said, 'Anyone has one good novel in him—it's the second one I'm interested in.' "[3] No composer was more attuned to the complex moral subtext of Hitchcock's work or better understood its origins. "He is essentially a puritan," Herrmann said. "Yet it's the puritanical artist that achieves real sexual expression because he conveys his ideas poetically through atmosphere."[4] Herrmann also empathized with the pessimism behind Hitchcock's urbane demeanor and superficially escapist films. Together, noted Hitchcock biographer Donald Spoto, the two men shared "a dark, tragic sense of life, a brooding view of human relationships, and a compulsion to explore aesthetically the private world of the romantic fantasy."[5]

But while Hitchcock's art was that of a disengaged observer looking into his own suppressed fears, Herrmann's was that of an outspoken participant whose art could be both passionately romantic and psychologically revealing. His musical idiom was the perfect complement to Hitchcock's often detached images, giving them an emotional center and reinforcing thematic purpose. "[Hitchcock] only finishes a picture 60%," Herrmann said in 1975. "I have to finish it for him."[6]

Although Herrmann later claimed that Hitchcock left all scoring decisions to him,[7] Hitchcock actually had much involvement in the scoring process (at least its earliest stages). For years he had provided his composers with extensive "sound notes" detailing each scene's sound design and the role of the music. His years with Herrmann differed in only one respect: Herrmann could—and often did—ignore Hitchcock's directions. (Two key disagreements illustrate both Hitchcock's trust and eventual disregard of Herrmann's opinion. Herrmann scored *Psycho*'s shower sequence, which Hitchcock originally wanted silent; and in 1966, Herrmann ignored Hitchcock's instructions for *Torn Curtain*, causing an irreparable breach between the two men. See Chapters 12 and 13, respectively.)

Although Hitchcock and Herrmann had already met at least twice, Lyn Murray has taken credit for bringing the two together after scoring Hitchcock's airy thriller *To Catch a Thief* in 1954. At the time Murray was working on *Thief*, Hitchcock was already looking for a composer for his next film, a black comedy called *The Trouble with Harry*. Murray suggested Herrmann.[8]

The rapport between the two was strong from the start. Soon Herrmann and Lucy were invited to spend the weekend at Hitchcock's secluded home in Bel Air, where days were spent in leisurely conversation and evenings with Alma Hitchcock's superb cooking. The Hitchcocks often played host to the Herrmanns, especially in the late 1950s. Recalled the third Mrs. Herrmann, Norma Shepherd, "Benny used to wash dishes with Hitch, and they'd talk about what they'd do if they weren't in the film business. Benny wanted to run an English pub, until somebody told him you actually had to open and close at certain hours. Benny asked Hitch what he would be. There was a silence. Hitchcock then turned to Benny, his apron folded on his head, and said solemnly, 'A hanging judge.' "[9]

Cementing their relationship was *The Trouble with Harry*, a very personal project for Hitchcock that required especially deft scoring. Its subject matter was essentially comic: Harry's trouble is that he is dead—a matter of grave inconvenience for the film's quartet of stars (Shirley MacLaine, John Forsythe, Mildred Natwick, and Edmund Gwenn), who repeatedly try to hide Harry.

Although it was the most static Hitchcock film Herrmann scored, *Harry* offers a bountiful variety of color—both literally, in Robert Burks's shimmering Vistavision photography that captures the beauty of a Vermont autumn, and in the sharp comic performances of its players. *Harry* also boasts Herrmann's one true comedy score, although the humor is naturally of the mordant flavor Hitchcock loved. ("I think I'd enjoy writing a good comedy score," Herrmann said in 1971, "but I've never had the luck to be offered such films. The nearest I got to it was Hitchcock's 'The Trouble with Harry,' and perhaps 'North by Northwest.' " And four years later: "One day I'm going to do a rip-roaring comedy, but without music that laughs.")[10] Yet Herrmann saw more in the film: "[It] is in many ways the most personal and the most humorous of Hitchcock's output," he wrote in 1968. "It is gay, macabre, tender, and with an abundance of his sardonic wit."[11]

Drolly commentative, Herrmann's score also contains passages of lyric tenderness and nostalgic beauty unique in his work with Hitchcock (the obsessive romanticism of *Vertigo* being entirely different). Like the film itself, the score is a balancing act of moods and whimsy. Its essential Englishness, such as Herrmann's jaunty main theme for muted brass, low winds, and harp that sums up the film's tone,* particularly delighted Hitchcock, who considered the score Herrmann's best.[12]

*Harry*'s undertone of autumnal gentility is personified in the wooing of the spinster Miss Gravely (Natwick) by the spry Captain Wilde (Gwenn). The couples' relationships blossom with the Vermont forest, inspiring Delian tone paintings from Herrmann that wisp their way through

---

*This theme, like several *Harry* cues, was originally written for "Crime Classics." Herrmann asked Elliott Lewis for permission to re-use the music, although he did not have to.

the film: a quirky valse for woodwinds for the captain's amiable lope; a lyrical ballade for oboe, harp, and strings to accompany the courting Wilde on his visits to Miss Gravely.

The unfortunate Harry is buried not once but four times in the film. Herrmann mocks each ceremony with a variety of accent-heavy ostinatos that mimic the physical action: a demented little waltz for dainty winds; a grotesque promenade that bounces from brass to cuckooing clarinet.

Less convivial was Herrmann's first experience with the Paramount Studios orchestra, no match for the concert-quality playing he was used to at Fox. On the first day of recording Murray introduced Herrmann to the orchestra, hoping to prevent the inevitable: "I told them he was an old friend of mine and that they'd have a good time together." But soon Herrmann was battling his oboist (a second-class but well-liked player) and railing at players, cutters, and dubbers alike. "Herrmann was very supe rior about our complaints about the acoustics at Paramount," Murray recalled. "He said, 'You guys who can't conduct always blame it on the acoustics!' After that first recording session, Paramount's head music cutter walked up to me and said, 'He may be a friend of yours, but he's still a prick.' After the dubbing sessions Herrmann finally admitted he was physically ill."[13]

Herrmann returned to Paramount in early 1955 for his second (and last) screen western, which also marked its star Burt Lancaster's directing debut. *The Kentuckian* was a surprisingly genteel film based on the novel *The Gabriel Horn*, its chief virtue being a cast of veteran scene-stealers (including John McIntyre, Una Merkel, and John Carradine) and one star-to-be, Walter Matthau as the villainous Boudine. Shot mostly on location in Kentucky in Cumberland Falls and Levi Jackson Wilderness State Park, the film was more authentic in texture than most westerns of the day— perhaps the reason producer Harold Hecht hired Herrmann to compose the film's vitally indigenous score. (According to writer Rory Guy, Herrmann visited the film's location shooting to absorb the forest's ambience, though neither Lancaster nor Lucy Anderson recalled such a trip.)[14]

Scored for four horns, strings, double woodwind, percussion, harp, and celeste (doubling piano), Herrmann's depiction of America's rural plains is unique among his film work. Unlike *All That Money Can Buy*, which blended folk tunes and dramatic scoring, *The Kentuckian* consists entirely of original music, combining Herrmann's individual style (especially horn and woodwind colors) with the native simplicity of traditional American scale patterns. Also fairly atypical is Herrmann's use of long, lyrical melody lines, mainly for strings, to describe Kentucky's unspoiled beauty (nicely captured in Ernest Laszlo's camera work). Besides reinforcing the wilderness setting, these themes serve as subtle catalysts for the relationship between Eli Wakefield (Lancaster) and Hannah (Diane Foster).

Much of Herrmann's portrait of nineteenth-century Kentucky is far from stately or tender, however. His prelude (adapted from his quintessentially *English* "Shropshire Lad" music of 1934) is a lively rondo that opens with a distant call-and-response dialogue for solo horn and oboe, becoming a vigorous fugue for full orchestra. For the film's dramatic high point, the tautly edited street fight between Wakefield and Boudine, Herrmann builds a tense two-note device for bass and horns to a grotesque fortissimo as Boudine challenges Wakefield; then music disappears as the fight begins, allowing the tense action to play "in the open."

What respect Herrmann had for Lancaster the actor did not extend to Lancaster the director. At the film's mixing, Lancaster insisted the score be dubbed at a volume lower than Herrmann wished. Herrmann stormed out (and either did or did not return, depending on the sources).[15] Lancaster would describe his one-time collaborator as "the most difficult man I ever worked with,"[16] but years later, more magnanimously, as "a genius."[17]

A smoother collaboration followed. Alfred Hitchcock had long wished to remake his 1934 British thriller *The Man Who Knew Too Much*, a film he once dismissed as "the work of a talented amateur."[18] When Hitchcock realized his ambition twenty-one years later, the result was a dazzling blend of visual storytelling and masterful pacing that, for many, topped the original.

Hitchcock and screenwriter John Michael Hayes retained much of the earlier film's story, a classic Hitchcock conflict in which the child of a traveling couple is kidnapped to prevent their revealing a planned assassination, to occur at London's Albert Hall. For the remake, characterizations were deepened, and, with a large Paramount budget, Hitchcock was able to shoot on location in Morocco and London and to enlist the London Symphony Orchestra, the Covent Garden Chorus, and Bernard Herrmann—now a member of Hitchcock's trusted inner circle—to recreate the Albert Hall climax.

The 1934 sequence was a rare showcase for British composer Arthur Benjamin (a favorite of Herrmann), whose cantata *Storm Clouds* was a perfect mix of concert hall splendor and dramatic scoring (the assassin's gunshot is fired at the work's climactic cymbal crash). Given the option in 1955 to write a new work for the sequence (to be filmed, unlike the original, in the Albert Hall), Herrmann chose not to: "I didn't think anybody could better what [Benjamin] had done."[19] Herrmann did reorchestrate the work, doubling several parts and adding expressive new voices for harp, organ, and brass. Benjamin was also commissioned to write an additional minute and twenty seconds of music for the film (and, at Herrmann's insistence, was paid £100 more than originally planned).[20]

Hitchcock made directorial revisions in the sequence as well, replacing the anonymous orchestra in the original with an identifiable musical protagonist as its conductor—and who would be better than Herrmann himself? Consequently, Herrmann was given the choicest screen appearance by a real-life conductor since Stokowski shook hands with Mickey Mouse. (Benjamin had recommended using English conductor Muir Matheson, while producer Herbert Coleman suggested another Englishman, Basil Cameron.[21] The final decision was probably Hitchcock's.)

To heighten the sequence's impact, Herrmann wrote fewer minutes of underscoring than for any previous film. His sparse cues are not linked thematically to the Benjamin cantata or to each other, but serve as brief catalysts for mood (exotic Moroccan scales for the mysterious Louis Bernard), action (the furious percussion–bass clarinet dialogue for the marketplace chase), and tension (a terse, hypnotic ostinato for harp, low winds, and muted strings as the kidnappers wait restlessly for the evening concert).

By the arrival of the climax, we have heard excerpts from the cantata during the assassin's planning of the shooting: we are ready and expectant. Hitchcock opens his cinematic ballet with a droll touch: as Jo McKenna (Doris Day) arrives at the hall to find her boy, we see a prominent banner outside announcing the evening concert by Bernard Herrmann and the London Symphony. Inside the theater, Jo is warned by the hired assassin that her boy will die if she tries to prevent the killing. As she begs to know where her child is, only the ominous tuning din of the orchestra answers her.

From the time Herrmann appears onstage (looking commanding in tails) and gives his downbeat, not a word of dialogue is heard on the soundtrack until the sequence's end. During the cantata's declamative opening, Hitchcock devotes nearly a minute of screen time to a high-angle montage of Herrmann, orchestra, and chorus, then introduces his other key visuals: the well-dressed assassin, his unsuspecting target, and Jo. Robert Burks's camera returns to Herrmann—then narrows, to inspect the orchestra's massive percussion section, its cymbalist, and finally the resting cymbals. (Hitchcock allows a last visual joke as the player eyes his written part—two pages of rests, interrupted in the score's last measure by a single cymbal crash.)

A thunderous timpani roll (in close-up) marks an abrupt transition: Hitchcock leaves his auditorium perspective as Ben (James Stewart) races into the lobby searching for his wife. A dialogue-free shot of the two urgently conferring and the orchestra's commentary explain all. Crosscutting rhythms accelerate as Ben and police search for the killer's box. The assassin poises his weapon as the cymbalist stands, instrument in hands. A snare-drum cadence builds excitement as Jo watches the gunman's barrel emerge from the box's curtain: chorus swells against a fast-paced montage of Herrmann vigorously conducting—his hand turning the score—a fast tracking shot of the same. As majestic organ pedal tones announce the coda, Hitchcock fixes his perspective on the assassin's gun . . . Ben's search . . . Jo's petrified stare. Chorus reaches its penultimate chord—the assassin squeezes the trigger—and Jo shatters the momentary silence before the cymbal crash with a scream. The gunman only wounds his target, and falls to his death from the balcony as the cantata comes to its triumphant close.

Both the 1934 and 1956 versions of *The Man Who Knew Too Much* face the formidable task of topping this high point. In both films, Hitchcock's solution is uniquely cinematic. While the original ends in an explosive gun battle between kidnappers and London police, the remake offers a more modest but equally suspenseful alternative: aware that her son is hidden in the foreign embassy, Jo creates a musical decoy by singing (and singing) "Que Será Será" while Ben makes his way up the mansion's staircase to find the boy.

Sensitive to accusations that Hitchcock was trying to sell a song as well as make a thriller, Herrmann rose to the director's defense: "It was imperative that he have something while he was panning down that staircase. So Doris Day came up with three songs, and this was the best. It was not a premeditated attempt at song-plugging. It was the same thing with 'The Third Man' theme, which was absolutely right for the postwar desolation in Vienna. At no time, I'm sure, were Carol Reed or Orson [Welles] hoping to push records. All pop hits are accidental. Like gold, it's where you find it."[22]

In fact, at least on Paramount's part, it was "premeditated song-plugging" that led to the hiring of Jay Livingstone and Ray Evans to write a song for the film. At their first meeting, recalled Livingstone, "Mr. Hitchcock proceeded to tell us that he did not want any songs in the picture, but since Doris Day was a singer, the studio was insisting on a song. . . . [Hitchcock] said, 'I need a song. I don't know what kind of song I want.' When we played 'Que Sera, Sera' for him, he said, 'Gentlemen,

I told you I didn't know what kind of song I wanted.' He hesitated, then pointed a finger at us and said, 'That's the kind of song I want.' Then he got up and walked out.''[23] The result was a rare instance of popular music well used in film—and, not incidentally to Hitchcock or Paramount, an Oscar-winning hit and promotional bonanza.

Herrmann's first encounter with the London Symphony during the filming of the Albert Hall sequence would be his happiest. During shooting breaks Herrmann entertained the musicians with Hollywood anecdotes and gained their respect with his knowledge of musical minutiae—so much so that at the end of filming, the orchestra presented him with a book on the Symphony inscribed ''To Bernard Herrmann, the Man Who Knows So Much.''[24]

Making his debut with the LSO that year was horn player Barry Tuckwell, who was delighted by Herrmann's affectionate tales of Stokowski. Herrmann suggested to the young Tuckwell that Stokowski be engaged as guest conductor to the Symphony. Management listened to the suggestion and invited Stokowski to conduct the following year.[25] It was an act of consideration by Herrmann that Stokowski soon reciprocated.

Also in London that spring was Orson Welles, then mounting the stage premiere of *Moby Dick: A Rehearsal*, Welles's free adaptation of the novel he and Herrmann knew so well. Welles visited Herrmann at the lavish Savoy Hotel and asked Herrmann to write an original score for the production. For reasons forgotten today, Herrmann declined.[26]

On his return to Hollywood, Herrmann embarked on a smaller-scale conducting project no less dear to him than the Hitchcock film. ''Music of the Georgian Era'' was the theme of five chamber recitals in July 1955 sponsored by the Los Angeles County Museum and featuring neglected music of Handel, William Boyce, Thomas Arne, Karl Ditters von Dittersdorf, and others. The performances were broadcast by local radio station KFAC, which must have made the ex–radio conductor feel at home. From orchestra to soloists, players were strictly ''pick-up'' but often first class, among them flutist Arthur Gleghorn (featured in Vivaldi's flute concerto *The Cardinal*) and Marilyn Horne, who sang arias by Handel (from *Jephtha*) and Thomas Arne. The latter selection, Arne's ''Water parted from the sea'' from *Artaxerxes*, was sung ''first in the manner in which we are accustomed to hearing [it], and secondly, in the style of the period as notated by Domenico Corri in his 'Select Collection of the Most Admired Songs' (1785).''[27]

Luck in soloists seemed to have run out by Herrmann's last broadcast of July 31. The program featured Johann Christian Bach's D Major Piano

Concerto with pianist André Previn, who had met Herrmann at MGM in the early fifties.* After learning the concerto—which to Herrmann's horror he confessed he had never heard—Previn committed a sin worse than ignorance: he came down with the mumps.[28] To Herrmann, who made a career out of misjudging Previn's motives, it was an unforgivable act of sabotage. Enter Fred Steiner:

One day Benny called me, very upset. He was going to do a piano concerto of the London Bach and he said André Previn had backed out on him. I told him, "C'mon, Benny, I haven't kept up my chops on the piano—I can't play that." He said, "Yes you can! It's *easy!*" Herrmann could be very persuasive, because the last thing I wanted to do was not only play a concerto in public but play it under the baton of Bernard Herrmann! My experience with him had been limited to playing Haydn symphonies for four hands and getting knocked off the piano bench. Benny sent me the music and finally persuaded me to do it—and we did. The piece was not terribly difficult, but I must confess mine was not a very good performance. But Benny was pleased, and very flattering. He said, "You played it *much* better than André could have—the cadenzas you played were just perfect! Did you write those yourself?" I said, "Yeah, sure." "They were terrific!"[29]

August saw the Herrmanns playing host (in Lucy's case, reluctantly) to Leopold Stokowski, who that year had become chief conductor of the Houston Symphony. After a three-day engagement in the Texas capital, Stokowski found the cool shade of Bluebell's eucalyptus trees and the Herrmanns' modest guest house a welcome change. Although Lucy tired of Stokowski's lord-of-the-manor demeanor, there was nothing but esteem between the two conductors, who spent many afternoons by the pool discussing music and listening to a singularly untalented trombonist down the block. "Father and Stokowski would listen keenly to every wrong note he played," Dorothy Herrmann recalled, "and they would say things like, 'I don't think he's gotten better' or 'Do you think he'll ever make it?' Then they would look at each other and shake their heads."[30]

---

*Recalled David Raksin: "I was having lunch in the MGM commissary with Bronislau Kaper and Miklós Rózsa, when in walked our youthful colleague André Previn. He sat down and said with the air of a man who has just seen a unicorn in his garden, 'I met the most amazing guy last night; I really think he should've been born in the eighteenth century.' Rózsa, Kaper, and I looked knowingly at each other, and I said, 'He was, and he's living in it.' When André asked how we were all so quick to guess whom he meant, we said, 'Who else but Benny Herrmann?' " (Raksin, from the radio show "The Subject Is Film Music"; Cinema Library USC).

Most of all Stokowski admired Herrmann's musical knowledge, as this 1955 letter illustrates:

Dear Bernardino

I enjoyed immensely your talk about the beauties of Handel. It came particularly well after a [recorded] performance of a symphony by Beethoven that was completely mechanical, although well done otherwise. It was as if a metronome started off the tempo and from that moment everything was as if a machine was playing. What you said about individual expression and about contributing to the composer, and particularly your choice of language in calling the singers of Handel's period "co-creators" was so just and illuminating. Also what you said about Bach's writing in his decorative phrases, whereas Handel, Gluck and other composers left such elaboration to the player and singer.

You made so clear the idea of collaboration between performer and composer, and what you said is so necessary today, when everything is becoming so materialistic and mechanistic in music. Thank you for having the courage to say it—and the clarity of mind to say it so well.

> Your friend
> Leopold[31]

Stokowski paid Herrmann an even greater compliment by asking him to guest conduct the Houston Symphony the following January—an offer Herrmann proudly accepted.

John and Evelyn Barbirolli also made Bluebell an overnight stop during their California visits. Long after their wives had retired for the night, Herrmann and the recently knighted Sir John entertained each other with musical anecdotes and analyses. Herrmann drew sharp analogies between their favorite composers—Elgar, Vaughan Williams, Delius—and a host of obscure English painters and authors, displaying "more knowledge than any Englishman," Evelyn Barbirolli recalled. "It used to terrify John!"[32]

One evening as the Barbirollis were going to bed, Herrmann brought one of his precious cats into the guest house and set it at the foot of their bed, explaining to the reluctant John that it was good luck to sleep with a cat at one's feet. Barbirolli agreed—then, certain Herrmann had gone, chucked the pet out the door "with great dispatch." The next morning, however, Herrmann was certain his efforts had been appreciated: "I've *converted* him," he told Lucy proudly.[33]

Barbirolli's opinion of Herrmann's opera was a more delicate matter. Confident that Sir John would produce *Wuthering Heights* in Manchester, Herrmann was crushed when Barbirolli told him the opera required more forces, orchestral and theatrical, than the Halle could manage. In fact, Evelyn Barbirolli recalled, "John didn't feel the work was entirely good. The economic problems he explained to Benny were true, but had John felt that the opera was *Moby Dick* plus, he would have made every possible effort."[34] Careful not to hurt his friend, Barbirolli never expressed his true feelings to Herrmann, who anticipated a Halle performance of his opera until Barbirolli's death in 1970.

By the mid-1950s, Bluebell Avenue was not only a second home to the famous; it was also the site of one of Hollywood's most remarkable private collections of music scores and manuscripts, and of a vast library of period and modern literature that filled every eighteenth-century bookcase and cabinet in Herrmann's study. Each volume was not only read and studied by Herrmann but expanded with a selection of relevant clippings, often haphazardly pasted into a book's front cover. ("I may be a slob," Herrmann once observed, "but I'm a slob with good taste.")[35]

Herrmann shared his collection with other musicologists, both amateur and professional, among them Ralph Kirkpatrick, harpsichordist and editor of a complete set of Scarlatti keyboard works. A letter to Kirkpatrick illustrates Herrmann's keen attention to historical detail: "A few weeks ago I had the good fortune to purchase, from a collector in Mexico City, some musical manuscripts. Among them was a letter of Domenico Scarlatti, a photostat of which I herewith enclose. . . . The letter seems to be a first draft of the letter that you reproduced in your book. If this letter is genuine, it brings out one important point—that the letter was addressed to the Duke of Alba and therefore must be of a much later period in Scarlatti's life than you attributed to the letter that you described. However, I am not an authority in these matters."[36]

Another beneficiary of Herrmann's scholarship was English bookseller Cecil Hopkinson. "Please forgive the delay in my writing to you to express my thanks and appreciation for your kindness and patience in regard to the Handel and Scarlatti manuscripts," Herrmann once wrote.

In regard to Mr. Kirkpatrick's opinion of your own work on Scarlatti, I should not take it to heart, as surely you must appreciate the fact that there are many interpreters and musicologists who regard the music they happen to perform or write about as being their own personal property, and who are fiercely jealous and possessive of it. It must be a form of compensation for, perhaps, a lack of their own real creativeness, and so, by a process of empathy, they reach the state of illusion that leads to such remarks as "Have you heard my Beethoven?" "My Wagner?" "My Scarlatti?" Or sometimes they even go further and simply take to themselves a whole period of time—middle-Renaissance, late-Renaissance, etc., etc., etc. But in spite of this, many of these people do contribute to the world's culture and understanding, and we must just overlook their eccentricities.[37]

Herrmann's final project of 1955 was his second and last "television opera" for CBS, a solemn retelling of the Christmas story called "A Child Is Born," based on a story by Stephen Vincent Benet. Written for "G.E. Theater" (hosted by Ronald Reagan, whose politics Herrmann loathed)[38] and just thirty minutes long, "Child" was actually more of an opera than Herrmann's earlier "Christmas Carol"; less song-oriented and almost continuously scored, it recalls *Wuthering Heights* in its use of fluid harmonic progressions and dark, low string colorations to achieve psychological (and here, spiritual) effects. The opera focuses on the middle-aged wife of a Bethlehem innkeeper, a woman who mourns the death of her only child. With her appreciation of Christ comes the realization that "life is not lost by dying—life can be lost without vision, but not by death."

Despite stilted dialogue and a stiff performance by Robert Middleton as the innkeeper, "A Child Is Born" is filled with affecting moments: Herrmann's gentle theme for the Virgin Mary, an ethereal cue for violins wrapped in delicate harp arpeggios; his solemn plagal setting of the wife's vision, "Something is loosed to change the shaken world"; the soft choral hymn of the wandering shepherds, a quiet carol brimming with humanity. "A Child Is Born" was performed live from Television City on December 23, 1955, and repeated the following year; among the original cast was a young Harve Presnell in the baritone role of Dismas the thief.

In January 1956, the Herrmanns left Hollywood for Houston (by car, in a grand, newly purchased Alvis) for Herrmann's debut with the Houston Symphony. The two concerts mixed popular, virtuoso works (the Tchaikovsky Violin Concerto with Erica Morini, Rachmaninoff's Third Piano Concerto with Van Cliburn) and more personal selections like Vaughan Williams's *London* Symphony and Liszt's *Faust* Symphony, both Herrmann favorites. Just as the English piece was a musical time machine to a long-vanished London, the Liszt symphony embodied the Romantic spirit and values Herrmann emulated as both composer and individual. Herrmann wrote in his perceptive program notes:

In this symphony Liszt has summoned up, not only musically but philosophically and psychologically, the Romantic attitude. The first movement is the portrait of Faust. It portrays the endless searchings, doubts and scepticisms of the aged Faust, and at the same time his eternal quest for an all-consuming and passionate fulfillment of life and youth. Of course, at the same time it is a true portrait of Franz Liszt and almost an autobiographical one. . . . The final movement, Mephistopheles, is one of the most remarkable achievements in all of Liszt's works, . . . for many years before the advent of Freud and his followers, Liszt understood that the evil which exists in man is not external but subjective. Hence Mephistopheles has no motives of his own but only the motives of Faust, which are twisted and tormented.[39]

*Faust's* theme of pervasive evil and the tragedy inherent in the human condition was also central to most of Herrmann's best work; it would find fullest realization in later scores for Hitchcock.

Despite Herrmann's enthusiasm for his program, the Houston trip was unhappy for most involved. According to John Houseman, Herrmann had successfully insulted most of the Symphony's board of trustees by the end of his stay.[40] Herrmann would later accuse the orchestra and its managers of anti-Semitism.[41] He would not return.

Back in California, Herrmann found film work and a final CBS radio project awaiting him. This last broadcast was appropriately grand: an adaptation of Aldous Huxley's classic science fiction novel *Brave New World* for the briefly revived "Columbia Workshop." Like CBS dramas of old, it was superbly acted (by a cast that included Joseph Kearns, William Conrad, and, as narrator, the soft-spoken Huxley himself) and skillfully adapted and directed by William Froug, with whom Herrmann had worked occasionally since the early fifties. Herrmann's score was typically (and necessarily) minimal, written for six percussionists and centering on a ticking, hypnotic ostinato for xylophone and organ that mirrored the childlike placidity of life in the twenty-third century.

Reviews praised the broadcast as an example of how exciting radio could be (and once was) and, in *Variety,* as an illustration of the forgotten art of radio scoring: "Old-timers will hail the return of composer-conductor Bernard Herrmann, once altar boy to Monsignor Norman Corwin and an old radio and Workshop hand. His contribution underscores the score's importance in radio—and music's relatively neglected status in video. It would not be far-fetched to argue that special music, written to supplement and implement story needs, often is better (and cheaper) than scenery."[42]

For Froug, the program was another chance to observe the odd, often pathetic mood swings that Herrmann could rarely control:

Beenie could laugh happily when listening to a playback in the control booth, but he also projected enormous vulnerability; you wanted to hug him and say, "It's okay." He'd throw his temper tantrums, pull out his hair, snort, and carry on, but you felt there was a wounded child underneath. Beenie didn't have any skin—just raw nerves, so the slightest thing could hurt him deeply. Those of us who worked with him wondered how he could survive.

Because of that extreme sensitivity you had to handle Beenie with kid gloves; if you just confronted him he'd storm out. Once over dinner at my house, a friend's wife tried to set him straight on something musical—I think she was trying to play one-upmanship with Bernard Herrmann. He just exploded: "How DARE you tell me that Mozart . . . "—he grabbed Lucy and said, "We're leaving." We just sat there in a state of shock. After a couple of these incidents it got to the point, frankly, where we just didn't invite him any more. My wife and I talked about it a great deal and decided that, as bright and charming as he could be, life was too short.

But Beenie could be a very sweet man—a lost child who wanted affection desperately. It was so clear; everything about him said, "Love me, please." Yet his behavior drove people away, the very people he wanted to love him.[43]

At the same time, a less temperamental composer sixteen years Herrmann's junior was building a reputation in CBS radio and television. After a brief internship in the network's music library, Jerry Goldsmith had become one of CBS's most imaginative and economical musicians. (For his first score, for the series "Romance," produced by Froug, he was paid an all-inclusive $50.)[44] Goldsmith had watched Herrmann conduct "Crime Classics" programs and, until 1956, had idolized him. But Goldsmith's success—and a radio programming error—led to a recurrence of Herrmann's now-familiar pattern of support followed by suspicion.

"I was doing a series at that time called 'Studio One,' " Goldsmith said.

We would score the show and then they would do a minute teaser or trailer of the next week's show. They would bring the cast and director from the studio . . . and have them do their bit as a trailer. There was never time to write music for these things . . . usually they would pick a piece of library music and play it. Unfortunately this week they picked a piece of Bernie's music that had been in the library and they used it as the underscoring for the trailer. Now the credits came up—"Music composed and conducted by Jerry Goldsmith." Well . . . he was going to sue everybody. He went around the studio demanding all sorts of incredible things: "There's Goldsmith! He's stealing my music!" and naturally I tried explaining to him. . . . Well, the more you explained it, it only exasperated the situation. So from that point on that was the end of our relationship."[45]

. As Goldsmith's star in Hollywood rose, Herrmann's bitterness grew in proportion. One afternoon in 1962 as he walked to the Universal lot, Goldsmith—then scoring his first major film, *Lonely Are the Brave*—heard the screeching voice of his ex-mentor from across the street: "You're like all the other Hollywood guys, using an orchestrator!" When a sour-faced Herrmann entered the recording stage where Joseph Gershenson was conducting Goldsmith's score, Goldsmith panicked: "But he did walk in at a very opportune time; it happened to be the best piece of music in the film, and it was quite exciting. [Herrmann] said, 'Don't use that music—it's too damn good for the picture! You save it, it's too damn good for the picture!'. . . . In spite of his own animosities and idiosyncracies, he was a musician to the core, and his own musical instinct could not be denied."[46]

In 1956, Herrmann had little cause for bitterness; never again would he juggle so diverse and rewarding a schedule. In addition to work for Hitchcock, CBS radio and television, and concerts with the London and Houston Symphonies, Herrmann found time to score one film for Fox, *The Man in the Gray Flannel Suit*, in February 1956.

It was a prestigious film (among the last supervised by Zanuck), and its themes—personal integrity, the pressure of conformity—were well suited to Herrmann. But Sloan Wilson's novel was an odd choice for the screen: the story has little action, centering on the inner conflicts of a New York advertising executive, Tom Raff (played with affecting restraint by Gregory Peck).

The film, 156 minutes of almost continuous dialogue, required little music. Most intriguing is Herrmann's handling of the many flashback sequences; as in *Snows of Kilimanjaro*, Peck's character retreats into his past to find meaning for the present, and Herrmann frames these transitions with subtle, concise musical bridges. A remembrance of a violent confrontation with Nazis in World War II is scored with muffled timpani, then low winds and brass, which remain a tightly rhythmic, nerve-racking murmur—until Raff fatally stabs a young guard, and the suppressed emotion explodes in a terrific orchestral scream.

Herrmann uses extremely delicate, fragmented devices for strings to encourage empathy with Raff, whose guilt over a wartime affair has left him barely able to communicate with his wife, Betsy, and his children. A restrained contrapuntal dialogue for strings adds a musical correlation to his confrontations with Betsy (tinnily played by Jennifer Jones); passion is reserved for Raff's thoughts of Maria, the Italian peasant girl whose family had been killed in the war—and whom Raff leaves pregnant. Here,

Herrmann writes music for strings that combines an almost religious transcendence with secular rapture, evoking both Maria's gentleness and her desperation. ("You have no idea how lonely I was," she tells Raff, in a line that Herrmann could not have ignored.)

After his happy experience with the London Symphony on *The Man Who Knew Too Much*, Herrmann was eager to return to England and the LSO to conduct a series of genuine concerts and convince London audiences of his talent. To make his services more attractive he offered to pay his own expenses during the trip;[47] Symphony management accepted. Four concerts at the Royal Festival Hall and one BBC broadcast were scheduled, the radio concert to feature the British premiere of a work Herrmann had long championed: after twenty years, the British were ready for Ives.*

The most conventionally structured of Ives's major works and filled with accessible American melodies, the Second Symphony was ideal for introducing Ives in England. Herrmann's performance was authoritative and affectionate, with an unpretentious dynamism that Ives would have enjoyed. Those who had puzzled over Herrmann's photocopies of the score could now judge for themselves: "We listened in with tremendous enjoyment to your broadcast," English composer Edmund Rubbra wrote his friend. "The *Falstaff* [a shrewd programming counterpoint] was splendid, and revealed things that I had never heard before. I liked the Ives Symphony very much. It was easier on the ear than I had imagined it would be and was full of entrancing material."[48]

Herrmann's championing of *Falstaff* is also worth noting. Since childhood it had been one of his favorite compositions: he once described it as "Elgar's supreme orchestral work, in spite of the special difficulty it presents of relating the music to the understanding of the audience. . . . [For] besides the arduous and exacting musical demands that it makes upon the conductor and performers, the audience must bring an understanding of the play to it."[49]

To American ears especially, Elgar's Shakespearean portrait was as foreign as Ives's barnyard dances and hymns were to the English, and from his first conducting days with the New Chamber Orchestra Herrmann had tried to convince his countrymen what they were missing. His passion for the work may be better understood through another remark, describing *Falstaff* as "a portrait in many ways of the composer: his deep sense of the

*In 1946 Herrmann had conducted the Fugue from the Fourth Symphony on the BBC; it was also broadcast in the mid-1930s, but to scant notice. Herrmann's broadcast of April 25, 1956, was the first complete performance of an Ives symphony in England.

country scene and pastoral tranquility, his enjoyment of ceremony and pomp, his intellectual cynicism and, at the same time, emotional unity with his fellow-man."[50] The eighteenth-century Briton in Herrmann had found his anthem.

The four LSO concerts at Festival Hall were far less convivial. Insecure and defensive on his London concert debut, Herrmann was not the genial scholar he had been during his Hitchcock visit, but an argumentative pedant. During one rehearsal the symphony's soft-spoken oboist raised his hand with a question. "Mr. Herrmann, my part is penciled in mezzoforte, but it's only penciled in. Do you wish me to observe it?"

"SURE I do," barked Herrmann. "Whaddaya want it in, NEON?"[51]

Eventually, violinist Henry Greenwood recalled, "Benny did so many things like that that the orchestra got tired of him—and when he did things wrong they let him wallow in his mistakes. In the end he was desperate, saying, 'Will ya quit *gettin'* at me?' But they just let him sink into the enormity of his egotry. I was so sorry for him, but he asked for all of it."[52] During breaks, Greenwood offered Herrmann suggestions and encouragement; through his loyalty he won the composer's lasting friendship and admiration.

During the concerts themselves, Herrmann worked himself to the brink of collapse, emerging wringing wet at each intermission for a quick change of dress; yet when an actual crisis arose, he astonished everyone with his coolness. One night, only minutes before the concert's start, Herrmann discovered his conducting score had been left in his car; he tapped his forehead and said, "If you haven't got it up here, what's the point in coming?"—and proceeded to conduct the lengthy piece from memory.[53]

Despite the friction between Herrmann and the orchestra and Herrmann's often awkward direction ("Benny wielded his baton like a poker," recalled Greenwood's wife, Joan),[54]* some of the Festival Hall performances were outstanding. Two highlights were the U.K. premiere of Russell Bennett's Concerto for Violin and Orchestra (in the Popular Style), with old friend Louis Kaufman, and a performance of Vaughan Williams's *London* Symphony, with its increasingly deaf composer present in the front row. As one critic noted, the evening's most touching moment came after the music: "As the epilogue gently faded out Herrmann held his baton for a few moments in silence. The composer stepped forward and

---

*Joan Greenwood provides another insight: "One day Benny sat down at our piano and played very, very modern music which he was making up as he went along. He then said to Henry, 'You think I can't write this kind of music—well, I can' " (Joan Greenwood to SCS, 5-13-85).

shook his hand. The exhausted conductor was obviously deeply moved."[55] (Herrmann considered the event "a supreme moment.")[56]

On the eve of his return to Hollywood another note of appreciation arrived, from the Composers Guild of Great Britain. "The Executive Committee . . . have asked me to convey to you our very sincere thanks for all the work you do, and have done, for British contemporary music," wrote Chairman Guy Warrick. "Your programmes both in America and while over here have been a great source of joy to British composers whom we have the honour to represent, and I send you our sincerest gratitude."[57]

Nevertheless, Herrmann would not be invited back by the London Symphony.

Another casualty of Herrmann's temper was *Wuthering Heights*, as yet unproduced in any medium. Not all music directors were unimpressed with the work, but in each case Herrmann's insistence on total artistic control—and his unwillingness to trim the three-and-a-half-hour work— brought the same frustrating results. A typical case involved the San Francisco Opera Company, which initially agreed to produce the work. Herrmann's friend Victor Bay, who had moved from CBS to conduct the Santa Monica (California) Symphony, witnessed the outcome:

One day while I was at Benny's house there was a telephone call—it was San Francisco. He took the call in his music room. I was sitting in the living room, but I could tell it was going from bad to worse. Finally Benny said in a high-pitched voice, "Well, I gotta HEAR her before we give her the part"—the part of Cathy. Benny kept yelling, and it ended apparently with the director saying, "To hell with you and your opera. We won't produce it." I felt sorry for Benny. San Francisco was a good opera company, and the opera would be *heard*. But Herrmann spoiled it himself. It was his character; he couldn't help it.[58]

A more diplomatic champion of the opera was music publisher Irving Broude, a friend of Herrmann's. Through Herrmann, Broude met Miklós Rózsa, and on Herrmann's recommendation he later published several of Rózsa's concert works. Recalled Rózsa:

Broude told me he was trying to help Benny with the opera. He talked to Julius Rudel, the director of New York's City Center. Rudel liked it, and it looked as if he was going to produce it, but Rudel said he wanted some changes. Benny exploded: "I'm not gonna change a NOTE!" So Rudel said forget it.

At that time, I was teaching film music at USC, so I asked Benny, "How about a USC performance?" . . . He snapped no. I asked why not.

He told me that when "Invitation to Music" came to an end, CBS had asked universities to write letters of support, and none did. I said, "You can't punish USC for that; they probably never even knew about it." "No," he said, "I don't want that." Two days later he called me and asked, "What did you say about USC?"

I told him they had a very good student orchestra and good singers. "I've heard them give performances of very difficult operas," I said, "and they have an excellent conductor, Walter Decloux." Benny said, "All right, well, how do we manage this?" I said, "Let me do it. I'll invite you for dinner with Dr. Decloux." I talked to Decloux, who was interested, so we decided to meet at the Beachcombers restaurant.

Decloux and I were there at 8:00. No Benny. 8:15, no Benny; 8:30, no Benny. At about a quarter to nine, Benny and Lucy arrived, quarreling. I sat Benny next to Decloux and we ordered. "Have you heard any new music here?" Benny asked Decloux. "Oh yes," Decloux replied, "we go to the Philharmonic. They have very good programs." . . . Benny said, "That's not music—those are IDIOTS conducting there! Mrs. Chandler only invites NAZIS!" "Mr. Herrmann," Decloux replied, "For me the war is over. I was in the war for four years as a soldier for the United States. Were you in the war?" Herrmann said, "Aww, who cares about the war? I did music!"

Afterwards, we came home, and I said, "Benny, will you bring in your score?" He brought in three big volumes. Decloux said, "Yes, fine . . . " —but it could have been *Die Meistersinger,* and he wouldn't have done it. [59]

Rózsa tried to interest another colleague, Georg Solti, who subsequently visited California and invited Herrmann to one of his concert rehearsals. As Solti began conducting a Schumann symphony, Herrmann entered and began berating Solti's reading: "The whole beginning is wrong—you should be doing it more slowly! Which version are you conducting?" "Schumann's version," Solti replied coolly. "No changes." "DON'T gimme that—I know that piece!" Herrmann answered.

Solti stood quietly on the podium. "Mr. Herrmann, will you please leave?" To Herrmann it was another betrayal. "What kind of friend is *that?*" he later asked Rózsa. [60]

A happier occasion that October was Herrmann's first of two conducting visits to the newly formed Glendale Symphony in Southern California, in a lengthy concert that included the "Von Nürnberg" Prelude from *Die Meistersinger,* Dvořák's *New World* Symphony, Sibelius's tone poem *En Saga,* Delius's *Walk to the Paradise Garden,* and the March and Dances from Borodin's *Prince Igor.* After the concert a party was held in

Herrmann's honor; but as his secretary Elsa Clay recalled, "He didn't so-
cialize at all but remained absorbed, along with some of the musicians, in
listening and commenting on a tape of the concert."[61]

Herrmann's own return to composition that year came at the behest of
Hitchcock, whose relationship with the composer continued to grow on an
intuitive level. As in *The Man Who Knew Too Much*, music played a key
role in *The Wrong Man*, Hitchcock's somber dramatization of the true-life
arrest and imprisonment of a New York musician, Manny Balestrero
(Henry Fonda), for a crime he did not commit; yet Hitchcock's unusually
straightforward approach to the story (though not without its baroque
touches) suggested to both director and composer that scoring should be
kept to a minimum. Source music, as in the Albert Hall climax of *The
Man Who Knew Too Much*, would be especially important because of
Manny's job as a bassist at New York's Stork Club.

In contrast to the whimsy of *The Trouble with Harry* and the taut es-
capism of *The Man Who Knew Too Much*, *The Wrong Man*—shot in oppressive black and white—is unremittingly bleak in its vision of society
at its most callous. Its theme of miscarried justice was a favorite not only
of Hitchcock but also of Herrmann, whose limited success in the world of
concert music was adding darker hues to his art and character.

Herrmann's score for *The Wrong Man* is his most terse, yet its claus-
trophobic power, created through cumulative shadings of orchestral color,
is inescapable. His instrumentation is an enlarged version of Manny's jazz
combo; but unlike the Latin-tinged, syncopated energy of Herrmann's
source music (first heard under the film's titles and our first glimpse of the
glamorous Stork Club, a cue that suggests Manny's profession and the
film's dark tone through subtle emphasis of bass), *The Wrong Man*'s score
is almost uniformly gray and cold.

Its effects are simple: eerie unison chromatics for muted brass, dark
clusters of low winds, and the thumping, monotonous rhythm of bass, hu-
morlessly mimicking Manny's past (as a musician) and present (the tedious, horrifying formalities of his arrest and imprisonment). Rarely does
Herrmann's color palette vary, except to add the dolorous, cobweb hush
of harp (most chillingly as Manny enters his dark prison cell, the harp's
color echoing both the setting and Manny's confusion) or a sighing dialogue for flutes and clarinets as Manny tells his eldest son of his arrest.
Simplicity of timbre, repeated rhythmic device, and simple harmonic dissonance (as in the arid clash of winds when Manny's wife loses her sanity)
are all that Herrmann needs to reinforce Hitchcock's stark textures—a
sensibility tempered only slightly by the film's finale as an epilogue tells

us of Rose's recovery after Manny's vindication. At last, mutes are removed (freed?) from Herrmann's trumpets, which are finally allowed to sing in round, open bell tones.

Herrmann's experience at Warner Brothers, the film's studio, was not a happy one. With *The Wrong Man* Herrmann raised his salary from its longtime $15,000 to $17,500—a figure Warners initially refused to pay.[62] After several days of pressure from Hitchcock and producer Herbert Coleman, the studio gave in, but Herrmann never worked there again. One year after the film's release, Herrmann sent Hitchcock a review from Australia, underlining the following paragraph: "The film is a certainty for our 10-best list for 1957—if for no other reason than that it is a classical demonstration of the uses of extreme quietness in developing suspense. The gaunt sound-track music, for instance, is a series of plucked low notes from the musician's own double-bass, always in a rhythm to suggest footfalls of a ghost—and this gives a weird feeling that ghastly intangibles are stalking the 'hero' into a world of eerie bewilderment and horror."[63]

Then and in later years, Herrmann took no chances in having his contribution overlooked.

A few weeks after scoring *The Wrong Man*, Herrmann undertook a smaller film project that was probably his favorite of the year: a short subject produced by Paramount titled *Williamsburg: The Story of a Patriot*, made to be shown to visitors of that city's historic sites. Set in early 1770s America, it charted a colonial family's growing support of the revolutionary movement, and allowed Herrmann to express his love of eighteenth-century music for the first time in film. (It also anticipates the Georgian idiom of his music for *The Three Worlds of Gulliver* in 1960.)

The score for *Williamsburg* not only adds a tremendous sense of period, but contains some of Herrmann's loveliest music: a spirited Georgian dance for the main title; singing, elegant melodies for strings and woodwind soli; and finally, a set of rousing, canonic variations on "Yankee Doodle" as America moves toward war. Composing it was such a pleasure that Herrmann declined a fee; however, when a pane of glass broke in one of his own eighteenth-century cabinets, Herrmann requested a replacement pane as his compensation. The producers gladly agreed.[64]

If Herrmann's primary medium was now film, the composer was still intrigued by its shadow, television. Herrmann's first two entries into the medium had been auspicious; now, as episodic TV became ingrained in Hollywood production schedules, Herrmann began writing music both for specific broadcasts and for CBS's stock music library (which also used many of his original radio scores, newly recorded).

Much of Herrmann's TV music was for a genre he was associated with only twice in film, the western. The themes for "Have Gun, Will Travel" and "Ethan Allen," as well as scores for episodes of "Have Gun," "Gunsmoke," and "The Virginian," all came from Herrmann between 1956 and 1965. Most imaginative was a series of "suites"—actually collections of cues written for no specific program, under such genre titles as "The Outer Space Suite" and "Western Suite." Masterfully illustrative of Herrmann's technique, their regular use in CBS television programs provided the composer with lucrative royalties for decades. Before long, however, the cues' interpolation into other composers' television scores—a practice within CBS's rights—became so frustrating to Herrmann that, with Fred Steiner, he authored a written complaint to CBS executive Guy Della Cioppa.[65] The letter's history is now forgotten; if it did reach CBS, it made no difference in their scoring practices.

1957 began on a note of both tragedy and promise.

Englishman Gerald Finzi was not only one of Herrmann's favorite modern composers; he had become a dear, if rarely seen, friend with whom Herrmann often corresponded. Finzi's death at age fifty-five from leukemia inspired one of Herrmann's most eloquent letters to the composer's widow.

Dear Mrs. Finzi:

I was deeply moved and shocked to hear from Louis Kaufman of the death of Gerald. Although he and I had very scant opportunities of seeing each other personally, his music was always very close to me, and through it I felt that I was in close touch with him.

The few times we had an opportunity of meeting always gave me the feeling of having seen a friend of long standing, and as though the time lapses were of no importance.

His music has deeply enriched my life, and its uniqueness and lyrical utterance have been a source of inspiration to me. As you know, I have frequently performed as much of Gerald's music as I could, and I wish to assure you that in the future I shall at all times be aware of any opportunity that allows me to play it.

I feel that though Gerald would have gone on to write many more wonderful works, those which he has left behind are a monument to the sensitivity and exquisite perception of a superb musical poet; certainly, "Dies Natalis" and "Farewell to Arms" are imperishable masterpieces of their kind. It is true that a man may die but an artist never does, for the works he leaves behind are the quintessence of his true personality and soul—and so he is always with us, perhaps in greater reality than ever before.

My wife and I shall be coming to London again this spring. I hope that you will afford us the opportunity of visiting you, for I would like ever so much to visit his home and grave. We both join you in your sadness and sorrow and can only assure you of our affectionate understanding and devotion.[66]

At the same time came an apparent offer, from Germany's Heidelberg Opera, to produce *Wuthering Heights*, as well as a request from English music publishers Novello & Co. for a short essay on Elgar, to offer "an American's impressions" on the composer's work. Herrmann's good-spirited reply to Novello's Richard Avenall:

Please forgive the delay in answering your kind letter. It arrived during my most busy season for television and radio work—the Christmas holidays—and I have just arrived at a breathing space. I will do my very, very best to write you a short essay on Elgar. . . . My secretary promises, faithfully, to nag me to death to get it done, and this is a sure guarantee that you will get it.

I have been invited to conduct in Johannesburg, but as of this moment have not quite made up my mind to go. If I do, I hope to do Falstaff there. As of this writing, I am scheduled to be in London for the month of May to do some concerts for the L.S.O. and for the B.B.C.; programs are still vague.

I think you will be pleased to learn that my opera, *Wuthering Heights*, has been accepted, contracts signed and all, by the Heidelberg Opera for presentation in April of 1958. They plan to do it with dual casts in both German and English, and also to transmit it via television. I shall be conducting and am, of course, most excited at the prospect.

Until we meet, Lucille and I join in wishing you a most prosperous, healthful and stimulating New Year. With kindest and most cordial greetings,

Bernard Herrmann[67]

Neither the Johannesburg nor the London visit would take place (the first presumably by choice, the second because Herrmann had been over-confident about an LSO invitation); nor did the Heidelberg offer come through. But in his essay for Novello, Herrmann provided a lasting tribute to his idol, Elgar; the piece also nicely articulates Herrmann's perception of the conductor's role as interpreter:

Throughout my musical career the music of Elgar has been a constant source of joy and inspiration. For in conducting his music, one was left with the feeling of exhilaration and excitement that only great music can bestow. And as a composer, the study of his music has been a deep and satisfying experience, and at the same time has served as a lesson from a superb master. It is from these two points of view that I should like to put down my impressions and observations.

I have always felt that one of the reasons why the bulk of Elgar's music is so little performed outside of England lies in that most mysterious sense that a conductor must have for the flexibility and nuances of tempo which it demands. His works almost seem to perish if a rigid tempo is imposed on them. This seems to me to arise from the essential nervousness, and at the same time the utmost poetic feeling, with which his music is so generously imbued. The tempo variations that arise in the course of an Elgar work are so subtle and elastic that they demand from the conductor and performer an almost complete infatuation with the music. For Elgar's music will not play by itself; merely to supervise it and give it professional routine playing will only serve to immobilize it.

It may well be, in the Enigma Variations, that the problem is more readily understood by conductors of different nationality and musical background owing to the shortened musical form, while his music of extended length, such as the symphonies and Falstaff, has remained a closed book. If conductors would only realize that these works, too, demand the same fluidity that the Enigma demands, there would be no difficulty at all in achieving a more universal audience for Elgar's music . . . .

It is . . . in the Second Symphony that Elgar achieved, perhaps, his most intimate and personal expression, particularly in the first movement, which I feel is unlike any other opening movement of any symphony ever written. For this movement, with its vibrancy and ecstatic flood tide of sound and the great urgencies of its innumerable lyrical themes, brings to my mind the Spring landscapes of Van Gogh and Samuel Palmer. Its embracing of joy and delight, which he wished to capture, have certainly resulted in a most unique and personal vision.

One could go on to describe the transparency and pliant quality of his orchestral technique, and one could devote many pages to the skill and ingenuity of his counterpoint and harmonic subtleties, but to me one of the most splendid things about this music is the pleasure and joy that sweeps over the faces of the players as one of the great climaxes of his music is reached. This certainly is one of the finest tributes that can be paid to a composer.[68]

Herrmann's next film was strikingly similar to *The Wrong Man* in style and tone, if not in quality. *A Hatful of Rain,* based on Michael Vincente Gazzo's successful play and directed by Fred Zinnemann, is the stark tale of a New York drug addict, Johnny Pope (Don Murray), who hides his double life from his wife, Celia (Eva Marie Saint). Although it was producer Buddy Adler who recommended Herrmann for the film, Zinnemann was pleased with the choice;[69] while true collaboration between director and composer was minimal (Zinnemann was out of town during most of the film's scoring), both men later spoke highly of the other's craftmanship and erudition. (Herrmann cited Zinnemann as one of the few directors who understood the function of music in film[70]—a slightly surprising remark, considering Herrmann's contempt for Tiomkin's song-oriented score for *High Noon*.) Unfortunately, the two never worked together again.

Today *A Hatful of Rain* seems very dated, its force lessened by more realistic, better acted versions of the same theme. Its chief attractions now are Joe MacDonald's marble-sharp black-and-white photography and Herrmann's sinister score.

The title music is a prelude in the truest sense: against a shot of Brooklyn skyscrapers, Herrmann constructs his own edifice of mounting tension as a simple, unrelenting ostinato for winds builds to a screeching climax—a musical signature for Johnny Pope's addiction, and a theme that haunts the entire score. (Herrmann's original, more hysterical version of the prelude was rejected by Fox as too frightening.)[71] Rarely does Herrmann shift emphasis from this pervasive motive; his few deviations (like a desolate passage for high strings soli, echoing Celia's monotonous clerical job) are equally despairing. Even Herrmann's coda for the film's overwrought finale is hardly optimistic: as Celia reports her husband's illness, we are left with a mournful sequence for woodwinds, its shift to a major-key resolution for strings coming only under the film's final credit.

Despite his work in Hollywood, Herrmann kept a close eye on comings and goings in the concert world. On October 16, 1957, the Halle Orchestra celebrated its centennial, an occasion that also recognized the key role John Barbirolli had played in the orchestra's regeneration. More than any other English ensemble, the Halle had been Herrmann's staunchest supporter, and its conductor one of Herrmann's closest friends. Herrmann's longtime acquaintance Irving Kolodin, now chief music critic of *Saturday Review*, asked the composer to write a *Review* cover story on the orchestra "to explain just what place the Halle has in musical life, and . . . to deal with the motivating theory—namely that a one-man orchestra can do more for music than a succession of guests."[72] As Kolodin had expected, the piece was no mere valentine from one admiring artist to another, but a skillful overview of twentieth-century conducting and Barbirolli's place as "one of the few remaining poet-conductors":

Today we have hundreds of conductors, many of whom are efficient, professional, and accurate so far as their limited imagination allows, but they can hardly be considered as creative conductors, for in reality they are kapellmeisters, subservient to prevailing musical fads and fashions, and in some cases interested in music only as a means to personal aggrandizement and career. But they can hardly be called co-creators, which is, in reality, what a conductor should be. He is the partner—the artist who, through musical empathy and poetic imagination, is able to enter into the creator's mind and to arrive at an understanding of how that composer's work should be projected. . . .

Today the orchestras of the world are beginning to assume a monochromatic greyness of sound. It is considered unfashionable for orchestras to have resplendent tonal sound—for climaxes to be brilliant and thrilling—for strings to sing—for woodwinds to be the principal actors on the stage. Today all is resolved into a uniformity and conformity of sound that makes the orchestra perform as though it were an organ with one set of registers pulled out for the entire evening . . .

But partly to blame for this paucity of imaginative playing is the fact that present-day orchestras have perpetual guest conductors; they are no longer led—they, in reality, lead, and the guest for a few days must accept overcooked or undercooked playing, as the case may be. For an orchestra without a permanent conductor cannot become a really great orchestra. Someone must give it a style, a tonal palette, and a source of vitality. . . .

Recently I had the pleasure of hearing Barbirolli conduct a performance of Rossini's Overture to "The Italian in Algiers" that so bubbled and effervesced with joyous good humor and witticisms that the audience at Festival Hall chuckled with pleasure. What a rare tribute to a performance. At the same concert, Bartók's Concerto for Orchestra was done as effortlessly as though it were some simple work instead of the formidable one that it is. Then a performance of Brahms' Fourth Symphony that conveyed all the tragedy and autumnal eloquence inherent in this great work. . . . When I complimented Sir John on this splendid performance he replied, "As Hazlitt said of Shakespeare's 'King Lear,' 'it is a great rock of granite, and all we can hope to do is chip off a fragment or two.' "

I was privileged to be present at one of the rehearsals of Vaughan Williams' Eighth Symphony and to sit beside the composer. In the opening set of variations, Sir John made a slight pause between each one, and when it was suggested to the composer that it might be a good idea to incorporate these pauses in the published score, Vaughan Williams replied, "Oh no! Everyone else will make it too long. Sir John does it just right, and that length is impossible to indicate." . . .

In all the years I have known Sir John, I have never heard him refer to himself in relation to a piece of music—never has he said "my interpretation," "my music," but always his comment has been about the joy and excitement of the music at hand. One has the impression that he is rediscovering the music anew and afresh every day of his life.[73]

Shortly after the article was published, Herrmann received a short handwritten note:

My dear Benny,

Your article has just arrived, and I confess I am in tears as I read it. If you really think that of me (and I believe in your complete sincerity) much of what I have had to go through to arrive there will have been worth while.

My love and blessings on you,

Ever,
John[74]

Barbirolli's letter clearly meant more to Herrmann than his check from *Saturday Review*, which he gave intact to his secretary, Elsa Clay.[75]

Ursula Vaughan Williams, a friend of both Herrmann and Barbirolli, provides a final insight on the artistic bond between the two men: "John was to conduct a recording of Ralph's Fantasia on a Theme of Thomas Tallis. 'It must be done in a stone building, not a studio,' said Benny. (The work had been commissioned for a Three Choirs Festival at Gloucester, and had its first performance in the cathedral in 1910.) He suggested the Temple Church, one of London's oldest churches—and there we went for a session that started at midnight to avoid any traffic noises. Coats and bags and thermos flasks were piled round the effigies of Crusader Knights. Benny was there, listening to the balance, listening to the music, and the resulting record is by far the best ever made of the work."[76]

Herrmann himself returned to the concert podium a month later in October, in his second and last concert with the Glendale Symphony, still a pick-up orchestra that on a good day included many of Hollywood's best musicians. In addition to studio regulars like horn players James Decker and Alan Robinson and bassoonist Don Cristlieb, Herrmann was joined by Louis Kaufman, who gave the West Coast premiere of Russell Bennett's Violin Concerto in the Popular Style. Also on the program were Wagner's *Tannhäuser* Overture, Sibelius's Second Symphony, and the beloved *Enigma* Variations of Elgar.

Despite the presence of many of Herrmann's favorite players, rehearsals began disastrously. When told that the third trombonist would be absent for a studio call, Herrmann exploded, berating the unprofessionalism of everyone and threatening to leave. Yet by the evening concert, Herrmann had evolved into the first-rate conductor he always thought himself to be. Lost in the beauty of the Elgar he almost danced on the podium, and throughout the concert his readings were imaginative and finely shaded. It was the finest West Coast concert Herrmann ever gave and, for many of the musicians, the most skillfully conducted *Enigma* Variations they had ever heard.[77]

Nevertheless, Herrmann's conducting career was virtually at an end. His countless rows with orchestra heads and musicians had taken their toll, coupled with Herrmann's erratic baton technique and predilection for slow, sometimes ponderous playing. But if his inability to find concert work would inspire great bitterness in later years, Herrmann still had many of his finest scoring achievements before him—none greater than his fourth collaboration with Hitchcock.

# ELEVEN

[It is a story] of endless yearning, the bliss and wretchedness of love, world, power . . . loyalty and friendship all blown away like an insubstantial dream; one thing alone left living—longing, longing unquenchable . . . one sole redemption—death, surcease, a sleep without wakening.

*Richard Wagner, Notes to* Tristan and Isolde

*Vertigo* is Alfred Hitchcock's most uncompromising film, and Bernard Herrmann's fullest realization of his favorite dramatic themes: romantic obsession, isolation, and the ultimate release of death. In Hitchcock's poetic vision, "human life, relationships, individual identity . . . become a quicksand, unstable, constantly shifting, into which we may sink at any step in any direction"[1]—an emotional trap that Herrmann's score makes all the more inviting, drawing us into the troubled mind of Scottie Ferguson (James Stewart) through depthless pools of color and shadow; for, despite the importance of lyrical fragments in Herrmann's score, it is the shifting hues of orchestration that give much of this score its tension and tragic grandeur.

If both the film and its music seem operatic in their urgent romanticism, it is hardly coincidental. *Vertigo*'s source, *D'Entre les Morts* by Pierre Boileau and Thomas Narcejac, was a modern version of the Tristan myth on which Wagner based his great work. Hitchcock's free adaptation of the French novel (reset in a ghostly, poeticized San Francisco) is complex, implausible, and spellbinding: retired from the police force after an attack of acrophobia (or vertigo), Scottie Ferguson is hired by his college friend Gavin Elster to follow Elster's wife, Madeleine (Kim Novak), who is apparently convinced she is the reincarnation of a dead Spanish ancestor, Carlotta Valdez. Scottie becomes obsessed with Madeleine, and, despite her insistence that she is destined to die, pursuer and pursued fall in love. Her prophecy is seemingly fulfilled: after Scottie takes her to the Spanish mission she has seen in a dream, Madeleine falls to her death from the church's bell tower, Scottie's vertigo preventing him from stopping her.

Months later Scottie meets Judy Barton, a young woman who except in dress and manner is Madeleine's double. Unknown to Scottie, Judy *is* Madeleine—or rather the girl who posed as Madeleine after Elster murdered his actual wife. Still in love with Scottie, Judy allows him to transform her into his fantasy Madeleine—until Scottie recognizes Judy's necklace as Madeleine's. Forcing Judy to return with him to the mission, Scottie pieces the crime together and overcomes his vertigo; but as Judy pleads for forgiveness, a wraithlike figure appears in the tower's shadows, and Judy tumbles to her death, this time for real. The intruder, a nun, rings the tower bell in mourning as Scottie gazes helplessly over the building's precipice, his Madeleine killed a second time.

*Vertigo* has been seen as a mirror of Hitchcock's own insecurities and his desire to manipulate the beautiful women he loved and feared.[2] It was Herrmann's own favorite of his Hitchcock collaborations, although he felt Hitch had made two mistakes: "They should never have made it in San Francisco, and not with Jimmy Stewart. . . . I don't believe that he would be that wild about any woman. It should have been an actor like Charles Boyer. It should have been left in New Orleans, or in a hot, sultry climate. When I wrote the picture, I thought of that."[3]

During preproduction meetings with Herrmann and cameraman Robert Burks, Hitchcock was extremely precise about the impressionistic tone he wanted, citing Vermeer paintings to Burks and discussing with Herrmann which sequences should feature music without dialogue. Hitchcock even located the original music for a 1920 stage production of James Barrie's *Mary Rose*, which he had seen in London at age twenty-one, a score that "used very effectively a background sound effect, probably a record, off stage, of eerie music, angels singing and low moaning wind."[4]

Hitchcock's sound and music notes were more specific than ever; but as usual, the directions were flexible. Hitchcock planned on using more music than in his previous films. For the "recognition" scene in which Scottie finally embraces Judy as Madeleine, Hitchcock writes: "when [Judy] emerges and we go into the love scene we should let all traffic noises fade, because Mr. Herrmann may have something to say here." Similarly, Hitchcock concludes his lengthy notes on the film's rooftop prologue with the words, "All of this will naturally depend upon what music Mr. Herrmann puts over this sequence."[5]

*Vertigo's* score, like Burks's cinematography, is filled with its own allusions, mainly to Wagner's *Tristan* and the doomed passion of its "Liebestod" (a favorite piece of Herrmann). But its sensuous orchestration is uniquely Herrmann's, infusing his elusive theme for Madeleine and his long, ostinato-based sequences for Scottie's pursuits with an urgent poignancy and hypnotic allure. Herrmann's prelude (recalled once in miniature, as Judy undergoes her cosmetic transformation into Madeleine) is a brilliant synthesis of the score's themes and its most important instrumental colors. Like artist Saul Bass's swirling geometric patterns, Herrmann's music finds beauty in strangeness and movement: the fixated woodwind ostinato; the eerie precision of solo harp (our introduction to Carlotta); Herrmann's sweeping love theme that shatters into a muted brass dissonance.

Titles and music segue into a churning moto perpetuo for strings and the film's first, confusing image, of a horizontal gray bar; a hand grabs it—a ladder rung—as our perspective is restored. The man, a criminal, is being chased across the rooftops of San Francisco by Scottie and a policeman, but it is the latter who falls to his death, his screams echoed in Herrmann's crashing chords for timpani and low brass (a motive of emotional devastation that recurs after each death). This sequence also contains the film's most innovative blend of image and music, to simulate Scottie's vertigo: as Ferguson looks down from his hold on the building's edge, the camera dollies forward as its lens backtracks, creating a sense of simultaneous forward and backward movement. On the soundtrack, a crossfire of overlapping harp glissandos opens a bottomless pit beneath Scottie's feet, the harps' spaciousness echoed in Herrmann's tonal contrasts of high wind triads and low brass dissonances.

A similar contrast of timbre distinguishes Carlotta's theme, a seductive habanera recalling the spirit of the dead woman and the ghosts of the old San Francisco she represents. Again Herrmann's material is almost childishly simple: a repeating syncopated rhythm for harp against a rising-and-falling chromatic pattern for strings; yet together the delicacy of the orchestration (whispering low woodwinds, veiled string harmonics) and the rhythmic ostinato create a remarkable sense of mystery and temporal imbalance. (The effect recalls a remark by poet Edith Sitwell: "Rhythm is one of the principal translators between dream and reality. Rhythm might be described as, to the world of sound, what light is to the world of sight. It shapes and gives meaning.")[6]

*Vertigo's* collision of fantasy and reality climaxes with Judy's physical transformation into Madeleine, what Herrmann called "the recognition scene." Using heightened, symbolic colors (luminous greens for the "evergreen, ever-living" Madeleine, softer lavenders for the suppressed Judy) and Herrmann's paraphrase of the "Liebestod" instead of dialogue ("We'll just have the camera and you," Hitch told Herrmann),[7] the five-minute sequence is perhaps cinema's most powerful evocation of romantic longing. Herrmann's echo of Wagner is allusive, not plagiaristic, using (in Wagner's apt, emotive words) "one long succession of linked phrases to let that insatiable longing swell forth from the first timidest avowal to sweetest protraction, through hopes and fears, laments and desires, bliss and torment, to the mightiest forward-pressing, the most powerful effort to find the breach that will open out to the infinitely craving heart the path into the sea of love's endless delight."[8]

In the first of many clashes over the scoring of a Hitchcock film, Paramount tried to persuade the director to include an exploitable pop theme in the movie, hiring Jay Livingstone and Ray Evans to write a song using Vertigo's enigmatic title.[9] Fortunately Hitchcock rejected the idea and used only Herrmann's music in the film. (The score's love theme was later arranged by Jeff Alexander and lyricist Larry Orenstein into a popular song that proved anything but.)[10]

After winning this battle, Herrmann was forced to admit defeat on another front. Because of a musicians' union strike, unresolved until late 1958, the Vertigo score could not be recorded in America. Instead it was recorded in Vienna by English conductor Muir Mathieson, much to the resentment of Herrmann, who later criticized Mathieson's performance as sloppy and error ridden.[11] At the time, however, producer Herbert Coleman wrote the following to Vienna music assistant Max Kimental: "Mr. Hitchcock and Mr. Herrmann, the composer, are very happy with the result. . . . You remember the commotion about the heavy bowing sound from the strings? Well, Mr. Herrmann said this was the effect he was after and is difficult to get here or in England because of the different techniques."[12]

The accomplishment and uniqueness of the film were well ahead of its time (though it did enjoy a lengthy run in France). Most critics dismissed it as a disorganized, if beautifully shot, failure ("another Hitchcock-and-bull story," Time sneered).[13] "We liked it," Herrmann told a reporter in 1961, "but even in the States, people thought [Vertigo] was a backache or something."[14]

Vertigo was not only the high point of Herrmann's work with Hitchcock; it was also the first in a series of film and TV scores that marked, arguably, Herrmann's most prolific and inventive period, from 1958 to 1963. While his Hitchcock scores of this time (North by Northwest and Psycho) would be his best known, his concurrent work, especially with American special effects wizard Ray Harryhausen, was no less distinguished.

By 1958, Hollywood had produced several great original fantasy scores, most notably Steiner's *King Kong* (1933) and Franz Waxman's *The Bride of Frankenstein* (1935). Miklós Rózsa's score for *The Thief of Bagdad* (U.K., 1940) was also among the genre's best. Herrmann's own entries in fantasy had been surprisingly few, considering his taste for the bizarre and supernatural; but in 1958, with Harryhausen's *The Seventh Voyage of Sinbad*, the tide turned dramatically and continued for several years, with scores for *Journey to the Center of the Earth, The Three Worlds of Gulliver, Mysterious Island, Jason and the Argonauts*, and television's "Twilight Zone."

It was Harryhausen producer Charles Schneer who selected Herrmann for *Sinbad* in late 1957 (Harryhausen's own first two choices being Steiner and Rózsa).[15] As a teenager Schneer had listened in awe to CBS's "Columbia Workshop," in which Herrmann played so key a role:

I told myself, if someday I produce a movie, this is the man I want to use. It took me twenty years. Professionally it was one of the most challenging and exciting relationships I've ever had.

I first met Herrmann at the Napoli Restaurant in Hollywood to ask him to score *Sinbad*. He didn't want to do it, but then every answer of his to a question began with "no"; you'd have to convince him to do something he really wanted to do all along. Harryhausen and I then showed him the film, at a screening room at Columbia that had three seats. It was a black-and-white print of the film—in those days, printing color rushes was very expensive—and the muddiness of the black-and-white print gave no indication of the brilliance of the movie's color.

Herrmann still didn't want to do it. He said, "It's not for me, it's something I've never done, I don't want to do it." After we had known each other for about six months, he finally consented to do it.[16]

Herrmann's true interest in the film is clear in *Sinbad*'s score, one of his most exciting and orchestrally ingenious. "I worked with a conventional sized orchestra," he later wrote, "augmented by a large percussion section. The music I composed had to reflect a purity and simplicity that could be easily assimilated to the nature of the fantasy being viewed. By characterizing the various creatures with unusual instrument combinations . . . and by composing motifs for all the major characters and actions, I feel I was able to envelop the entire movie in a shroud of mystical innocence."[17]

Herrmann's clearest antecedent here is Rimsky-Korsakov's *Scheherazade*, the definitive Arabian Nights narrative for orchestra that Hollywood musicians had long used for inspiration or outright theft. Herrmann's score is much more: its derivations are formal, its specific material unmistakably Herrmann's own. Orchestral timbre is used to create both mood and a sense of scale, a world in which evil is characterized by low, "heavy" instruments and in which heroism and beauty are depicted through light or traditionally balanced textures.

The heroic aspect of Sinbad's adventures—and the film's sense of escapist fun—is quickly established in Herrmann's overture, which shifts from an emphatic three-chord opening for brass and orchestra to a mysterious Arabesque. (Herrmann would reuse this second theme, slightly altered, as *Marnie*'s love theme six years later; both versions are surprisingly similar to the main theme of Leonard Rosenman's 1957 score for *Rebel Without a Cause*.) The film's first scene finds Herrmann at his most subtle, creating tension and menace through the queasy repetition of a simple string chromatic as Sinbad's ship sails through a dense fog. A gradual crescendo and inversion of the figure, with eerie high-strings harmonics, give the scene its basis in an inescapable reality—the quality that gives the best fantasies their capacity to disturb.

Strings also provide the exotic, Rimskian theme for Princess Parisa (Kathryn Crosby), Sinbad's fiancée. Just as the color of violas, cellos, and basses conveys the first scene's palpable mystery, Herrmann's motive for violins gives the princess an ethereal grace and beauty (qualities less evident in Crosby's likable but earthy performance).

But it is Herrmann's menagerie of musical monsters that offers *Sinbad*'s most thrilling moments. Herrmann gives Harryhausen's creatures a sense of gigantic scale through the density of his orchestration: the earth-shaking timpani rolls, cymbal crashes, and grunting brass of the Cyclops; the thumping timpani and bass crawl of the dragon. Elsewhere Herrmann uses strange instrumental juxtapositions for droll effect, as in the cobra woman's dance, which pits shrieking piccolos, brass, and glockenspiel against the seductiveness of low descending woodwinds, or the hatching of the giant birds, a chirping wind and bells figure that grows to encompass low brass and harp as the creatures emerge. Best known is Herrmann's dazzling "Duel with the Skeleton," a diabolically propulsive scherzo for low brass, trumpets, castanets, and xylophone (an instrument historically associated with skeletons, for obvious reasons). Here, Herrmann rarely "catches" the visual action, but creates a dynamic sense of forward motion, giving Harryhausen's creation a musical frame of heightened drama and wit.

Herrmann's own comments on the score to Harryhausen and Schneer were surprisingly terse and negative.[18] The reason, both men felt, had nothing to do with the music; like *Vertigo, Sinbad* was recorded without Herrmann's participation (this time in Germany, with the Graunke Orchestra) because of the musicians' strike. (Herrmann's belief that Schneer was excessively tight with production and music budgets helped to erode their relationship over the next six years.)

Herrmann's last score that year was, like the film itself, his least interesting. By the time Norman Mailer's war novel *The Naked and the Dead* reached the screen in 1958, Mailer's strong prose and thematic ambiguities had been replaced by screenwriters Dennis and Terry Sanders with censor-pleasing clichés and flat characterizations. Despite Raoul Walsh's solid direction, the film was a standard World War II programmer that only hastened RKO's closure (by the time the film was released, the studio was no longer in existence).

Herrmann's cynically militaristic score creates an underpinning of hellish brutality that the film scarcely reflects. Written almost entirely for low instruments, it rarely speaks louder than a threatening murmur (except in the frenzied title prelude for timpani and brass, which endlessly repeats the same hysterical figure). Attempts to add dimension to the film's shallow characters are few: a questioning three-note figure for muted brass mirrors the cold, enigmatic General Cummings (Raymond Massey), but Herrmann is given virtually nothing to respond to.

Herrmann was now forty-seven years old, active in film, more financially successful than ever, but increasingly dissatisfied. His frustrations over conducting and the opera were further exacerbated by the rise of new, young screen composers like Goldsmith, Rosenman, and Henry Mancini. Song-oriented scores were increasingly prevalent. A handful of successful years lay ahead for Herrmann, but he was already anticipating an unhappy future.

The concert world was also changing. In Europe, "new music" referred almost exclusively to modernism, a school that Herrmann mostly rejected as emotionally hollow. Another symbol of music's ticking clock was the death of Vaughan Williams on August 6, 1958. His passing, like that of Ives four years earlier, prompted nostalgic reflection for Herrmann—on his New York childhood, and his first discovery of the Englishman's works in the 58th Street Music Library. His remembrances took the form of an article, this time for London's *Musical Times*:

In reading the warm and affectionate tributes paid to the late Vaughan Williams by his many friends, I began to think about the personal enrichment that his great art had brought to my musical life and about the six bars of music from the original version of the slow movement of his London Symphony. . . .

When I first began to perform the work, the only set of parts and score available to New York was that of the first version. The slow movement at that time possessed six remarkable bars at the letter K, which later the composer omitted, and I wish to say a few words here about those bars. It has always been my intense reaction, and of course a subjective one, that these bars were one of the most original poetic moments in the entire Symphony. It is at this moment as though, when the hush and quietness have settled over Bloomsbury of a November twilight, that a damp drizzle of rain slowly falls, and it is this descending chromatic ponticello of the violins that so graphically depicts it.

Years later this set of parts was withdrawn by the New York agents and a new set of the revised version of the Symphony was sent out with, alas, these magical six bars omitted. On one occasion I spoke to Vaughan Williams about these bars and expressed my deep regret about their deletion. He replied that he had revised this work three times—"Oh, it's much too long, much too long, and there was some horrid modern music in the middle—awful stuff. I cut that out—couldn't stand it." And that was as far as I could ever get with him to discuss the possibility of restoring those bars.

I, for one, shall always regret this deletion, for it remains in my memory as one of the miraculous moments in music, and its absence in the present version is felt like the absence of a dear, departed friend. It will always be an enigma to me why these bars were removed, for in their magic and beauty they had caught something of a London which Whistler captured in his Nocturnes.[19]

Herrmann returned to the present with another stunning film score. *North by Northwest*, Hitchcock's grand summation of every "wrong man" thriller, reunited the talents of Herrmann, Robert Burks, and editor George Tomasini for what became Hitchcock's most entertaining blend of sophisticated humor and suspense. Cary Grant, who had served as the director's cinematic alter ego in three earlier films, had one of his best roles, as Roger Thornhill, a Madison Avenue executive caught in a deadly espionage game of cat-and-mouse; and Hitchcock's visual mastery was never more apparent than in his rousing Mount Rushmore climax, and in the battle between Grant and a lone, gun-blazing crop duster. Much has been written about the film and Herrmann's crackling score; less well known is an equally important nonmusical contribution by the composer, made long before the film's shooting, in 1957.

"It was Benny who, as my friend and acquaintance, once said to me,

'I've got to get you and Hitch together. I think you would hit it off very well,' " recalled screenwriter Ernest Lehman. "Before too long, I found myself invited to lunch in Hitchcock's office at Paramount, with Benny joining us, and Hitch and I *did* hit it off well. Within a year, Hitchcock was asking MGM, to whom I was under contract, to assign me to Hitch's next project [*The Wreck of the Mary Deare*]. But instead we abandoned that film, and I wrote *North by Northwest*." To Lehman, Herrmann's seesaws between genius and genius temperament added up to a fascinating character study: "Benny was *very* likable, very irritable, exceedingly iconoclastic, had little use for Hollywood ways, loved to ruffle feathers, to speak with anger in his voice, and above all, be provocative. I suspect, however, that he was a highly gifted, somewhat unappreciated pussycat."[20]

For *North by Northwest*, the "pussycat" voiced himself with a roar— quite literally, from the precredits growl of Leo the Lion (integrated into the score's opening bars to create, in Christopher Palmer's words, "a unique musical feeling of *menace*")[21] to the triumphant orchestral finale that carries Roger Thornhill from the brink of Mount Rushmore to the arms of heroine Eve Kendall (Eva Marie Saint). Best remembered (and most imitated) is Herrmann's dazzling, dizzying overture, described by the composer as "a kaleidoscopic orchestral fandango designed to kick off the exciting rout which follows."[22] Using furious South American rhythms of alternating 3/4 and 6/8, Herrmann bandies instrumental voices back and forth in a breathless evocation of "the crazy dance about to take place between Cary Grant and the world."[23] (MGM originally wanted conventional, Gershwinesque city music for the opening—one of several ill-advised proposals that included Sammy Cahn's "hit theme" for the film, "The Man on Lincoln's Nose.")[24] Deft variations of the fandango recur throughout the film like a terpsichorean chorus, most thrillingly in the Mount Rushmore climax, a cue Herrmann drolly titled "On the Rocks."[25]

Thornhill's romance with the mysterious Eve allows Herrmann some musical breath catching, as he introduces a lyrical duet for oboe and clarinet over gently propulsive string rhythms (suggesting the steady cadence of train travel), in a sequence reminiscent of the similarly constructed first movement of Shostakovitch's Fifth Symphony. (Herrmann also quotes from his own *White Witch Doctor* score, recalling the lovely "Nocturne" for the love duet's bridge section.)

For the film's most harrowing set piece, the crop duster scene, Herrmann does something equally dramatic: he remains silent. If Hitchcock was relatively unsophisticated about music, his use of sound was often brilliant, as it is here. Thornhill waits by a quiet, empty roadway for the nonexistent "George Kaplan"; suddenly the sequences's languid rhythm is shattered by the swooping plane and its staccato gunfire. As Thornhill runs into a dense cornfield, only the sounds of the approaching duster and the rustling brush are heard, the absence of scoring thus reinforcing Hitchcock's sense of heightened reality. Only at the sequence's climax, the crop duster's explosive crash into a flammable truck, does music begin—an emotional release after its absence for so many minutes. "If you're a painter, it doesn't mean that you can't use black—and that is a sound: black," Herrmann said in 1975.[26] The success of the (non)scoring technique was not lost on Hitchcock, who encouraged Herrmann to use the effects-as-music device four years later more extensively with *The Birds*.

To no one's surprise, *North by Northwest* was Hitchcock's greatest popular and critical success to date. The director wasted no time in starting his next project—but for Herrmann, there would be two film scores and his finest television works in the interim.

Four years after Disney's *20,000 Leagues Under the Sea*, Fox brought Jules Verne back to movie houses with *Journey to the Center of the Earth*, an old-fashioned, entertaining adventure yarn starring James Mason and Pat Boone. Alfred Newman wisely chose Herrmann to provide what the film's comic-book narrative needed most: a measure of credibility. Again, Herrmann responded on his own wondrously inventive terms: "I decided to evoke the mood and feeling of inner Earth by using only instruments played in low registers. Eliminating all strings, I utilized an orchestra of woodwinds and brass, with a large percussion section and many harps. But the truly unique feature of this score is the inclusion of five organs, one large Cathedral and four electronic. These organs were used in many adroit ways to suggest ascent and descent, as well as the mystery of Atlantis."[27]

As Herrmann's self-appreciative notes suggest, the score is pure, malevolent color, bringing a power and diversity to the film's good-naturedly shoddy visuals. Thematic material is stripped to the bone (as it increasingly would be in Herrmann scores): Herrmann's favorite two-note semitone device dominates much of the film's score. His title prelude captures this blend of imposing strength and impressionistic wonder with mighty timpani crashes (imitating the volcanic explosions onscreen), fortress-tall brass declarations, and thick, sinister organ chords, which plunge deeper and deeper in their respective registers until they hit orchestral bottom.

"I wanted to create an atmosphere with absolutely no human contact," Herrmann said in 1975. "This film had no emotion, only terror."[28]

For *Journey's* serial-style climax, in which our heroes are threatened by Titan-sized lizards, Herrmann revives the grotesque whine of the medieval serpent (again played by Don Cristlieb), which in this context seems a droll Herrmann comment on the less-than-convincing fleet of cosmetically altered garden chameleons. Strings make a fleeting appearance in Herrmann's interpolation of one of the song score's loveliest themes, James Van Heusen's melody for Robert Burns's "My Love is Like a Red, Red Rose" (sung here by Boone). A caressing string fragment of the theme recalls the Edinburgh the travelers have left, and gives hints of dimension to *Journey's* superficial romance between Alec McEwen (Boone) and Professor Lindenbrook's daughter, Jenny (Diane Baker).

Enhancing the richly textured score was Fox's stereo mix of the soundtrack ("I had speakers all over the place," Herrmann recalled),[29] which preserved every lush harp glissando and eerie vibraphone reverberation (a particularly apt color for the echoing caverns at the Earth's core).

Considering the variety and excellence of his other work in this period, Herrmann's score for the Fox film *Blue Denim* is a pardonable aberration. A turgid teen pregnancy drama starring Carol Lynley and Brandon de Wilde, it was directed by Herrmann's friend Philip Dunne, who later confessed he didn't know why Herrmann agreed to score the film.[30] Herrmann's music is sophisticated, dramatic—and surprisingly heavy-handed in its lush romantic echoes of *Vertigo* for a story of two immature teens who Should Have Known Better. One cue, a self-consciously comic accompaniment to a poker game, was dropped by Dunne; Herrmann, who never wasted a note, reused it as the theme for an Alfred Hitchcock TV episode, "Nothing Happens in Linvale."[31]

Far superior was Herrmann's work for another medium, in a genre with which he was far more comfortable. On October 2, 1959, the pilot episode of "The Twilight Zone," an anthology series created and written by Rod Serling, aired on CBS.

The secret of Serling's "fifth dimension, beyond that which is known to man," was insight, perceptions of the human experience, told through allegories, fables, and nightmares. In its five-year, 156-episode run, "The Twilight Zone" eschewed television's usual predictability in favor of the ironic and unexpected. Usually Serling and his collaborators succeeded, producing a series of imagination, suspense, and surprising moral gravity.

No television vehicle was better suited to Bernard Herrmann's own vision of the fantastic and the tragic. Although his involvement with the series was limited mainly to its first season, Herrmann would play a substantial role in bringing its special universe to life, painting musical portraits of great impressionistic beauty, horror, and poignance.[32]

Herrmann's work on the series began early in 1959, when producer William Self and director Robert Stevens mounted "Twilight Zone"'s impressive pilot. "Where Is Everybody?" was the first of many studies by Serling of a basic fear, isolation, as amnesia victim Mike Ferris (Earl Holliman) finds himself in a deserted town devoid of people—only to learn that his experience was actually a nightmare, suffered while inside an isolation booth in rehearsal for a U.S. space flight.

As in radio, Herrmann's scoring time was limited to a few days (a restriction he accepted in television but rarely in film); nevertheless, the results were superb. Serling's theme of alienation struck of chord with the composer. Like most subsequent scores for the series, Herrmann's music is largely atmospheric, its material derived almost entirely from the questioning three-note device for muted brass heard at the opening. (This simple, eerie fragment became one of CBS's most-used pieces of cue music, particularly on later "Twilight Zone" episodes.) What changes the music undergoes are mainly orchestral, yet through subtle shifts in color a sense of tension is carefully enforced. By the story's end, the unanswered question of Herrmann's opening remains unresolved (giving this rather conventional episode some sense of ambiguity), but in the transference of the theme from brass and vibraphone to the warmer color of strings, an emotional, if not musical, resolution is reached.

Not surprisingly, both CBS music head Lud Gluskin and Buck Houghton, producer of "Twilight Zone"'s first three seasons, were eager for Herrmann to score more episodes. Recalled Houghton:

Bernard was a cross, wonderfully pleasant man, which made him a pleasure to work with, because he was *not* mealy-mouthed. He went away from a picture and said, "Don't worry, I'll fix it!" He looked upon every picture as a cripple that needed his fine hand to make it work better—and he *did* improve most everything he did. He had very, very strong opinions and fought very aggressively for things that he felt, and I fought very aggressively for things that I felt. He resigned from "Twilight Zone" several times when we came to disagreements!

One fun thing about Herrmann was that when you went to the scoring session you never knew what set of musicians you were going to see. You'd walk on the stage, and there would be an alliance of instruments you'd never heard of in your life. And every time was a very agreeable surprise, because there was nothing conventional about Herrmann at all. I don't think he undertook the show to be bizarre, but "Twilight Zone" was bizarre in its own way, and Bernard seemed to love it. It gave him the opportunity to try and do things outside the norm, just as Hitchcock gave him the opportunity to do things he couldn't do otherwise. And Bernard contributed a great deal to the total effect.[33]

Like "Where Is Everybody?" Serling's next teleplay, "The Lonely," dealt with isolation. Here, the situation is not a surreal nightmare but a moving character study. Convict James Corry (Jack Warden) knows the location of his deserted prison: it is a distant, barren asteroid where he serves a life sentence for killing in self-defense. Corry's existence changes with the arrival of Alicia (Jean Marsh), a lovely, seemingly human robot left as a companion for Corry by a visiting supply officer. Suspicious at first of his companion, Corry gradually falls in love with Alicia. Eleven months later, the supply ship returns with the news that Corry has been pardoned; they are to leave for Earth immediately— but the ship is too heavy to bring Alicia. To convince Corry that Alicia is not human, the supply chief shoots the replicant; her face mechanisms explode as her body lies on the empty sand. Corry, now free, is again alone.

"There were two things you had to confirm rather quickly," Houghton said; "number one, how strange the setting was, and number two, that this was a love story."[34] Herrmann's score establishes both elements in its first minutes; unlike "Where Is Everybody?" his music employs several motivic devices that develop throughout the drama. His instrumentation is small and strange: brass, winds, organ, vibraphone, and percussion are heard at the drama's opening, sensuous yet alien. Eerie, reverbatory vibraphone chords echo above a somnolent harp, reflecting the empty desert around Corry and the prisoner's crushed spirit. Softly, unobtrusively, a low, unchanging pedal tone on organ emerges under the duet, joined by languid brass chords whispering a dissonant lament of despair. The calm becomes cacophony as the supply ship lands, bringing its mysterious cargo; a plaintive four-note trumpet motive identifies its contents, in Herrmann's first allusion to Alicia.

The couple's love is finally acknowledged in "The Stars," one of Herrmann's loveliest evocations of the mystical beauty of the heavens, suggesting in its elemental richness the transcendentalism of Ives. As Corry points out the constellations to Alicia under an alien sky, Herrmann introduces a prismatic harp arpeggio; shimmering vibraphone colors fall like crystals of light; a hushed, muted brass chorale is added, and finally a soaring organ solo rises ethereally above the ensemble. (Throughout the piece, the dynamic level remains a glowing mezzo-piano.)

The lover's relationship ends with the gun blast of Allenby, the supply officer; as Alicia's mechanisms explode Herrmann strikes with equally ugly brass dissonances, harp and vibraphone sadly mimicking Alicia's voice, which repeats Corry's name like a broken record. As Corry leaves the wrecked figure, Herrmann recalls the dead chords of the story's opening, now especially poignant as we see the body of Alicia, forgotten and alone.

Herrmann's third "Twilight Zone" episode offered the fullest realization of Serling's recurring theme of emotional longing. "Walking Distance" is generally considered the series' high point, the best example of Serling's poetic style. It also inspired Herrmann's most moving score for television, a score that ranks with his best work for any medium.

The story is both semiautobiographical and universal in its portrait of a harried executive's "errant wish" to reexperience his fondly remembered childhood. Gig Young (whose own life ended in suicide) starred as Martin Sloane, the businessman who returns to his boyhood town of Homewood, to find it unchanged after twenty-five years. His enchantment turns to disbelief, however, when he sees a boy carving his name on a merry-go-round: it is Martin Sloane at age twelve; the year is 1934. Rejected by his unbelieving parents, Sloane searches for his boyhood self to tell him how special this time of his life will be, that it will never come again. Frightened by the strange, obsessed man, young Martin falls from the merry-go-round, twisting his leg. As the elder Martin sits alone by the silent carousel, his father—now convinced of his identity—approaches him to explain "there's only one summer to each customer": he must return to his own time. Martin reluctantly agrees, leaving Homewood with a limp he acquired in a childhood fall from a merry-go-round.

Serling's affection for the symbolic Homewood was shared by his collaborators. Robert Stevens's direction is subtle and eloquent, as is George Clemens's dreamlike camera work. But none felt the story's message more deeply than Herrmann, whose longing for a similarly romanticized childhood and the beauty of the past grew stronger with each year. Unlike his previous "Twilight Zone" scores, Herrmann's orchestration here is neither strange nor fantastic; employing strings and celeste, it is warm, immediate, and human. (Its nearly pure-strings instrumentation makes it a fascinating companion piece to 1960's *Psycho*. Together they demonstrate Herrmann's virtuosity in creating distinct psychological attitudes through limited means.)

As with "The Lonely," Herrmann's music unfolds in narrative fashion, from the sighing phrase that echoes Martin's wish to return home to a more expansive, lyrical theme for violas and cellos as he recalls the simple pleasures of his youth. A distantly heard valse wafts through the score like an elusive breeze, recalling "the magic of a band concert on a summer night" (a fragment of this cameolike melody can be heard in *The Ghost and Mrs. Muir*). Herrmann recalls this motive as twelve-year-old Martin falls from the carousel; here, however, it is almost unrecognizable in its brutal anguish.

Most poignant is the long musical sequence that follows Martin's accident. As the boy is gently carried away, each child silently climbs off the merry-go-round and follows as if hypnotized. Clemens's lighting isolates Sloane from this eerie procession, contrasting the drama's clash of reality and fantasy in a single shot. It is a powerful moment of poetic beauty and sadness, reinforced in an elegiac requiem for violas and cellos that suggests A. E. Housman, one of Herrmann's favorite poets:

> That is the land of lost content,
> I see it shining plain,
> The happy highways where I went
> And cannot come again.[35]

It also recalls (in style, not theme) one of Herrmann's favorite pieces of film music: Walton's passacaglia for Falstaff's death in Olivier's *Henry V*.

According to Buck Houghton, Herrmann's original scoring of Martin's dialogue with his father differed from the sequence finally used: "Herrmann had a lovely melody going behind the dialogue. I said, 'Bernard, we just can't use it—it's competing.' 'WELL!' he snarled, and stormed out. Eventually he came back and said, 'Most producers don't know what they're doing, and you're no different!' "[36] The final scoring of the scene ranks with Herrmann's most sensitive dialogue music in *Muir* and *Vertigo*, delicately weaving its thematic strands around—but never over—Serling's words.

A year later, after two projects with Hitchcock, Herrmann returned to score another of "Twilight Zone"'s best episodes. In "Eye of the Beholder," Serling tackled another brand of alienation: social conformity, and the price paid by those who resist. Probably the most famous program in the series, it was certainly the most intricately crafted, from the meticulous choreography of its camera work to its scoring.

Serling's teleplay is deliberately ambiguous as to time and place. A hospital patient awaits the removal of the bandages that conceal her deformed face; Douglas Heyes's direction and George Clemens's photography make her limited point of view ours as doctors and nurses move in and out of frame, their faces obscured by lighting or blocking sleight-of-hand. Finally the bandages are removed: the "hideous" woman is beautiful, while the doctors and other members of this conformist state are revealed to be monstrous, piglike mutations.

Filming the drama so that its twist ending would not be obvious posed a special challenge for Heyes and Clemens; scoring posed another. "Bernard realized something needed to tell you there was a trap door at the end of the hallway," Houghton observed.[37] His solution was particularly apt for the anticonformity theme: he based his sparse score on an unvarying ostinato. Harp and vibraphone intone repeated chromatic fragments with disturbing seductiveness; distant muted brass rise and fall without resolution. (Only one motivelike device, a sinister pattern for low brass, is used, first inferentially, then explicitly, to identify the grotesque pig-men.) The resulting score is hypnotic, chilling, and oddly beautiful— a dichotomy that reflects Serling's advocacy of social diversity.

Herrmann's last three scores for the series, written in the summers of 1962 and 1963, were similarly atmospheric, using evocative color blends rather than developed musical ideas to achieve their dramatic ends. Richard Matheson's "Little Girl Lost," directed by ex–Mercury Theatre actor Paul Stewart, was quintessential "Twilight Zone" in its drama of ordinary people fighting the supernatural. Reworked twenty years later as the film *Poltergeist*, Matheson's modest original concerns a little girl who falls out of bed—and into the fourth dimension.

Again, the story's supernatural element was implied more than visualized. " 'Little Girl Lost' runs the danger of being a little incomprehensible," Houghton later said. "The actors are trying to find a little girl in the fourth dimension—and since they don't say anything about it, who's speaking for the odd things going on?"[38] Herrmann's instrumentation offers a solution: flutes, oboe, bass clarinet, and solo viola evoke the weirdness and beauty of the alien world, augmented by vibraphone and percussion in the story's last moments. The simplest of Herrmann's "Twilight Zone" scores in its impressionistic use of harp arpeggios and shifting flute patterns, its fluid textures (including a plaintive viola solo that deliberately recalls *Wuthering Heights*' lost Cathy)[39] are both seductive and chilling. ("Little Girl Lost" was the only "Twilight Zone" episode to give Herrmann main title credit, an indication of Houghton's delight with the score.)

By the series' last season in 1963, William Froug was producing. "I would call Beenie up and say, 'Would you do a "Twilight Zone"?' " Froug recalled. "The typical Beenie answer would be, 'For you, Frougie, of course,' The implication was, not for anybody else, but I'll do you a favor! You had to laugh." Like Houghton, Froug attended Herrmann's recording sessions, as colorful as the music being performed: "Benny would snap his baton and say, 'Pick up your goddamn feet over there!' And more than once I saw the musicians looking over at each other, quietly smiling."[40]

"Living Doll," the purest horror story of the series, allowed Herrmann to respond to the series' most nightmarish elements. Jerry Sohl's teleplay pits cruel stepfather Erich Streator (Telly Savalas) against a lethal toy doll, who threatens to kill Erich whenever he alone is in earshot. Herrmann's miniature ensemble takes musical sides on the battle, juxtaposing a menacing device for solo bass clarinet against a macabre, dissonant waltz for harp and vibraphone that mimics Talking Tina's stilted movements and lifelike glare. Sardonically childlike in structure but tense and horrific in execution, the score is unique among Herrmann's "Twilight Zone" work in its single-minded evocation of evil.

Herrmann's last score for the series was his most conventional and genteel, as its story dictated. "Ninety Years Without Slumbering," written by Richard deRoy from a story by George Clayton Johnson, was a charming variation on another favorite series theme, the rejuvenation of the aged through renewed self-faith. Here tempo is as important as Herrmann's themes or orchestration (for very English winds, harp, and vibraphone). Based on the traditional melody that provides the episode's title, Herrmann's music emulates the slow, inevitable pendulum swing of the grandfather clock that keeps Sam Forstman (Ed Wynn) alive. Herrmann's use of the English tune is typically fragmentary until the drama's climax, when Forstman overcomes his dependence on the antique clock and chooses life, his last soliloquy celebrated in a straightforward, moving version of the theme that radiates compassion and tenderness.

It was on "Twilight Zone"'s recording stages at Goldwyn Studios that Herrmann found the next great love of his life: a flea-ridden stray pup whom he adopted and named Twilight (Twi for short). As even Herrmann's wives acknowledged, his passion for animals often seemed to dwarf his relations with humans. No pet received more of Herrmann's childlike love than Twi, with whom he posed in a portrait modeled especially after a photo of Elgar and *his* pet. Herrmann also played host to three cats: Puss, Boots, and Inchie. Two neighbors' cats, Papa and Dapper Dan, spent most of their afternoons at the Herrmanns' as well because of the adult food he served them—for, despite the protests of friends and wives, Herrmann insisted that "all animals are gourmets."[41]

# TWELVE

I have the imagination of disaster—and see life indeed as ferocious and sinister.

*Henry James*

As Herrmann's "Twilight Zone" association began, Alfred Hitchcock was completing what would be his most notorious (and successful) film. If *Psycho* is a black comedy (as its director insisted),[1] it is also Hitchcock's most extreme exercise in nihilism; its impact comes not only from its famous murder sequence but also from its apparent lack of moral center. "We're all in our private traps, clamped in them," one character remarks, "and none of us can ever get out. We scratch and claw, but only at air—and for all of it, we never budge an inch." Life becomes a series of arbitrary events that clash with brutal urgency; and perhaps as a result of Hitchcock's Catholic upbringing, sin cannot be redeemed through guilt—as the death of repentant thief Marion Crane (Janet Leigh) and the madness of Norman Bates (Anthony Perkins) demonstrate.

*Psycho* was not only the film that made Hitchcock infamous; it also made him rich.[2] Its huge box office success was the greater for Hitchcock's cost-cutting production methods, inspired by his lack of confidence in the film. But although he insisted on inexpensive actors, a five-week shooting schedule, and television shooting methods (using his TV series cameraman, John L. Russell), Hitchcock was adamant that Herrmann write the score, despite the composer's non-reduced fee. Still, the overall music budget was small, and although Herrmann initially protested the cutback, he would use the restriction to memorable advantage.

*Psycho* was their collaborative masterwork, a film that, as Hitchcock admitted at the time, depended heavily on Herrmann's music for its tension and sense of pervading doom.[3] It remains Herrmann's best-known score, unprecedented in its use of strings soli to match the texture of the cinematography, and featuring probably the most famous (and most imitated) cue in film music.

At the time of its making, *Psycho* was hardly considered classic material. Based on a grisly novel by Robert Bloch, it included such sordid elements as mass murder, body snatching, and matricide. (The plot concerns the murder of a Phoenix secretary who, after stealing $40,000 from her employer, is stabbed to death in an isolated hotel—apparently by the elderly mother of its owner, but in fact by the psychotic young man himself, who wore his dead mother's clothes for this and other killings.) Paramount disliked the film,[4] and after editing the final cut with George Tomasini in December 1959, Hitchcock too was disappointed.[5]

Fortunately, before recutting the film he screened it for Herrmann. "Hitchcock . . . felt it didn't come off," Herrmann recalled. "He wanted to cut it down to an hour television show and get rid of it. I had an idea of what one could do with the film, so I said, 'Why don't you go away for your Christmas holidays, and when you come back we'll record the score and see what you think.' . . . 'Well,' he said, 'do what you like, but only one thing I ask of you: please write nothing for the murder in the shower. That must be without music.' "[6]

Herrmann's idea made cinema history. In thirty film scores he had used a wider, more successful diversity of orchestral combinations than any screen composer; but in limiting his *Psycho* score to strings alone, "to complement the black-and-white photography of the film with a black-and-white score"[7] (and to accommodate the budget restriction), Herrmann created his most audacious and brilliant challenge. "In addition to the purely musical problem induced by a limitation of orchestral color," wrote Fred Steiner in his study of the score, "Herrmann's selection of a string orchestra deprived him of many tried and true musical formulas and effects which, until that time, had been considered essential for suspense-horror films: cymbal rolls, timpani throbs, muted horn stings, shrieking clarinets, ominous trombones, and dozens of other staples in Hollywood's bag of chilly, scary musical tricks. . . . [Additionally,] when one thinks of strings, one usually thinks of romance—above all, in film music."[8]

Yet as Rimsky-Korsakov observed in *Principles of Orchestration*, "Stringed instruments possess more ways of producing sound than any other orchestral group. They can pass, better than other instruments from one shade of expression to another, the varieties being of an infinite number." Comparing the wide gradation possibilities of black-and-white photography with Rimsky's statement, Steiner concludes that "just as the 'no color' images of a black and white film are able to convey all the emotions and visual effects the director wishes to express, so the string orchestra has the capability—within the limits of its one basic *color*—to produce an enormous range of expression and a great variety of dramatic and emotional effects, with all the gradation in between."[9]

After conceiving his orchestration, Herrmann devised ways of using it to tighten the film's deliberate pace. First came the credits sequence. "In film studios and among filmmakers, there is a convention that the main title has to have cymbal crashes and be accompanied by a pop song—no matter what," Herrmann said in 1973. "The real function of a main title, of course, should be to set the pulse of what is going to follow. I wrote the main title to 'Psycho' before Saul Bass even did the animation. They animated to the music. . . . After the main title, nothing much happens in the picture, apparently, for 20 minutes or so. Appearances, of course, are deceiving, for in fact the drama starts immediately with the titles. . . . I am firmly convinced, and so is Hitchcock, that after the main titles you know that something terrible must happen. The main title sequence tells you so, and that is its function: to set the drama. You don't need cymbal crashes or records that never sell."[10]

After the strident, contrapuntal urgency of the prelude (which is recalled three times in the score), Herrmann abruptly shifts tone with a series of placid, descending string chords as Hitchcock's lazy montage of downtown Phoenix begins—and the audience begins its wait for action. Rather than accelerate the images' languid rhythm, Herrmann's music further slows it down, making the effect all the more agonizing and drawing us vertically down "as if into a vortex" as Russell's camera descends into an open hotel window.[11] (*Psycho*'s most striking images reinforce Hitchcock's running theme of voyeurism; often, as Bates peers at Marion through a peephole, Herrmann writes music of chilling austerity to hold us at a distance from what we—and Bates—see.)

The first scene, our introduction to the frustrated Marion and her lover, Sam (John Gavin), gives Herrmann a rare opportunity in the film for lyricism—but even here strings only intone a desolate falling pattern that is, at best, a melodic fragment. (Notes Steiner, "Analysis of the 'Psycho' score reveals a marked absence of tunes, or melodies, in the sense in which those terms are generally used . . . imparting to it a special, disturbing quality.")[12]

Throughout *Psycho* Herrmann maintains the prelude's promise of violence through a favorite device, the ostinato, subtly altered within a cue by shifting instrumental textures. Typical is an early scene that would probably have been cut had Hermann not interceded, Marion's decision to steal the $40,000 entrusted to her. Two minutes long, it consists of only two visual elements—Leigh and the money on her bed—and contains no dialogue. Yet Herrmann's quietly agitated device for violas against long, ascending-and-descending violin chords transforms the scene into one of enormous tension, the uneasy chromatics of the strings giving Marion's temptation a Mephistophelian persuasiveness.

The next sequence, in which Marion makes her escape—and the film's nightmare begins—was the most problematic. Observed Herrmann: "What you actually saw was a very good-looking girl driving a car. She could have been driving it to the supermarket, to her mother-in-law's; she could have been just going for a ride before going back to work. Hitch said to me, 'Well, we'll put in voices occasionally from her mind—that they're missing the money now. . . .' I said, 'That's all right, but that still doesn't make it terrible.' That's when we both agreed to bring back the music we'd related to the opening of the film, which again tells the audience, who don't know something terrible is going to happen to the girl, that it's *got* to."[13]

Few viewers have ever forgotten after seeing *Psycho's* much-analyzed shower sequence, visually outlined by Saul Bass and requiring seventy-eight camera setups.[14] But as Hitchcock realized after watching the scene in dubbing, its impact was not all he had hoped for with only Leigh's screams and the sound of running water on the soundtrack. Herrmann silently agreed and without Hitch's knowledge wrote *Psycho's* most celebrated cue, a "return to pure ice water."[15] "Many people have inquired how I achieved the sound effects behind the murder scene," Herrmann said. "Violins did it! People laugh when they learn it's just violins, and that's interesting to me. It shows that people are so jaded that if you give them cold water they wonder what kind of champagne it is. It's just the strings doing something every violinist does all day long when he tunes up. The effect is as common as rocks."[16] Yet its usage was unique in film music, linked powerfully to *Psycho's* visuals: the violin bridge slashes relate not only to the stabbing motion of Bates's knife and Marion's cries, but also to the imagery of Bates's stuffed birds, which hover throughout the film's design. (When asked for his own description of what the cue signified, Herrmann chose one word: "Terror.")[17]

Having written the cue, Herrmann next had to convince Hitchcock it was key to the scene's success. "When Hitchcock returned [from his vacation] we played the score for him in the mixing and dubbing studio. . . .

We dubbed the composite without any musical effects behind the murder scene, and let him watch it. Then I said, 'I really do have something composed for it, and now that you've seen it your way, let's try mine.' We played him my version with the music. He said, 'Of course, that's the one we'll use.' I said, 'But you requested that we not add any music.' 'Improper suggestion, my boy, improper suggestion,' he replied."[18]

*Psycho* contains less dialogue than any other sound Hitchcock film, allowing Herrmann's music to play almost totally "in the open." Yet Herrmann's sensitivity for scoring dialogue is apparent during Marion and Norman's conversation in Norman's office, which begins without music. As Marion suggests Norman put his mother in a home, a menacing three-note device emerges on the soundtrack, evolving into a dissonant, eerie fugue that echoes the third movement of Bartók's *Music for Strings, Percussion, and Celesta,* a piece alluded to in Bloch's novel. (It is worth noting again that the "Madhouse" theme was first written for Herrmann's 1935 *Sinfonietta for Strings,* provides the coda in the cantata *Moby Dick,* and reappears in Herrmann's last film score, *Taxi Driver.* Clearly it was one of the composer's favorite signatures for madness and desolation.)

Hitchcock was delighted with the psychological and dramatic impetus that Herrmann's music gave the film, and had only one complaint: he wanted more—specifically, for Bates's last attack, on Marion's sister Lilah, which Herrmann had not scored. The composer agreed, adding the shower music to the sequence.[19]

Released with a clever publicity campaign that allowed no one into a theater once the film had begun, *Psycho* surpassed everyone's expectations financially (critically it was generally panned as an exploitation film unworthy of its director). Within weeks Hitchcock had made $2 million from the film;[20] yet as his revenue increased, so did his desire for power. In an act that would become typical, Hitchcock offered Herrmann a car and a smaller fee instead of his full salary of $17,500. Herrmann refused, and never forgot what he considered Hitchcock's condescension.[21]

Shortly after the film's release, Herrmann received a letter from a Mrs. Donald Werby praising the *Psycho* score: "I thought it was an excellent film that fully accomplished what it set out to do, and the music magnificently abetted this purpose. . . . I realized at the second viewing how much the building of mood, the growing sense of terror, owes to your music."[22]

Replied Herrmann:

Thank you for your appreciative letter about "PSYCHO."

Composing music for films (and television) is in many ways a very un-
rewarding artistic endeavor. So often one's efforts are scarcely even noticed, not because the music is unworthy, nor that the picture may be
more or less successful, but because it is frequently just taken for granted.
Therefore, to receive a letter such as yours is always a great compliment
and a stimulus to continue to do one's best, knowing that there are people
who listen sensitively and objectively and who take the time to express
their appreciation.

Again, my sincere thanks for your kindness in writing, and with all
good wishes, I am

> Sincerely yours,
> Bernard Herrmann[23]

Herrmann sent copies of both letters to Hitchcock.[24]

*Psycho*'s scoring planted another seed for future disagreement. After
his success in convincing Hitch that the shower music was essential, and
after Hitchcock's remark that "33% of the effect of 'Psycho' was due to
the music"[25] (recalled *Psycho* screenwriter Joseph Stefano: "Hitchcock
gave [Herrmann] more credit than anyone else he ever spoke of"),[26] Herrmann had come to believe that the director trusted his judgment implicitly, and that Hitchcock's instructions were not inviolable.

For five more years, Herrmann remained a welcome presence at Hitchcock's office (first at Paramount, then at Universal), whose staff increased
that year with the hiring of secretary Sue Gauthier. "One day Benny
called on the phone, said he didn't know me, demanded to know who I was
and why I was there and what my name was!" Gauthier recalled. "I was
scared to death of this man; he really intimidated me. Well, when he came
into my office, Benny gave me a big bear hug. In our office refrigerator
we always had snacks we'd brought in for lunch, and Benny would come
in, sit in front of that refrigerator and eat whatever we'd brought from
home. He always had a cigarette hanging out of his mouth, with all the
ashes dribbling down his front, and he'd never brush them off. He was
temperamental, but Benny had a sweet old heart, and I loved him."[27]

Somewhat surprisingly, Hitchcock received an Oscar nomination for
*Psycho*'s direction the next January, as did John Russell for cinematography, but as usual Herrmann's contribution was ignored.

Hitchcock's economizing on *Psycho*'s score was salt in an increasingly
sore wound to Herrmann: his dissatisfaction with the slim residuals paid
by the American Society of Composers, Arrangers, and Publishers
(ASCAP) for film music (despite their generous royalty payments for film

songs). On January 1, 1960, Herrmann changed his affiliation from ASCAP to the rival Broadcast Music Incorporated (BMI), with whom he would stay for the last fifteen years of his life. It was BMI chief Dick Kirk who convinced Herrmann to make the switch: "I had never met a man as outspoken as Bernie. Generally when people meet, they feel each other out first; but Bernie either liked or disliked you immediately. He criticized anyone he wanted to, but there was also a great kindness in him. When we went out to his car after our first lunch, during which he'd been very irascible, he introduced me, literally, to his little dog Twi, and his face grew very soft when he saw her."[28]

Herrmann's resentment of Hollywood songwriters was based not only on revenue; he rightly perceived their role in film as growing and his own scoring idiom on the wane. At the first meeting of the Composers' Guild in 1955, Herrmann raged against pop composers to the embarrassment of all,[29] and few composers in Hollywood escaped a lecture on the topic. Elie Siegmeister, who unlike most of the Young Composers had remained in New York, came to Hollywood in 1959 to score the Columbia film *They Came to Cordura*. Recalled Siegmeister: "On arriving I was delighted to have a message at my hotel, 'Call Bernard Herrmann.' I hadn't seen him in quite a few years. On making the phone call, [I realized] good old Benny was still delivering his one-two 'get-em-boys' invectives. . . . He wasted no time in quizzing me. 'Siggy, are you doing the theme song?' I wasn't exactly clear what a theme song was, but he quickly finished it off in spicy terms—something like, 'Godammit, if they hire some pop punk to write the lousy song instead of letting you do it, I'd throw it in their faces, can the whole thing, and go straight back to New York.' I thanked him as politely as I could under the circumstances for his kind advice and hung up."[30]

Herrmann's next film, made and scored in London, could not have offered a greater contrast in spirit or subject matter. After *Psycho*, *The Three Worlds of Gulliver*—which reteamed Herrmann with Ray Harryhausen and Charles Schneer—would be a high-spirited English lark.

"When once you have thought of the big men and the little men," Samuel Johnson sniffed in response to Jonathan Swift's 1726 novel *Gulliver's Travels*, "it is very easy to do all the rest."[31] For Harryhausen and Schneer, the big men and the little men were enough. Written and directed by Jack Sher (who like other Harryhausen directors had no involvement in scoring), *Gulliver* was the most engaging blend to date of Harryhausen's Dynamation effects and Herrmann's music. Just as Herrmann's knowledge of American folk music made him ideal for *All That Money*

Can Buy, the English wit characterizing Swift's satire played an equally key role in the composer's make-up. (Similarities between composer and author are worth noting. Like Herrmann, Swift's irascibility and sharp tongue were often construed by peers as signs of misanthropy; but, noted scholar H. W. Nevinson, "it was not any spirit of hatred or cruelty but an intensely personal sympathy with suffering that . . . kindled [in Swift] that furnace of indignation against the stupid, the hateful and the cruel . . . a furnace in which he himself was consumed.")[32]

This second Herrmann-Harryhausen collaboration was almost prevented by Columbia's music director, Max Stoloff, reluctant as many were to deal with Herrmann's irascibility, and by Columbia executives, who insisted on an "exploitable" composer who could generate record sales.[33] A compromise was reached with the hiring of George Duning and Ned Washington, whose dispensable songs "Gentle Love" and "What a Wonderful Fellow Is Gulliver" were reduced to seconds in the final cut. Surviving intact is Herrmann's delightful score, a cinematic *Nutcracker* that contains Herrmann's most charming music while retaining much of Swift's sharp humor.

While Sher's adaptation of *Gulliver* softened the novel's sardonicism, Herrmann's score—using separate orchestral ensembles for Lemuel Gulliver's three worlds of England, Lilliput, and Brobdingnag—remained a droll parody of Swift's main targets: English pride and vanity. Tidily summarizing Gulliver's travels is Herrmann's rousing overture for large twentieth-century orchestra, staunchly British in its bold brass theme and stirring percussion, but slightly tongue-in-cheek; eighteenth-century pomp becomes a dainty miniature for harps and celeste as Herrmann introduces the diminutive Lilliputians; then contrabass tubas and winds mimic the gigantic Brobdingnags, before Herrmann returns to the overture's brilliant opening with a stately Georgian flourish. Significantly, however, the thematic material in the overture never really changes: "The music I composed for the giants and the Lilliputians is exactly the same," Herrmann explained. "All I did was change the emphasis." As Herrmann and Swift realized, scope is totally subjective. "There is no world of small people, and there is no world of giants—only in one's head. But poor Gulliver. He was so levelheaded he thought he knew differently."[34]

Herrmann's depiction of the Lilliputians (Swift's metaphor for tradition-steeped England) pokes sober-faced fun at British institutions and pomp, with a delicate trumpet processional for the indecisive Lilliput emperor, a jolly sailor's hornpipe as Gulliver catches fish in his "giant" cap, and a bedrock-solid *minuetto pomposo* for the Englishman's pragmatic uprooting of a Lilliputian forest to grow crops. Best of all is "The Tightrope," a sparkling orchestral tour de force describing the acrobatic contest between Lilliput's two ministerial candidates (a Swiftian jab at campaigning). A "virtuoso juggling match"[35] between woodwinds and pizzicato strings, with sideline commentary by ethereal piano glissandos and harp arpeggios, it recalls Tchaikovsky or Rimsky Korsakov at their most whimsical.

Some Lilliputian-style squabbling spilled into the film's scoring as well, with constant financial arguments flaring between Schneer and Herrmann. Recalled London Symphony violinist Henry Greenwood, "During the recording Benny stopped and yelled at Schneer, 'I TOLD ya we oughta have more strings—this isn't coming through the way I wanted it to. If ya don't get more I'm gonna clear off.' Schneer replied, 'All right, Benny. Clear off.' Benny just went silent. Luckily it was about time for a break, so we took him to a pub. He always calmed down with a bit of Scotch whiskey—and sure enough, he decided to go on."[36]

As usual, Herrmann and Lucy spent their London stay at the lavish Dorchester Hotel, in keeping with the composer's self-perceived honorary membership in the nobility. (That year Herrmann joined the Saville Club, a quintessentially English all-male club in London. He rarely visited it in later years; the act of belonging was enough.)[37] At the nearby Westbury was another visiting American conductor, twenty-seven-year-old Charles Gerhardt. Gerhardt was then embarking on what would be a highly successful recording and producing career with RCA:

As a teenager I had listened to Herrmann's CBS broadcasts and loved hearing all those pieces one didn't know, like the Raff symphonies. When I called Benny at the Dorchester he was very open and said to come on over. I went to his hotel room, and he got lists out of his briefcase— single-spaced, typed lists of repertoire that he had done or wanted to do. He knew I was a producer for a record company, and I said I hoped I could record some things with him sometime.

Benny liked all kinds of repertoire; he was no snob. A lighter piece by Sibelius could interest him just as much as something else. To find any similar musical figure to Benny you'd have to go to Ives. Ives was a more primitive Grandma Moses of music. Benny was more schooled, but you find in Benny's scores things that look like they were written by a man who didn't know as much as he did, and that was because of his tremendous ability to turn off his experience and seek something new. Music was music to him, be it written for film or TV or the concert hall. As he said, Haydn wrote a piece for the Esterházys' dinner party, played it on the balcony, and then had to eat in the kitchen. "At least I don't have to eat in the kitchen," he'd say.

Sometimes when people start studying something as complex as music they get lost; there's so much, and everything gets pigeonholed. This man had no rules. Everything was fresh and open. One minute he'd say he didn't like a piece of music—it could be one of the great masterpieces, and everyone would be shocked—and then he could change his mind.

He was a great friend of Barbirolli's, and one night he called me and said, "C'mon, we gotta go to a concert; I've got tickets, we're gonna hear Mahler Two. J. B.'s doing it at the Festival Hall." So we went to the concert. We had discussed Mahler; of course, Benny was very knowledgeable about him. In those days Mahler just wasn't played, so Benny championed him. But when Mahler became more popular, Benny had no time for him; Mahler didn't need him anymore. Herrmann started to pick on the Second Symphony by the second movement; he leaned over and said, "Jewish wedding—it's a Jewish wedding!" I'd whisper, "Be quiet, Benny." Later, during the long chorales in the fourth movement, he'd say, "Nothing but the pedal point! He's been on that D natural for an hour!" That concert was the turning point; Mahler wasn't any good from then on.

Benny was completely unembarrassed by the way he dealt with people. But if he started to go into a tantrum over dinner at *my* home I could say, "Benny, shut up, stop saying such rubbish" and he'd start to giggle as if to say, "Did I go too far?" Then he'd be fine again. But there weren't enough people strong enough to do that. He hated weaklings.

Benny's one big blind spot was that he loved conductors who were difficult. He adored Koussevitsky. If he heard gossip on the phone about Munch coming to London to record he'd tell all about it—"The Philharmonia was there, and Munch said to them, 'You know, you don't inspire me!' and he walked out and went home!" To Benny that was a success. What he admired most about Toscanini were his rages; he had a 78 recording he always played of Toscanini exploding at the musicians. I always thought, when a conductor walks out there is no music; you don't produce anything. But Benny had a great love of the glamor image of the cantankerous conductor—which he himself was.[38]

Another enduring friendship was made in London that summer, with a soft-spoken English composer of television and film music, Laurie Johnson. Johnson was a former dance band arranger whose path to film music was wildly different from Herrmann's; yet the two men shared a common attitude about the scoring process:

I met Benny at Technicolor, where film prints are run. "Did you record at such-and-such studios?" he asked me. I said yes. "How'd ya find it?" I said, "Not very good." He replied, "That's what I think. It's the only place where they can make ninety musicians sound like thirty. But, they tell me, 'Joe Bloggs' is such a nice guy. I don't want a nice guy! When I go to the dentist I go to him because he's a good dentist!" He never suffered fools gladly, and he sometimes misunderstood people's motives. But he was the kindest man I've ever known. My family and I never saw that brusque side at all.

Our friendship became very special because our family lives, like our professional lives, became totally intertwined. Our approaches to music and to life were very similar. We shared favorite authors—Poe, Stevenson, Dickens. He had a great feel for Victorian London, Sherlock Holmes. One day Benny said to me, "We should buy an old pub, dress it up with gaslights, we'll have a fog machine outside, and then we'll have just us and the family in it!"

He liked Victorian values in some ways. One day he decided he was going to have an ulster, a sensible English garment. One morning he was out walking in Regent Park with this thick cloak and a walking stick. A woman walked up to him and said, "What a pleasure it is to see a perfect English gentleman walking through Regent Park." He turned and in his heavy New York accent said, "Oh, YE-EAH?"

Herrmann knew exactly what the function of music in cinema was. Most composers just think of their one aspect of the film, but he was thinking of the whole. The only irritations I was aware of him having occurred when he felt people weren't subscribing to his strict code of understanding and respect for the medium. And time and time again I would hear him say, "So-and-so did a good score for that film." If Rózsa or North did a good score he would praise it. Sometimes his comments would be in shorthand, like "He's got talent," or "He hasn't."

Some would say Benny was too unbending in his standards, but there were times when he could suddenly bring things down to a very fundamental level. If someone were ill, he'd say, "What does this matter? It's only a film." That sounds like a complete contradiction to a life spent defending this delicate art, but if it were a question of health, that took precedence. Once when I wasn't feeling very well he said, "Tell me what the cues are—I'll write them." He was screaming on the phone for me to go to bed and said, "You'd do the same for me, wouldn't ya?"—which was perfectly true. Nobody ever wrote a note for anybody else, but it was a gesture. "It's only a film," he'd say.[39]

Herrmann's return to Hollywood was little more than a visit. A decade of continuous work and royalty checks had made Herrmann wealthy; but as he discovered after each return from London, the trend of film offers was gradually reversing itself. The "hit"-mania that plagued his career

since *The Man Who Knew Too Much* and the eagerness of some composers (like Tiomkin) to satisfy producers' demands for pop music had reinforced Herrmann's outsider status in Hollywood, as had his extended trips
abroad. Also, Herrmann's associations with Hitchcock and Harryhausen
were blinding many filmmakers to Herrmann's skill in other genres, a ste-
reotyping to which Herrmann became very sensitive.

A more basic impediment to Herrmann's career was his temper. Remarked David Raksin in 1967: "Benny is capable of stalking out of a projection room and saying to the producer who is considering hiring him for
the film being screened: 'Why do you show me this *garbage?*' At one time
or another he has insulted nearly everyone within earshot. While it is to
his credit that he has not spared his friends, whether they needed it or not,
he has not always borne resulting ruptures of friendship with the grace
one might expect from a man so willing to give the initial provocation. . . . Anyone who has a friend like him doesn't need a hair shirt."[40]
As Herrmann's fuse shortened in the 1960s, a growing number of friends
and potential employers decided his abusiveness outweighed the rewards
of associating with him.

In the spring of 1961 Herrmann eagerly returned to England, for a series of concerts in Manchester with the Halle* and in London with the
BBC Northern Orchestra and the Royal Philharmonic (the result of his
friendship with the widowed Lady Beecham, whose husband had founded
the orchestra), as well as for a new collaboration with Harryhausen and
Schneer.

Herrmann's trip that spring was one of his happiest, not only because
of his concert appearances but for the uniquely English indulgences the
composer loved. In London, he and Lucy finally purchased a large, inviting flat on Cumberland Terrace, a tree-lined street near the London Zoo
in Regent's Park. The contrast with Hollywood could not have been sharper,
as a Herrmann letter to Norman Corwin, dated April 4, illustrates:

Dear Norman and Kate:

Please forgive the delay in telling you how much your cable meant to
me—it seemed to make me go forward to the stage entrance instead of
running for the Exit sign. My concerts have been really first class—and
full houses everywhere—and the youngsters line up to see me as if I were

*Wrote John Mapplebeck in a profile of Herrmann in the *Manchester Guardian* (3-
30-61): "At least half the interview was taken up by his interrogation of his interviewer on
the failure of the city to support its orchestra. With that brisk American enthusiasm for doing something about it, he suggested a referendum on putting up the rates to subsidize the
Halle, and brushed aside any objections that the result might not be quite what he expected."

a movie star. I made a speech about Sir Thomas Beecham at my first concert and every one was pleased with it. Have been twice to Manchester and had a wonderful time there—the orchestra gave me a standing ovation—which means that I will not be asked again for at least ten years—that's the trouble with being a guest conductor—be good—but not too good. We shall see . . .*

Had a long talk about you and your offers to come to England to do a series with Lindsay Wellington, director of Sound Service. . . . I shall advise you of my progress in the matter. . . . Also shall be seeing Sydney Bernstein, head of Granada TV—and discuss the possibility of a Corwin TV series . . .**

We love our flat and it is very splendid—and all our English visitors call me "your Grace" and Lucy "your Ladyship." We went to the Thames yesterday to watch the Oxford-Cambridge [boat] Race—Oxford lost by 4½ lengths. We're served drinks and cold turkey by full dressed butlers. What a life!!! The weather has been sunny—warm and in full spring blessings for the last month—not a drop of rain—might be in Palm Springs—if not for the wonder full surroundings. I do another concert tomorrow night—and only wish you were both here with us.

> Love,
> Bernard

Herrmann's account of his conducting success was hardly exaggerated; but despite good attendances and glowing notices, these concerts represented the beginning of the end of his conducting career. Offers became scarce, mainly because of Herrmann's temperament. After Beecham's death that March, Herrmann was confident he would be offered a conducting post with the Royal Philharmonic.[41] He was not.

Herrmann's 1961 English visit had an ironic footnote. While conducting the BBC's Northern Orchestra near Liverpool, his curiosity took him to hear a little-known pop band that had recorded a few German singles. "I came back from England and brought back the early records of the Beatles that they made for Deutsche Grammophon [actually Polydor]. Nobody would record them in England. They were turned down by every major company. . . . They were playing in a nightclub there; I met them, and they gave me their records. I took them to all the big powers in [Hollywood] and they laughed at me. . . . I took [the music] to Universal and CBS and played it for the big mandarins of jazz in this town and they said, 'There's nothing in that crap.' I said I thought the Beatles had something

---

*Herrmann returned to the Halle a final time in 1964.
**These projects did not materialize.

new and different to offer. But nobody agreed."[42] A few years later, of course, Hollywood not only discovered rock music but *insisted* on it— alienating Herrmann further from the film industry.

For the rest of 1961 at least, Herrmann's spirits were high, as was his scoring sensitivity. *Mysterious Island*, his third collaboration with Harryhausen and Schneer, was a loose adaptation of Jules Verne's sequel to *20,000 Leagues Under the Sea* and the most handsomely produced of Harryhausen's fantasies to date. Its visual set pieces—a storm-tossed balloon escape; a world of gigantic crabs, bees, and octopi—were dazzling in scope and wryly humorous.

Complementing Harryhausen's virtuosity was Herrman's ingenious potpourri of odd orchestral settings. As with *Sinbad* and *Gulliver*, Herrmann could vary his musical palette from scene to scene in a way "most realistic pictures do not allow."[43] Consistent in his score is an impressionistic theatricality, as in the film's rousing opening, the prison escape of four Civil War soldiers by balloon during "the greatest storm in American history." Herrmann summons the full, God-fearing power of the London Symphony in a furious dialogue of strings, woodwind glissandos, and biting brass declamations that climb higher and higher as the balloon takes flight. (Noted Christopher Palmer: "If Delius is the quiet poet of nature in her tranquilities, Herrmann deals quite as successfully with the elements in clash and convulsion.")[44]

In a lighter vein are Herrmann's portraits of the island's gargantuan wildlife. "The Giant Crab" is an instrumental battle between an artillery of thunderous, whooping horns and brittle wind and string responses, all to a jagged seven counts to the bar. "The Giant Bees" are represented by flutter-tonguing brass that make Rimsky-Korsakov's villain a benign gnat in comparison. Best is "The Giant Bird"—or more accurately, "phororhacos," a prehistoric mutation that is a comedic high point for animator and composer. For this grotesquely amusing, chickenlike beast, Herrmann borrowed an eighteenth-century fugue for organ by Johann Ludwig Krebs (after playfully suggesting to Harryhausen the American standard "Turkey in the Straw"!).[45] Herrmann's orchestration for low winds, pizzicato strings, and fluttering high reeds is not only a wickedly funny counterpart to the film's visual, but a skillful reworking of Krebs's original as well.

That spring Herrmann received another English film offer, Stanley Kubrick's *Lolita*. Insightful as Kubrick was in choosing Herrmann to score Nabokov's tale of erotic obsession and death, the collaboration was doomed by Kubrick's preexisting concept of the music. Recalled Herrmann: "When I agreed to do it, [Kubrick] said, 'But there's one thing I've forgotten to tell you—you've got to use a melody of my brother-in-law's.' So I told him to forget it."[46] Kubrick did, hiring Nelson Riddle instead to write a score incorporating Bob Harris's "Lolita Theme."

With the retirement of Alfred Newman as Fox music director in 1960, one of Herrmann's longest career associations came to an end. Scoring decisions in the 1960s were increasingly made by the producer, not the music head, and few chose to work with Herrmann. His last Fox project, *Tender Is the Night,* was his unhappiest—a film wrecked by miscasting, bad writing, and lazy production.

The project had been developed by David O. Selznick, who then sold it to Fox as he had *Jane Eyre;* as usual, however, he gave much unsolicited advice from the sidelines. "It is my hope . . . that 'Tender is the Night' will be the definitive picture about the twenties," Selznick wrote producer Henry T. Weinstein in February 1961.

Every other film about the twenties, without exception, has failed
to capture the period—in its costuming, in its detail, in its *music.* If
Scott Fitzgerald, the great symbol of the twenties, and Scott Fitzgerald's
semiautobiographical masterpiece, are to be realized on the screen in such
a manner as to really capture the mood that one can see in the
documentaries of that time, the music is of course essential. . . . Now as to the
title song. . . . The difficulty is that most of the better composers of scores
are not necessarily equally talented at composing popular songs. . . . A
notable exception is Dimitri Tiomkin, who of course has done many of
the great scores of the better pictures for many years, and whose principal
themes for these pictures have been converted by him into hugely successful
songs in a great many cases.[47]

When Tiomkin proved unavailable, Herrmann was chosen with the resulting necessity, the producers felt, of hiring songwriters Sammy Fain and Paul Francis Webster. (According to Lyn Murray, Herrmann turned down the film when he learned of its title song stipulation. After the film was assigned to Murray, however, Herrmann returned to Fox and pleaded to director Henry King, "with tears in his eyes," to be reassigned to the film—which he was.)[48]

Even had Fox's quest for a hit song paid off, *Tender Is the Night* would still have been a poorly acted, superficial treatment of Fitzgerald that wasted the talents of Jason Robards and director King. Barely surviving the two-and-a-half-hour debacle was Herrmann's eloquent score, which battled Fain and Webster's maudlin title song for screen time. (The film's credit sequence is the dreariest of any Herrmann-scored film, with melo-

dramatic piano glissandos and Muzakesque chorus—*not* arranged by Herr
mann—aping the giant letters of the titles.)

Clearly, what attracted Herrmann was not the lackluster film but the
Fitzgerald story of madness and disillusionment among post–World War
I expatriates. Again Herrmann uses primarily strings, with dark brass
touches, to suggest Nicole Diver's mental illness, most affectingly in an
early party sequence that ends in Nicole's breakdown. As Richard Diver
(Robards) tries to convince Nicole (Jennifer Jones) that her fears are imaginary, Herrmann introduces a muted, unresolved pattern in the violins'
lowest register, then repeats it an octave higher, then an octave higher, as
Richard gives his grinning wife a glass of water. Despite the stasis of the
scene, on the soundtrack tension increases until strings become a screeching, dissonant sound effect as Nicole hurls the glass at Richard, shattering
a mirror behind him. (Throughout the film, Jones's histrionic performance
is aided by Herrmann's far more persuasive understatement.)

Largely ignoring the film's European locales, Herrmann focuses on the
intimate character drama with a gentle theme for strings and woodwinds,
reminiscent in its quiet, doomed passion of *Tristan*'s "Liebestod." Some
Herrmann déjà vu is also apparent: for the film's water-skiing opening the
composer uses a slightly fuller orchestration of his "train station" music
from *The Ghost and Mrs. Muir*.

That the score was one of the film's few virtues was lost on Selznick,
who later complained that "some of the best scenes in the picture were infinitely better in the picture's rough cut, because they did not suffer the
destructive underscoring."[49] Released in January 1962, *Tender Is the
Night* was primly heralded by Fox as "an adult love story without
smut . . . it contains no nudity, no pornography or semipornography, no
language of the gutter, no scenes of unmarried couples in bed together. It
will not require Supreme Court approval to be shown publicly."[50]

The film died a quick box office death.

Complicating Herrmann's scoring of *Tender Is the Night* was his concurrent work on another film, a practice he hated. *Cape Fear*, an adaptation of John MacDonald's novel *The Executioners* directed by J. Lee
Thompson, was Herrmann's only film score for Universal away from the
auspices of Hitchcock (though he did work with Hitch's editor, George
Tomasini, on the project). Herrmann's increasingly bad relations with the
studio were due only partly to the composer's irascibility; like MGM,
Universal disliked using nonstaff composers—especially those whose
commercial potential was virtually nil.

Yet Herrmann was perfect for *Cape Fear*. A brutal psychological thriller starring Gregory Peck as Sam Boden, a Florida attorney, and Robert Mitchum as Max Cadey, a psychotic ex-convict seeking revenge, it depicts a society in which law seems useless and terrorism reigns supreme. Its methodical, humorless escalation of the war between Boden and Cadey finally builds to an upbeat resolution—but not before a hundred minutes of emotional and physical violence in a style that would increasingly characterize the cinema of the 1960s.

Herrmann's score reinforces *Cape Fear*'s savagery. Mainly a synthesis of past devices, its power comes from their imaginative application and another ingenious orchestration for only flutes, horns, and strings (the absence of trumpets, low brass, and other woodwinds being a rehearsal for his similar orchestration on Hitchcock's *Torn Curtain* in 1966). Like earlier "psychological" Herrmann scores, dissonant string combinations suggest the workings of a killer's mind (most startlingly in a queasy device for cello and bass viols as Cadey prepares to attack a prostitute). Herrmann's prelude searingly establishes the dramatic conflict: descending and ascending chromatic voices move slowly toward each other from their opposite registers, finally crossing—just as Boden and Cadey's game of cat-and-mouse will end in deadly confrontation. (Herrmann would use a similarly intellectual but highly dramatic device in his music for *Sisters* in 1972.)

Herrmann's double film commitments that winter were the exception to the rule. Few producers would tolerate his seemingly unmotivated tantrums—especially since a new guard of composers, less expensive and less difficult, was replacing him and his generation. While Herrmann was busy battling producers over *Tender Is the Night*, Jerry Goldsmith wrote outstanding scores for *Lonely Are the Brave* and John Huston's *Freud*; Elmer Bernstein wrote one of his best scores for *To Kill a Mockingbird*; Henry Mancini composed songs and scoring for Blake Edwards's films *Breakfast at Tiffany's* and *The Days of Wine and Roses* (which won the Oscar for best song in 1962);* and Maurice Jarre began his long association with David Lean on *Lawrence of Arabia* (1962's Oscar winner for best score).

Two filmmakers, Ray Harryhausen and Alfred Hitchcock, remained loyal to Herrmann, although these relationships too would soon end. In the meantime, Hitch still involved Herrmann in each project from its earliest stage, including *Marnie*, an adaptation of Winston Graham's romantic novel about a compulsive thief who is blackmailed into marrying her

---

*Of the four songs nominated in 1962, only one—that for *Tender Is the Night*—was not written by the same composer as wrote the accompanying film score.

intended victim. When its intended star, Grace Kelly, later Princess of Monaco, chose not to return to Hollywood, the project was abandoned—though Hitchcock remained obsessed with the idea of filming the book.[51]

Instead Hitchcock turned to a short story by Daphne DuMaurier, whose novel *Rebecca* had been the subject of his first American film. His version of DuMaurier's *The Birds* was far less faithful to its source. At Hitch's instruction, the first third of Evan Hunter's screenplay dealt not with the antagonists of the film's title but with the romantic billing-and-cooing of its human stars, with only hints at dark events to come. This choice was made in part because of Tippi Hedren, a television model turned actress (*The Birds* was her film debut) and Hitchcock's latest discovery and fixation. Hedren lacked the confidence of past Hitchcock stars like Kelly or Ingrid Bergman; but the director assured his new leading lady that it would come with time.

Herrmann was more skeptical. To him, Hedren was both untalented and exploitive of Hitchcock's obvious infatuation; still, he had no choice but to tolerate the situation. In terms of scoring, at least, *The Birds* offered interesting options. But it was Hitchcock who (with Herrmann's agreement) decided on the film's unusual scoring approach.

"Film music is a kind of emotional scenery passing through a film," Herrmann said in 1961. "Very few films can dispense with it altogether. Hitch did it in 'Rope' and 'Rear Window,' and Clouzot in 'Les Diaboliques'; but they are rare."[52] *The Birds*, Hitchcock and Herrmann decided, was such a film. Rather than an orchestral score, the realistic sound of bird cries would create a musiclike rhythm and pace. Sounds would be "orchestrated" in terms of tempo and dynamics. "After all," Hitchcock remarked, "when you put music to film, it's really sound, it isn't music per se."[53]*

Herrmann's role on the film was largely advisory since he could neither "write" the sounds nor create them. The first challenge was to find out who could. "It wasn't possible to get a thousand birds to make that sound," he recalled. "I guess you could if you went to Africa and waited for the proper day."[54] In April 1962, Hitchcock received a letter from German avant-garde composer Remi Gassmann, codesigner of the Studio Trautonium, an electronic keyboard instrument first used commercially

---

*Electronic scoring was not unheard of by 1961. Herrmann had used amplified instruments for *The Day the Earth Stood Still* in 1950, and six years later Louis and Bebe Barron used electronic music more abstractly in their *Forbidden Planet* soundtrack. *The Birds*, however, was unprecedented in its use of realistic sounds recorded electronically but used musically.

by the New York City Ballet. Wrote Gassmann: "Familiar sounds—from common noises to music and esoteric effects—as well as an almost limitless supply of completely unfamiliar sounds, can now be electronically produced, controlled and utilized for film purposes. The result is much like a new dimension in film productions."[55] That December Herrmann and Hitchcock traveled to West Berlin (Herrmann's first trip to Germany, and a surprisingly happy one) to hear for themselves. Delighted with the Trautonium's bizarre, atonal squawks that sounded amazingly like actual bird calls, Hitchcock hired Gassmann to record the film's soundtrack.

"I just worked with him simply matching it with Hitchcock," Herrmann said in 1971, "but there was no attempt to create a score by electronic means."[56] Even so, Herrmann was as proud of his contribution as he was of any more conventional work. "It was the one Hitchcock film he talked about a lot," recalled Alastair Reid, a later Herrmann collaborator. "He regarded himself one of its prime movers, almost a codirector because of his role in creating the soundtrack."[57]

Throughout production, sequences were carefully planned in both visual and aural terms. Tippi Hedren recalled the shooting of the lengthy bird attack on the Brenner house: "When we arrived on the set, we saw this drummer sitting there with a huge drum. We didn't know Hitch had planned this. In the scene, the tension is supposed to slowly build as the birds start to attack the house. Even Hitchcock, as fine a director as he is, couldn't get a bunch of birds to act that way, so he got the idea of using the drum roll to help us react and to build up the tension. For me, it was the most effective scene in the film."[58]

In this and other sequences, electronic bird effects contrast with long stretches of almost total silence, a device Hitchcock particularly liked. The extended quiet before the attack on the Brenner home "was one of the most satisfying scenes for me personally," he said. "You have a boarded-up room with four people in it, sitting there in silence, just waiting for the birds to come. I kept the silence going quite a bit."[59]

A similar starkness of sound design is used in several of the most violent scenes, replacing more customary tension devices like music or sound effects. In the film's climax, the attack on Melanie (Hedren) in the Brenner attic, Hitchcock and Herrmann chose to keep their feathered assassins silent; only the sounds of their beating wings accompany this attempted "silent murder."[60] For the film's unresolved finale, in which the Brenners and Melanie drive cautiously out of Bodega Bay as thousands of birds look on, Gassmann created an eerie electronic murmur (resembling a hushed string tremolo) to suggest both the birds' muted squawks and their thoughts as they sit planning—perhaps—another attack. The sound builds to a dissonant fortissimo as the last inconclusive image fades out, an effect reminiscent of Herrmann's hanging chords for *Psycho's* ending without (emotional) resolution.

Another, more contrapuntal sound device in *The Birds* was a special Hitchcock favorite: "You can have, if you get the right setting, a man come into a room and murder a woman and have somebody across the road playing the piano, playing pop music—which is even more dramatic, to hear this giggly music playing."[61] Here, as Melanie sits outside the Bodega school playground we hear only the song of the children in the schoolhouse, their innocent self-occupation contrasted with the menace of the crows gathering on the playground jungle gym. (The song was recommended by screenwriter Hunter, whose own children liked singing it.)[62]

*The Birds* was another huge box office success for Hitchcock, especially when rereleased with *Psycho*. Hitchcock's popularity had reached a new high—making his fall from grace one year later all the more shattering.

From *The Birds*, Herrmann turned to his first real film score in over a year, and his last collaboration with Harryhausen and Schneer. Although the filmmakers would remain socially cordial with Herrmann, by 1963 their professional relationship had soured. Herrmann was particularly impatient with what he perceived as Schneer's miserly handling of the films' music budget[63]—an unhappiness that can be sensed in his score for *Jason and the Argonauts*, the most lavish and literate of the Harryhausen films to date. Again Herrmann's score is based on an ingenious orchestral corollary: an enormous ensemble of brass, winds, and percussion (but no strings) to create a militaristic sheen and feeling of power.

*Jason's* title overture, recalled from Herrmann's 1944 radio music for Corwin's "Untitled," is the score's most distinctive sequence: a heroic, stirring battle march, Wagnerian in its militaristic grandeur and chorus-like brass voices. Its theme dominates Herrmann's score, the most monochromatic and self-derivative of his work for Harryhausen. By limiting himself to the simplest of orchestral devices, Herrmann sacrifices much of the freshness and ingenuity of *Sinbad, Gulliver,* and *Mysterious Island*; in fact, many of *Jason's* most effective moments are borrowed from earlier pieces (the clawing strings device for the flying Harpies comes from the darkroom scene in *Five Fingers*; the skeleton warriors music is lifted from *Nocturne and Scherzo*).

Despite its paucity of inventiveness, *Jason's* synthesis of past devices works well as music drama, especially the relentless march for brass, low winds, and timpani to evoke the giant Talos and yet another sinister variation on the Dies Irae for the skeleton warriors (perhaps the most exhilarating sequence in Harryhausen's work).

After the completion of *Jason and the Argonauts*, Herrmann returned to California for what would be his last American concert appearance. At least it partly fulfilled a long-frustrated ambition: to conduct at the Hollywood Bowl. To his disappointment, however, thirteen other conductors joined him; it was the first of the Bowl's "Music from Hollywood" concerts, featuring an impressive roster of film music talent that included Elmer Bernstein, David Raksin, John Green, Miklós Rózsa, Alfred Newman, and Franz Waxman. Jerry Goldsmith and John Williams were represented in a medley of TV themes that also included Jerome Moross's "Wagon Train." But Herrmann made a strong impression with a shrewd undercut of programming: amid the roar of Roman festivals and western overtures, the quiet of *The Snow of Kilimanjaro's* "Memory Waltz" was deafening. With the Bowl audience successfully lulled, Herrmann then launched into the fierce overture to *North by Northwest*, the evening's showstopper.[64]

Before the end of 1963 Herrmann was again working on a Hitchcock project—but not with the director himself. MCA chief Lew Wasserman first conceived of exploiting Hitchcock's droll persona in a weekly TV series;[65] the result, the half-hour anthology "Alfred Hitchcock Presents," made its debut on October 2, 1955.

Hitchcock's involvement with the series was mainly as adviser and as its sardonic host. The artistic directors were old Hitch colleagues, Norman Lloyd (of the Mercury Players, and a memorable villain in Hitchcock's *Saboteur*) and Joan Harrison, Hitchcock's personal assistant for many years. Lloyd and Harrison produced the series, both together and separately, over the next ten years.

The series' packaging of Hitchcock was slick and smart, from the use of Gounod's "Funeral March for a Marionette" as its theme to Hitchcock's mordant introductions. Several of the director's favorite actors worked on the program during its long run, among them John Williams, Vera Miles, and Leo G. Carroll. But it was not until 1963, during the show's eighth season, that Herrmann began to write original music for the series; until then the scores were put together by Hitchcock's Shamley Productions, with stock music provided by producer David Gordon.[66]

In 1963, after the series was expanded into "The Alfred Hitchcock Hour," a new union ruling allowed Lloyd and Harrison to use a variety of original composers, including Lyn Murray, Leonard Rosenman, Lalo Schifrin, and, most importantly, Herrmann. During the program's last two seasons, Herrmann scored seventeen of the hour-long shows; his music would also be reused often as tracked scoring for other episodes.

Herrmann's first Hitchcock television score was the Robert Bloch–scripted "A Home Away from Home," a variant on the Marat/Sade theme of madmen who incarcerate their keepers. Ray Milland starred as a patient who kills the sanatorium's chief doctor and assumes his identity, but then must entertain the victim's suspicious niece, Natalie (Claire Griswold). Moodily directed by Howard Doughtery, the episode featured Herrmann's most developed Hitchcock TV score.

Herrmann uses mainly strings (with harp and vibraphone) to convey psychological disorder and menace. And as in Bloch's *Psycho*, Herrmann uses thematic fragments rather than melodies to suggest alienation and madness. Most effective is a tense four-note pizzicato dialogue between violas and celli as Natalie investigates the sanatorium; additional string harmonics and other instruments combine in a steadily crescendoing four-note pattern, climaxing with Natalie's discovery of her murdered uncle's body.

Death haunts each scene of "The Life Work of Juan Diaz," an affecting Ray Bradbury teleplay set in Mexico about a courageous woman's battle to save her husband's corpse from a cheating gravedigger. The episode was a favorite of its director, series producer Lloyd, who by this time had some reservations about using Herrmann: "Stanley Wilson [music supervisor for the series] felt Benny would be good for 'Juan Diaz'; Stanley was a beautiful man and a great defender of Benny's. I said, 'Benny is an old friend of mine, but I won't put him on the picture unless he sketches out some music for me, plays it on the piano, and tells me what he's going to do. Benny really doesn't take television seriously; he's inclined to fasten on four bars and just repeat them.' Benny was absolutely shocked that I would make this request, but we had a meeting and he played me a few things."[67]*

Herrmann's entire score is based on a single seductive habanera (the same device used in *Vertigo*'s nightmare sequence); like the specter of death that haunts the villagers' lives, the theme is insistent and all-pervasive. Only in the last moments of this dark, poignant score does

---

*Lloyd's criticism is debatable. If Herrmann employed ostinatos more often in television than in film, his choices were either sound dramatically or based on time restrictions.

Herrmann offer a major-key resolution of hope, as the mummified body of Juan Diaz, now a popular tourist attraction, stands watchfully over his family, finally providing the security he could not provide in life.

With his score for "The Jar," James Bridges's chilling adaptation of a Ray Bradbury story, Herrmann wrote his last great score for a medium he treated as seriously as film or the concert hall. Like the original tale, set in a remote rural town where the mysterious contents of a carnival jar exert a strong influence over the townspeople, Herrmann's music looks at the commonplace through a glass darkly, finding evil of doomsday magnitude. The score is provocative and inferential: quietly, slowly, its ideas ferment and grow, from a lulling, seductive calliope theme to a triumphant chorale on the Dies Irae, heralding—like Berlioz's *Fantastique* witches—the presence of unleashed demons.

Like the music for *Psycho* and most of Herrmann's fantasy films, the score's effectiveness is greatly enhanced by its orchestral omissions. Eliminating strings and woodwinds, Herrmann uses only organ, vibraphone, and brass to create a timbre of cathedrallike reverberation and pureness, applied here to the antithesis of liturgical celebration. The episode's first scene is a superb example of Herrmann's ability to reinforce changing dramatic elements with the subtlest shifts of orchestration: as Charlie Hill (Pat Buttram) stares at the jar in a carnival sideshow, a sinuous calliope tune modulates up, then down, as the silent contents move (turn?) in their murky container. Muted brass add distant flourishes like heralds for the rising dead; the music remains fixed yet elusive, as enigmatic as the jar itself. When Charlie displays his new possession for his grasping wife, Thedy, gradually, cautiously, the calliope intones a new, more somber theme: the Dies Irae chant of death.

For the townspeople, Charlie's jar becomes an entity of religious significance, a new god that presumably replaces the old—the "heart of all life," as one local proclaims. The Dies Irae now reigns supreme on the soundtrack. Herrmann's Black Mass is complete, for now the jar rules its disciples, one of whom will be driven to kill.

Another busy composer in Universal's television department was Johnny (later John) Williams, whose work and sincerity Herrmann greatly admired.

Friendship is a difficult word to use with Benny, because there were always adversarial aspects in every Herrmann relationship. If they weren't there he put them there. But I can use the word, because Benny was quite warmly friendly to me, more so than with most people. One big reason, I think, was that he was very fond of my late wife. If he began to be abusive, she would say, "Benny, stop that—behave yourself!" He would giggle and get flustered, even blush sometimes. It was comfortable and nice. I was really just a youngster then. While I knew about his work, I don't think I knew enough about him to have the kind of reverential respect I would have had if I had been older.

Benny was encouraging; he came to some of my recording sessions. He was never flattering, but he encouraged me. In the early sixties I wanted to write a symphony. One day at lunch I complained to Benny about wanting to write some music other than film music. He answered, "Who's STOPPING ya?" His answer was so blatant and direct—and *right*—that I went home and spent the requisite four or five months writing this piece. In my life, Benny represented some kind of avuncular push that remark illustrates so well—a man of few words, but the right ones at the right time for a young person. . . .

As I grew in experience, our friendship continued. I did a score for a television production of *Jane Eyre* in 1970, and Benny was very taken with that score. About ten years after the writing of my symphony, in 1972, André Previn performed the work at the Royal Festival Hall with the LSO. Benny said he wasn't coming because he didn't like Previn. Well, because I didn't have seats, André and I were running around the front of the box office side of the Festival Hall—and as we were fussing around, we turned to see Benny slinking into the hall, not wanting to be seen by us! He rang me up the next morning . . . and said, "It's a good piece. I like the first movement, you have a good tune in there. What did ya cover it up for with all those effects, all that excessive orchestration?" He was critical, yet supportive.

Herrmann was probably not a good conductor. He took things too slowly, generally, but he was good in that even if a piece were too slow, he would approach it with genuine conviction; he had a definite point of view. He'd say, "It's *meant* to go this tempo, and everybody's taking it too fast; they're all off the freeway in a rush. This is my conviction about the piece." Even if you didn't agree with him, his interpretation had conviction. I think that for anybody, that's a very attractive quality. Benny was sure of himself, secure in his opinions, and in some sense almost fatherly.[68]

The year 1964 was one of diminishing prospects not only for Herrmann but also for his most influential supporter. Despite the success of *Psycho* and *The Birds*, Alfred Hitchcock's standing at Universal was shrinking as studio executives tried desperately to be "hip" and capture young audiences. Their demands were hard to ignore, as Norman Lloyd recalled: "By this time Hitchcock, who was having health problems and couldn't assert himself as he had in previous years, tolerated interference he would have dealt with before. [MCA president] Lew Wasserman had a 'hatchet man' named Edd Henry, who was his liaison to Hitchcock. Henry talked like a bookie and was the tough guy. He intruded into Hitchcock's office without even knocking, and when I complained about this to Hitch he said, 'How can I stop them?' "[69]

The making of *Marnie* reflected these and other problems. In February 1964, Hitchcock's pathetic infatuation with Tippi Hedren and his attempts to control her social life ended in a row on the set. Hitchcock's description of the flare-up was characteristically terse: "She did what no one is permitted to do—she referred to my weight."[70] According to Hitchcock biographer Donald Spoto, the director had blatantly propositioned Hedren.[71] In any case, Hitchcock and Hedren did not speak for the rest of production.

Rancor spilled into postproduction that spring. Universal/MCA management were voicing presages of doom to the frustrated Hitchcock and demanding that he not hire the irascible, "old-fashioned" Herrmann to score the film, or that he at least insert a potential hit song over *Marnie's* titles. Hitchcock insisted on Herrmann, but the pressure for a marketable tune remained. Not surprisingly, Herrmann's more sympathetic colleagues suffered the brunt of his anger at Universal as he stormed through friends' homes repeating his diatribes against the corporate powers.[72]

To Herrmann, *Marnie's* most serious liability was not its lack of a pop theme but Tippi Hedren (an opinion that could hardly have endeared him to Hitchcock). Throughout Herrmann's aggressively romantic score (written for large symphony orchestra) one senses the composer trying to conceal this perceived inadequacy. His emotive theme for Marnie, a semi-quotation from the prelude for *The Seventh Voyage of Sinbad*, dominates most sequences in Herrmann's forty-seven-minute score, a repetition that prevents *Marnie* from ranking with Herrmann's best work for Hitchcock. The lush romanticism also softens one of Hitchcock's darkest films, with its art-imitates-life story of compulsive behavior and sexual blackmail.

But the score's dramatic power is undeniable, especially in the film's much-discussed fox hunting scene, which ends in the death of Marnie's beloved horse. Herrmann opens the sequence on a note of rousing cheer, with a lively riding theme for strings answered by the call of huntsman's horn. But clouds soon gather: as the phobia-beset Marnie races from the crowd, Herrmann's gallop becomes a relentlessly driving, nightmarish variant of her theme, building momentum until horse and rider tumble over a brick wall. Admittedly, the sequence's murky rear-screen projection works against credibility, but Herrmann and editor George Tomasini's expert rhythms create a heightened sense of drama that suspends most viewer disbelief.

As Herrmann expected, viewers were not convinced by Hedren's performance or the film's simplistic psychology. It was Hitchcock's first major flop in years—although, like most of the master's "failures," its reputation has steadily improved. At the time, however, *Marnie* was a foreshadowing of battles to come. The deaths of Hitch's long-time cameraman, Robert Burks (in a domestic fire), and George Tomasini (of a heart attack) shortly after the film's completion were sad reminders that an era was over.

A more devastating event awaited Herrmann that spring. None of the composer's three wives would characterize her years with Herrmann as easy, but for Lucy Anderson, unable to endure Herrmann's constant, irrational attacks on her and others, life was especially difficult. In fifteen years of marriage their relationship had paralleled Herrmann's worsening melancholia and professional jealousy; and while Herrmann seemed able to withstand emotional stress, even considering it an impetus to work, Lucy found it painfully impossible to endure.*

William Froug was one of many witnesses to the collapse of Herrmann's second marriage. "He was terrible to Lucy. My wife and I would go home from dinner with them and ask, 'How can she take this?' I remember going backstage after one of Beenie's London concerts, and there was Lucy—an attractive, sweet woman—sweating profusely. I could just see the nerves and the tension she was going through, and I thought, What can it be like to be married to this volcano that can erupt at any moment? As Thoreau would say, she lived a life of quiet desperation."[73] Joan Greenwood, wife of violinist Henry Greenwood, was among those who tried to convince Lucy to stand her ground, with little success: "Lucy died a little death every time Benny got into one of his tantrums."[74]

Returning to Bluebell one night shortly after finishing the *Marnie* score, Herrmann found only Twi and a vacated home awaiting him. Slowly realizing that Lucy had left him, he began an urgent, pathetic series of phone calls to friends that began with the same childlike question: "Why did she leave?"[75]

Elsa Clay (whose secretarial work for Herrmann ended amicably that year) was one whom Herrmann sought for guidance: "I think Benny felt that if he could persuade us that Lucy should not be leaving him, then he

---

*Although Taffy Herrmann still spent summer vacations at Bluebell, Wendy decided in 1963 not to leave her home in Maryland with Lucille Fletcher and Douglas Wallop. Relations between Herrmann and both daughters grew increasingly strained in the next decade.

might be able to convince her; and I remember his frequently using the phrases 'to look after me' and 'to take care of me.' "[76]

For Herrmann, the next months were times of desperate loneliness and anger. His few surviving friendships were tried to the extreme. "Benny was always yelling about something," Joan Greenwood said, "because he so desperately didn't want to be divorced from Lucy. He didn't want to be alone."[77] After years of abstinence, Herrmann began to drink heavily. Days were spent numbly by the pool at Bluebell in his dressing gown, nights at friends' doorsteps on the pretense of being an invited dinner guest.

"My suffering is only because of my deep love for you—and if I must let you go —in order to give you happiness—I love you deeply enough to do so," Herrmann wrote Lucy, during what would be two years of attempts at reconciliation. "So please dear heart—allow all pressures to be lifted and bask in the sun and enjoy our dear pets and have a triumphant life. . . . We have had a wonderful fifteen years together and I['d] like to spend the rest of my life with you. I married you in happiness and I cannot bear to leave you in sorrow and torment."[78]

The eloquence of Herrmann's letters contrasted sharply with the bitter tirades that possessed him during his meetings with Lucy. One lunch at a seafood restaurant became so disruptive that dining patrons approached the Herrmanns' table, prepared to intercede on Lucy's behalf if necessary.[79] Herrmann's behavior with others was hardly better. Recalled John Houseman: "He was consumed with rage and envy and malice and hatred. It got so that he was virtually unfrequentable; you couldn't spend an evening with Benny without his spending half of it in a terrible diatribe about one of the young musicians who'd gotten a job. It was boring, unbearable."[80]

Only a conducting trip to Manchester that spring—Herrmann's last— redeemed 1964. Yet he discovered that concertgoers no longer packed Free Trade Hall as they had in the thrilling postwar days of Britain's cultural revival; in fact, these would be the most sparsely attended of Herrmann's Halle appearances.

The first, on April 19, was unique for the presence of an important listener: Sir John Barbirolli. It was no coincidence that Herrmann conducted the first Halle program Sir John attended as a member of the audience since becoming the orchestra's director in 1943. Ironically, while Herrmann's selections were typically Anglo-oriented (Delius's *Walk to the Paradise Garden*, Handel's *Water Music*), Barbirolli's own request was American: Bennett's *Symphonic Pictures from "Porgy and Bess."*[81] Reviews were extremely favorable (Herrmann's Delius was "like a second Beecham," his Handel "as though he had been on the river himself that afternoon," according to the *Daily Express*), but it was Barbirolli's description of the concert as "a wonderful experience" that meant most to Herrmann.[82]

His May 20 concert with the Philharmonia Orchestra at London's Festival Hall was equally praised. The Delius piece again appeared ("full of fine shading and delicacy," wrote the *New Daily*), along with Wagner's *Tannhäuser* Overture, Tchaikovsky's Sixth Symphony, and the *Enigma* Variations—"a moving and beautiful reading," in which "almost every possible idea that piece could have was extracted and projected."[83]

Yet Herrmann's personal life was reaching new lows. "I am not trying to upset you or agitate you," he wrote Lucy that May, "but I am so exhausted from the strain of all the work—the divorce suit and its problems and the concerts—that I am slowly but surely reaching a point of no return—that is I cannot begin to consider any work of any kind—I live in a daze and concern—for both of us. I bless you dear one—keep well— you are ever in my heart and thoughts."[84]

Little work awaited Herrmann on his return to Hollywood. As Hitchcock prepared his next film, a cold war thriller to be filmed in 1965, Herrmann returned to CBS and Universal television to score his last "Twilight Zone" and Hitchcock episodes, as well as several ill-fated pilots. The jobs were not enough to alleviate his frustration. In an act of self-pride and defiance, Hermann raised his fee as work offers dwindled, even to Ray Harryhausen and Charles Schneer. After reading the script for their next project, a version of H. G. Wells's *First Men in the Moon*, "Herrmann gave us a price twice what he'd asked for before," Schneer recalled. "We couldn't afford it—we just didn't have the money—and he was very upset, with me in particular. One day he walked into my office, threw the script on the waiting-room chair, and slammed the door without saying a word. That's when we broke."[85] Herrmann's friend Laurie Johnson scored the film.

"The Americans" was one of CBS's most ambitious new series in 1965, a Civil War drama whose pilot benefited greatly from Herrmann's theme and score. Coincidentally, former Fox music editor Ralph Ives was among those on the Goldwyn lot during scoring: "When Benny saw me, he asked me to work on the program with him. During the editing we talked a lot together. I learned it was a lean period for him. He was very depressed; he told me he was in the middle of a divorce and that no one was hiring him. He also felt he'd been a little too outspoken with some of the people who were hiring composers."[86]

"The Americans" was canceled shortly after its fall premiere.

Herrmann scored just one film in 1965. *Joy in the Morning* was a depressing reflection of how low Herrmann's film career had sunk. Based on Betty Smith's novel about troubled newlyweds in the 1920s, the MGM film was amateurishly acted (especially by stars Richard Chamberlain and Yvette Mimieux as Carl and Annie), badly written, and hideously directed by Alex Segal. Predictably, MGM insisted that Herrmann's score share screen time with a title song by Sammy Fain and Paul Francis Webster (a surprisingly pleasant melody, warbled by Chamberlain under the film's credits).

To offset the film's unrelenting mawkishness, Herrmann offers a score of gentle lyricism, much of it for strings soli. Thematically, the score is rarely original: the hypertensive romanticism of *Marnie* is echoed throughout (as in Herrmann's plaintive string harmonics when Carl and Annie set foot in their first home). The music's quiet intensity and occasional humor (for example, the jaunty pizzicato promenade as Annie eyes a female rival) are all the film has to offer.

Under the terms of his divorce settlement, Herrmann left Bluebell; the furniture remained with Lucy, as did Twi and the cats. (Months later, Lucy and Herrmann agreed to share the house: Lucy would stay at Bluebell during Herrmann's six-month trips to England.) Alone and unemployed, Herrmann followed in the steps of other divorced composers and filmmakers by moving into Sportman's Lodge. He turned to composition and his first concert work in fourteen years, "a series of nostalgic emotional remembrances" for string quartet titled *Echoes*. (Given Herrmann's depression, the work's title may also recall a feeling the composer expressed to Lucille Fletcher at the time of their separation: "More and more I feel that perhaps I am not possessed of any real great talent. It is perhaps an echo of a talent—that is why I can conduct and do all kinds of musical activities—they are all echoes—never the real voice.")[87]

The piece itself is bleak and confessional. While many of its memories remain private (making *Echoes*, in an unassuming way, Herrmann's own *Enigma* Variations), others can be guessed by allusions to past works. Running through each of the work's ten sections is Herrmann's typical disregard for formal development or long melody lines in favor of an affecting simplicity of expression. Most of Herrmann's favorite devices appear: a sad *valse lente*, a lyrical barcarole, a habanera with its allure of Latin syncopation, each briefly recalling happier occasions through the melancholy vision of the present. Some episodes seem deliberately to impart no feeling at all, like the Prelude, its "cool objectivity . . . the expression not of an emotional neutrality but of a state of mind in which the nerves have ceased to vibrate with their former frequency and register impulses only as remembered echoes."[88]

The origins of the Allegro are unmistakable: the plucked signature of its opening is *Psycho*'s violent prelude, the crying violin harmonics of its coda, *Vertigo*'s lost Madeleine. Soon this brief outburst of emotion gives way, inexorably, to the solemn epilogue-prelude, the dark, low tones of viola and cello forming a stepladder for the violins' climbing harmonics, abandoned at the peak of their range in a last, poignant expression of isolation. (The work's dedication, "To N. S.," was not, as some believed, to the next Mrs. Herrmann, Norma Shepherd—whom he met in 1966—but to Nancy Sanderson, a California friend who also had gone through a painful separation at the time *Echoes* was composed.)[89]

The quartet received its premiere on December 2, 1966, in London's Great Drawing Room in St. James Square, in a recital that also featured Edmund Rubbra's Third String Quartet. (Herrmann had long been one of Rubbra's greatest champions in America and England.) The concert received scant notice, although a 1967 recording of *Echoes* inspired a positive notice in *The Gramophone*: "The quartet repertory . . . is surely badly in need of other pieces which are something other than fully serious large-scale works; here is such a piece, and it includes many passages of real beauty into the bargain."[90]

If *Echoes* helped to channel Herrmann's pain, it hardly replaced its cause. With nothing but Hitchcock's next film, *Torn Curtain*, to look forward to, Herrmann decided to go on a cruise, to find the diversion he sought with increasing desperation. During the trip he met Kathleen MacDuffy, a former model also traveling alone to escape unhappiness in California. The discovery of a beautiful, lonely traveler was a perfect tonic for Herrmann's spirits, inspiring his most gallant and erudite behavior after months of self-pity. Another result of the trip was Herrmann's unlikely hiring of a Japanese maid to look after Cumberland Terrace, after a wealthy Asian couple who befriended Herrmann on the voyage decided a servant was the cure for his ills. Their recommendation, a quiet young girl of allegedly noble ancestry, also met with Herrmann's approval, although her refusal to do housework in the presence of her male employer would cause minor havoc during Herrmann's London stays.[91]

Herrmann's sea journey recharged his energies. Sullen fits of anger still interrupted his routine and friendships, but with the promise of a new film ahead Herrmann was determined to remain in Hollywood.

The fates, however, were against him. As Herrmann realized, times had changed: good scores were becoming "as rare as whales in telephone booths," he complained to the *Hollywood Reporter*. "In my 24 years in Hollywood the standard of movie music has gone down, down. A large percentage of producers today are so unaware of their pictures they're looking for a musical gimmick to lure the public. Like the hit title tune, a harmonica surrounded by a choral group, the twanging sound of an electric zither, or the wail of a kazoo in an espresso cafe. Stuff like that. It only takes away from what's happening on the screen." Ironically, perhaps defensively, Herrmann put his faith in one director: "There are still a handful of producers like Hitchcock who really know the score and fully realize the importance of its relationship to a film."[92]

From London that November he also wrote Lucy a cautiously optimistic note: "One does run into these rough times—and the new year looks much better. I shall be doing Hitch's new film 'Torn Curtain' and shall be back in L.A. after Christmas to begin work on it . . . so here's for a better year."[93]

# THIRTEEN

JOHNSON: If an architect says, "I will build five stories," and the man who employs him says, "I will have only three," the employer is to decide.

BOSWELL: Yes, Sir, in ordinary cases. . . .

*Boswell*, Life of Johnson

*Torn Curtain* was the prophetic title of Alfred Hitchcock's fiftieth film, a box office disaster that also ended cinema's most distinguished director-composer relationship. The reasons for Herrmann's famous breakup with Hitchcock, after twelve years of collaborative masterpieces, are as complex as the two strong egos at the conflict's center.

Some rancor existed between the two as early as *Psycho*, when Hitchcock's attempt to reduce Herrmann's usual fee was met with resentment by the composer. *Psycho* made a fortune, as did Hitchcock's television series; but the more the director's wealth increased, the more obsessively he tried to keep it all for himself. The change in Hitch, Herrmann believed, was due to Universal and MCA chief Lew Wasserman: "They made him very rich," Herrmann later said, "and they recalled it to him."[1]

From the early 1960s Herrmann had little but contempt for Universal's priorities in film music. Some time earlier, recalled David Raksin, "Benny had turned down a job from Wasserman, who got angry and said, 'All right, Benny, when you get hungry you'll come to see me.' Herrmann said, 'Lew, when I get hungry I go to Chasen's.' "[2] By the time of *Marnie* Universal wanted little to do with the "old-fashioned" composer,[3] and tried to convince Hitchcock to agree with them. *Marnie* had been a flop—and part of the reason, they told the director, was the lack of marketable music. That year "A Hard Day's Night," the soundtrack to the Beatles' first movie, had outgrossed the film's profits . . . and so the argument went.

Hitchcock had changed as well, becoming more egocentric as well as insecure.[4] In his dealings with Universal he was an apologetic child facing

267

a stern master, but with film collaborators he became increasingly cruel and begrudging of any suggestion that they had contributed to his success. Hitchcock's secretary, Sue Gauthier, recalled a typical incident: "George Tomasini had been told by his doctor his cholesterol level was too high and that he had to change his diet, so George was given a vacation. Before leaving he sat for two and a half hours outside Hitch's office to say goodbye—but Hitch never interrupted what he was doing, and he knew very well George was waiting to say goodbye. Hitch never saw him again; a short time later George was dead. George had idolized Hitch, and they had had a long, very good association. It was a terribly cruel thing to do."[5]

By 1965 Herrmann was receiving similar treatment. Despite his championing of Herrmann to Universal executives, Hitchcock was tiring of the composer's abrasive personality, even though the latest outbursts, Hitch knew, were partly the result of his divorce from Lucy. Nevertheless, for Hitchcock, Herrmann had become "a very difficult man."[6] Hitchcock was also convinced that Herrmann was recycling past compositions. Listening to Herrmann's *Joy in the Morning* score in a private screening, Hitch told his assistant, Peggy Robertson, that Herrmann was using music that rightfully belonged to his films.[7]

The only person who seemed to anticipate disaster was Herrmann. Now in England, he relied mainly on Robertson as his liaison with Hitchcock—and her descriptions of what Hitchcock wanted in the *Torn Curtain* score were not encouraging. Herrmann became convinced that Hitchcock no longer planned to use him. He was probably right, considering the improbable (for Herrmann) demands Hitchcock stipulated in a lengthy cable of November 4, 1965:

DEAR BENNY

TO FOLLOW UP PEGGY'S CONVERSATION WITH YOU LET ME SAY AT FIRST I AM VERY ANXIOUS FOR YOU TO DO THE MUSIC ON TORN CURTAIN. HOWEVER I AM PARTICULARLY CONCERNED WITH THE NEED TO BREAK AWAY FROM THE OLD FASHIONED CUED-IN TYPE OF MUSIC THAT WE HAVE BEEN USING FOR SO LONG. I WAS EXTREMELY DISAPPOINTED WHEN I HEARD THE SCORE OF JOY IN THE MORNING, NOT ONLY DID I FIND IT CONFORMING TO THE OLD PATTERN BUT EXTREMELY REMINISCENT OF THE MARNIE MUSIC. IN FACT, THE THEME WAS ALMOST THE SAME. UNFORTUNATELY FOR WE ARTISTS, WE DO NOT HAVE THE FREEDOM THAT WE WOULD LIKE TO HAVE, BECAUSE WE ARE CATERING TO AN AUDIENCE AND THAT IS WHY YOU GET YOUR MONEY AND I GET MINE. THIS AUDIENCE IS VERY DIFFERENT FROM THE ONE TO WHICH WE USED TO CATER; IT IS YOUNG, VIGOROUS AND DEMANDING. IT IS THIS FACT THAT HAS

BEEN RECOGNIZED BY ALMOST ALL OF THE EUROPEAN FILM MAKERS WHERE THEY HAVE SOUGHT TO INTRODUCE A BEAT AND A RHYTHM THAT IS MORE IN TUNE WITH THE REQUIREMENTS OF THE AFORESAID AUDIENCE. THIS IS WHY I AM ASKING YOU TO APPROACH THIS PROBLEM WITH A RECEPTIVE AND IF POSSIBLE ENTHUSIASTIC MIND. IF YOU CANNOT DO THIS THEN I AM THE LOSER. I HAVE MADE UP MY MIND THAT THIS APPROACH TO THE MUSIC IS EXTREMELY ESSENTIAL, I ALSO HAVE VERY DEFINITE IDEAS AS TO WHERE MUSIC SHOULD GO IN THE PICTURE AND THERE IS NOT TOO MUCH. SO OFTEN HAVE I BEEN ASKED, FOR EXAMPLE BY TIOMKIN, TO COME AND LISTEN TO A SCORE AND WHEN I EXPRESS MY DISAPPROVAL HIS HANDS WERE THROWN UP AND WITH THE CRY OF "BUT YOU CAN'T CHANGE ANYTHING NOW, IT HAS ALL BEEN ORCHESTRATED." IT IS THIS KIND OF FRUSTRATION THAT I AM RATHER TIRED OF. BY THAT I MEAN GETTING MUSIC SCORED ON A TAKE IT OR LEAVE IT BASIS. ANOTHER PROBLEM: THIS MUSIC HAS GOT TO BE SKETCHED IN, IN ADVANCE, BECAUSE WE HAVE AN URGENT PROBLEM OF MEETING A TAX DATE. WE WILL NOT FINISH SHOOTING UNTIL THE MIDDLE OF JANUARY AT THE EARLIEST AND TECHNICOLOR REQUIRES THE COMPLETED PICTURE BY FEBRUARY FIRST.

SINCERELY,<br>HITCH

(Blank carbon copy sent to Edd Henry, Tower building.)

Cut from Hitchcock's typed draft of the cable was the sentence "Will you please cooperate and do not bully me."[8]

The film was already in trouble. *Torn Curtain* was a thriller without thrills, a tedious script worsened by dull performances from its stars, Julie Andrews and Paul Newman. Hitchcock was aware of its problems, and probably considered the soundtrack its most viable commercial venue.

Herrmann later claimed to have turned down the film initially. "I knew they were wrong," he said in 1975, "and I was the wrong man to do what they wanted."[9] Perhaps he did decline prior to Hitchcock's November cable. But on receipt of Hitchcock's instructions, Herrmann sent a surprisingly conciliatory reply: "DELIGHTED TO COMPOSE VIGOROUS BEAT SCORE FOR TORN CURTAIN ALWAYS PLEASED HAVE YOUR VIEWS REGARDING MUSIC FOR YOUR FILM PLEASE SEND SCRIPT INDICATING WHERE YOU DESIRE MUSIC CAN THEN BEGIN COMPOSING HERE WILL BE READY RECORD WEEK AFTER FINAL SHOOTING DATE GOOD LUCK, BERNARD."[10] The cable did not satisfy Hitchcock, who sensed an attempt at compromise. Hitchcock told production associate Paul Donnelly to restress to Herrmann his position on the score.

November 11, 1965

Dear Benny:

Delighted to hear you will again be associated with Hitch on his current production "Torn Curtain." . . .

Benny, there is one point that Hitch asked me to stress and that is the
fact that you should not refer to his "views" toward the score, but rather
his requirements for vigorous rhythm and a change from what he calls
"the old pattern."

If these terms meet with your approval, please write or cable me upon
receipt of this letter.

By the following week, Herrmann had worked himself into a state of
near emotional collapse. He had not received the script and had heard
nothing. His worst suspicions returned:

November 18, 1965

Dear Peggy:

Nearly two weeks ago I replied to Hitch's cable. . . . As of today I have
not received the script and am anxious to have it as it will allow me to get
down to work on it. I would also like to have Hitch indicate where he
wishes music and also his ideas about the kind of music for each cue. If he
could describe these in the same manner as he does when he gives the
sound dept. his notes on sound. However, if he is too busy to do this
now—could you at least send me the script as soon as possible. Also, bear
in mind that I can quickly compose the score so as not to be too far behind Hitch's shooting. When would he like me to return to begin on the
film? I could start on *December 27* (Monday) and be ready to record on
*19th of January*—which gives us the week of *January 24th* for dubbing
and therefore making the Technicolor date of February 1st. This plan
allows me 3½ weeks for composing, 2 or 3 days for the orchestra
scoring—and a full week for dubbing—or if needed one could start dubbing
on Friday January 21. Please let me know how the above plans meet
with Hitch's plans and approval. . . .

I have been asked to do Truffaut new film next May or June. I am
certain that this is because of Hitch and I thank him for it. . . .

I send to all my greetings and all the best for the TORN CURTAIN.
Indeed I feel certain it will be one of Hitch's greatest films. I just know
it will be so.

Love
Benny

Herrmann received the script a week later and wrote an encouraging
letter to Robertson and Hitchcock. On December 3 Robertson replied:

"Was so glad to get your letter and reactions to the TORN CURTAIN screenplay. Am really looking forward to the time when you screen the film which is really and truly marvellous—I think it will be Hitch's greatest. I read your letter to him and he was most pleased, as you can imagine."

Hitchcock did not write the requested music notes until February 15, 1966. Curiously, considering the trepidations he and Herrmann shared about scoring, the notes consisted only of stop/start indications, with the exception of the main title: "On opening of 'TORN CURTAIN' I feel that the Main Title should be an exciting, arresting and rhythmic piece of music whose function would be to immediately rivet the audience's attention. Irrespective of the abstract designing of the titles and their background, the music could be, and should be, written before this is achieved."[11] Herrmann complied, on his terms: his prelude was exciting, rhythmic, and riveting. But it was not jazz or pop music.

Herrmann returned to Los Angeles on December 27, still fighting deep fits of depression. At a meeting with Hitchcock, he played his sketched themes for *Torn Curtain*, a series of short, oppressive devices that Hitchcock decided were too "heavy."[12] Hitchcock also demanded there be no music for the film's lengthy murder sequence; he stressed the need for a melodic love theme; and, according to Norman Lloyd, he told Herrmann there was to be "no Richard Strauss" this time.[13] (If this quote is correct, it demonstrates Hitchcock's limited understanding of Herrmann's music, which usually was as thematically and orchestrally understated as Strauss's could be excessive.)

Communication between the two men during the next month was almost nonexistent. Working in isolation at Sportsman's Lodge, Herrmann wrote a score that he believed would save Hitch's mediocre film—a score that, like *Psycho*'s, would give the narrative new focus and tension.

And in doing so, he disobeyed most of Hitchcock's instructions.

"What 'Torn Curtain' needed was music that didn't make these people into ludicrous TV characters, but into reality," Herrmann said in 1971;[14] and to achieve that he devised, somewhat paradoxically, one of his most outlandish and texturally unusual orchestrations: sixteen french horns, twelve flutes, nine trombones, two tubas, two sets of timpani, eight cellos, eight basses, and a small group of violins and violas. The bizarre mosaic of mainly brass and woodwinds, Herrmann felt, would be as disturbing as *Psycho*'s pure strings: "The sound of twelve flutes," he told Laurie Johnson with quiet excitement, "will be *terrifying*."[15] Thematically repetitious (simple scale devices are repeated and inverted), the score would achieve its effect from the chilly blend of the horns' austerity and the woodwinds' sensuous harmonics.

Herrmann's prelude introduces this startling color with a leaping, dissonant horn fanfare, which against spiraling flute chromatics becomes a huntlike theme of pursuit. The horn-flute juxtaposition reappears even more harshly in the murder sequence (as with *Psycho*, Herrmann believed Hitchcock would at least try it his way). Built on the familiar interval of the minor third (a popular device for danger or fear), the sequence builds to a pitch of brutal horror through a canonical horn pattern, echoing flutes, and driving timpani. Only once in the entire score does the instrumentation soften to hint at lyricism—although unlike the exploitable tune Hitchcock clearly wanted, Herrmann offers a melancholy valse for viola d'amore, similar (but inferior) to his "Memory Waltz" from *The Snows of Kilimanjaro*.

Overall, Herrmann's music for *Torn Curtain* evokes a deliberate steeliness and aridity, an emotional gray versus the black-and-white contrasts of *Psycho* or the colorful romanticism of *Vertigo*. It was a brave tactic to score Hitchcock's "TV characters" with music that seems, at least when heard apart from the film, monochromatic in texture. Hearing the score on its own, one cannot accurately assess its success; but considering Herrmann's past record of brilliant audacity, the chances were highly in his favor.

By late March 1966 the score was finished. Two days for recording were booked at Goldwyn Studios. Horn and flute players were astonished to find their sections expanded to four times their usual size, but after recording the title sequence the orchestra gave Herrmann a spontaneous ovation, a rare honor from session musicians.[16]

The murder sequence and at least half of the score had been recorded when Hitchcock, dour and silent, arrived with Peggy Robertson.[17] Herrmann, pleased with the day's work, asked the engineer to play back his prelude. Hitchcock listened—then told Herrmann it was exactly what he had not wanted. Then the director learned that Herrmann had scored the murder sequence: another breach of agreement. Herrmann began to panic. A studio break was quickly called, but only a few terse words were left to be exchanged between director and composer.

"I heard the first segment," Hitchcock later said, "and I said, 'Finished, no other way, finished; goodbye, here's your money, sorry.' "[18] The actual scene was no less patronizing or abrupt. Hitchcock left Goldwyn, drove directly to Universal, apologized to the studio heads for his error, canceled the next day's scoring, and reportedly offered to pay Herrmann's fee with his own money.[19]

A brilliant twelve-year collaboration, and one of Herrmann's proudest friendships, had collapsed. Alone at Goldwyn Studios, Herrmann's reaction was initially disbelief, then growing anger. Later that day Hitchcock called, more demonstrably angry than at the session, and Herrmann was his verbal match: "I told him, 'Hitch, what's the use of my doing more with you? Your pictures, your mathematics, three zeros. My mathematics, quite different.' So it meant forget about it; I said, 'I had a career before, and I will afterwards. . . . He said he was entitled to a great pop tune. I said, 'Look, Hitch, you can't outjump your own shadow. And you don't make pop pictures. What do you want with me? I don't write pop music.' "[20] Both voices were rising, and the conversation quickly ended. It was Hitchcock and Herrmann's last.

Herrmann's pride in standing his ground was soon replaced by a depression unmatched since Lucy's walkout. Norman Lloyd was at his Universal office that afternoon when the telephone rang:

It was Benny, completely shattered. He said, "I've got to see you immediately." I asked him to come to my office. He said, "It would be very bad if I go on the lot." So we met at a little hamburger joint on Ventura Boulevard. And to sit at a deserted hamburger joint on Ventura Boulevard at 2:30 in the afternoon, on a sunny California day, was like being relegated to a corner of Dante's hell. Benny arrived and told me what had happened—and that day I saw him as an almost totally destroyed human being. To Benny, his relationship with Hitchcock and his history with Welles were the two greatest things in his life. He considered himself a very good friend of Hitchcock's, and he felt it was over.

So we debated the issue—was there anything that could be done? Could we enlist the music department at Universal? Then we realized they were the ones who had set up the whole situation, so there was no hope there. And there was no way that Hitch was going to listen to another note of the score. So one just held Benny's hand; the situation was one of total destruction.[21]

Word of the falling out spread quickly among composers, and at least one—Dimitri Tiomkin—wasted no time in offering his services as a replacement.[22] But it was English composer John Addison (winner of 1963's Best Score Oscar for *Tom Jones*) who was hired to quickly write a more "appropriate" score. Despite Addison's eagerness to work closely with Hitchcock, the director left for London to begin promoting the film, limiting their communication to telephone. When Addison called to play prospective cues, "most of the time [Hitchcock] would just say 'Right.' "[23] On his return, Hitchcock decided that Addison's score still

lacked the hit theme Universal now insisted on, so Jay Livingstone and
Ray Evans were drafted to join Addison in writing a new song for the film,
"The Green Years." After much indecision on Hitchcock's part, the song
was not used.[24] Hitchcock's battle for a pop score had failed—and *Torn
Curtain* was indeed the box office bomb everyone expected.

For years Hitchcock was noncommittal about the entire episode, and
for an equally long period Herrmann rose to the director's defense. "It's
not Hitch's fault," he told David Raksin and cellist Edgar Lustgarden the
night of his firing, as the two men tried to coax out his pent-up
resentment.[25] In fact, both director and composer felt deeply betrayed by
the other. As far as Hitchcock was concerned, Herrmann had defiantly
broken their agreement, despite explicit instructions. For his part, Herrmann believed that after their trust of twelve years, Hitch owed him the
chance to prove his approach: "A patient goes to a doctor because he isn't
well. That's what music is—music is part of helping a picture. And the patient gets well and goes back to the doctor and says, 'Well, I know I got
well, but you didn't make me rich!' Today a composer must not only write
a film score, he must also make everybody rich."[26]

Neither viewpoint was subject to change. "Obviously they were both
on different courses before the collision," said John Williams, who worked
with both. "They were two men whose characters may have permitted a
lot of irritating things to have gone unnoticed longer than they should."[27]

When asked about the breakup, Herrmann sometimes told a light-
hearted story about Toscanini and Puccini. After a falling out, he said,
each removed the other from his Christmas panatoni list. When one of
the two men's assistants accidentally sent the other a plate of the forbidden bread, the sender immediately followed the gift with a telegram:
"Panatoni sent by mistake." Replied the recipient: "Panatoni eaten by
mistake."[28] In Herrmann's case, however, such a scenario was wishful
thinking. Despite unusually humble peace overtures from the composer,
Hitchcock never forgave. Years later while speaking at USC, Hitchcock
was asked if he would work with Herrmann again; he replied with thick
condescension, "Yes—if he'll do as he's told."[29]

As usual, Hitchcock got his laugh.

Financially, Herrmann was secure, thanks to royalties from past film
and television work. Professionally and emotionally he had reached a na-
dir. The television series "Twilight Zone" and "Alfred Hitchcock Presents" had been canceled (though Herrmann probably would not have
worked on the latter), and Alfred Newman had been succeeded at Fox by
his brother Lionel, who viewed Herrmann's talent differently: "Benny

was a marvelous orchestrator, but he couldn't write a tune to save his ass."[30] Besides, Lionel told Herrmann at the time, producers didn't want him anymore; they were "running with the new kids."[31] It was a phrase Herrmann never forgot.

In his private life, Herrmann still pathetically sought reconciliation with Lucy. His letters to her—unlike their meetings—remained loving and supportive; they also convey gentle advice that Herrmann could not accept himself:

There is no need for you to ever consider cutting back as you put it. You will have the funds to continue to live as you now are. I promise you this—I do not wish you to add to your other fears—the one of thinking that you will not be able to continue to live as you now are doing. . . . It gives me great comfort to know that you are in a lovely flat surrounded by the things that you love and that mean so much to you. I bear you no anger but only concern for your welfare and happiness. What ever you may think—at all times I have remained your friend and have and still have your care and contentment at heart. There is no need for you to work unless the job gives you pleasure and enriches your life. So please chase the bears out [of] the forest—except the cubs—I know how much you love them. Please don't allow new fears and anxieties to add to those you already are fighting. So be of good cheer—good heart—and keep remembering that your welfare is a deep concern of mine—and always will be so. . . .

Please take care of yourself—be of good heart and allow your spirits to sing the day along.

Bernard[32]

One happy film project remained for Herrmann that April, as France's premier director, François Truffaut—who that year would publish a book of interviews with his idol Hitchcock—prepared his debut in English-language cinema.

*Fahrenheit 451* was an adaptation of Ray Bradbury's 1953 novel set in a futuristic society where books have been outlawed and Gestapo-like firemen start fires to destroy the thought-provoking contraband. For Truffaut, the leap from French cinema to work in English was premature. Compounding his difficulties with the language (Truffaut could barely communicate without an interpreter)[33] were the inherent problems of dramatizing a fantastic yet psychological novel. The result was a film that faithfully evoked Bradbury's austere social vision (with some memorably droll touches) but conveyed less of the intended message of hope and courage for the future.

If *Fahrenheit* was not totally successful in visualizing Bradbury's poetic universe, it did produce one major victory. Smarting from rejection and convinced that his days of film scoring were over, Bernard Herrmann found himself sought out by the best of young filmmakers, as well as a cineaste who shared his love for the genius of Welles and Hitchcock. "Usually young men tell the old fellows to get the hell off the boat," Herrmann remarked. "Truffaut and Hitchcock are highly complementary to each other. Hitchcock is known as the master of suspense but what is most characteristic of him is his romantic attitude. Truffaut is also a romanticist. He's an extension of Hitchcock and his only heir apparent."[34]

Herrmann was deeply touched by Truffaut's offer, but when the two men met in London he was outwardly suspicious, as usual: "When Truffaut spoke to me about doing the score for the film, I said to him, 'Why do you want me to write you "Fahrenheit"? You're a great friend of Boulez and Stockhausen and Messaien, and this is a film that takes place in the future. They're all avant-garde composers. Why shouldn't you ask one of them?' 'Oh no, no,' he said. 'They'll give me music of the twentieth century, but you'll give me music of the twenty-first.' "[35]

Herrmann's idea of the film's score, however, differed from Truffaut's: "I felt that the music of the next century would revert to a great lyrical simplicity and that it wouldn't have truck with all this mechanistic stuff. Their lives would be scrutinized. In their music they would want something of simple nudity, of great elegance and simplicity. So I said, 'If I do your picture, that's the kind of score I want to write—strings, harps and a few percussion instruments. I'm not interested in all this whoopee stuff that goes on being called the music of the future. I think that's the music of the past.' "[36]

Deeply heartfelt and rich in impressionistic nuance, *Fahrenheit 451* was the composer's finest screen work since *Psycho* and proof, for those who needed it, that Herrmann did not need a Hitchcock thriller to write a brilliant score. Like the novel and film, Herrmann's score is a long emotional crescendo that charts, with initial uncertainty, the emancipation of Montag, the rebellious fireman (Oskar Werner). "In the plot of *451* the hero reads a book and the heroine makes love, and they are persecuted for it," Herrmann said in 1975. "Well, these things set to absolutely pure music become horrifying. But if the music was to have been nervous and excitable, it would not have worked. That was my approach. I tried to make it beautiful, the idea that people meet in one place and at one time, prisoners because they read. They therefore have fine thoughts, and I felt that through music I could transfigure them and their lives into something really hauntingly beautiful."[37]

*Fahrenheit's* clever title sequence—in which credits are spoken over a chilly montage of twenty-first-century Britain—gives the first musical hint of this emotional inhibition: life as "some kind of fantastic nursery game,"[38] with childlike, crystalline glockenspiel chimes falling through a lush cascade of harp arpeggios and muted strings. But despite Herrmann's sensuous orchestration (which recalls Delius's *A Song of Summer*), the music remains emotionally neutral: "There's a greyness about it," Herrmann noted. "This was purposely done."[39]

Herrmann's description of the stormtrooper-firemen continues this "aimless music for an aimless life," though more brutally, its strident, monotonous theme for strings and percussion "a kind of parody of lots of avant-garde music."[40] Significantly, Herrmann's first suggestion of compassion comes midway in the film, as Montag secretly reads his first book, *David Copperfield*. By *Fahrenheit's* moving conclusion, in which the ex-fireman joins the renegade book people in the hills (a sequence enhanced by a magical, real-life snowfall), this simple melodic fragment has blossomed into what Herrmann described as "a full song of humanity."[41] Like the film's uncertain finale, the poignancy of the music is intensified by the hint that the book people's efforts may be in vain (a point Truffaut makes with a young boy's stammering recitation of his dying grandfather's book). Like many of Herrmann's best works, the cue ends on a pattern of sensuous, jarring chords that hang unresolved as the last image fades. Of this finale Ray Bradbury said, "Every time I hear the music Benny composed for it I burst into tears."[42]

At least one Shepperton Studios executive, however, demanded that Herrmann's finale be thrown out and replaced by a pop song. "He didn't get his way, of course," Herrmann recalled. "This same executive also said to Truffaut in my presence, 'I don't like your picture at all.' Truffaut replied, 'I didn't ask your opinion, did I?' Such rare integrity is seldom encountered. It is difficult to find two people who stick together on a film."[43]

Herrmann and Truffaut's mutual admiration survived to the end of Herrmann's life, though their two collaborations were not without problems. "The thing that tried Benny's patience to the utmost was the language problem between them," Laurie Johnson recalled. "I went to one of the *Fahrenheit* recording sessions at Denham [in London's Pinewood Studios] and it was very funny. Benny couldn't speak French, and at that time Truffaut could hardly speak any English. We were in the control room running the music back, and Truffaut said something about the harp glissandos fighting each other in the fire engine sequence. Benny was saying, 'Take the harps out.' I was just standing there, and suddenly Benny turned to me and said, 'Laurie, you know what I mean—YOU tell him!' 'I can't speak any French either!' I told him—but Truffaut turned silently to me as if to say, 'You can tell me?' "[44]

That year Herrmann worked on one more film project of sorts. Although he was not asked to score *The Family Way*, a gentle English comedy starring Hayley Mills and Hywell Bennett, Herrmann did give scoring advice to its first-time film composer, Beatle Paul McCartney, as a favor to producers John and Roy Boulting. In exchange for the consultation, Herrmann was given a Chagall.[45]

Regenerated by his work on *Fahrenheit 451*, Herrmann turned to another project almost as therapeutic. He was still deeply frustrated by lack of interest in *Wuthering Heights*; the most recent rejection of the opera, this time by a German company, was because of its non-"problematic" style in an era of experimentalism.[46] If no one was interested, Herrmann decided, he would produce it himself—on disc.

No record company was interested in financing such a venture: who would listen to an album of an opera no one had ever heard, or heard of? Undaunted, Herrmann formed a cofinancing arrangement with Pye, an obscure London record company, in which he paid most of the expenses. Next came the selection of vocalists, which Herrmann tightly controlled. A brunette soprano named Morag Beaton was chosen as Cathy, baritone Donald Bell as Heathcliff.

By the time rehearsals began in the late summer of 1966, Herrmann, excited by the recording, had become a less-than-benevolent dictator, as his good friend Ursula Vaughan Williams recalled:

Benny was in a very nervous and edgy state, and without a piano, so the rehearsals for *Wuthering Heights* took place at my home in Gloucester Crescent. This was an obvious venue, because I had Ralph's Steinway. A young composer named Jeremy Dale Roberts (Benny thought he was called Jeremiah), who was a good pianist, lived in a flat in the basement, and Morag Beaton was staying with me. Joseph Ward ([cast as] Edgar Linton) was already my friend, and with Donald Bell and Elizabeth Bainbridge (Isabel Linton) he came to rehearse; I think it was all much calmer when Miss Bainbridge was there. Benny was perhaps more passionate about his opera than any other of his works, and conducted Jeremy as if he were a full orchestra; Morag was deeply nervous, Donald seemed to get taller and paler as the hours passed, Joseph thinner and thinner, and Morag frequently cried. I brought in gallons of coffee when the strife was at crisis point.

At the recording sessions in Barking Town Hall, there were more storms and tears; Benny behaved atrociously to Morag and made her dreadfully nervous. He had collected a wonderful ad hoc orchestra [the Pro-Arte]; one of the players asked me, "What are you doing here?" "Prisoner's friend," I said.

After those ghastly sessions, the record was lovely.[47]

In London, Herrmann gave the work its "premiere" with a listening playback for friends, including Truffaut and singer Marni Nixon. That evening he also met Gerard Schurmann, a thirty-nine-year-old composer whose modern idiom was very different from Herrmann's style. Nevertheless, Herrmann admired and championed his work, finding him a publisher in Novello & Co. (who had recently begun publishing Herrmann's music).

Months earlier Herrmann had met Schurmann's companion (and future wife), Carolyn Nott, a writer who had interviewed Herrmann for a London music publication; almost desperately, he had sought her friendship. In person and in letters he began giving her professional and personal advice: "No person can be a purpose or meaning in life—to allow this to happen can only lead to bitter frustration and in the end a sense of wasted time. . . . And of your talent I have no doubts—I feel you should work on a novel—a play or even short stories . . . do not write from your head—but from your heart. Novels and plays that are of emotions and people who are vivid is what matters. Not ideas—ideas become dated—but feelings are always the same."[48] The Schurmanns became close friends of Herrmann's for the next five years—until, as always, the inevitable breach occurred.

Returning to California, Herrmann held another private playback of the opera for friends, among them Norman and Kathryn Corwin, CBS executive Guy Della Cioppa, and Ray Bradbury. Said Bradbury:

It was a very exciting evening. When the opera was over after three and a half hours, we all sat there, stunned and moved. And because our applause was ten seconds in coming—as happens when you suddenly realize something is over—Herrmann was very upset with us, that we didn't leap to our feet and thunder our warmth! He whirled around, hurt, and started to leave the studio. We went over to him; I patted him on the back and said, "There, there, everything's okay, we still love you!" Everyone smothered him with affection, this little boy trapped in a large body. I think we all have these same feelings; we just pay more attention to them in talented, famous persons, and we notice how easily they are hurt. Maybe it's true of everyone who ever existed in the world, and we just don't notice it.

I had written a play called *Leviathan 99: Moby Dick in Outer Space* which I thought would make a wonderful opera, so I invited Mr. Herrmann to have lunch with me and told him the story. At lunch we discussed it—I had given him a copy of the script a few days before—and he said, "What I really want to do is the story of Lady Godiva as an opera." I sat there stunned: "Jesus God, what do you do when she gets off the horse?" It's a story like Don Quixote that defies adaptation. I pleaded with Herrmann, saying, "Please, I don't want to do Lady Godiva; I wouldn't know what to do with it. Please look at my material again, because to me you're the bastard son of Puccini, if you'll accept that as the compliment I mean it to be." Fortunately he took it as a compliment, but he never got back to me. It's a great shame; I think we could have done something quite wonderful.[49]

Copies of *Wuthering Heights* found their way into the homes of nearly everyone Herrmann visited. One afternoon during a social gathering at cellist Lucien Laporte's home, Herrmann played the entire recording; but few guests remained by the time of Cathy's dying breath. Two exceptions were Louis and Annette Kaufman, who tried to persuade Herrmann to record his other concert works—*Moby Dick* perhaps, or the symphony with its exciting scherzo.[50] On the surface, Herrmann disagreed, but the idea—probably already in his mind—stayed with him.

While most listeners were no doubt grateful to hear *Wuthering Heights* in a form other than Herrmann's croaking recitations,* few were entirely satisfied. After a Sunday listening to the opera (during which Herrmann "conducted" the entire piece) Alfred Newman remarked privately to his wife, Martha, what an extremely long work it was. His words to Herrmann were naturally congratulatory.[51] Another well-known composer conveyed little more than polite encouragement:

Dear Bernard Herrmann:

I spent most of yesterday playing over the records of "Wuthering Heights" that you very kindly had sent me, and following the opera in the vocal score. Yours is a very dramatic score, powerful and lyrical by turns,

---

*Music critic Page Cook was discussing the opera with Herrmann in 1966 when, "totally unexpected, in a rather full dining room, Herrmann began to sing 'Now art thou fair, my golden June' from the opera, in something of a very craggy baritone. I was a little disencountenanced but then, realizing this was Bernard Herrmann, just sat back and listened, trying to make something out of the noises he was producing" (Cook to Craig Reardon, 11-12-78).

and I do hope you will have the satisfaction before long of seeing it staged somewhere, so that the full impact of the work can be felt.

> With best wishes for it
> Yours sincerely
> Arthur Bliss[52]

Other responses were less kind. According to Herrmann the BBC returned its copy (submitted by the composer), the album wrapper unopened, with a terse note saying it was "not appropriate" for broadcast.[53]

Nevertheless, Herrmann considered the recording a complete triumph. "After so many years of it being in my head and on paper it finally now lives on sound for all to hear," he wrote Lucy Anderson that May. "It is a fine performance and very exciting. It all sounded exactly as I had imagined—nothing needed to be changed or rewritten—the work is really an original one—and certainly is the best I have done. It plays nearly 3 hours [in fact, nearly 3½]—and as such it is really a big impressive work. The singers and orchestra were first rate—and were most taken with it. . . . I had many years of torment and anguish to bring this work into being—but I am certain that it had to be done and I feel that you will agree. Some how now my purpose in life seems to make sense."[54]

Through the opera's recording, his travels to Europe, and his work with Truffaut, Herrmann had found short-term distractions from the loneliness that plagued him. A more permanent solution was discovered that December of 1966 in London, at a party given by a perfume saleswoman Herrmann had met at Fortnam's and her husband. Among the guests was Norma Shepherd, an attractive twenty-six-year-old journalist and Oxford graduate, who was warned early on by her hosts about an amusingly outspoken American who would interrupt any conversation when he became bored. Later, when she was formally introduced to Bernard Herrmann, Norma realized they had already met:

Benny and his friends used to go to an Italian restaurant in Soho owned by a young man who had been at Oxford with me and whom I had been going out with on and off for years. That New Year's Eve Benny and I met again at the party, and it was very hard to get taxis afterwards. Benny was leaving at the same time I was; we were both going in the same direction, so we got in the same taxi and he said, "You two have been hanging around together so long you should either get married or not get married—I mean, what's going on?" That's the way he'd speak to a stranger.

I told him, "Oh, we're not going to get married; I know him too well—he's like a brother now." Benny then invited me to lunch. He used to invite all sorts of people out; he adored young ladies. He would go to Christian Dior and chat up all the salesgirls, then come back with Christian Dior beads for me! He knew all about each of the girls' love lives, their mothers and families. He was always great on giving everyone advice, which is what he was doing with me in the first place.

Over lunch that January he'd say to me, "What kind of a life do you lead? Don't you know any interesting people—poets and actors, not all these faceless gray people at the BBC."* It was a kind of rudeness. I said, "I'm sorry, I don't know any poets, but I do know a few actors."[55]

As Herrmann learned, Norma was equally good at giving what she got, and in spite of his mocking jabs at women jouralists, he admired her sharp sense of humor and Yorkshire spirit. (Recalled Joan Greenwood: "Benny was sitting in our garden, looking in amazement at some of our birds. I said, 'We have wrens, magpies, bluetits, greytits, coldtits. . . . ' With the most wicked grin Benny said, 'The *sto*-ry of my life.' Norma snapped, 'Get BACK into the gutter from whence you came!'—and Benny loved every second of it.")[56] In turn, Norma saw through Herrmann's pretenses: to her he was "a toffee-apple, all crusty on the outside and soft on the inside":[57]

The first time I went to Benny's flat in Cumberland Terrace, I was forced to listen to *Wuthering Heights* from beginning to end. I knew the book from start to finish, but I'm not musical. What do you say when someone forces you to listen to three and a half hours of his life's work? I was sitting in a corner, on an uncomfortable seat, thinking, What does he expect me to say? I don't know what I finally said—something probably very disappointing.

Benny loved to buy things for young women. He actually had the nerve of buying another girl friend of his a little bottom piece of an eighteenth-century necklace, and the top part and a brooch for me. Well, one day she came over, produced her half, and said, "Do you remember this eighteenth-century—" asking Benny how to get it mended. I just gulped, and was naive enough to say, "Hey, wait a minute, that's my broo. . . . " She was terribly embarrassed. Benny went pink and bit his lip; then his shoulders started shaking like a child caught doing something. He giggled [to] himself all evening.[58]

Herrmann's *Souvenirs de voyage*, written in January 1967 for string quartet and solo clarinet, reflects this rise in the composer's spirits. Like the string quartet it is nostalgic and often melancholy, but its romanticism and tonal colors are immeasurably warmer—a change attributable to Herr-

*Norma would become a writer at the BBC in 1973.

mann's two key relationships of the period: his professional one with Truffaut and especially his personal one with Norma.

The quintet's more specific inspirations come from three distinct artistic sources. The first movement owes its origin to A. E. Housman's poem "On Wenlock Edge the wood's in trouble" (from the *Shropshire Lad* collection, the source of musical settings by Herrmann twenty-three years earlier). Unlike Vaughan Williams's song adaptation of the poem in his cycle *On Wenlock Edge*, Herrmann's use of the verse is more suggestive than literal, evoking, in Palmer's phrase, "the force which plays havoc with the minds of men, now as in the days when Wenlock Edge was part of a Roman encampment."[59] Herrmann alternates a tumultuous setting, filled with gusty clarinet arpeggios and fluttering string tremolos, with a lovely *valse triste* for violin; the coda suggests Housman's last stanza:

> The gale, it plies, the saplings double,
> It blows so hard, 'twill soon be gone;
> To-day the Roman and his troubles
> Are ashes under Uricon.

The second-movement Berceuse also carries Vaughan Williams allusions, shifting to Ireland's Aran Islands, site of John Millington Synge's novel *Riders to the Sea*, which had inspired an opera by the English composer. In the Berceuse one can envision a cloud-drenched, autumnal sunset off the Irish west coast, Herrmann's swaying, dreamlike rhythm for strings and sighing clarinet appogiaturas rising like wave crests against their foundation.

These dark colorations of "remembered loss" make way for a third movement that is contrastively lush and romantic—not surprisingly, given that Turner's dazzling Venetian watercolors served as the movement's inspiration. (This is Herrmann's only "official" Turner setting, though the artist's influence can be heard throughout Herrmann's music, especially *Moby Dick*.) A love theme is sung by violins, its gentle ripples heard in viola and clarinet arpeggio responses; "as the lagoons shimmer in the evening sunlight, echoes of a trumpet summons from a distant barracks are born in the wind"—a remote clarinet shanty, one of Herrmann's loveliest and most simple depictions of nature's enticement. A lively tarantella for strings suggests far-off revelry, but Herrmann's lovers ignore it; their theme reappears in blissful solitude, "left to die peacefully into the still of the night."[60]

The clarinet quintet was Herrmann's last concert work, but hardly his last word on the medium. Encouraged by the recording of *Wuthering*

*Heights,* he decided similarly to preserve other of his concert works, again mainly at his own expense. Pye agreed to distribute two more albums, *Moby Dick* and the suites *Welles Raises Kane* and *The Devil and Daniel Webster,* which were recorded in May and June, respectively. The orchestra was the London Philharmonic, always ready to bolster its income by recording the music of film composers, if not to give them public concerts.

The summer sessions were far less tense than those for the opera, but for the rest of his life Herrmann approached his London recording sessions with an abrasiveness that masked insecurity. In the case of *Moby Dick,* his apprehension was shared by John Amis, a BBC radio personality who often hosted Herrmann on his program, and who was then taking singing lessons:

[Benny] was interested in my singing venture, scolded me for continuing with my lessons instead of getting out there onstage to sing. "Why the heck don't you open your mouth in public?"

"Because no one will pay me to sing as yet."

"Well, I will," says he. . . .

Didn't he want to hear me first—to see if I was right? "Damn it, no, just say which part you want and you're engaged."

I took a look at the score and decided on Ishmael. Who wouldn't like to deliver some of those lines: "Call me Ishmael"? Before the recording he did at last hear me. "Having difficulty with that G sharp, huh? Well, sing any damn note you like, provided it fits the harmony and the declamation." Interestingly, almost word for word what Brahms said to the young George Henschel when singing a solo baritone part in one of the master's choral works.

Came the recording day, Barking Town Hall; that great recording engineer Bob Auger in charge; . . . a small professional male chorus [the Aeolian Singers]; David Kelly, a helpful old friend, as Ahab. I was considerably beset by nerves as may be imagined but . . . , I hope, not showing it too much. I sang it reasonably accurately, but on the rare occasions when I listen to it, I can't say I like it.[61]

Most critics agreed with Amis's assessment, although the cantata on disc received far more praise than it had in 1940. "On this rehearing it seems quite evident that Herrmann's response to the arrangement by W. Clark Harrington of salient passages from Melville's novel produced quite the strongest, best music of his known to me," wrote Irving Kolodin in *Saturday Review.* "Its straightforward, non-complicated musical style is, in itself, a pertinent commentary on musical 'innovation.' Who cares now whether it was first performed in 1940, 1920 or 1910? Its continuing existence depends not on how it sounded when it was new, but how it sounds now that it is old. In my judgment, very well indeed."[62]

*Welles Raises Kane* and *The Devil and Daniel Webster* was Herrmann's best album to date, with sharp playing and lively tempi (later conducting by Herrmann would be increasingly lethargic). Another *Saturday Review* colleague, former CBS director Oliver Daniel, had kind words for both the music and its composer, in a page-long "Perspective on Herrmann":

While not pretending to be a magnum opus, [the Daniel Webster suite] is one of the most sprightly bits of nostalgic Americana in the entire orchestral repertory. . . . Unlike Copland, who in similar situations strove constantly to impress his individuality by various harmonic devices, Herrmann pours out his music with a total lack of self-conscious identification and achieves a naturalism of such high order that one accepts it as a mainstream piece. . . .

Those who have worked with [Herrmann] know that he can be insulting, vehement, raucous, and even brutal. But those who know him better are aware that he can also be kind, sentimental, tender, and loving. He has withal a capacity to inspire devotion as well as anger. I can attest to that. And it is no surprise to find Sturm und Drang—Herrmann fashion— abruptly alternating with almost sentimental serenity in his works.[63]

Herrmann sent a copy of the album to the dedicatee of the *Daniel Webster* suite, William Dieterle, now a resident of Liechtenstein. Replied Dieterle:

Dear Benny:

The record is fantastic! I played it several times the first evening and would have played it all through the night but the neighbors! The music brought back so many sweet memories—thank you ever so much for it. I also want to thank you for the clipping about my film, "The Last Flight." It would be wonderful if we could meet again . . .

All the best wishes
Bill[64]

Despite his revivifying activity in the recording studio, Herrmann's return to film that year, on his second and last collaboration with Francois Truffaut, was a surprising disappointment. This time the director did not have to explain his choice of composer: *The Bride Wore Black* was Truffaut's homage to Hitchcock, an adaptation of a story by Cornell Woolrich (author of *Rear Window*'s source material) about an obsessed woman avenging the death of her bridegroom, who was accidentally shot on their wedding day. Jeanne Moreau led an excellent French cast, and Truffaut's knowledge of Hitchcock's oeuvre, as well as his own body of work, promised an exciting film.

Yet for the most part, *The Bride Wore Black* proved an uncompelling misfire. Perhaps Truffaut was too genteel an artist to film what Herrmann rightly described as "a story of emotional revenge . . . an emotional *Monte Cristo*."[65] The motive of the anonymous avenger (Moreau) is revealed midway through the film, and the story's vein of macabre humor, as Moreau methodically kills the five men responsible for her groom's death, goes largely untapped.

As with *Fahrenheit 451*, Herrmann's challenge was to enliven a sterile film with a layer of psychological complexity. "It was a rather simple film to work on," he told the BBC during the film's scoring. "The process of musical thinking was to try to enter into the psychic thinking of a woman who is motivated by one motive, and that is to revenge the dead."[66] Herrmann's intellectual focus on the story was as sharp as ever; but his score is oddly lifeless. Mendelssohn's "Wedding March" is its chief motive, recalled, in a ghoulish organ fortissimo, with each flashback to the doomed wedding procession; it also provides witty, ironic punctuation in the film's final moments, when Moreau stabs her last victim in prison and her *Liebestod* is consummated. But Herrmann's own music rarely moves beyond the superficial violence and agitation of his main title, as throbbing, dissonant horns and percussion suggest the single-minded death wish of the protagonist.

So morbid a tale was bound to inspire some inventive moments. A nervous pizzicato device for strings against falling brass and winds describes Moreau's cross-country travels to each murder with economy and excitement; and the "Miser's Waltz" from *All That Money Can Buy* is echoed in a mordant dance of death as the bachelor Corale, freshly poisoned, watches Moreau waltz around him: a vibraphone intones the Dies Irae, mocking Corale's drugged state, and churning brass and winds mimic both dancer and the nausea that "tears apart" the dying man.

The recording session in Paris, a city that Herrmann loved, was especially frustrating for the composer. On *Fahrenheit* he had had to deal only with a non-English-speaking director; now he faced French musicians, conductor (André Girard), and recording engineers as well. Truffaut did not hear the score until the session, which was documented by BBC television cameras filming a segment on Herrmann. Truffaut's remarks about the score were implicitly favorable ("[The film] includes fity-six minutes of music, and all fifty-six minutes are absolutely necessary").[67] Privately, though, he was disappointed.[68] At the session Truffaut asked Herrmann to rescore one scene, the poetic journey of the scarf that wafts from the balcony off which Moreau has pushed her first victim. Herrmann's original cue was a long, ethereal, and haunting melody for strings; its hasty replacement was a neobaroque, simple guitar tune whose obvious humor contrasts awkwardly with Herrmann's consistently somber approach. Later, Truffaut moved and shortened other cues in the film; most peculiarly, he replaced Herrmann's jaunty scoring for the sympathetic victim Corale's first appearance with a brooding ostinato for harp and winds. (Truffaut did send the Herrmanns a note, with a dozen roses for Norma: "François Truffaut is very happy man with music of Bride Whore [sic] Black and he say thank you very very much for you and Norma your inspiratrice. Amitiés à vous 2, François.")[69]

Herrmann was angered both by Truffaut's score tampering and by the reediting of the film in its dubbed U.K. release. "I feel that it's a remarkable film," he said in 1971, "but it has been mucked around in both English and French versions. . . . When I last saw [Truffaut], he was talking about recutting 'Les Quatre Cents Coups.' He feels that a director can go back and recut. He doesn't like to leave a film just as he has finished it, contrary to Orson who says 'That's it' and Hitchcock who never looks at his films again. He runs them for people but he always leaves the room. When it says 'The End' he comes back with a cigar. He says, 'Why do I want to see it? I see all the things that are wrong with it. There's nothing I can do now.' "[70]

A happier bride entered Herrmann's life on November 27, 1967, when the fifty-six-year-old composer and twenty-seven-year-old Norma were married at London's Marylebone Register Office, with Joan and Henry Greenwood in attendance. The short ceremony was followed by a trip to a West End cinema to see *Far from the Madding Crowd*—"but it was so crowded we left before the end," Norma said. "Later we went clothes shopping in Bond Street. Benny always liked to go into a shop and pretend he was a gentleman, saying, 'Bring that' and 'Why don't we buy that.' Our salesgirl that day obviously thought she was on to a good thing and said to me, 'Would your father like a chair?' Benny loved that story."[71]

Less convivial were Herrmann's living arrangements, for although he now worked almost exclusively in England, he could not bring himself to subject his beloved pets to England's twelve-month quarantine. The result was an annual six months in England, and six months of inactivity at Bluebell Avenue.

The Hitchcockian parallels of *The Bride Wore Black* underscored a sad irony in Herrmann's career: despite twenty-seven years of film scoring and the breadth of his skills, he was now being hired or considered almost solely on the basis of his eight scores with Hitchcock, with whom he would never work again. In 1965 William Wyler thought of using Herrmann for his film *The Collector* but decided he did not want "a Hitch man";[72] Maurice Jarre—who would score Hitchcock's 1969 film *Topaz*—was hired instead.

If Hollywood's old guard had forgotten Herrmann, a new generation on the fringe was just becoming interested. Cumberland Terrace became a pilgrimage for "hip" young directors, all eager to work with the master but rarely having the money to talk seriously. Few left, however, without constructive advice from Herrmann or a meal from Norma. A typical case was Wim Verstappen, a young Dutch director of low-budget exploitation films, who showed Herrmann his latest "sex and psycho suspense mystery" *Obsessions* (co-written by a young Martin Scorsese). A 1969 press release captures the tone of this and other films screened for the composer:

A hole in the wall. The beginning of an exciting erotic adventure. Through the hole, in the next apartment, a man and a woman are seen, making love. Next, this man is giving the girl injections. She gets unconscious. An innocent young medical student, who has watched all this through the hole, wants to know more about the mysterious behaviour of his neighbor. He wants to know what's wrong with the girl. When his neighbor is out, he breaks into the room and finds a second girl, lying naked in the bathtub, also unconscious. . . . Suspense mounts, and the plot reaches some breathtaking climaxes, coming to a surprisingly shocking finale.[73]

Neither content nor budget put the film in Herrmann's league, but because the composer liked Verstappen he directed him to the CBS music library, where his stock music could be acquired more cheaply;[74] hence the curious place of *Obsessions* in the composer's filmography as a Herrmann score that isn't.

His film career at a standstill, Herrmann began reconsidering the project he had discussed with Ray Bradbury months earlier. The story of Lady Godiva's ride through medieval Coventry was a favorite of Herrmann's and one that (apparently to him alone) had musical and dramatic potential. With empty appointment diaries for 1968 before him, Herrmann decided he had both the time and means to adapt the English legend, for a medium he had previously avoided: musical comedy. It was an odd choice, to say the least; but after the droll Truffaut film, and perhaps eager to prove his diversity, Herrmann began a light-hearted experiment.

For a collaborator Herrmann's friend, BMI executive Richard Kirk, recommended New York lyricist Diane Lampert.[75] Initially Lampert, who had written lyrics for fifties rock 'n' roll, contemporary pop, country, jazz, folk opera, and film, seemed an odd choice. But the forthright songwriter was in some ways a perfect complement to Herrmann with his mix of cantankerousness and vulnerability. Lampert found him to be "like seven bears bitten by twenty-one bees," melancholy yet inexhaustible: "Some people drink coffee to get their machinery going before work. Benny cranked himself up to emotional outbursts that exhausted me. Then he'd try revitalizing, with charm, wit, warmth, sensitivity and intellectual stimulation. . . . Benny introduced me to London and appointment books—so afraid of being alone, he was obsessed with filling empty pages. On Christmas he accepted three invitations thinking each might cancel."[76]

Working in London and Los Angeles, they prepared an outline for the musical (titled *Ride a Cock Horse*), several song lyrics, and some music. But as others expected, the project was doomed. Somehow the English legend about charity and honor (Godiva rode nude to force her husband, Leofric, to reduce city taxes) became a sophomoric burlesque show, heavy on sexual innuendo. A sample of its outline:

Leofric attempts to cajole his uncooperative wife into his bedchamber. . . . (I WILL NOT BE SEDUCED [TILL TAXES ARE REDUCED]). . . . Leofric and his Ministers now muse upon the Good Old Days . . . when one just banged his woman over the head and dragged her off to bed (A CAVE, A CLUB & A WISE). . . .

[Godiva discusses] the re-decoration of her Castle with Chintz, Secretary of Interior and Restoration. . . . Chintz's assistants Minuet in displaying bolts of material—wool from virgin lambs—linen from gently flagellated flax. . . . The trio section of the Minuet becomes a jazz madrigal. . . .

Leofric . . . consults with his three advisors: the Apothecary, the Astrologer, and the Magician. . . . In a mystical, magical setting, his three Advisors trying to impress him, sing: HOCUS-POKUS, HANKY-PANKY, CRYSTAL-BALLING. . . .

Chintz has bought out the Chastity Belt Factory and has converted it into the manufacturing of his new discovery the *bed spring* . . . a new bounce to sex. Chintz and Godiva . . . giggling like two children at play, gayly Can Can as they test out the mattress (CAN TO CAN—CAN CAN). . . .

Lord Leofric bursts into the room in a rage of jealousy. . . . He accuses her of being a harlot in the song: (A TART FROM NOTTINGHAM).

Lady Godiva furiously replies that inasmuch as he has accused her of being a harlot . . . she will justify his accusations by walking nude through the streets of Coventry. He sarcastically and bitterly replies—"A Lady always rides!" . . . Suddenly all her need for recognition, adulation and love is completely illuminated, and she is triumphant and ecstatic at the prospect that those who already adore her and her beauty can now feast their eyes on her nakedness.

Leofric . . . issues an edict that anyone who has the effrontery to peep at his gorgeous wife in the nude will be blinded. . . .

A STABLE. . . . Two stable boys are grooming Lady Godiva's horse for the big ride. . . . The frustration of the stable boys and the populace are voiced in a sensuous song about her long glowing golden hair, and soft white derriere riding on *almost* the luckiest horse in the world, for he too must wear "blinkers" . . . (RIDE A COCK HORSE). . . .

The ride is about to begin! (Our Program Book informs the audience that there is a pair of dark spectacles available for those who do not wish to run the risk of having their eyes blinded by witnessing the ride). . . . The music that will accompany her ride is a hush sex waltz—blending into a strip Minsky Burlesque tempo. . . .

[Godiva] removes a piece of clothing every time she goes behind a building, a tree, etc.—until she reaches almost complete nudity. We never see her below the waist until she comes practically at the footlights.

At this point, the maid who is leading the horse . . . screams "someone has peeked!" The maid is very agitated and so is the music as the curtain descends on Act One.[77]

After *Horse*'s demise, Herrmann chose a more adaptable source for a musical, again with Lampert as collaborator. Since childhood Herrmann had loved Israel Zangwill's *The King of Schnorrers*, a satirical tale of rival Sephardic and German Jews in eighteenth-century London. The 1893 novel had been adapted into both musical and nonmusical plays (in New York in 1905, and in London in 1925 and 1930), but by 1968 no version was still being performed. After months of copyright investigations (the novel had become a viable property after the success of *Fiddler on the Roof*), Herrmann obtained story rights and began work with Lampert and writer Shimon Wincelberg. (Wincelberg had worked at Twentieth Century Fox in the 1950s and written many CBS television scripts, but he did not meet Herrmann until work began on *Schnorrers*).

Wincelberg's book caught the spirit of Zangwill's lively 1790s London and its roguish schnorrers (Jewish beggars who have turned their "profession" into an art). Its dialogue captured (albeit lightheartedly) much of the resentment felt by Sephardic and Russian Jews toward their German counterparts—a resentment that Herrmann remembered from his own childhood.

Herrmann's score, rooted in the energetic, minor-key Yiddish music of his teenage years, evokes a similar if less explicit air of cultural pride, both in idiom and in titles like "Long Live He," "It's a Long Walk from Here to Jerusalem," and "It Is Writ." Absent, however, are a sense of light-heartedness and extended lyricism: solemnity shadows most of the nineteen songs in *Schnorrers*. Attempts at operetta-style comedy, like the ironic servants' ode "What the Butler Sang" and the Georgian dressers' dance "Ducks and Drakes," misfire. For years Herrmann had vilified other composers' reliance on melody for musical effect. It is not surprising, then, that Herrmann's own attempts at popular melody writing seem halting and incomplete. (Three songs from *Cock Horse* found their way into *Schnorrers*: "The Ballad of Lady Godiva" became the lovely final duet between young lovers Yankel and Deborah, "Epithalamium"; "An Olive from Spain" evolved into the droll habanera "It Is Writ"; and "Swans and Swains" became "Ducks and Drakes.")

Some of Herrmann's longer, more lyrical melodies (for example, the valse-ballad "A Tree Without Sun" and the gentle love theme "Before I Was Born") are genuinely touching and skillfully crafted. ("A Tree Without Sun" was Herrmann's favorite song in the score, a theme that reduced him to tears when he played it for others.)[78] Other songs, like the plaintive soprano solo "You Mind Your Own Heart," just seem unfinished; throughout, Herrmann resists conventional song forms and relies on mere chorus repetitions. As a musical, *The King of Schnorrers* was hardly a triumph; but it was certainly an improvement on *Ride a Cock Horse*. The writing process, however, had taken its toll. By the time the work was completed Herrmann and Lampert had fallen out (the lyricist's new husband, Fred Stewart, had little patience for his wife's occupation, which led to group friction); and when director Mel Shapiro mounted a production of *Schnorrers* at Connecticut's Goodspeed Opera House in 1970, none of its creators were on speaking terms.[79]

Even in happier circumstances, the Goodspeed production would not have pleased them. Shapiro disliked the *Schnorrers* book, while Goodspeed music director Lynn Crigler reportedly disliked the score.[80] Herrmann knew changes were being made in the musical and could have stopped the production, but chose not to.[81] His own disinclination to discuss the project in later years seems a tacit admission of disappointment. Heavily rewritten in an attempt to make the story more accessible, the production lost what distinction *Schnorrers* had had, despite an excellent performance by Raul Julia, a late casting choice, as the king.

# FOURTEEN

He, for his part, had a countervailing grudge against the world, fancying the work he did for it but feebly remunerated.

*Israel Zangwill*, The King of Schnorrers

Although Herrmann's relationship with Hitchcock would never improve, one Hitchcock-related project remained for the composer: "The Great Movie Thrillers," Herrmann's first of twelve recordings for Decca and the affiliated London Records. A much larger label than Pye, Decca was uninterested in recording Herrmann's concert works,[1] but it did release more commercially viable albums of his film music. Herrmann chose five scores for the Hitchcock album, each adapted for the new medium. Some changes were merely interpretive, like the more expansive tempi of the *Vertigo* suite. Two scores, for *Marnie* and *The Trouble with Harry*, were arranged into one-movement concert suites; nine *Psycho* cues were linked in a "Narrative for Orchestra"; and the rousing *North by Northwest* overture was expanded in length.

Herrmann's intentions in recording the album (besides promoting music he rightly considered neglected) were painfully clear to those still close to him: it was a rare attempt at reconciliation. "Most people think of Hitchcock as a master of mystery and suspense," Herrmann wrote in his liner notes. "Although this is fundamentally true, he is also a great romantic director, his films allowing enormous scope for sensual and lyrical musical treatment. This record displays many of his diversified talents." *Harry*'s score became an eight-minute tribute to Hitchcock: "The film is in many ways the most personal and the most humorous of Hitchcock's entire output. It is gay, funny, macabre, tender and with an abundance of his sardonic wit, and I hope my interpretation of these moods will in turn be transformed into a portrait of 'Hitch.' "[2]

As a collection of Herrmann's best Hitchcock scores, "The Great Movie Thrillers" (recorded with the London Philharmonic in December 1968) was a satisfying testament to the composer's work. As an olive branch it was a total failure. Earlier that year Herrmann and Norma had made an unannounced visit to Hitchcock's Universal office. With a copy of Truffaut's Hitchcock volume in hand, Herrmann approached the director's assistant Peggy Robertson and asked to see Hitch. She told him Hitchcock was out. His voice rising, Herrmann demanded that Hitch sign his book, since Truffaut had had "the decency" to sign a copy.[3] He and Norma left the studio, never to return, unaware that Hitchcock had been standing just feet away, behind the ajar door of his office to avoid Herrmann.[4]

Three years later Hitchcock was back in London to film his last exceptional thriller, *Frenzy*. Henry Mancini was hired to write the music; but after its recording, Hitchcock rejected the score later commenting, "If I want Herrmann, I'd *ask* Herrmann."[5] (Mancini never understood the experience, insisting that his score sounded nothing like Herrmann.)[6] Composer Ron Goodwin replaced him—"And you know what?" Herrmann said in 1975, clearly hurt: "Hitchcock told Ron Goodwin . . . he thought his was the greatest score ever written."[7]

Another sad echo of the break was Herrmann's only film of 1968, *Twisted Nerve*, a feeble English thriller far removed from Hitchcock's masterworks. Another Boulting Brothers film starring Hayley Mills and Hywell Bennett, it inspired Herrmann's most self-derivative score to date. Although the simplicity of the main theme (for solo whistler, the score's one novelty) is a commentary on the film's retarded protagonist-killer, the main impression is one of boredom. No doubt because of studio pressure, Herrmann's theme recurs in the film as a jazz piece, arranged by English composer Howard Blake. "There were two great remarks Herrmann would always make," Blake recalled. "If you tried to suggest a cue was a little weak, he'd say, 'Film music is a mosaic art.' And on anything he didn't like: 'We live in a *sub*culture.' I once asked him what his favorite instrumental lineup was. He said, 'Strings, and one vibraphone.' I asked, 'How many times have you used that?' He said, 'In five hundred radio shows with Orson Welles.' "[8]

Another reminder of Herrmann's CBS days came one afternoon as the composer lunched with John and Roy Boulting at Shepperton Studios. Also in the commissary was John Green, then working on the musical *Oliver!* (1968's winner for best picture): "Benny walked in wearing an enormous Ragland overcoat and a big muffler around his neck, although it was a nice English day. By this time he was already carrying a walking stick. I hadn't seen him in years and was thrilled. I jumped up, damn near knocked my chair over, and said, 'Benny! How are you?' Well, if he'd been Hitler and I'd been a Jew, he couldn't have been less friendly. He castrated me with a look. Sir John Woolf, the producer of *Oliver!*, was sitting next to me. With perfect timing, over a mouthful of sole, John said to me, 'Who's your friend?' "[9]

Herrmann's next Decca album, "Great Tone Poems," offered revealing strokes of the conductor's personality behind a conservative program of Sibelius's *Finlandia*, Dukas's *The Sorcerer's Apprentice*, and Liszt's *Les Préludes*. Each work had played a role in forming Herrmann's own musical vocabulary, and if his readings were often leaden, his love of the music helped give them dramatic viability. Herrmann's version of the Sibelius must be the bleakest of all Finlandian landscapes; no other conductor would make so much of its ferocious, declamatory opening. The Dukas and Liszt offer similar pleasures of orchestral color at the cost of rhythmic drive, but both also emphasize the links between Herrmann and his material, as in the mordant wit of Dukas's writing for woodwinds or the jabbing string downbeats that terrorize the mischievous apprentice.*

If Herrmann's studio albums were rarely first-rate, at least they kept him occupied. That October, discouraged by a continual lack of film offers, Herrmann found new representation with English agent Liz Keyes, whom Hollywood orchestrator Herbert Spencer had recommended. Yet little changed; recalled Keyes, "Producers were trying anything other than a symphonic score."[10]

If anything, the gap between Herrmann and Hollywood was widening. In late 1967 he resigned from the Academy of Motion Picture Arts and Sciences: "I do not approve of music being listed as a technical credit," Herrmann told the *Los Angeles Times*. "And there's no point to belonging to an organization in which one is judged by one's inferiors—not one's peers. It was Tolstoy who said 'Eagles fly alone and sparrows fly in flocks.' But I'm afraid we eagles of the world are being pushed into sanctuaries."[11]

His view of Hollywood producers remained equally dim:

If I were starting now I'd have no career in films. I don't like the "new look" in film scores. They have nothing to do with the movie. Or, a

---

*Herrmann conducted one public concert with the Philharmonic in Hastings on December 10; the program was Wagner's *Tannhäuser* Overture, Delius's *Walk to the Paradise Garden*, Elgar's *Enigma* Variations, and the Tchaikovsky Sixth. It was the last time Herrmann would conduct any of those pieces.

movie can be nothing but $2½ million spent to promote a disc Producers should ask themselves, "Will I get a record or a fine picture?" Pictures have become a promotional gimmick for music publishers and recording companies. I can't understand how you can make a sophisticated film, then proceed to the lowest common denominator in the score, which will turn out to be rubbish. . . .

Everybody's looking for a new sound, which means taking an old sound and jacking it up and amplifying it till your ears hurt. There are no new sounds, only new ideas, and they don't come along very often. . . .

Yet it is almost impossible to make movies without music. Movies need the cement of music: I've never seen a movie better without it. Music is as important as the photography.

My only real complaint is that cinema music is not reviewed in the press, yet it reaches the greatest audience in the world. A film score will live longer than any other kind of music. I predict the 21–22nd centuries may not be interested in our art but will be interested in our cinema. Wouldn't you like to see a movie made in 1860? Yet because there's no critical attention to movie music it's left to producers who are musical ignoramuses. . . .

What has happened in music today is that it's become highbrow. If more than two people understand it, it's passé. Composers feel it means moral degeneration to their souls to do a film. Such preciousists! Stravinsky was once asked by Selznick if he would be interested in doing a score. Stravinsky said yes—for $100,000. Selznick said, "We never spend that much on music." Stravinsky replied, "My music's cheap—it's my *name* that's expensive."

America is the only country in the world that has so-called "film composers." Every other country has composers who sometimes do films. You have to be a good composer before you can be a "film composer," and I wouldn't call most of my colleagues composers. If there weren't any money in films they wouldn't do it. [12]

Yet for Herrmann, England was scarcely better. Once, orchestras like the Halle and the BBC had considered him an important force in American concert music; but neither organization would invite him again to conduct. Herrmann blamed the BBC's rebuff on the odd coincidence that *another* Bernard Herrmann, an English conductor of music hall songs and pop music, led the BBC's Northern Orchestra and that the two men had become confused. The BBC denied any confusion—though that did not prevent the American Herrmann from receiving the Englishman's BBC income forms year after year. [13]

One year, after BBC radio announced that the Beatles were visiting arranger Bernard Herrmann at London's Broadcasting House, Norma and

Herrmann found teenage girls scaling the walls of Cumberland Terrace in search of the moptops. Herrmann also received fan mail intended for the Northern Orchestra conductor, and delighted in reading it; recalled Norma: "He said how wonderful it was to read how people loved you, even though you knew it was for the wrong person."[14]

Herrmann's last scoring project of 1968 was for another marginal suspense drama, notable mainly as the only television movie Herrmann scored. *Companions in Nightmare* was directed by Norman Lloyd, former coproducer of the Hitchcock TV series and Herrmann's friend; its impressive cast (Melvyn Douglas, Anne Baxter, Gig Young, Patrick O'Neal, Dana Wynter, and Leslie Nielsen) enhanced a mystery that would have been equally well served as an hour Hitchcock episode. The theme of repressed madness (Young's character is actually a psychotic murderer) was well suited to Herrmann, and his music was genuinely suspenseful, if streamlined like several of his television scores. The score is most interesting as a partial blueprint for *Sisters* four years later: both the murder music, with its clanging percussion and wailing horns, and the finale, in which unresolved high strings are answered by the chilling toll of a bell, anticipate Herrmann's music for the De Palma film.

Without Norman Lloyd's involvement it is unlikely Herrmann would have been asked to score the TV film. Hollywood continued to ignore its reluctantly resident composer, which left Norma without friends or interests and Herrmann in his Bluebell study with his books and pets. In addition to caring for his own three cats and the beloved Twi, Herrmann often lured the stray animals of North Hollywood to his home with expensive food, then trapped them, had them neutered, and set them free.[15] One dog that remained was Alpy, a ragged half-breed named after the American dog food Alpo. Strange and wolflike, Alpy softened around the master who loved her: "When God made all the dogs, he had little bits left over and put them in a drawer," Herrmann would say. "When he pulled the drawer out, there was Alpy."[16]

Herrmann's 1941 Packard, long undriven, had become a permanent nest for squirrels. When Norma asked to use the car (she had none of her own), Herrmann refused: "It's their home." Later, Norma recalled, "A man came from an exterminator company and said he could get rid of all our squirrels—we were overrun with them. Benny yelled and screeched and chased the man down past our front gate, and he didn't get over it for the rest of the day. He told everyone he met this story about the man who wanted to exterminate the squirrels, and every time he'd get just as angry as he'd been."[17]

Ida Herrmann, almost eighty but as cantankerous as ever, still came out from New York to see her favorite son. Her visits were stressful for both Herrmann and Norma, as they had been for the previous Mrs. Herrmanns: now, Ida demanded to know why Benny's union wasn't doing something about getting him work.[18]

Still, as this letter from Norma to Carolyn Schurmann illustrates, the doldrums at Bluebell Avenue had a lighter side:

I personally am dying to get back to England. . . . I am getting bored with the ghost of ex–Mrs. Herrmann. The post office sent my letters back to England saying Mrs. Herrmann left five years ago. He hasn't bothered to tell anybody he's married, and all sorts of things happen with people who think she's moved in again. The best of all is with the gardener who is 93. He cornered me under the lemon trees and told me how he couldn't stand Herrmann, how difficult he was to work for, and how did *I* find him? He ended up by saying how glad he would be when THEY went back to England, and asked me if I'd be glad. So I said I was anxious for THEM to go. That gardener chops down trees (he says Mrs. Herrmann likes them that way) and doesn't bother to tell people to get out of the way and he hosed me down fully clothed with freezing cold water because I was in his path at the time. He writes leaflets about Jesus Christ and gives them out on street corners, saying that The End is Nigh.[19]

Herrmann wrote no music in 1970. Early that year he was offered Robert Fuest's remake of *Wuthering Heights*. "There wasn't one word of Brontë in it," he said in 1971. "They said, 'Oh, we don't have to use that crappy old-fashioned language. It's not relevant today.' . . . The way their version starts off, the first thing [Cathy and Heathcliff] do is have a great sex life. Well, the story of *Wuthering Heights* is that Cathy and Heathcliff didn't have a sex life together; they had other things that existed for them that were much more important in their lives—the way they both responded to the living environment of nature. . . . I don't need the new way of looking at *Wuthering Heights*. I like the old way. The great way."[20]

Instead Herrmann returned to the recording studios of Decca, for four albums of varied quality. That Herrmann wished to record Gustav Holst's *The Planets* is not surprising; it was perhaps the single work to which Herrmann was most indebted as a composer. Its dramatic, neoimpressionist textures had found their way into Herrmann works as diverse as Norman Corwin's "Seems Radio Is Here to Stay" and *Journey to the Center of the Earth*. As always, Herrmann scrupulously researched the work before recording, consulting Imogen Holst on her father's original score; [21]

but the performance itself, made at London's Kingsway Hall with the London Philharmonic, was more earthbound than ethereal. Always a believer in expansive tempi, Herrmann had lost his inner sense of timing as a conductor. Unlike the fluid rubatos of Beecham and Barbirolli, Herrmann's slow tempi were simply dull.

The Philharmonic musicians responded to Herrmann's direction with sloppy playing few conductors would have accepted; but if Herrmann liked the "atmosphere" of a cue, he was loath to rerecord it no matter what inaccuracies it contained. One incident suggested the gods were not on Herrmann's side: as organist Leslie Pearson and the orchestra played the climactic fortissimo of "Mars" during rehearsal, the Kingsway ceiling began first to crack, then collapse in plaster lumps around the organ. The organ parts were later recorded elsewhere and dubbed in.[22]

Despite its flaws, Herrmann's *Planets* is intriguing as a reflection of Herrmann's own style: a distracted listener hearing the four-note "Uranus" theme might mistake it for the brass opening of *The Trouble with Harry*, "Saturn"'s mysterious chords for a passage from *Journey to the Center of the Earth*. Despite mixed reviews, the album sold well, though not as well as Herrmann boasted.[23] (Herrmann once requested the album in a London record shop, and was told by a young employee—moments before the withering blast—that the store did not carry that recording: "We don't recommend it.")[24]

Herrmann's next two albums were much better. On February 16, 1970, he recorded "Music from Great Film Classics," another London Philharmonic album for Decca of his own film music. Handsomely packaged with notes by the composer, the album was a mix of previously unrecorded material (a fine suite based on the "*Jane Eyre*" score, the first stereo recordings of *Kilimanjaro*'s "Memory Waltz" and Interlude) as well as music recorded just two years earlier (excerpts from *Daniel Webster* and the *Kane* suites, slower here but stunningly recorded). Most critics, unfamiliar with the scores, were pleasantly surprised by their inherent musicality, and the disc sold well in both England and America.

Herrmann's third recording project of 1970 was his most imaginative and, for its maker, the most satisfying. Perhaps Herrmann's own period of relative neglect brought him back to the music of Joachim Raff, the once-renowned German composer Herrmann had championed at CBS following Raff's swift decline in popularity after World War I. "It was as if Raff was an old friend who had been done an injury," Norma recalled. "When he got upset over it he was upset in the most noble way. Michael Mannes, a translator of Ibsen, wrote a biography in which he said that Ibsen's daughter had married an obscure composer named Raff. Years later when Benny met Mannes at a party he attacked him in a rather nice way, saying, 'You must *never* make that mistake again. Raff was important.' Benny would tell me that other composers like Tchaikovsky used to copy Raff. Finally he said he was going to do something for him and record his Fifth Symphony. He was terribly excited over that—more excited than anything I ever saw him do."[25]

Inspired by a 1773 lyric-ballad by poet Gottfried August Bürger, in which a slain soldier reappears to take his lover on a nightmarish midnight horse ride, Raff's *Lenore* Symphony was a work of romantic sensitivity and supernaturalism, ranking in Herrmann's esteem with Berlioz's *Symphonie Fantastique*, Liszt's *Faust* Symphony, and Tchaikovsky's *Manfred* Symphony.[26] Record companies did not agree; no one had heard the work or saw a market for it. Eventually, through a young English music critic and fan named Edward Johnson, Herrmann learned of Unicorn Records, a small London company interested in recording the symphony if Herrmann covered the bulk of expenses.[27]

An afternoon meeting between Herrmann, Johnson, and Unicorn executive John Goldsmith was arranged. When Goldsmith was ten minutes late, "Benny was immediately crabby. I wasn't sure I wanted any association with this character; but I learned that on a first meeting Benny tended to be defensive and withdrawn." With a commitment from Unicorn to record the symphony, their relationship quickly improved, the start of both a friendship and several memorable recording collaborations:

Benny loved to visit people; he and Norma came to see my wife and me fairly regularly. One afternoon he called and said, "Can we come around this evening? 'The Big Country' is on TV and ours isn't working." So they came over and we all watched it. He was always full of praise for what he considered to be the best work of other film composers, and he thought Jerome Moross's "Big Country" score was tremendous.

Benny also had a tremendous sense of humor. On one occasion he came to stay with us in Leicestershire, in our manor home about a hundred miles north of London. After I picked him up at the coach station we passed a cinema which was showing two big disaster movies, *Earthquake* and *Volcano*. Benny said in his growly voice, "Reminds me of a bakin' powder we have at home called Shake 'n' Bake." Right off the cuff, and very funny.[28]

The *Lenore* recording was made that May, with the London Philharmonic at Barking Town Hall in East London. As usual, Herrmann's rehearsal was little more than a read-through; the recording itself made with few interruptions. Herrmann was eager to hear the Philharmonic's opinion of his rediscovery; recalled Norma: "During the first tea break Benny asked the fixer, 'What are they saying?'—he thought the music would excite the orchestra. The fixer replied, 'Oh, they're saying that at this rate they'll be done at four o'clock.' "[29]

Despite their disinterest Herrmann was ecstatic about the album, from its performance to its liner notes (by Edward Johnson, under Herrmann's guidance) and jacket design (which used Fuseli's Romantic masterpiece *The Nightmare*, also at Herrmann's suggestion).[30] Despite poor sales (which surprised no one), the album received encouraging reviews and was a lasting source of pride for its creator, who also felt it had satisfied a higher critic. "Within a few days of the recording Benny got a letter at Cumberland Terrace," Norma said. "For years he had been having correspondence about not receiving royalties for his 'Christmas Carol' television opera, and this morning Benny said to me, 'You'll never guess what this is.' It was a royalty check that was almost to the penny of what he had paid for the Raff recording. 'You see?' he said. 'I told you. *I* did something for him, and he did something for *me*.' "[31]

Herrmann's last album that year was an affectionately chosen collection of French and Swiss music for Decca titled "The Impressionists," which finally applied Herrmann's conducting to its proper métier. Here his doting emphasis on color was ideal: Satie's delicate *Gymnopédies* nos. 1 and 3, with their gemlike woodwind soli and lush harp arpeggios, emerge as cameos of fragile beauty, as does "Clair de lune," iridescent and fresh in a Debussy-approved orchestration by André Caplet. Equally lyrical is Herrmann's interpretation of Debussy's "La plus que lente," performed with an engaging rubato that savors each phrase of the cimbalom-laced romance.

In January 1971, Herrmann began scoring his first film in over two years. A young director named Alastair Reid had requested him for *The Road Builder* (in America, *The Night Digger*), a psychological love story adapted by Roald Dahl from Joy Cowley's novel *Nest in a Falling Tree*. It was also the first quality film Herrmann had worked on since *The Bride Wore Black*. Conceived as a vehicle for Dahl's wife, Patricia Neal, who was still recovering from a stroke that had left her partially paralyzed, the film was a slightly arid character study of a cloistered, middle-aged spinster named Maura (Neal) whose life with her blind foster mother is shattered by a young motorcyclist (Nicholas Clay) with whom Maura falls in love—and who she learns is a psychotic killer.

Herrmann apparently liked Dahl's script; but when director and composer met at Twickenham Studios, the collaboration, like many before it, seemed doomed. Recalled Reid:

At this stage the film was still an independent production; later it was picked up by MGM. But everything depended on whether Bernard wanted to do the music. When he first walked in to Twickenham, and I saw this big, gruff person with a Brooklyn accent, he immediately reminded me of a gangster from some Hollywood film. We ran the picture, and as the lights came up, Bernard's one comment was, "You'll have ta change the ending."

"To what?" we asked—and he told us, although I don't remember now how it differed from the film [in which the cyclist Billy falls to his death after Maura confronts him]. There was never any money on that film, so even if we had a better ending we couldn't have shot it. But Bernard said we had to go out and film new scenes.

"Would you like a cup of coffee, Mr. Herrmann?" we asked.

"No!"

The producer and I eased our way out of the viewing theater and asked ourselves, "Does he mean we've got to change the ending before he'll do it?" We walked back into the theater—and saw Bernard had had the projectionist rewind the film to the first reel and was already scribbling music down.[32]

Disagreements continued between Herrmann and Dahl, who was angered to see his script pared down to emphasize Herrmann's score. "This is Pat's film!" Dahl told the mild-mannered Reid, a remark that sent Herrmann into paroxysms: "Do you think they're gonna line up outside the box office in the cold and say, 'Can I have two seats please for *Pat's* film?'! I know they could have a good picture," he told Norma, "but they won't listen."[33]

None of Herrmann's frustration is evident in his beautiful score for strings, harp, and solo harmonica, in which he explores a favorite theme, romantic alienation, against a Hitchcockian backdrop of psychological horror. (Allusions to the master abound in the film, both in its camera borrowings and black sexual humor.) Like Maura, trapped by guilt in the home of her tyrannical benefactor, Herrmann's score is most eloquent in its muted passages of longing: the mournful viola d'amore soli, which capture the essence of Maura's loneliness; the naive scale patterns of Billy's harmonica, which mask a psychotic. Herrmann's prelude is a brilliant synthesis of several narrative elements—a stabbing, modulating bass figure is followed by the musical introduction of Billy via harmonica, then the pathetic Maura, whose theme is heard on viola d'amore in a melancholy quote from Herrmann's *Echoes* quartet (recalling the composer's own bout with loneliness).

As the titles end, Herrmann segues into a sighing passage for strings as Maura returns from her hospital job to her foster mother's home, the violins' desolate lyricism noting each ancient wall display and framed photo the blind woman cannot see. Maura's enervating routine, and Herrmann's commentary, are interrupted by the enigmatic Billy, introduced leitmotiv-style by a dangling minor third figure for cellos against a sustained bass chord, as economic and chilling as any of *Psycho*'s string devices. (Herrmann frequently uses suspended chord patterns in this score to create psychological and sexual tension, as in the seductive ostinato for harp and muted strings that reflects the sheen of Billy's motorcycle straps.)

Director Reid employs Billy's harmonica as a symbol of the stranger's inarticulateness. Musically it becomes an eerie herald of death, blended with swirling violin bridge effects and harp glissandos during each of Billy's killings, to suggest the arrested development of the boy's mind and his concealed brutality. Yet Billy's kindness is also genuine, and as Maura falls in love with her young helper Herrmann transfers Billy's harmonica theme to strings in a subtle orchestral analogue to their deepening relationship.

The *Echoes* habanera phrase returns with increasing passion as Maura vows never to leave Billy, then blossoms into the score's emotional climax as the two escape to a new life in the Scottish highlands. Their happiness is brief: under Reid's wordless finale, in which Billy hurtles off a clifftop as Maura watches helplessly, Herrmann reprises the prelude's wistful melody for viola d'amore; he then adds harmonica, the lonely sound of the ocean waves echoing its question of what might have been. It is a coda of intense, poetic sadness, deftly obscuring the film's abrupt and somewhat inconclusive finale.

The score's recording was done not at Twickenham but, to Reid's surprise, at Barking Assembly Hall, "way out in the middle of nowhere, in a creepy, seedy area where you don't walk alone at night. I thought, well, that's typical—here's a Brooklyn gangster type who wants to record at a gangster's hideout. Of course, he chose it because Barking was the only place in London that had the correct acoustics; so we converted the hall into a dubbing theater, putting up a big screen and soundproof projection boxes." As Herrmann conducted with his large baton, Reid jokingly recalled the fate of Jean Baptiste Lully, who fatally injured himself with his conducting stick—a quip "that went down like a lead pipe in water."[34]

After dubbing at Twickenham (which Herrmann "overlorded very carefully"), the film was released to generally good reviews in New York, then pulled from distribution by MGM, shelved in the studio vaults, and written off as a tax deduction. "Patricia Neal, Roald Dahl, and I were never paid a penny, since we all deferred our payments to royalties," Reid said in 1984, "and to this day we've never received a penny. The only guy who came out okay was Bernard Herrmann, who insisted on money up front. And he was dead right."[35] Years later, the film was rereleased and did nicely for MGM.

It was Herrmann's next film that belonged on a studio shelf. The history of *The Battle of Neretva*, a $12 million Yugoslavian World War II epic filmed in 1969, is almost as long and convoluted as the film itself. From the outset its multicountry financing suggested disaster: Yugoslavia, Italy, Germany, and the United States all had a hand in the making of the film, through multi-international production companies. The next step to chaos was the casting of worldwide superstars, each seemingly in a different film (the cast included Yul Brynner, Franco Nero, Curt Jurgens, and Orson Welles). No cost was spared, except in getting a coherent script. Consequently, the three-hour film was a succession of celebrity cameos, propaganda, and Götterdämmerung-scale battle scenes.

Several versions of *Neretva* were prepared for the various participating nations, each with its own nationalistic bias and omissions (most references to Tito were cut from American and English prints). Producers Henry T. Weinstein and Steve Previn (André's brother) were given the thankless task of making the hodgepodge palatable to Americans (the English saw yet *another* version); and while their version was even less coherent than the original, the bright decision of hiring Herrmann was theirs.[36]

Herrmann never had any pretensions about *Neretva*. "What it is," he growled to Norma, "is a great big roast beef—and everybody cuts off the bit they like. The Russians get a cut, the British get a cut; one bit is well done, another bit's overdone. A great big roast beef, and everybody's happy." Herrmann's bit included a higher salary than usual (his stipulation) and a trip for him and Norma to Yugoslavia, where a favorite Herrmann jibe about his wife's liberalism found new variations. When two men in dark glasses met the couple in Zagreb, Herrmann pointed to Norma and said, "It's all right—she's one of *them*."

After seeing the original film, they were escorted by two solemn envoys to a popular Yugoslavian restaurant, which was closed. Two Tito sidemen arrived, and the kitchen was quickly opened and readied for service. "Benny found it all an amazingly amusing experience," Norma recalled. "In a period when funny young directors with long hair and no money were coming around to see him, here were these people waving lots of cash and a trip to Yugoslavia."[37]

The film may have been a fiasco, but Herrmann took the assignment as seriously as his best screen projects. Indeed, its ineptitude presented an even greater challenge to the composer, who dressed much of the celluloid corpse so successfully it almost seemed to walk.

*Neretva*'s instrumentation is larger than in any other Herrmann score; in sheer rhetoric it almost makes static film jump. (The London Philharmonic was again used, giving their best performance for Herrmann.) The title theme, a somber Balkan-style hymn set against a furious percussion cadence, immediately creates a sense of rushing momentum that distracts the viewer (at least initially) from the numbing repetitiveness of director Veljko Bulajic's images. Majestic and terrifying, its expansive melody, orchestrated for low strings and brass, evokes like nothing in the film a sense of war's tragic waste and the patriotism of Yugoslavia's partisans.

Two previous Herrmann compositions fit seamlessly into the score: the minor-third "murder" device for *Torn Curtain*'s evil Russians now becomes a signature for Nazis, and the Venetian melody of Herrmann's clarinet quintet, a spiritual idée fixe for Franco Nero's Italian captain. Herrmann's last major motive (there are others for the endless company of fighters) is related to his prelude, except here the neo-Russian hymn is a grinding, deliberately labored march that imparts genuine poignance to the partisans' exodus across their homeland. (The cue is also an excellent example of when to *slow* images down for maximum effect.)

As Herrmann predicted, all the participants in the battle of *Neretva* returned to their native lands satisfied with either a propagandist tool or a thicker billfold. The less fortunate critics dubbed the film confused and tedious, and, like most international film ventures, *The Battle of Neretva* vanished into cinematic obscurity.

By 1971 Herrmann's personal and professional life had reached an impasse. Although he had rarely worked in California during the last five years, he remained stranded at Bluebell, unwilling to subject his precious pets to a year's quarantine in London; yet the few film offers he received invariably came from England. Even more than her husband, Norma was eager to leave the United States.[38]

Herrmann continued to express his frustration through all the wrong channels. Interviewers were especially susceptible to abuse: most typical is Herrmann's encounter with *Los Angeles Free Press* writers Greg Rose and Leslie Zador (son of film orchestrator-composer Eugene Zador), a dialogue that found the composer alternately terse, perceptive, and explosive:

HERRMANN:    Whether you write occasionally for television, for films, or for symphony, I don't see that they're any different. It's all part of the life of being a composer. Pardon me, I don't think that even a great man like Mozart, a great genius like that, thought he was not being a composer when he wrote some ballroom music. . . . Most people in this town who say they're film composers aren't composers at all. They just farm the music out to ghost writers. . . . I get telephone calls all the time from people who want me to ghostwrite for them. . . . It's the great unsung profession. . . .

ROSE:    But you say your concert music comes first?

HERRMANN:    I DIDN'T SAY THAT AT ALL! . . . What makes concert music so great? YOU live in this city—how often does the orchestra play anything by anybody? . . . They have [the] courage of amoebas—they don't believe in anything! Why don't they play their contemporaries? I played Charlie Ives when it was a filthy word to mention his name! . . . Why can't they play commissioned works every year the way the Boston Symphony did or the New York Philharmonic before Lenny Bernstein got there? You're making something holy about concert music that isn't.

ZADOR:    To give an example of what Mr. Herrmann is talking about, he wrote an opera called *Wuthering Heights*. Part of the music from act one, scene one, was in a film called *The Ghost and Mrs. Muir*.

HERRMANN:    No I didn't, that's completely false.

ZADOR:    But it sounds just like it . . .

HERRMANN:    THAT'S BECAUSE IT HAPPENS TO BE ME! I WAS THE COMPOSER OF BOTH! I SOUND LIKE MYSELF! It didn't come from that picture and I resent that. I mean, I have certain earmarks as a composer! And if it shows up in my film music or in my opera, in my symphony or in my string quartet, that's MY music! Hell, Copland sounds like Copland no matter what he's writing! . . . Where did you find out that it sounded like *The Ghost and Mrs. Muir*? That interests me. Where did you get this—startling bit of information?

ZADOR:    I saw *The Ghost and Mrs. Muir* on television a couple of times, and then I listened to your opera. . . .

HERRMANN:    Well, there might be a couple of phrases that might sound alike, but so what! Who the hell cares! What's that got to do with one or the other!

ZADOR: They're both good.

HERRMANN: BUT THAT HAS NOTHING TO DO WITH IT! I didn't take somebody else's music, it's my OWN music! . . .

ZADOR: I think that your connection with Orson Welles would be of interest to our readers.

HERRMANN: I don't want to go into all of that. I'm not interested in doing my life's story. . . .

ZADOR: Did you find him easy to get along with?

HERRMANN: I always find difficult people easy. I only find glad-Harrys difficult and vacuous. Nice guys are difficult. It's because they're a bunch of empty-heads, that's why they're nice guys! They pretend to be nice guys, but it's a disguise. They're not nice. They're vicious, vindictive people who try to make sure that anything good HASN'T GOT A CHANCE!

ZADOR: Then Orson Welles, who's a difficult person, gave you a chance. . . .

HERRMANN: HE DIDN'T GIVE ME ANY CHANCE! I gave HIM a chance! I had a job and he was just an actor who we used. . . . What the hell . . . he didn't give me any JOB!

ZADOR: Well, for *Citizen Kane* and *The Magnificent Ambersons*. . . .

HERRMANN: He didn't give me a job! It was to his advantage to have me do the music for him! He didn't give me a job or break or anything. . . . For chrissake, what's working in there, an accounting department? . . .

ZADOR: Did you select the various passages to be scored?

HERRMANN: Yes, I do that. It's my profession and not theirs.

ZADOR: [after a pause]: Well, you're sure good at it.

HERRMANN: WELL THAT'S MY TALENT! WHADDA I NEED SOME HALF-WIT TO TELL ME WHAT HE THINKS! . . .

ZADOR: How did [your association with Hitchcock] begin?

HERRMANN: He asked me to do *The Trouble with Harry*. That was it. You seem to have an idea that you need a patronage to get yourself a film.

ZADOR: No I don't.

HERRMANN: They asked me because they thought I was the right man to do it! Today it's not done by people who got the right man. Every job is an opportunity for your friends who have as little talent as you have! That's how you get a job. The first requisite is that you have absolutely no talent. You're a nice guy who won't rock their boat. . . .

ZADOR: Which scores do you care for the most of the ones you've done?

HERRMANN: I like them all, but I don't have any favorites. I forget about them after I do them. . . . It's a surprise to me when I hear them again. You can't think about old music and go on to write new music. . . .

ROSE: [Current] films seem to lack a point of view, an emotional focus. It would help to have a better score for a contemporary picture; but as you seem to say, it's just part of the pop culture we're in.

HERRMANN: Yeah, and besides that it has to do with other things. Today's world is all full of sensationalism. . . . A picture like *Jane Eyre* wouldn't make any sense today. Today it would be either she goes to bed with him or she doesn't. All the nuances, people's relationships with one another, it's not portrayed. Therefore, the music that they have that goes along is primitive music that suits the inarticulateness of the story itself. Look at the language. It all comes from the drunken dance bands of back rooms. It has become the current language of intellectual communication. "Get with it." "Get off it." You tell me what the hell it means. . . .

ROSE: Do you think it's a passing phase? Do you think the higher standards will return?

HERRMANN: No, I don't think it's a passing phase. . . . It'll only pass when the new generation of young people come in and they have different attitudes towards life. . . . It's like the Dark Ages have settled on the arts, and just a few people have got to preserve the text. It's important to preserve the past, because you can't have a present and a future if you don't have a past. Just because you have people that have no training and have no ability to transmit their ideas in a great art form, there's no reason that the art must be destroyed. It would be like if nobody could paint a decent picture, we would burn Titian. . . .

ZADOR: Which film composers do you admire?

HERRMANN: Who, in film music? I like William Walton, Prokofiev . . .

ZADOR: *Alexander Nevsky?*

HERRMANN: One of the greatest scores ever written. I thought Copland did a lot of interesting film music. I don't admire music that panders beneath itself. I like music that is proud of itself. I don't like a guy that says, "It's a good idea, but it's too good for these creeps who come in and look at a movie, so I'll debase it."

ZADOR: Well, that's not always done by choice.

HERRMANN: NO! It IS done by choice! You don't *have*-ta do it! You can walk away from it! You say, I'm not your man, get somebody else! Don't tell ME that he has to make a buck—look what Schubert put up with. I never cheapened a piece because somebody said that's what they want! That to me is where you separate the composers from the frauds. . . . The only hard luck I ever had was my disagreement with Hitchcock over *Torn Curtain,* and we never recorded the music. So somebody else wrote a new score, which is fair enough. . . . See, I wasn't willing to debase my music because Universal Studios and Alfred Hitchcock said, "This is what we have to do."

ROSE:            Then there's so much justice in the fact that . . .

HERRMANN:    WHAT JUSTICE! You talk like a kid!

ROSE:            Listen to me a second.

HERRMANN:    You talk like a kid.

ZADOR:          Mr. Herrmann, I have a plane to catch.

HERRMANN:    Oh well, okay. I've given you enough crap anyhow.[39]

Late one evening in August 1971, the Herrmanns received a telephone call from Laurie Johnson in London. English quarantine restrictions had been reduced from one year to six months.

"Benny began to pace and pace," Norma said, "and then a few hours later he decided it was on. Goodbye to Hollywood. He bought the dogs new harnesses and said to me, 'Look at this, they're getting excited! They're saying, "What's all this about—new straps?" They're thinking, something's going to happen!' "[40]

To Norma, it was clear who couldn't wait.

# PART THREE

# London

## 1971–1975

# FIFTEEN

Once in awhile the best believer recognizes the impulse to set his religion in order, to sweep the temple of his thoughts and trim the sacred lamp. It is at such hours as this that he reflects with elation that the British capital is the particular spot in the world which communicates the greatest sense of life.

*Henry James,* English Hours

In sixty years that seemed both physically and intellectually many more, Bernard Herrmann had repeatedly been in the right place at the right time. In the connecting train of events that took him from New York's East Side to radio conducting to Hollywood, his last destination was perhaps inevitably England. Herrmann's last years in California had seemed like premature retirement; but his life in Britain would be a period of rediscovery, both in England and in America, as if the absence of his vocal presence had created an evident void.

It was almost two years, however, before a true reappreciation of Herrmann's work came about. In the meantime, apart from Herrmann's move from Bluebell Avenue and Cumberland Terrace to 31 Chester Close in North London,* little had changed—apart from the worsening health of Twi, riddled with cancer in her old age.

In the summer of 1971 the animals were flown to their six-month quarantine in London, a change the cats and Alpy scarcely minded but that weakened Herrmann's favorite pet. Recalled Norma: "I tried to warn Benny when we were moving that the vet said she wouldn't live much longer, but he refused to believe it. He never saw her very ill, because he refused to see the pets in quarantine; instead he sent me every day on a forty-minute drive to bring back news. He insisted I bring them delicacies and take them beds from Harrods, although the quarantine man said the

---

*The spacious home had once been the residence of Christine Keeler, infamous for her role in Britain's Profumo scandal (Norma Shepherd, Spring 1985).

straw they used was healthier. But Benny, who wanted to provide them with something, said, 'To hell with the straw.' We actually stored the beds from Harrods off to one side of the cage, and Benny never knew."[1]

Four months into quarantine, Twi died. Herrmann was desolate; he wandered the rooms of Chester Close in his dressing gown for two days, seldom speaking. Eventually bereavement gave way to the excitement of a new residence and the full-time commitment of a new film.

Herrmann's friendship with John and Roy Boulting led to his scoring *Endless Night*, a muddled adaptation of Agatha Christie's 1968 thriller by writer director Sidney Gilliatt, whose past work included *Green for Danger* and coauthorship of Hitchcock's *The Lady Vanishes*. The new film reteamed Hayley Mills and Hywell Bennett in the last of their pairings.

Initially Herrmann expressed enthusiasm for his collaboration with the veteran Gilliatt: "I like to work on a film from the very beginning, but very few producers or directors think of that. They bring you in when the picture is near its final cut and they want you to do it within a very short time—always the least amount of time in which you can possibly do it. 'Endless Night' is an exception. . . . Sidney Gilliatt is a very experienced director who understands the problems, and he asked me to talk with him and consider what we should do musically at a very early stage. I find that the younger generation of directors think you can write an hour of music in two days. The film business today is full of bikini manufacturers."[2]

But *Endless Night* was another disappointment, an ineptly crafted mystery whose denouement left more questions than answers. As usual, Herrmann turned to the film's source material for inspiration, conceiving his score along similarly literary lines: like Christie's deceptively romantic prose that masks a murder scheme, Herrmann's music is misleading in design, a "musical decoy" that "leads you to believe that you're seeing a romance, but you're not. You're seeing a cold-blooded murderer at work. You can't believe this lush, romantic music accompanies such an evil person."[3]

Against sensuous orchestration Herrmann decided to juxtapose a strange, jarring instrument to suggest the menace of Gypsy Acre, the story's South England setting. After considering, then rejecting, a theremin, he chose a Moog synthesizer, an instrument introduced to him by Howard Blake, the young jazz arranger of *Twisted Nerve*.[4] Herrmann was delighted with the Moog's wailing, alien sound colors and featured it in three film scores, in the process rediscovering a more conventional keyboard instrument, the organ.

For all of Herrmann's imaginative choices, his idea of the music as a dramatic red herring was almost too conceptual to be a total success, though the score does help mask the film's lack of cohesion. After recording and dubbing were finished, Herrmann was eager to put the film behind him. Recalled Norma: "When the film was finished EMI rang up and invited us to a screening; Agatha Christie's husband, Sir Max Mallowan, was going to be there. But Benny wouldn't go. I thought it was terribly rude, so I went by myself. It turned out there were just two of us in an empty studio, Agatha Christie's husband and me. After the film Sir Max said, 'I think Agatha would be upset by all the violence'—although you didn't actually see any violence in the film at all."[5] Reviews were poor, the film's distribution almost nonexistent.

*Endless Night* was Herrmann's last film score for almost a year. What few offers he received were thwarted for either artistic or financial reasons (Herrmann agreed to score Stephen Frears's detective satire *Gumshoe*, starring Albert Finney, but his fee proved too high).[6] Writing concert music no longer interested him, as he was convinced no one would perform it.[7] Instead Herrmann returned to recording. "The Four Faces of Jazz," a compendium of jazz-influenced concert works by Kurt Weill, Gershwin, Milhaud, and Stravinsky, seemed an odd choice for a musician who had little good to say about the jazz idiom—until one realized Herrmann had known all four composers, and in 1934 had given the East Coast premiere of Milhaud's *Creation of the World* and one of the first performances of Gershwin's "I Got Rhythm" Variations (both featured on the Decca album, played by the London Festival Recording Ensemble).

As usual, the West Hampstead recording session was a blend of Herrmann tantrums and imprecise conducting ("I Got Rhythm Variations is *right*," said one musician),[8] but the final recording was appealingly played and handsomely engineered.

Conductor Charles Gerhardt remembered the album for other reasons. Long estranged from Herrmann (they had fallen out years earlier, ostensibly because Gerhardt had recorded an album of popular film music without including any Herrmann), Gerhardt was a frequent visitor to Decca and happened to be in the Hampstead studios that August:

I heard some music coming from the control room and recognized Gershwin's "I Got Rhythm" Variations. As I stood listening, the door flew open and Benny ran right into me as he came out. I said, "Oh, umm, Mr. Herrmann, sorry—I just heard the music . . . " He said excitedly, "Yes, it's being recorded—it's a wonderful piece—I'm delighted you're here—ya gotta hear it, come on in." He was carrying on like mad with the woodwinds: "What the hell is this—this is the blues! Do I have-ta TELL ya?" When it was over, Benny looked at me and said, "Come in and listen to the playback." As he showed me the score he said, "You're comin' over for dinner tonight; come ta my place and we'll talk about it." It was as if nothing had happened. I went to his home that night and met Norma; we had a lovely evening and talked about many things.

The next morning Norma called, laughing. She said, "Benny told me as soon as he got up this morning to call and ask you for dinner again on Friday. At breakfast I said, 'Listen, this chap who came to dinner last night was a nice guy. You've always told me what a monster he was.' 'I NEVER SAID ANYTHING OF THE KIND—HE'S ONE-A MY BEST FRIENDS!' "

Benny could be a loyal friend, too; he wouldn't hear a word against anyone he liked. If someone said something against a friend he'd say, "So whadda you? You got no faults?" It was all a question of whether you knew anything or not. If you were an idiot he didn't like you. If you knew something or had any talent, he'd forgive you for a lot. For some people, being with Benny was a chore, but I didn't find him difficult to be with; I liked him for what he was. He liked to be pampered, but I didn't mind—the man had such insight, and there seemed to be no limit to his knowledge.

Benny often called to say he had to take Alpy for a walk in the park and he didn't want to go by himself, so I'd drive over and we'd go together. He was at his best when you were alone with him; he'd often get bored or irritated in a group and find it necessary to make some outrageous remark. But when you were alone with him he'd tell you things that had happened to him in his life, and he'd ask you questions. It was not a one-way conversation; quite the contrary. When he was alone with you he was very interested in your point of view—which he'd be very quick to disagree with if he felt you didn't know what you were talking about![9]

When a "Twilight Zone" or "Hitchcock" program appeared on English airwaves, Herrmann would sit transfixed in front of his small black-and-white television at Chester Close, wrapped in his dressing gown with Alpy or a cat at his knee.[10] Not every (perceived) rediscovery of a past score was so happy:

Mort Stevens
CBS TV Centre
Hollywood

Dear Mort:

During the month of November the Hawaii 5-0 television show appeared here over ITA as it has done for some years. I was astonished to hear that on three of these shows (devoted to the Vashon family) the music used was based on a piece of mine entitled "The Ambush," and that no credit was given to me, nor has it ever appeared on the clearance sheets of BMI. . . .

Now let me make one thing clear. Although CBS has every right to use this music which is in their tape library, as they see fit, they have no right to give somebody else credit for composing it. . . .

I should appreciate your attention in this matter, and your advising me promptly of your reactions. I should like these before I proceed further to protect my legal and artistic rights. . . .

With best regards,
Bernard Herrmann[11]

Stevens replied:

Dear Bernie:

In answer to your letter of January 23rd . . . I must say that I fail to see any evidence to support your suggestion that the theme . . . was based on one of yours entitled "Ambush." I find no more similarity between \*\*\*'s theme and your theme of "Ambush" than between your "Ambush" theme and the first few notes of "Fuer Elise" by Beethoven or the first fragment of Mozart's "Overture to the Marriage of Figaro."

Nevertheless, I am happy that you reminded me of your piece entitled "Ambush" because in listening to it again I find a new appreciation of the marvellous way in which you made such a few notes build a level of tension which was extraordinary.[12]

Enraged by Stevens's "condescending and snide" answer,[13] and convinced CBS had committed a moral if not legal violation, Herrmann battled the network over the issue for years without success.

A better reminder of Herrmann's CBS days came with a visit in early 1972 from his boyhood friend Jerome Moross. "After ten minutes we were right back to being two adolescents," Moross recalled. "We spent two days together. He wanted to monopolize my time, just as we monopolized each other's time when we were adolescents. As we wandered down the street, he had a pipe and a cane, which he didn't need, and we went to his club—but he didn't know anyone there! Since he'd been a Mahler devotee in his youth, I asked him, 'By the way, Benny—Mahler is suddenly in. How do you feel about Mahler now?' He said, 'Mahler? He's *vulgar!*' "[14]

Herrmann's next album was another look back, to the Ives performances of his New York days and to his English premiere of Ives's Second

Symphony with the LSO in 1956. Herrmann was to make his first record of the composer now hailed as an American poet in music; the debut recording, appropriately, was of Ives's Second Symphony with the London Symphony Orchestra.

Appalled by Leonard Bernstein's version of the piece, which he considered overblown and inaccurate,[15] Herrmann turned to his own photocopies of the original score with corrections by Ives (the edition Herrmann had retrieved from the closet of Walter Damrosch twenty-five years earlier). Herrmann's "new" version created some confusion among musicians at Kingsway Hall that January, but the London players were becoming used to "the usual Ives mess"[16] of college songs, patriotic hymns, and, in the case of the Second, overtones of Brahms and Bruckner.

The recording was also noteworthy for its reunion, after a decade, of Herrmann and the London Symphony, whose snubbing of the conductor after his 1956 visit and appointment of "that jazz boy"[17] André Previn as chief conductor in 1970 had enraged Herrmann. "Benny came back to the LSO a bit grudgingly," said first violinist Henry Greenwood, whose friendship with Herrmann had endured the professional battles, "but I think he realized he could get a better job from us than the London Philharmonic."[18] Herrmann did: the recording was superbly engineered, the performance an improvement on the 1956 premiere—more leisured, yet more rhythmically focused than Herrmann's other recent recordings.

Herrmann's recording was invariably reviewed in comparison to Bernstein's, and often won higher marks. "[Herrmann] parades his affection less obviously, is less of a weekend visitor from the Big City," noted London's *Financial Times*.[19] And in *Stereo Review*: "So carefully detailed is Herrmann's performance—with microphoning to match—that one could virtually copy the notes back onto score paper from a hearing of this recording. . . . Herrmann's . . . delineation of the counterpoints from the beginning to the end of [the Finale] would be the envy of any New England stitchery expert."[20] Both the Ives and Herrmann's "Impressionists" album (released in 1971) were chosen by *Saturday Review* as among the best classical recordings of 1972.

Another, wider audience was taking notice of Herrmann as well. Not surprisingly, the first steps toward a Herrmann revival were made by those most interested in cinema's past: film historians (who had been growing in number since the 1960s, partly because of television's airing of older films). On June 11, 1972, after having published a lengthy interview with the composer in its magazine *Sight and Sound* that winter, the prestigious British Film Institute (BFI) hosted Herrmann in what would be his only London lecture, held at the National Film Theatre and chaired by Canadian writer Ted Gilling. Despite a large, receptive audience and Gilling's intelligent questions (the two had met in 1964 and remained friends), a clear streak of bitterness accompanied Herrmann's informed commentary:

In spite of all new fashion and aesthetic theories, film is one medium that needs other arts, because it's a cooperative, mosaic enterprise, and the use of music has always been necessary even from silent days to the present day. People always ask me this question, "Why does a film need music?" Well, I'd like to say this: I've never met a producer who said to me, "I've just finished a film, and I don't need you!" They say, "You must come and see what you can do to help us!" . . . Music is a sort of cement, or veneer, that finalizes the art of making a film. . . . I think that Jean Cocteau said once that in films, one is never fully aware whether it's the music that's propelling the film or the film propelling the music.

And I would like to say that many times directors who receive great credit and applause for the marvelous scenes at the crucial time of recognition seem to forget the contribution that the composer has made to the film. I wish it were possible historically to see some films the way they were given to the composer, and if they were given to the world that way, whether they would be regarded with the same esteem. . . .

Today there is no mention of film music made by film critics in England or New York. It's completely ignored. . . . Nobody seems to mention whether it was good, tasteless, sensitive, evocative; either way, they've regarded the film medium as a free-for-all to have the most, the greatest vulgarity that the human race has ever achieved, perpetrated on the screen, with the point of view that it's music that'll make money, and nobody'll notice it anyhow! . . .

I must make it very clear that all remarks made by me only refer to my own attitude. I have colleagues who would dispute everything I say, who would say film is a way to make a buck—never mind what the film is about. . . . Most of the film directors I've had the good luck and good fortune to work with have regarded music as something that had to be created *with* the film—but I have worked for people who regard music as just a sort of you-take-it-to-Harrods-gift-wrapping-department. In this case there is no latitude given to you, and the picture's not elastic, it's set. . . .

The art of writing a film score is fast becoming equivalent to having been a medieval enameler—you know, making beautiful jewelry. It's not needed anymore. Today they just hope for a pop song—nothing to do with the film, the actors, just get us a pop song, that's all! . . . But I think that film music is an art, and that films need music—and music needs films. I think that composers who think it beneath them—I feel sorry for them, because they haven't had the chance. A composer with an attitude that radio or TV or film music is beneath him is doomed to oblivion. Real composers welcome any opportunity to write music.

Later that year Miklós Rózsa also addressed BFI members, in a lecture attended by his old friend. Recalled Rózsa:

I arrived at 2:30 that afternoon, shortly before I was to speak, and Benny was waiting for me. He said, "I have to talk to you." I asked, "What is it, Benny? They're waiting for me." He said, "I heard a recording of Bartók's 'Music for String Instruments' conducted by Boulez." Benny hated Boulez.

At that moment someone said, "Mr. Rózsa, the audience is all here." I said, "Benny, I have to . . . "

"No, no, wait. This was so wonderfully conducted . . . " He went on and on, and the people kept calling me—"Please come on." "Benny," I said, "I have to go."

"No, no, wait."

He went on praising Boulez, and I finally said, "Benny, I'm glad." Then he said, "NOT like your friend ORMANDY, that IDIOT! That STUPID FOOL!"

"Bye bye, Benny!" It was all a big buildup for Ormandy to get it.

Afterwards there was a reception. A little man, eighteen or nineteen years old, came to me. He was a butcher boy who loved music. He said he had come from Sheffield to hear me, and would I please sign these records? I said of course. He looked across the room and said, "Is that Mr. Herrmann?" I said yes. "Could I talk to him?" I said of course, go over to him. Seconds later I heard Benny's voice screeching "WHADDAYA WANT FROM ME? GO AWAY! GO AWAY!" This boy came back, shaking his head, and asked, "Why is he so mad at me?" He just wanted to tell Herrmann he liked his music.

Benny would call me whenever I was in London and curse every other conductor for half an hour. After one of these rages he said, "By the way, Norma and I are going out to dinner. Come with us." I said I'd have to think about it. I just couldn't take it all the time, listening to bad things about everybody. [But] I went with them—and Benny was the most charming man you could imagine. It was a party of ten people, and he was laughing, telling jokes. It was not the same person.[21]

As usual, Herrmann's diatribes and mood swings were symptoms of deeper frustrations: his inactivity as a composer and conductor, and the growing sense that his career had come to an end.

Herrmann was both right and wrong. An exciting, final phase of his career was about to begin.

# SIXTEEN

"Sir, I love the acquaintance of young people; because, in the first place, I don't like to think myself growing old. In the next place, young acquaintances . . . have more generous sentiments in every respect. I love the young dogs of this age. . . . "

Samuel Johnson, quoted in Boswell, Life of Johnson

In the spring of 1972, a twenty-six-year-old film editor named Paul Hirsch sat watching the dailies of *Sisters,* a low-budget horror film directed by Brian De Palma, in a New York cutting room. Hirsch realized something was missing:

*Sisters* was an independent production, and the producer, Ed Pressman, wanted to have a screening of some of the material already shot for some potential backers so they could finish the picture. Brian wanted to show the murder sequence, which had already been filmed. This was only the second picture I'd ever done, and frankly, when I saw the dailies I was disappointed, although that was due in part to my inexperience.

That night by a curious coincidence, *Psycho* was being shown on television in New York. I was watching the scene in which Janet Leigh is driving and is being followed by the motorcycle cop, and I thought, wow—this scene is fantastic. I turned off the sound to analyze the shots, and I realized the entire scene was made up of three camera set ups: a close-up of Janet Leigh's face, a close-up of her view of the road ahead, and a point-of-view shot of the rearview mirror. They were very ordinary, very boring shots. Then I turned the sound back on and realized it was the music that was making it so tense and compelling.

I went to Colony Records in Manhattan and asked them for the music from *Psycho.* I had to spell Benny's name for them, and they had to look it up in the catalogues. Finally they dug up a copy of "The Great Movie Thrillers," and I transferred the *Psycho* music onto the soundtrack of *Sisters* and presented it to Brian as a sort of fait accompli.[1]

De Palma (who oddly enough had not considered using Herrmann for his Hitchcock-inspired thriller) loved the results but guessed that Herrmann was dead; the last film De Palma remembered him scoring was *The Birds* in 1963.[2]

Hirsch determined that Herrmann was not only alive but also very available. After contacting Liz Keyes, Ed Pressman sent Herrmann the script. A few weeks later Herrmann agreed to score the film; by this time financing had been secured and his fee—the single largest item on the budget[3]—could be met. "I could hardly believe the genius who had scored 'Vertigo,' 'North by Northwest' and 'Psycho' was really going to write our music," De Palma said:

That day finally came and still my faith that the mythical Herrmann would emerge from an elevator at the Movielab screening room to see my movie was faint. I was right only about one thing—he didn't emerge from the elevator. Rather, when we came off the elevator at 10 A.M. he was waiting for us. He was a short, stout man, with silver gray hair plastered down [on] his head, thick glasses, and he carried an ominous-looking walking stick. Ed apologized for being late (we weren't) and asked how his flight had been. Herrmann impatiently mumbled, oh, all right, but I'm staying on London time and all I want to do is see the film, have dinner, and go to bed. I got the impression there was something unpleasant about New York time and, in fact, about everything New York, including ourselves. But I wasn't sure because I couldn't see Herrmann's face (he never looked up at us, keeping his head straight down, his eyes never leaving the floor) to determine if he was kidding us or not. Undaunted, Ed launched into an apology for the present rough state of the film.

Herrmann's impatience broke into anger. "I flew here not to talk about the film but to see it!" he shouted, waving his cane like an enraged Mr. Magoo. "For God's sake—let's get on with it!"

As I came to learn later, no matter how loud or brutally frank Herrmann was, he was almost invariably right. And if you disagreed with him about anything, you'd have to weather the blast. But then if you had a good point, he would subside and begrudgingly come around to your point of view. . . .

For ten minutes the screening seemed to be going along all right (at least he wasn't shouting at us), but then the first music cue arrived. On the screen, Danielle (Margot Kidder) and her black lover embraced on the deck of the Staten Island Ferry. As they kissed, the room was filled with Herrmann's own love theme from Hitchcock's "Marnie." It was a beautiful moment.

"What's that!" shrieked Herrmann with unbelievable horror. "That's where the first music cue is," I frantically explained. "I just wanted to show you the type of music I had in mind for this sequence . . . ''

"Stop it," he cried, his cane thumping the floor in rage.

"But I thought . . . ''

"You thought!" he rasped contemptuously. "That's 'Marnie,' not your movie!''

"But 'Marnie''s perfect," I argued.

"Turn it off," he ordered. "I don't want to hear 'Marnie' when I'm looking at your movie. How can I think about anything new with that playing?' By this time, his feet had joined his drumming cane and I feared for his heart. But fortunately Paul had raced around to the projection booth and switched the accursed music off. . . . *

When the film was over, silence ensued. After what seemed an eternal pause Herrmann started to reminisce. He wasn't shouting now.

"I remember sitting in a screening room after seeing the rough cut of 'Psycho.' Hitch was nervously pacing back and forth, saying it was awful and that he was going to cut it down for his television show. He was crazy. He didn't know what he had. Wait a minute, I said. I have some ideas. How about a score completely for strings. I used to be a violin player, you know . . . ''

If Herrmann was comparing my film to "Psycho" maybe he liked it.

"But let's talk about the music while the film is fresh in my mind," continued Herrmann.

Fine, I replied, and launched into an eager ten minute explanation of why I didn't want any title music. The first scene in "Sisters" is a long set-up shot from a hidden camera in a bathhouse changing room. The partition separating the women's room from the men's has been removed. Over the scene of a blind girl undressing I wanted to fade in and fade out four titles with the primary screen credits . . . to make the credits short without any dramatic music. After I finished, Herrmann exploded.

"No title music? Nothing horrible happens in your picture for the first half hour. You need something to scare them right away. The way you do it, they'll walk out.''

"But in 'Psycho' the murder doesn't happen until forty . . . ''

"You are not Hitchcock! He can make his movies as slow as he wants in the beginning! And do you know why?''

I shook my head.

"Because he is Hitchcock and they will wait! They know something terrible is going to happen and they'll wait until it does. They'll watch your movie for ten minutes and then they'll go home to their televisions.''

Herrmann was brutal and, of course, right.

"What do you think we should do?" I asked.

*Truffaut had also used Herrmann music as a "dummy" soundtrack when showing him *Fahrenheit 451*—with the same results.

"I will write you one title cue, one minute and twenty seconds long. It will keep them in their seats until your murder scene. I got an idea using two Moog synthesizers."[4]

Since the story was about Siamese twins, he would compose "Siamese twin music," Herrmann announced to their immediate apprehension—until he explained he would write an ascending string line against a descending part, which would parallel each other and cross. De Palma and Hirsch were awed.

"Benny was also very sensitive to the idea that music didn't have to do it all in a film," Hirsch said:

When we were spotting the music, he'd have these fantastic ideas for *not* using music where you would expect to use it, and using it where you didn't expect it. In *Sisters* there's a scene where Margot Kidder is backed into a corner by Bill Finley, and he's trying to shock her into recalling the murder. He's holding a knife in front of her, and unbeknownst to him she's reaching for a scalpel on the table. When we looked at this, my idea had been to play it as a suspense cue. The cutting had been designed to create a sense of anticipation, getting faster and faster leading to a climax when she cuts him.

My idea had been to reflect this in the music; there would be this growing tension building to a crescendo. But Benny said, "No. Watch—this is what I want to do." We reran the scene and I asked, "You bring in the music here?" He said, "No, not yet . . . not yet . . . " We played the whole scene through, and suddenly when she cuts him he said, "*That's* where I start the music." Instead of playing the whole buildup he let that play silent; then at the release, where you might have ended the music, he started it. I later noticed he did the same thing in the famous crop duster scene in *North by Northwest*. He was brilliant in his sense of how silence was an effect also.[5]

Over his first lunch with De Palma, Pressman, and Hirsch, Herrmann carefully outlined his instrumentation and the musicians' fees. Pressman, who had wanted Michael Small (*Klute*) to write a jazz score that would be economical in both senses of the word, became increasingly alarmed. Herrmann erupted: "Let me tell you something—if you get a Rolls Royce, you don't ask how many miles it gets to the gallon. It gets nine; I should know, because I've got one!"[6]

The *Sisters* score was all the filmmakers had hoped for, a stunning fusion of flamboyant horror, bitterly ironic wit, and poignance. Throughout, Herrmann interweaves strange, contrasting orchestral textures, vivid and disturbing from the score's first moments to its last. Not since *Psycho*'s jarring prelude had Herrmann so arrestingly geared an audience for terror. Against an eerie montage of two growing fetuses, horns blare a four-note motif—a familiar children's chant—accompanied by wailing Moog synthesizers, a hysterical, descending string line, and, most drolly, the childlike patter of glockenspiels.

The film's first images, like many of Hitchcock's, are deliberately disorienting: the voyeuristic scene of a man watching a blind woman undress becomes a slick TV program, "Peeping Toms." The shock of realization is all the greater because Herrmann's scoring has been in deadly earnest: a questioning phrase for woodwinds echoes despairingly in strings and harp, becoming a lyrical, sad fragment for high strings soli. As in *Psycho's* seemingly innocuous early scenes, Herrmann confirms that there is more here than meets the eye. De Palma's parodic game show is in fact the first step toward a brutal, senseless murder.

This feeling of impending tragedy haunts *Sisters*'s most affecting moments, including Philip and Danielle's quiet conversation on the Staten Island Ferry. Again, a lyric, incomplete phrase for strings is made poignant by dark woodwind harmonies and harp, a color blend that is recalled in a gentle, hopeless valse when the couple first kiss. But as they make love at Danielle's apartment, Herrmann's romanticism gives way to a jagged pattern for ascending violins, then a frenzied wash of strings, horns, and Moogs as we see Danielle's scarred hip, the legacy of her dead twin. Again, these scenes' emotional focus comes almost entirely from Herrmann's score.

Recurring motivic devices are sparingly used but illuminating. As Philip prepares Danielle's birthday cake, we hear a childlike, celebratory anthem for glockenspiels soli; low, sustained woodwind harmonies and vibraphone provide the menace and irony. Just as the cake will be a dangerous reminder for Danielle of Philip's existence, this simple, sad motive will remind us of Philip's kindness and the wastefulness of his death.

Philip's murder—long and explicitly grisly—inspires Herrmann's wildest murder sequence. As Danielle thrusts a knife into her victim's groin, mouth, and body, a shriek of Moogs, horns, and strings cries in pain and terror, the tinny chime of glockenspiels rising pungently above all. In this disparate musical blend—traditional Herrmann brass and woodwind colors, with glockenspiel and the shrill, otherworldly synthesizers—Herrmann heightens the scene's brutality to an almost unbearable pitch, mocks our expectations about the "appropriateness" of music (as with the dainty glockenspiel), and pulls us into a vortex of chaos, death, and futility.

Herrmann's epilogue to Danielle's last murder and Grace's recovery, while no less despairing, is among the composer's most intense and moving. As the brainwashed Grace (who earlier tried to prove Danielle is a killer) now insists that she witnessed no murder, a soft, dissonant wash of winds and synthesizer whisper on the soundtrack. A slow tracking shot transports us to an empty railroad station in Quebec, where the couch containing Philip's body—covered with a shroudlike sheet—lies, observed by a man perched on a nearby telephone pole—the detective hired by Grace. Against this final shot Herrmann recalls Philip's quiet glockenspiel theme, now against dark, swelling string harmonics and the dirgelike toll of a bell, which rise to an intense crescendo, then diminuendo. This scene, observed critic Royal S. Brown, "is ironic enough: here is the piece of evidence that will no longer serve any purpose, the piece of evidence which contained 'the body that wasn't there.' . . . But the music used here—the 'birthday cake' theme . . . darkens the humor with a border of bitter poignancy. For the music resurrects, at the moment when he was the most alive, the most warm, the most human, a man who is now a forgotten, hidden cadaver."[7]

The score was recorded at London's Denham Studios. "As I entered the recording booth and looked out onto the studio floor, [Herrmann] was on the podium, standing over a full orchestra, berating the two young men on his left who were frantically trying to get the two Moog synthesizers in tune with the rest of the orchestra," De Palma recalled:

"We can't wait any longer. We'll play without them," Herrmann grumbled bitterly.

"Please, Mr. Herrmann," pleaded one of the young men, "It will just take a second."

"You said that five minutes ago and still we wait! It's an undisciplined instrument and should not be allowed in the orchestra."

The room filled with unearthly squeals as the Moogs reeled through the scales in search of the right key. Finally, the two young men managed to settle them down into a shrill sound.

"All right. That's good enough. Let's try it!"

Herrmann raised his baton and the orchestra sprang to attention. He looked up at the large time clock overhead, counted eight beats, and jerked his baton down. The Moogs wailed out and I got that same chill I'd had in the editing room a few months before. Herrmann had done it again. He was right. I couldn't leave my seat.[8]

One of the Moog players was arranger-musician Howard Blake, who gives a different description of Herrmann that afternoon: "During a break

I said to him, 'Bernie, why are you doing crap like this?' and sort of laughed. He burst into tears."[9]

The soundtrack's mixing at New York's Reeves Studio was both instructive and devastating for Paul Hirsch, whose pupil-like admiration for Herrmann was dealt a heavy blow:

As Benny walked into the studio he said, "First I have to get used to the room." I had thought he was going to be very impatient, but he wasn't. That was another thing I learned from him: when you go into a new mixing theater and you don't know the place, it takes a while to adjust to the room.

When we were dealing with dialogue and effects, Benny just snoozed, but finally we got to the murder sequence, and the music mixer forgot to turn on Benny's score. He sailed right into where the cue should have begun and there was no music. I was sitting between Brian and the mixer, and Benny was sitting up front with his back to us, facing the screen. He called out over his shoulder, "Where's the music? Isn't there music there, Paul?"—addressing me. The mixer said, "No, I just forgot to . . . "

All Benny heard was no. And since he was addressing me, he thought I was saying, "No, there's no music there." He stood up and flew into a volcanic rage, screaming at me, "How DARE you tell me there's no music there! I WROTE the music! I CONDUCTED it! I RECORDED it! You're INSOLENT! Don't you DARE speak to me in that way! I'm going to report you to the union!" And I had not said a word.

I was crushed. Here was a guy I idolized, turning on me for no reason. I looked at Brian, and I looked at the mixer, and he just shrugged. Benny went on and on; he was spitting, the veins were standing out on his forehead. Everyone was in shock. Finally Benny calmed down, and at the end of the day the mixer went over to him and said, "It was nobody's fault but my own, Benny." But for the rest of the mix, I could not open my mouth without Benny saying, "NO, NO, absolutely not!" It finally got to the point where I'd make my suggestions to Brian, who would say, "Benny, do you think we should . . . ," and Benny would say, "Yeah, we can do that." There was no way anything I said could be any good.

I was really wounded by this. Brian said to me, "Look, you handled it absolutely right. There's nothing to do. If he's crazy, just try to ignore it; he's delivering a great score to us."

Benny told me an interesting story either before or subsequent to that incident. It was from Dostoyevski, in which two men are walking down the street and one says to the other, "Oh no, here comes Nicholas. Let's cross the street, I don't want to see him." "Why?" his friend asks; "Nicholas is such a nice fellow; he's never done anything to anybody." The other man replies, "Well, I once did a terrible thing to him, and now

I can't stand him." It was like that between me and Benny. I think he knew he had erred, but he couldn't stand me because he had done a terrible thing to me. [10]

Despite the friction, Herrmann continued to make incisive contributions to the film, both musical and structural. Recalled Hirsch, "Even though he'd read the script and seen the film, while we were mixing one of the later reels Benny said, 'Brian, stop for a second. Look, if you have this scene in the picture, we may as well go home right now. She tells everything in this scene—think about it! Everything's been revealed.' We went back to the editing room, thought about it, and we finally said, 'Hey, he's right.' So we started pulling things out; we recut the scene, and it worked much better." [11]

De Palma and Hirsch were no less grateful for Herrmann's musical contributions, and in a *Village Voice* article De Palma wrote a long, lively account of Herrmann's irascibility and unerring dramatic skill. [12] But as review after review demonstrated, the score spoke for itself. "Herrmann, composer of many great scores for Hitchcock, has contributed a textbook example of filmmusic," *Variety* observed. "The main title theme gets the 92-minute film off to a great start, and in the reels to follow the music smooths out many rough edges and actually lends dramatic viability to scenes which otherwise would have fallen flat. Herrmann is one of the many rarely utilized musicians whose screen work is sorely missed." [13]

The commercial and critical success of *Sisters* in 1973 put Herrmann in his most positive state of mind since his move to London. His spirits raised and his bank account fortified, he convinced Norma that summer it was time for a vacation. As a member of England's Byron Society he had been invited on a two-week tour of Italy, to retrace Byron's countryside travels. Norma's initial reluctance to spend two weeks moderating between Herrmann and their fellow travelers was based on experience:

But Benny said it would be a lark, so I agreed. We were the craziest group of people imaginable; Benny called us the Byron Rabble. We descended on dignified patricians in beautiful country houses, poking all over their homes, just because they lived where Byron had once spent the night with a mistress. Benny was overweight and on a strict diet, so I kept all the money to make sure he didn't go off and buy sweets. He didn't understand foreign currency anyway, so I doled him about twenty-five cents to get a bread roll, since he got up much earlier than I did.

But Benny would go begging for money. If he could get two shillings out of one of the group he'd sneak off to get a gelato and come back grinning. Once I returned in time to see Lady Longford, who was a member of the group, standing on the top of a country hill with two dripping ice cream cones. Benny then appeared and shot up that hill in an amazing way for a man who couldn't walk without his walking stick.

Our coach driver was an Italian who couldn't speak English very well, so wherever we went he told people we were the Bible Society. When we reached the Tower of Lucca, this same coach driver pointed out a cinema and said, "Lovely town; today everareebodee go to de cinema and see *Pisco.*" Benny hissed, "*Psycho.*" The chap got angry—"*Pisco!* Everareebodee in Etaly know *Pisco!*" Afterwards I said to the driver, "This man knows all about *Pisco* because he wrote the music." But he didn't believe me—"These Amereecans, they know nothing," he'd say.

It was such a fast-moving trip it was rare one had time to go see "Pisco." Once we stopped in a seaside town for lunch only; then we were to get back on the coach. We entered the restaurant, which was not really prepared for us (we were not such a wonderful group to have). Benny got really cross; he was on his diet, and the waiter brought him minestrone soup as thick as porridge. On a very, very hot day. When Benny told them he didn't want it, they said it had been ordered for the whole group. They didn't seem eager to please him, so he stormed out of the restaurant and disappeared.

I thought, I'm not chasing after him this time, because this is getting really bad. So I sat and ate this appalling minestrone, which left a lump in my stomach for weeks after. Finally, since the group had deadlines, I set out to find him. The restaurant was slightly outside the town, and there was one long road leading to it. He wasn't on it. There was very little time before we had to leave. I went dashing down toward the town; it was a crowded seaside resort crammed with people, and Benny was wearing khaki shorts like everybody else, but I had to find him. I went looking everywhere, running inside four or five restaurants.

I don't know how I found him, but finally there he was, sitting at a table at an outside restaurant just finishing a dessert of cheesecake and large blackberries. And he had the biggest smile I had ever seen on his face. I stood there livid, and he was laughing like a child, with his shoulders shaking. I said, "How could you do this, with all those people waiting! And what's more, how the hell can you come here and order a meal— you don't speak Italian!" He pointed at this grinning waiter, who didn't speak any English, and said, "Ah, my friend and I have an understanding." I said, "But you've got no money! How were you going to pay for it?" Benny smiled and said, "I knew you'd come and find me."[14]

Their return on the Italian liner *Michelangelo* was no less eventful:

We were in first class, which was very formal indeed—different evening dresses every night and lots of rich Americans. After dinner we went to the ballroom, where people danced and you were waited on hand and foot. A dance band started playing at the other end of this big room, and Benny suddenly got up from our table. Everyone else was quietly sitting when they saw this solitary figure walking from one end of this huge, polished dance floor to the other. Everybody's attention was now on him because he looked as if he was going to do something.

Benny stood right in front of the band and made this horrible gesture of covering his ears, waving the band away and looking pained as he pointed at the bass player, a look of total contempt. After doing this he walked very slowly back to our table. I was always slightly ashamed of behavior like that in front of people, so I asked, "What on earth did you do that for?" He stood and pointed from across the room at the bass player and said, "HE knows!"

Benny adored music on its own level. He never expected great musicianship of anybody in a low-class band, in restaurants when a gypsy fiddler came around to his table he'd clap and put his thumb in the air. I remember a village band in Sorrento, which consisted of the village blacksmith and butcher and all that. It was an Easter carnival, and all those old men were playing bass drums and going, "*Oompa oompa.*" Benny said, "Oh, Charlie Ives woulda loved this." He wouldn't criticize them, and he certainly wouldn't criticize the gypsy fiddler. But there was something that chap in the dance band was doing, and I never found out what it was.[15]

During the Byron trip, the Herrmanns met a professor from the University of Western Ontario, who asked Herrmann to guest lecture that fall at his college. The composer agreed; he also accepted an invitation from Eastman House in Rochester to speak at their seminar "Sound and the Cinema" (which hosted RKO soundman James G. Stewart as well). At both appearances Herrmann was in top form, witty, informed, and opinionated. "The whole subject of film music is one of great mystery, not only to film makers, but also to critics and audiences," he told the university audience. "I don't like to call cinema music 'music,' because its existence is shaped by the film. But so we can understand each other, we'll use that word."[16]

But by the trip's end, Herrmann's recollections of past triumphs seemed to have brought on a renewed melancholia. "The spirit was tiring as much as the body," recalled Ted Gilling, who moderated the Eastman seminar. "A couple of hours before he left for England . . . he said to me, 'I'm an old man.' There was no anger in it. That was what worried me. It was the deep disappointment of recognition."[17]

Life had again reached a pace the young Herrmann would have thrived on but that exhausted the sixty-two-year-old man who seemed a decade older. By 1973 he was greatly overweight, yet he resisted every diet. "You lose weight in the grave," he would remark.[18] Although Herrmann still read voraciously, it was increasingly difficult for him. His lifelong poor eyesight had led to dyslexia: letters became reversed in his mind, and a Herrmann-scrawled grocery list for apples now read "sleppa" instead.[19]

As Herrmann's self-reliance declined, Norma's gained new strength. In 1973 she began working for the BBC, an institution that now ignored Herrmann almost completely (apart from John Amis, who still invited the composer to discuss music on his radio program). Herrmann's feelings about Norma's work as a BBC television writer were typically ambivalent:

Benny didn't want to hear about it at all. When I eventually presented a program on BBC-2, he totally ignored it. I would have a week of deadlines, writing the scripts and going on live every Thursday, then get ready to open the door at Chester Close to eight people for a dinner I'd cooked. And none of his friends knew I worked. But Benny was marvelous in that if anybody ever upset me, he'd have me convinced in five minutes that they were entirely inadequate, and how silly of me to let it bother me. If I came home in tears he'd say, "The world's full of stupid people. Don't worry." And I believed all of it.

But Benny had a habit of sounding out new people to see how far he could get with them, like children do—to see how far he could push them in a boxing match before they'd submit to make a row. One afternoon we had to go to a birthday party for Esther Rantzen [host of "That's Life," Norma's first program], and I knew Benny would meet my boss, who was head of the department. I said to Benny, "Now look, this is a young man, but he is important, and he's my boss, so don't insult him. Don't treat him like a young whippersnapper. Though he may look like one, he's not."

Benny wasn't responding at all—there was just silence—so I'd have another go: "Just for me, just this once, be a little humble." He never said a word until we got in and he was introduced to Desmond. Benny walked up to him and yelled, "Well, WHO THE HELL DO YOU THINK YOU ARE ANYWAY?" Fortunately, I think Desmond had been warned.

Esther Rantzen's mother loved Benny and he loved her, but they used to have terrible fights over trivial things. I always felt uncomfortable, so one day I had the same go I'd had about Desmond: "Can't you be nice to Mrs. Rantzen for once?" When we got there, Esther's mother gave us sherry, and I had mine on a chair arm and spilled a little bit—and as I was rubbing it off Benny suddenly yelled, "JUST LOOK AT WHAT YOU'VE DONE! All the way here ya say ta me, 'Be polite to Mrs. Rantzen, don't tell her off even if she's talking rubbish, even though she doesn't know anything about art,' and YOU go and spill sherry!''

By now Benny was expecting these behavior lectures from me every time we were going somewhere. As we were getting ready to go to the writer Mervyn Jones's home I shouted up the stairwell at Chester Close, "Umm, can I have a word with you before we go?" Benny's voice came down the stairwell, "I know, I know, EAT the rabbit!"—which summed up my whole lecture about putting up with anything, because he couldn't eat rabbit.

Of course, that was the only time in my life of eating out that dinner turned out to be rabbit.[20]

In addition to De Palma, other young filmmakers, in America and abroad, were discovering Herrmann's work. Among them was another of the young New York directors whose work was changing the business: brash and talented William Friedkin had scored a popular and critical success with *The French Connection* and was completing his screen version of William Peter Blatty's novel *The Exorcist* when he saw *Sisters*. Friedkin decided Herrmann was perfect for his film, and the two men met in New York. The outcome is best documented in a series of recollections that begins with Friedkin:

[Herrmann] flew in from England; I showed him the rough cut and he loved the picture, and he wanted to do it, except he said he would not work in California. He didn't like California's musicians. He didn't want to work in Hollywood. He had been through all that and to hell with it. He had to record it in London and he had to get St. Giles Church which has the greatest sound in there. I thought that was a marvellous idea if I had six months to finish the movie and let him just mail me a score. But I was making changes in the picture throughout . . . and I wanted to dub the picture [in New York] because I love the facilities here. . . . I couldn't be in London and here, so I had to not use Bernard Herrmann. I didn't know who the hell to use then.

Friedkin's remarks, published in Elmer Bernstein's magazine *Filmmusic Notebook* in late 1974, prompted a reply by Christopher Palmer, writing on the ailing Herrmann's behalf:

In the first place, Herrmann hated the film and never really wanted to do it. Second, Friedkin wanted credit as co-composer and musical director *and* a share in the music royalties; the idea was that Herrmann should call upon Friedkin with his previous day's work, play it over for him and then Friedkin would do his thing—which . . . would no doubt have led to some very interesting results. Third, Herrmann never made any such disparaging remarks about Los Angeles musicians; he wanted to record in St. Giles Cripplegate, London, because of the peculiar acoustic there and because he wanted its pipe organ. William Friedkin objected to this on the grounds that he didn't want any "Catholic" music in his film.

"It was a very quick decision," Laurie Johnson recalled. "It was all resolved within one afternoon. Benny returned to London, and as we sat in the sun at my home, he said, 'It's too tough—I don't want to touch it.' That was it; there was no further discussion about it."[21]

Finally, director Larry Cohen: "Friedkin said to Benny, 'I want you to give me a better score than you wrote for *Citizen Kane*.' Benny replied, 'Well, why didn't ya make a better PICTURE than *Citizen Kane?*' and walked out of the screening room. That's when I heard he was available."[22]

The Herrmann-Friedkin debacle was a blessing for Cohen, a young writer-director of successful exploitation films. His latest was *It's Alive*, a low-budget horror movie about a deformed killer baby and its murderous rampages around Los Angeles. Gory and bizarre, this film was not *Citizen Kane* either, but it was undeniably offbeat. "I called Benny in London," Cohen said,

and he told me to send him a print of the film, so I made a black-and-white dupe and shipped it to London. Subsequently I called him back, and he said both he and Norma liked the picture and he was interested. I said, "Go ahead and write whatever you think is good for the picture. I'm sure it'll be great. I'd love to meet you, but since I'm here in L.A. I probably won't." So basically we made a package deal; Benny would score the film, supply the musicians and recording studio, and I would pay him a flat fee for everything.

Sometime later I called him back. There was a little sequence in which a TV set was playing a Road Runner cartoon, and I asked Benny, "Could you possibly write a little music for the cartoon?" He yelled back, "I don't WRITE music for cartoons! If ya want that, ya got the wrong composer, get somebody else!" I said, "Wait a minute, don't get mad at me! If you don't want to write music for the cartoon don't do it, okay?" He said okay. That was the only argument we had.

A few weeks later I got a call from him; he said he was going to be scoring the picture over Christmastime in England. He asked me, "Aren't you coming over?" I said, "Well, I'd love to come. I didn't know if you wanted me to." He said, "Of *course* I want you to. When are you coming? We'll have to make plans. We want to make sure you have a place to be on New Year's Eve, we want to introduce you to people we know in London . . ." I said to my wife, "We can't pass on this; he wants us to come."

At that time there was a power shortage in London; the oil embargoes were going on, and England was dimming all its lights. After a certain hour they turned off the lights in Picadilly and put candles in the store windows. It was terrific; you felt like you were there during the war. Benny had rented St. Giles for the recording and had recorded some of the music the day before Christmas, but the big session was the day after Boxing Day.

The first day we met, we went to a studio and listened to some of the music he had already done. I'd talked to him about the picture's main titles, and he said he was writing an overture for it. "Give me ninety seconds to tell the audience what to expect," he said. I said I'd come up with some sort of title design. He wrote the overture in London, and in the meantime I shot the title sequence in California, a scene of flashlights going on in the dark—first one or two, then six, eight, twenty, forty flashlights going through the darkness. I brought this roll of film to London in my pocket, we ran it with the score, and it fit perfectly; the beats happened right as the flashlights went on. I suppose that cemented our relationship; it made it seem meant to be.[23]

It was a collaboration Herrmann genuinely enjoyed; what glaring weaknesses existed in the film were more than compensated by Cohen's enthusiasm for Herrmann's music and the working freedom the film offered.

Unfortunately, the score itself is Herrmann's most self-derivative. As in *Sisters*, Herrmann experiments with electronic sounds to evoke a sense of the abnormal and horrific; the odd blend of bass guitar and viola also enhance Herrmann's trademark use of low woodwinds and brass (no strings are used; instead Herrmann enlarges his usual brass instrumentation to give a sense of weight and power). Yet the music is tediously repetitive and overscaled for the low-budget film it accompanies.

Herrmann's title prelude is the most effective sequence, with thick clusters of brass and Moog counterbalancing a melancholy viola solo and quietly pulsating bass. Equally memorable in the film (for camp, not musical, reasons) is the infant's bloody murder of a Carnation milkman in the back of his delivery truck—a scene whose cue Herrmann drolly titled "The Milkman Goeth."[24] Herrmann's own favorite moment in *It's Alive* comes at the film's conclusion, as police drive the parents (John Ryan and Sharon Farrell) from their baby's last slaughter site, only to learn that an identical infant has been born in Seattle—and, Herrmann would whisper with glee, "you know it's going to happen all over again!"[25]

The first recording session, on December 24, was a near disaster: the musicians were tired and often inattentive; St. Giles was cold and damp; the film projector was loud; and the nearby pubs (saviors of many a tense recording session) were closed. Herrmann was depressed and almost in tears.[26] But the next session, on the 27th, Larry Cohen recalled, was more positive:

During the session Benny stayed very close to me, telling me everything he was doing and asking my opinion. Finally he said, "What are you doing for dinner?" He wanted to take us to Laurie Johnson's for New Year's Eve. We went and had a wonderful time; there was a big, roaring fireplace, all kinds of family—old people, young people, people who'd lived through the war and could tell great stories. Another night he took us to his favorite London restaurant, Goodies'; he said it had the best Dover sole in London.

Occasionally we would take him to L'Ambassador or some bigger restaurant, but he always hated it if there was an orchestra or group playing. He despised bad musicians and bad music—"Make them stop!" he'd yell, tapping his cane. "Make them stop!"

Every couple of days he would call on our house. If we hadn't called in a day or two he'd call and say, "What's the matter? Are the children all right?" He was like a relative. Finally he said to us, "Why don't you come and live in England? You'd love it over here." I was tired of the sameness of Los Angeles, and I'd made some pictures that had made money, so I said to my wife, "Why don't we take the kids"—we had five—"and go to England for a year?" We ended up moving to London, all because of Benny.[27]

Cohen and Herrmann's friendship also led to a free trip for both to Paris, and perhaps the strangest movie double bill in cinema history:

André Langlois of the Cinémathèque wanted to show *It's Alive*, so he called and asked me if I could come over [to Paris]. I said sure and asked, "Would you like it if Bernard Herrmann also came?" Langlois said they would love it. . . . I called Benny, and he and Norma decided they would go; they would have a good time, see Truffaut. And sure enough, Truffaut did come to our hotel to see them. We then went to the screening at the Cinémathèque. They had two shows there, an eight o'clock and a ten o'clock show. We were supposed to run *It's Alive* at ten and answer questions after it.

Well, for the eight o'clock show they'd put on *Citizen Kane!* I said, "Oh my God, we have to follow the greatest movie ever made! This is going to be terrible." Benny arrived, saw what they were showing, and said, "Oh no, not again." I asked him, "Don't you want to go in?" He said, "Nah, I've seen it." Then all of a sudden, I looked around, and he was gone. Finally he came out of the theater and said, "They're not playing it loud enough!"

While we were riding in a taxi in Paris, my wife and I made the mistake of mentioning that we were going to pick up a maestro, a conductor. The cab driver turned out to be a self-styled opera singer, and as soon as Benny got into the car the cabbie began to sing opera as he drove! Benny started screaming for him to shut up—we thought he was going to hit him with his cane—but the guy wouldn't stop; he thought Benny was kidding. Finally at a stoplight, Benny opened the door and started to get out, and the driver finally shut up. It was like a comic scene from a movie.[28]

On returning to London, Herrmann found several Hollywood offers awaiting him, but his unwillingness to forget the past was as great as his desire to work. Recalled Charles Gerhardt:

People would call from California to ask him something and he wouldn't even come to the phone. Universal Studios was not exactly high on his list. Frank Perry directed a film with Joel Grey called *Man on a Swing* which he wanted Benny to score, and since Perry had no intro to him Frank asked me to talk to Benny. I did, and when Benny asked me what studio it was for and I told him Universal, he exploded: "Those sons-a bitches, I don't care WHO it is . . ." I said, "Look, it's a whole new ball game now. They're doing a lot of good things and they've got a lot of new people in there." He finally said, "Yeah, you're probably right." But he never did the Perry film.

One night at Chester Close a producer called from California and asked Benny to score a picture. "Do this for old Sam Spiegel," the man said— and Benny . . . said, "Why the hell should I do something for Sam Spiegel? What the hell did he ever do for me? Just because he's an old man now I gotta be kind to him?" And Benny was quite right; a lot of producers would get favors out of people because they were ninety, but they would have cut anybody's throat before then. Benny wouldn't buy that. Also, they wanted the score in five weeks, and Benny wouldn't be pressured. He needed time to do what he did well, and he wouldn't bring in an orchestrator. The thing he hated most of all was that the music was the last thing to be done and it would get short shrift.[29]

Mike Nichols, director of *The Graduate* and *Who's Afraid of Virginia Woolf?*, flew to London to screen his thriller *The Day of the Dolphin* for Herrmann (on the recommendation of Stephen Sondheim, a staunch Herrmann admirer since his 1945 fan letter about *Hangover Square*). When Nichols demanded that the score be completed in six weeks to satisfy the studio release date and producer Joseph Levine, Herrmann reportedly ordered him out of Chester Close.[30]

Not all directors fared so poorly. Through Brian De Palma and Dutch producer Pim de la Parra, Herrmann met Martin Scorsese, whose stylized depictions of New York street life the composer greatly admired ("Take 'Mean Streets,' " Herrmann told an interviewer; "Scorsese did 'Mean Streets' like an Italian opera").[31] In June 1974 Scorsese sent the composer the script of his next project, *Taxi Driver.* Herrmann agreed to score the film.

A prestigious picture for a major studio (Columbia), *Taxi Driver* was a triumphant turning point for Herrmann, who had become not only a cult figure among cineastes but also a composer again sought out by Hollywood's best directors. "The new guys, they want me!" he told Ted Gilling with glee. "Usually in the past, the young guys would tell all the old guys to get the hell off the boat—but since I'm in vogue again, I can tell *them* where to go!"[32]

And to Norma, in an echo of Lionel Newman's remark of a decade past: "*I'm* running with the kids now."[33]

# SEVENTEEN

BOSWELL:    But is not the fear of death natural to man?

JOHNSON:    So much so, Sir, that the whole of life is but keeping
            away thoughts of it.

                                        *Boswell,* Life of Johnson

The 150th anniversary of the death of Lord Byron in April 1974 was the occasion of Herrmann's first public concert in over five years. It was also his last. But if the evening ranked among the most forgettable of Herrmann's conducting career, at least it took place in the nineteenth-century magnificence of Drury Lane, whose 1812 opening Byron himself had commemorated.

The April 21 concert came at the invitation of the Byron Society, with whom Herrmann had traveled the previous year; and while the concert's failure was unquestionably Herrmann's fault, it was not because he lacked knowledge and understanding of his subject. In a program essay Herrmann wrote:

Although Byron has been dead 150 years, he still exerts as vibrant and forceful an influence on the creative mind as ever he did. We present this programme, not in any spirit of any sycophantic homage-making or arid antiquarianism, but as a testimony to our belief in Byron as a living presence, a vital source of fascination and inspiration for artists in all media of creativity. His dynamic zest for life, his fearless iconoclasm, his love of liberty and hatred of oppression, the richness of his poetic technique, his intense interest in nature, in the supernatural, in the magical, his feeling for drama as an integral part of life—all are as meaningful and relevant today as when they first burst like a bombshell on the contemporary scene of life and letters. We speak of a "Byronic attitude"; in relation to a man's character as a whole, not just to some particular facet. Byron has become a part of all our lives, whether we are consciously aware of it or not. If he'd never existed we'd have had to invent him, to paraphrase Voltaire.

Musically speaking, Byron's following has been enormous, and we can do no more here than offer a representative cross-section of those composers whose muse has been fired by Byron's own. . . . Our concert is thus intended, not as a random compilation of works associated with Byron, but as an attempt to recreate the living presence of Byron in music which grew out naturally from his influence and ambience.[1]

Sadly, the result more closely resembled an autopsy. Herrmann's ambitious program (Berlioz's *Harold in Italy*, Richard Arnell's Symphonic Portrait of Byron, Liszt's tone poem *Tasso*, a specially commissioned choral work by Elizabeth Maconchy, and more) simply tackled more than the Royal Philharmonic could digest in one rehearsal. While Maconchy's *Isles of Greece* was amply practiced, the Liszt and Berlioz works were almost ignored until the concert itself—all too obviously.

A second problem was Herrmann's increasing lack of strength, which rendered his rudimentary baton technique almost invisible. His entrance that evening was that of a feeble old man who reached the podium long after the applause had ended. From the rostrum Herrmann took a labored bow, which elicited a second pathetic smattering of applause from the audience.[2] Reviews ranged from dismissive to scathing. "The 'dead' acoustics of an orchestra seated flat on the theatre stage, instead of raised in tiers . . . made the Royal Philharmonic sound like an ancient gramophone record," one critic wrote. "The other [handicap] was the pedestrian conducting of its American guest, Bernard Herrmann, whose performance of Berlioz's 'Harold in Italy' was plodding in character, wrong-headed in tempo, and thereby wasteful of the talents of Frederick Riddle as the viola soloist."[3] According to the *Daily Telegraph*, Herrmann "was content to beat time without ever raising his eyes from the score."[4] For Herrmann's friends—who, unlike the critics, were aware of his poor health—it was an equally depressing evening, and a sad finale to a conducting career that in its prime was innovative and exciting.

A happier event followed in June. In 1972 RCA had launched a series of newly recorded "Classic Film Scores" under the baton of Charles Gerhardt. The first album, a selection of Korngold works, topped the classical charts for weeks. Eight editions and two years later, Gerhardt was ready to record an album of Herrmann, and was delighted to find the composer enthusiastic about the project.

Gerhardt lived in New York, but by telephone the two men mapped out each aspect of the recording. Most of the selections were made by Gerhardt: a *Citizen Kane* suite, including the opening and finale, the "Rosebud" music, the breakfast montage, and *Salammbô*; the *Hangover Square*

concerto; *Beneath the 12-Mile Reef* and *White Witch Doctor.* The last selection was Herrmann's: "Benny said, 'I've got this one piece—ya gotta
hear it, I think it would be very interesting.' It was the "Death Hunt"
from *On Dangerous Ground;* he had a very good acetate of the piece from
the soundtrack. I fell in love with it and said we had to use it."[5]

Gerhardt traveled to California and returned with microfilm copies of
the *Kane* score: "I wrote a little transitional passage for the *Kane* suite
about five bars long, and I was a little worried since the score was one of
his great works. I tried to be as Herrmannesque as I could, but I was afraid
to show it to him; I thought he might hand me my head. He looked at
it and saw I was anxious to show I knew something about his music. He
frowned at me with those evil eyes, then took a pencil, and over the first
of the three bars for strings he wrote 'Sul tasto.' I thought, I didn't think
of that; he wants it played on the violins' fingerboard so it's ghostly. A
lot of people would think that's not very important, but I realized that the
man was *constantly* concerned with the sound that's going to come out.
He changed a little thing in the flutes, did something in the trombones—
he put his signature on it and made it Herrmann."

The three-day recording session was held in London's Kingsway Hall,
with Herrmann present and George Korngold (Erich's son) producing. For
the *Salammbô* aria, Gerhardt engaged Kiri Te Kanawa, who had recently
made her debuts at the Metropolitan Opera and Covent Garden. Unlike
the unfortunate Mrs. Kane, Te Kanawa had no difficulty hitting the aria's
climactic top D. Recalled Gerhardt, "As we finished the recording, her
agent came up as she stood with me and Benny. As he bustled her up and
put her coat on, he said, 'Pure MGM, my dear.' Benny heard that. I've
never had much respect for that man since."

Illness forced pianist John Ogdon to cancel as soloist for the *Hangover
Square* concerto, but as usual Herrmann had an idea: he would conduct,
and Gerhardt would play piano. Recalled Gerhardt: "It wasn't a bad idea,
but I said, 'Benny, we've got four days, and I don't play it.' 'You can do
it,' he said. 'I'll change things if it's too difficult. Who cares about that—
you're a great pianist.' Great pianist! But I thought, there's so much else
to worry about, and what if he starts conducting and I can't follow him.
The Spanish pianist Joaquin Achucarro was free at the time and said he'd
do it. I told him it was not long, it was certainly within his technique, and
it had the very unusual quality of being the only piano concerto that starts
and ends with solo piano. Achucarro thought it would be some modern
thing with alternating meter, so he was really nervous by the time he got
to London. When we met and I handed him the score, he said, 'Thank

God, it's Romantic—real piano music!' We worked very hard those four days; he sight-read the piece straight off, and turned in a very good performance."

The virtuosic "Death Hunt" was the most challenging piece to record, especially since, to the dismay of its nine horn players, it was the first item to be tackled in an early-morning session. Next was *Beneath the 12-Mile Reef:*

At one point Benny told me, "Don't take *12-Mile Reef* music too fast, especially the main title. I know it's fast in the picture, but I had no time, and I got into the rut of writing too much music." I said yes, yes, yes, every day on the phone. Then came the first rehearsal, with nine harps behind me on the stage. Benny was standing next to me with his cane, and as I gave the upbeat to begin he yelled, "It's too FAST!" Of course, we hadn't played yet, and the whole orchestra collapsed with laughter. It's like the old joke about Tiomkin giving an upbeat and saying before they played, "Too loud, was!"

Then Benny made one of his great malapropisms: he looked at the harps and said, "After all, they've only got ten fingers!" You can't have nonsense like that when you're working, so I said, "*Out!* Back in your control room!" He sulked away—"Aww, all right . . . " It was a big act which might have looked like a row, but it was just the usual horseplay to relieve tension.

Nine harps made way for a battery of percussion and the recording of *White Witch Doctor.* "Benny drove everybody crazy, because he wanted just the right sound for the clang in the opening. . . . He finally ended up using [an automobile] brake drum in the film. . . . Tris Frye, the head of percussion, . . . brought brake drums to the session, plus an enormous anvil which weighed a ton—all this to just try things. Here we were, waiting to record the main title, and Benny was over in the percussion section clanking away. We had one from a Rolls Royce; that didn't make it. Then one from a Volkswagen—and Benny said, 'That's it!' It was as if an oboe player were changing his reed."

The finished album was a triumph, from Korngold's superb production to Christopher Palmer's literate program booklet (a young university graduate, Palmer became one of Herrmann's most articulate champions and closest friends). Reviews were generally ecstatic. Wrote Royal S. Brown in *High Fidelity:* "In addition to the excitement, gloom, exuberance, terror and other moods generated by the five highly diversified Herrmann scores recorded here, and in addition to the marvellously expansive, rich sonics and stereo effect . . . I must say that a great deal of my enthusiasm for the music on this disc is inspired by Charles Gerhardt's almost unbelievably intense and exhilarating interpretations. Very simply, these are some of the most captivating performances of film music I have ever heard."[6]

Throughout the year Herrmann had been not only weak and exhausted but suffering from shortness of breath as well, which he attributed to flu. That July, Laurie Johnson recommended that Herrmann see his doctor and friend D. L. Griffiths, who realized Herrmann's condition was more serious than anyone had thought. A consultant cardiologist confirmed Griffiths's diagnosis of hypertensive cardiac failure or, more simply, a deteriorating heart condition.[7]* Two days later Herrmann was admitted into London's St. George's Hospital, his feisty unwillingness to cooperate masking a childlike terror of his own mortality. "Benny was so frightened he was rigid," Norma recalled:

He had always been very scared about anything happening to him, the slighest pimple or finger cut, like a child. Those two days at home he stayed in his dressing gown and didn't speak, he was so terrified. I called Chris Palmer, who came over and tried to cheer him up; they'd just sit together and not say anything. Then Benny went into the hospital, and when I went to see him later that day we were actually laughing, because it wasn't as bad as he thought.

But Benny would never get into his hospital bed. I think he thought that if he got under the sheets he was a patient and was ill. He ran around the whole ward in his bare, dirty feet and tried to start an argument with every heart patient. It was during the last stages of Watergate, and Benny would insist to all the old English gentlemen, "Nixon WON'T resign!" When they all agreed with him, he went around saying, "Nixon WILL resign!"

Then I started hearing from the nurses that there were marauders in the hospital. Well, Benny would nick all the fruits and things people took each other in the heart patients ward. He used to laugh as if he were four years old, because he was on a strict diet and he was getting fat on other people's goodies. I was in a panic all through that period, but the hospital staff and Griff said to me, "Oh, he's all right, he's just got to take it easy."[8]

In retrospect, Norma was glad Griffiths had not told her what he knew: Herrmann's heart condition was irreversible. He had one, perhaps two years left to live.

---

*A 1989 medical report described heart disease as most prevalent in workaholics and those having "mistrust of the motives of others, and who openly and frequently expressed their anger" (cited in Janny Scott, "Hostility Seen as 'Toxic Core' in Behavior of Type A People," Los Angeles Times, 1–17–89, pt. 1, p. 3).

Herrmann went home two weeks later, after the completion of tests. His confidence restored, he returned to film, and his second and last collaboration with De Palma.

*Obsession* is Bernard Herrmann's cinema requiem, a summation of his film skills and an affirmation of the human spirit. More than any other Herrmann film, *Obsession*'s power and narrative focus come almost entirely from the composer's score, "a marvellously evocative choral work," wrote critic Alexander Walker, "on which the story often floats wordlessly like a picture in a river's reflection."[9] In fact, *Obsession* owes more to Herrmann than its score alone; like *Sisters* its story construction and script benefited from Herrmann's suggestions.

Paul Schrader's original screenplay (entitled *Déjà Vu*) was a free paraphrase of *Vertigo*'s Tristan and Isolde story, with Hitchcock's San Francisco setting changed to New Orleans. Sixteen years after the kidnaping and death of his wife, Elizabeth, and his daughter, tycoon Michael Courtland (Cliff Robertson in the film) meets Elizabeth's double (Genevieve Bujold) in the Florentine church where he first met his wife. They fall in love, but on the eve of their marriage the nightmare repeats itself: the girl, Sandra, vanishes, apparently the victim of an identical kidnapping.

But unkown to Courtland, it is a scheme between his business partner, LaSalle, and Court's daughter, Amy, who did *not* die but was flown by LaSalle to Italy where she grew up believing her father had caused Elizabeth's death. Court learns of the plot, kills LaSalle, and is sent to prison, while the guilt-ridden Amy is incarcerated in a madhouse. Years later, both are released and reconciled.

Herrmann's reaction to the script's final third: "Get rid of it," he told De Palma in 1974; "that'll never work."[10]

De Palma listened, and drastically condensed the finale into a more immediate and upbeat reunion of Courtland and Amy after LaSalle's death. After financial backing was assembled by producer George Litto, *Obsession* (as it was finally titled) was filmed in late 1974. De Palma now insisted on Herrmann as composer, but George Litto proposed John Williams (after Williams's enormous success with *Jaws*). Again, as he had done with *Sisters*, Paul Hirsch used Herrmann's music to convince a producer: "I laid the *Vertigo* score against the sequence of Robertson following Bujold through the streets of Florence. The material itself was very neutral, but the music made it seem as if Robertson was dying of love for this woman—which was the whole idea. Litto said, 'What's that, *Romeo and Juliet*?' We said, 'No, it's Bernard Herrmann!' From then he was sold."[11]

His respect for Herrmann aside, Hirsch was not looking forward to another meeting after their falling-out on *Sisters:* "Our relationship had started so great and then turned into a nightmare. But when Benny came to New York to see *Obsession* and saw me, he walked over, gave me a warm handshake, and said, 'Paul, my boy, how *are* you? It's good to see you.' I just stood there wondering what was going on. Obviously he had read Brian's *Village Voice* article and realized I had been responsible for his getting *Sisters.* So from being the whipping boy I had become the golden boy."

De Palma and Hirsch were further startled to hear Herrmann chuckling throughout the *Obsession* screening. They asked, with some apprehension, why he was laughing. Herrmann smiled. "I'm laughing because I can hear the music already—but you'll have to wait."[12]

In Genevieve Bujold Herrmann found a contemporary Lucy Muir, a lost romantic with whom he became boyishly infatuated. "I identified with the girl, how she felt," he told Royal S. Brown. "It's a very strange picture, a very beautiful picture [with] a Proustian, Henry Jamesian feeling to it. The only other score I ever felt this way about was 'The Ghost and Mrs. Muir'; there's the same feeling of aloneness, of solitude."[13]

Back in London (with a small transparency of Bujold that he carried in his wallet until his death),[14] Herrmann quickly began work on the score, writing all night with an ease that amazed him: "It just came to me, I don't know where from. This I did in a month."[15]

Herrmann's score itself is very much about time—remembered love and tragedy, the past echoing through events that cross-refer and blur into fantasy. It is filled with remembrances of Herrmann's own past as well, with allusions to *Vertigo, Fahrenheit 451,* and a last setting of the Dies Irae chant of death.

The core of *Obsession*'s score is heard in the film's first frames, in a title sequence of Herrmann's own devising. "During lunch one day Benny stopped eating, went straight to the phone, and called De Palma," Laurie Johnson recalled. "He said, 'This is Benny. I've got the idea for the main titles. Don't argue, just listen.' And he outlined the whole sequence, telling De Palma the number of frames for each shot."[16]

Against the film's first image—the Florentine church, viewed from a climbing point-of-view shot—brass and organ declaim Herrmann's two-note theme with a grandeur that recalls the similarly liturgical opening of *Moby Dick.* But as a cross-cutting montage of photos of Courtland and Elizabeth arrests our ascent to the church, Herrmann's epic forces disappear, replaced by a remote, sighing echo of the phrase for voices and harp. The juxtaposition of past and future continues to the credits' end, alternating brutality with ghostly lyricism, until we hear only the sound of nocturnal crickets and distant voices; it is New Orleans 1959, at the elegant plantation home of the Courtlands, "the last romantics." As Vilmos Zsigmond's camera gracefully spins around the dancing lovers, Herrmann's two-note theme is transformed into an ethereal *valse lente* that evokes, like the swirling images, the "Proustian, Henry Jamesian feeling" of dislocated time that Herrmann loved about the film.

The following montage, of Court's ransom delivery, is, like many Hitchcock sequences, dramatically flat and detached without Herrmann's score. With maniacal precision, Herrmann denotes both the scene's literal and psychological elements—the ferry boat's whirring paddle and Court's fears—in a stabbing moto perpetuo for strings against the weighty counterpoint of cathedral organ. As De Palma observed, "It was his music which gave that sequence all its complexity."[17]

As in *Vertigo*, *Obsession*'s most stunning musical passages are dialogue-free. One accompanies De Palma's most subtle use of his revolving camera metaphor as Court watches the construction of Elizabeth and Amy's memorial in his vast, empty park. As the tracking camera leaves Court staring at the monument, the park's tall ferns rocked gently by the wind, the breeze is reflected in dreamy harp and choral sighs; when we pass the great shrine a title tells us it is now sixteen years later—a vigil Herrmann notes with a quote from his love theme from *Vertigo*.

Soon Court returns to Florence and the church where he first met Elizabeth; it is, of course, the church of the film's credits and the original of Courtland's monument. As he enters—the hollow sound of his footsteps echoing Scottie Ferguson's lonely walk through the San Francisco mission—an organ intones a solemn plagal melody; it is joined by a caressing countertheme for violins, suggesting that the sounds emanate from Court's mind. Strings gradually build in suspended excitement until he sees, as in a dream, his dead wife, a moment expanded by De Palma's half-speed images and Herrmann's sighing, diminuendo chorus. ("My 'Obsession' score has two distinct elements: romance and tension," Herrmann said. "They usually go hand-in-hand.")[18]

Significantly, Herrmann's *valse lente* first recurs while Court and Sandra walk together through Florence after their first dinner together. Like Schrader's dialogue, the theme here is tentative and delicate, adding an emotional luster to Court's playful description of Elizabeth's "Bryn Mawr walk." As their relationship deepens the melody undergoes textural variations (if not actual development) until the couple's (imagined) wedding, when it becomes an exultant statement of romantic fulfillment.

As in *Vertigo*, this narrative and musical climax triggers a return to *Obsession*'s tragic first act. Deceived into believing that Sandra has been kidnaped, Court again carries out the ransom instructions of sixteen years earlier, Herrmann's agitated ferry music recalling the trauma of the film's opening. Again LaSalle's plot backfires; as the two men struggle to the death, Herrmann employs a brilliant instance of dramatic counterpoint: a slow, mounting rhythm for bass pizzicatos and organ against an overlaying theme for horns, creating an amazing sense of impending doom.

*Obsession*'s denouement, unlike *Vertigo*'s, is triumphant, at least to Herrmann. Court embraces "Sandra," then realizes that she is his daughter, Amy; Zsigmond's camera spins breathlessly around the couple, and Herrmann, in a joyous reprise of the valse—now for orchestra and chorus, melding past and present—conveys the emotions that the dazed Court cannot (at least, not in Robertson's bland performance). It is the sequence of which Herrmann was especially proud. "[Herrmann] was the master of giving a whole emotional subtext to the characters," De Palma said. "That is what makes the film work."[19]

Appropriately for such a spiritualistic score, *Obsession* was recorded at St. Giles, in July 1975 with the National Philharmonic. At lunch before the session Herrmann told Paul Hirsch, "John Milton is buried at St. Giles about six feet from where I conduct. If I do a good job, he'll whisper to me."[20] The recording, however, was anything but smooth. Although he was surrounded by friends—De Palma, Hirsch, Laurie Johnson, Charles Gerhardt—Herrmann was tired, his conducting erratic; the situation was not improved by the extreme heat of one of London's warmest summers. Recalled Gerhardt:

There were some wrong notes in the horn parts, and Benny wasn't too quick to spot an E natural instead of an E flat at that time of his life, so when they questioned him he got annoyed and said the score was right, he was right, so just play it. The Philharmonic's former first horn, who was then playing second horn, was having a drinking problem; he was a superb player but it was getting out of hand. At the end of the morning session, Benny started to leave the podium and said, "I've never heard such lousy horn playing in my life." The third man, a Welshman who was trying to keep the second horn player in shape, couldn't take it any more and said, "And I've never seen such lousy conducting in my life."

It was really like a truck driver and a taxi driver who roll down their windows and yell at each other but never get out—but their leader, Sidney

Sax, got very upset and told Benny he'd take care of everything. He sacked the Welshman from the orchestra, although he finished the sessions.

But the acoustic of St. Giles was magical. Benny put the eight female singers up in the organ loft at the back of the church without a microphone. Then the strings, four horns, one oboe, two harps, and timpani were in the front. All the sound from the organ loft was recorded just through the strings mike; that was Benny's idea.[21]

By 9:45 that evening, with only the last sequence left to record, Herrmann was too exhausted to continue. At Herrmann's request, Laurie Johnson conducted the long cue.[22] A surprise but welcome visitor at the sessions was Genevieve Bujold. Recalled Gerhardt: "As she spoke to Benny in a heavy French accent I could tell he was about to get the hanky out. She told him of all the trouble she'd had with Cliff Robertson because he spent all his time in makeup and didn't make their love scenes meaningful. She said, 'Mr. Herrmann, he wouldn't make love to me—but you made love to me with your music.' And Benny started to cry. He would tell that story over and over at dinner, and start crying again every time."[23]

Herrmann's good spirits continued into the film's dubbing in New York the next month, a period spent revisiting the city with De Palma, Martin Scorsese, and Hirsch. Hirsch later said:

The year before *Obsession* my godfather had died. He was a violinist in a famous quartet of the twenties and played for Toscanini for many years, and he had always been a very close grandfatherlike figure to me. So when Benny and I became friends again it was like a renewal of that relationship, listening to stories about classical music and the early twentieth century.

We went to Sam Goody's record store together, and in just the two years between *Sisters* and *Obsession,* where they originally had to look up his name in a catalogue and search the back room, there was now a whole case of Herrmann recordings. He was very proud that he had his own section, and told me about each album—"This one's a rip-off . . . This one's very good. . . . "

After dubbing was finished we screened the film, and it's an extraordinary moment when you see a picture for the first time. Several people were there—record executives, Brian, myself, Benny, and others. As the picture ended the lights came up, and Benny was sobbing. He cried for about ten minutes. I was very moved by this. Nobody knew what to say, so everyone went ahead and left me with him. After a while we went outside and got into a taxi. Benny was still sobbing occasionally, and I put my hand on his arm. He said, "I don't remember writing it. All I know is

I woke up one night and said, 'It's got to have a chorus.' " Later, after he died, I thought about this. The next day Benny and I had dinner at Sardi's, and he said, "I want to tell you why I was so upset yesterday. When I saw the picture all finished, I felt as if those characters had left me."

Benny gave the actual score to Brian and inscribed it, "With thanks for the finest film of my musical life." We were very startled at first, because in his scrawl it looked as if he had written "the *final* film of my musical life."[24]

Herrmann's work on *Obsession* may have been finished, but De Palma and Hirsch's was not. No distributor would release the film because of its story element of incest (in the original film the marriage is consummated before "Sandra"'s disappearance). Hirsch "thought it was a mistake to drag incest into what was basically a romantic mystery, so I suggested to Brian, 'What if it never happened? What if instead of having them get married Court only dreams of getting married? We have this shot of Cliff Robertson asleep. We could use that and then cut to the wedding sequence.' And that's what we did. It became a projection of his desires rather than actual fact."[25] The changes helped the film gain a distributor (Columbia) but required recutting Herrmann's score—done in the composer's absence, and resulting in often jarring music cuts that he would hardly have approved. But he was never to see the film in its reedited form.

Even before *Obsession*'s completion Herrmann was busy arranging his next two recording projects for Unicorn. The inexorable passage of time was the apt theme of "A Musical Garland of the Seasons," which combined Herrmann's *Fantasticks* (in its first recording) and *For the Fallen*, Delius's *A Late Lark*, and Warlock's *Four Motets* (for chorus) to trace an approximate chart of the seasons in transition. The album was a charming tribute to three composers who shared a common love of nature and the beauty of English poetry. Ironically, time was a key element in the recording itself; conceived as an interim project between the writing and recording of *Obsession*, it was hastily organized and was recorded in a single afternoon.[26]

In addition to soprano Gillian Humphreys and alto Meriel Dickinson (a champion of Ives, Lord Berners, and other Herrmann favorites), the composer enlisted for *The Fantasticks* bass Michael Rippon and sometime tenor John Amis, both of whom had sung on the 1967 *Moby Dick* recording. The years had not been kind to Amis's marginal singing voice; but when Amis declined Herrmann's offer, "Benny's voice went up in pitch

that dangerous fourth, and he yelped at me, 'Look I did you a favor way
back over "Moby Dick," di'n' I? Now do me one, cos I want your voice,
and nobody else's, singing these two numbers. And the Delius title is
kinda suitable. It's called "A Late Lark." ' Irresistible."[27]

The session, on a beautiful June afternoon in St. Giles, was the usual
mix of Herrmann cantankerousness and unchecked emotionalism: as
Amis recalled, "when the Delius got beautiful, Benny blubbed." Amis's
account of his own performance was less charitable but accurate: "The
'Late Lark' is just a bit too late on my part, veering towards the Peter Sell-
ers record of the old man in the bathtub singing 'You are the promised kiss
of springtime.' "[28]

Herrmann's next Unicorn album was organized that same week, when
Christopher Palmer, acting at the composer's request, asked Herrmann's
old friend Fred Steiner to assemble the complete *Psycho* score and send
copies to London. The package arrived in September, along with a letter
from Steiner expressing concern about Herrmann's health. Herrmann
replied:

Dear Fred,

The music and score arrived safely yesterday and we are now in the
process of making sufficient duplicates of the string parts. We will record
on October 2nd and the fact that we are doing so is by no means without
the knowledge of your valuable contribution. It is certainly a great relief
to have the parts and score under this roof. Many thanks. . . . My plans
have now altered and my trip to California for 'Taxi Driver' recording will
be January 1976. . . .

I have just received the Elmer Bernstein magazine [*Filmmusic Notebook*] and, needless to say, I am more than pleased with your splendid article ["Bernard Herrmann: An Unauthorized Biography"]. It is the only
one written about me which was not full of rumor, anecdotes and fictitious
rubbish. At least you tell about me the way you knew me which is more
than your colleagues care to do. . . .

Thank you again for your kindness.

Best wishes,
Bernard[29]

The clarity and excitement of the new *Psycho* recording—made at
Barking Assembly Hall with the National Philharmonic's string section—
hardly seemed possible at the outset of the one-day session, at which Herrmann was weak and tense. "Benny started rehearsal with the prelude,"
John Goldsmith recalled, "and although he was never the world's greatest

conductor, he certainly wasn't himself healthwise. He began conducting the opening at a crawl—and Laurie Johnson and I just looked at each other. Benny turned to us and said, 'Whaddaya think?' I said, 'A bit slow.' 'Whaddaya mean?' he said. 'This ain't the film!' 'Well, I *know* it's not the film, Benny; but it's *much* slower.' So he did it again, and Laurie jollied him on a bit more. Benny kept doing it, and doing it, and finally gave the baton to Laurie and said, 'Awww, Christ—*you* do it!' After Laurie recorded the first track, Benny woke himself up and did better."[30] In the end the score was brilliantly performed and engineered, and the album sold well after its Christmas release. It was Herrmann's last recording for Unicorn.

While the *Psycho* score was in production, *The Ghost and Mrs. Muir*, Herrmann's own favorite, was being recorded commercially for the first time by Elmer Bernstein. Although the album was made at Wembley, a mere half-hour from Herrmann's Chester Close home, Bernstein chose not to consult the composer: "I knew if I opened that can of beans we'd never get the job done." Sensitively performed and faithful to the spirit of Herrmann's original, the recording pleased both film music aficionados and Herrmann—"and that was big news," Bernstein said, "although Benny was really too ill by that time to dislike things."[31]

After his long-standing feud with Bernstein, Herrmann decided it was time to make peace; some weeks before the album's recording the two met for lunch at Chester Close. "It was really very sad," Bernstein said. "On that last meeting all Benny wanted to talk about were the composers he knew in Hollywood that had once been his friends. He wanted to know everything I could tell him about these people—Jeff Alexander, Lyn Murray, Hugo Friedhofer—composers about whom he had had relatively little good to say when he was in Hollywood." To Bernstein's astonishment Herrmann began to reminisce about his childhood on 14th Street in New York, his parents, his days as a pit violinist in the Yiddish Theater. It was a side Bernstein had never seen before. Herrmann also made some revealing comments on the scoring process:

I remarked to Benny how much I enjoyed Richard Rodney Bennett's score for *Murder on the Orient Express,* which was a kind of pastiche score with a wonderful waltz for the train. When I mentioned my approval Benny went livid—"How could he have done that? No! I hated it—it was silly, terrible." I asked why. Herrmann replied, "That train was a train of *death.*" That gives you a major clue to Benny's thinking. You couldn't take that film seriously, and something in Bennett sensed that. But I might have done something exactly like Herrmann. Although he was older than I, we both came from a generation that took life quite seriously. There was the Depression in the United States, Hitler on the horizon; it was a very serious time. And to a certain extent that has affected the way we score films. To us, life is serious—and when there's going to be a murder on a train, *that's* serious business.[32]

During lunch Herrmann also expressed his appreciation for the recognition given him in Bernstein's *Filmmusic Notebook* articles and recent recordings of his work. At the meeting's end, although clearly tired, Herrmann walked with Bernstein to the gate of Chester Close mews, as happy and as melancholy as his colleague had ever seen him.

Another reminder of the passing years came that September in a lengthy letter to Herrmann from former CBS producer Davidson Taylor. It proved a touching farewell to one of Herrmann's oldest friendships:

Last night I glanced at some issues of *Modern Music* and read again your admirable 1945 piece on the four Ives symphonies. You have had a great gift for the English language ever since we have known you, and not only for music. My debt to you for your music and for the introduction to other music is paralleled by the pointers you have made me in English literature. . . .

It has been too long since we saw you. . . . I feel at age 63 a renewed concern about friends, always all too few and fewer now. . . . Our friends are dropping right and left, though we have no intention of doing so. . . .

We play records and seldom go to the opera or concerts. I did an account of the hymn tunes in the Ives SECOND SYMPHONY. . . . How we value your magisterial recordings of that Symphony. The version you did on CBS almost parallels the technically superior discs with the London Symphony Orchestra. It is a bloody shame that the music world does not acknowledge your recognition, understanding, mastery of Ives 30 years before he became the rage on his 100th birthday. But we know about the infrequent and almost accidental justice. . . .

And now along the bookshelves I see Sitwells, never met them but through you. The record shelves: Lord Berners, Warlock. I am in your debt, San Bernadino. . . .

Parmenides wrote, "Why is there not nothing?" I used to think this meant that someone or something had made it. Not at all. He meant that the human mind cannot conceive of nothing.

I wish to thank you for an invaluable part of my education, and to send you our sustenance.

Dave[33]

The fear of nothingness—the void of isolation—was also on Herrmann's mind that fall; for although he was generally happy, his next—
and last—film, *Taxi Driver*, was the most chilling and nihilistic of his
career.

For years Martin Scorsese, whose knowledge of film was exhaustive,
had been an avid admirer of Herrmann's work. In 1968, at a screening in
Paris of *The Bride Wore Black* and *Marnie*, Scorsese was excited by the
impact of four hours of Herrmann's music; that same year Scorsese co-
scripted *Obsessions*, the film that had used CBS tracks to create a "new"
Herrmann score. *Taxi Driver*, in Scorsese's mind, would fuse brooding images and music to create a style the director called "New York gothic." Before production began, Scorsese told coproducer Michael Phillips that Herrmann was his first and only choice for the score.[34]

Herrmann was typically quarrelsome when Scorsese approached him
by phone: "I don't know anything about taxi drivers," he snapped at the
director. Scorsese sent Herrmann the script; its rich, tragic character study
proved irresistible. (Herrmann told Scorsese at their first meeting he was
particularly intrigued by the fact that the story's protagonist ate cereal
with peach brandy.)[35]

Over the next months, the two men continued to discuss the score;
Herrmann even visited on location in New York.* By the time he saw the
finished film in October 1975, Herrmann told Laurie Johnson and Christopher Palmer that the score was almost complete in his mind.[36]

If Paul Schrader's *Obsession* script was a love story haunted by death,
his screenplay for *Taxi Driver* is its darkest antithesis, a study of fueled
hate and alienation in which death is the inevitable outcome. Robert De-
Niro portrayed Travis Bickle, a New York cabbie whose isolationism and
mounting hatred lead to an all-out bloody assault on the city's "scum."
Throughout, Schrader and Scorsese maintain a disturbing ambivalence toward Bickle and his actions—even at the film's close, when the cabbie is
hailed as a hero after slaughtering several lowlifes. *Taxi Driver* is the most
graphically violent and unpleasant of Herrmann's films ("it makes *Sisters*
look like a Sunday picnic," Herrmann told Paul Hirsch);[37] but, like so
many of his best screen projects, it is also a brilliant psychological portrait
of festering evil.

*Columbia music head Richard Berres was also visiting the city: "I'll never forget an aw-
ful cab ride I had with Benny. There were bars between us and the driver, and Benny started
pounding his cane on the window, yelling 'I don't like the way you drive!' The cabbie looked
like he could have pulled out a knife and killed both of us, and I said to Benny, 'Forget it,
it'll just be another minute'—but Benny said, 'NO! I don't like the way he drives, and he
*must know*' " (Berres to SCS, 8-1-84).

Following Herrmann's death, the score for *Taxi Driver* was both overpraised (as Herrmann's masterpiece) and unjustly dismissed by critics who considered the music too dynamic for a contemporary film. Yet it is difficult to recall Scorsese's nightmare vision of New York without hearing Herrmann's music. Although light years away from the beauty and romanticism of *Obsession*, *Taxi Driver*'s score was a similarly felt, intuitive experience for Herrmann, who was still obsessed with the darkest and saddest sides of human nature.

Each element of the film's orchestration creates a precise psychological effect; combined, the instrumentation is brittle and horrific yet eerily sensuous. Herrmann's prelude, heard against a hallucinatory montage of mist-filled streets seen through the eyes of Travis Bickle, blends each motivic fragment of the score in its own glaze of indistinctness, a reflection of Bickle's cloudy mind. After a fierce, accelerating snare drumbeat—sounding the battle between Travis and his world—we enter a gray collage of muted trumpets (listlessly rising and falling), the chilly hush of suspended cymbal, basses ticking a pizzicato rhythm like a time bomb, and, most evocatively, a lovely jazz theme for saxophone, piano, bass, and vibraphone.

This theme, *Taxi Driver*'s recurrent motive and most famous musical sequence, was written only partly by Herrmann. When asked to compose a jazz source cue for a scene between the pimp Sport (Harvey Keitel) and his young prostitute Iris (Jodie Foster), Herrmann asked Christopher Palmer to adapt an existing Herrmann piece for the purpose, since his own skill in writing jazz was limited. Palmer took the first four bars of the soprano solo "As the Wind Bloweth" from *The King of Schnorrers*, then continued the melody line in a piece he titled "So Close to Me Blues." Herrmann was so delighted with the result that the theme became a key part of the score.[38]

The jazz idiom pervades the film, as Travis's taxi rides and monologues are echoed by the pulsating rhythm of cymbal and snare. The device, perhaps the score's most psychologically astute element, works on several levels: the increasingly brutal battery of percussion could mirror the steady tick of Travis's meter, his throbbing mind ("twelve hours of work and I still can't sleep"), the meaningless beat of the passing city dwellers, or simply the mounting tension that Scorsese methodically builds.

*Taxi Driver*'s intermittent flashes of beauty—personified by the campaign worker, Betsy (Cybill Shepherd)—are isolated further from their surroundings by Herrmann's sensual scoring for harp and jazz combo. But as Travis hardens his mind and body ("every muscle must be tight"), the score grows colder, more aloof and chilling. "Especially in the exercising scene, Herrmann wanted strength—brass and percussion," Scorsese recalled. "He wanted the idea of a solid image, a sense of something strong, like metal—the unstoppable quality of this character, the unstoppable quality of the tragedy itself."[39] Descending clusters of muted brass and low woodwinds replace the romantic jazz theme, even quote it ironically as Travis prepares for his climactic bloodbath. (Herrmann also alludes to *Psycho*'s madhouse theme moments before Travis's shooting of a liquor store thief, and again as Travis lurks among a crowd at a political rally.)

Bickle's mad slaughter, one of the most explicit and repulsive in cinema, is left unscored (the images speak for themselves), but Herrmann's epilogue to the scene is unforgettable. As a long, steady tracking shot explores the body-littered site, a throbbing percussion solo fills the soundtrack; weird harp glissandos and muted brass follow the vertiginous, bird's-eye camera through blood-drenched corridors; horns wail a grotesque rendition of the jazz theme as we move down staircases and across the body of Sport.

Herrmann's use of the jazz theme here is particularly symbolic. "Benny explained that the reason he did it was to show that this was where Travis' fantasies about women led him," said coproducer Michael Phillips. "His illusions, his self-perpetuating way of dealing with women had finally brought him to that bloody, violent outburst. . . . I had never thought of it in terms of what Benny said, but Bobby [DeNiro] and I both said, 'God, he's right.' Absolutely. Perfect."[40]

*Taxi Driver*'s ending is ambiguous and disturbing. Now local hero, Bickle is back on the streets in his taxi, apparently cured of his madness. But in our last glimpse of Bickle through his taxi's rearview mirror, his eyes dart uncertainly—and "you *know*," Herrmann would whisper to Norma, "he's going to do it *again*."[41] For the last time, Herrmann recalls the madhouse theme (although as finally dubbed it is not heard until well into the film's end titles).

Scorsese loved Herrmann's contribution. "If the film is successful, a great deal of it has to do with the score," he later said. "It supplied the psychological basis throughout. I once had a young man in Beijing following me around at a cocktail party. He kept talking to me about the loneliness that the music and the film evoked . . . asking me how I dealt with the loneliness."[42]

That Herrmann could complete the score at all in his failing condition amazed those around him. "I knew he was dying when he came to New

York and took me to Martin Scorsese's birthday party," Dorothy Herrmann recalled. "He was just a shadow of his former self, and it was remarkable that he could have written 'Taxi Driver' under the circumstances. How he did it I'll never know, but I think it must have had something to do with the fact that he wanted to keep on working right up until the end of his life."[43]

Exhausted and overworked, Herrmann still insisted on overseeing the score's recording. "I've got to go to California to do it," he told Laurie Johnson. "I don't mind going, but the worst part is I won't be here for Christmas."[44] The two agreed they would hold their traditional holiday celebration when Herrmann returned on January 3.

By the time of his departure for California, Herrmann's schedule for 1976 was nearly full. After completing *Taxi Driver* he would score Herbert Ross's Sherlock Holmes pastiche *The Seven Per Cent Solution*, from a screenplay by Nicholas Meyer. (That the film was to be produced at Universal, once the focus of Herrmann's contempt for Hollywood, was another sign of how times had changed.) After reading the script, a fanciful account of Sherlock Holmes's disappearance after battling his nemesis Moriarty, Herrmann was filled with ideas for both his score (to incorporate Viennese waltzes, Hungarian czardas, and other period dance forms) and the film itself. "Benny had a great idea for the title sequence," Larry Cohen recalled. "He wanted to open the film with an overture, showing an orchestra playing in a huge symphony hall. As the credits rolled, the camera would move closer and closer into the orchestra, until at the titles' end it would focus on one of the violinists—Sherlock Holmes, working as a pit musician. And that, Benny said, would be the answer to what happened to Holmes at the end of the picture. 'They're never gonna listen to me,' he said, 'because they never do.' "[45] (Ross and Meyer did choose another approach.)

After *The Seven Per Cent Solution* would be another De Palma film, an adaptation of Stephen King's horror best-seller *Carrie*; after that, a return to concert music and an opera based on Henry James's *Sense of the Past*, with librettist Ursula Vaughan Williams.[46] There would be recordings for Unicorn, Entracte, and Decca: an album of the complete *Kane* score (introduced by Welles, Herrmann promised, with Joan Sutherland his hope for *Salammbô*); a disc of great adventure scores (*Five Fingers, Garden of Evil, King of the Khyber Rifles*); suites from *The Kentuckian* and *The Night Digger*; a second album of British film scores featuring Rawsthorne, Bliss, and Alwyn; more Ives and Cyril Scott; perhaps Caplet's little-known *The Mirror of Jesus*; and, most intriguingly, an album of unused film scores including *Torn Curtain* and Walton's *Battle of Britain*.[47] In early December he received an invitation from the American Film Institute to address a film symposium at the John F. Kennedy Center in Washington, D.C., that spring.[48] Herrmann now found himself in the enviable position of turning down work not on aesthetic grounds but because of other commitments.

Shortly before his departure for Hollywood, Herrmann phoned his agent, Liz Keyes, who was now busily juggling the composer's 1976 calendar. "Goodbye, dear," he said, "and thank you for everything."[49]

On December 20 Herrmann and Norma left London for California. The flight was long and tiring, but Herrmann was eager to see friends and colleagues in Los Angeles. Unfortunately, the trip and his already precarious health precluded Herrmann's conducting the *Taxi Driver* sessions. "Benny started taking indigestion pills because he felt a tightness in his stomach," Norma recalled. "We were riding in Janelle Cohen's Rolls the day before the sessions, and Benny said, 'Open the window, I can't breathe.' I did, and he said, 'CLOSE the window, I can't breathe with all that wind.' Then he said, 'OPEN the window, I can't breathe without any air.' I kept opening and closing the window, and feeling a little worried."[50]

A conductor and assistant in Los Angeles was clearly needed. Herrmann requested Jack Hayes, one of Hollywood's best (and most diplomatic) arranger-conductors. "I went into the job with some trepidation," Hayes recalled, "but Benny was just a pussycat through the whole thing."[51] For the sessions, which began on December 22 at the Burbank Studios, contractor Marian Kline assembled many of Herrmann's favorite musicians, among them horn player James Decker, bassoonist and serpent player Don Cristlieb, horn player Alan Robinson, his wife, flutist Marnie Robinson, and cellist Eleanor Slatkin (widow of Fox concertmaster Felix Slatkin). Herrmann also made arrangements to spend the last week of his stay at the Robinsons' home after Norma returned to work in London.[52]

From the beginning, everyone realized *Taxi Driver* was to be no ordinary two days' work. Visitors filled the studio. "It was an emotional homecoming in many ways," Scorsese recalled. "The first day on the recording stage, all the musicians came around just to greet him and pay their respects."[53] Herrmann remembered them all; as Cristlieb stooped to speak to the seated composer, whose walking stick was now an obvious crutch, Herrmann asked with a grin when Cristlieb was bringing his serpent to England.[54] Another attendant was Steven Spielberg, who had just had his first major success with *Jaws*. Spielberg told the composer how greatly he admired his music—to which Herrmann snarled in mock anger,

"Yeah? Well, if ya admire *my* music so much, why do ya always use Johnny Williams for your pictures?"[55]

To Norma it was clear Herrmann was in his element. "All sorts of curious people came to take a look at him, as he sat mopping his brow with a handkerchief—and because there was no place to sit and talk to him, they were *kneeling*. He looked around all of them, and as he leaned on his cane it was just as if he were Henry VIII in his court."[56]

Throughout the recording Herrmann was unusually receptive to suggestions. For the last film's shot, in which Travis looks nervously into his taxi's rearview mirror, Scorsese wanted the music to suggest that Bickle remained a walking time bomb. Herrmann directed a percussionist to hit a "sting" on the glockenspiel. Scorsese thought the result was "too direct, too obvious." "Play it backwards," Herrmann instantly replied. They did; the effect was perfect.[57]

Only twice, during the last session, did traces of his irascible wit surface. When a musician questioned a broken musical pattern in the score, Herrmann answered, "Whaddaya want—linoleum?" His final criticism concerned a lifelong bane, the timpanist's unsatisfying sticks: "Hit 'em harder!" he shouted over the control room intercom. "If ya break the damn things, I'll buy ya a new pair!" Music editor Erma Levin turned to Marian Kline and whispered, "Take a good look at Bernard Herrmann. It's the last time any of us will ever see him."[58]

Shortly before 5:00 P.M. that day, December 23, all cues had been recorded except one, the original theme for small jazz ensemble. Although Kline said it could be recorded after the Christmas holidays, Herrmann disagreed: "Let's do it now." Hayes again conducted.

After affectionate goodbyes from the musicians, Hayes drove Herrmann and Norma back to their hotel, the Sheraton Universal, which overlooked the old *Psycho* set on the Universal lot. As he got out of the car, Herrmann asked Hayes, "Why don't you come to dubbing?" and said goodnight.[59]

Although Herrmann and Norma had intended to meet Fred Steiner for dinner, plans were changed when Larry Cohen asked the couple to see his just-edited film *God Told Me To* (which Herrmann was to score) at Goldwyn Studios, the site of the ill-fated *Torn Curtain* sessions nine years earlier. Steiner promised to meet them at the Sheraton for breakfast the next morning instead. Taking a taxi from the hotel, the Herrmanns met Larry and Janelle Cohen at Goldwyn. Herrmann like the film, made notes during the screening, and told Cohen he planned to use choral voices in the score: "I've already worked it out in my mind."[60] He made some suggestions for recutting, and the four left for dinner at an Italian restaurant in Santa Monica.

"When we got there, we learned they'd had a fire earlier in the evening," Cohen recalled. "Talk about omens." But since the restaurant had reopened, they decided to stay: "It wasn't a particularly good meal— Benny sent a few plates back, as usual—but the company was nice."[61] During their conversation Herrmann proudly demonstrated a new digital watch with a battery light: "They'll have to put one in my coffin so I'll know what time it is in the grave," he chortled.[62]

After dinner, the Herrmanns returned to the Sheraton. Although it was past midnight—now Christmas Eve—Herrmann stayed sitting up in bed, carefully planning each day of his California visit. "What are we doing here," Norma heard him sigh, moments before he closed his eyes, drifted to sleep, and surrendered all battles with the world.

By 8:15 the next morning, Fred Steiner was convinced Herrmann had forgotten their appointment. From the Sheraton restaurant he phone upstairs; Norma, whom he had never met, answered. "Oh God, he's still asleep," she said, and promised to wake Herrmann.

Moments later, a dazed young woman approached Steiner in the restaurant. "Fred?" she asked. Steiner nodded.

Norma tossed him the room keys. "I think he's dead," she said blankly.[63]

The rest of the day was a confusion of reporters, coroners, and detectives fingerprinting the dead man's belongings. It was later determined he had died of congestive heart failure. But to all appearances Herrmann was still sleeping, with a look of contentment that had escaped him throughout life.

# Postlude

On December 28 a memorial service was held in a small church near RKO Studios in Hollywood. Among those present were François Truffaut, Martin Scorsese, Miklós Rózsa, John Williams, and Larry Cohen, as well as others who knew Herrmann only through his work. The eulogizers were Fred Steiner, Elmer Bernstein, David Raksin, and Norman Corwin; all spoke candidly, to the embarrassment of some and the appreciation of many. Recalled Raksin:

In what might have remained the traditional hush of sorrow and reticence there was from time to time an affectionate laughter when we made reference to his awesome tirades, so impartially bestowed upon friend or foe that some were moved to wonder whether he always knew the difference. Looking out at that distinguished assemblage as I spoke, I felt emanating from them a needful affirmation that the life we were gathered to celebrate had had its share of greatness, of fulfillment, and of love given and reciprocated. Benny was not one of those passive people who are content to be acted upon by events, who are in the end grateful to take leave of this world. He was an artist, and a warrior in the cause of his art.[1]

After twenty-nine years without a single nomination, in 1977 Herrmann was recognized doubly by the Academy of Motion Picture Arts and Sciences, with Oscar nominations for both *Taxi Driver* and *Obsession*—just as Herrmann's first two film scores had competed against each other. (The winner was Jerry Goldsmith's score for *The Omen*.) A more poignant tribute concludes the Scorsese film: a title card reads simply, "Our gratitude and respect, Bernard Herrmann, June 29, 1911–December 24, 1975."

Ida Herrmann lived long enough to see her first son precede her in death. She never recovered, and followed him one year later. Her last words, to Louis Herrmann, were "When are you taking me to see my son?"[2] Louis and Rose both died in 1985.

Lucille Fletcher remained married to writer Douglas Wallop until his death in 1985. Lucy Anderson also remarried. Norma Shepherd continued at the BBC as a writer; years after Herrmann's death she entered a new, happy relationship and had a son.

In November 1982, *Wuthering Heights* received its world premiere by the Portland Opera Company. The performance would not have taken place had Herrmann been alive: forty minutes of the opera were cut, its ending changed to the upbeat resolution Julius Rudel had fought for nearly thirty years before. Most reviews were unenthusiastic, but for those who had followed the work from its beginnings it was, in part, a vindication of Herrmann's faith.

In the years after his death, parodies, pastiches, and plagiaristic thefts all paid "homage" to the legacy of Bernard Herrmann. In 1984 three of his collaborations with Hitchcock (*The Trouble With Harry, The Man Who Knew Too Much,* and *Vertigo*) were rereleased to great critical and box office success. The majority of Herrmann's music—for radio, television, and film—has been released on new or original recordings.

The last word belongs to Herrmann himself. In 1973, Herrmann addressed Eastman College as part of a symposium on the function of sound and music in film. The following are his introductory remarks, an analysis of dramatic music from a historical and critical perspective, as well as an appropriate summary of Bernard Herrmann's art.[3]

My subject is film music. I should like firstly to indicate how the sound film was an ideal back in the days of classical Greece. I should like secondly to say something about the contemporary use of music in films. . . .

Drama, as we know it, began with the Greeks. Less well known is the fact that the Greeks projected and kept alive a vital part of the theatre which they called the "melodram." The melodram was theatre with the spoken word accompanied by music.

Unfortunately we know very little about Greek music, except that whatever music they did create must have been of great simplicity; perhaps some harps, some string sound, some woodwind sound and some choral music. But in the melodram the Greeks encountered a problem that has remained with us from that day to this: whenever people get on the stage and start to talk, and some instrument in the pit begins to play, you can't hear what the people are saying. This has been one of the great recurring problems in theatre, and we shall see how it was solved.

Although modern drama really doesn't have music in the pit (it's been done away with), the idea of using music with drama has persisted since the time of the Greeks. The notion was essentially reborn with Monteverdi, whose first attempt at what we now call "opera" consisted in deciding that the voice could speak at specific pitches which could be accompanied and underlaid by sound. That was the beginning of opera as we know it—the opera which, departing from melodram by taking another direction, soon left the word and became more interested in music. But the idea of drama with accompanying music (melodram) still remained. In the 18th century Gluck worked at melodram, Mozart attempted it, and it persisted through the 19th century in little isolated works. Even in the present day certain works by Carl Orff might be considered melodram, while a great part of Berg's "Wozzeck" is really a melodram rather than opera.

But along the way in the early part of the 20th century Claude Debussy became fascinated by the concept of melodram. He faced the same problem as the Greeks, but he, of course, created the form of his kind of vocal music—as evidenced in "Pelleas"—which is practically spoken drama with music. Debussy's dream was to write pure melodram, and he lived long enough to see some early examples of the cinema! He saw early experiments in the cinema in which an orchestra sat behind the screen and played specially composed music. He felt that this was the art of the future. Debussy said that the cinema would allow the perfect creation of poetry, vision, and dreams. If Debussy had lived long enough into the era of the sound film, who knows what he would have created. Who knows what we've lost.

With the invention of the sound film, the problem of the Greeks was solved; for by separately recording music and sound and voice, we are able to mix them together at the proper volume. The speaking voice and the music can achieve a perfect balance. That is the greatest contribution of the genuine sound film.

Nobody attempted to write music for silent films. They simply played existing music, good or bad. And when early sound came in, they could only draw upon what had been commercially viable in the past in the theatre. This was the situation until a film called "The Brothers Karamazov" was made by the Soviet director Fedor Ozep working in Germany in 1931. The film starred Fritz Kortner and Anna Sten. Ozep employed a composer by the name of Karol Rathaus who did the score. This, to me, was the first great realization of the dream of melodram. Rathaus, who remains relatively unknown, was to become a refugee in New York and to teach at Queen's College. Nobody gave him an opportunity to write any further films. But the music of "The Brothers Karamazov" is one of the most imaginative achievements in sound film.

What did Rathaus do? He treated for the first time the music of a film as an integral part of the whole, not as decoration. Because the film deals with one of the Karamazovs falling in love with a prominent harlot and visiting her in her establishment wherein a gypsy orchestra plays, the music of the picture begins with a gypsy orchestra simply playing Russian gypsy music. But as the picture progresses and the brother becomes more and more involved with the harlot, the music stops being ornamental and becomes an emotional mirror of him. It becomes more and more tragic and more and more hysterical. It reaches its greatest moment, I think, when the brother hysterically drives a troika through a raging blizzard accompanied musically by a great battery of percussion instruments. Remember: this was done way back in the early 1930s! It is one of the great genuine achievements of using music for the first time as an integral emotional accompaniment—not as decoration, and not to achieve the sale of phonograph records!

I don't know why, today, a film has to cost four million dollars to push a record costing 70 cents, but it does. Film music ought not to be written so that people going to cocktail parties can say, "Play me that bit." Music for film should no more be noticed than the camerawork. If you sit and admire the camerawork of a picture the first time, there's something wrong. And the music of a film oughtn't to be admired either. Cinema is only one thing: an illusion of *many* arts working together. The minute *one* aspect begins to dominate, and subordinate everything else to it, the film is doomed. I know personally some great directors who've gotten to the point where they don't even need a camera!

The use of music in films is a completely unstudied territory. In the old days there used to be atlases of the world with unexplored regions marked in white and labeled "unknown." Well, that's still what cinema music is like. Some of the most sensitive directors are complete ignoramuses concerning the use of music in their own films, while sometimes an inferior director will have a great instinct for it. Whatever music can do in a film is something mystical. The camera can only do so much; the actors can only do so much; the director can only do so much. But the music can tell you what people are thinking and feeling, and that is the real function of music. The whole recognition scene of "Vertigo," for example, is eight minutes of cinema without dialogue or sound effects—just music and picture. I remember Hitchcock said to me, "Well, music will do better than words there."

Remember also, whenever speaking of music in the cinema, that the ear deludes the eye as to what it is seeing. It changes time values. What you think is long may be only four seconds, and what you thought was very short may be quite long. There's no rule, but music has this mysterious quality. It also has a quality of giving shape to a mundane stretch of film. Let me explain that to you.

You can cut a scene ABA, or BCA—any way you like. But if you put music from one point in a film to another, there is no alternative to that music as it is in itself. Music is a kind of binding veneer that holds a film together, and hence is particularly valuable in the use of montage. It's really the only thing that seals a montage into one coherent effect. That's why it was used in the newsreel in its most primitive form. (Have you ever watched a newsreel without music? Try it!) This sort of binding is one of the mysterious things that music can do.

The other thing that the sound film permitted music to do for the first time is to give a musical close-up (analagous to the way the camera can give a visual close-up). Let me explain this to you. A lone clarinet playing one note in a concert hall means nothing; but given the way you can manipulate its sound on a soundtrack, it can be made to take over the whole auditorium. This is another valuable way of using music.

There are some directors who say, "We can make a film without music—we don't need it." A wonderful example of this attitude was Richardson's "Mademoiselle," a film with Jeanne Moreau. Jeanne Moreau, I believe, portrays a schoolteacher who's a pyromaniac. As great an actress as she is, however, she couldn't do anything to give the audience a sense of her inner turmoil. Mr. Richardson, who was so sure that he'd gotten it all on film, had no score prepared, and so the picture went no place. When you saw Moreau's face in the film while her emotions supposedly burnt within her, you heard just silence and some crickets. But with the proper score that would have been a most moving and exciting film!

There's no reason why you can't have a film with sound effects and no music. "The Grapes of Wrath," "A Tree Grows in Brooklyn," and "Les Diaboliques," for example, had no music. Every once in awhile there's an exception—a good film without music. But generally the odds are against it. I've been associated with so many films whose music pulled them through. Not only me, but many colleagues of mine have saved films in a similar way by making them acceptable for an hour or two.

Music really is something that comes out of the screen and engulfs the whole audience in a common experience. It isn't something away from the screen. I've spent a long life in films, trying to convince people of this. They don't see it. It's partly because making a film is a cooperative effort of many talents and gifts working together. But, you see, at the present time there's this hysterical cult of the director. No director can make a film by himself. No one man can do it. The nature of the cinema requires cooperative pulsation. And I, having had the privilege and pleasure of working for many great directors, can tell you: the ones who have the greatest humility in this way achieve the greatest films.

I have the final say about my music; otherwise I refuse to do the music for the film. The reason for insisting upon this is that all directors—other than Orson Welles, a man of great musical culture—are just babes in the woods. If you were to follow the taste of most directors, the music would be awful. They really have no taste at all. I'm overstating a bit, of course; there are exceptions. I once did a film, "The Devil and Daniel Webster," with a wonderful director, William Dieterle. He was a man of great musical culture. Hitchcock is very sensitive; he leaves me alone! (Fortunately, because if Hitchcock were left by himself, he would play "In a Monastery Garden" behind all his pictures!) It depends on a composer, and I'm not making a rule about it. But for myself, personally, I'd rather not do a film than have to take what a director says. I'd rather skip it, for I find it's impossible to work that way. . . .

It shows vulgarity, also, when a director uses music previously composed. I think that "2001: A Space Odyssey" is the height of vulgarity in our time. To have outer space accompanied by "The Blue Danube Waltz," and the piece not even recorded anew! They just used gramophone records. . . . ("Death in Venice" is a different kind of thing altogether.) . . .

Hitchcock generally was very sensitive about the use of music. He sometimes said to me, "I'm shooting this scene tomorrow. Can you come down to the set?" I'd come to the set and watch, and he'd say, "Are you planning to have music here?" I'd say, "Well, I think we should have it." "Oh, good," he would say, "then I'll make the scene longer; because if you were not going to have music, then I would have to contract it." Some directors are considerate about things like that. Hitchcock, at least, likes people to work with him through the shooting of a film. So do Welles and Truffaut. But there are many directors whom I never even met until the picture was completely shot. They're not even interested enough to care.

Of course there are disappointments in this business, but most are unintentional. Things just don't fuse together sometimes. People go off in different ways. Generally what happens is that somebody's ego, usually the director's, is so great that everybody else becomes superfluous to him. His attitude becomes "I can do it without you." This attitude has been the reason for some of Hitchcock's greatest films, and, unfortunately, one of the reasons why Hitchcock and I don't get along any more. . . .

There are no fixed rules in this business. There is nothing, for example, in the nature of a film that says we should use what they call an "orchestra" on the soundtrack. An orchestra was a device developed over several hundred years—an agreed representation of certain instruments to play a certain repertoire. If you wish first to play the music of Haydn at Esterházy, and then to play it in Paris, you have to use the same kind of instruments. But music for film is created for one performance—for that one film—and there is no law that says it has to be related to concert music. As a matter of fact, such an opportunity to shift the complete spectrum of sound within one piece has never before been given to us in the history of music. You can't do this in an opera house. I know! If you write an opera and you request something a little unusual they say, "Well, we can't do Wagner if we do yours." Or, "For Puccini we use this, why can't you use that?" But not with film. Each film can create its own variety of musical color.

The screen itself dictates musical forms: the way a picture is cut, or the way it's shaped. I myself am very flexible to the demands of the screen itself. I don't think, for example, that one can do a film score that has the musical vitality of, say, a work by Richard Strauss, and get away with it. I mean that in all seriousness. If you could do a score for a picture, and *really* play Strauss' "Don Juan," no one would watch the picture. The music would completely sweep you away and the film would not be seen. Sound and music, after all, are only part of the illusion which is cinema, not all of it. Filmed opera, therefore, won't work because film is primarily visual, while opera is not primarily a visual art. Film aims at melodram, not opera—at an integration of all the arts, not one in isolation.

You may have noticed that the tempi of the gramophone recordings of my film scores frequently differ from the tempi of the soundtracks themselves. Why? The tempo of the music on the film is dictated by the film itself; on a film everything is dictated by the screen. But the tempo of the music on a record is dictated by musical reasons which have nothing to do with cinematic reasons. After all, there is no "right" tempo for a piece of music. Even with great classic music there is a difference of opinion concerning tempi. (I hate to think what Toscanini would think of Karajan's tempi!)

Now I must discuss a terrible thing, namely, most of the people who write music for films! I would say—and I'd go to the gallows for saying it—that roughly 98 out of every 100 persons making film music would have no more interest in making films if it weren't for the money. Only about 2% are interested in the cinema, and the cinema is a very demanding art form. The rest have figured out how to cheat. Most film music is created by assembly line: one fellow sketches it, another fellow completes it, another one orchestrates it, and yet another adapts it. Consequently the music is dissipated; it has no direction. Then some man of the lowest denomination says, "It'll be a hit!" I don't see what merit this approach has for the creation of a film, but that's the way it is.

There is enormous pressure to write film music which can be exploited afterwards. Out of every 100 film scores we make, the producers would want a gramophone record of 99 of them. "Dr. Zhivago" is a good example. Notice: nobody ever talks about the *film*. David Lean said recently in London that without its wonderful music his film would have been nothing. If that's what he feels about his film, too bad! But do you see what a terrible and really revolting circle it is? What does that piece of harmless legitimate music have to do with a big saga of the ending of the aristocracy in Russia? Nothing! But to the studio it's great!

I have a friend who was denied a film music contract from a studio and asked for the reason. "Oh," they said, "we're using so-and-so. His music sold over a million records." My friend replied, "But I've sold three-quarters of a million records!" "Yes," they said, "but it wasn't a million, was it?" This is what I've hated all my life. The cinema is a great vehicle for contemporary expression, and a contemporary *art* form. Yet I was recently in the Museum of Modern Art—the museum *called* the Museum of Modern Art!—and the people working there are not interested in music for the cinema at all—not at all. One museum after another is devoted to the contemporary cinema, yet uninterested in film music. And they're proud of it, too, because they don't understand. Even the people who should understand cannot comprehend what's happening to them. I've spent my entire career combating ignorance.

# Appendix:
# The Music of Bernard Herrmann

FILMOGRAPHY

Films are followed by date of composition, director, principal cast, original running time, and studio. Year headings correspond to release dates.

## 1941

*Citizen Kane* (summer 1940). Dir.: Orson Welles. Cast: Orson Welles, Joseph Cotten, Everett Sloane, Agnes Moorehead, Dorothy Comingore, Ray Collins, George Coulouris, Ruth Warrick, William Alland, Paul Stewart, Erskine Sanford. 119 mins. RKO. [Academy Award nominee.]

*All That Money Can Buy* [a.k.a. *The Devil and Daniel Webster*] (July 1941). Dir.: William Dieterle. Cast: Edward Arnold, Walter Huston, James Craig, Anne Shirley, Jane Darwell, Simone Simon, Gene Lockhart. 112 mins. RKO. [Academy Award winner.]

## 1942

*The Magnificent Ambersons* (Jan.–Feb. 1942). Dir.: Orson Welles. Cast: Tim Holt, Joseph Cotten, Dolores Costello, Anne Baxter, Agnes Moorehead, Ray Collins, Richard Bennett, Erskine Sanford. 88 mins. RKO. [Additional music for RKO's recut version of the film was written by Roy Webb.]

## 1943

*Jane Eyre* (July–Aug. 1943). Dir.: Robert Stevenson. Cast: Orson Welles, Joan Fontaine, Margaret O'Brien, Peggy Ann Garner, John Sutton. 96 mins. Fox.

## 1945

*Hangover Square* (July–Dec. 1944). Dir.: John Brahm. Cast: Laird Cregar, Linda Darnell, George Sanders, Glenn Langan, Faye Marlowe, Alan Napier, Frederic Worlock. 77 mins. Fox.

*1946*

*Anna and the King of Siam* (Feb.–Apr. 1946). Dir.: John Cromwell. Cast: Irene Dunne, Rex Harrison, Linda Darnell, Lee J. Cobb, Gale Sondergaard, Mikhail Rasummy. 128 mins. Fox. [Academy Award nominee.]

*1947*

*The Ghost and Mrs. Muir* (Jan.–Apr. 1947). Dir.: Joseph L. Mankiewicz. Cast: Gene Tierney, Rex Harrison, George Sanders, Edna Best, Vanessa Brown, Anna Lee, Robert Coote, Natalie Wood. 104 mins. Fox.

*1948*

*Portrait of Jennie* (no existing score). Dir.: William Dieterle. Cast: Jennifer Jones, Joseph Cotten, Ethel Barrymore, Lillian Gish, David Wayne, Henry Hull. 86 mins. Selznick International. [Herrmann composed Jennie's theme only; the remainder of the score was adapted by Dimitri Tiomkin from themes of Debussy. Herrmann does not receive music credit but is listed under special acknowledgments.]

*1951*

*The Day the Earth Stood Still* (June–July 1951). Dir.: Robert Wise. Cast: Michael Rennie, Patricia Neal, Hugh Marlowe, Sam Jaffe, Billy Gray, Frances Bavier, Lock Martin. 92 mins. Fox.

*On Dangerous Ground* (Nov.–Dec. 1950). Dir.: Nicholas Ray. Cast: Robert Ryan, Ida Lupino, Ward Bond, Ed Begley, Cleo Moore, Charles Kemper. 82 mins. RKO.

*1952*

*Five Fingers* (Oct.–Dec. 1951). Dir.: Joseph L. Mankiewicz. Cast: James Mason, Danielle Darrieux, Michael Rennie, Richard Loo. 108 mins. Fox.

*The Snows of Kilimanjaro* (May–June 1952). Dir.: Henry King. Cast: Gregory Peck, Susan Hayward, Ava Gardner, Hildegarde Neff, Leo G. Carroll. 117 mins. (color). Fox.

*1953*

*White Witch Doctor* (Feb.–Mar. 1953). Dir.: Henry Hathaway. Cast: Susan Hayward, Robert Mitchum, Walter Slezak, Timothy Carey. 96 mins. (color). Fox.

*Beneath the 12-Mile Reef* (July–Aug. 1953). Dir.: Robert Webb. Cast: Robert Wagner, Terry Moore, Gilbert Roland, J. Carroll Naish, Richard Boone, Peter Graves. 102 mins. (color, stereo). Fox.

*King of the Khyber Rifles* (Oct.–Nov. 1953). Dir.: Henry King. Cast: Tyrone Power, Terry Moore, Michael Rennie, John Justin. 100 mins. (color, stereo). Fox.

*1954*

*Garden of Evil* (Mar.–Apr. 1954). Dir.: Henry Hathaway. Cast: Gary Cooper, Susan Hayward, Richard Widmark, Hugh Marlowe, Cameron Mitchell, Rita Moreno. 100 mins. (color, stereo). Fox.

*The Egyptian* (May–June 1954). Dir.: Michael Curtiz. Cast: Edmund Purdom, Jean Simmons, Victor Mature, Gene Tierney, Michael Wilding, Peter Ustinov. 140 mins. (color, stereo). Fox. [Co-composed with Alfred Newman.]

*Prince of Players* (Nov. 1954). Dir.: Philip Dunne. Cast: Richard Burton, Maggie McNamara, Raymond Massey, Charles Bickford, John Derek, Eva Le Gallienne, Mae Marsh, Sarah Padden. 102 mins. (color, stereo). Fox.

## 1955

*The Trouble with Harry* (Dec. 1954–Jan. 1955). Dir.: Alfred Hitchcock. Cast: Shirley MacLaine, John Forsythe, Edmund Gwenn, Mildred Natwick, Mildred Dunnock, Jerry Mathers, Royal Dano. 99 mins. (color). Paramount.

*The Kentuckian* (score undated). Dir.: Burt Lancaster. Cast: Burt Lancaster, Diana Lynn, Dianne Foster, Walter Matthau, John McIntire, Una Merkel, John Carradine. 104 mins. (color). Paramount.

## 1956

*The Man Who Knew Too Much* (score lost). Dir.: Alfred Hitchcock. Cast: James Stewart, Doris Day, Brenda De Banzie, Bernard Miles, Ralph Truman, Alan Mowbray, Carolyn Jones, Hilary Brooke. 120 mins. (color). Paramount. [Herrmann appears in the film's Albert Hall sequence, conducting the London Symphony Orchestra in Arthur Benjamin's *Storm Clouds* cantata.]

*The Man in the Gray Flannel Suit* (Feb. 1956). Dir.: Nunnally Johnson. Cast: Gregory Peck, Jennifer Jones, Fredric March, Marisa Pavan, Lee J. Cobb, Ann Harding, Keenan Wynn. 153 mins. (color, stereo). Fox.

*The Wrong Man* (Sept.–Oct. 1956). Dir.: Alfred Hitchcock. Cast: Henry Fonda, Vera Miles, Anthony Quayle, Harold J. Stone, Nehemiah Persoff. 105 mins. Warner Brothers.

*Williamsburg: The Story of a Patriot* (Nov. 1956). Dir.: Geroge Seaton. (color). Paramount [A short subject.]

## 1957

*A Hatful of Rain* (Mar.–Apr. 1957). Dir.: Fred Zinnemann. Cast: Eva Marie Saint, Don Murray, Anthony Franciosa, Lloyd Nolan, Henry Silva. 109 mins. Fox.

## 1958

*Vertigo* (Jan.–Feb. 1958). Dir.: Alfred Hitchcock. Cast: James Stewart, Kim Novak, Barbara Bel Geddes, Tom Helmore, Henry Jones, Ellen Corby, Raymond Bailey, Lee Patrick. 128 mins. (color). Paramount.

*The Naked and the Dead* (Mar.–Apr. 1958). Dir.: Raoul Walsh. Cast: Aldo Ray, Cliff Robertson, Raymond Massey, William Campbell, Richard Jaeckel, James Best, Joey Bishop, L. Q. Jones, Robert Gist, Lili St. Cyr, Barbara Nichols. 131 mins. (color). RKO.

*The Seventh Voyage of Sinbad* (May–June 1958). Dir.: Nathan Juran. Cast: Kerwin Mathews, Kathryn Grant, Richard Eyer, Torin Thatcher. 87 mins. (color). Columbia.

*1959*

*North by Northwest* (Jan.–Mar. 1959). Dir.: Alfred Hitchcock. Cast: Cary Grant, Eva Marie Saint, James Mason, Leo G. Carroll, Martin Landau, Jessie Royce Landis, Philip Ober, Adam Williams. 136 mins. (color). MGM.

*Blue Denim* (May–June 1959). Dir.: Philip Dunne. Cast: Carol Lynley, Brandon de Wilde, Macdonald Carey, Marsha Hunt, Warren Berlinger, Roberta Shore. 89 mins. (stereo). Fox.

*Journey to the Center of the Earth* (Sept.–Nov. 1959). Dir.: Henry Levin. Cast: James Mason, Pat Boone, Arlene Dahl, Diane Baker, Thayer David, Alan Napier. 132 mins. (color, stereo). Fox.

*1960*

*Psycho* (Feb.–Mar. 1960). Dir.: Alfred Hitchcock. Cast: Anthony Perkins, Janet Leigh, Vera Miles, John Gavin, Martin Balsam, John McIntire, Simon Oakland, John Anderson, Frank Albertson, Patricia Hitchcock. 109 mins. Paramount.

*The Three Worlds of Gulliver* (score undated). Dir.: Jack Sher. Kerwin Mathews, Jo Morrow, June Thorburn, Lee Patterson, Gregoire Aslan, Basil Sydney. 100 mins. (color). Columbia.

*1961*

*Mysterious Island* (Jan.–Feb. 1961). Dir.: Cy Endfield. Michael Craig, Michael Callan, Gary Merrill, Joan Greenwood, Herbert Lom. 101 mins. (color). Columbia.

*1962*

*Tender Is the Night* (score undated, late 1961). Dir.: Henry King. Cast: Jennifer Jones, Jason Robards, Jr., Joan Fontaine, Tom Ewell, Jill St. John, Paul Lukas. 146 mins. (color, stereo). Fox.

*Cape Fear* (Aug.–Dec. 1961). Dir.: J. Lee Thompson. Cast: Gregory Peck, Robert Mitchum, Polly Bergen, Martin Balsam, Lori Martin, Jack Kruschen, Telly Savalas. 105 mins. Universal.

*1963*

*Jason and the Argonauts* (June–Aug. 1962). Dir.: Don Chaffey. Cast: Todd Armstrong, Gary Raymond, Nancy Kovack, Honor Blackman, Nigel Green. 104 mins. (color). Columbia.

*The Birds* (no written score). Dir.: Alfred Hitchcock. Cast: Rod Taylor, Tippi Hedren, Suzanne Pleshette, Jessica Tandy, Veronica Cartwright, Ethel Griffies, Charles McGraw. 120 mins. (color). Universal. [Herrmann's role in the film was supervisory; postproduction, on which Herrmann worked, was from July to December 1962.]

*1964*

*Marnie* (score undated). Dir.: Alfred Hitchcock. Cast: Tippi Hedren, Sean Connery, Diane Baker, Martin Gabel, Louise Latham, Alan Napier. 129 mins. (color). Universal.

## 1965

*Joy in the Morning* (score lost). Dir.: Alex Segal. Cast: Richard Chamberlain, Yvette Mimieux, Arthur Kennedy, Sidney Blackman. 103 mins. (color). MGM.

## 1966

*Torn Curtain* (Jan.–Mar. 1966). Dir.: Alfred Hitchcock. Cast: Paul Newman, Julie Andrews, Lila Kedrova, David Opatoshu, Ludwig Donath. 128 mins. (color). Universal. [This score was not used; it was replaced with music by John Addison.]

*Fahrenheit 451* (May–June 1966). Dir.: François Truffaut. Cast: Julie Christie, Oskar Werner, Cyril Cusack, Anton Diffring, Jeremy Spencer, Bee Duffell, Alex Scott. 111 mins. (color). Universal.

## 1968

*The Bride Wore Black* (Sept.–Oct. 1967). Dir.: François Truffaut. Cast: Jeanne Moreau, Claude Rich, Jean-Claude Brialy, Michel Bouquet, Michel Lonsdale, Charles Denner. 107 mins. (color). Lopert.

*Twisted Nerve* (score lost). Dir.: Roy Boulting. Hywell Bennett. (color). Rank.

## 1971

*The Night Digger* (Jan. 1971). Dir.: Alastair Reid. Cast: Patricia Neal, Pamela Brown, Nicholas Clay, Jean Anderson, Graham Crowden, Yootha Joyce. 100 mins. (color). MGM.

*The Battle of Neretva* (score undated). Dir.: Veljko Bulajic. Cast: Yul Brynner, Sergei Bondarchuk, Curt Jurgens, Sylva Koscina, Hardy Kruger, Franco Nero, Orson Welles. 102 mins. (color). AIP.

*Endless Night* (Oct.–Nov. 1971) Dir.: Sidney Gilliatt. Cast: Hywell Bennett, Hayley Mills, Britt Ekland, George Sanders, Per Oscarsson, Peter Bowles, Lois Maxwell. 99 mins. (color). Rank.

## 1972

*Sisters* (May–June 1972). Dir.: Brian De Palma. Cast: Margot Kidder, Jennifer Salt, Charles Durning, Barnard Hughes, William Finley, Mary Davenport, Lisle Wilson. 93 mins. (color). AIP.

## 1974

*It's Alive* (Nov.–Dec. 1973). Dir.: Larry Cohen. Cast: John Ryan, Sharon Farrell, Andrew Duggan, Guy Stockwell, James Dixon, Michael Ansara. 91 mins. (color). Warner Brothers.

## 1976

*Obsession* (June–July 1975). Dir.: Brian De Palma. Cast: Cliff Robertson, Genevieve Bujold, John Lithgow, Sylvia Kuumba Williams, Wanda Blackman. 98 mins. (color). Columbia.

*Taxi Driver* (Oct.–Dec. 1975). Dir.: Martin Scorsese. Cast: Robert DeNiro, Cybill Shepherd, Harvey Keitel, Peter Boyle, Jodie Foster, Albert Brooks, Leonard Harris, Joe Spinell, Martin Scorsese. 113 mins. (color). Columbia.

## CONCERT WORKS

As a teenager Herrmann wrote many small-scale works that remain unpublished; several were not finished. The following is a selective list of his concert works. Published scores are indicated by an asterisk; unless otherwise noted, the publisher is Novello and Co. Ltd., London. Dates are given when known.

### 1929

*The Forest:* A Tone Poem for Large Orchestra (Jan.). [This is probably Herrmann's first complete work for large orchestra.]

*November Dusk* [a.k.a. *Late Autumn*]: A Tone Poem for Large Orchestra (Oct.–Dec.).

"Tempest and Storm: Furies Shrieking!" (Nov.). [A piano piece inscribed to "H. Heine."]

Two Songs for Medium Voice and Small Chamber Orchestra: "The Dancing Faun" [after Paul Verlaine] and "The Bells" [after Paul Bourget] (Apr.–Sept.). [These works were probably written two years earlier than the score's date.]

"Requiescat" [after Oscar Wilde] (Nov.). [A short piece for voice and piano.]

"Twilight": Pastoral for Violin and Piano (May).

### 1932

Ballet music for *Americana Revue* (fall).

"Marche Militaire."

Aria for Flute and Harp (May).

"A Shropshire Lad" [after A. E. Housman] (Feb.).

### 1933

Orchestral Variations on "Deep River" and "Water Boy."

Prelude to "Anathema" for 15 Instruments.

Aubade for 14 Instruments (July). [In the 1970s Herrmann retitled this work "Silent Noon," after a Rossetti poem.]

### 1935

"The Body Beautiful."

*Nocturne and Scherzo* (Sept.).

*\*Sinfonietta for Strings* (New Music Orchestra Series).

*Currier and Ives* Suite.

*1937*

Violin Concerto. [Not completed.]

*1938*

*Moby Dick:* A Cantata for Male Chorus, Soloists, and Orchestra (Feb. 1937–Aug. 1938). [Dedicated to Charles Ives.]

*1940*

*Johnny Appleseed:* A Cantata. [Not completed.]

Fiddle Concerto. [No score survives; may be another title for the 1937 violin concerto.]

*1941*

*Symphony (Oct. 1939–Mar. 1941). [Dedicated to Lucille Fletcher.]

*1942*

*The Fantasticks* (Mar.). [Dedicated to Dorothy Herrmann, with the inscription "For Bungles."]

*The Devil and Daniel Webster* Suite (July). [Dedicated to William Dieterle.]

*1943*

*For the Fallen* (Broude Brothers)

*Welles Raises Kane* (Mar.). [Dedicated to Orson Welles.]

*1951*

*Wuthering Heights:* An Opera (Apr. 1943–June 1951).

*1965*

*Echoes* for String Quartet. [This work was peformed as a ballet with the title *Ante Room* in 1971. Dedicated to Nancy Sanderson.]

*1967*

*Souvenirs de voyage:* Clarinet Quintet. [Dedicated to Norma Shepherd.]

*1968*

*The King of Schnorrers:* A Musical Comedy; lyrics by Diane Lampert, libretto by Shimon Wencelberg.

At the time of his death Herrmann had begun sketching an Organ Symphony "after Four Visions by John Martin." Herrmann also arranged several film scores for recording in the 1960s and 1970s. Because these works were not rewritten for concert performance, they are not listed here.

RADIO WORK

It is impossible to list all of Bernard Herrmann's radio music. Much has been lost, and what survives would fill a book of its own. The following includes the highlights.

### 1934

"In the Modern Manner"—a series of poetry settings, incl. "La Belle Dame sans merci," "The City of Brass," "Annabel Lee," "Cynara," and "A Shropshire Lad."

### 1937

"The Columbia Workshop"—a series of experimental broadcasts, incl. "The Fall of the City," "The Tell-tale Heart," "Ecce Homo," "The Broken Feather," "Macbeth," "The Wedding of the Meteors," "The Devil and Daniel Webster," "Daniel and the Sea Serpent," "Surrealism," "Wet Saturday," "Mr. Sycamore," and "Melodrams."

### 1938–1939

"The Mercury Theater on the Air"—Welles's famous hour-long series, incl. "Dracula," "Treasure Island," "A Tale of Two Cities," "The War of the Worlds," "Sherlock Holmes," "The Magnificent Ambersons," "Heart of Darkness," "The Thirty-nine Steps," "Oliver Twist," "Julius Caesar," John Drinkwater's "Abraham Lincoln," "The Man Who Was Thursday," "Around the World in Eighty Days," "Life with Father." In December 1938 the program's name was changed to "The Campbell Playhouse"; subsequent broadcasts included "Rebecca," "Jane Eyre," "A Christmas Carol," and "The Hitchhiker."

### 1941

"We Hold These Truths"—an hour-long special written and directed by Norman Corwin. Also "Samson," part of "26 by Corwin."

### 1942

"Suspense"—the long-running mystery series, incl. "The Cave of Ali Baba," "Menace in Wax," and "August Heat."

### 1944

"Columbia Presents Corwin"—incl. "The Moat Farm Murder," "Untitled," "Savage Encounter," "An American Trilogy," and "There Will Be Time Later."

### 1945

"On a Note of Triumph"—Corwin's hour-long celebration of V-E Day. Broadcast May 8, performed again May 13.

### 1952

"Crime Classics"—a thirty-minute series directed by Elliott Lewis; Herrmann used a maximum of four musicians.

*1956*

"Brave New World"—an hour-long broadcast of the "Columbia Workshop" directed by William Froug.

## TELEVISION MUSIC

As with radio, Herrmann wrote a large amount of stock television music for CBS's music library. The following is a selective compilation of specific scores and CBS stock cues that Herrmann arranged in "suites."

*1954*

"A Christmas Carol"—an hour-long "television opera" with lyrics by Maxwell Anderson (CBS).

*1955*

"A Child Is Born"—a half-hour television opera presented on "G.E. Theater" (CBS).

*1956–1959*

"The Ethan Allen Story"—a CBS pilot.

"Western Suite," "The Outer Space Suite," "The Desert Suite": CBS cue music.

"Gunsmoke," "Have Gun Will Travel": original themes.

"Kraft Suspense Theater": miscellaneous scores.

"Studio One," "The Virginian": miscellaneous scores.

*1959–1964*

"The Twilight Zone": original theme, as well as original scores for "Where Is Everybody?" "The Lonely," "Walking Distance," "Eye of the Beholder," "Little Girl Lost," "Living Doll," "90 Years Without Slumbering" (CBS).

*1963–1965*

"The Alfred Hitchcock Hour": original scores for "A Home Away from Home," "Terror at Northfield," "You'll Be the Death of Me," "Nothing Ever Happens in Linvale," "Body in the Barn," "The Jar," "Behind the Locked Door," "Change of Address," "Water's Edge," "The Life Work of Juan Diaz," "The McGregor Affair," "Misadventure," "Consider Her Ways," "Where the Woodbine Twineth," "An Unlocked Window," "Wally the Beard," "Death Scene" (Universal-MCA).

*1968*

*Companions in Nightmare.* Dir. Norman Lloyd. Universal-MCA. [Herrmann's only television movie.]

## RECORDINGS CONDUCTED BY BERNARD HERRMANN

Recording dates and original record company follow title. Listed by year of release. Unless otherwise noted, music is by Bernard Herrmann.

*1966*

*Wuthering Heights:* An Opera in Four Acts and a Prologue (May 11–13). Pro Arte Orchestra and the Elizabethan Singers, chorus master Louis Halsey. Soloists: Morag Beaton, Donald Bell, John Kitchiner, Pamela Bowden, Joseph Ward, Elizabeth Bainbridge, Michael Rippon, David Kelly, Mark Snashall. Pye, reissued Unicorn.

*Echoes* for String Quartet (June 20–22). The Amici Quartet. Pye, reissued Unicorn. [With Edmund Rubbra's String Quartet no. 2.]

*1967*

*Moby Dick:* A Cantata for Male Chorus, Soloists, and Orchestra (May 24–25). London Philharmonic Orchestra and the Aeolian Singers, chorus master Sebastian Forbes. Soloists: John Amis, David Kelly, Robert Bowman, Michael Rippon. Pye, reissued Unicorn.

Suites: *The Devil and Daniel Webster* and *Welles Raises Kane* (June 6). London Philharmonic Orchestra. Pye, reissued Unicorn.

*1968*

"Music from the Great Movie Thrillers": *Psycho:* A Narrative for Orchestra; *Marnie* Prelude and Hunting Scene; *North by Northwest* Overture; *Vertigo* Prelude, "The Nightmare," and *Scène d'amour;* and "A Portrait of Hitch" from *The Trouble with Harry* (Dec. 12). London Philharmonic Orchestra. Decca.

*1969*

"Great Tone Poems": Sibelius, *Finlandia;* Dukas, *The Sorcerer's Apprentice;* Liszt, *Les Préludes* (May 20, 23). London Philharmonic Orchestra. Decca.

*1970*

*The Planets* by Gustav Holst (Feb. 23–25). London Philharmonic Orchestra. Decca.

Symphony no. 5, *Lenore,* by Joachim Raff (May 27–29). London Philharmonic Orchestra. U.K., Unicorn; U.S.A., Nonesuch.

"The Impressionists": Satie, *Gymnopédies* nos. 1 and 3; Debussy, "Clair de lune"; Ravel, "Five o'Clock Foxtrot"; Fauré, "Pavane"; Honegger, *Pastoral d'été* (Dec. 21). London Philharmonic Orchestra. Decca.

*1971*

"The Four Faces of Jazz": Weill, Songs from *The Threepenny Opera;* Gershwin, Variations on "I Got Rhythm"; Stravinsky, "Ragtime"; Milhaud, *Creation of the World* (Aug. 16–18). London Festival Recording Ensemble, with David Parkhouse, piano. Decca.

"Music from Great Film Classics": *Jane Eyre* Suite, *The Snows of Kilimanjaro* Interlude and "Memory Waltz," *Welles Raises Kane* excerpts, *The Devil and Daniel Webster* Suite excerpts (Feb. 16). London Philharmonic Orchestra. Decca.

1972

Symphony no. 2 by Charles Ives (Jan. 4). London Symphony Orchestra. Decca.

"Erik Satie and His Friend Darius Milhaud": Satie, Ballet *The Adventures of Mercury*, Music Hall Music *La Belle eccentrique*, *Jack in the Box*; Milhaud, *Saudades do Brasil* (Oct. 17–18). London Festival Players. Decca.

1973

"The Fantasy Film World of Bernard Herrmann": Suites, *Journey to the Center of the Earth*, *The Seventh Voyage of Sinbad*, *The Day the Earth Stood Still*, and *Fahrenheit 451* (Nov. 28–30). National Philharmonic Orchestra. Decca.

1974

Symphony (Jan. 10). National Philharmonic Orchestra. Unicorn.

Clarinet Quintet: *Souvenirs de voyage* and *Echoes* (Jan. 12). The Ariel Quartet, with Robert Hill, clarinet. Unicorn.

"Music from Great Shakespearean Films": Shostakovich, Suite from the Incidental Music to *Hamlet*; Walton, Prelude to *Richard III*; Rózsa, Suite from the Incidental Music to *Julius Caesar* (March 28). National Philharmonic Orchestra. Decca.

Piano Concerto no. 1 by Cyril Scott (April 2–3). London Philharmonic Orchestra, with John Ogdon, piano. Lyrita.

1975

"The Mysterious Film World of Bernard Herrmann": Suites, *Mysterious Island*, *Jason and the Argonauts*, and *The Three Worlds of Gulliver* (Feb. 6–7). National Philharmonic Orchestra. Decca.

*Psycho:* The Complete Score (Oct. 2). National Philharmonic Orchestra. Unicorn.

1976

"A Musical Garland of the Seasons": *The Fantasticks*; *For the Fallen*; Delius, "A Late Lark"; Warlock, Four Motets (June 26, 1975). National Philharmonic Orchestra and the Thames Chamber Choir, conducted by Louis Halsey, with Stephen Hicks, organ. Soloists: Michael Rippon, Meriel Dickinson, Gillian Humphreys, and John Amis. Unicorn.

"Great British Film Music": Lambert, *Anna Karenina* Suite; Bax, *Oliver Twist*, Two Lyrical Pieces; Benjamin, *The Ideal Husband* Waltz and Gallop; Walton, *Escape Me Never* Ballet; Vaughan Williams: *The 49th Parallel* Prelude; Bliss, *Things to Come* Suite (Nov. 5–6, 1975). National Philharmonic Orchestra. Decca.

Piano Concerto no. 2 and *Early One Morning* by Cyril Scott (Apr. 2–3, 1974). London Philharmonic Orchestra, with John Ogdon, pianist. Lyrita.

# Notes

NOTES TO PRELUDE

1. The verb *to score*, as in *to score a film*, refers in this book to the *original composition* of music for a film.
2. Vaughan Williams to SCS, March 1985.
3. Quoted by Kevin Thomas, "Film Composer Settles a Score," *Los Angeles Times*, 2–4–68, p. 17.
4. Joan Greenwood to SCS, 5–13–85.
5. Corwin to SCS, 2–18–84.

NOTES TO CHAPTER ONE

1. Lucille Anderson to SCS, spring 1986; also Louis Herrmann to Martin Silver, Dec. 84.
2. For an account of Jewish immigration to America in the early twentieth century, see Irving Howe, *World of Our Fathers* (New York: Harcourt Brace Javanovich, 1976); also Arthur A. Goren, *New York Jews and the Quest for Community* (New York: Columbia University Press, 1970).
3. Unless otherwise noted, information on Abraham Herrmann comes from interviews with Louis Herrmann, by Craig Reardon (6–4–79) and Martin Silver (Dec. 1984); corroborated wherever possible by interviews with family members.
4. Louis Herrmann to Silver, Dec. 1984.
5. Ruth Herrmann to SCS, spring 1988.
6. Information on Abraham and Ida's courtship is taken primarily from SCS interviews with Norma Shepherd (spring 1985).
7. Ibid.

8. Louis Herrmann to Reardon, 6–4–79.

9. Joan Greenwood, 5–13–85.

10. Ruth Herrmann, spring 1988.

11. Louis Herrmann to Reardon, 6–4–79.

12. Goren, *New York Jews*, p. 25.

13. Norma Shepherd, spring 1985.

14. Louis Herrmann to SCS, spring 1984.

15. Quoted by Henry Gleitman, *Psychology* (New York: W. W. Norton, 1981), p. 475.

16. Ruth Herrmann, spring 1987.

17. Norma Herrmann to SCS; also Ruth Herrmann to SCS.

18. Louis Herrmann to Reardon, 6–4–79.

19. Norma Shepherd, spring 1985.

20. Letter from BH to Lucille Fletcher, 5–18–48.

21. Lucille Fletcher to SCS, 1–12–88.

22. BH quoted from notes made by Lyn Murray, 4–18–54.

23. See Gleitman, *Psychology*, p. 465.

24. Lyn Murray notes, 4–18–54.

25. Louis Herrmann to Silver, Dec. 1984.

26. Cited in radio commentary by Deems Taylor, from an interview with BH, CBS radio, 4–14–40.

27. CBS press release, "Bernard Herrmann—Composer and Orchestra Leader," 2–24–38.

28. Norma Shepherd, spring 1985.

29. Ibid.

30. Louis Herrmann to Silver, Dec. 1984.

31. DeWitt Clinton school records, 1931.

32. Louis Herrmann to Reardon, 6–4–79.

33. DeWitt Clinton school records, 1928–1931.

34. Moross interview with Craig Reardon, 1979.

35. Laurie Johnson to SCS, 6–4–84.

36. Moross to Reardon, 1979.

37. Score in BH collection, University of California Santa Barbara (UCSB).

38. Cited in BH press bio from the 1940s, and in album notes supervised by BH; also by Louis Herrmann to Reardon, 6–4–79.

39. Score in BH collection, UCSB.

40. Ibid.

41. Polonsky to SCS, 1985.

42. BH, "An American Voice," in *Edward Elgar Centenary Sketches*, ed. H. A. Chambers (London: Novello, 1957), pp. 20–21.

43. BH, letter to *Musical Times*, Jan. 1959, p. 24.

44. Quoted by Harold Atkins and Archie Newman, *Beecham Stories* (New York: St. Martin's Press, 1979), p. 60.

45. Charles Reid, *Beecham: An Independent Biography* (London: Victor Gollancz, 1961), p. 240.

46. Ibid., p. 195.

47. Cited by Deems Taylor, CBS radio, 4–14–40.

## NOTES TO CHAPTER TWO

1. For a definitive account of Ives's life and music, see Frank R. Rossiter, *Charles Ives and His America* (New York: Liveright, 1975).

2. BH, "Charles Ives," *Trend: A Quarterly of the Seven Arts* 1, no. 3 (Sept.–Nov. 1932): 99–101.

3. BH, lecture on Ives, UCSB, 1969.

4. Quoted by Vivian Perlis, *Charles Ives Remembered: An Oral History* (New Haven: Yale University Press, 1974).

5. BH discussed his meeting with Copland in the UCSB lecture, 1969. See also Aaron Copland and Vivian Perlis, *Copland* (New York: St. Martin's Press/Marek, 1984), p. 204.

6. BH interview with John Amis, BBC radio, 3-12-71.

7. DeWitt Clinton school records, 1929.

8. Louis Herrmann to Reardon, 6-4-79.

9. Irving Kolodin to SCS, Jan. 1986.

10. Bernstein to SCS, Oct. 1985.

11. Dorothy Herrmann to SCS, Jan. 1986.

12. Polonsky, 1985.

13. BH diaries, from collection of Norma Shepherd.

14. Gould to SCS, 7-29-84.

15. Scores in BH collection, UCSB.

16. See BH chapter in *Sound and the Cinema*, ed. Evan Cameron (Pleasantville, N.Y.: Redgrave, 1980).

17. Moross to Reardon, 1979.

18. Louis Herrmann to Reardon, 6-4-79.

19. School records.

20. Louis Herrmann to Reardon, 6-4-79.

21. DeWitt Clinton school records, 1931.

22. Norma Shepherd, spring 1985.

23. BH lecture, UCSB, 1969.

24. BH, "Recorded and Neglected Russian Music (The Five)," *New Music* (date unknown).

25. Arthur Berger, *Aaron Copland* (New York: Oxford University Press, 1953), p. 21.

26. Heilner to SCS, Apr. 1984.

27. Siegmeister to SCS, 7-3-84.

28. Moross to Reardon, 1979.

29. Kolodin to SCS, Jan. 1986.

30. Louis Herrmann to Reardon, 6-4-79.

31. Reviewed in the *Daily Mirror*, 2-15-32.

32. From undated Juilliard clipping.

33. Oscar Levant, *A Smattering of Ignorance* (New York: Doubleday, Doran, 1940), pp. 225, 230.

34. Green to SCS, 6-23-84.

35. Moross to Reardon, 1979.

36. BH interview with Max Wilk, Oct. 1971.

37. "New York Artists Reshape America over the Week End." *New York Herald Tribune*, 7–10–32, sec. 1, p. 14.

38. Description from contemporary press cited by John Bird, *Percy Grainger* (London: P. Elek, 1976), p. 23.

39. Ibid., pp. 204–205.

40. Ibid., p. 204.

41. Ibid., p. 205.

42. Louis Herrmann to Reardon, 6–4–79.

43. Ibid.

44. Norma Shepherd, spring 1985.

45. BH to Elmer Bernstein; EB to SCS, 11–14–84. No other confirmation, however.

46. Siegmeister, 7–3–84.

47 Siegmeister letter to Copland, 12–22–32.

48. Siegmeister, 7–3–84.

49. "Musical Events," *New Yorker*, 1–28–32.

50. "Young Composers Group Together," *Musical Leader*, Jan. 1933.

51. "Junior Group of Composers Offer Concert," *New York Herald Tribune*, 1–16–33.

52. "Young Composers' Group Concert," *Musical Courier*, 1–21–33.

53. Siegmeister, 7–3–84.

54. Heilner, Apr. 1984.

55. Dorothy Herrmann, Jan. 1986.

56. Cohn interview with Wayne Bryan, 9–12–84.

57. Norma Shepherd, spring 1985.

58. Julian Seaman, *Daily Mirror*, 5–19–33.

59. "New Chamber Orchestra Offers Modern Works," *New York Herald Tribune*, 5–18–33.

60. Robert A. Simon, *New Yorker*, May 33 (exact date unknown).

61. Henry Cowell, *American Composers on American Music: A Symposium* (Stanford: Stanford University Press, 1933).

62. BH lecture, UCSB, 1969.

63. Ibid.

64. Levant, *A Smattering of Ignorance*, p. 232.

65. BH to John Amis, BBC Radio, 3–12–71.

## NOTES TO CHAPTER THREE

1. See Laurence Bergreen, *Look Now, Pay Later: The Rise of Network Broadcasting* (Garden City, N.Y.: Doubleday, 1980).

2. Robert Metz, *CBS: Reflections in a Bloodshot Eye* (Chicago: Playboy Press, 1975), p. 45. Unless otherwise noted, the history of CBS's early days is drawn from chapter 5 of Metz's book. See also William S. Paley, *As It Happened* (Garden City, N.Y.: Doubleday, 1979).

3. Green to SCS, 6–23–84.

4. Ibid.

5. Ibid.

6. Ibid.

7. Ibid.

8. Lucille Fletcher, "One Iceberg Please: The Strange Story of Radio's Musical Cue Man," *Detroit Free Press*, 5–14–39.

9. Irving Kolodin, "The Wide Screen World of Bernard Herrmann," *Saturday Review*, 3–6–76, pp. 35–38.

10. Bay to SCS, 5–9–84.

11. Green, 6–23–84.

12. See Hugh MacDonald, *Hector Berlioz* (London: J. M. Dent, 1982), chap. 5.

13. Norma Shepherd, spring 1985.

14. CBS press release, "Bernard Herrmann—Composer and Orchestra Leader," 2–24–38.

15. Siegmeister, 7–3–84.

16. Raksin to SCS, 1–25–84.

17. Morris Hastings, "Bernard Herrmann: A CBS Institution," CBS press release, 1943.

18. Lucille Fletcher, Jan. 1988.

19. Ibid.

20. Harrington to SCS, Sept. 1984.

21. Ibid.

22. BH, "On Composing a Setting of *Moby Dick*," *New York Times*, April 1940 (exact date unknown).

23. Ibid.

24. *Moby Dick* program, New York Philharmonic, 4–14–40.

25. BH interview with Vivian Perlis, 11–12–69.

26. Quoted by John Houseman, *Run-Through* (New York: Simon & Schuster, 1972), p. 366.

27. "Exploring Music," *The Billboard* (date unknown).

28. Harmony Ives letter to BH, 10–7–36.

29. Charles Ives letter to BH, 10–19–36.

30. CBS memo, Fassett to BH (undated).

31. Murray to SCS, 3–1–84.


NOTES TO CHAPTER FOUR

1. Fletcher, "One Iceberg Please."

2. Ibid.

3. Ibid.

4. Lloyd to SCS, 5–11–84.

5. "If Background Stays in Back, Just Thank Cue," *New York Herald Tribune*, 7–17–38.

6. BH interview with John Amis, BBC radio, ca. 1974.

7. Lucille Fletcher, Jan. 1988.

8. Recalled by Abe Polonsky, 1985.

9. Ibid.

10. Letter to BH from Polonsky, 3–8–37.

11. Victor Bay, 5–9–84; also John Houseman, *Run-Through*, p. 365.
12. Houseman, *Run-Through*, p. 365.
13. Ibid., pp. 365–366.
14. Ibid., p. 366.
15. Quoted in ibid., pp. 366–367.
16. Ibid., p. 364.
17. Ibid., pp. 390–392.
18. Ibid., p. 393.
19. Paul Stewart to SCS, 1984.
20. Houseman, *Run-Through*, pp. 399–400.
21. Liz Keyes to SCS, 5–2–85.
22. Houseman, *Run-Through*, p. 404.
23. Lucille Fletcher, Jan. 1988.
24 Paul Stewart, 1984.
25. Corwin to SCS, 2–17–84.
26. Fletcher to Vivian Perlis, 8–18–72.

NOTES TO CHAPTER FIVE

1. Lucille Fletcher, Jan. 1988.
2. Norma Shepherd, spring 1985.
3. See Richard B. Jewell and Vernon Harbin, *The RKO Story* (New York: Arlington House, 1982).
4. Quoted by Don Wardell, "Music to Commit Murder By," *Soho Weekly News*, 9–9–76. Herrmann fee from BH records.
5. George Coulouris and BH with Ted Gilling, "The *Citizen Kane* Book," *Sight and Sound* 41 (Spring 1972).
6. Cameron (ed.), *Sound and the Cinema*, p. 119.
7. BH, "Score for a Film," *New York Times*, 5–25–41.
8. Houseman, *Run-Through*, p. 365.
9. See BH, "Barbirolli and the Halle," *Saturday Review*, 11–30–57.
10. Quoted by Michael Kennedy, *Barbirolli, Conductor Laureate* (London: MacGibben & Kee, 1971), pp. 144–145.
11. CBS press release, "Herrmann Cantata on 'Moby Dick' Chosen by Philharmonic for 1940 Premiere," 4–26–39.
12. Olin Downes, "*Moby Dick* Sung in Cantata Form," *New York Times*, 4–12–40.
13. Francis D. Perkins, "Moby Dick to Music," *New York Herald Tribune*, 4–12–40.
14. Barbirolli to SCS, Mar. 1985.
15. Lucille Fletcher, Jan. 1988.
16. Quoted by Marc Scott Zicree, *The "Twilight Zone" Companion* (New York: Bantam Books, 1982), p. 65.
17. Lucille Fletcher, Jan. 1988.
18. For more on *Kane* and Welles's earlier film ideas, see Robert L. Carringer, *The Making of "Citizen Kane"* (Berkeley and Los Angeles: University of California Press, 1985).

19. Quoted by Kolodin, "Wide Screen World of Bernard Herrmann."

20. BH, "Score for a Film."

21. Quoted by Ted Gilling, "The Colour of Music: An Interview with Bernard Herrmann," *Sight and Sound*, Winter 1971–1972, p. 37.

22. For an overview of the development of film music, see Roy M. Prendergast, *Film Music: A Neglected Art* (New York: W. W. Norton, 1977).

23. Mark Evans, *Soundtrack: The Music of the Movies* (New York: Hopkinson & Blake, 1975), p. 22.

24. Quoted by Gilling, "Colour of Music," p. 36.

25. BH, "Score for a Film."

26. Quoted by Gilling, "Colour of Music," p. 37.

27. BH radio interview with Misha Donat, Feb. 1973.

28. BH lecture, National Film Theatre, 6–11–72.

29. BH, "Score for a Film."

30. Royal S. Brown, "An Interview with Bernard Herrmann," *High Fidelity*, Sept. 1976, pp. 64–67.

31. BH lecture, National Film Theatre, 6–11–72.

32. Cameron (ed.), *Sound and the Cinema*, p. 126.

33. Coulouris, BH, and Gilling; "Citizen Kane."

34. For the *Citizen Kane* script, see Pauline Kael, *The "Citizen Kane" Book* (Boston: Atlantic Monthly Press, 1971). Kael's essay on the film is filled with inaccuracies, however, including her remarks about the film's scoring.

35. Cameron (ed.), *Sound and the Cinema*, pp. 127–128.

36. Quoted by Peter Bogdanovich, "The Kane Mutiny," p. 189. *Esquire*, Oct. 1976.

37. Lucille Fletcher, Jan. 1988.

38. Houseman, *Run-Through*, p. 461.

39. BH, "Score for a Film."

40. Cameron (ed.), *Sound and the Cinema*, pp. 129–130.

41. BH lecture, National Film Theatre, 6–11–72.

42. Quoted by Brown, "Interview with Herrmann," p. 66.

43. Cristlieb to SCS, 7–11–84.

44. James G. Stewart to SCS, 3–28–84. For the fate of the cue that Stewart and Welles nixed, see Prendergast, *Film Music*, p. 54.

45. Wise to SCS, 2–21–84.

46. Carringer, *Making of "Citizen Kane,"* p. 134. Welles said his most important collaborators on *Kane* were Mankiewicz, Herrmann, Toland, and art director Perry Ferguson.

47. Jaglom to SCS, Feb. 1988.

48. BH lecture, National Film Theatre, 6–11–72.

NOTES TO CHAPTER SIX

1. Bruno David Ussher, "Sounding Board," unidentified clipping, 1941; from the collection of Norma Shepherd.

2. James G. Stewart, 3–28–84.

3. Quoted by Ted Gilling, "Benny," *Main Title*, Spring–Summer 1976.

4. BH lecture, National Film Theatre, 6–11–72.

5. Larry Cohen interview with Craig Reardon, 2–17–77.

6. Quoted by Page Cook, "Bernard Herrmann," *Films in Review* 18, no. 7 (Aug.–Sept. 1967).

7. Jewell and Harbin, *The RKO Story*, p. 166.

8. Leslie Zador, "Bernard Herrmann Remembered," *Cue Sheet* 2, no. 1 (Jan. 1985).

9. "Bernard Herrmann Will Direct His Symphony No. 1 This Sunday," unidentified New York newspaper, 1941; from collection of Norma Shepherd.

10. Murray, 3–1–84.

11. Christopher Palmer, "Symphony" album notes, Unicorn Records, 1974.

12. Ibid.

13. BH program notes, "Symphony no. 1," July 1941.

14. Unidentified clipping, July 1941; from the collection of Norma Shepherd.

15. Unidentified clipping, July 1941; ibid.

16. Unidentified clipping, July 1941; ibid.

17. Norman Corwin, *More by Corwin: 16 Radio Dramas* (New York: Henry Holt, 1944), pp. 228–229.

18. Ibid., p. 92.

19. Quoted in ibid.

20. MacLeish letter to BH, 12–29–41; from the collection of Norma Shepherd.

21. Corwin eulogy, BH memorial service, 12–28–75.

22. BH lecture, National Film Theatre, 6–11–72.

23. Richard Wilson to SCS, 3–17–84.

24. For more information on *The Magnificent Ambersons*, see Carringer, *Making of "Citizen Kane,"* chap. 6.

25. CBS press release, April 1943.

26. BH lecture, National Film Theatre, 6–11–72.

27. James G. Stewart, 3–28–84.

28. Louis Kaufman to SCS, 2–24–84.

29. Ibid.

30. According to Peter Bogdanovich, BBC-TV interview, spring 1985.

31. Jewell and Harbin, *The RKO Story*, p. 142.

32. Quoted by Elsa Clay to SCS, Sept. 1984.

33. RKO records.

34. Quoted by Gilling, "Colour of Music," p. 38.

35. Scorsese to SCS, 1–24–89.

36. Collins letter to BH, 8–4–42.

37. Daniel interview with Craig Reardon, 3–18–79.

38. Certificate in the collection of Norma Shepherd.

39. Brown, *High Fidelity*, Dec. 1976.

40. Edward Johnson to SCS, 3–22–85.

41. Ormandy letter to BH, 9–10–42.

42. Ormandy letter to BH, 9–21–42.

43. BH, Philharmonic concert program, 12–16–43.

44. Quoted by Miklós Rózsa to SCS, 6–20–84.

45. Unidentified clipping from collection of Norma Shepherd.

46. Quoted by William A. Taylor, "English Audiences Keenly Interested in Modern Music," *Musical Courier*, p. 14.

47. Hyams to SCS, 3–27–84.

48. Ben Hyams, "Herrmann: He Opened My Eyes and My Ears," *Honolulu Magazine*, Feb. 1976.

49. Ben Hyams, *Honolulu Magazine*, July 1979.

50. Hyams, 3–27–84.

51. From Leslie T. Zador and Greg Rose, "A Conversation with Bernard Herrmann," in *Film Music 1*, ed. Clifford McCarty (New York: Garland Publishing Co.); copyright 1989 by the Society for the Preservation of Film Music.

52. Louis and Annette Kaufman to SCS, 2–24–84.

53. Hyams, *Honolulu Magazine*, July 1979.

54. Oliver Daniel, *Stokowski: A Counterpoint of View* (New York: Dodd, Mead, 1982), p. 536.

55. Greenhouse to SCS, 7–1–84.

56. Finzi letter to BH, 8–29–43.

57. Ben Hyams, "Lo the Poor Oboe, Clarinet with a Cold," *Honolulu Magazine*, Aug. 1971.

58. Annette Kaufman, 2–24–84.

59. Miklós Rózsa, 6–20–84.

60. Houseman, *Run-Through*, p. 478.

61. David Raksin, *Filmmusic Notebook*, no. 2 (1976).

62. David Raksin, quoted by Tony Thomas, *Music for the Movies* (New York: A. S. Barnes, 1973), p. 54.

63. Rudy Behlmer, ed., *Memo from David O. Selznick* (New York: Viking Press, 1972), p. 325.

64. Stravinsky used music sketched for *Jane Eyre* in his concert work *Ode* (1943).

65. BH letter to Lucille Fletcher, 12–7–42.

66. Steiner to SCS, 9–9–84.

67. Gilling, "Colour of Film," p. 38.

68. Williams to SCS, 9–6–84.

69. Lyn Murray, 3–1–84.

70. Page Cook, *Films in Review*, 1971.

71. Wardell, "Music to Commit Murder By."

72. Paul Bowles, "Music for 'Jane Eyre,' " *New York Herald Tribune*, 12–26–43, p. 7.

73. BH, "Music from Great Film Classics" album notes, Decca, 1971.

74. Norma Shepherd, spring 1985.

75. Raksin to SCS, 7–11–84.

76. Norma Shepherd, spring 1985.

77. Morris Hastings, "Bernard Herrmann, a CBS Institution," CBS press release, 1943.

78. Lucille Fletcher, Jan. 1988.

## NOTES TO CHAPTER SEVEN

1. BH to Zador and Rose, fall 1970.
2. Norma Shepherd, spring 1985.
3. Gray letter to BH, 4–11–43.
4. CBS press release, Apr. 1943.
5. BH, "*Wuthering Heights*" album notes, Pye, 1966, p. 5.
6. Notes on the composing of *Wuthering Heights* are in the collection of Norma Shepherd.
7. Books are in the collection of Norma Shepherd.
8. Quoted by Frank Kinkaid, "Scaling the Heights," *Opera News*, Nov. 1982, p. 17.
9. BH, "*Wuthering Heights*" album notes, Pye, 1966, p. 5.
10. Ibid.
11. Lucille Fletcher, *Wuthering Heights* libretto (included with album), act 1, scene 1.
12. Dated sketches of the *Wuthering Heights* score are in the BH collection, UCSB.
13. Fletcher, *Wuthering Heights* libretto, act 2.
14. Louis Kaufman to SCS, 2–24–84.
15. Robson to SCS, 1984.
16. Corwin, 2–17–84.
17. Norman Corwin, '*Untitled*' *and Other Radio Dramas* (New York: Henry Holt, 1947), p. 307.
18. Ibid., p. 72.
19. Christopher Palmer, "*Citizen Kane:* The Classic Film Scores of Bernard Herrmann" album notes, RCA, 1974.
20. Brahm interview with Craig Reardon, 2–22–79.
21. Napier to SCS, 5–8–84.
22. Sondheim to SCS, 1986.
23. Quoted by Donald Spoto, *The Dark Side of Genius: The Life of Alfred Hitchcock* (New York: Little, Brown, 1983), p. 293.
24. Miklós Rózsa, *Double Life* (New York: Hippocrene Books, 1982), p. 131.
25. Corwin, "*Untitled*" *and Other Radio Dramas*, p. 490.
26. Ibid., p. 495.
27. BH telegram to Corwin, 5–10–45; from the collection of Norman Corwin.
28. Ibid.
29. BH telegram to Corwin, 5–14–45.
30. Erich Leinsdorf, "Some Views on Film Music," *New York Times*, 6–17–45.
31. BH, "Music in Motion Pictures—A Reply to Mr. Leinsdorf," *New York Times*, 6–24–45.
32. BH, "The Symphonies of Charles Ives," *Modern Music*, May–June 1945.
33. Harmony Ives letter to BH, 6–15–45.
34. BH lecture, UCSB, 1969.
35. Elsa Clay to SCS, Sept. 1984.
36. Quoted by Cook, "Bernard Herrmann," p. 403.

37. Louis Kaufman, 2–24–84.

38. Murray, 3–1–84.

39. Berres to SCS, 8–1–84.

40. Mildred Norton, undated article (1946) from the collection of Norma Shepherd.

41. Win Sharples, Jr., "Bernard Herrmann 1911–1975," *Filmmakers Newsletter*, Oct. 1976.

42. Harmony Ives letter to BH, 6–4–46.

43. Ernest Bean, *"Wuthering Heights"* album notes, Pye, 1966, p. 4.

44. Quoted by Kinkaid, "Scaling the Heights."

45. BH, "Musical England," *New York Herald Tribune*, Dec. 1946.

## NOTES TO CHAPTER EIGHT

1. Norma Shepherd, spring 1985.

2. Philip Dunne, Audio History, Special Collections Dept., Doheny Library, University of Southern California, Los Angeles.

3. BH to Zador and Rose, fall 1970.

4. BH to Adolph Deutsch; recalled by Hugo Friedhofer to Craig Reardon, 3–12–77.

5. Bernard F. Dick, *Joseph L. Mankiewicz* (Boston: Twayne, 1983), p. 53.

6. Lucille Fletcher, Jan. 1988.

7. *New York Herald Tribune*, 7–29–47.

8. Unidentified newspaper clipping, 7–30–47.

9. Annette Kaufman, 2–24–84.

10. Daniel interview with Craig Reardon, 3–18–79.

11. Lucille Fletcher, Jan. 1988.

12. Letters from the collection of Lucille Fletcher.

13. BH letter to Lucille Fletcher, quoted to SCS, Jan. 1988.

14. BH letter to Lucille Anderson, undated (1948).

15. Lucille Fletcher, Jan. 1988.

16. BH letter to Lucille Fletcher, fall 1947.

17. BH letter to Lucille Fletcher, Oct. 1947.

18. James G. Stewart, 3–28–84.

19. Lucille Fletcher, Jan. 1988.

20. Selznick memo to James G. Stewart, 7–24–47.

21. Christopher Palmer to SCS, May 1985.

22. Hunt to SCS, 3–13–84.

23. Polonsky, 1985.

24. Corwin, 5–16–84.

25. BH, "From Sound Track to Disc," *Saturday Review*, 9–27–47, p. 42.

26. Ernest Bean letter to BH, 10–28–48.

27. Combs letter to Paley, 3–21–49.

28. Schoenberg letter to BH, 6–8–49.

29. Schoenberg letter to BH, 7–27–49.

30. BH, *Stokowski: Essays in Analysis of His Art*, ed. Edward Johnson (London: Triad Press, 1973), pp. 38–40.

31. Stokowski letter to Oliver Daniel, 9–6–49.

32. Louis Biancolli, "Stokowski Conducts a 4-Nation Program," *New York Telegram*, 2–11–49.

33. Letters from the collection of Norma Shepherd.

34. Daniel to Reardon, 3–18–79.

35. "The Halle Concerts," *Manchester Guardian*, 11–7–49.

36. Barbirolli letter to BH, 12–5–49.

37. RKO memo quoted by John Houseman, *Front and Center* (New York: Simon & Schuster, 1979), p. 317.

38. Nicholas Ray, *Movie*, no. 9 (May 1963).

39. Houseman to SCS, 4–20–84.

40. Houseman, *Front and Center*, p. 178.

41. Quoted by Gilling, "Colour of Music," p. 37.

42. Gilling, "Colour of Music," p. 37.

43. Houseman, *Front and Center*, p. 326.

44. Quoted by Black Lucas, notes for *On Dangerous Ground*, Los Angeles County Museum of Art series "The RKO Years."

45. In BH collection, UCSB.

46. Barbirolli letter to BH, 8–31–51.

47. Lyn Murray notes, 1951.

48. Ibid.

49. Barbirolli letter to BH, 8–31–51.

50. Charles Gerhardt to SCS, 6–4–84.

## NOTES TO CHAPTER NINE

1. Lucy Anderson to SCS, spring 1986.

2. Hunt, 3–13–84.

3. Quoted by Murray to Craig Reardon, 4–27–77.

4. Presnell to SCS, 3–13–84.

5. Wise to SCS, 2–21–84.

6. Gilling, "Colour of Music," p. 37.

7. BH lecture, National Film Theatre, 6–11–72.

8. Wise, 2–21–84.

9. Lionel Newman to SCS, 7–16–84.

10. BH lecture, National Film Theatre, 6–11–72.

11. BH, "The Fantasy Film World of Bernard Herrmann" album notes, Decca 1973.

12. Wise, 2–21–84.

13. Lewis to SCS, 6–26–84.

14. Fred Steiner to SCS, 3–3–84.

15. Shirley Steiner to SCS, 3–3–84.

16. Lyn Murray notes, 1954.

17. BH, "Music from Great Film Classics" album notes, Decca 1971.

18. Ernest Hemingway, "The Snows of Kilimanjaro," in *The Complete Short Stories* (New York: Scribner's, 1987), p. 54.

19. Gilling, "Colour of Music," p. 37.

20. Raksin, 1–25–84.
21. Gene D. Phillips, *Hemingway and Film* (New York: Frederick Ungar, 1980), p. 119.
22. Bosley Crowther, New York Times, 9–19–52.
23. Friedhofer interview with Craig Reardon, 3–12–77.
24. Clay to SCS, Aug. 1984.
25. Dorothy Herrmann, Jan. 1987.
26. Green interview with Craig Reardon, 1977; Green to SCS, 6–23–84.
27. Rózsa to SCS, 6–20–84.
28. Wardell, "Music to Commit Murder By."
29. Rózsa, *Double Life*, p. 141.
30. David Raksin, "The Subject Is Film Music," syndicated radio program; Cinema Library, USC.
31. Zanuck, quoted in Otto Lang letter to BH, 6–1–53.
32. Notes accompanying score, in BH collection, UCSB.
33. Christopher Palmer, *"Citizen Kane"* album notes, RCA, 1974.
34. Ibid.
35. Zanuck memo to Alfred Newman, 12–11–53.
36. Engel to SCS, 7–17–84.
37. John Mapplebeck, "Bernard Herrmann," *The Guardian*, 3–30–61.
38. Friedhofer to Reardon, 3–12–77.
39. Philip Dunne, 5–15–84.
40. Philip Dunne, *Take Two* (New York: McGraw Hill, 1980), p. 64.
41. Quoted by Cook, "Bernard Herrmann," p. 405.
42. BH's cues are in the BH collection, UCSB.
43. Quoted by Gilling, "Colour of Music," p. 38.
44. Ibid.
45. Cristlieb to SCS, 7–11–84.
46. Hathaway to SCS, spring 1984.
47. Paul Hirsch to SCS, 3–21–84.
48. Dunne, 5–15–84.
49. Ibid.
50. Dunne, *Take Two*, p. 272.
51. Bernstein to SCS, 11–14–84.
52. Ibid.
53. Murray, 3–1–84.
54. Corwin, 2–17–84.
55. Raksin, 1–25–84.
56. Score in the collection of Victor Bay.
57. Wagner to SCS, Dec. 1985.

NOTES TO CHAPTER TEN

1. Michael Ratcliffe, "Composing the 'Emotional Scenery' for the Screen," *Sheffield Telegraph*, 3–25–61.
2. See Spoto, *Dark Side of Genius*.
3. Quoted by Kevin Thomas, "Film Composer Settles a Score," p. 17.

4. Quoted in *Newsweek*, Hitchcock obituary, 5–12–80.

5. Spoto, *Dark Side of Genius*, p. 381.

6. Brown, "Interview with Herrmann," p. 65.

7. Cameron (ed.), *Sound and the Cinema*, p. 121.

8. Murray, 3–1–84.

9. Norma Shepherd, spring 1985.

10. "Colour of Music," p. 36; Wardell, "Music to Commit Murder By."

11. BH, "Music from the Great Movie Thrillers" album notes, Decca, 1969.

12. Hitchcock interview with Adriano, 9–26–72.

13. Lyn Murray diary, 1954; read to SCS, 3–1–84.

14. *The Kentuckian* album notes, Entracte, 1976; Lancaster to SCS, 9–11–85; Anderson to SCS, spring 1986.

15. Larry Cohen (to SCS, 6–16–84) believes Herrmann did not return; Lancaster (9–11–85) recalled that he did.

16. Quoted by Larry Cohen, 6–16–84.

17. Lancaster, 9–11–85.

18. John Russell Taylor, *Hitch: The Life and Times of Alfred Hitchcock* (New York: Pantheon Books, 1978), p. 237.

19. Quoted by Gilling, "Colour of Music," p. 38.

20. Undated cable; from Hitchcock collection, Academy of Motion Picture Arts and Sciences.

21. Benjamin note, 3–18–55; Coleman letter to Hitchcock 3–12–55; from Hitchcock collection, Academy of Motion Picture Arts and Sciences.

22. Quoted by Kevin Thomas, "Film Composer Settles a Score," p. 21.

23. Quoted by Alan Gelb, *The Doris Day Scrapbook* (New York: Grossett & Dunlap, 1977), pp. 88–90.

24. Book in the collection of Norma Shepherd.

25. Daniel, *Stokowski: A Counterpoint of View*, p. 669.

26. Lucy Anderson, spring 1986.

27. From program booklet accompanying the series.

28. Previn to SCS, May 1985.

29. Fred Steiner, 3–3–84.

30. Zador, "Bernard Herrmann Remembered," p. 2.

31. Daniel, *Stokowski*, p. 637.

32. Barbirolli to SCS, March 1985.

33. Ibid.

34. Ibid.

35. Joan Greenwood, 5–13–85.

36. BH letter to Kirkpatrick, 10–10–54.

37. BH letter to Hopkinson, 1–11–55.

38. Dorothy Herrmann, Jan. 1986.

39. BH, program notes, 1–17–56 concert.

40. Houseman, 4–20–84.

41. Lucy Anderson, spring 1986.

42. *Variety*, 2–1–56, p. 30.

43. Froug to SCS, 3–6–84.

44. Ibid.

45. Goldsmith interview, *Filmmusic Notebook*, no. 2 (1977): 20.
46. Ibid.
47. Lucy Anderson, spring 1986.
48. Rubbra letter to BH, 4–30–56.
49. BH, "An American Voice," p. 19.
50. Ibid.
51. Henry Greenwood to SCS, 5–13–85.
52. Ibid.
53. Joan Greenwood, 5–13–85.
54. Ibid.
55. Unidentified London clipping, 1956; from the collection of Norma Shepherd.
56. Lyn Murray diaries, 1956.
57. Warrick letter to BH, Apr. 1956.
58. Bay, 5–9–84.
59. Rózsa, 6–20–84.
60. Ibid.
61. Clay, Aug. 1984.
62. Herbert Coleman letter to BH, 1–21–56.
63. BH letter to Hitchcock, 2–21–58.
64. Norma Shepherd, May 1985.
65. Copy of letter in collection of Fred Steiner.
66. BH letter to Mrs. Gerald Finzi, 1–2–57.
67. BH letter to Richard Avenall, Jan. 1957.
68. BH, "An American Voice," pp. 17–20.
69. Zinnemann to SCS, Feb. 1984.
70. Cook, "Bernard Herrmann," p. 409.
71. Len Engel to SCS, 7–17–84.
72. Kolodin letter to BH, 10–16–57.
73. BH, "Barbirolli and the Halle."
74. Barbirolli letter to BH, 12–8–57.
75. Clay, Aug. 1984.
76. Vaughan Williams to SCS, Mar. 1985.
77. Robert Stone (7–11–84) and Don Cristlieb (7–11–84) to SCS.

## NOTES TO CHAPTER ELEVEN

1. Robin Wood, *Hitchcock's Films* (New York: Castle Books, 1965), p. 91.
2. See Spoto, *Dark Side of Genius*, pp. 427–435.
3. Brown, "Interview with Herrmann," p. 66.
4. See *Vertigo* notes, Hitchcock collection, Academy of Motion Picture Arts and Sciences.
5. Ibid.
6. Edith Sitwell, "Some Notes on My Own Poetry," *London Mercury*, 31, no. 185 (Mar. 1935): 448–454.
7. Gilling, "Colour of Music," p. 38.
8. Richard Wagner, notes on *Tristan and Isolde*.

9. Livingstone and Evans to SCS, 9–21–84.

10. "Madeleine," published by Famous Music, 1958.

11. Steve Harris, "An Afternoon with Bernard Herrmann," *RTS*.

12. Coleman letter to Kimmental, 3–31–58.

13. Quoted by Robert A. Harris and Michael S. Lasky, *The Films of Alfred Hitchcock* (Secaucus, N.J.: Citadel Press, 1976), p. 186.

14. Ratcliffe, "Composing 'Emotional Scenery.' "

15. Harryhausen to John Morgan.

16. Schneer to SCS, 2–11–85.

17. BH, "The Fantasy Film World of Bernard Herrmann" album notes, Decca, 1973.

18. Schneer, 2–11–85.

19. BH, *Musical Times*, Jan. 1959, p. 24.

20. Lehman to SCS, 3–5–84.

21. Christopher Palmer, *North by Northwest* album notes, Varese-Starlog, 1980.

22. BH, "Music from the Great Movie Thrillers" album notes, Decca, 1968.

23. BH radio interview with Misha Donat, Feb 1973.

24. Ibid.; Taylor, *Hitch*, p. 253.

25. Score in BH collection, UCSB.

26. Wardell, "Music to Commit Murder By."

27. BH, "The Fantasy Film World of Bernard Herrmann" album notes, Decca, 1973.

28. Wardell, "Music to Commit Murder By."

29. Quoted by Charles Gerhardt to SCS, 6–4–84.

30. Dunne, 5–15–84.

31. The deleted cue is in the BH collection, UCSB.

32. See Zicree, *"Twilight Zone" Companion*.

33. Houghton to SCS, 11–16–84.

34. Ibid.

35. Houseman, *A Shropshire Lad*, poem 40 (first published 1896).

36. Houghton, 11–16–84.

37. Ibid.

38. Ibid.

39. Norma Shepherd, spring 1985.

40. Froug, 3–6–84.

41. Diane Gleghorn to SCS, 7–4–84.

## NOTES TO CHAPTER TWELVE

1. Taylor, *Hitch*, p. 258.

2. Spoto, *Dark Side of Genius*, p. 467.

3. Ratcliffe, "Composing 'Emotional Scenery.' "

4. Gillling, "Colour of Music," p. 39.

5. Cameron (ed.), *Sound and the Cinema*, p. 132.

6. Ibid.

7. BH, "Music from the Great Movie Thrillers" album notes, Decca, 1969.

8. Steiner, "Herrmann's 'Black-and-White' Music for Hitchcock's 'Psycho,'"
*Filmmusic Notebook*, Fall 1974, part 1, pp. 31–32.

9. Ibid., p. 33.

10. Cameron (ed.), *Sound and the Cinema*, p. 132.

11. Misha Donat, in radio interview with BH, 1973.

12. Steiner, "Herrmann's 'Black-and-White' Music," pp. 33–34.

13. BH to Misha Donat, 1973.

14. Stephen Rebello, "Psycho," *Cinefantastique*, Oct. 1986, p. 49.

15. Gilling, "Colour of Music," p. 37.

16. Cameron (ed.), *Sound and the Cinema*, p. 133.

17. *"Pscyho"* album notes, Unicorn, 1975.

18. Cameron (ed.), *Sound and the Cinema*, p. 133.

19. Peggy Robertson to SCS, fall 1985.

20. Spoto, *Dark Side of Genius*, p. 264.

21. Dorothy Herrmann, Jan. 1986.

22. Werby letter to BH, Nov. 1960.

23. BH letter to Werby, 11–25–60.

24. *Psycho* file, Hitchcock collection, Academy of Motion Picture Arts and Sciences.

25. Ratcliffe, "Composing 'Emotional Scenery.'"

26. Rebello, "Psycho," p. 74.

27. Gauthier to SCS, 10–30–84.

28. Kirk interview with Craig Reardon, 2–15–77.

29. Elmer Bernstein, 11–14–84.

30. Siegmeister, 7–3–84.

31. Quoted by Michael Foot, introduction to Jonathan Swift, *Gulliver's Travels* (Harmondsworth, Eng.: Penguin Books, 1967), p. 10.

32. Ibid., p. 17.

33. Harryhausen to SCS, 6–2–84.

34. Quoted by Wardell, "Music to Commit Murder By."

35. Christopher Palmer, "The Mysterious Film World of Bernard Herrmann" album notes, Decca, 1975.

36. Henry Greenwood, 5–13–85.

37. Norma Shepherd, spring 1985.

38. Gerhardt, 6–4–84.

39. Johnson to SCS, 6–4–84.

40. Quoted by Cook, "Bernard Herrmann," p. 398.

41. Norma Shepherd, spring 1985.

42. BH to Zador and Rose, fall 1970.

43. BH lecture, National Film Theatre, 6–11–72.

44. Christopher Palmer, "The Mysterious Film World of Bernard Herrmann" album notes, Decca, 1975.

45. Harryhausen, 6–2–84.

46. Cameron (ed.), *Sound and the Cinema*, p. 122.

47. Behlmer (ed.), *Memo from David O. Selznick*, pp. 475–478.

48. Murray to Reardon, 4–27–77.

49. Behlmer (ed.), *Memo from David O. Selznick*, p. 487.

50. From 1962 publicity material; Cinema Library, USC.

51. Spoto, *Dark Side of Genius*, pp. 481–482.

52. Ratcliffe, "Composing 'Emotional Scenery.' "

53. Quoted in "*The Birds:* Hitchcock's Most Unconventional Film Score," *Cinefantastique*, Fall 1980.

54. Quoted by Gilling, "Colour of Music," p. 37.

55. Gassmann letter to Hitchcock, 4–18–62.

56. Quoted by Gilling, "Colour of Music," p. 37.

57. Reid to SCS, 6–6–84.

58. "*The Birds.*"

59. Ibid.

60. Ibid.

61. Hitchcock to Adriano, 9–26–72.

62. "*The Birds.*"

63. Norma Shepherd, spring 1985.

64. James Decker to SCS, 6–13–84.

65. Taylor, *Hitch*, p. 232.

66. Norman Lloyd, 5–11–84.

67. Ibid.

68. Williams to SCS, 9–6–84.

69. Lloyd, 5–11–84.

70. Taylor, *Hitch*, p. 279.

71. Spoto, *Dark Side of Genius*, p. 504.

72. Guy Della Cioppa to SCS, 7–25–84.

73. Froug, 3–6–84.

74. Joan Greenwood, 5–13–84.

75. Martha Ragland to SCS, 11–29–84.

76. Clay, Aug. 1984.

77. Joan Greenwood, 5–13–84.

78. BH letter to Lucy Anderson, 4–12–64.

79. Lucy Anderson, spring 1986.

80. Houseman, 4–20–84.

81. Gerard Dempsey, "Sir John Joins Audience to Hear Halle Concert," *Daily Express*, 4–20–64.

82. Ibid.

83. Denis Miniver, *New Daily*, 5–20–64, p. 12.

84. BH letter to Lucy Anderson, 5–17–64.

85. Schneer, 2–11–85.

86. Ives to SCS, 10–24–84.

87. BH letter to Fletcher, Nov. 1947.

88. Christopher Palmer, "Clarinet Quintet" album notes, Unicorn, 1974.

89. Norma Shepherd, spring 1985.

90. *The Gramophone*, Oct. 1967, p. 213.

91. Norma Shepherd, spring 1985.

92. "Herrmann Says Hollywood Tone Deaf as to Film Scores," *Hollywood Reporter*, 7–14–64, p. 5.

93. BH letter to Lucy Anderson, 11–28–65.

## NOTES TO CHAPTER THIRTEEN

1. Brown, "Interview with Herrmann," p. 65.
2. Raksin, 1–25–84.
3. Taylor, *Hitch*, p. 285.
4. Spoto, *Dark Side of Genius*, chap. 14.
5. Gauthier to SCS, 10–30–84.
6. Hitchcock to Adriano, 9–26–72.
7. Robertson to John Williams; JW to SCS, 9–6–84. See also Hitchcock telegram to BH, 11–4–65.
8. Telegram and typed draft in Hitchcock collection, Academy of Motion Picture Arts and Sciences.
9. Brown, "Interview with Herrmann," p. 65.
10. BH telegram to Hitchcock, 11–5–65.
11. From Hitchcock collection, Academy of Motion Picture Arts and Sciences.
12. Taylor, *Hitch*, p. 286.
13. Lloyd, 5–11–84.
14. BH to Zador and Rose, fall 1970.
15. Johnson, 6–4–84.
16. According to David Raksin, "The Subject Is Film Music," syndicated radio series; Cinema Library, USC.
17. Musicians who discussed the session with SCS include Don Cristlieb (7–11–84), James Decker (6–13–84), Alan Robinson (6–13–84), and Mr. and Mrs. Dominic Fera (7–1–84).
18. Hitchcock to Adriano, 9–26–72.
19. Taylor, *Hitch*, p. 286.
20. Brown, "Interview with Herrmann," p. 65.
21. Lloyd, 5–11–84.
22. Tiomkin Telegram to Hitchcock, Hitchcock collection, Academy of Motion Picture Arts and Sciences.
23. Addison to Elmer Bernstein, *Filmmusic Notebook*, 1978.
24. A copy of the song and relevant correspondence are in the Hitchcock collection, Academy of Motion Picture Arts and Sciences.
25. Raksin, 1–25–84.
26. BH lecture, National Film Theatre, 6–11–72.
27. Williams, 9–6–84.
28. Norma Shepherd, spring 1985.
29. Excerpt from Hitchcock lecture played by David Raksin, "The Subject Is Film Music," syndicated radio series.
30. Lionel Newman to SCS, 7–16–84.
31. Norma Shepherd, spring 1985.
32. BH letter to Lucy Anderson, 4–15–66.
33. Norma Shepherd, spring 1985.
34. Quoted by Kevin Thomas, "Film Composer Settles a Score," p. 17.
35. Cameron (ed.), *Sound and the Cinema*, p. 130.
36. Quoted by Gilling, "Colour of Music," p. 38.
37. Quoted by Wardell, "Music to Commit Murder By."

38. BH lecture, National Film Theatre, 6–11–72.

39. Cameron (ed.), *Sound and the Cinema*, p. 131.

40. BH lecture, National Film Theatre, 6–11–72.

41. Cameron (ed.), *Sound and the Cinema*, p. 131.

42. Quoted by David Raksin, "The Subject Is Film Music," syndicated radio series.

43. Cameron (ed.), *Sound and the Cinema*, p. 131.

44. Johnson, 6–4–84.

45. Norma Shepherd, spring 1985.

46. BH to Zador and Rose, fall 1970.

47. Vaughan Williams, Mar. 1985.

48. BH letter to Schurmann, 1–10–67.

49. Bradbury to SCS, 12–14–84.

50. Louis and Annette Kaufman, 2–24–84.

51. Martha Ragland to SCS, 11–29–84.

52. 1967 note from the collection of Norma Shepherd.

53. Recalled by Edward Johnson to SCS, 3–22–85.

54. BH letter to Lucy Anderson, 5–28–66.

55. Norma Shepherd, spring 1985.

56. Joan Greenwood to SCS, 5–13–85.

57. Quoted by Edward Johnson, *Bernard Herrmann: Hollywood's Music-Dramatist* (London: Triad Press, 1977).

58. Norma Shepherd, spring 1985.

59. Christopher Palmer, "Clarinet Quintet" album notes, Unicorn, 1974.

60. Ibid.

61. John Amis, *Amiscellany: My Life, My Music* (London: Faber & Faber, 1985), pp. 195–196.

62. Irving Kolodin, *Saturday Review*, 1–27–68, p. 55.

63. Oliver Daniel, "A Perspective of Herrmann," *Saturday Review*, 7–13–68, p. 49.

64. Dieterle letter to BH, 6–29–68.

65. Quoted by Thomas, "Film Composer Settles a Score," p. 17.

66. BBC interview, fall 1967.

67. Ibid.

68. Georges Delerue to SCS, Oct. 1985.

69. 1967 note from the collection of Norma Shepherd.

70. Quoted by Gilling, "Colour of Music," p. 38.

71. Norma Shepherd, 1985.

72. Brown, "Interview with Herrmann," p. 65.

73. *Obsessions* press release, May 1969.

74. Norma Shepherd, spring 1985.

75. Kirk to Reardon, 2–15–77.

76. Diane Lampert, "Herrmann—Madman in Filmdom," *Los Angeles Herald-Examiner*, 1–18–76.

77. In BH collection, UCSB.

78. Louis Herrmann to Silver, Dec. 1984.

79. Fred Stewart to SCS, Jan. 1986.
80. Shimon Wincelberg to SCS, 12–24–86.
81. Norma Shepherd, spring 1985.

NOTES TO CHAPTER FOURTEEN

1. John Goldsmith to SCS, 5–17–85.
2. BH, "Music from the Great Movie Thrillers" album notes, Decca, 1969.
3. Norma Shepherd, spring 1985.
4. Spoto, *Dark Side of Genius*, p. 521.
5. Brown, "Interview with Herrmann," p. 65.
6. Mancini to SCS, Jan. 1988.
7. Brown, "Interview with Herrmann," p. 65.
8. Blake to SCS, spring 1985.
9. Green to SCS, 6–23–84.
10. Keyes, 5–2–85.
11. Quoted by Thomas, "Film Composer Settles a Score," p. 21.
12. Ibid.
13. Norma Shepherd, spring 1985.
14. Ibid.
15. Joan Greenwood, 5–13–85.
16. Norma Shepherd, spring 1985.
17. Ibid.
18. Ibid.
19. Norma Herrmann letter to Carolyn Schurmann, undated.
20. Zador and Rose, "A Conversation with Bernard Herrmann."
21. Correspondence with Imogen Holst; collection of Norma Shepherd.
22. "Mars Barred," *London Times*, 2–26–70.
23. Decca producer Ray Few to SCS, 5–1–85.
24. Gerard Schurmann, 1988.
25. Norma Shepherd, spring 1985.
26. Raff, "Symphony no. 5" album notes, Unicorn, 1971.
27. Johnson to SCS, 3–22–85.
28. Goldsmith to SCS, 5–17–85.
29. Norma Shepherd, spring 1985.
30. Edward Johnson, 3–22–85.
31. Norma Shepherd, spring 1985.
32. Reid, 6–6–84.
33. Norma Shepherd, spring 1985.
34. Reid, 6–6–84.
35. Ibid.
36. Liz Keyes, 5–2–85.
37. Norma Shepherd, spring 1985.
38. Ibid.
39. Zador and Rose, "A Conversation with Bernard Herrmann."
40. Norma Shepherd, spring 1985.

## NOTES TO CHAPTER FIFTEEN

1. Norma Shepherd, spring 1985.
2. Quoted by Gilling, "Colour of Film," p. 38.
3. Brown, "Interview with Herrmann," p. 64.
4. Blake to SCS, spring 1985.
5. Norma Shepherd, spring 1985.
6. Liz Keyes, 5–2–84.
7. Gerard Schurmann, 1988.
8. Charles Gerhardt, 6–4–84.
9. Ibid.
10. Norma Shepherd, spring 1985.
11. BH letter to Stevens, 1–23–73.
12. Stevens letter to BH, 2–14–73.
13. BH letter to Dick Kirk, 4–1–73.
14. Moross to Reardon, 1979.
15. BH lecture, UCSB, 1969.
16. Edward Greenfield, "Ives from England," *High Fidelity*, Apr. 1972, p. 20.
17. Quoted by Miklós Rózsa, 6–20–84.
18. Henry Greenwood, 5–13–85.
19. Max Loppert, "American Masters (and Others)," *Financial Times*, 5–31–73.
20. *Stereo Review*, Nov. 1972, p. 113.
21. Rózsa, 6–20–84.

## NOTES TO CHAPTER SIXTEEN

1. Hirsch to SCS, 3–21–84.
2. Brian De Palma, "Murder by Moog: Scoring the Chill," *Village Voice*, 10–11–73.
3. Ibid.
4. Ibid.
5. Hirsch, 3–21–84.
6. Ibid.
7. Royal S. Brown, *"Sisters"* album notes, Entracte, 1974.
8. De Palma, "Murder by Moog."
9. Blake, spring 1985.
10. Hirsch, 3–21–84.
11. Ibid.
12. De Palma, "Murder by Moog."
13. *Variety*, 3–14–73.
14. Norma Shepherd, spring 1985.
15. Ibid.
16. Quoted by Gilling, "Benny."
17. Ibid.
18. Norma Shepherd, spring 1985.
19. Ibid.

20. Ibid.
21. Johnson, 6–4–84.
22. Cohen, 6–16–84.
23. Ibid.
24. Score in BH collection, UCSB.
25. Norma Shepherd, spring 1985.
26. Pauline Hamer to SCS, 5–2–85.
27. Cohen, 6–16–84.
28. Ibid.
29. Gerhardt, 6–4–84.
30. Larry Cohen to SCS, 6–16–84.
31. Quoted by Brown, "Interview with Herrmann," p. 66.
32. Gilling, "Benny."
33. Norma Shepherd, spring 1985.

NOTES TO CHAPTER SEVENTEEN

1. BH, "Byron To-day," program book for Byron Society concert, 4–21–74.
2. Miklós Rózsa, 6–20–84.
3. Noel Goodwin, "Byron Concert: Drury Lane Theatre," unidentified clipping, 4–22–74.
4. Martin Cooper, "Eloquence of Maconchy at Byron Concert," *Daily Telegraph*, 4–22–74.
5. This and the following recollections of the "Classic Film Scores" project were made by Gerhardt to SCS, 6–4–84.
6. Royal S. Brown, "Theater and Film," *High Fidelity*, Jan. 1975.
7. Griffiths to SCS, 9–3–84.
8. Norma Shepherd, spring 1985.
9. Alexander Walker, "The Lady Vanishes (Twice!)," *Evening Standard*, 9–23–76.
10. Michael Pye and Lynda Myles, *The Movie Brats* (New York: Holt, Rinehart & Winston, 1979), p. 163.
11. Hirsch, 3–21–84.
12. Ibid.
13. Brown, "Interview with Herrmann," p. 66.
14. Norma Shepherd, spring 1985.
15. Quoted by Brown, "Interview with Herrmann," p. 66.
16. Johnson, 6–4–84.
17. Quoted by Pye and Myles, *The Movie Brats*, p. 164.
18. Quoted by Wardell, "Music to Commit Murder By."
19. Quoted by Pye and Myles, *The Movie Brats*, p. 164.
20. Hirsch, 3–21–84.
21. Gerhardt, 6–4–84.
22. Johnson, 6–4–84.
23. Gerhardt, 6–4–84.
24. Hirsch, 3–21–84.
25. Ibid.

26. Meriel Dickinson to SCS, 2–20–85.

27. Amis, *Amiscellany*, p. 196.

28. Ibid.

29. BH letter to Steiner, 9–14–75.

30. Goldsmith, 5–17–85.

31. Bernstein, 11–14–84.

32. Ibid.

33. Taylor letter to BH, 9–13–75.

34. Scorsese, 1–24–89.

35. Ibid.

36. Johnson, 6–4–84.

37. Hirsch, 3–21–84.

38. Palmer, May 1985. Score sketches support Palmer's account.

39. Scorsese, 1–24–89.

40. Quoted by Carmie Amata, "Scorsese on *Taxi Driver* and Herrmann," *Focus on Film*, Summer–Autumn 1976.

41. Norma Shepherd, spring 1985.

42. Scorsese, 1–24–89.

43. Quoted by Zador, "Bernard Herrmann Remembered."

44. Johnson, 6–4–84.

45. Cohen, 6–16–84.

46. Vaughan Williams, Mar. 1985.

47. Brown, "Interview with Herrmann," p. 65.

48. Letter from Michael Webb, Film Programming Manager, to BH, 12–8–75.

49. Keyes, 5–2–85.

50. Norma Shepherd, spring 1985.

51. Hayes to SCS, 10–15–84.

52. Alan Robinson to SCS, 6–13–84.

53. Quoted by Amata, "Scorsese on *Taxi Driver*."

54. Cristlieb to SCS, 7–11–84.

55. Williams, 9–6–85, and Scorsese, 1–24–89, to SCS.

56. Norma Shepherd, spring 1985.

57. Scorsese, 1–24–89.

58. David Raksin, "The Subject Is Film Music," syndicated radio series; Cinema Library, USC.

59. Hayes, 10–15–84.

60. Cohen, 6–16–84.

61. Ibid.

62. Norma Shepherd, spring 1985.

63. Steiner, 3–3–84.

## NOTES TO POSTLUDE

1. David Raksin, "Bernard Herrmann," booklet, 1976.

2. Louis Herrmann to Reardon, 6–4–79.

3. Printed in Cameron (ed.), *Sound and the Cinema*.

# Selected Bibliography

Amata, Carmie. "Scorsese on *Taxi Driver* and Herrmann." *Focus on Film*, Summer–Autumn 1976.

Barrett, Gavin. "Scoring in Films." *Guardian*, 3–3–70.

Bazelon, Irwin. *Knowing the Score: Notes on Film Music.* New York: Van Nostrand Reinhold, 1975.

Behlmer, Rudy, ed. *Memo from David O. Selznick.* New York: Viking Press, 1972.

Berger, Arthur. *Aaron Copland.* New York: Oxford University Press, 1953.

Bergreen, Laurence. *Look Now, Pay Later: The Rise of Network Broadcasting.* Garden City, N.Y.: Doubleday, 1980.

Bird, John. *Percy Grainger.* London: P. Elek, 1976.

Bogdanovich, Peter. "The Kane Mutiny." *Esquire*, Oct. 1976.

Bowles, Paul. "Music for 'Jane Eyre.' " *New York Herald Tribune*, 12–26–43.

Broeck, John. "Music of the Fears." *Film Comment*, Sept.–Oct. 1976.

Brown, Royal S. "Bernard Herrmann and the Subliminal Pulse of Violence." *High Fidelity and Musical America* 26 (Mar. 1976).

———. "Herrmann, Hitchcock and the Music of the Irrational." *Cinema Journal* 21 (1982).

———. "An Interview with Bernard Herrmann." *High Fidelity*, Sept. 1976.

Bruce, Graham. *Bernard Herrmann: Film Music and Narrative.* Ann Arbor: UMI Research Press, 1985.

Cameron, Evan, ed. *Sound and the Cinema.* Pleasantville, N.Y.: Redgrave, 1980.

Carringer, Robert L. *The Making of "Citizen Kane."* Berkeley and Los Angeles: University of California Press, 1985.

Cook, Page. "Bernard Herrmann." *Films in Review* 18, no. 7 (Aug.–Sept. 1967).

Copland, Aaron, and Perlis, Vivian. *Copland.* New York: St. Martin's Press/Marek, 1984.

Corwin, Norman. *More by Corwin: 16 Radio Dramas.* New York: Henry Holt, 1944.

———. *"Untitled" and Other Radio Dramas.* New York: Henry Holt, 1947.

Coulouris, George, and Bernard Herrmann, with Ted Gilling. "The *Citizen Kane* Book." *Sight and Sound* 41 (Spring 1972).

Cowell, Henry. *American Composers on American Music: A Symposium.* Stanford: Stanford University Press, 1933.

Daniel, Oliver. "A Perspective of Herrmann." *Saturday Review,* 7–13–68.

———. *Stokowski: A Counterpoint of View.* New York: Dodd, Mead, 1982.

De Palma, Brian. "Murder by Moog: Scoring the Chill." *Village Voice,* 10–11–73.

Dick, Bernard F. *Joseph L. Mankiewicz.* Boston: Twayne, 1983.

Donat, Misha. "Music in the Cinema. *Listener,* 10–28–71.

Dunne, Philip. *Take Two.* New York: McGraw-Hill, 1980.

Evans, Mark. *Soundtrack: The Music of the Movies.* New York: Hopkinson & Blake, 1975.

Ewen, David. *Dictators of the Baton.* New York: Ziff-Davis, 1948.

Fletcher, Lucille. "One Iceberg Please: The Strange Story of Radio's Musical Cue Man." *Detroit Free Press,* 5–14–39.

Foreman, Lewis. "Bernard Herrmann" (Obituary). *Gramophone,* Feb. 1976.

Gilling, Ted. "Benny." *Main Title,* Spring–Summer 1976.

———. "The Colour of Music: An Interview with Bernard Herrmann." *Sight and Sound,* Winter 1971–1972.

Goren, Arthur A. *New York Jews and the Quest for Community.* New York: Columbia University Press, 1970.

Greenfield, Edward. "Ives from England." *High Fidelity,* Apr. 1972.

Herrmann, Bernard. "An American Voice." In *Edward Elgar Centenary Sketches.* London: Novello, 1957.

———. "Barbirolli and the Halle." *Saturday Review,* 11–30–57.

———. "Bernard Herrmann: A John Player Lecture." *Pro Musica Sana* 3, no. 1 (Spring 1974); 3, no. 2 (Summer 1974).

———. "Charles Ives." *Trend: A Quarterly of the Seven Arts* 1, no. 3 (Sept.–Nov. 1932).

———. "From Sound Track to Disc." *Saturday Review,* 9–27–47.

———. "Musical England." *New York Herald Tribune,* Dec. 1946.

———. "Music in Motion Pictures—A Reply to Mr. Leinsdorf." *New York Times,* 6–24–45.

———. "On Composing a Setting of *Moby Dick.*" *New York Times,* April 1940 (exact date unknown).

———. "Score for a Film." *New York Times,* 5–25–41.

———. "The Symphonies of Charles Ives." *Modern Music,* May–June 1945.

"Herrmann Says Hollywood Tone Deaf as to Film Scores." *Hollywood Reporter,* 7–14–64.

Houseman, John. *Front and Center.* New York: Simon & Schuster, 1979.

———. *Run-Through.* New York: Simon & Schuster, 1972.

Howe, Irving. *World of Our Fathers.* New York: Harcourt Brace Jovanovich, 1976.

Hyams, Ben. "Herrmann: He Opened My Eyes and My Ears." *Honolulu Magazine,* Feb. 1976.

Jewell, Richard B., and Vernon Harbin. *The RKO Story*. New York: Arlington House, 1982.

Johnson, Edward. *Bernard Herrmann: Hollywood's Music-Dramatist*. London: Triad Press, 1977.

———. ed. *Stokowski: Essays in Analysis of His Art*. London: Triad Press, 1973.

Kael, Pauline. *The "Citizen Kane" Book*. Boston: Atlantic Monthly Press, 1971.

Kennedy, Michael. *Barbirolli, Conductor Laureate*. London: MacGibbon & Kee, 1971.

Kinkaid, Frank. "Scaling the Heights." *Opera News*, Nov. 1982.

Klein, Howard. "The Man Who Composed 'Citizen Kane.' " *New York Times*, 6-27-71.

Kolodin, Irving. "Great Whales and Little Pieces." *Stereo Review*, May 1974.

———. "Ives by His Prophet, Bernard Herrmann." *Saturday Review*, 9-9-72.

———. "The Wide Screen World of Bernard Herrmann." *Saturday Review*, 3-6-76.

Lampert, Diane. "Herrmann—Madman in Filmdom." *Los Angeles Herald-Examiner*, 1-18-76.

Levant, Oscar. *A Smattering of Ignorance*. New York: Doubleday, Doran, 1940.

———. *The Unimportance of Being Oscar*. New York: Putnam, 1968.

MacDonald, Hugh. *Hector Berlioz*. London: J. M. Dent, 1982.

Mapplebeck, John. "Bernard Herrmann." *Guardian*, 3-30-61.

Metz, Robert. *CBS: Reflections in a Bloodshot Eye*. Chicago: Playboy Press, 1975.

Murphy, A. D. "Bernard Herrmann, 64, Dies." *Variety*, 12-31-75.

Paley, William S. *As It Happened*. Garden City, N.Y.: Doubleday, 1979.

Palmer, Christopher. "Bernard Herrmann, 1911-1975: A Personal Tribute." *Crescendo International*, Feb.–Mar. 1976.

———. "The Music of Bernard Herrmann." *Monthly Film Bulletin* (British Film Institute), Oct. 1976.

Perlis, Vivian. *Charles Ives Remembered: An Oral History*. New Haven: Yale University Press, 1974.

Prendergast, Roy M. *Film Music: A Neglected Art*. New York: W. W. Norton, 1977.

Pye, Michael, and Lynda Myles. *The Movie Brats*. New York: Holt, Rinehart & Winston, 1979.

Ratcliffe, Michael. "Composing the 'Emotional Scenery' for the Screen." *Sheffield Telegraph*, 3-25-61.

Rebello, Stephen. "Psycho." *Cinefantastique*, Oct. 1986.

Reid, Charles. *Beecham: An Independent Biography*. London: Victor Gollancz, 1961.

Rossiter, Frank R. *Charles Ives and His America*. New York: Liveright, 1975.

Rózsa, Miklós. *Double Life*. New York: Hippocrene Books, 1982.

Shales, Tom. "Perfectionist, Iconoclast, Maverick." *Washington Post*, 1-18-76.

Sharples, Win, Jr. "Bernard Herrmann 1911-1975." *Filmmakers Newsletter*, Oct. 1976.

Spoto, Donald. *The Dark Side of Genius: The Life of Alfred Hitchcock* (Boston: Little, Brown, 1983).

Steiner, Fred. "Bernard Herrmann: An Unauthorized Biographical Sketch." *Film-music Notebook* 3, no. 2 (1977).

———. "Herrmann's 'Black-and-White' Music for Hitchcock's 'Psycho.'" *Filmmusic Notebook,* Fall 1974.

Taylor, John Russell. *Hitch: The Life and Times of Alfred Hitchcock.* New York: Pantheon Books, 1978.

Thomas, Kevin. "Film Composer Settles a Score." *Los Angeles Times,* 2–4–68.

Thomas, Tony. *Music for the Movies.* New York: A. S. Barnes, 1973).

Wardell, Don. "Music to Commit Murder By." *Soho Weekly News,* 9–9–76.

Wood, Robin. *Hitchcock's Films.* New York: Castle Books, 1965.

Zador, Leslie. "Bernard Herrmann Remembered." *Cue Sheet* 2, no. 1 (Jan. 1985).

Zador, Leslie T., and Greg Rose. "A Conversation with Bernard Herrmann." In *Film Music 1,* ed. Clifford McCarty. New York: Garland Publishing Co., 1989.

Zicree, Marc Scott. *The "Twilight Zone" Companion.* New York: Bantam Books, 1982.

# Index

Academy of Motion Picture Arts and Sciences, 87, 88, 108, 126, 357; Herrmann's resignation from, 294
Achucarro, Joaquin, 338–39
Addison, John, 273–74
Adler, Buddy, 215
"Alfred Hitchcock Presents" (television series), 229, 256–58, 263, 274, 314
*All That Money Can Buy* (*The Devil and Daniel Webster*, film), 85–88, 90, 148, 165, 194, 242, 284, 285, 286, 362
Alpy (pet dog), 296, 311, 314
American Society of Composers, Arrangers, and Publishers (ASCAP), 241–42
"Americans, The" (television series), 263
Amis, John, 284, 329, 346–47
"Amour à la Militaire" (dance), 34
Anderson, Lucille, 133–35, 136, 137, 141, 145–46, 163–64, 188, 266, 275, 281, 297; divorce from Herrmann, 263–64; marriage to Herrmann, 155; remarriage of, 358; separation from Herrmann, 261–62
Anderson, Maxwell, 59, 189
Andrews, Julie, 269
*Anna and the King of Siam* (film), 124–26
Arnold, Edward, 85
Avenall, Richard, 213

Bainbridge, Elizabeth, 278
Baker, Diane, 228
Barber, Samuel, 56, 102, 129
Barbirolli, Evelyn, 73, 74, 158–59, 201

Barbirolli, Sir John, 73–74, 127, 150, 156, 215–17, 245, 262–63; and Halle Orchestra, 95; visits to Herrmann, 200–201; and *Wuthering Heights*, 158–59, 200–201
Barlow, Harold, 42, 46, 56, 57, 58, 98, 100
Bartok, Bela, 102, 168, 216, 240
Bass, Saul, 221, 238, 239
*Battle of Neretva, The* (film), 303–4
Bax, Arnold, 44, 62, 71
Bay, Victor, 46, 189, 208
Bean, Ernest, 127–28, 150, 156
Beatles, The, 165, 248–49, 267, 295–96
Beaton, Morag, 278–79
Beecham, Sir Thomas, 64, 98, 247, 263, 298; death of, 248; influence on Herrmann, 20; radio appearances of, 102
Bell, Donald, 278
"Belle Dame Sans Merci, La" (incidental music), 45, 61
*Beneath the 12-Mile Reef* (film), 178–79, 181, 338–39
Benet, Stephen Vincent, 59, 85, 97, 202
Benjamin, Arthur, 195–96
Bennett, Hywell, 293, 312
Bennett, Richard Rodney, 348
Bennett, Robert Russell, 32, 36, 43, 207, 217, 262
Berg, Alban, 18, 359
Berger, Arthur, 30
Berlioz, Hector, 14–15, 20, 178, 188, 299, 337
Berners, Lord, 62, 346, 349

Bernstein, Elmer, 186–87, 252, 256, 330, 348–49, 357
Bernstein, Leonard, 100–101, 135, 305, 316
Berres, Richard, 126, 350n
Bezzerides, A. I., 156, 158, 178
Birds, The (film), 191, 253–55, 320
Blacklisting, 19, 148, 186
Blake, Howard, 312, 324–25
Bliss, Arthur, 62, 77, 353; on Wuthering Heights, 280–81
Blitzstein, Marc, 61
Bloch, Ernest, 23
Blue Denim (film), 229
Boone, Pat, 228
Boulanger, Nadia, 30
Boulting, John, 278, 293, 312
Boulting, Roy, 278, 293, 312
Bowles, Paul, 108
Bradbury, Ray, 257, 258, 275–77, 288; on Wuthering Heights, 279–80
Brahm, John, 118–19, 159
Brandt, Henry, 30, 32
Bride Wore Black, The (film), 285–86, 350
British Film Institute (BFI), 316–18
Britten, Benjamin, 129, 131
Broadcast Music Incorporated (BMI), 242, 289
Brothers Karamazov, The (film), 359–60
Broude, Irving, 208
Brown, Royal S., 98, 324, 339–40
Brynner, Yul, 303
Bujold, Genevieve, 341, 342, 345
Burks, Robert, 193, 196, 220, 226, 261
Burton, Richard, 184
Buttram, Pat, 258
Byron, George Gordon, Lord, 326, 328, 336–37

"Campbell Playhouse" (radio series), 67–68, 74–75
Cape Fear (film), 251–52
Carradine, John, 194
Carroll, Leo G., 256
CBS Symphony, 3, 42–44, 46, 47, 48, 56, 66, 71, 89, 95, 96, 101–4, 119, 126, 135, 150, 155; disbanding of, 159, 163
Chaplin, Charles, 125
Chávez, Carlos, 30
"Child Is Born, A" (television opera), 202
Christmas Carol, A (radio play), 67–68
"Christmas Carol, A" (television opera), 189–90
Citizen Kane (film), 2, 47, 72–84, 85, 87, 88, 91, 92, 104, 131, 147, 171, 306,

.331, 333, 337–38, 353; leitmotivs in, 78–79, 81; premiere of, 84
Clay, Elsa, 173, 210, 217, 261
Clemens, George, 232, 233
Cohen, Janelle, 354, 355
Cohen, Larry, 331–34, 353, 355–56, 357
Coleman, Herbert, 222
Collins, Anthony, 79, 96, 137; film music of, 122
Columbia Artists (management corporation), 101–2
Columbia Broadcasting System (CBS), 42–44, 52–53, 58–69, 89–90, 95–96, 100–104, 166–168, 189–90, 202–4, 229–30
"Columbia Presents Corwin" (radio series), 115
"Columbia Workshop" (radio series), 58, 59–61, 203
Combs, Ralph L. F., 150
Companions in Nightmare (television movie), 296
Composers' Guild, 242
"Concerto Macabre" (film concerto), 117, 118
"Congo Rhapsody" (ballet), 31
Conrad, William, 203
Cook, Page, 280n
Cooper, Gary, 183
Copland, Aaron, 23, 40, 86n, 285, 305; film music of, 122, 126, 307; and Young Composers Group, 29–33
Cortez, Stanley, 91–92
Corwin, Kathryn, 149, 279
Corwin, Norman, 4, 93, 247, 279; activism of, 164; at CBS, 43, 115–16, 120–21; collaborations with Herrmann, 68–69, 89–91; eulogy of Herrmann, 357; on Herrmann's temper, 188; during McCarthy era, 148
Cotten, Joseph, 91, 109
Cowell, Henry, 22, 29, 33, 38
"Crime Classics" (radio series), 166–68, 193n, 204
Cristlieb, Don, 81–82, 183, 217, 229, 354
Crosby, Kathryn, 224
Crowther, Bosley, 172–73
Currier and Ives (suite), 47
Curtiz, Michael, 181

Dahl, Roald, 300–303
Damrosch, Walter, 20, 24, 124, 316
Daniel, Oliver, 96–97, 136, 155; on Herrmann's orchestral music, 285; and "Invitation to Music," 101
Dardick, Abraham. See Herrmann, Abraham

Darnell, Linda, 118, 125
Day, Doris, 196–97
*Day of the Dolphin, The* (film), 334
*Day the Earth Stood Still, The* (film), 164–66, 171, 253n
"Death Hunt" (*On Dangerous Ground*), 157–58, 338, 339
Debussy, Claude, 4, 10, 19, 38, 58, 100, 108, 131, 179, 300, 359
Decker, James, 217, 354
Decloux, Walter, 209
De la Parra, Pim, 335
Delius, Frederick 20, 40; Herrmann's admiration of, 34, 52, 56, 100, 101, 102, 135, 200, 209, 249, 262–63, 277, 294, 347; and *Wuthering Heights*, 111
Della Cioppa, Guy, 166, 212, 279
DeNiro, Robert, 350, 352
De Palma, Brian, 319–25, 330, 335, 341–46, 353
Depression (1929), 25, 27, 41, 349
*Devil and Daniel Webster, The.* See *All That Money Can Buy*
*Devil and Daniel Webster Suite*, 101, 153, 284–85
Dickinson, Meriel, 346
Dieterle, William, 148, 285, 362; and *All That Money Can Buy*, 85–87
Donnelly, Paul, 269
Downes, Olin, 73
*Dr. Zhivago* (film), 363–64
*Dracula* (radio play), 64–65, 68
"Duel with the Skeleton" (*Seventh Voyage of Sinbad*), 224
Dukelsky, Vladmir (Vernon Duke), 32, 36
Duning, George, 243
Dunne, Irene, 124
Dunne, Philip, 131–33, 181, 184–86, 229

*Echoes* (String quartet), 87, 264–65, 302
*Egyptian, The* (film), 181–83
Elgar, Edward, 10, 36, 73, 129, 168, 200, 213–14; Herrmann's performances of, 206; influence on Herrmann, 19–20
*Endless Night* (film), 312–13
Engel, Lehman, 30, 32
Engel, Len, 179–80
*Enigma Variations* (Elgar), 19, 214, 217, 218
Evans, Ray, 197, 222
*Exorcist, The* (film), 330–31
"Exploring Music" (radio series), 56
"Eye of the Beholder" ("Twilight Zone"), 233–34

*Fahrenheit 451* (film), 275–78, 286, 321n, 342
"Fall of the City" (radio play), 60–61
*Falstaff* (Elgar), 19, 36, 168, 206–7, 214
*Fantasia* (film), 119
*Fantasticks, The* (choral work), 97–98, 189, 346
Farrell, Eileen, 80, 96, 103
Farrell, Sharon, 332
Federal Symphony Orchestra, 58
Film music, early, 2, 76–77, 359–60
Fine, Vivian, 30, 32, 35
Finley, Bill, 320
Finzi, Gerald, 129; death of, 212–13; friendship with Herrmann, 103
*Five Fingers* (film), 170–71, 255, 353, 366
Fletcher, Lucille, 45, 50–53, 60, 75, 89, 90, 125, 133, 261n, 358; courtship by Herrmann, 51–53; divorce from Herrmann, 112, 136–146; marriage to Douglas Wallop, 146; marriage to Herrmann, 71–72; on Orson Welles, 109; profile of Ives, 69; trip to England (1946), 127–28; writing career of, 59, 74, 90, 95, 124, 134; and *Wuthering Heights*, 111–15
Fonda, Henry, 210
Fontaine, Joan, 104
Forsythe, John, 193
*For the Fallen* (orchestral work), 71, 100, 154, 156, 346
Foster, Jodie, 351
"Four Faces of Jazz, The" (recording), 313–14
Friedhofer, Hugo, 173, 181, 348
Friedkin, William, 330–31
Froug, William, 203–4, 234–35, 261

Gabel, Martin, 120
*Garden of Evil* (film), 183–84, 353
Garney, Jay, 34–35
Gassmann, Remi, 253–55
Gauthier, Sue, 241, 268
Gavin, John, 238
*Gentle Art of Making Enemies, The* (Whistler), 14, 59, 191
George Peabody Citation, 129
Gerhardt, Charles, 244–45, 313–14, 334, 337–40, 344–45
Gershwin, George, 23–24, 40–41, 43, 313
*Ghost and Mrs. Muir, The* (film), 48, 97, 131–34, 178, 233, 251, 342; recording of, 348; and *Wuthering Heights*, 113, 131, 305
Gilliat, Sidney, 312
Gilling, Ted, 317, 328, 335
Girard, André, 286

Glans, Harry, 56
Glendale Symphony, 209–10, 217–18
Gluskin, Lud, 95, 120–21, 230
Goldsmith, Jerry, 204–5, 252, 256, 357
Goldsmith, John, 299, 347–48
Goodman, Benny, 46
Goodwin, Ron, 293
Gordon, David, 256
Gorenstein, Ida. *See* Herrmann, Ida
    Gorenstein
Gorenstein family, 9
Gould, Morton, 27–29
Grainger, Percy, 33–34, 36–37
Grant, Cary, 226
Gray, Cecil, 62, 110
"Great Movie Thrillers, The" (recording),
    292–93, 319
"Great Tone Poems" (recording), 294
Green, John, 32, 43–45, 256, 293–94;
    at CBS, 43–45, 47, 49; at MGM,
    175–76
Greenhouse, Bernard, 103
Greenwood, Henry, 207, 244, 261, 287,
    316
Greenwood, Joan, 9, 207, 261, 262, 282,
    287
Griffiths, D. L., 340
Gwenn, Edmund, 193

Halle Orchestra, 95, 127, 128–29, 155–
    56, 215, 247, 248n, 262–63, 295
Hammerstein, Oscar, 126
*Hangover Square* (film), 97, 117–19, 334
"Hangover Square" (film concerto), 338
Harms (music company), 32
Harrington, Clark, 53, 54, 284
Harris, Roy, 23
Harrison, Joan, 256–57
Harrison, Rex, 124, 131
Harryhausen, Ray, 222–24, 242–43, 247,
    249, 252, 255–56, 263
Hart, Moss, 185
*Hatful of Rain, A* (film), 214–15
Hathaway, Henry, 183
"Have Gun, Will Travel" (television se-
    ries), 212
Hayes, Jack, 354, 355
Hayes, John Michael, 195
Hayward, Susan, 172, 177, 178, 183
Hayworth, Rita, 109
Hearst, William Randolph, 75
Hecht, Harold, 194
Hedren, Tippi, 253, 254, 260–61
Heifetz, Jascha, 86–87
Heilner, Irwin, 30, 35, 36
Heine, Gustav, 19, 20
Hemingway, Ernest, 171

Henry, Edd, 260, 269
Henry Hadley Citation, 129
Herrmann, Abraham, 7–12, 14, 15, 18–
    19, 29, 37, 41
Herrmann, Bernard: academy award of,
    87–88; Anglophilia of, 3, 12, 50, 93,
    97, 190, 246; awards received by, 129,
    130; birth of, 7, 10; breach with
    Hitchcock, 267–73, 293; at CBS, 44–
    47, 48–50, 96, 115–17; and Charles
    Ives, 21–22, 38–39, 53, 123–24, 305,
    349; childhood of, 10–13, 348; collab-
    oration with Alfred Newman, 181–83;
    collaborations with Hitchcock, 3, 191–
    94, 195–97, 210–11, 219–22, 226–28,
    236–41, 252–55, 259–61, 267–74,
    306; collaborations with Orson
    Welles, 3, 63–68, 72–84, 91–94, 147,
    306; and "Columbia Workshop," 59–
    62; as conductor, 3, 24, 27, 31, 81–
    82, 100, 115, 135–36, 139, 155–56,
    174, 187–88, 209–10, 217–18, 247,
    256, 262–63, 336–37; correspondence
    with Ives, 57–58, 123–24; correspon-
    dence with Lucille Anderson, 145–46,
    275; correspondence with Lucille
    Fletcher, 136–40, 141–46; correspon-
    dence with Leopold Stokowski, 154;
    courtship of Lucille Fletcher, 51–53;
    critical notices of, 38, 73–74, 108,
    172–73, 203, 265, 284–85, 316, 326,
    339–40, 341; death of, 356–57; debut
    as conductor, 34–35; diary of, 25–27;
    divorce from Lucille Anderson, 263–
    64, 268, 275; divorce from Lucille
    Fletcher, 112, 136, 140, 145; early
    compositions of, 17, 28; education of,
    12–13, 15–16, 24, 29; on Elgar, 213–
    14; on English composers, 128–30;
    family of, 7, 18–19, 37; fear of death,
    174, 350; on film music, 76, 78, 122–
    23, 126, 149–50, 241, 253, 266, 294–
    95, 305, 307, 317, 358–64; film music
    of, 2, 74–84, 92, 104–5, 107–9, 117–
    19, 124–26, 236–41, 322–24, 332,
    342–44, 350–52; friendships of, 3, 4,
    148–49, 258–59; on George Gersh-
    win, 40–41; and Glendale Symphony,
    209–10, 217–18; and Halle Orchestra,
    127, 128–29, 155–56, 247; heart con-
    dition of, 340–41, 352–53, 354; on
    Hollywood, 294–95; Hollywood
    homes of, 75, 125, 163, 201; and
    Houston Symphony, 202–3; interest
    in psychology, 14; interviews of, 305–
    8; on jazz, 187; on John Barbirolli,
    216–17; knowledge of cinema, 72–73;

lectures of, 177, 316–17, 328, 358–64;
London home of, 247; and London
Symphony Orchestra, 197, 206–8,
316; love of animals, 51, 149, 235,
296, 304, 311–12; and Manchester
Symphony, 262; marriage to Lucille
Anderson, 155, 156; marriage to Lucille Fletcher, 71–72; marriage to
Norma Shepherd, 287; during McCarthy era, 148; melodic facility of, 172;
and Mercury Theatre, 63–68; move
to London, 311; musical training of,
11–13, 15, 19, 23, 28–29, 31, 33; and
New Chamber Orchestra, 36–38; and
New York Philharmonic, 88, 135–36;
on opera, 359; orchestrations of, 34,
81, 271–72, 304; Oscar nominations
of, 87–88, 126, 357; parents of, 7–10;
and Philharmonia Orchestra, 263; political opinions of, 69, 164; radio music of, 45–46, 56–57, 59–62, 63–68,
89–91, 95, 115–17, 120–21, 166–68;
reading habits of, 11, 12–14, 18, 50,
201, 329; recordings of, 149–50, 284,
292–93, 294, 297–300, 313–14, 337–
40, 346–48, 353–54, 358, 363; relationship with mother, 10–11; religious
views of, 142–43, 146; reuse of
themes, 47–48, 113, 116, 117, 193n,
233, 251, 255, 264, 304, 342; romanticism of, 4, 14, 25, 131–34; and
Royal Philharmonic, 337–38; screen
appearance of, 196–97; separation
from Lucille Anderson, 261–62; sib-
lings of, 10; television music of, 179,
189–90, 211–12, 229–35, 256–58;
temper of, 174, 188–89, 204, 247,
248; trip to England (1937), 62; trip
to England (1946), 127–30; trip to
England (1949), 155–56; trip to England (1964), 262–63; trip to Italy
(1973), 326–28; trip to Yugoslavia
(1971), 303–4; at 20th Century Fox,
104–8, 117–19; use of folk music, 2,
242; use of leitmotivs, 2, 107, 118,
132; use of ostinato, 108, 113, 170,
172, 186–87, 221, 234, 238, 257n; use
of sound effects, 60, 87, 165, 253–55,
339; views on women, 145; and
Young Composers Group, 30. Works:
*All That Money Can Buy*, 85–88,
165, 242, 362; "Amour à la Militaire"
(dance), 34; "Anathema," 36, 38;
*Anna and the King of Siam*, 124–26;
*The Battle of Neretva*, 303–4; "La
Belle Dame Sans Merci," 45; *Beneath
the 12-Mile Reef*, 178–79, 181, 339;

*The Birds*, 253–55, 320; *Blue Denim*,
229; *The Bride Wore Black*, 285–86;
*Cape Fear*, 251–52; "A Child Is
Born," 202; *Citizen Kane*, 2, 74–84,
306, 333; "Concerto Macabre," 117,
118; "Congo Rhapsody" (ballet), 31;
*Currier and Ives Suite*, 47; *The Day
the Earth Stood Still*, 164–66, 253n;
*Devil and Daniel Webster Suite*, 101,
153, 284–85; *Echoes*, 87, 264–65,
302; *The Egyptian*, 181–83; *Endless
Night*, 312–13; *Fahrenheit 451*, 275–
78, 286, 342; *Fantasticks*, 97–98, 189;
*Five Fingers*, 170–71; *For the Fallen*,
100, 154, 156; *Garden of Evil*, 183–
84; *The Ghost and Mrs. Muir*, 131–
34, 233, 251, 342; *Hangover Square*,
117–19, 334; *Hatful of Rain*, 214–15;
*It's Alive*, 331–33; *Jane Eyre*, 67,
104–5, 107–9; *Jason and the Argonauts*, 117, 223, 255–56; *Journey to
the Center of the Earth*, 223, 228–29,
297; *Joy in the Morning*, 264, 268;
*The Kentuckian*, 16, 117, 194–95;
"The King of Schnorrers," 35, 290–
91, 351; *King of the Khyber Rifles*,
180–81; *Late Autumn, The Forest*
(tone poem), 28, 38; *The Magnificent
Ambersons*, 91–94, 306; *The Man in
the Gray Flannel Suit*, 205–6; *The
Man Who Knew Too Much*, 109, 195–
98, 247; *Marnie*, 224, 252–53, 260–
61, 320–21; *Moby Dick*, 28, 53–56,
73–74, 76, 240, 283, 342; *Mysterious
Island*, 223, 249–50; *The Naked and
the Dead*, 225; *The Night Digger*,
300–303; *Nocturne and Scherzo*, 56,
57, 58; *North by Northwest*, 158,
226–28; *Obsession*, 182, 288, 341–46,
350, 351, 357; *On Dangerous
Ground*, 156–58, 171; *Prince of Players*, 184–85; *Psycho*, 47, 116, 158,
192, 236–41; *Ride a Cock Horse*,
288–90, 291; *The Road Builder*, 300–
303; *The Seven Per Cent Solution*,
353; *The Seventh Voyage of Sinbad*,
223–25, 260; "Sinfonietta for
Strings," 47, 240; *Sisters*, 252, 296,
319–26, 332, 350; "The Skating
Rink," 47; *The Snows of Kilamanjaro*,
171–73, 205; *Souvenirs de voyage*,
282–83; *Symphony*, 88–89, 98–100;
*Taxi Driver*, 240, 335, 347, 350–52,
357; *Tender Is the Night*, 250–51,
252; *The Three Worlds of Gulliver*,
211, 223, 242–44; *Torn Curtain*, 116,
192, 252, 265, 266, 267–72; *The*

Herrmann, Bernard (*continued*)
    *Trouble with Harry*, 191–94; *Twisted
    Nerve*, 293; *Vertigo*, 4, 193, 219–22,
    257, 342–44, 360; *Welles Raises
    Kane*, 110, 154, 284–85; *White Witch
    Doctor*, 177–78, 227, 339; *The Wrong
    Man*, 210–11, 214; *Wuthering
    Heights*, 48, 54, 111–15, 127–28, 129,
    136, 138, 139, 150, 200–201
Herrmann, Dorothy, 88, 89, 98, 124, 146,
    173, 261n, 353; recollections of Herr-
    mann, 174–74, 199
Herrmann, Ida Gorenstein, 8–9, 10, 18,
    37, 41, 62, 74, 297, 358
Herrmann, Louis, 9, 10, 13, 37, 62, 358
Herrmann, Lucille Anderson. *See* Ander-
    son, Lucille
Herrmann, Lucille Fletcher. *See* Fletcher,
    Lucille
Herrmann, Norma Shepherd. *See* Shep-
    herd, Norma
Herrmann, Rose, 10, 37, 62, 358
Herrmann, Wendy, 124, 146, 173–74,
    261n
Heyes, Douglas, 233
Hindemith, Paul, 102
Hirsch, Paul, 319–22, 325–26, 341–42,
    344, 345–46, 350
Hitchcock, Alfred, 4, 108–9, 119, 163,
    239–40, 293; breach with Herrmann,
    267–73, 293; childhood of, 191; col-
    laborations with Herrmann, 191–94,
    195–97, 210–11, 219–22, 226–28,
    236–41, 252–55, 259–61, 306; meet-
    ing with Herrmann, 106; musical
    taste of, 362; and *Psycho*, 321; on
    *Vertigo*, 360
Hitchcock, Alma, 192
"Hitchhiker, The" (radio play), 74
Holliman, Earl, 230
Hollywood Bowl, 175, 256
Holst, Gustav, 69, 297–98
"Home Away from Home, A" ("Alfred
    Hitchcock Presents"), 257
Hopkinson, Cecil, 201–2
Horne, Marilyn, 190, 198
Houghton, Buck, 230–31, 233–34
Houseman, John, 156, 157, 203, 262; and
    *Citizen Kane*, 80; and *Jane Eyre*, 104;
    and Julius Caesar, 175, 176; and Mer-
    cury Theatre, 63, 64; and *War of the
    Worlds*, 65–67
Houston Symphony, 200, 202–3
Humphrey, Doris, 34
Humphreys, Gillian, 346
Hunt, Marsha, 148, 163–64
Huston, Walter, 85, 87

Huxley, Aldous, 203
Hyams, Ben, 101–2, 103–4

Immigrants, 23, 71; Jewish, 7, 8
"Impressionists, The" (recording), 300,
    316
"Invitation to Music" (radio series),
    101–4, 126–27, 209
*It's Alive* (film), 331–33
Ives, Charles, 10, 20, 21–23, 44, 55–56,
    244; correspondence with Herrmann,
    57–58, 123–24, 346, 353; Fourth
    Symphony, 153n; Herrmann's perfor-
    mances of, 39, 57, 69–70, 206, 315–
    16; influence on Herrmann, 19, 33,
    53; meeting with Herrmann, 38–39;
    *114 Songs*, 20, 22, 31; Second Sym-
    phony, 123–24, 127, 206, 315–16,
    349; Third Symphony, 126–27; *Three
    Places in New England*, 29
Ives, Harmony, 57, 123–24, 127

James, Philip, 24, 97
*Jane Eyre* (film), 48, 54, 67, 97, 104–9
"Jane Eyre" (suite), 298
"Jar, The" ("Alfred Hitchcock Presents"),
    258
Jarre, Maurice, 252, 288
*Jason and the Argonauts* (film), 117, 223,
    255–56
Johnson, Edward, 299, 300
Johnson, George Clay, 235
Johnson, Laurie, 245–46, 263, 271, 308,
    331, 333, 342, 344–45, 348, 353; on
    François Truffaut, 277; and
    Herrmann's illness, 340
Jones, Jennifer, 148, 205, 251
Jones, Mervyn, 330
*Journey to the Center of the Earth* (film),
    223, 228–29, 297, 298
*Joy in the Morning* (film), 264, 268
Judson, Arthur, 42, 43, 73
Juilliard School of Music, 31, 33–34
Julia, Raul, 291
*Julius Caesar* (film), 175–76
Jurgens, Curt, 303

Karajan, Herbert von, 152–53, 164, 363
Kaufman, Annette, 93, 104, 125, 135, 280
Kaufman, Louis, 125, 184, 207, 212, 217;
    and *Magnificent Ambersons*, 93; and
    *Wuthering Heights*, 280
Kearns, Joseph, 203
Kelly, Grace, 253
*Kentuckian, The* (film), 16, 117, 194–95,
    353
Keyes, Liz, 294, 320, 354
Kidder, Margot, 320

King, Henry, 171, 250
"King of Schnorrers, The" (musical comedy), 35, 290–91, 351
*King of the Khyber Rifles* (film), 180–81, 353
Kirk, Dick, 242, 289
Kirkpatrick, Ralph, 201
Kline, Marian, 354, 355
Knight, Arthur, 188
Koerner, George, 93–94
Kolodin, Irving, 215, 284–85
Korngold, Erich Wolfgang, 77, 96, 102, 338
Korngold, George, 338, 339
Koussevitsky, Serge, 17, 245
Krebs, Johann Ludwig, 249
Kubrick, Stanley, 249–50

Lambert, Constant, 44, 62, 129
Lampert, Diane, 289–91
Lancaster, Burt, 16, 194, 195
Landowska, Wanda, 102
*Late Autumn, The Forest* (tone poem), 28, 38
Laughton, Charles, 115–16
Lean, David, 364
Lehman, Ernest, 227
Leigh, Janet, 236
Leinsdorf, Erich, 121–22
Levant, Oscar, 31–32, 39–40, 63, 174
Levin, Erma, 355
Lewis, Elliott, 166–68, 193
"Liebestod" (Wagner), 220–21, 222, 251
"Life Work of Juan Diaz, The" ("Alfred Hitchcock Presents"), 257–58
"Little Girl Lost" ("Twilight Zone"), 234
Litto, George, 341
Litvak, Anatole, 134
"Living Doll" ("Twilight Zone"), 235
Livingstone, Jay, 197, 222, 274
Lloyd, Norman, 61; and "Alfred Hitchcock Presents," 256–57; on Hitchcock, 259–60, 271, 273, 373; as television director, 296
London Philharmonic, 284, 298, 299–300, 304, 316
London Symphony Orchestra, 195, 198, 206–8, 244, 249, 315–16
"Lonely, The" ("Twilight Zone"), 231–32
Lorentz, Pare, 60
Los Angeles Philharmonic, 174
Lupino, Ida, 157

MacDuffy, Kathleen, 265
MacGowan, Kenneth, 107
MacLaine, Shirley, 193
MacLeish, Archibald, 59, 60, 90

*Magnificent Ambersons, The* (film), 47, 91–95, 147, 165, 306
Mahler, Gustav, 10, 153; *Das Lied von der Erde*, 26; Herrmann's interest in, 16, 52, 245, 315
Mallowan, Sir Max, 313
Mancini, Henry, 252, 293
*Man in the Gray Flannel Suit, The* (film), 205–6
Mankiewicz, Herman, 75, 131
Mankiewicz, Joseph L., 131, 132, 133, 170–71, 175, 176
Mann, Thomas, 86
Mannes, Michael, 298–99
*Man Who Knew Too Much, The* (film), 109, 191, 195–98, 210, 247
March, Frederic, 116, 189
*Marnie* (film), 191, 224, 252–53, 260–61, 267, 320–21, 350
Marsh, Jean, 231
Mason, James, 170–71, 228
Massey, Raymond, 225
Matheson, Richard, 234
Mathieson, Muir, 222
Mattfeld, Julius, 52, 101
Matthau, Walter, 191
McCarthy era, 148, 186
McCartney, Paul, 278
McCormick, Harold, 76
McIntyre, John, 194
Melodram, 358–59
"Melodrams" (radio program), 61
"Memory Waltz"(*The Snows of Kilimanjaro*), 87, 171, 256, 272
Mercury Theatre, 61, 63–68, 75, 91
Merkel, Una, 194
Middleton, Robert, 202
Miles, Vera, 256
Milhaud, Darius, 39, 102, 313
Miller, Mitch, 56, 103–4
Mills, Hayley, 293, 312
"Miser's Waltz" (*All That Money Can Buy*), 87, 286
Mitchum, Robert, 177, 178, 252
"Moat Farm Murder, The" (radio play), 115–16, 117
*Moby Dick* (cantata), 28, 53–56, 201, 240, 283, 284, 342; performance of, 73–74, 76, 346
*Moby-Dick* (novel), 53, 54
Monteverdi, Claudio, 359
Moog synthesizer, 312, 322–24, 332
Moore, Terry, 178, 180
Moorehead, Agnes, 92, 96
Moreau, Jeanne, 286, 361
Moross, Jerome, 16–17, 256, 299, 315; at CBS, 49; and Charles Ives, 22–23; in

Moross, Jerome (*continued*)
    Hollywood, 62–63; and Young Com-
    posers Group, 30–31, 32
Murray, Don, 214
Murray, Lyn, 46, 58, 88, 159, 187–88,
    194, 250, 348; diary of, 158n; and
    Hitchcock, 192; television music of,
    257; visits to Herrmann, 164
"Music from Great Film Classics" (re-
    cording), 298
Musicians' strike (1958), 222, 225
"Music of the Georgian Era" (recitals),
    198–99
*Mysterious Island* (film), 223, 249–50,
    255

*Naked and the Dead, The* (film), 225
Napier, Alan, 118–19
National Philharmonic, 344, 347–48
Natwick, Mildred, 193
Neal, Patricia, 300, 303
Nero, Franco, 303
New Chamber Orchestra, 36–38, 39, 206
Newman, Alfred, 77, 79, 82, 124, 165,
    178, 180, 256; collaboration with
    Herrmann, 181–83; retirement of,
    250, 274; at 20th Century Fox, 105–
    7; and *Wuthering Heights*, 280
Newman, Lionel, 274–75, 335
Newman, Paul, 269
New York, 8, 10
New York Philharmonic, 73, 88, 89, 95,
    100, 135–36, 153
New York School of Music, 13
Nichols, Mike, 334
*Night Digger, The* (film), 116, 300–303,
    353
"Ninety Years Without Slumbering"
    ("Twilight Zone"), 235
Nixon, Marni, 279
*Nocturne and Scherzo*, 56, 57, 58, 255
North, Alex, 29, 246
*North by Northwest* (film), 158, 178, 191,
    193, 226–28, 256, 320
Norton, Mildred, 126
Nott, Carolyn, 279, 297
Novak, Kim, 219

*Obsession* (film), 182, 341–46, 351, 357
*Obsessions* (film), 288, 350
Odets, Clifford, 125
"On a Note of Triumph" (radio play),
    120–21
*On Dangerous Ground* (film), 156–58,
    171, 178
*114 Songs* (Ives), 20, 22, 31

Orff, Carl, 359
Ormandy, Eugene, 98–100, 101, 318
Ozep, Fedor, 359

Paley, William S., 42–43, 45, 48, 95,
    101, 151, 159
Palmer, Christopher, 88–89, 117, 179,
    227, 249, 330–31, 339, 340, 347, 351
Paramount Studios, 194, 195, 197, 222,
    237, 241
Peck, Gregory, 171, 205, 252
Perkins, Anthony, 236
Perkins, Francis D., 74
Perry, Frank, 334
Philharmonia Orchestra, 263
Phillips, Michael, 350, 352
Piston, Walter, 23, 30
Polonsky, Abraham, 17–19, 62–63, 148
Polonsky, Charlotte, 19, 26
Presnell, Harve, 202
Presnell, Robert J., 164
Pressman, Ed, 319–20, 322
Previn, André, 199, 259, 303, 316
Previn, Steve, 303
*Prince of Players* (film), 184–85
*Principles of Orchestration* (Rimsky-
    Korsakov), 237–38
Prokofiev, Serge, 307; film music of, 72,
    77, 122, 150
*Psycho* (film), 47, 55, 116, 158, 191, 192,
    232, 236–41, 242, 255, 267, 272, 276,
    319, 320, 322, 323, 327; recording of,
    347–48; reuse of themes, 352
Purcell, Henry, 36
Purdom, Edmund, 181

Radio, 1, 15; concerts on, 42–47, 101
Raff, Joachim, 56, 244, 298–300
Raksin, David, 49–50, 63, 172, 178, 188–
    89, 199n, 247, 267, 274; on Alfred
    Newman, 105; eulogy of Herrmann,
    357; *Laura*, 108–9
Rantzen, Esther, 329
Rathaus, Karol, 72, 359–60
Rathbone, Basil, 189
Ray, Nicholas, 156–58
Reagan, Ronald, 202
*Rebecca* (radio play), 67
Reid, Alastair, 254, 300–303
Reis, Irving, 59
Rennie, Michael, 165
*Ride a Cock Horse* (musical comedy),
    288–90, 291
Rimsky-Korsakov, Nikolai, 223, 224, 237–
    38, 244
Rippon, Michael, 346

RKO (studio), 72, 79, 81, 82, 85, 88, 91–95, 156, 225

*Road Builder, The* (film). See *Night Digger, The*

Robards, Jason, 250, 251

Roberts, Jeremy Dale, 278

Robertson, Cliff, 341, 345

Robertson, Peggy, 268, 270–72, 293

Robinson, Alan, 217, 354

Robson, William, 59

Rodgers, Richard, 126, 154

Rose, Greg, 305–8

Rosenman, Leonard, 224, 257

Ross, David, 43, 45, 61

Ross, Harold, 35

Ross, Herbert, 353

Royal Philharmonic, 247, 248, 337

Rózsa, Miklós, 100, 119, 149, 150, 165, 177, 223, 246, 357; on Herrmann, 208–9, 318; *Julius Caesar*, 176

Rubbra, Edmund, 129, 206, 265

Rudel, Julius, 208, 358

Russell, John L., 236, 241

Ryan, John, 332

Ryan, Robert, 156

Saint, Eva Marie, 214, 227

*Salammbô (Citizen Kane)*, 79–80, 337–38

"Samson" (radio play), 89–90

Sanders, George, 117, 118–19

Sanderson, Nancy, 265

Sarnoff, David, 42

Savalas, Telly, 235

Schaefer, George, 90; and *Magnificent Ambersons*, 91, 93; and Orson Welles, 72

Schneer, Charles, 223, 224, 225, 242, 244, 247, 249, 255, 263

Schoenberg, Arnold, 21, 22, 43, 151–52

Schrader, Paul, 341, 350

Schurmann, Gerard, 279

Scorsese, Martin, 94, 288, 335, 350–55, 357

"Seems Radio Is Here to Stay" (radio program), 69, 297

Selznick, David O., 104, 105, 119, 147–48, 250, 251, 295

Serling, Rod, 229–34

*Seven Per Cent Solution, The* (film), 353

*Seventh Voyage of Sinbad, The* (film), 223–25, 249, 255, 260

Shapiro, Mel, 291

Shepherd, Cybill, 351

Shepherd, Norma, 163, 265, 281–83, 295–96, 326–28, 335, 352, 355; at BBC, 329–30, 358; in California, 297; and death of Herrmann, 356; and

*Endless Night*, 313; and Herrmann's illness, 340–41; and Herrmann's pets, 311–12; and Hitchcock, 193; liberalism of, 303; marriage to Herrmann, 287; and *Wuthering Heights*, 282

Sher, Jack, 242

Siegmeister, Elie, 49; in Hollywood, 242; and Young Composers Group, 30–31, 35–36

"Sinfonietta for Strings," 47, 55, 240

*Sisters* (film), 252, 296, 319–26, 330, 332, 350

"Skating Rink, The," 47

Slatkin, Eleanor, 354

Slonimsky, Nicholas, 22, 29

*Snows of Kilamanjaro, The* (film), 171–73, 205, 256

Solti, Georg, 209

Sondheim, Stephen, 119, 334

"Sorry, Wrong Number" (radio play), 95–96

*Sorry, Wrong Number* (screenplay), 134, 140, 143

*Souvenirs de voyage* (quintet), 382–83

Spialek, Hans, 36

Spielberg, Steven, 354

Spoto, Donald, 192, 260

Stahl, John M., 131

Stefano, Joseph, 241

Steiner, Fred, 212, 347, 355–56; eulogy of Herrmann, 357; on Newman and Hellmann, 106; as piano soloist, 199; on *Psycho*, 237–38; visits to Herrmann, 167–69

Steiner, Max, 2, 72, 77, 83, 84, 132, 223

Steiner, Shirley, 169–70

Stevens, Mort, 314–15

Stevens, Robert, 232

Stevenson, Robert, 104

Stewart, James, 197, 219–20

Stewart, James G., 85–86 147–48, 328; on *Citizen Kane*, 82–83; and *Magnificent Ambersons*, 91, 92

Stewart, Paul, 57, 66, 234

Stoessel, Albert, 24, 28, 29, 97

Stokowski, Leopold, 24, 46, 103, 119, 198; Herrmann's early admiration of, 17; Herrmann's essay on, 152–53; and Herrmann's works, 153–54; visits to Herrmann, 199–200

Stoloff, Max, 243

Stravinsky, Igor, 21–22, 102, 105, 111, 295

Studio Trautonium (keyboard instrument), 253–55

"Suspense" (radio series), 95–96

Swift, Jonathan, 243

Tashlin, Frank, 164
Taxi Driver (film), 157, 240, 335, 347, 350–57
Taylor, Davidson, 43, 63, 96, 123n, 135, 349
Taylor, Deems, 43, 97
Te Kanawa, Kiri, 42, 338
Tender Is The Night (film), 250–51, 252
Thirty-nine Steps, The (film), 72n
Thirty-nine Steps, The (radio play), 65
Thompson, J. Lee, 251
Thomson, Virgil, 23, 111, 307
Three Worlds of Gulliver, The (film), 211, 223, 242–44, 249, 255
Tierney, Gene, 131
Tiomkin, Dimitri, 2, 148, 149, 173, 247, 250, 269, 273
Tippett, Michael, 129
Toland, Gregg, 76, 81, 91
Tomasini, George, 226, 236, 251, 260–61, 268
Torn Curtain (film), 116, 192, 252, 265, 266, 267–74, 274, 304, 308, 353, 355
Toscanini, Arturo, 12, 17, 20, 24, 43, 97, 274; Herrmann's opinion of, 46, 93, 245, 363
"Treasure Bandstand" (radio series), 150
Treatise on Orchestration (Berlioz), 14
Trouble with Harry, The (film), 178, 191–94, 210, 298, 306
Truffaut, François, 270, 279, 283, 333, 357, 362; The Bride Wore Black, 285–87; Fahrenheit 451, 275–78, 321n
Tuckwell, Barry, 197
Twentieth Century Fox (studio), 104–7, 117–19, 177, 250
"Twilight Zone, The" (television series), 4, 229–35, 263, 274, 314, 373
Twi (pet dog), 235, 242, 261, 264, 296, 311–12
Twisted Nerve (film), 293

Unicorn Records, 299, 346, 347–48
Universal Studios, 241, 251, 259, 260, 263, 273, 308, 334, 353; musical policies of, 267–68

Varèse, Edgar, 29, 31
Vaughan Williams, Ralph, 2, 26, 39, 71, 73, 103, 129, 168, 200, 217, 283; death of, 225; Eighth Symphony, 216; Herrmann's performances of, 207–8; Herrmann's tribute to, 225–26; Herrmann's visit to, 62; influence on Herrmann, 20
Vaughan Williams, Ursula, 2, 217, 278, 279, 353

Verstappen, Wim, 288
Vertigo (film), 4, 54, 191, 193, 219–22, 257, 272, 320, 342–44, 360
Villa-Lobos, Hector, 102

Wagenaar, Bernard, 29
Wagner, Robert, 178
Wagner, Roger, 190
Walker, Alexander, 341
"Walking Distance" ("Twilight Zone"), 232–33
Wallop, Douglas, 146, 261n
Walsh, Raoul, 225
Walton, William, 72, 77, 129, 233, 307, Henry V, 150
Ward, Joseph, 278
Warden, Jack, 231
War of the Worlds, The (radio play), 65–67
Washington, Ned, 243
Wasserman, Lew, 256, 260, 267
Waxman, Franz, 77, 122, 223
Webb, Roy, 79, 84, 94
"We Hold These Truths" (radio play), 90
Weidman, Charles, 34
Weinstein, Henry T., 303
Welles, Orson, 3, 54, 84, 109, 197, 198, 293, 303, 353; Citizen Kane, 72, 75–76, 80, 82–84; collaborations with Herrmann, 63–68, 77–84, 147, 306; and "Columbia Workshop," 61; film career of, 72; in Jane Eyre, 104–6; The Magnificent Ambersons, 91–94; during McCarthy era, 148; and Mercury Theatre, 63–68; musical taste of, 362; and RKO studio, 94–95
Welles Raises Kane (suite), 110, 154, 284–85
Werner, Oskar, 276
"Where Is Everybody" ("Twilight Zone"), 230
Whistler, James McNeill, 14, 59, 191
White Witch Doctor (film), 177–78, 227, 339
Widmark, Richard, 183
Williams, John, 256, 355, 357; on Herrmann, 258–59; on Hitchcock, 274
Williamsburg: The Story of a Patriot (short subject), 211
Wilson, Stanley, 257
Wincelberg, Shimon, 290
Wise, Robert, 83–84, 85, 91, 94, 165, 166
Wrong Man, The (film), 191, 210–11, 214

*Wuthering Heights* (film), 297
*Wuthering Heights* (opera), 48, 54, 107, 110–15, 127–28, 129, 130, 131, 136, 138, 139, 150, 200–201, 305; atttempts at production, 208–9, 213; completion of, 158; leitmotivs in, 112–13; libretto of, 111, 113; premiere of, 358; recording of, 278–81, 283–84
Wyler, William, 288
Wynn, Ed, 235

Yaddo Festival, 31–32
Yiddish Music Theater, 35, 348
Youmans, Vincent, 32
Young Composers Group, 30, 32, 35–37, 242

Zador, Leslie, 305–8
Zanuck, Darryl, 104, 105, 131, 178, 179, 181, 183, 205
Zinnemann, Fred, 163, 173, 214–15
Zsigmond, Vilmos, 343, 344

Compositor: BookMasters, Inc.
Text: 10/13 Aldus
Display: Aldus
Printer: Malloy Lithographing, Inc.
Binder: John H. Dekker & Sons

黎廉圖書社
LIM M. LAI
PRIVATE LIBRARY